Introduction to
Sociological Theory

Introduction to Sociological Theory

Theorists, Concepts, and Their Applicability
to the Twenty-First Century

THIRD EDITION

Michele Dillon

WILEY Blackwell

This third edition first published 2020
© 2020 John Wiley & Sons Ltd

Edition History
John Wiley & Sons Ltd (2e, 2014); Blackwell Publishing Ltd (1e, 2010)

Registered Offices
John Wiley & Sons, Inc., 111 River Street, Hoboken, NJ 07030, USA
John Wiley & Sons Ltd, The Atrium, Southern Gate, Chichester, West Sussex, PO19 8SQ, UK

Editorial Office
9600 Garsington Road, Oxford, OX4 2DQ, UK

For details of our global editorial offices, customer services, and more information about Wiley products visit us at www.wiley.com.

Wiley also publishes its books in a variety of electronic formats and by print-on-demand. Some content that appears in standard print versions of this book may not be available in other formats.

Library of Congress Cataloging-in-Publication Data
Name: Dillon, Michele, 1960– author.
Title: Introduction to sociological theory : theorists, concepts, and their
    applicability to the twenty-first century / Michele Dillon.
Description: Third edition. | Hoboken, NJ : John Wiley & Sons, Ltd, [2020] |
    Includes bibliographical references and index.
Identifiers: LCCN 2019016119 (print) | LCCN 2019018838 (ebook) | ISBN
    9781119410928 (Adobe PDF) | ISBN 9781119410898 (ePub) | ISBN 9781119410911
    (pbk.)
Subjects: LCSH: Sociology. | Sociology–History.
Classification: LCC HM585 (ebook) | LCC HM585 .D55 2019 (print) | DDC
    301–dc23

Cover Design: Wiley
Cover Image: © A. Astes/Alamy Stock Photo

Set in 10/13pt Minion by SPi Global, Pondicherry, India
Printed and bound in Singapore by Markono Print Media Pte Ltd

10   9   8   7   6   5   4   3   2   1

CONTENTS

LIST OF BOXED FEATURES

TIMELINES

CONCEPTUAL BOXES

CONTEMPORARY TOPICAL APPLICATIONS

LIST OF ANALYTICAL PHOTOS

ACKNOWLEDGMENTS

I am very grateful to Justin Vaughan at Wiley-Blackwell for persuading me to write this book and to embark on subsequent revised editions. I appreciate his support throughout the process. I also appreciate the editorial production assistance of Annie Rose and Ben Thatcher and Sandra Kerka's attentive copyediting. I am very grateful to James Tucker, Jennifer Esala, Jared del Rosso, Erin Anderson, Inger Furseth, Erin Steuter, and anonymous reviewers for their helpful comments; and to Jordan Burke for his editorial assistance and suggestions. I also benefited greatly from Andrew Wink's photography skills.

The information in the timelines is derived from various sources including: Colin McEvedy (1985), *The Macmillan World History Factfinder*, New York: Macmillan; H. E. L. Mellersh (1999), *Chronology of World History*, volumes 1–4, Santa Barbara, CA: BC-CLIO; Derrick Mercer, ed. (1996), *Chronicle of the World*, London: Dorling Kindersley; Hans-Albrecht Schraepler (1997), *Directory of International Economic Organizations*, Washington, DC: Georgetown University Press; and Caroline Zilborg and Susan Gall, eds. (1997), *Women's Firsts*, Detroit, MI: Gale.

HOW TO USE THIS BOOK

As you read through the individual chapters in this book, you will find the following features designed to help you to develop a clear understanding of sociological theory and to apply it to everyday life.

Key Concepts   Each chapter opens with a list of its key concepts, presented in the order in which they appear in the chapter. They are printed in blue when they first appear in the text, and are defined in the glossaries at the end of each chapter and at the end of the book.

Chapter Menu   A menu gives you the main headings of the chapter that follows.

Biographical Note   These provide background information on the main theorists discussed in the chapter. Their names are given in bold when they first appear in the chapter.

Theorists' Writings   Each of the first three chapters has a chronological list of the major writings of the theorists discussed: Marx, Durkheim, and Weber.

Timelines   Where a historical framework will aid your understanding of the chapter, timelines list major events with their dates.

Conceptual Boxes   These introduce additional theoretical ideas or summarize points relevant to the chapter.

Contemporary Topical Applications   These features draw on information reported in the news about an event or issue that has particular salience for the concepts being discussed in the chapter. The stories highlight how particular everyday events can be used to illustrate or probe larger social processes.

Summary   The text of the chapter is summarized in a final paragraph or two.

Points to Remember   These list in bullet note form the main learning points of the chapter.

Glossary   At the end of each chapter its key concepts are listed again, this time in alphabetical order, and defined. The glossary at the end of the book combines the end-of-chapter glossaries to define all the key concepts covered in the book.

Questions for Review   At the end of each chapter, questions are listed that prompt you to discuss some of the overarching points of the chapter.

ABOUT THE WEBSITE

The *Introduction to Sociological Theory: Theorists, Concepts, and Their Applicability to the Twenty-First Century* companion website contains a range of resources created by the author for instructors teaching this book in university courses. Features include:

- Instructor's manual for each chapter, including
  - Note to the Instructor
  - News Resources that can be used to stimulate classroom discussion
  - Essay Assignment Questions
  - Exam Short Answer Questions
  - Multiple choice questions (and answers)
- PowerPoint teaching slides with contemporary analytical photographs and video links
- List of complementary primary readings
- Quote Bank

Instructors can access these resources at www.wiley.com/go/dillon

INTRODUCTION

SOCIOLOGICAL THEORY: A VIBRANT, LIVING TRADITION

KEY CONCEPTS

sociological theory	classical theory	scientific reasoning
concepts	canon	empiricism
conceptual frameworks	contemporary theory	positivist
pluralistic	Enlightenment	objectivity
macro	democracy	interpretive understanding
social structures	reason	emancipatory knowledge
micro	rationality	double-consciousness
culture	inalienable rights	
culture	utilitarianism	

CHAPTER MENU

Introduction to Sociological Theory: Theorists, Concepts, and Their Applicability to the Twenty-First Century,
Third Edition. Michele Dillon.
© 2020 John Wiley & Sons Ltd. Published 2020 by John Wiley & Sons Ltd.
Companion website: www.wiley.com/go/dillon

Timeline I.1	Major pre-Enlightenment influences, and events from the Enlightenment to the establishment of sociology
500 BC–AD 999 The Classical World 1000–1490 The Feudal Age 1490–1664 The Age of Discovery	
1599	Francis Bacon, *Essays*
1620	English Pilgrims arrive at Plymouth Rock, Massachusetts
1633	Galileo summoned by the Inquisition to defend his theory that the earth moves around the sun
1636	Harvard College founded
1637	René Descartes, "I think, therefore, I am"
1665–1774 The Enlightenment	
1670	Blaise Pascal, "Man is only a reed, the weakest thing in nature; but he is a thinking reed"
1687	Isaac Newton explains laws of motion and theories of gravitation
1689	John Locke, *On Civil Government*
1702	Cambridge University establishes faculty chairs in the sciences
1733	Voltaire praises British liberalism
1752	Benjamin Franklin invents a lightning conductor; demonstrates the identity of lightning and electricity
1762	Jean-Jacques Rousseau, *The Social Contract*
1771	The right to report parliamentary debates established in Britain
1775–1814 The Age of Revolution	
1775	American War of Independence; battles of Lexington and Concord (Massachusetts)
1776	British troops evacuate Boston; Declaration of Independence
1776	Adam Smith, *The Wealth of Nations*
1788	Bread riots in France

1789	Fall of the Bastille; beginning of the French Revolution; new French Constituent Assembly abolishes feudal rights and privileges
1791	Bill of Rights in America; first 10 amendments to the US Constitution
1792	Mary Wollstonecraft, *Vindication of the Rights of Woman*
1796	Freedom of the press established in France
1805	First factory to be lit by gaslight (in Manchester, England)
1807	Air pump developed for use in mines
1813	Jane Austen, *Pride and Prejudice*
1823	Jeremy Bentham, utilitarianism
1831	John Stuart Mill, *The Spirit of the Age*
1835–1840	Alexis de Tocqueville, *Democracy in America*
1837	Harriet Martineau, *Society in America*
1839	Comte gives sociology its name
1855	Harriet Martineau translates Comte's *Positive Philosophy*
1859	Charles Darwin, *The Origin of Species* (modern evolutionary theory)
1861–1865	American Civil War, the South (Confederates) versus the North (Union)
1865	US president Abraham Lincoln assassinated
1865	Thirteenth amendment to the US Constitution, abolishing slavery

Welcome to **sociological theory**. Theory, by definition, is abstract. This book illustrates the richness of sociological theory by emphasizing how its breadth of **concepts** or analytical ideas have practical application and explanatory relevance to daily life. It will introduce you to the major theorists whose writings and **conceptual frameworks** inform sociological thinking. It will equip you with the theoretical vocabulary necessary to appreciate the range of perspectives found in sociological theory. It will give you confidence to apply these ideas to the many sociological topics you study (e.g., inequality, crime, medical sociology, race, political sociology, family, gender, sexuality, culture, religion, community, globalization, etc.) and help you to think analytically about the many occurrences in daily life far beyond the classroom.

Topic I.1   Hotel rooms get plusher, adding to maids' injuries

"Some call it the 'amenities arms race,' some 'the battle of the beds.' It is a competition in which the nation's premier hotels are trying to have their accommodations resemble royal bedrooms. Superthick mattresses, plush duvets and decorative bed skirts have been added, and five pillows rather than the pedestrian three now rest on a king-size bed. Hilton markets these rooms as Suite Dreams, while Westin boasts of its heavenly beds. The beds may mean sweet dreams to hotel guests, but they mean pain to many of the nation's 350,000 hotel housekeepers. Several new studies [by unions and health scientists] have found that thousands of housekeepers are suffering arm, shoulder, and lower-back injuries … it is so strenuous a job that [housekeepers have] a higher risk of back disorders than autoworkers who assemble car doors … The problem, housekeepers say, is not just a heavier mattress, but having to rush because they are assigned the same number of rooms as before while being required to deal with far more per room: more pillows, more sheets, more amenities like bathrobes to hang up and coffee pots to wash. Ms. Reyes [a hotel housekeeper] complained that some days she must make 25 double beds, a task that entails taking off, and putting on, 100 pillowcases … Housekeepers who earn $17,300 a year on average, invariably stoop over to lift mattresses, some of which are only 14 inches off the floor. They frequently twist their backs as they tuck in the sheets, often three of them rather than the two of yesteryear. Since it can take 10 to 12 minutes a bed, a housekeeper who makes 25 beds a day frequently spends four to five hours on the task, lifting mattresses 150 to 200 times … [A Hilton spokesman] said the company had increased training to try to minimize harm to housekeepers … [and to ease] workloads … [and said that the unions are] pushing the injury issue as a smoke screen, largely to pressure hotel companies to agree to procedures making it easier to unionize workers."

Steven Greenhouse, "Hotel Rooms Get Plusher, Adding to Maids' Injuries." *New York Times* (April 21, 2006). © 2006 The New York Times. All rights reserved. Used by permission and protected by the Copyright Laws of the United States.

ANALYZING EVERYDAY SOCIAL LIFE

This short excerpt (Topic I.1) on housekeepers and hotel mattresses provides a single snapshot of contemporary society, but its elements can be used to highlight the different ways that sociological theorists approach the study of society. Karl Marx (1818–1883), a towering figure in the analysis of modern capitalism (see chapter 1), would focus on the forces of economic inequality and exploitation that underlie hotel maids' injuries. Marx's theory would highlight the extent to which capitalist pursuit of profit structures the service production process: Corporate executives develop efficient work practices that dictate how maids will work, and they also determine the low wage paid for such work. Ultimately, Marx would say, the pursuit of profit consolidates the economic or class inequality that is part and parcel of capitalism (see also Romero 1992; Sherman 2007). You might suggest that if the maids are unhappy, they should leave the hotel. But if they leave, what are their options? Very limited, Marx would respond. Because hotel maids (and other workers) have to live, they need money in order to survive (especially in a "welfare-to-work" society in which there is very little government economic support available to those who are unemployed long term). Therefore, although the maids are free to leave a particular hotel they are not free to withhold labor from every hotel – they must work someplace. Hence wage-workers must sell their labor on the job market, even if what they receive in exchange for their labor will always be significantly less than the profit the capitalist will make from their work. Although hotel owners must pay the many costs associated with the upkeep and running of a hotel, a large gap remains between the hotel maids' minimum wage (and waitresses, etc.; approx. $7 an hour) and the price paid by hotel guests for a one-night stay in the luxury hotel room ($399 and upwards) the maids clean.

Further, the competitive nature of capitalism and the economic competition between hotels mean that the profit-driven working conditions in one luxury hotel will not vary much from those in another. If a hotel company were to lose "the battle of the beds" in the competition for affluent customers, a decline in the hotel's profit may spell its demise. Low wages and occupational injuries, therefore, are what maids can expect, regardless of the particular hotel (whether the Westin or the Hilton). Moreover, if hotel maids aren't able to work as a result of their injuries, there will always be others waiting to take their place; one of the effects of globalization (a topic discussed in chapter 14) is to increase the competition between low-wage workers whose pool is expanded by the increasing numbers of immigrant and migrant workers available to the low-paying service industries (e.g., Chen 2015; Ehrenreich and Hochschild 2002; Sassen 2007).

In focusing on the profit and economic relations within capitalist societies, Marx also alerts us to how ideology, that is, a society's taken-for-granted ideas about work, achievement, freedom, consumption, luxury, etc., determines how we explain and justify all sorts of social phenomena, whether social inequality, the Olympic Games, or the latest consumer fad. Marx – and more recent theorists influenced partly by Marx, such as Critical Theorists (see chapter 5) – would argue that the ideology of freedom – typically used to denote political freedom and democracy – has in today's world become the freedom to shop. We all (more or less) want the plush consumer lifestyle that we associate with luxury hotels, a pursuit promoted by the (globalizing) capitalist class, and especially by advertising, mass media, and pop culture industries. Thus the popularity of, for example, "Louie," a Blood Raw/Young Jeezy song celebrating Louis Vuitton merchandise. Similarly, Kanye West's "Flashing Lights" reminds us that consumption trumps everything else. Indeed, Marx would argue that it is largely because hotel housekeepers (and their families and neighbors) buy into the allure of consumption that they consent to work as hard as they do, despite their injuries, and without fully realizing or acknowledging the inequality of the capitalist system with its ever-growing gap between the rich and the poor.

Max Weber (1864–1920) (his last name is pronounced *vayber*), also offers an analysis of modern capitalism. But unlike Marx, he orients us to the various subjective motivations and meanings that lead social actors – either individually, or collectively as workers, hotel companies, trade unions, religious organizations, states, or transnational alliances (e.g., the European Union [EU]) – to behave as they do (see chapter 3). Weber, like Marx, highlights strategic or instrumental interests among other motivating forces underlying social behavior. In particular, hotel owners and unions pursue their own economic and political interests by making cost–benefit assessments of which courses of action are the most expedient given the respective objectives of each group. Hotel companies, for example, are suspicious of the union's objectives beyond the specific issue of housekeeper injuries: The companies are concerned that their strategic interests (in making money, hiring particular workers, and competing with other hotel chains) will be undermined if their work force is unionized. And union leaders, too, are concerned if they think that workers can garner a good wage deal without the union's intervention. Not surprisingly, as some contemporary theorists highlight (e.g., Ralph Dahrendorf; see chapter 6), intergroup conflict is common in democratic societies as various economic and other interest groups compete for greater recognition of their respective agendas.

Life, however, is not all about economic and strategic interests. One of Weber's theoretical achievements was to demonstrate that values and beliefs also matter. Values orient social action, a point subsequently emphasized by Talcott Parsons, an American theorist who was highly influential from the 1940s to the 1980s in shaping sociological thinking and research (see chapter 4). Individuals, groups, organizations, and whole countries are motivated by values – by commitments to particular understandings of friendship, family, patriotism, environmental sustainability, education, religion, etc. Subjective values, such as commitment to their family and providing for their children, may explain why hotel housekeepers work as hard as they do; indeed many immigrant women leave their children and families in their home country while they work abroad earning money to send home so their children can have a more economically secure life (e.g., England 2005; Sassen 2007). The strong cultural value of individualism in the US, for example, also helps to explain why labor unions have a much harder time gaining members and wielding influence in the US than in Western European countries such as the UK, Ireland, and France. The historical-cultural influence of Protestantism in the US and its emphasis on self-reliance and individual responsibility means that Americans tend to believe that being poor is largely an individual's own responsibility (and a sign of moral weakness), a belief that impedes the expansion of state-funded social welfare programs.

As recognized by both Marx and Weber, differences in economic resources are a major source of inequality (or of stratification) in society, determining individuals' and groups' rankings relative to one another (e.g., upper-class, middle-class, lower-class strata). Additionally, Weber, unlike Marx, argues that social inequality is not only based on differences in income but also associated with differences in lifestyle or social status. Weber and contemporary theorists influenced by his conceptualization of the multiple sources of inequality – such as Pierre Bourdieu (see chapter 13) – argue that individuals and groups acquire particular habits that demonstrate and solidify social class differences. Such differences are evident not only between the upper and lower classes but also between those who are closely aligned economically. This helps to explain why affluent people stay in premier rather than economy hotels and why some affluent people prefer the Ritz Carlton to the Westin. For similar status reasons, some women will spend hundreds of dollars on a Louis Vuitton handbag rather than buy a cheaper, though equally functional one by Coach.

The cultural goals (e.g., consumption, economic success) affirmed in society are not always readily attainable. Children who grow up in poor neighborhoods with underfunded schools are disadvantaged by their limited access to the social institutions (e.g., school) that provide the culturally approved means or pathways to academic, occupational, and economic success (e.g., MacLeod 2008). Thus, as the American sociologist Robert Merton (see chapter 4) shows, society creates deviance (e.g., stealing) as a result of the mismatch between cultural goals (e.g., consumer lifestyle) and blocked access to the acceptable institutional means to attain those goals.

Deviance is a social fact and is "normal" – as classical theorist Emile Durkheim (1858–1917) emphasizes, that is, normal because it comes from society and exists in all societies as indicated by crime rates. Yet "too much" deviance (or crime) may threaten the social order. Social order and cohesion are Durkheim's core theoretical preoccupation (see chapter 2). He is basically interested in what knits society together, that is, what binds and ties individuals into society. Therefore, rather than focusing on what Marx, for example, would see as exploitation, Durkheim would highlight the social interdependence suggested in our story of the hotel maids. For Durkheim, hotel owners, workers, guests, unions, and occupational health scientists are all part of the social collectivity, a collectivity whose effective functioning is dependent on all doing their part in the social order. In like manner, Talcott Parsons sees social institutions such as the economy, the family, and the political and legal systems as working separately but also interdependently to produce an effectively functioning society (see chapter 4).

Social interdependence for Durkheim is underscored by the fact that without guests, for example, there would be no hotel maids and no hotel owners. This is well understood by people living in seaside towns; business is seasonal and when hotels/restaurants close for the winter, there are fewer work opportunities. Durkheim is not interested in analyzing (unequal) economic relations in the hotel industry or the historical origins of tourism. Rather, what is relevant is how collective social forces (e.g., occupations, hotels, tourism, consumption patterns, and all other social things) shape, constrain, and regulate individual, group, and institutional behavior. In the process, these social forces tie individuals, groups, and institutions into interdependent social relationships.

Tipping hotel maids and restaurant servers is not required by law. But we are nudged into doing so – even though no one other than the maid can tell whether or not you left money for her in the hotel room – by the strong collective force of social custom. As Durkheim would stress, all social customs (and laws) both come from society and function to affirm and bolster the interdependence of social relations. Moreover, as contemporary network theorists demonstrate, even *weak* ties among individuals, among acquaintances who occasionally share information either on Facebook or when they run into each other on the street, are socially beneficial to individuals (in finding a good restaurant, or a job, etc.) and to enhancing community well-being (e.g., in mobilizing people to participate in neighborhood projects; see chapter 7).

In contrast to Durkheim, exchange theorists such as George Homans and Peter Blau (see chapter 7) emphasize the use value of social exchange. We tip and give gifts and invite friends to dinner with the expectation that this will yield some specific return to us. Therefore, when I tip the hotel maid even though I don't expect to return to that hotel (and with the tip-related expectation of better service), I must be getting something in return, such as the validation of my own status relative to the maid – perhaps found in the slight nod of the head or smile when passing the maid and her cart in the corridor. For exchange theorists, exchange relationships are not just those based on money (as for Marx). They are also based on the exchange of status (see also Bourdieu, chapter 13), information, friendship, advice, housework, political influence, etc., and the power imbalances in relationships (e.g., between friends, spouses, governments, etc.) that they reflect and perpetuate. In all relationships, rational choice theorists contend, we assess what we get and what to give on the basis of its probable use value to us as individuals (i.e., resource maximization; see chapter 7).

So far I have not commented on the fact that the hotel worker quoted in our excerpt is a woman. Indeed, "maid" is a gendered word, that is, used to denote a woman and "women's work." Male domestic servants, by contrast, are referred to in more elegant language as "butlers." They, as depicted in *Downton Abbey*, have a higher status and more independence even as they are, nonetheless, at the beck and call of their masters/superiors. Today, despite advances in women's equality, women comprise a disproportionate share of low-wage service workers. Feminist standpoint theorists such as Dorothy Smith and Patricia Hill Collins draw attention women's inequality (see chapter 10). In particular, they highlight the day-in/day-out routines and experiences of women who make 25 beds a day, and who, after the paid workday ends, make the beds and cook dinner and do many other chores for their families. Feminist theorists also underscore that women's chores, experiences, and opportunities are typically different from men's, and when similar, women's work is rewarded very differently than men's work (at work and at home); women continue, for example, to remain on the margins of the decision-making power elites in society (see C. Wright Mills; see chapter 6).

The phenomenological tradition (see chapter 9) emphasizes the significance of ordinary everyday knowledge in defining individuals' concrete "here-and-now" social realities. Partly influenced by phenomenology, feminist standpoint theorists (e.g., Smith) underscore how the knowledge deriving from women's everyday experiences is very different from the knowledge that is recognized as the legitimate, objective knowledge in society. Whether in politics, in corporate offices, in law courts, or even among sociologists, the knowledge that comes from women's experiences – as mothers, homemakers, and in the "man-made" world of work and public life – tends to be demeaned. It does not fit well with the male-centered (see chapter 10) and indeed heterosexist bias (see chapter 11) that characterizes sociology and other established sources of knowledge.

Feminist theorists (e.g., Collins), along with race theorists (see chapter 12) and globalization scholars (see chapter 14), would also highlight that it is not just women but particular types of women who tend to be employed in the low-wage service sector, namely, women of minority racial and ethnic background, many of whom are immigrants. Many feminist scholars, therefore (e.g., Collins), focus on exploring how the multiple intersecting experiences of inequality – of gender, race, class, immigration, sexuality, etc. – shape the life chances and experiences of women. Feminist and postcolonial theorists (e.g., Paul Gilroy; see chapter 12) further attend to how advertising and mass media promote particular cultures of femininity and masculinity conveying gender- and race-based messages that perpetuate social inequality.

Feminist scholars also draw attention to the fact that a lot of women's work is not just physical body work (e.g., lifting heavy mattresses) but emotion work, whether in mothering (e.g., Chodorow 1978), or as work for pay (e.g., Arlie Hochschild; see chapter 10). Hotel housekeepers do mostly "backstage" work (as elaborated by Erving Goffman; see chapter 8) – that is, cleaning toilets, making beds, etc. – preparing bedrooms whose presentation will impress guests and their supervisors. Hotel housekeepers have fewer opportunities than receptionists and waitresses to smile at guests. But it is women far more than men who are expected to smile – at home, at work, and *as* work – irrespective of body pain or of how they are actually feeling (e.g., Hochschild; see chapter 10). This is what is entailed in "doing gender," as ethnomethodologists would argue (see chapter 9) – the everyday procedures or methods that women use on an ongoing basis to establish their credibility as women (as mothers, wives, teachers, colleagues, friends, etc.) in a society where women are still unequal relative to men. Women in Western society have achieved great advances in equality. Yet gender-specific roles and role expectations (see Parsons; chapter 4), are still powerful forces, a point underscored by controversies over gender inequities and stereotyping at Google and other high-tech companies (see chapter 4, Topic 4.3); and more generally by the fact that in 2016 women earned 80.5 percent of the wages of men for comparable work (Leubsdorf 2017). Moreover, as Paula England's research shows women predominate in caregiving occupations (England 2005) and working wives do more housework than their husbands (Bittman et al. 2003). And there are gender-subordinated ways of self-presentation; in advertisements, for example, women still smile up at men, and men smile down at women, thus reaffirming the gender-role hierarchy (see Goffman; chapter 8). This is a social order that, when disrupted by a successful woman business executive or politician, for example, may provoke negative comments that seek to put them in their (gendered) place; a response that helps illustrate the relative fragility of the collectively produced order that underlies all social life (see Harold Garfinkel; chapter 9).

Although the self-presentation of bodies is a core part of everyday social behavior (underscored by the rising prevalence of cosmetic surgery and dermatology; see Chapter 8), Michel Foucault sees the body more generally as a targeted object of social control. For Foucault, all social institutions – the church, the prison, the school, the clinic, the government – have made control of the body, what bodies do, and what bodies are allowed to do with other bodies (e.g., sexual practices) a primary objective, the results of which inform what we regard as "normal" sexuality (see chapter 11). Just think, for example, of the public controversies about shared gender-neutral bathrooms; these debates convey assumptions about the nature of gender, sexuality, bodies, and what particular bodies do and can (or should) do.

Finally, the hotel excerpt (see Topic I.1) also points to something that many sociologists emphasize: facts (i.e., the data) do not speak for themselves. Regardless of whether the facts are presented by Twitter users, media reporters, business leaders, unions, scientists, or academics, their presentation and interpretation will depend on the purpose for which they are being used. Thus, the occupational injury data referenced in our hotel excerpt are contested by those (unions and hotel companies) who have a particular interest in the meaning and implications of those facts. Whereas some see the maids' annual income of $17,300 as clear evidence of exploitation (e.g., Marx), others construe it as a sign of great job opportunities in the US compared, let's say, to Guatemala, where an average woman's wage might be $2,000 a year. Yet other researchers might consider the issue of wages less relevant given that it is not money but an individual's social ties and community support, for example, that buffer against despair and suicide (e.g., Durkheim; chapter 2).

The same objective facts, therefore, may be interpreted differently depending on the political context in which they are being discussed. Importantly too, the interpretation of facts depends on the theoretical lens used. Different theorists make different assumptions and prompt us to focus on some things and not others, and they may therefore interpret the same apparent reality quite differently. Thus theorists such as Jean Baudrillard, for example, would argue that luxury hotels comprise not an authentic reality but an artificial and glossy "hyperreality" in which ordinary, everyday routines (e.g., eating a hot dog) are made into lavish, Disney-like fantasies and spectacles (see chapter 15). Other theorists emphasize a "risk society" confronting individuals and society as a whole with insecurities and dilemmas that are not easily resolved (e.g., Beck; Giddens, see chapter 15).

IMMERSION IN THEORY

By getting to know the array of theorists and ideas that comprises sociological theory, you will develop the competence to thoughtfully analyze the complexity of social life. Theoretical immersion will enable you to adopt an analytical attitude – to see beyond your own experiences and impressions in ways that help you recognize how social patterns and forces shape the phenomena characterizing our world. One of the advantages of knowing sociological theory is that it allows us to try to make sense of virtually any aspect of social behavior we might be interested in. Although different theorists tend to emphasize different aspects of society and social behavior, there is conceptual overlap in their ideas and in the subject matter they address (e.g., economic inequality). Overall, as a body of interrelated analytical ideas, sociological theory provides a **pluralistic** and varied though comprehensive resource by which we can understand and explain social life.

Sociological theory focuses on how **macro**, or large-scale, **social structures** such as capitalism (e.g., the economic structure of the hotel industry); bureaucracies; occupational, gender, political, and racial structures; and migration shape the organization of the social environment; how these structures constrain the choices and opportunities available to any individual, family, or larger collectivity (e.g., a particular social class or gender or geographically located group); and thus how they shape the patterns of social action and interaction that occur. Theorists also pay attention to the **microdynamics** of individual experience (e.g., of particular hotel workers in particular hotels) and interpersonal interaction in and across the diverse contexts of everyday life. Sociological theorists emphasize the constraining force exerted by social structures on individual, group, organizational, and collective behavior, as well as on the **culture**(s) – the strategies of action and the ways of thinking and feeling – in any particular society (or among any particular group, region, or class in society). At the same time, they are attentive to the impact of culture (e.g., ideas, habits, customs, and beliefs) in shaping social structures and institutions (e.g., the economy, law, education, government, religion, family, mass media). Sociological theorists affirm, moreover, the **agency** that individuals exert personally (e.g., voting, choosing an occupation or a spouse) and collectively (e.g., through social movements) in responding to, reworking, creatively resisting, and transforming (highly stable) social structures and social processes (e.g., the gendered character of inequality); though as sociologists we are also highly cognizant of the tension that invariably exists between individual agency and structural and cultural constraints.

CLASSICAL AND CONTEMPORARY THEORY

It is customary in sociology to talk about classical theory and contemporary theory. The term **classical theory** refers primarily to the writings of Karl Marx (1818–1883), Emile Durkheim (1858–1917), and Max Weber (1864–1920). Their writings produced what sociologists acknowledge as the classic or foundational texts in sociology; their ideas constitute the **canon** or body of conceptual knowledge that all sociologists are expected to know. Hence, this book begins with Marx, Durkheim, and Weber, and I give their individual ideas greater elaboration than contemporary successors. Other early sociologists include **Harriet Martineau** (1802–1876) and Georg Simmel (1858–1918) whose important contributions I acknowledge throughout the book. Previously overlooked early theorists, such as Charlotte Perkins Gilman (1860–1935), and the black sociologist William E.B. Du Bois (1868–1963), are also recognized for their groundbreaking sociological analyses, especially of gender (see chapter 10) and racial inequality (see chapter 12).

BIOGRAPHICAL NOTE

Harriet Martineau (1802–1876) was born in England into a relatively prosperous Unitarian family, which suffered a great economic loss upon the death of her father. Under pressure to support herself, but constrained by her own weak health – she was deaf by age 20 – Harriet worked as a dressmaker before succeeding as a writer. As well as translating Comte and writing sociology she also wrote nonfiction. Martineau was popular in London's intellectual and literary circles; she was close, for example, to Charles Darwin (founder of biological evolutionism) and his brother (see Hoecker-Drysdale 1992).

What comprises **contemporary theory** is more open ended. Although called *contemporary*, the theorists who are customarily referred to in this way include sociologists such as Talcott Parsons, Max Horkheimer, C. Wright Mills, George Homans, and Erving Goffman, who wrote in the decades around the mid-twentieth century (1940s–1970s), as well as those whose ideas came to prominence during and after the 1980s such as Dorothy Smith, Patricia Hill Collins, Arlie Hochschild, James Coleman, Michel Foucault, Pierre Bourdieu, and Immanuel Wallerstein. Many of these theorists are dead, but like the classical theorists, their ideas are still relevant in helping us understand contemporary society. A survey of current sociology professors asking whom they would categorize and how they would rank the importance of contemporary theorists would undoubtedly produce some variation. Nonetheless, there would be a fairly strong consensus that sociology students should have familiarity with the ideas of all or at least almost all of the theorists included in this book, though depending on a given sociologist's particular areas of interest, some might give greater prominence to the ideas of some theorists over others.

The relevance of particular theorists or of a particular concept will necessarily vary depending on the specific issue you are interested in understanding/explaining. This book aims to provide you with sufficient grounding in sociological theory so that you will be confident in evaluating and applying the theorists/constructs that offer the strongest explanatory framework for the specific questions of interest to you.

SOCIETAL TRANSFORMATION AND THE ORIGINS OF SOCIOLOGY

Sociology is a relatively recent discipline. Unlike philosophy, theology, astronomy, and mathematics, for example, all of which have their origins in medieval times, sociology had its birth in the nineteenth century. Why is this the case? For a scientific discipline to emerge as an independent field of study, certain conditions have to be present. If you think for a moment about what sociology does, you will begin to see that it could not really have emerged any earlier than it did. Sociology is about analyzing (and evaluating and critiquing) social structures. For this to happen, social structures have to be seen as having a *social* existence – they have to be seen as human-social creations and thus amenable to criticism and change – rather than being seen as natural or divinely ordained structures. This may seem like an obvious point, but from a historical perspective it is not so obvious. For many centuries, in both the East and the West, monarchs and emperors were seen as deriving their authority from divine sources. Can you contemplate an imaginary sociologist in the twelfth century trying to analyze the legitimacy or the foundation of such authority?

Just think of the current situation in North Korea or in Syria: political leaders go to great lengths to suppress any challenge to their authority, even refusing entry to foreign aid workers trying to distribute food supplies to famine-threatened or displaced people. Or think of China. Although a major player in the global economy, it routinely represses individuals' basic rights, including the freedom of speech. In some societies today, the freedom to probe social reality, and to identify the social forces that underlie economic and social inequalities, is severely constrained. You can imagine, then, how even more preposterous it would have seemed in earlier historical eras, when the divine right of kings was accepted as a natural and obvious truth, to suggest that it is social rather than divine or natural forces that structure the order and organization of social life. Thus it is not accidental that the seeds allowing sociology to emerge as a discipline were sown during the eighteenth century, the era of the **Enlightenment** and democratic revolutions in France and America.

Though the eighteenth century was still characterized by a power structure consolidated among relatively few wealthy landowners and members of the nobility, the nineteenth century witnessed a radical shift of power associated with the Industrial Revolution. The rise of large factories and the rapid expansion of trade meant an increase in the middle class and a large migration of people from the rural countryside to the city. These shifts in socioeconomic arrangements accelerated democracy and the power struggles regarding voting rights and the status of the monarchy that dominated the late eighteenth century.

The French Revolution and the storming of the Bastille (July 14, 1789) marked the revolt of the nonprivileged masses of ordinary people against the feudal privileges and rights long enjoyed by the monarchy and the aristocracy in France. It overturned the inherited privileges of the few in favor of equality and freedom for all. It rejected the long-standing practice whereby what family you were born into determined your lifelong status, whether among the monarchy, nobles, and aristocrats or among the peasants. The French Revolution also marked the beginning of the decline of the power of the established Catholic Church in France and its alliance with the monarchy and ushered in the political ethos so important in French and American law, that church and state are separate spheres.

The American Revolutionary War (1775–1783) was motivated by a similar rejection of the inherited authority of kings and queens; indeed, by boldly proclaiming independence from Britain with the Declaration of Independence in 1776 (July 4), the Americans affirmed political equality. These were radical political events. Up until the American and French revolutions, individuals were accustomed to thinking that it was normal and right that they should be subject to a ruling power that was not of their choosing. And for most people, this ruling power was represented by kings and queens. Instead, the revolutionaries argued, the authority of government leaders should derive from the will of the people; hence the opening line in the US Constitution: "We the People …"

THE ENLIGHTENMENT: THE ELEVATION OF REASON, DEMOCRACY, AND SCIENCE

The ideas that American and French revolutionaries had about the will of the people, and the authority of **democracy** over monarchy, came from Enlightenment thought (e.g., Ham 1999, p. 856). Although Enlightenment thinkers (e.g., Jean-Jacques Rousseau, Immanuel Kant, David Hume, Thomas Jefferson) came from different countries and different family backgrounds and wrote about different things, they all emphasized the importance of **reason** *and* **rationality**. Enlightenment writers argued that reason was the individual's naturally endowed gift; that each of us, by virtue of being human, possesses the innate ability to think or to reason about things and about ourselves. Reason gives the individual **inalienable rights** (human rights) that no external authority (e.g., a monarch, the church, the state) can strip away. In the Enlightenment view, therefore, individuals should use reason to determine their destiny and to achieve the political freedom and social progress worthy of their humanity. For Enlightenment philosophers, reason not only allows but *requires* humankind to "see the light" and thus to move away from reliance on the nonrational explanations represented by religion, myth, and tradition.

THE INDIVIDUAL AND SOCIETY

Given the innate human ability to reflect on and reason about things, Enlightenment thinkers argued that humans should be able to use reason to govern themselves as individuals and in their relations with others. In this view, collective life (i.e., society and its governance) should be based on principles of reason rather than deference to nonrational forces such as those exemplified by the traditional power of the monarchy. This principle may seem obvious – it is, after all, the core principle of democratic societies. It is not self-evident, however, how society ought to protect and support individual freedom while simultaneously bolstering the well-being of society as a whole. The complex relation of the individual to society is an underlying theme of both classical and contemporary sociology. Sociologists examine the autonomy of the individual in relation to social institutions (e.g., the economy, education, law, marriage, etc.), social relationships, and other social forces (e.g., sexism, immigration, racism, globalization, heteronormativity, etc.).

Individual rights

Prior to the establishment of sociology, early political theorists debated the issue of individual rights vis-à-vis the state and society.[1] The seventeenth-century English philosopher Thomas Hobbes (1588–1679) believed that individuals are necessarily selfish and, if left to their own devices, would produce social chaos and disorder. The Hobbesian view is well depicted in William Golding's novel *The Lord of the Flies*, where a group of adolescents, shipwrecked on a desert island, create a society full of viciousness and mayhem. Hobbes used his view of human nature as brutish to argue in favor of a strong monarch who would have very few limits on his power to control individuals; this view sat well with monarchical feudal Europe.

Hobbes's view contrasts with that of John Locke (1632–1704), another English philosopher, writing less than 100 years after Hobbes. According to Locke, humans are born basically good and, therefore, they should not have to surrender their rights to a strong monarch in order to survive. Rather, Locke argued, individuals yield certain rights to, or make a contract with, a government that is responsible to them and that performs functions that maintain social order (e.g., regulating crimes against private property). This view of the protective role of the state fitted well with the growing wealth and power of the English middle classes resulting from the Industrial Revolution (see Smelser 1959).

Utilitarianism

Another important strand in Locke's philosophy was **utilitarianism**. This thesis argues that rational, self-determining individuals act on their own rational self-interests and by doing so, they simultaneously ensure their own individual well-being and that of society as a whole. If individuals can be trusted to make decisions that are useful to advancing their own self-interests, then by extension, the government does not need to intervene and regulate human-social behavior. These ideas, often referred to as liberal enlightenment thought, were also expressed by Adam Smith (1723–1790), the eighteenth-century Scottish economist who emphasized the self-interested nature of individual economic exchange. Similarly, too, English philosophers John Stuart Mill (1806–1873) and Harriet Taylor Mill (1807–1858) advocated an understanding of society based on self-interested action. Both

Mills believed that women should have the right to vote not only as a way to maximize their own particular self-interests but also to constrain men's self-interests. (Self-interest is a prominent theme in many political and economic debates today, and in sociological theorizing emphasizing exchange and resource maximization behavior; see chapter 7.)

Social contract

The French philosopher Jean-Jacques Rousseau (1712–1778) focused on the larger community rather than individual self-interests. He argued that the best way to regulate individuals' different interests was through the voluntary coming together of individuals as citizens committed to the common good. He envisioned individuals adhering to a social contract – principles about the collective political life of society as a civic community – that gave priority to the good of the whole community rather than to advancing particular self-interests. Of course, what constitutes the common good is itself something that is highly contested today. On any issue, questions regarding what rights and whose rights to favor are necessarily complicated. Reasonable solutions tend to be those that aim for some sort of balance among competing interests and that work in practice toward producing social consensus.

Figure I.1 With social progress comes a preoccupation with social order. Source: Author.

Socially situating the individual

Sociological theory fully affirms the Enlightenment view of individual rationality and the related belief that political and social structures emerge from society rather than being divinely prescribed. At the same time, sociologists depart from the Enlightenment emphasis that the self-determining, rational individual alone is largely responsible for his or her destiny. Sociologists emphasize that although individuals have free will, their behavior in society is not freely determined by them alone. Rather, it is shaped and constrained by social structures and by how particular norms and ideas get structured into everyday ways of thinking about and doing things. In other words, the sociological lens frames the individual within their social context, that is, the social environment that always and necessarily surrounds, envelops, and is acted on by the individual. Sociologists thus examine how particular social circumstances and forms of social organization produce particular social outcomes.

SCIENTIFIC REASONING

Enlightenment thinking, as I have highlighted, brought recognition to the human-social origins of political structures. Another corollary of its emphasis on human rationality was the elevation of science – **scientific reasoning** – as the canon of truth, that is, as the only valid explanatory logic in a modern society. Like the idea of democracy, the Enlightenment affirmation of scientific reason was also grounded in the work of earlier philosophers. One particularly important influence was the emphasis placed on **empiricism** by Francis Bacon (1561–1626) and other British philosophers (including Locke and David Hume, 1711–1776). Empiricism gives primacy to observation and experience rather than abstract reasoning. It maintains that knowledge based on scientific data-gathering methods is the only knowledge that matters. In this view, scientific principles and scientific explanations have a necessary superiority over the use of any other type of argument including appeals, for example, to nonrational arguments based on tradition, religious faith, or some superstition. Scientific reasoning requires visible, demonstrated evidence or positive proof that something exists or happened and that x causes y, or that x offers a reasonable explanation as to why y occurred or is likely to happen.

These principles of scientific reasoning are at the core of modernity, and they may seem somewhat obvious. But only 400 years ago Giordano Bruno (1548–1600), an Italian priest and philosopher, was sentenced to death, in part for advocating that the sun (rather than the earth) is the center of our planetary system. Copernicus (1473–1543) and Galileo (1564–1642) had to recant similar views in order to escape censure by the Catholic Church. It was not that Galileo was led astray by being a bad scientist or a poor empiricist. He was, after all, the inventor of the telescope, and by pointing it at the moon and showing the moon's craters, he was able to disprove the erroneous belief – held since the time of Socrates and the ancient Greeks – that heavenly bodies (planets, moons) were simply well-polished crystal balls (Feyerabend 1979). Galileo got into trouble because he dared to challenge beliefs that were held as core truths grounded in a religiously based worldview that was accepted as being beyond empirical refutation. The conflict between religion and science did not end with the Enlightenment, as highlighted by public debates over evolution and creationism in the US, for example, and in Turkey (where the government in 2017 prohibited the teaching of evolution in high school). In any event, our contemporary view of science as being able to refute nonempirically grounded beliefs is a relatively new development (and not without controversy, even today; see Topic I.2).

In sum, the Enlightenment was of critical importance for sociology. Its emphasis on reason meant that reason could be applied not only to reflect about the self but also to reflect about and study the self in society, and the social structures that characterize any given society. Further, by emphasizing the acquisition of knowledge through scientific empirical reasoning, it opened up a unique place for what would come to be defined as sociology. Sociology was envisioned as a discipline that would provide a reasoned, scientific analysis of social life: it would illuminate the impact of social forces on societal processes, thus displacing the pre-Enlightenment view that society was divinely ordained.

THE ESTABLISHMENT OF SOCIOLOGY AS SCIENCE: AUGUSTE COMTE AND HARRIET MARTINEAU

The Enlightenment's affirmation of scientific rationality, and the notion of social authority derived from a social contract among individuals, paved the way for the emergence of sociology as an intellectual discipline. **Auguste Comte** (1798–1857), the figure most associated with the initial establishment of sociology, embraced the Enlightenment's scientific approach and adapted it to the study of human society. Comte was a French philosopher and truly a child of the Enlightenment. He believed that a science of society was not only possible but necessary to social progress.

Topic I.2   "Post-truth" society, and what to call untruths

The process of gathering and analyzing data, and inferences about what the data mean and how they should be understood, are open to different approaches. But the truth uncovered – what the facts or the data show – is accepted as impartial, evidence-based truth. Evidence-based truth is accepted unless subsequently proven false by a changing social reality and/or a new scientific discovery that may temper the known facts; we thus say that science, including social research, is an inductive, empirically grounded process.

For years before he himself ran for political office, Donald Trump frequently asserted that Barack Obama was not born in America (though he was: in Hawaii on August 4, 1961). Obama was dogged by this false accusation, one that was not denounced as false by other leading Republicans, and it continued even though he released his birth certificate demonstrating proof of his US birth. Trump's penchant for "uttering untruths" was a routine part of his own presidential campaign and pervaded his presidency from his inauguration onwards, so much so that amid the whirls of misinformation, the notion of **post-truth society** gained currency. Among other falsehoods, Trump and his senior staff repeatedly overstated the size of the crowd at his inauguration even though various official figures contradicted these assertions. One of his senior aides in a television interview defended these assertions as "alternative facts." The interviewer Chuck Todd responded that "alternative facts are not facts. They are falsehoods." How to deal with the issue of "provable falsehoods" has become controversial among reputable journalists and news organizations. Concerns about how to distinguish between "truth" and "lies" intensified due to the Trump administration's attacks on the "fake journalism" of reputable mainstream media and its denial of the scientific consensus on climate change as well as its more general attack on science as "fake science." These attacks prompted a broad array of scientists (including sociologists) to participate in an unprecedented March for Science, in Washington, D.C., and in similar rallies in several other cities on Earth Day, April 22, 2017. Fact-checker columns (used for many years by the *New York Times*) comparing Trump's assertions and objective data became more pervasive as various news outlets as well as scientific organizations, including the American Sociological Association, emphasized that "now more than ever" we need evidence-based analysis and policymaking.

Reputable journalists and editors struggle, however, over whether and how to draw a line between "falsehoods" and "lies." Unlike the *New York Times* and CNN, for example, who use both words, *The Wall Street Journal*'s editor in chief Gerard Baker (2017, p. A15) explained why he would "be careful about using the word 'lie.' Lie implies much more than just saying that something is false. It implies a deliberate intent to mislead….It's not because I don't believe that Mr. Trump has said things that are untrue. And nor is it because I believe that when he says things that are untrue we should refrain from pointing them out. This is exactly what the Journal has done. Mr. Trump has a record of saying things that are, as far as the available evidence tells us, untruthful…[and] it's reasonable to infer that Mr. Trump should know that these statements are untrue….[but] The word 'lie' conveys a moral as well as a factual judgment….If we are to use the term "lie" in our reporting, then we have to be confident about the subject's state of knowledge and his moral intent….What matters is that we report the story and find the truth… and to point out when [people] say things that are untrue. But I'm content for the most part to leave the judgment about motive – and mendacity – to our readers who are more than capable of making up their own minds about what constitutes a lie." *The Economist* (2017, p. 71) similarly pointed out that although Mr. Trump says things that are "nakedly false" and nonsense – and may actually be deluded in believing them as true because of his grandiosity and attachment to conspiracy theories – there is a difference between a false statement and a lie (intent to deceive). Citing the Oxford English Dictionary, it noted that "Falsehood is…the wider word" because it "covers lying and 'uttered untruth in general.'"

EVOLUTIONARY PROGRESS AND AUGUSTE COMTE'S VISION OF SOCIOLOGY

Comte had a highly ambitious vision for sociology. In this he was influenced by his intellectual collaborator, Claude Henri de Saint-Simon (1760–1825). Though a French aristocrat, Saint-Simon renounced his privileges during the French Revolution and fought as a soldier with the French army against the British in the American War of Independence (Taylor 1975: 14–15). He was driven by "the desire to do what is of most use to the progress of the *science of man*" (Saint-Simon 1813 in Taylor 1975: 111, italics in original). Toward this end, he praised the superiority of science and empiricism – positive science, that is, "a doctrine based on observation" (1810 in Taylor 1975: 107), and argued for a science of society, one whose knowledge would provide a blueprint, a map, for implementing progressive forms of social organization.

Building on Saint-Simon's trust in the power of science to produce calculated results to advance social progress, Comte believed that sociology could be the science of humanity. He envisioned a **positivist** sociology – paralleling Saint-Simon's emphasis on the superiority of an observation-based "positive science." In Comte's view, sociology would focus only on *observable* data; it would approach its subject matter with the same **objectivity** and impartiality of physical scientists, with the same systematic attention to processes and causes, just like biologists studying plants. We don't expect biologists' empirical observations of plant life to be affected by their values or social background. And so too, Comte believed that social life could be similarly studied, that is, objectively, by sociologists who would approach their subject matter with the same detachment a biologist or a physicist brings to laboratory experiments. Sociology would be what Comte called the "Positive Philosophy" – a field whose knowledge of humanity would be determined by empirical findings, not speculation, and by the affirmation only of that which is discoverable and objectively evident in society. Comte explained:

> All good intellects have repeated, since Bacon's time, that there can be no real knowledge but that which is based on observed facts. This is incontestable, in our present advanced age … the first characteristic of the Positive Philosophy is that it regards all phenomena as subjected to invariable natural *Laws*. Our business

BIOGRAPHICAL NOTE

Auguste Comte (1798–1857) was born into an aristocratic Catholic family in France; he studied science and for many years was the private secretary and collaborator of Claude Henri de Saint-Simon (1760–1825), who emphasized an observation-based, positivist social scientific method. Comte elaborated a "Positive Philosophy" for the study of humanity, and won renown for coining the term "sociology," a word designed to capture his belief that a "social physics," a science that would emulate the natural sciences, could discover laws explaining society (see Blumberg 1974).

is … to pursue an accurate discovery of these Laws, with a view to reducing them to the smallest possible number … Our real business is to analyze accurately the circumstances of phenomena, and to connect them by the natural relations of succession and resemblance … Theologians and metaphysicians may imagine and refine about such questions [about the nature of life]; but positive philosophy rejects them … Now that the human mind has grasped celestial [astronomy] and terrestrial physics [physics, chemistry, and physiology] … there remains one science, to fill up the series of sciences of observation – Social physics. This is what men have now most need of. (Comte 1855/1974: 28–30)

In Comte's view, sociology – what he calls "social physics" in the quotation – would represent a progressive advance on all other disciplines. Just as each new generation tends to think of themselves as being more advanced, more liberated, more sophisticated than their parents' generation, this view of a constantly evolving progress was very much a part of how Enlightenment thinkers thought about humanity. It was also present (in different ways) in how Marx and Durkheim thought about society and its forms of social organization. There is thus a deep-seated presumption in intellectual and scientific thought (across all disciplines) that progress invariably occurs along with the march of time. This perspective is often referred to as an evolutionary view of progressive social change: in this understanding, changes that occur in society are not simply changes, but are changes that are better than what existed previously.

Comte championed an evolutionary-progressive view of science, and indeed, he embraced sociology as a superior science precisely because of its newcomer status on the scientific scene. Sociology would develop more quickly as a discipline because it could mimic existing scientific observational methods—then improve upon them. Comte also emphasized sociology's focus on observable data across *all* aspects of society, a feature that further bolsters its superiority. Physicists, chemists, and biologists, for example, are confined to specialized domains of *physical-biological activity*, whereas sociology is not. Similarly, economists, political scientists, anthropologists, and psychologists are confined to studying *compartmentalized social activity*, but sociologists suffer no such restrictions. Comte believed, therefore, that sociology could offer a highly elaborated synthesis of the human-social condition. In short, sociology would be *the* science of humanity, *the* science of society. It would outline "the most systematic theory of the human order" (Comte 1891/1973: 1).

Thus Comte saw himself as "the founder of the religion of humanity" (1891/1973: 26), of a scientific sociology whose knowledge would guide society. He believed that once sociology discovered the scientific laws of humanity/society and thus demonstrated how society works or how it functions, humans could then move society progressively forward and impose some order on its organization and development. Humans could then rightfully, in his view, turn their backs on all the inferior and speculative knowledge that had preceded their era.

Comte's positivism was, and still is, a hotly debated issue. This is the case because most social phenomena cannot be observed in the way that scientists observe phenomena in biology, physics, or chemistry. You can see bacteria grow in a biology experiment, but you cannot actually see social cohesion no matter how hard you try. Consequently, in order to study social phenomena you have to first operationalize them – you have to devise a working definition of the indicators representing the particular social thing you will observe and measure, that is, count. The positivist tradition is exemplified in the work of one of sociology's founding theorists, Emile Durkheim (see chapter 2). It is most apparent today in the quantitative methodology of sociologists who use surveys and other large data sets and sophisticated statistical techniques to study particular topics (e.g., education, migration, and income inequality) and

Figure I.2   Sociology is, and for, science. Source: Courtesy of Nina Bandelj and Megan Brooker.

the relations between them. One way sociologists measure social cohesion is by simply counting the number of friends individuals see during the week. We devise similar indicators of other things; for example, one index of gender inequality is to measure the difference in women's and men's wages in a particular occupation. As we will see, however, many theorists (e.g., Max Weber, chapter 3; Dorothy Smith, chapter 10) have misgivings about this approach; their concern is that we miss out on the lived context in which – and how – such things occur and the various meanings given by individual and groups to their experiences.

HARRIET MARTINEAU: SOCIOLOGY AS THE SCIENCE OF MORALS AND MANNERS

Comte's vision of scientific sociology was translated into English by the prolific English writer and feminist Harriet Martineau, the "first woman sociologist" (Hoecker-Drysdale 1992). Martineau regarded Comte's *Positive Philosophy* as "one of the chief honors of the [nineteenth] century" (1855/1974: 3), and considered its dissemination crucial to the march of social progress. She wrote: "The law of progress is conspicuously at work throughout human history. The only field of progress is now that of Positive Philosophy … whose repression would be incompatible with progress" (p. 11).

In addition to translating Comte, Martineau also wrote a detailed instructional booklet explaining the systematic way in which "morals and manners" – her definition of sociology's subject matter – should be scientifically observed. In *How to Observe Morals and Manners* (1838), she emphasized that "The powers of observation must be trained, and habits of method in arranging the materials presented to the eye must be acquired before the student possesses the requisites for understanding what he contemplates" (p. 13). Paralleling the scientific methodology of the natural scientist, Martineau advised:

> The traveler must not generalize on the spot … Natural [scientists] do not dream of generalizing with any such speed as that used by the observers of men … The geologist and the chemist make a large collection of particular appearances before they commit themselves to propound a principle drawn from them though their subject matter is far less diversified than the human subject, and nothing of so much importance as human emotions, – love and dislike, reverence and contempt, depends upon their judgment. (Martineau 1838: 18–19)

Martineau's perception of the breadth of sociology's subject matter was underscored by the range of topics in her research manual (and in her other writings). She included social class, religion, suicide, health, family, crime, newspapers, popular idols, and the arts. Moreover, long before it was fashionable for sociologists to discuss the relevance of the researcher's own social context and personal biases for the research conducted (see chapter 10), Martineau warned researchers not to be judgmental regarding people's habits and not to evaluate the observed behavior in terms of their own or their society's values (1838). She cautioned that "every prejudice, every moral perversion dims or distorts whatever the eye looks upon" (p. 51).

Martineau was committed to sociology as an observation-based science. At the same time, however, she recognized, unlike Comte, that the subject matter of sociology is different from what is studied by natural scientists. Because it includes the study of human emotions and values, it presents different challenges than those encountered by biologists and physicists. Given the relevance of the human-emotional element in the study of social life, Martineau thus emphasized the need for sociologists to adopt an attitude of empathy and understanding toward those they were observing. She stated:

> The observer must have sympathy; and his sympathy must be untrammeled and unreserved. If a traveler be a geological inquirer he may have a heart as hard as the rocks he shivers, and yet succeed in his immediate objects … if he be a statistical investigator he may be as abstract as a column of figures, and yet learn what he wants to know: but an observer of morals and manners will be liable to deception at every turn, if he does not find his way to hearts and minds. (Martineau 1838: 52)

INTERPRETIVE UNDERSTANDING

With this empathic approach, Martineau articulated the second strand of research methodology in sociology: the emphasis on **interpretive understanding** (or hermeneutics) elaborated by the German philosopher Wilhelm Dilthey (1833–1911). Unlike Comte, who argued for the unity of all sciences, namely, the idea that sociology is a science methodologically similar to the natural sciences, Dilthey maintained that there is a distinction between the natural and the human sciences (Outhwaite 1975). In his view, sociology as a human science is different from physics (and other natural sciences) as a result not of its logic but of its *content* – its concern with social life and the lived experiences of individuals. Unlike atoms, humans engage in mental activity; they experience everyday reality, and mentally and emotionally internalize this reality.

Therefore, Dilthey argued, the study of social life requires a different methodology than that applied to the study of natural phenomena; it requires a method of empathic understanding (or *Verstehen*, the German word for understanding). This requires us to enter with empathy into the lived experiences of those whom we are studying and to seek to understand those individuals' interpretation of their reality (Outhwaite 1975). This interpretive methodological tradition was consolidated in sociology by Dilthey's fellow German, Max Weber who emphasized the importance of tracing and understanding the meanings underlying individual, group, and institutional behavior (see chapter 3). It is the method embraced by sociologists when they conduct historically grounded research (using diaries, letters, sermons, archival materials, etc.), or when they conduct ethnographic studies and in-depth interviews, an influence richly apparent today across several sociological topics and subfields.

Sociology, therefore, is characterized by two dominant methodological approaches to the study of society: (1) a positivist tradition that focuses on the explanation of social reality using various measures as indicators of particular social phenomena and demonstrating the statistical relations between them (e.g., education and income); and (2) an interpretive tradition that focuses on explaining social phenomena through understanding the everyday contextualized reality of individuals/ groups and organizational cultures. Although there is some tension between these two research traditions, they are not mutually exclusive, and both are necessary to studying social life. Moreover, whether using statistical (positivist) or interpretive methods, sociologists frequently pursue research topics that have the additional purpose of contributing to the empowerment of individuals and groups. Sociological inquiry can be used to advance **emancipatory knowledge** – research findings that can help liberate people from the various historical and social structural barriers that hinder their full acceptance or participation in society (Habermas 1968/1971). Emancipatory research (such as documenting the overrepresentation of migrant women in low-wage service jobs; for example, Ehrenreich and Hochschild 2002) provides knowledge that in turn can be used by workers, activists, and policy-makers to change some of the conditions underlying particular patterns of inequality. It can also be used by individuals such as gay and lesbian Catholics (e.g., Dillon 1999) to understand that their particular realities are far more normal than might sometimes be conveyed by various stigmatizing discourses and practices. Whatever the research topics we pursue, all sociological theorizing prompts us to ask questions, though the questions asked and the assumptions informing them vary. The very act of asking questions about the social and cultural forces that structure individual behavior, social relations, and the organization of society invariably prompts us to rethink our existing assumptions about the world and how it works. As such, sociological theory provides intellectual and analytical resources for critical thinking. It directs us to ask questions and to look for patterns and variation in a given societal context. At the same time, the data sociologists gather and the empirical patterns they find help to challenge and refine sociological theory. There is thus an ongoing conversation between theory and data. And, as I noted at the beginning, good sociological theory offers constructs that help us make sense of social reality.

SOCIAL INEQUALITY AND CONTEXTUAL STANDPOINTS: DU BOIS, DE TOCQUEVILLE, AND MARTINEAU

Inequality is a central focus in sociology today, and it has long preoccupied sociologists. A pioneer in articulating its variously intersecting contours was William E.B. Du Bois. In this final section, I highlight some of his important insights and then consider how two other perceptive early observers of America life, Harriet Martineau and Alexis de Tocqueville, construed social inequality. The different lenses of these scholars alert us to how an observer's social identity and background prompt attentiveness to different dimensions of a given reality and/or to a different framing or interpretation of it.

WILLIAM E. B. DU BOIS: SLAVERY AND RACIAL INEQUALITY

BIOGRAPHICAL NOTE

William Edward Burghardt Du Bois was born in Great Barrington, Massachusetts, in 1868. Though he was admitted to Harvard University, he could not afford to go and, instead, with funding from local white community leaders in Great Barrington, went to Fisk University in Nashville, Tennessee, for his undergraduate education. During the summers at Fisk, he traveled through rural Tennessee teaching summer school and getting to know the everyday details of life for rural black southerners. He subsequently studied at Harvard, where he received a second BA and an MA and a PhD in history. While there, he was awarded a fellowship to study in Berlin, Germany, for two years. After completing his PhD, Du Bois spent the bulk of his academic career as professor of sociology at Atlanta University. He was a prolific book writer and magazine editor. Among his many political activities, he was a founding member of the National Association for the Advancement of Colored People (NAACP) and highly involved in it and in other race-based groups. In 1945, Du Bois was a consultant to the US delegation at the founding of the United Nations. An avowed socialist, he made frequent visits to the Soviet Union and to other countries. He died in Ghana in 1963, at the age of 95 (Marable 1986). His biographer, the sociologist Manning Marable, states: "Few intellectuals have done more to shape the twentieth century than W.E.B. Du Bois. Only Frederick Douglas and Martin Luther King, Jr., equaled Du Bois's role in the social movement for civil rights in the United States" (1986: viii).

William Du Bois (1868–1963), a Harvard-trained black sociologist, writer, and political activist, is widely recognized as "the prime inspirer, philosopher, and father of the Negro protest movement" (Marable 1986: 214–215). He is among the most influential pioneers in black sociology, though he was marginalized within sociology for many decades (Marable 1986; Morris 2015). A prolific ethnographic researcher and writer, he devoted much attention to slavery's legacy on black racial inequality and identity. Du Bois argued that slavery (which ended in the 1860s) produced a black **double-consciousness**, meaning that blacks as ex-slaves must invariably see themselves through the eyes of the white master. In *The Souls of Black Folk*, one of his most renowned books, he elaborated:

> The Negro is … born with a veil … [one that] only lets him see himself through the revelation of the other world. It is a peculiar sensation, this double-consciousness, this sense of always looking at one's self through the eyes of others, of measuring one's soul by the tape of a world that looks on in amused contempt and pity. One ever feels his twoness, – an American, a Negro; two souls … two unreconciled strivings; two warring ideals in one dark body … The history of the American Negro is the history of this strife, – this longing to attain self-conscious manhood, to merge his double self into a better and truer self. In this merging he wishes neither of the older selves to be lost. He would not Africanize America, for America has too much to teach the world and Africa. He would not bleach his Negro soul in a flood of white Americanism, for he knows that Negro blood has a message for the world. He simply wishes to make it possible for a man to be both a Negro and an American, without being cursed and spit upon by his fellows, without having the doors of Opportunity closed roughly in his face. (Du Bois 1903/1969: 45–46)

Black men, Du Bois argues, were emasculated by slavery, by the violence of the Civil War conflict over its resolution, and by the economic terms and context of their freedom during Reconstruction (Du Bois 1903/1969). As freed ex-slaves *some* blacks were able to take advantage of the relatively cheap parcels of land made available by the US War Department's Freedmen's Bureau (established in 1865) and the Southern Homestead Act (1866) and were able to acquire "40 acres and a mule" (e.g., Oubre 1978). These early resources were critical to the long-term economic success of some black families. Overall, however, as Du Bois argues, the legal emancipation of slaves did not ensure their economic and social emancipation. Emancipation, though welcomed by some in the South who felt "that the nightmare was at last over" (Du Bois 1934/2007: 549), was followed by the economic and political enslavement of the freed slaves, whose new-found legal freedoms competed with the economic goals of white landowners, white laborers, and white small farmers.

Du Bois thus gives particular emphasis to the economic sources and consequences of racial inequality and elaborates on the significance of slavery in the creation of capitalist profit through the exploitation of blacks (Du Bois 1934/2007). He states:

> It must be remembered and never forgotten that the civil war in the South … was a determined effort to reduce black labor as nearly as possible to a condition of unlimited exploitation and build a new class of capitalists on this foundation. The wage of the Negro worker despite the war amendments, was to be reduced to the level of bare subsistence by taxation, peonage, caste, and every method of discrimination. This program had to be carried out in open defiance of the clear letter of the law. (Du Bois 1934/2007: 549; see also 1903/1969: 54–78)

Consequently, Du Bois argues, the economic exploitation of the freed slaves underscored the deep racial wedge of division between ex-slaves and their white ex-masters. Further, racial divisions were used by white capitalists to drive a competitive wedge between black and white laborers; white land-owners encouraged white laborers to regard black laborers as obstacles impeding their chances for economic advancement – the white workers' "chance to become capitalists" (e.g., Du Bois 1934/2007: 14–15). White racism, and the mechanisms in place to suppress ex-slaves' economic advancement (e.g., through low, subsistence wages), converged not only to undermine blacks' social and economic progress but, symbolically, to consolidate for whites the idea that blacks are racially inferior (Du Bois 1903/1969).

Although preoccupied with the slavery/postslavery economic and social conditions of blacks, Du Bois's vision of social equality was not confined to the plight of blacks alone. He contended: "The emancipation of man is the emancipation of labor" (Du Bois 1934/2007: 11), and he envisioned a democracy in which "all labor, blacks as well as white, became free" (p. 9), free of capitalist exploitation. He argued that this vision was best realized through the creation of a socialist society, which, despite its many shortcomings, offered a more just alternative for blacks and for society in general, irrespective of race (Marable 1986). Therefore, although Du Bois was intellectually and emotionally engrossed in the problem of race, he believed that the inequalities produced by the color line were exacerbated by capitalism, that is, the use of racial differences to divide the working class and to suppress their realization that under capitalism, all wage-workers, regardless of race, are exploited and disposable (as Karl Marx elaborates, see chapter 1).

Du Bois was critical of all forms of racism – in economic and labor relations, education, religion, culture, and the arts, but he was especially critical of the labor movement (Du Bois 1935/1996). He argued that the American labor movement's own racism prevented it from recognizing capitalist exploitation of labor as a whole. Its racism, he maintained, made it side with the "captains of industry who spend large sums of money to make laborers think that the most worthless white man is better than any colored man" (p. 434). In short, emphasizing the intersecting effects of both economic and racial inequality, he concluded that, "To be a poor man is hard, but to be a poor race in a land of dollars is the very bottom of hardships" (Du Bois 1903/1969: 49–50).

RACIAL AND GENDER EQUALITY

Prophetic for his time, Du Bois also emphasized the ways in which social class, race, and gender intersect in the reproduction of inequality (on intersectionality, see also chapter 10). As early as 1915, when the issue of women's suffrage was gaining momentum in the US, he argued:

> The statement that woman is weaker than men is sheer rot. It is the same sort of thing that we hear about "darker races" and "lower classes." Difference, either physical or spiritual, does not argue weakness or inferiority. That the average woman is spiritually different from the average man is undoubtedly just as true

as the fact that the average white man differs from the average Negro; but this is no reason for disenfranchising the Negro or lynching him. It is inconceivable that any person looking upon the accomplishments of women today in every field of endeavor … could for a moment talk about a "weaker" sex … To say that men protect women with their votes is to overlook the testimony of the facts. In the first place, there are millions of women who have no natural men protectors: the unmarried, the widowed, the deserted and those who have married failures. To put this whole army out of court and leave them unprotected is more than unjust, it is a crime … [Moreover] a woman is just as much a thinking, feeling, acting person after marriage as before. (Du Bois 1915/1996: 378)

Du Bois is clear that women are not a subspecies, dependent on and inferior to men. He was also emphatic that democracy required equality for all discriminated groups, and hence the project of claiming equality for blacks entailed not just equality for black men, but for black and white women too. Thus: "The meaning of the twentieth century is the freeing of the individual soul; the soul longest in slavery and still in the most disgusting and indefensible slavery is the soul of womanhood" (Du Bois 1915/1996: 379).

ALEXIS DE TOCQUEVILLE: CULTURE AND SOCIAL INSTITUTIONS

Alexis De Tocqueville (1805–1859), a French aristocrat, was among the first observers to highlight the dynamic relation between cultural ideas and individual and institutional practices. Traveling across the eastern part of America in the 1830s, he made extensive notes in his journals based on what he observed about everyday habits and learned from conversations with ordinary Americans. His account resulted in his two-volume work, *Democracy in America* (1835–1840/2004). Coming from a country with a long history of nondemocratic, hierarchical power (e.g., the monarchy and the church), de Tocqueville was especially interested in the way in which democracy, and its ideals of freedom, took hold and were expressed in American society.

De Tocqueville's account has become highly influential among successive generations of sociologists because it shows how individuals engage in the life of their community/society while simultaneously realizing their own individual aspirations (e.g., Bellah et al. 1985). De Tocqueville showed that family, religion, and politics – the social institutions to which he gave most attention – are strong in America. He argued that these institutions provide the backbone of American community-civic activities precisely because they allow individuals a great deal of freedom and autonomy; and individuals use this freedom not to abandon but to participate in community. He was impressed, for example, with the way in which religious institutions and individual freedom intertwined in American society rather than, as was the French experience, being opposed to one another. The classical French idea is that in a modern (Enlightened) democratic society, freedom should mean freedom *from* the controlling power of religion. But in America, de Tocqueville found, individual freedom and church participation went hand in hand.

Unlike post-Revolutionary France (and its antireligious ethos), the everyday habits and norms that American democracy established provided opportunities for religious as well as political and economic fulfillment. De Tocqueville argued that these freedoms and opportunities produced an order in America that simultaneously allowed for both individual fulfillment and strong institutions amidst the turmoil of economic transformation and social change. In this view, Americans could realize their new political and economic ambitions while also maintaining their (traditional) religious and family commitments.

HARRIET MARTINEAU: CULTURAL VALUES AND SOCIAL CONTRADICTIONS

Harriet Martineau visited America around the same time as de Tocqueville, 1834–1836. She similarly traveled through the eastern, southern and midwestern states (Martineau 1837/1981), and with a similar intent: a "strong curiosity to witness the actual working of republican institutions … [and] with a strong disposition to admire democratic institutions" (p. 50). Martineau marveled at the hospitality she received from a broad array of Americans, including the president, members of Congress and the Supreme Court, and slave owners, clergy, lawyers, merchants, and farmers. She was also impressed with the many institutions (factories, hospitals, prisons, schools, etc.) and families she visited, and with her interactions with women and children in kitchens, nurseries, and boudoirs – "all excellent schools in which to learn the morals and manners of a people" (p. 53).

Martineau commented approvingly on the honesty and kindness of Americans, but unlike de Tocqueville, she was also very critical of many of the things she observed. She took particular note of the contradictions she witnessed between American ideals of democratic equality and everyday practices. She wrote at length about slavery – the division of society "into two classes, the servile and the imperious" (Martineau 1837/1981: 220) – and criticized the oppression and degradation to which slaves were subjected. She also noted the prejudices against "people of colour" in the North, evident, for example, in families "being locked out of their own hired pew in a church, because their white brethren will not worship by their side" (pp. 122–123). Beyond racial issues, she commented on the mass conformity, apathy, and timidity in political opinion; the mass disapproval of religious skepticism and atheism; the many social status hierarchies and cliques that existed, even among children; and the inequalities in wealth and luxury e.g., arguing that "enormous private wealth is inconsistent with the spirit of republicanism" (p. 263).

De Tocqueville too commented at length on racial inequality in America and the oppressed status of both the Negro and the Indian (e.g., 1835–1840/2004: 365–476). He argued that slavery "can not endure in an age of democratic liberty and enlightenment" (p. 419).He found it hard, nonetheless, to imagine an American society in which blacks and whites would be equal. He believed that the consequences of slavery (even after abolition) would continue to foster servility among blacks and lead them to abuse freedom, with the overarching consequence that blacks and whites would invariably be in conflict. He wrote:

> Plunged into this abyss of woe, the Negro scarcely feels his affliction. Violence made him a slave but habituation to servitude has given him the thoughts and ambitions of one. He admires his tyrants even more than he hates them and finds his joy and his pride in servile imitation of his oppressors … Should he become free, independence will often strike him as a chain heavier to bear than slavery itself … You can make the Negro free, but you cannot make him anything other than alien vis-à-vis the European … those who believe that the Negroes will one day blend in with the Europeans are nursing a chimera [an illusion]. (De Tocqueville 1835–1840/2004: 367, 394, 395)

De Tocqueville conveyed a similarly passive, though a far more praising (and highly idealized) view of the status of women in America. He commented approvingly that Americans believe in a democratic equality which recognizes the complementary "natural differences" between men and women (1835–1840/2004: 705), something that accounted for women's comportment. Thus, he stated, "American women, who often display a manly intelligence and an energy that is nothing less than virile, generally maintain a very delicate appearance and always remain women in manners, although they sometimes reveal themselves to be men in mind and heart" (p. 706). American women, he further observed, did not "topple the husband from power and confuse lines of authority within the family"; instead, they "prided themselves on the voluntary sacrifice of their will and demonstrated their greatness by freely accepting the yoke rather than seeking to avoid it. That, at any rate, was the sentiment expressed by the most virtuous among them" (p. 706). Indeed, so admiring was de Tocqueville of American women, he concluded that the "superiority of their women," most of whom "seldom venture outside the domestic sphere," was "primarily responsible for the singular prosperity and growing power of this people" (p. 708).

In stark contrast to de Tocqueville's assessment, Martineau was especially critical of the contradictions between democratic ideals of equality and women's inequality. She underscored the "political non-existence of women" (1837/1981: 125–128) due to their lack of voting rights. She also commented on the narrowness of women's interests, a narrowness forced by their general exclusion from the public sphere of economics and politics: "Wifely and motherly occupation may be called the sole business of woman there [in America]. If she has not that, she has nothing" (p. 301).

Anticipating an argument elaborated by Karl Marx with regard to economic class inequality (see chapter 1), Martineau exhorted women to collectively take responsibility for their own emancipation; she argued this freedom was necessary to the realization of American ideals of equality:

> The progression or emancipation of any class usually, if not always, takes place through the efforts of individuals of that class: and so it must be here. All women should inform themselves of the condition of their sex and of their own position. It must necessarily follow that the noblest of them will, sooner or later, put forth a moral power which shall [expose hypocrisy], and burst asunder the bonds (silken to some, but cold iron to others,) of feudal prejudices and usages. In the meantime, is it to be understood that the principles of the Declaration of Independence bear no relation to half of the human race? … how is the restricted and dependent state of women to be reconciled with the proclamation that "all are endowed by their Creator with certain inalienable rights; that among these are life, liberty, and the pursuit of happiness?" (Martineau 1837/1981: 307–308)

In sum, as a woman and a feminist sensitized to inequality, Martineau readily saw and highlighted the various ways in which women were excluded from full democratic participation in society (denied access to voting/the public sphere). Similarly, coming from his minority status as a black man, Du Bois articulated a penetrating critique of racial domination and inequality. Yet, both Du Bois and Martineau, unlike de Tocqueville (a privileged white male aristocrat), were able to transcend their own particular gender/racial identities: Du Bois was also able to transcend a male standpoint to recognize the intersecting character of gender and racial (and economic) inequality; and Martineau was able to transcend her white identity to recognize the oppression of black people.

SUMMARY

The intent of this book is to provide you with a thorough grounding in sociological theory. It discusses the conceptual frameworks elaborated by sociology's core founding theorists – Marx, Durkheim, and Weber – as well as the broader range of ideas and concepts that comprise contemporary theory. My approach is to demonstrate the applicability of sociological theory and its relevance in helping us make sense of the complexity of the social world in which we live. This chapter highlighted the historical background to the emergence of sociology as an intellectual discipline. I discussed the influence of Enlightenment thought, and Auguste Comte's vision of sociology as a scientific field of social inquiry, and also highlighted how the subject matter of sociology – human-social behavior and social processes – complicates its analysis and interpretation.

POINTS TO REMEMBER

- Sociological theory:
  - Aims to explain empirical social phenomena
  - Focuses on social structures, culture, and institutional practices
  - Incorporates both macro- and micro-level approaches to the study of society
  - Addresses the interplay between individual/collective agency and structural forces
  - Enhances students' critical analytical thinking skills
- Sociology is a relatively new discipline – its origins date to the mid-nineteenth century
- The Enlightenment (eighteenth century) set the scene for the emergence of sociology. The Enlightenment:
  - Emphasized human reason and social progress
  - Moved away from the explanatory forces of the past (myth, tradition, despotism)
  - Reason in politics translates onto ideals of equality democracy, and collective self-governance
  - US Declaration of Independence, 1776
  - French Revolution, 1789
  - Scientific reasoning emphasizes observable, empirical phenomena
- Auguste Comte: sociology as the empirical, positive science of society
  - Positive sociology: scientifically discoverable laws of society
- Harriet Martineau: sociology as the scientific study of morals and manners
  - Subject matter of sociology different to that of natural science
  - A positive scientific method that includes sympathetic understanding of individuals
- Wilhelm Dilthey: sociology as interpretive understanding
- Du Bois was the first sociologist to systematically draw attention to racial inequality
- The subjects addressed by Du Bois, Martineau, and de Tocqueville, and their interpretations, highlight how an observer's social background and theoretical questions influence the content/social processes that are observed/critiqued

GLOSSARY

agency individuals, groups, and other collectivities exerting autonomy in the face of social institutions, social structures, and cultural expectations.

canon established body of core knowledge/ideas in a given field of study.

classical theory the ideas, concepts, and intellectual framework outlined by the founders of sociology (Marx, Durkheim, Weber, Martineau).

concepts specific ideas about the social world defined and elaborated by a given theorist/school of thought.

conceptual framework the relatively coherent and interrelated set of ideas or concepts that a given theorist or a given school of thought uses to elaborate a particular perspective on things; a particular way of looking at, framing, theorizing about, social life.

contemporary theory the successor theories/ideas outlined to extend and engage with the classical theorizing of Marx, Durkheim, Weber, and Martineau.

culture beliefs, rituals, ideas, worldviews, and ways of doing things. Culture is socially structured, that is, individuals are socialized into a given culture and how to use it in everyday social action.

democracy political structure derived from the ethos that because all individuals are endowed with reason and created equal they are entitled (and required) to participate in the political governance of their collective life in society.

double-consciousness the alienation of blacks' everyday identity/consciousness as a result of slavery such that blacks invariably see themselves through the eyes of (superior) whites, the dominant race.

emancipatory knowledge the use of sociological knowledge to advance social equality.

empiricism use of evidence or data in describing and analyzing society.

Enlightenment eighteenth-century philosophical movement emphasizing the centrality of individual reason, scientific rationality, and human-social progress; and the rejection of nonrational beliefs and forms of social organization (e.g., monarchy).

inalienable rights Enlightenment belief that all individuals by virtue of their humanity and their naturally endowed reason are entitled to fully participate in society in ways that reflect and enrich their humanity (e.g., freedom of speech, of assembly, to vote, etc.).

interpretive understanding *Verstehen*; task of the sociologist in making sense of the varied motivations that underlie meaningful action; because sociology studies human lived experience (as opposed to physical phenomena), sociologists need a methodology that enables them to empathically understand human-social behavior.

macro analytical focus on large-scale social structures (e.g., capitalism) and processes (e.g., class inequality).

micro analytical focus on small-scale, interpersonal, and small group interaction.

objectivity positivist idea (elaborated by Comte) that sociology can provide an unbiased (objective) analysis of a directly observable and measurable, objective social reality. This approach presumes that facts stand alone and have an objective reality independent of social and historical context and independent of any theories/ideas informing how we frame, look at, and interpret data.

pluralistic simultaneous coexistence of, and mutual engagement across, diverse strands (of thought, of research, of people).

positivist the idea that sociology as a science is able to employ the same scientific method of investigation and explanation used in the natural sciences, focusing only on observable data and studying society with the same objectivity used to study physical/biological phenomena.

post-truth society a term that has gained currency amid the whirl of misinformation and false statements disseminated on social media and by partisan news outlets; it conveys that objectively validated, evidence-based statements are displaced by distorted or contrary assertions adjusted to suit the interests of the individual or group making particular, untruthful claims.

rationality emphasis on the authority of reason in deliberating about, and evaluating explanations of, the nature of reality/social phenomena.

reason human ability to think about things; to create, apply, and evaluate knowledge; and as a consequence, to be able to evaluate one's own and others' lived experiences and the socio-historical contexts that shape those experiences.

scientific reasoning emphasis on the discovery of explanatory knowledge through the use of empirical data and their systematic analysis rather than relying on philosophical assumptions and faith/religious beliefs.

social structures forms of social organization (e.g., capitalism, democracy, bureaucracy, education, gender) in a given society that structure or constrain social behavior across all spheres of social life, including the cultural expectations and norms (e.g., individualism) that underpin and legitimate social institutional arrangements.

sociological theory the body of concepts and conceptual frameworks used to make sense of the multilayered, empirical patterns and underlying processes in society.

utilitarianism idea from classical economics that individuals are rational, self-interested actors who evaluate alternative courses of action on the basis of their usefulness (utility) or resource value to them.

QUESTIONS FOR REVIEW

1   What is sociological theory and what does it do?
2   Why does it make sense that the discipline of sociology emerged *after* rather than *before* the Enlightenment?
3   What does it mean to say that sociology is a social science? Why social? And why science?
4   How might subjectivity and the social context of a sociologist influence what they study/see and how they interpret what they see?

NOTE

1   A helpful introduction to the various philosophers and other thinkers associated with the Enlightenment can be found in the *Cambridge Dictionary of Philosophy*, edited by Robert Audi (1999).

REFERENCES

Audi, Robert, ed. 1999. *The Cambridge Dictionary of Philosophy*. 2nd edition. New York: Cambridge University Press.

Baker, Gerard. 2017. "Trump, 'Lies' and Honest Journalism." *Wall Street Journal* (January 5), p. A15.

Bellah, Robert, Richard Madsen, William Sullivan, Ann Swidler, and Steven Tipton. 1985. *Habits of the Heart: Individualism and Commitment in American Life*. Berkeley: University of California Press.

Bittman, Michael, Paula England, Liana Sayer, Nancy Folbre, and George Matheson. 2003. "When Does Gender Trump Money? Bargaining and Time in Household Work." *American Journal of Sociology* 109: 186–214.

Blumberg, Abraham. 1974. "Introduction." Pp. i–xi in *Auguste Comte: The Positive Philosophy*. Translated and condensed by Harriet Martineau. New York: Calvin Blanchard.

Chen, Victor T. 2015. *Cut Loose: Jobless and Hopeless in an Unfair Economy*. Berkeley: University of California Press.

Chodorow, Nancy. 1978. *The Reproduction of Mothering: Psychoanalysis and the Sociology of Gender*. Berkeley: University of California Press.

Comte, Auguste. 1855/1974. *The Positive Philosophy*. Translated and condensed by Harriet Martineau. Introduction by Abraham Blumberg. New York: Calvin Blanchard.

Comte, Auguste. 1891/1973. *The Catechism of Positive Religion*. 3rd edition. Translated by Richard Congreve. Clifton, NJ: Augustus M. Kelley.

De Tocqueville, Alexis. 1835–1840/2004. *Democracy in America*, volumes 1 and 2. Translated by Arthur Goldhammer. New York: Library of America.

Dillon, Michele. 1999. *Catholic Identity: Balancing Reason, Faith and Power*. New York: Cambridge University Press.

Du Bois, W.E.B. 1903/1969. *The Souls of Black Folk*. Introductions by Nathan Hare and Alvin Poussaint. New York: New American Library.

Du Bois, W.E.B. 1915/1996. "Woman Suffrage." Pp. 377–379 in Eric Sundquist, ed. *The Oxford W.E.B. Du Bois Reader*. New York: Oxford University Press.

Du Bois, W.E.B. 1934/2007. *Black Reconstruction in America*. New York: Oxford University Press.

Du Bois, W.E.B. 1935/1996. "A Negro Nation Within the Nation." Pp. 431–438 in Eric Sundquist, ed. *The Oxford W.E.B. Du Bois Reader*. New York: Oxford University Press.

Economist. 2017. "A Taxonomy of Dishonesty." (February 18), p. 71.

Ehrenreich, Barbara, and Arlie Russell Hochschild, eds. 2002. *Global Woman: Nannies, Maids, and Sex Workers in the New Economy*. New York: Holt.

England, Paula. 2005. "Emerging Theories of Care Work." *Annual Review of Sociology* 31: 381–399.

Feyerabend, Paul. 1979. *Against Method*. London: Verso.

Greenhouse, Steven. 2006. "Hotel Rooms Get Plusher, Adding to Maids' Injuries." *New York Times* (April 21).

Habermas, Jürgen. 1968/1971. *Knowledge and Human Interests*. Boston: Beacon Press.

Ham, J. 1999. "Social Contract." Pp. 855–856 in Robert Audi, ed. *Cambridge Dictionary of Philosophy*. 2nd edition. New York: Cambridge University Press.

Hoecker-Drysdale, Susan. 1992. *Harriet Martineau: First Woman Sociologist*. Oxford: Berg

Leubsdorf, Ben. 2017. "New Record for Household Incomes." *Wall Street Journal* (September 13), p. A2.

MacLeod, Jay. 2008. *Ain't No Makin' It: Aspirations and Attainment in a Low-Income Neighborhood*. 3rd edition. Boulder, CO: Westview Press.

Marable, Manning. 1986. *W.E.B. Du Bois: Black Radical Democrat*. Boston: Twayne.

Martineau, Harriet. 1837/1981. *Society in America*. Edited, abridged, and with an introduction by Seymour Martin Lipset. New Brunswick, NJ: Transaction Books.

Martineau, Harriet. 1838. *How to Observe Morals and Manners*. London: Charles Knight.

Martineau, Harriet. 1855/1974. *The Positive Philosophy of Auguste Comte*. Freely translated and condensed. New introduction by Abraham Blumberg. New York: AMS Press.

Morris, Aldon. 2015. *The Scholar Denied: W. E. B. Du Bois and the Birth of Modern Sociology*. Berkeley: University of California Press.

Oubre, Claude. 1978. *Forty Acres and a Mule: The Freedmen's Bureau and Black Land Ownership.* Baton Rouge: Louisiana State University Press.

Outhwaite, William. 1975. *Understanding Social Life: The Method Called Verstehen.* London: Allen & Unwin.

Romero, Mary. 1992. *Maid in the USA.* New York: Routledge.

Sassen, Saskia. 2007. *A Sociology of Globalization.* New York: Norton.

Sherman, Rachel. 2007. *Class Acts: Service and Inequality in Luxury Hotels.* Berkeley: University of California Press.

Smelser, Neil. 1959. *Social Change in the Industrial Revolution.* Chicago: University of Chicago Press.

Taylor, Keith, ed. 1975. *Henri Saint-Simon: Selected Writings on Science, Industry and Social Organisation.* London: Croom Helm.

CHAPTER ONE

KARL MARX (1818–1883)

KEY CONCEPTS

capitalism
bourgeoisie
inequality
mode of production
means of production
proletariat
private property
exploitation
historical materialism
class relations
class consciousness
dialectical materialism
communism
subsistence

species being
capital
profit
use-value
commodification of labor
   power
false consciousness
surplus value
exchange-value
division of labor
alienated labor
alienation from products
objectification

alienation in the production
   process
alienation from our species
   being
alienation of individuals
   from one another
standpoint of the proletariat
ideology
fetishism of commodities
superstructure
economic base
ruling class
ruling ideas

Introduction to Sociological Theory: Theorists, Concepts, and Their Applicability to the Twenty-First Century,
Third Edition. Michele Dillon.
© 2020 John Wiley & Sons Ltd. Published 2020 by John Wiley & Sons Ltd.
Companion website: www.wiley.com/go/dillon

CHAPTER MENU

Timeline 1.1	Major events spanning Marx's lifetime (1818–1883)
1818	First steamship (the *Savannah*) to cross the Atlantic Ocean, taking 26 days
1819	British Factory Act prohibiting employment of children under 9 in the cotton industry; and 12-hour days for those ages 10–16.
1821	US population: 9.6 million
1830	Revolution in France, fall of Charles X and Bourbons
1833	Britain abolishes slavery in its empire
1837	US Congress passes a "gag" law to suppress debate on slavery
1840	Railway-building boom in Europe
1841	First university degrees granted to women in America
1842	Depression and poverty in England
1842	British Mines Act forbids underground employment for women and girls and sets up inspectorate to supervise boy labor
1843	Skiing becomes a sport
1845	Engels, *The Condition of the Working Class in England*
1845	Florida and Texas gain statehood
1846	Height of potato famine in Ireland
1848	Revolutions against monarchy/aristocracy in Europe (Paris, Berlin, Prague, Budapest)
1848	Marx and Engels, *The Communist Manifesto*
1848	California Gold Rush
1850	Sydney University established
1854	Charles Dickens, *Hard Times*
1859	Peaceful picketing during a strike legalized in Britain
1862	Abraham Lincoln issues Emancipation Proclamation declaring slaves free
1862	Lincoln issues the first legal US paper money
1862	Victor Hugo, *Les Misérables*
1866	National Labor Union (crafts union) established in the US
1867	Marx, *Capital* (*Das Kapital*)
1871	Trade Union Act in Britain secures legal status for trade unions, but picketing illegal
1872	Penny-farthing bicycle in general use
1876	Alexander Graham Bell invents the telephone
1877	US railroad strike; first major industrial dispute in US
1879	Thomas Edison produces incandescent electric light
1882	Standard Oil Company controls 95 percent of US oil-refining capacity

BIOGRAPHICAL NOTE

Karl Marx was born in Germany (in Prussia, in 1818) into a middle-class family and completed several years of university education studying law, history, languages, and philosophy. Rather than pursue an academic career, Marx turned to journalism and devoted his attention to business and economics, writing about labor conditions during this era of rapid industrialization. The year 1848 was the "Year of Revolutions" in Europe, as workers and ordinary people rebelled against the ruling monarchies in Germany, Italy, Austria, Hungary, and France. Marx himself had participated in the German revolutionary movement, and that same year he and Friedrich Engels published their famous treatise *The Communist Manifesto*. Marx was expelled from Germany and subsequently also from France because of his revolutionary views. He eventually settled in England in 1849, with his German wife, Jenny von Westphalen. For many years subsequently, they and their six children suffered abject poverty, relying on money from Engels and small fees from Marx's political articles for the American radical newspaper the *New York Daily Tribune*. He died in 1883, predeceased by his wife and three of their children (Tucker 1978: xvii; Kimmel 2007: 170).

Marx's Writings
1844a: "Alienation and Social Classes," ASC
1844b: *Economic and Philosophical Manuscripts of 1844*, EPM
1846: *The German Ideology* (with Engels), GI
1847: *Wage Labour and Capital*, WLC
1848: *The Communist Manifesto* (with Engels), CM
1852: "The Eighteenth Brumaire of Louis Bonaparte," Bru
1858: *The Grundrisse: Foundations of the Critique of Political Economy*, Gru
1859: "Preface to 'A Contribution to the Critique of Political Economy,'" Preface
1867: *Capital* (*Das Kapital*), Cap

EXPANSION OF CAPITALISM

When you hear the name **Karl Marx** it is tempting to wonder why you should be studying his ideas. Marx has been dead for almost one hundred and forty years, and communism, the social system with which his theoretical vision is associated, has all but disappeared around the world. The dominant communist power of the twentieth century, the Soviet Union, collapsed – an event captured literally by the fall of the Berlin Wall on November 9, 1989. Today, the largest ex-Soviet republic, Russia, is in the throes of **capitalism**, crystallized by the development of shopping malls even in Siberia and by the expanding global economic reach of Russian millionaires and billionaires. One, for example, owns the world-famous Chelsea (England) Football (soccer) Club; another was an early capital investor in Facebook; and another owns the Brooklyn Nets professional basketball team, whose home arena – the spectacular Barclays center in Brooklyn, New York – is a venture in which Jay-Z is also an investor. Such developments would have been unimaginable 25 years ago. Capitalism is steadily expanding too in China (see Topic 1.1); China occupies a major role in the global economy and it is expected to be the world's number one economy by 2030, displacing the US.

Lest you think that this capitalist expansion is all the more reason not to study Marx, you might be surprised to know that Marx, in fact, predicted it:

The need of a constantly expanding market for its products chases the **bourgeoisie** [the capitalist ownership class] over the whole surface of the globe. It must nestle everywhere, settle everywhere, establish connections everywhere … The bourgeoisie, by the rapid improvement of all instruments of production, by the immensely facilitated means of communication, draws all, even the most barbarian, nations into civilization. The cheap prices of its commodities are the heavy artillery with which it batters down all Chinese walls, with which it forces the barbarians' intensely obstinate hatred of foreigners to capitulate. It compels all nations, on pain of extinction, to adopt the bourgeois mode of production; it compels them to introduce what it calls civilization into their midst, i.e., to become bourgeois themselves. In one word, it creates a world after its own image. (CM 83–84)[1]

Thus writing in the mid-nineteenth century, Marx envisioned today's global economy! The expansion of capitalism and its need to have bigger and bigger global markets for its commodities create capitalist societies whose progress is defined by the extent of their bourgeois capitalist culture. These societies must continuously adapt to meet the demands of capitalism by producing commodities for domestic and global consumption. Hence the expansion of Western capitalism has created a globalizing capitalist world in which consumer goods are the common global cultural currency, a theme I discuss further in chapter 15.

Topic 1.1   Contemporary China: Consumer capitalism in a state-controlled society

The successful summer Olympics in Beijing, China, in 2008 showcased a highly modern and resourceful city well able to blend old cultural traditions with hypermodern architecture and technologically sophisticated art. The Olympics provided the world with a bright look at the new China as it weaves together authoritarian state control and, since the 1980s, core elements of market capitalism. Today, China is the new global juggernaut, competing with the US for the label of the world's largest economy. A Chinese company, for example, owns Volvo (the quintessential European/Swedish car), and it is vying to buy Jeep (an iconic American brand). With 731 million Internet users, rising personal incomes, and an expanding middle class, there is booming demand within China for such staples of capitalist consumption as cars, real estate, the latest household appliances, and imported fresh oysters (from New Zealand), fresh blueberries (from Chile), and fresh tulips (from the Netherlands). Consumer demand for personal technology items is intense, making China the fastest growing market for Apple products. China's own technology companies are also rapidly growing. Alibaba, one of China's largest Internet, e-commerce, and social media titans, has more sales than Amazon and eBay combined, and it can track the spending habits of more than 450 million customers through its popular phone-pay app. Chinese online consumer spending is already strong and is expected to continue rapid growth, especially in entertainment, beauty and hygiene products, travel, and dining (Lin 2017a). Chinese tourism to destinations outside of China is increasingly popular and will be further accelerated by Alibaba's new travel-service website, a joint venture with the US Marriott hotel chain, already well-known in China where it owns over 600 hotels (Lin 2017b).

More than 87 percent of Chinese families own or partially own property, and more than one-tenth own more than one property (Wong 2013: A9). Income inequality is a growing problem: households in the top 5 percent income bracket earn a quarter of all China's household income (Wong 2013: A9). Many of China's super-rich families send their children abroad to study – to the US, Vancouver (Canada), and England (e.g., Fan 2016) – and their affluent lifestyles, whether abroad or at home, contrast starkly with the lives of China's middle class and especially the poor. Despite the strong-armed and well-funded domestic security forces that police everyday life, labor unrest in China is increasingly common. In 2017 alone, there were about 600 strikes or protests by blue-collar workers, a figure that experts suggest probably represents about 10–15 percent of the actual number. The government keeps a close eye; in Beijing, if as few as ten workers show up at a protest, the police break it up (*The Economist*, "Workers Disunited," August 19, 2017, p. 37).

CAPITALISM AS STRUCTURED INEQUALITY

Many people across the world enjoy the wide range of consumer goods made available by capitalism. Cubans, for example, take a 13-hour flight to Moscow not to visit the Kremlin but to "bring back bags of jeans, haberdashery and car parts to a Communist island starved of consumer goods" (Kurmanaev and Sharoyan 2017). (Miami is closer, just 300 miles, but US border restrictions are an impediment to Cuban visitors/shoppers.) Marx, however, emphasizes the cost of capitalism: the **inequality** that inheres in it. Capitalism is one way of organizing production in order to meet the needs of our existence; it is the **mode of production** that characterizes the organization of society. From a long historical perspective, capitalism is not the only mode of production known to society; medieval Europe (for approximately five hundred years, from 1000 to 1490), for example, was characterized by a feudal mode of production whereby serfs worked and cultivated the land of medieval lords, who, in turn, assumed responsibility for the everyday welfare of the serfs and their families.

Capitalism is a mode of production based on unequal private ownership of the means of production (in contrast, for example, to state ownership in socialist societies, e.g., North Korea). Under capitalism, a minority of capitalists, the bourgeoisie, own and monopolize the **means of production**, that is, property – land, oil wells, railroads, factories, corporations, and increasingly today, intellectual property (including computer algorithms). Company owners and executives (the bourgeoisie) accumulate profit based on the labor of employees. The employees are the **proletariat**, the wage-workers who must work hard to meet production demands in factories, farms, mines, corporate offices, and hotels (see Introduction), and who through their work produce commodities, including services, information, computer software, that are sold by the capitalists for profit. In turn, capitalists use this profit to expand their ownership of **private property** (including financial capital) while the property-less workers – like hotel housekeepers (cf. Introduction, Topic I.1) – continue to toil for minimal wages.

As Marx argued, this **exploitation** maintains the ever-growing economic and social gap between capitalists and workers. Indeed, even Britain's Prime Minister Theresa May has acknowledged the severity of this gap. In announcing her candidacy for leadership of the Conservative Party in 2016, she declared that the wage gap between employers and workers is "irrational, unhealthy, and growing." But such inequality is inherent in capitalism; according to Marx, it is both necessary to, and a consequence of, capitalism's profit accumulation logic.

MARX'S THEORY OF HISTORY

Marx understands history as the progressive expansion of the material or economic forces in society, that is, in the advances made by societies in organizing their material production (e.g., agriculture, manufacturing, services). Marx's theory is referred to as **historical materialism** because he focuses on the material (economic) conditions in society and on how these conditions determine social structures and social relations. As elaborated by Marx's intellectual collaborator, Friedrich Engels,

> The materialist conception of history starts from the proposition that the production of the means to support human life and, next to production, the exchange of things produced, is the basis of all social structure; that in every society that has happened in history, the manner in which wealth is distributed and society divided into classes or orders is dependent upon what is produced, how it is produced, and how the products are exchanged. (Engels 1878/1978: 700–701)

History, Marx emphasizes, does not simply evolve independently of individuals and of the objective social relations (e.g., unequal **class relations**) that condition their lives. Rather, Marx argues that historical change, that is, change in the material conditions of society and in how economic-social relations are organized, emerges out of the perceived *contradictions* in existing economic and social arrangements. Thus, in Revolutionary France, the bourgeoisie overthrew the despotism of feudal monarchs and the aristocracy to create progressive economic and social institutions grounded in democratic principles (see Introduction).

As part of a similar historical logic, Marx predicted that the expansion of capitalism with its endless pursuit of profit, would lead to its downfall. Capitalism produces economic crises that threaten its very foundations. These crises include recessions; the collapse of stock markets; severe financial losses for banks, companies, and households; high levels of unemployment; worker unrest; and the depletion and degradation of natural resources. Marx argued that these ongoing crises would create polarized class antagonisms (between the bourgeoisie and the proletariat). They would also lead the working class to develop a **class consciousness**: individual wage-workers would come to recognize that their exploitation is part of the mass exploitation of all wage-workers, and that such exploitation is inherent in the structural organization of capitalism. Class consciousness would propel the working class to revolt against capitalism. Thus, in Marx's construal, the downfall of capitalism is contingent on both the bourgeoisie and the proletariat. The bourgeoisie, through their constant efforts to expand capitalist markets, sow the seeds of their own downfall and of capitalism's destruction; they are its "grave-diggers" (CM 94). And the proletariat is the "revolutionary class" – the "special and essential product" of modern industrial society (CM 91) – the class that would develop the revolutionary consciousness that would lead to the overthrow of capitalism and usher in new societal arrangements. We saw a glimmer of this revolutionary potential in the US in the 1920s with the rise of the antiestablishment Anarchist Party and a surge in labor union protests against factory owners. This disruption was relatively short lived, however, dampened in part by the social-democratic New Deal policies of the Roosevelt government that provided economic benefits to those hardest hit by the Depression. More recently, the Occupy Wall Street movement and the Occupy groups it spawned in various US, European, and Asian cities are another example of an attempt to disrupt capitalism (see chapter 14). It is hard, however, for these actions to gain political momentum due, as Marx also recognized, to the overarching economic and ideological constraints that impede the overthrow of capitalism (discussed later in this chapter).

Despite the ongoing crises that capitalism produces, it has also evolved in ways that Marx did not anticipate, and these developments mitigate against its (predicted) downfall. One, Marx assumed that the expansion of capital (and profit accumulation) would also require the expansion of the proletariat (i.e., that more laborers are needed to produce more commodities), which would produce a subsequent increase in workers' mass association and unionization (CM 89–90). Two, he assumed that the expanding proletariat would remain poor (CM 87–88) and thus would be further motivated to revolt against the capitalists. These conditions did not occur. Technological advances have made commodity production less contingent on manual labor than Marx anticipated, and while there is persistent poverty and substantial class inequality in well-developed capitalist societies such as the US, the working class is relatively well off. Wage-workers avail themselves of many of the economic and consumer opportunities in society: The shopping mall has become an equalizer of sorts, because we can all (more or less) go shopping. Thus the working class, like the capitalist class, has a major stake in the ongoing success of capitalism. We explore the reasons for this in a later section of this chapter when we discuss ideology.

DIALECTICAL MATERIALISM

For Marx, history does not progress smoothly. Rather, "revolution is the driving force of history" (GI 29). Each historical-economic epoch (e.g., slave society, feudalism, capitalism) is characterized by tensions or contradictions. Change emerges only when these contradictions, and the social forces and relations that reproduce these contradictions, are exposed and ruptured through social revolution. Marx's view of history emphasizes how the human-created economic conditions at a given historical moment give rise to particular economic and social practices. These practices motivate particular groups (like Occupy Wall Street) to challenge the unequal conditions of their existence, and such activism opens the possibility for the emergence of new material (economic) conditions and social relations.

This historical process, for Marx, is **dialectical materialism**. "Dialectic" derives from the Greek word *dialegein*, meaning "to argue." Philosophers from Plato to Hegel used its method to draw out the contradictions in the logic used in intellectual ideas. Dialectical method does not outline a linear argument. It instead works back and forth like a pendulum: posing a thesis, followed by its antithesis, and the integration of the two into a synthesis. Marx emphasized the importance of focusing on *real* history, that is, the history not of ideas but of "the production of material life itself" (GI 16). And he used "dialectical materialism" to convey the human-social activity involved in the historical transformation of contradictory or antithetical economic forces and relations. In this framing, existing material conditions (e.g., capitalist class inequality – the thesis) would produce opposition (class revolution – the antithesis), which in turn ushers in a new economic system (communism – the synthesis). In an earlier historical transformation, slave-based economies gave way to feudalism with indentured peasants only to be superseded by capitalism with its rising middle class of small shop owners.

Although the dialectic sounds complicated, we basically see a dialectical process in the regular cycle of democratic politics. In the US, for example, no one political party dominated the White House for more than 12 years or so over the course of the twentieth century, partly because when Republicans are in power, their policies (thesis) eventually produce a backlash (antithesis) among the electorate that contributes to the Democrats gaining power. Once in power, Democrats have to deal with the new reality created by Republican policies and thus modify their own agenda, producing new policies (synthesis), which, after creating a temporary balance, lead eventually to disaffection among the electorate, who then return the Republicans to power; and the back-and-forth cycle of adjustment and change continues. Though there are more than two parliamentary parties in the UK, a largely similar dynamic occurs with a back-and-forth swing in whether the Conservative or the Labour Party are in government. For Marx, dialectical materialism means that historical change (i.e., material/economic change) is the result of conscious human activity, which is conditioned by economic forces. Human conscious activity emerges from material/economic conditions, and as human consciousness acts upon those conditions and their contradictions, it produces new form of social existence:

> History is nothing but the succession of separate generations, each of which exploits the materials, the forms of capital, the productive forces handed down to it by all preceding ones, and thus on the one hand, continues the traditional activity in completely changed circumstances, and on the other, modifies the old circumstances with completely changed activity … It shows that circumstances make men just as much as men make circumstances. (GI 38, 29)

COMMUNISM

In Marx's historical-evolutionary thesis, **communism** is the type of society that would emerge following the overthrow of capitalism. He did not outline a blueprint of how the transition to communist society would be worked out or how communism would be organized. And indeed the economic and social realities both in the late nineteenth century and today make the practical imagining of such a society an excessively hypothetical exercise. For Marx what was important was that the transcendence of capitalism would produce a society characterized by the abolition of private property/capital, profit, the division of labor, and social classes. All of these concepts have very particular meanings in Marx's analysis and need to be understood in terms of his construal of human/social existence, as I elaborate later. But in essence, the logic of material production in communist society would be based on individual/social needs and talents rather than profit accumulation. It would require each person to contribute their creativity and labor to the everyday material and social good of the community on the basis of their diverse and multifaceted abilities. Communism would deprive

> no man of the power to appropriate the products of society: all that it does is to deprive him of the power to subjugate the labour of others by means of such appropriation … In place of the old bourgeois society, with its classes and class antagonisms, we shall have an association [a community] in which the free development of each is the condition for the free development of all. (CM 99, 105)

In contrast, therefore, to the unequal relations of capitalist production between owners and wage-workers, there would be equality between people (no one would be particularly rich or poor). This would end the structural conflict that inheres in capitalism: The asymmetrical division between the property-owning bourgeoisie and the property-less proletariat. Marx outlined this vision in *The Communist Manifesto*. Labor, he argued, would "no longer be converted into capital, money, or rent, into a social power capable of being monopolized" (CM 98). Instead, all individuals would be entitled to "appropriate the products of society" (CM 99), because the division of labor, private property, profit, and class inequality would disappear (CM 104–105; GI 21–23).

Consequently, communism would represent the "end of history," so to speak; it would mark the end of the periodic historical ruptures from ancient times, through the slave-owning Roman and Classical epoch (from 500 BCE to AD 999), the Feudal Age (1000 to 1490), and through the various stages of capitalism. In communist society – that is, a society in which the division of labor, private property, profit, and inequality would be eliminated, no one class (e.g., slave owners, feudal lords, capitalists) would control the means of production (e.g., slaves, land, capital). Consequently, there would be no more tensions and contradictions to resolve, and the dialectic or pendulum of history (dialectical materialism) would come to a stop.

Marx's theoretical vision of communism, therefore, would entail the emancipation not only of the working class but of all people: Communism represents "universal human emancipation" (EPM 82). Thus: "All previous historical movements were movements of minorities, or in the interests of minorities. The proletarian movement is the self-conscious, independent movement of the immense majority, in the interests of the immense majority" (CM 92). It would produce a society wherein each person would have rights and responsibilities toward the maintenance of their shared material and social existence. Clearly, Marx's emancipatory principles have never been realized, especially in societies that are often referred to as communist. Rather, the Soviet Union and North Korea, for example, epitomize political oppression and economic and social inequality.

THE MILLENNIUM'S GREATEST THINKER

Capitalism has not collapsed and yielded to communism (or has not *yet* collapsed, as contemporary Marxists who have not ruled out its possible downfall might aver; e.g., Wallerstein; see chapter 14). Nevertheless, Marx's analysis provides an insightful critique of capitalism's structures and processes and how they work in the production of inequality. Capitalism has changed a lot over the past several decades, and especially since the late 1990s, propelled by the rise of Internet technology and wide-ranging globalizing forces. Today's capitalist structures are much more complex than they were in the mid- to late nineteenth century when Marx was writing. And there was a lot more economic and social deprivation and industrial strife than we see today in Western societies. Just think of America or England in the 1890s when child labor was a normal part of everyday life, a theme vividly portrayed in Charles Dickens's novels.

Despite the changes that have occurred over the last century, Marx's ideas continue to provide a highly salient lens for analyzing the many ways capitalism infuses everyday life. Even the highly influential *Economist* magazine, an active proponent of free-market capitalism, stated in May 2017 that "there is an enormous amount to learn from Marx. Indeed, much of what Marx said seems to become more relevant by the day" (2017a, p. 52). Appreciation for Marx's influence is also seen in British public opinion, which at the end of the twentieth century resoundingly favored Marx as the "millennium's greatest thinker," followed by Einstein, Newton, and Darwin.

The logic of capitalism is not restricted to just one domain of activity such as the economy or paid work. It also pervades sports, medicine, education, Hollywood, politics, and even romance and marriage. We can enjoy living in a capitalist society and the freedoms associated with capitalism, most especially the freedom to shop. But while reading Marx, we also have to step back from our complete immersion in capitalism and all that we take for granted about how society is organized. Instead, we begin to critique it, probing beneath surface appearances to discern the multiple ways in which capitalism matters in daily life. It makes us probe, for example, why hotel housekeepers receive low wages for their labor (see Introduction) whereas many chief executive officers (CEOs) receive multimillion dollar yearly salaries and bonuses. For example, the median pay for CEOs at the biggest US companies in 2016 was $11.7 million (a postrecession record); the chairman of the Walt Disney Company was paid $41 million; and Apple CEO Tim Cook collected a bonus of $89 million in 2017.

HUMAN NATURE

Marx's view of human nature is frequently misunderstood. Because Marx is critical of the inequality structured into capitalist society, people who have not studied him tend to think he is opposed to work. This is far from true. Marx, in fact, has a very positive view of work, of labor. Indeed, he saw the individual's productive skills as integral to what it means to be human. Through work, the ability to work with and transform nature, individuals demonstrate the higher consciousness of the human species. In *The German Ideology*, Marx celebrates those traits that are distinctively human:

> The first premise of all human history is, of course, the existence of living human individuals. Thus the first fact to be established is the physical organization of these individuals and their consequent relation to the rest of nature … Man can be distinguished from animals by consciousness … [Humans] begin to distinguish themselves from animals as soon as they begin to *produce* their means of **subsistence** [their livelihood]. (GI 7)

By creatively working with and transforming their physical-natural environment in order to produce a livelihood, individuals working together "are indirectly producing their actual material life" (GI 7). The creativity in producing material life – our actual physical, economic, and social existence – is something that whole populations have necessarily shown throughout history. The ability to adapt to and make use of the physical and material resources in any given environment is exclusive to the human species. Engagement in this process of transforming nature is integral to what Marx calls our **species being** (our humanity). We don't just simply perform basic bodily functions (e.g., eating, sleeping, procreating); we also creatively work in and on our physical (and social) environment and adapt it to our needs (for food, tools, education, entertainment, etc.).

The activities individuals do in order to live and in order to reproduce their mode of existence (their way of life) are what set humans apart from other species. We live with nature and we embrace our natural surroundings. But we also act on nature, and in acting on nature we produce and continually reproduce our means of economic (and social) life. We transform our natural environment through what we make of it and out of it, that is, what we produce. Marx elaborates:

> The way in which men produce their means of subsistence depends first of all on the nature of the actual means of subsistence they find in existence and have to reproduce. This mode of production must not be considered simply as being the reproduction of the physical existence of the individuals. Rather it is a definite form of activity of these individuals, a definite form of expressing their life, a definite *mode of life* on their part. As individuals express their life, so they are. What they are, therefore, coincides with their production, both with *what* they produce and with *how* they produce … This production … presupposes the intercourse of individuals with one another. (GI 7–8)

MATERIAL AND SOCIAL EXISTENCE INTERTWINED

Through production, we create and recreate a mode of existence that is compatible with who we are as a species. As humans, we are physical beings, but not that alone. Rather, we have a consciousness that makes us aware that we exist in relation to other individuals. As Marx emphasizes, we maintain a social existence by producing material goods and doing so in interaction with other individuals:

> In production men not only act on nature but also on one another. They produce only by co-operating in a certain way and mutually exchanging their activities. In order to produce, they enter into definite connections and relations with one another and only within the social connections and relations does their action on nature, does production, take place … Thus the social relations within which individuals produce, the social relations of production, change, are transformed, with the change and development of the material means of production, the productive forces. The relations of production in their totality constitute what are called the social relations, society, and specifically, a society at a definite stage of historical development, a society with a peculiar, distinctive character [e.g., ancient, feudal, bourgeois society]. (WLC 29–30)

Throughout history, individuals have always existed in relation to other individuals, both physically and socially. As Marx notes, Robinson Crusoe, the exemplar of the lone individual, is a fictional character. In historical fact, there is no Robinson Crusoe. Explorers, settlers, and immigrants have always adapted to their physical surroundings by working collectively to transform them and creating a society in the process. Society is made up of

> real individuals, their [practical] activity and the material conditions under which they live, both those which they find already existing and those produced by their activity ... Life is not determined by consciousness [ideas], but consciousness by life [everyday lived existence/experience]... the real living individuals themselves ...not in any fantastic isolation and rigidity, but in their actual, empirically perceptible process of development under definite conditions. (GI 7, 15)

Individuals' material existence, *what* people do in everyday life and *how* they do it, is therefore what matters; it is this "practical activity" (GI 15) that we need to focus on. Existence is not something abstract or philosophical. Questions about the meaning of existence have a place in human thinking, and many of us have some doubts about the meaning of existence (as seen in the novels of e.g., Jean-Paul Sartre and Albert Camus). But Marx is not interested in looking at the *idea* of existence. He wants us to focus on the *actuality* of our existence: the concrete things we do, the living conditions and practices that characterize everyday reality, because through practical activity "definite individuals who are productively active in a definite way enter into ... definite social and political relations" (GI 13). Therefore, if we want to understand what is going on in society - the nature of social structures and the forces that drive social relations – we must study the "life-process of definite [real] individuals ... [who] produce materially, and are active under definite material limits" (GI 13). This is what sociologists do. We don't simply philosophize about social life; we go out into society and investigate how real people live in and adapt to definite economic and social contexts.

CAPITALISM AS A DISTINCTIVE SOCIAL FORM

PRIVATE PROPERTY

Marx emphasizes that the notion of private property developed as the world became more populated and more complex in its social organization. Private ownership was the norm in ancient Rome (e.g., ownership of slaves), in the feudal system in medieval Europe, and it is a core characteristic of capitalism. In capitalist society, ownership of the means of production – of land, oil wells, factories, financial capital, computer software programs – differentiates the bourgeoisie from the proletariat. It is on this unequal division that the whole system of economic, that is, class, and social relations rests (GI 8–13). Society, therefore, has long been stratified (organized into unequal classes or strata). Inequality is not the result of the transition to capitalism, or the result of industrialized, factory production, and nor is it the result of the emergence of today's digital economy. Rather, inequality has characterized social organization and social relationships from as early as the slave-owning Roman Empire.

THE PRODUCTION OF PROFIT

Marx singled out capitalism for specific critique largely because in his assessment (and in accord with his view of the progressive march of history), capitalism had outlived its usefulness. Although he appreciated the economic and technological advances achieved by capitalism, and recognized it as a progression over previous modes of production (e.g., feudalism), he also emphasized its regressive aspects. In particular, he underscored the fact that capitalism is a system of commodity production. Its fundamental objective is the production of commodities whose sale in the marketplace produces **capital** (money/economic resources), which accumulates as **profit** for the capitalist. The primacy of capital and profit means that the ties among individuals in a capitalist society are purely determined by economic interests. Capitalism requires a mass of individuals who must sell their labor power, and the only relevance wage-workers have for the capitalist is the extent to which they can be used (employed) to produce profit for the capitalist.

This, according to Marx, is what sets capitalist social relations apart from those in ancient Roman or in feudal systems. In Roman society, slavery was common and inequality clearly existed between slaves and masters (and there was also inequality between free men and

Figure 1.1 Walmart is a fast-growing global retail corporation with over 10,000 stores in 27 countries (with Asda its store title in the UK). Its employee policies epitomize the low-wage, cost-reduction strategies required by contemporary capitalism. Source: © RiverNorthPhotography/iStockphoto.

women). Notwithstanding this inequality, however, slave-masters also had a certain commitment to the welfare of their slaves, as did feudal lords toward their serfs – even if these commitments were driven largely by self-interest. Feudal lords, for example, did not abandon the serfs in times of famine – they felt obliged to still feed them even though the serfs were (temporarily) unable to produce food for the manor.

Conversely, under capitalism, when there is an economic downturn or when profits are in decline, factory owners and corporations fire many of their workers; they downsize and retrench. Thus Pfizer laid off more than seven thousand workers in Brooklyn, New York, when its profits were hurt by other companies' sales of generic drugs. Notwithstanding any personal regrets that any individual capitalists might have, they are obliged to terminate a worker's employment. This is what "the economy," that is, capitalism requires – typically referred to in everyday conversation as "Wall Street," or "the City" (London's concentrated financial district). By using these terms, we reify capitalism and its financial institutions and processes. This language makes us think of economic processes as if they are *things* separate from and beyond the control of the collective economic and political decision making of powerful individuals, rather than a product of capitalist structures and social relations (see Marx, CM 97; Cap 83).[2] Capitalism as a system of profit production and profit accumulation requires the factory owner or corporation to maintain economic competitiveness vis-à-vis other companies, and thus to cut production costs (including employees) in order to maintain profitability, its economic viability.

WAGE LABOR: THE COMMODIFICATION OF LABOR POWER

In capitalist society, the capitalists (e.g., owners of capital, land, oil, factories, railroads, banks, technological systems, television networks, etc.), care about workers only insofar as they have **use-value**, that is, the extent to which they can be put to use in producing something useful, something that results in producing capital and profit for the capitalists. Marx elaborates: "The capitalist buys labour-power in order to use it; … The purchaser of labour-power consumes it by setting the seller of it to work … on something useful" (Cap 197). Thus, the extent to which use-value converts into capital, into profit, is the criterion determining social relations in a capitalist society. The ties between individuals are based

Georg Simmel (1858–1918), another important German figure in the founding of sociology, also wrote about the centrality of money, economic exchange, and how they shape the character of modern society and social relations. For Simmel, monetary transactions reflect and reinforce the coldness, utility, fluidity, and emotional detachment of modern social ties. He used the example of prostitution to illustrate the calculated and impersonal detachment that inheres in monetary exchange relations more generally. He argued that the money transaction allows for "a purely momentary relationship which leaves no traces … for money establishes no ties … Money serves most matter of factually and completely for venal pleasure which rejects any continuation of the relationship beyond sensual satisfaction: money is completely detached from the person and puts an end to any further ramifications. When one pays money one is completely quits, just as one is through with the prostitute after satisfaction is attained … Of all human relationships [prostitution] is perhaps the most significant case of the mutual reduction of two persons to the status of mere means … Money is concerned only with what is common to all, i.e., with the exchange value which reduces all quality and individuality to a purely quantitative level." (Simmel 1907/1971: 121–122; 1903/1950: 326).

on "naked self-interest," and sentiment and honor are displaced by the only value that matters in a capitalist society, the "callous 'cash payment'" (CM 82). In short, "Show me the money" is the catch-cry informing social relations under capitalism (see Box 1.1).

What is especially distinctive about capitalism vis-à-vis other historical systems of inequality is that under capitalism, workers are free. This is a mark of progress; workers are not owned by masters, even though historically, slavery was integral to the expansion of capitalism (e.g., Patterson 1982; see chapter 12). In democratic capitalist societies, political and economic freedom tend to be coupled (though there are historical exceptions, such as South African apartheid). The interrelation of economic and political freedom produces the historically unusual circumstance whereby in capitalist societies, free workers (must) sell their labor (their labor power) on the market. And in doing so, wage-workers themselves become commodities to be bought and sold. Capitalism thus requires and is built upon the **commodification of labor power**. Marx explains,

what [workers] sell to the capitalist for money is their labor *power*. The capitalist buys this labor power for a day, a week, a month etc. And after he has bought it, he uses it by having the workers work for the stipulated time. For the same sum with which the capitalist has bought their labor power, for example, two marks [German currency], he could have bought two pounds of sugar or a definite amount of any other commodity. The two marks with which he bought two pounds of sugar, are the *price* of the two pounds of sugar. The two marks, with which he bought twelve hours' use of labor power, are the price of twelve hours' labor. Labor power, therefore, is a commodity neither more nor less than sugar. The former is measured by the clock, the latter by the scales. Labor power is, therefore, a commodity which its possessor, the wage worker, sells to capital … Labor power was not always a commodity. Labor was not always wage labor, that is, free labor. The slave did not sell his labor power to the slave owner anymore than the ox sells its services to the peasant. The slave, together with his labor power, is sold once and for all to his owner. He is a commodity which can pass from the hand of one owner to that of another. He is *himself* a commodity, but the labor power is not *his* commodity. The serf sells only a part of his labor power. He does not receive a wage from the owner of the land; rather, the owner of the land receives a tribute from him … The free laborer, on the other hand, sells himself and indeed sells himself piecemeal … The worker belongs neither to an owner nor to the land, but eight, ten, twelve, fifteen hours of his daily life belong to him who buys them. (WLC 17–21)

The freedom under capitalism is really an illusion, Marx argues, because in reality capitalism is a coercive system of labor exploitation. In capitalist societies, the commodities produced are not solely the sorts of things we typically think of, such as manufactured goods, our clothes and food, or information and services. Labor power itself is a commodity. Wage-workers are exchanged and traded on the market and their market value, as with other commodities, is given a price. Unlike slaves and serfs, wage-workers are free to leave a particular employer if they don't like the price they get for their labor or don't like their general working conditions. This freedom, however, is always constrained. The movement of labor may appear to be done freely, but it is in fact required, demanded, and coerced by capitalism (see Topic 1.2). Marx explains:

> The worker leaves the capitalist to whom he hires himself whenever he likes, and the capitalist discharges him whenever he thinks fit, as soon as he no longer gets any profit out of him, or not the anticipated profit. But the worker, whose sole source of livelihood is the sale of his labor power, cannot leave the *whole class of purchasers*, that is, the capitalist class, without renouncing his existence. He belongs not to this or that capitalist but to the *capitalist class*, and, moreover, it is his business to dispose of himself, that is, to find a purchaser within this capitalist class. (WLC 21)

Accordingly, for Marx, wage-labor is, essentially, "forced labour" (EPM 74). Whereas slavery is "*direct* forced labour," wage-labor is "*indirect* forced labour." Under capitalism, workers are obligated to present their labor power – their usefulness to a prospective employer - as a commodity for sale. Laborers "live only so long as they find work, and … find work only so long as their labour increases capital. These labourers, who must sell themselves piecemeal, are a commodity, like every other article of commerce, and are consequently exposed to all the vicissitudes of competition, to all the fluctuations of the market" (CM 87). Wage-workers think they are free – they may even think of themselves as just trying to make a decent living – but the reality is that their labor power is a commodity bought and sold on the market for others' profit accumulation.

> What [a wage-laborer] produces for himself is not the silk that he weaves, not the gold that he draws from the mine, not the palace that he builds. What he produces for himself is wages, and silk, gold, and palace resolve themselves for him into a definite quantity of the means of subsistence, perhaps into a cotton jacket, some copper coins and a lodging in a cellar. And the worker who for twelve hours, weaves, spins, drills, turns, builds, shovels, break stones, carries loads etc., – does he consider this twelve hours' weeding, spinning, drilling, turning, building, shoveling, stone-breaking as a manifestation of his life, as life? On the contrary life begins for him when this activity ceases, at table, in the public house, in bed. The twelve hours labor, on the other hand, has no meaning for him as weaving, spinning, drilling etc., but as *earnings*, which bring them to the table, to the public house, into bed. (WLC 20)

PROFESSIONAL SPORTS: THE COMMODIFICATION OF LABOR POWER IN ACTION

The commodification of labor power is well demonstrated in professional sports. We see this in several ways. The very language that professional sports organizations and teams use in talking about their hiring practices ensures that there is no ambiguity about the fact that football or basketball players are evaluated as commodities. This is underscored in the US by the National Football League's

Topic 1.2   The sharing, on-demand economy

The rise of what's called the sharing or gig economy facilitated by computer apps (e.g., Uber and Lyft ride-hailing services, Airbnb home rentals, Postmates home delivery, TaskRabbits home-skills service) is changing the organization of work. On the one hand, it gives individuals more control of their schedules; they can make themselves available to drive for Uber on days and time slots that suit them (or to rent out a spare bedroom at their convenience). The popularity of these new options means that many workers can supplement their monthly income as Uber drivers, etc., and some even as a full-time job (with enough money to live on, and yet still on their own schedule). The sharing economy also encourages worker creativity. You decide what you are good at and what you enjoy, whether driving (e.g., Uber, Lyft), doing light household carpentry work (e.g., TaskRabbits) or minding pets (e.g., Dogvacay), and you opt for that kind of work, rather than being required (coerced) to do tasks that you find boring or restrictive.

Notwithstanding the advantages of the sharing economy for both workers (flexibility, creativity, income) and users (efficiency, personalized service, saved income), it also has the disadvantages or inequalities that are built into capitalist labor processes more generally. The sharing economy is a still a *competitive* marketplace. Though *you* know what you are good at (or what a beautiful home or bedroom you have to rent out), the customer ratings of the quality of the work/service you provide, and of your attitude while doing so, will affect whether you become a go-to person for the particular on-demand service. Prospective clients, as they review the online ratings and comments, might choose to give you a miss in favor of another. Similarly, although you can, in principle, set your own schedule, you still need to be available when customers/clients need you/your service. It is, after all, an *on-demand* economy and you must meet that demand, that is, share yourself (and do it well) in order to live, that is, in order to make enough money for yourself. On-demand also means that your work is contingent on the needs of others, and is therefore more unstable and uncertain than many other jobs, though seasonal (e.g., fruit-pickers) and adjunct (e.g., per-course college lecturers) work is also precarious. Further, because most gig workers are considered "independent contractors" rather than company "employees," they do not get health insurance and sick day benefits from the contracting company (e.g., Uber). They are useful to the company only as *workers*; it is their labor and services, not their unwell feelings, that get shared, that is, that are valued for profit.

Moreover, the app/contracting company also gets a cut of the money exchanged (via the app) for the service. Airbnb, for example, typically takes 10 percent of what a guest pays for leasing accommodation from a registered host. Although Airbnb, Uber, and other sharing companies have business costs (e.g., the costs of building and maintaining the app computer platform infrastructure, and administering and overseeing the details of everyday operations), each company still makes *surplus profit* at the expense of those who work for it (and those who use it too). Uber, for example, has had multiple corporate scandals: Some are over its work practices – in Singapore, for example, it knowingly leased unsafe SUVs with electrical problems to its drivers; others relate to its corporate culture, where sexual harassment is prevalent. Indeed, in September 2017, London's Transport Authority banned Uber from operating in London (where it has 3.5 million users), citing its "lack of corporate responsibility." Uber, nonetheless, is still valued at approx. $70 billion (and Airbnb at approx. $30 billion) (see, for example, Heller 2017; McMillan and Purnell 2017.)

(NFL) annual draft. We hear about the *trading* that occurs prior to draft day; one team exchanges their #5 pick for two lower-ranked choices from a different team. We hear how much money prospective players are willing to settle for, what price they will accept for their labor power, and we are left in no doubt that the quarterback (QB) is being selected (and subsequently assessed) not for his all-around athletic ability or leadership qualities, but for his *piecemeal* value – his arm, his ability to throw the ball, his "passing efficiency." Despite the glamour and the high salary (think of Tom Brady, the New England Patriots QB), the quarterback more than any other player – and especially compared to defensive backs whose entire bodies are commodified – is reduced to the value of one body piece, the usefulness of the arm. And the efficiency of the arm is determined statistically: the number of completed passes and the ratio of touchdowns to interceptions thrown (See Topic 1.3).

We see similar efficiency-evaluation scales used across other professional sports. Players' usefulness is determined by their productivity; their performance statistics, such as a baseball pitcher's velocity, the per-game shooting percentages of basketball and hockey players, the number of goals scored on the football field, etc., provide a shorthand metric determining their market value. Thus star football players like Tom Brady and David Beckham are paid millions of dollars not only to play ball and to expand a team's fan base but also for their off-the-field usefulness in promoting (and selling) their favored footwear (e.g., Adidas, UGGs), clothing, and bottled water brands, among other products. And although some players are "free agents," not bound by their contract to a previous team owner, they are nonetheless, as Marx reminds us, not really free; they must find another team owner to whom to sell themselves. Wage-workers, whether professional sports players or waitresses, must sell their labor power. Why do they sell it?

> In order to live. But the exercise of labor power, labor, is the worker's own life activity, the manifestation of his own life. And this life activity he sells to another person in order to secure the necessary *means of subsistence*. Thus his life activity is for him only a means to enable him to exist. He works in order to live. He does not even reckon labor as part of his life, it is rather a sacrifice of his life. It is a commodity which he has made over to another. (WLC 19)

Many professional sports players earn big salaries; their multimillion dollar contracts allow them to meet their subsistence needs far more easily than is the case for waitresses, sales people, skilled workers, and most professional workers (e.g., lawyers, doctors). Nonetheless, despite their exceedingly high

---

Topic 1.3   Scouting new football recruits

The evaluation of football players as efficient physical objects – as future profit-generating commodities – is the primary purpose of the NFL's annual Scouting Combine, the exhibition show for prospective professional football recruits. At the weeklong event, college football players are competitively evaluated by NFL coaches and scouts. Several tough physical tests assess the players' physical strength: how well they do in the broad jump, the vertical leap, the three-cone drill, lifting weights – and especially their speed – because in the NFL "each second makes a difference" to the player's and the team's success. It is not all about speed, however. At the Combine, "the least exhaustive test … often takes the longest to prepare for … the look test … During a medical exam, the prospects strip to their shorts to reveal whether they look the part of a football player." For some, this means bulking up, for others, slimming down (Packer 2007: C16).

incomes, professional sports players are commodities, and perhaps more than many other workers, they literally sacrifice their lives to work. Many sports players retire with a comfortable amount of money but are severely disabled from a career marked by repeated concussions (which lead, for example, to early onset of Alzheimer's disease) and other injuries that have long-term debilitating effects on the player's physical and mental functioning. This is a topic getting increased attention in football circles, and after decades of denial, even NFL owners/executives are acknowledging the negative long-term impact of sports injuries (see Topic 1.5).

Not only do professional athletes endure these injuries as part of their job, many feel the competitive pressure to actively harm their bodies over the long term by taking steroids to build up their short-term strength and endurance. As early as high school, young men are taking steroids – substances that over time build up cumulative negative effects on an individual's physical and mental health – in order to enhance the price they can get for themselves when (in actuality, *if*) they make it to draft day and a professional career.

WORK: LIFE SACRIFICE

There is compelling evidence from professional sports of workers' willingness to sacrifice their health for someone else's profit. Many other wage-workers also sacrifice their health, working in dangerous jobs in return for moderate earnings. Meat-packers, miners, firefighters, police officers, soldiers, and construction workers confront the threat of injury and death on a regular basis (see Topic 1.4). In any case, because all wage-workers sell their labor power "in order to live" (WLC 19), work becomes a means to an end rather than an end in itself. It thus loses its potential as a creative and cooperative activity reflective of humans' higher consciousness. Its value is instead determined by its usefulness in the production of capitalist profit.

Further, even if steroid-using athletes were assured of success – of getting drafted (bought) or getting a contract extension – a Marxist-derived analysis would argue that they are deluded by a **false consciousness**, a consciousness that is itself the historical product of capitalism. Because we embrace the "illusion" of the capitalist epoch in which we live (GI 30) – its affirmation and celebration of freedom, equality, money, and consumption (GI 40) – we willingly and freely sell ourselves because we believe that we are profiting through our particular actions.[3] But this is false, Marx tells us: The capitalist will always profit more than even the most highly paid professional athlete. The capitalist's profit, by definition, always comes at the expense of the wage-worker's life. Wage-workers, though consciously working to produce capital (and in the process, reproducing capitalism as a system), work under a false illusion. This is the historically produced illusion that capitalism is a natural economic system rather than a historically specific, and humanly produced, economic system that favors some (the owners/capitalists) at the expense of others (wage-workers). Under capitalism, therefore, wage-workers are unable to develop a true consciousness of how their economic interests are in contradiction with those of capitalism. They cannot see that their objective (unequal) class position is in contradiction with the class position and economic profit interests of the capitalists (for whom belief in the "naturalness" of capitalism aligns with their interests).[4]

WAGE-LABOR AND SURPLUS VALUE

What the high-income professional sports player and the low-income hotel housekeeper have in common is that **surplus value** is extracted from both by their respective employers. The logic of capitalism is the accumulation of profit, and this profit has to come from somewhere. It comes from

Topic 1.4   Occupational injuries in the meat-packing industry

In 2015, the US Bureau of Labor Statistics recorded 4,836 deaths sustained from injuries in the workplace, with the construction, warehousing/transportation, and agriculture/forestry/fisheries sectors the most hazardous (https://www.bls.gov/iif/oshcfoi1.htm). A report by Human Rights Watch vividly highlights the occupational hazards some workers confront: "Meatpacking work has extraordinarily and unnecessarily high rates of injury, musculoskeletal disorders (repetitive stress injuries), and even death. Whatever the inherent dangers of meatpacking work, they are aggravated by ever-increasing line speeds, inadequate training, close-quarters cutting, and long hours with few breaks … Almost every worker interviewed … for this report began with the story of a serious injury he or she suffered in a meat or poultry plant, injuries reflected in their scars, swellings, rashes, amputations, blindness or other afflictions." Among the meat-industry injuries recorded by the US federal Occupational Safety and Health Administration (OSHA) were the following:

- "Worker killed when hog-splitting saw is activated."
- "Worker dies when he is pulled into a conveyor and crushed."
- "Worker loses legs when a worker activates the grinder in which he is standing."
- "Worker loses hand when he reaches under a boning table to hose meat from chain."

(See "Blood, sweat, and fear: Workers' rights in US meat and poultry plants," https://www.hrw.org/sites/default/files/reports/usa0105.pdf.)

Meat-workers are further disadvantaged because many are illegal immigrants. Case Farms is a chicken plant in Ohio that produces nearly a billion pounds of chicken for Kentucky Fried Chicken and Taco Bell and deli meat for supermarkets and for the US federal government's school-lunch program. It is "among the most dangerous workplaces in America. In 2015 alone, federal workplace-safety inspectors fined the company nearly two million dollars, and in the past seven years it has been cited for two hundred and forty violations." Working conditions such as fast "line speeds and a procedure that required [workers] to cut three wings at a time by stacking the wings and running them through a spinning saw [meant that] occasionally the wings broke, and bones got caught in workers' gloves, dragging their fingers through the saw." When some employees protest against such procedures, however, the company typically uses their undocumented immigration status as a reason to fire them (Grabell 2017: 46, 51; see also Miraftab 2017).

the extra value – the surplus value or extra capital – created by wage-workers' labor. Supply and demand influence how much a given worker or a group or class of workers, electricians say, can earn in a given place at any given time. How well the economy is doing, and whether there is an under- or oversupply of qualified workers available to meet the market demand for a particular commodity (e.g., new housing, dentists, restaurant services at a seaside resort), have an impact on how much money workers get for their labor power.

Marx recognizes these factors in determining wages. But he also highlights an even more basic way in which wages are determined – the actual cost of production. Marx argues:

> ### Topic 1.5   "If I had a perfect place to die, I would die on the field."
>
> Injured bodies – in football, rugby, tennis, or golf – are part of professional athletes' exchange value. Chronic traumatic encephalopathy (CTE), a degenerative disease of the brain, is associated with repeated head traumas like concussion. In 2016, after years of dismissing the issue, a senior NFL official publicly acknowledged a connection between football and CTE, and the NFL and the NFL Players Association agreed to a new policy to enforce concussion protocol. Teams violating the policy are subject to discipline, through fines or losing upcoming draft picks. The league and its 32 club owners will provide $100 million in support of engineering advancements and medical research, in addition to $100 million it previously pledged to the National Institutes of Health (NIH) for medical and neuroscience research (a donation that was itself controversial because the NFL sought to have medical doctors with ties to the NFL supervise the NIH research).
>
> In July 2017, a study published in the Journal of the American Medical Association (JAMA) identified CTE in 110 of 111 deceased NFL players' brains that were donated to scientific research. A few days later, when asked at training camp about his concerns over CTE, the New York Jets rookie (and first-round draft pick) Jamal Adams said: "I'm all about making the game safer … but as a defensive player, I'm not a big fan of it [laughing]…But, I get it…..and I could speak for a lot of guys that play the game, we live and breathe [football] — this is what we're so passionate about. Literally, if I had a perfect place to die, I would die on the field. I would be at peace. Literally. That's not a lie" (http://www.espn.com/blog/new-york-jets/post/_/id/69973/jamal-adams-on-cte-field-is-perfect-place-to-die-fans-cheer). Jamal's is not a lone voice. Roy Keane, assistant manager of the Irish football team and renowned ex-Manchester United player, expresses a similar view: "We want players to put their bodies on the line. People have died for their country….they've done more than just break their leg" (*Irish Times*, June 9, 2017, https://www.irishtimes.com/sport/soccer/international/roy-keane-we-want-players-to-put-their-bodies-on-the-line-1.3113821).

the price of labor will be determined by the cost of production, by the labor time necessary to produce this commodity – labor power. *What then is the cost of production of labor power? It is the cost required for maintaining the worker as a worker and of developing him into a worker. … The price of his labor* will, therefore, be determined by the *price of the necessary means of subsistence* … Another consideration … in calculating the cost of production of simple labor power, there must be included the cost of reproduction, whereby the race of workers is enabled to multiply and to replace worn-out workers by new ones. Thus the depreciation of the worker is taken into account in the same way as the depreciation of the machine. The cost of production of simple labor power, therefore, amounts to the *cost of existence and reproduction of the worker*. The price of this cost of existence and reproduction constitutes wages. Wages so determined are called the *wage minimum*. (WLC 27–28; italics in original)

In other words, the capitalist pays the minimum necessary to ensure the worker's physical subsistence as an able-bodied worker, and enough to ensure the actual physical, social and biological reproduction of a new generation of workers. Today, in the US, the federally mandated minimum wage is $7.25 per hour (less than the cost of a large cheese pizza). Wage costs are necessary costs that the capitalist encounters in reproducing current and future workers who can be put to work creating capital and profit. In return for these wages, the capitalist receives "the productive activity of the worker, the creative power whereby the worker not only replaces what he consumes [as a worker] but gives to the accumulated labor a greater value than it previously possessed … he produces capital" (WLC 32). And, this capital has a surplus value for the capitalist above and beyond the worker's production cost (i.e., the cost to the capitalist of the worker's subsistence and reproduction as a worker).

Marx explains surplus value as the difference between a worker's **exchange-value** – that is, the market value of a worker's labor, or simply, their wages – and their use-value:

> The daily cost of maintaining [labor] and its daily expenditure in work, are two totally different things. The former [the cost of maintaining labor, i.e. the subsistence and reproduction of the worker] determines the exchange value of the labour-power, the latter [the living labor that it can call into action] is its use-value … Therefore, the value of labour power, and the value which that labour-power creates in the labour process are two entirely different magnitudes, and this difference of the two values was what the capitalist had in view, when he was purchasing the labour power … What really influenced him was the specific use-value which this commodity possesses of being a source not only of value, but of more value than it has itself. This is the special service that the capitalist expects from labour power, and in this transaction he acts in accordance with the "eternal laws" of the exchange of commodities. The seller of labour-power, like the seller of any other commodity, realizes [acquires] its exchange value, and parts with its use-value. He cannot take the one without giving the other. The use value of labour-power [labor] … belongs just as little to its seller, as the use-value of oil after it has been sold belongs to the dealer who has sold it. (Cap 215–216)

THE GAP BETWEEN EXCHANGE-VALUE AND USE-VALUE

Consequently, what workers are paid – their earnings/market value or exchange-value – and what they are paid for – their labor power/use-value, their usefulness in creating capital/profit – are two very different things. The capitalist pays the exchange-value (wages) of 20 hours' labor power but gets the use-value of 40 hours' labor; the wage-workers' usefulness in creating capital extends beyond what they are paid for, and this difference between their exchange-value (wages) and their use-value is what constitutes surplus value, or profit for the capitalist (Cap 207–217). For workers to subsist and to physically maintain themselves as workers, they may need to work for only 4 hours a day, but they work for 8 hours a day. A worker may need to prepare and cook 12 cheese pizzas every day in exchange for the wages they are paid by the restaurant owner, but in fact, the worker prepares 48 pizzas every day thereby creating surplus value for the owner because their labor produces 36 additional pizzas. The additional hours worked, or the additional pizzas prepared by the worker, over and above the capitalist's production cost (including the costs of the ingredients, electricity, building maintenance, etc.), represent surplus value for the capitalist. And it is this surplus value produced by the worker that constitutes the capitalist's profit.

Accordingly, the capitalist's surplus value is the worker's surplus labor (Cap 207–217). The production of surplus value is necessary for the pursuit and accumulation of capitalist profit. The more productive workers are, the more surplus value they create for the capitalist. Consequently, the proportional cost of their labor power becomes cheaper for the capitalist. As Marx states: "The worker becomes all the poorer the more wealth he produces … The worker becomes an ever cheaper commodity the more commodities he creates" (EPM 71). Workers' use-value to the capitalist increases but their exchange-value – the cost of maintaining them as workers (i.e., their wages) – decrease in inverse proportion to their use-value. In short, workers' use-value to the capitalist is greater than their exchange-value is to themselves (Cap 215–216). Notwithstanding the gap between the surplus value (profit) workers create and the wages they receive, employers continuously look to find ways to increase their profits at workers' expense. Caterpillar, the US-based multinational manufacturer of bulldozers and other heavy earth-moving equipment, for example, earned a record $5.7 billion profit in 2012. Its top-tier skilled machinists at its American plant in Indiana earn $55,000 a year whereas its junior employees earn $12 to $19 per hour; overall Caterpillar makes a profit of more than $40,000 per each employee. Nonetheless, it implemented a six-year wage and pension freeze and also requires workers to pay increased health-care contributions (up to $1,900 per year) (see Greenhouse 2012: A1, 3).

THE DIVISION OF LABOR AND ALIENATION

The **division of labor**, or economic and occupational specialization, is a dominant feature of modern capitalist society, and has evolved progressively over time (GI 8). The division of labor separates sectors (e.g., agriculture, manufacturing, services) and workers into discrete spheres of ever-more specialized activity. Adam Smith (1776/1925), the eighteenth-century Scottish philosopher and advocate of free market capitalism, emphasized the material advantages that derive from exchange based on occupational specialization and the division of labor. Marx, by contrast, underscores its negative, fragmentary effects. He argues that individuals have the human ability to do many things and have the capacity for many creative interests and hobbies. But the division of labor – as an objectified structure of capitalism – reduces the individual to the performance of the specialized activity that has the most use-value in the production of capital (e.g., the arm-throwing labor of football quarterback Tom Brady). Marx states,

> as soon as labor is distributed, each man has a particular exclusive sphere of activity, which is forced upon him and from which he cannot escape. He is a hunter, a fisherman, a shepherd, or a critical critic, and must remain so if he does not want to lose his means of livelihood…; while in communist society where nobody has one exclusive sphere of activity, but each can become accomplished in any branch he wishes … makes it possible for me to do one thing to-day and another to-morrow, to hunt in the morning, fish in the afternoon, rear cattle in the evening, criticize after dinner, just as I have a mind, without ever becoming hunter, fisherman, shepherd or critic. (GI 22)

THE PRODUCTION PROCESS

The organization of capitalist production – whether in factories, construction sites, or corporate offices – ensures the usefulness or efficiency of workers in the creation of surplus value (capitalist profit). Workers' tasks are divided into minute elements so that each individual is responsible for a very specific aspect of the production process. The diversity of occupations that exists in any industrialized country underscores that to make a living in today's economy, a worker must specialize in a highly defined activity. Just picking a random page in the US Census occupational code, we see the following specialized jobs: "aircraft cleaner, aircraft communicator, aircraft designer, aircraft electrician, aircraft engine specialist, aircraft instrument tester, aircraft lay out worker, aircraft log clerk, aircraft machinist, aircraft metalsmith, aircraft painter, aircraft riveter, aircraft stress analyst," and so on.

The fast-moving, assembly-line production we associate with the manufacture of goods (whether cars, pizzas, or candy) epitomizes the division of labor under capitalism. Assembly-line production assigns specific tasks to each worker (or worker team), whose speedy task accomplishment is essential to the smooth, uninterrupted operation of commodity production. A similar division of labor is evident in the production (construction) of houses: a primary contractor is hired to build the house and in turn hires a whole retinue of subcontractor specialists: laborers, plasterers, plumbers, tilers, carpenters, electricians, roofers, and landscapers. And intellectual labor is also highly specialized. Doctors typically specialize in one of a broad array of specialties (oncology, gynecology, dermatology, pediatrics, urology, cardiology, etc.). Lawyers also specialize: corporate law, family law, property law, estate law. Even sociologists are expected to specialize in a particular subfield: The American Sociological Association currently has 52 sections, reflecting the specialized topics and subject areas of its members: sociology of culture, medical sociology, sex and gender, political sociology, etc.

ALIENATED LABOR

The division of labor may seem necessary to distributing responsibility and expertise for the many complex jobs that need to be done in society. It ensures that labor is used efficiently to produce the vast amount of commodities (including knowledge commodities) that are needed to meet consumer demand. But Marx wants us to see it differently – to see it as dehumanizing of the individual and of society. He argues that the commodification of labor power reduces workers to commodities (with exchange- and use-value) and produces alienation, or **alienated labor**. Alienated labor is thus objectively inherent in the economic and social organization of capitalism; it is entwined with the production objectives (e.g., profit) and processes of capitalism such as the division of labor (see EPM 71–81; Box 1.2).

Box 1.2   Alienation inheres in capitalism

(a)   Alienation of wage workers from the products produced
(b)   Alienation through the production process
(c)   Alienation of individuals from their species being (their human essence)
(d)   Alienation of individuals from one another

(a)   Alienation of workers from the products they produce
Workers are alienated or estranged from the **products** their labor produces; their labor and the product of their labor are *external* to them, both literally and in terms of ownership. Workers' labor is not their own but is "forced labour" (EPM 74); it belongs to the employer. Similarly, the products of the worker's labor do not belong to the worker but to someone else – the employer who sells the product/commodity and the consumer who buys it. The commodities that workers produce are not theirs to use despite their having made them; they are only theirs to buy. Thus the product of a worker's labor (like the labor itself) becomes a force that is external to the worker. Rather than being the objective reflection of the worker's transformation of raw materials into something new – an object available to the worker – the product of the worker's labor becomes an object for someone else's disposal on the market. Marx writes, "it exists outside him, independently, as something alien to him; … it becomes a power of its own confronting him: it means that the life which he has conferred on the object confronts him as something hostile and alien" (EPM 72). He refers to this process as the **objectification** of labor. The products produced by a worker's labor exert a power over the worker; the worker must keep producing more and more products (and service workers must serve more and more customers; hotel housekeepers must clean more rooms, change more beds; and university lecturers must teach more students, etc.) – but the value of this extra work returns to the employer and not to the worker.

This idea fits with Marx's thesis (discussed previously) that the more commodities the worker produces the relatively poorer the worker becomes. Wages can increase, but the profit return to the capitalist from the wage-worker's labor will always be proportionally greater than the wages paid to (for) the worker. Wage-labor thus differs from the labor done, for example, under feudalism, where the farmer-serfs plowed the land, planted the seeds, tilled and cultivated the furrows, and then harvested the crops and kept what was necessary for their family's subsistence. The farmers experienced the complete cycle of production and produced for their own needs while also producing for others, as did craft workers and others under the feudal lord's tutelage.

(b)   Alienation of workers in the production process

The worker is also alienated through the **production process** itself. The process of production is "active alienation," whereby the "worker's own physical and mental energy" is turned against him (EPM 74, 75). Labor is not an end in itself that is freely chosen by the worker. Rather, it is coerced by and performed for someone else, most immediately, the capitalist employer. Wage-labor is "activity performed in the service, under the dominion, the coercion and the yoke of another" (EPM 80). In short, wage-workers do not determine what they produce or how they produce it; they are simply objects in the production process. As those of you who have worked in restaurants know, your daily schedule and the number of tables/customers you serve are not spontaneously determined by you but by your supervisor/employer. And the speed with which you serve the customers is also not yours to decide; each employer sets prior standards and rules that you have to abide by, irrespective of how much energy you might have on a given day (see Topic 1.6).

(c)   Alienation of workers from their species being

By reducing workers to objects with use-value in commodity production, the production process **alienates them from their species being** – from the creativity and higher consciousness that distinguish humans from animals (EPM 76–77). Wage-labor coerces us to use work – our life activity – as a means to our physical existence, rather than using our physical existence to realize our humanity and to engage in the freely chosen physical and mental activities of which our species is capable. In principle, work can be a creative extension of our selves: "the productive life is the life of the species. It is life-engendering life" – but under capitalism, "life itself appears only as a means to life" (EPM 76). In other words, we work to live (to subsist) rather than working to fully actualize our human-social life. Alienated labor strips work of its intrinsic human meaning and its potential to express human creativity. In this process, humans are reduced essentially to an animal-like status; they are alienated from the very characteristics that distinguish them as humans. Marx writes:

> First, the fact that labor is external to the worker, i.e., it does not belong to his essential being; that in his work, therefore, he does not affirm himself but denies himself, does not feel content but unhappy, does not develop freely his physical and mental energy but mortifies his body and ruins his mind. The worker therefore only feels himself outside his work, and in his work feels outside himself. He is at home when he is not working, and when he is working he is not at home. His labor is therefore not voluntary, but coerced; it is *forced labor*. It is therefore not the satisfaction of a need; it is merely a *means* to satisfy needs external to it … man (the worker) no longer feels himself to be freely active in any but his animal functions – eating, drinking, procreating, or at most in his dwelling and in dressing-up, etc.; and in his human functions he no longer feels himself to be anything but an animal. What is animal becomes human and what is human

becomes animal. Certainly eating, drinking, procreating, etc., are also genuine human functions. But in the abstraction which separates them from the sphere of all other human activity and turns them into sole and ultimate ends, they are animal. (EPM 74)

(d)   Alienation of individuals from one another

Although humans are a social species who relate to and cooperatively interact with others, capitalism produces "the *estrangement of man* from *man*" (EPM 78; italics in original), of **individuals from one another**. Work becomes the individual's life, rather than the means to enjoy life with others. The demands of work, whether for wage-laborers or for salaried professionals, are not conducive to workers' family life or to their participation in community activities; the demands of work require that work rather than nonwork activities receive priority. At many companies – including Starbucks, Gap, Abercrombie & Fitch, and Victoria's Secret – on-call and erratic scheduling means that workers can't make plans for nonwork activities. At Walmart, for example, workplace policies "create a cheaper, more flexible work force by capping wages, using more part-time workers and scheduling more workers on nights and weekends," meaning that workers are pressured to be available 24/7 (Greenhouse and Barbaro 2006). This enables Walmart to have more part-time than full-time employees, thus reducing its wage costs, expanding its profits, and increasing its stock price on Wall Street. On-call, open-ended scheduling demands have a negative impact on employees' family and other commitments, making it difficult for them to care for their children, to attend school functions, or to go to church. One worker said, "it makes it hard to establish routines like reading to your kids at night or having dinner together as a family" (Greenhouse and Barbaro 2006). Walmart, moreover, "routinely refuses to accept doctors' notes, penalizes workers who need to take care of a sick family member and otherwise punishes employees for lawful absences" (Abrams 2017).

And at work, the alienation of workers from one another is accomplished through the production process. Its demands of speed and efficiency – the number of beds made, of customers served, of hours billable to a client – require workers to work rather than to socialize. Another way in which workers are alienated from one another is through the competitive nature of the workplace. Who will be the employee of the month? Who will get a bonus? Who will get the most valuable player award? These are competitive awards for which there are winners and losers, thus pitting workers against one another, and they exist across all work sectors, from fast-food restaurants to the banking industry. The worker who receives an award will be the one who has been the most productive, that is, delivers the most pizzas, sells the most condominiums, sees the most patients thereby creating the most surplus value/profit during a given time interval. So, even when it seems that employers (including universities) are being nice to workers by giving them bonuses and awards, from a Marxist perspective, these incentives are a capitalist strategy to ensure that more and more surplus value, more and more profit is being produced by workers for their respective employers and for the capitalist class as a whole.

Capitalist production, moreover, is structured so that the livelihoods of employed workers are in constant threat from those on the sidelines (e.g., because of seasonal work, unemployment, immigration flows). The capitalist always has access to the labor power of the unemployed, especially when employees can be fired and replaced by other workers who must necessarily find work in order to make a living wage. This is yet another way in which labor is coerced and by which capitalism sets individuals against one another. Further, interworker competition is globalized. Workers in the US or the UK, for example, are stripped of sympathy for their fellow workers in the sweatshops of China and Bangladesh, because they see them as a threat to their own continuing employment. This, in turn, further dampens the development of the class consciousness of the proletariat envisioned by Marx.

Topic 1.6   Laboring in the poultry factory

Chicken processing plants exemplify the how the capitalist production process produces not just commodities but objectively alienated labor. At these plants, there is a highly specialized division of labor; the women who work in the plant's "deboning line" are not just *poultry* workers, but, more specifically, chicken deboners or "wing cutters." Their personal identity is reduced to this highly specific wing-cutting activity such that they are described as if they were machines, as objects rather than humans (i.e., alienated in the production process and from their human species being). In 2017, with growing consumer demand for chicken, the National Chicken Council (which represents poultry companies) asked the government for permission to increase line speeds from 140 to 175 birds a minute. Even at 140 per minute, the line speed pressure means that workers are not allowed to have bathroom breaks. (Walmart and other workplaces have similar restrictions on employee rest breaks.) Nor clearly is there time for chatting with other workers on the line. These demands produce alienated labor: The workers' physical and social needs are subjugated to the demands of profit production. Workers make approximately 18,000 deboning cuts during a typical shift (eight hours), preparing chicken pieces for supermarket sales to consumers. The deboned chicken breasts, fillets, etc. thus come to exist as objects that have an external, controlling power over the workers; they are not for the workers' consumption, for satisfaction of their physical hunger, but are tallies of the workers' speed and productivity (thus producing workers' alienation from the products of their labor power). Most chicken deboners, even those with a lot of experience, earn less than $8 an hour. Given that a packet of chicken tenders sells in the supermarket for about $7, we can readily see that, even taking account of the expense incurred in raising a chicken, and the production costs and profit margins in the distribution chain from factory owners to shop owners, there is a substantial gap between the worker's exchange-value (approx. $8 per hour) and their use-value (deboning over 2,000 chickens per hour) – the surplus value or profit their labor produces for the factory owner. Chicken-cutters produce a lot of surplus value. Nevertheless, their profit usefulness is lessened if they take bathroom breaks – thus this activity is regulated. It is not the workers who decide when they need to go to the bathroom; like the amount of wing-cuts required, this need is determined externally – by factory owners who are mindful only of the production of profit. Reflecting global capitalism's competitive nature, the Chicken Council argues that a line speed increase would increase both worker and plant efficiency, and help the US reclaim international meat sales lost to competitors like Brazil, which has surpassed the US in chicken export sales (Bunge 2017). And pork plants too are expecting new rules to allow faster line speeds. (See also Topic 1.4 and Topic 2.4, chapter 2.)

THE OPPRESSION OF CAPITALISTS

In Marx's analysis of capitalism, it is not just wage-workers who are objectively alienated. Business owners and corporate executives are also in servitude to production demands, that is, the production of capital. Companies and all employers (e.g., meat plants, hospitals, universities) must compete with others in their sector to cut production costs and increase profits and market share.

Capitalists' relation to capital – as owners of land, factories, corporations – is quite different to that of workers, and the production process is organized to maximize the capitalists' accumulation of capital. Nevertheless, capitalists themselves are controlled by capital, though it may seem that they are its masters. In actuality, their life activity is driven toward the accumulation of capital. To succeed as capitalists they must defer their noneconomic interests and activities to the pursuit of profit; this activity takes on a life of its own and renders the capitalists "under the sway of [the] inhuman power" of capital (EPM 125).

There is much evidence of this in the business world. For example, James Kilts, the retired, highly successful former chairman and chief executive of Gillette, accepted a postretirement appointment managing a private investment firm. He commented that, unlike some of his peers at other firms who work *part time* (i.e., five days a week), his was a 24/7 commitment. The need for Mr. Kilts to work seven days a week was not driven by his lack of personal wealth; when Gillette was sold to Procter & Gamble (P&G) in 2005, he received $175 million, and an additional $19.1 million subsequently as vice chairman of P&G. Yet, despite his extensive economic assets, he is still enchanted by the prospect of making even more money; this is the lure of capitalism and capital accumulation.

The pressure toward ever-more capital accumulation on the everyday, capital-accumulation habits of corporate executives gives flesh to Marx's argument:

> The less you eat, drink and read books; the less you go to the theater, the dance hall, the public house; the less you think, love, theorize, sing, paint, fence etc., the more you save – the *greater* becomes your treasure which neither moths nor dust will devour – your *capital*. The less you *are*, the more you *have*; the less you express your own life, the greater is your *alienated* life – the greater is the store of your estranged being … all passions and all activity must therefore be submerged in *avarice*. (EPM 118–119; italics in original)

This avarice is not necessarily a personal trait of any individual capitalist but is demanded by capitalism: The accumulation of capital and profit is a ceaseless task, a 24/7 commitment.

And the capitalist who fails to serve capital, who fails to accumulate it in an ever-greater amount, must leave the capitalist class. Or, in today's more differentiated corporate structure, must leave its higher echelons, at least for a while. Any action that threatens to reduce the stock price of a company, whether faulty financial management or a CEO's lapse in personal behavior (e.g., sexual harassment, embellishing one's résumé), can spell the demise of its corporate leader. As the business news attests, the "resignation" and management "restructuring" (i.e., the firing or demotion) of corporate executives are quite common. The everyday, profit-oriented activities and the personal reputation of corporate executives are beholden to "Wall Street" and "the City." Corporate value and the profit productivity of companies and their executives are the objects of several economic indexes and ratings. Therefore, just as the productivity of factory workers and football players is easily assessed, we can also readily see the stock performance and capital rankings of corporations, indicators that signal whether company executives are making the profit-oriented decisions that satisfy corporate owners/shareholders.

Corporate executives are thus subservient to Wall Street's capital growth demands; each business quarter – three months, or the length of one semester – brings the threat of failure, of having a profit sheet that shows less capital than anticipated by shareholders and investors. In sum, although capitalist owners/executives are much wealthier than workers, they are nonetheless self-alienated because of the hold of capital accumulation on their lives. The objective alienation that capitalism produces is all the more dehumanizing given, as Marx recognized, the vast resources that capitalism generates. These could be used to create a society in which individuals are free to pursue goals that are not incessantly tied to the unrelenting obligation to produce surplus value/profit. But under capitalism, capitalists and workers alike are servants of capital.

Recognizing exploitation

It is more difficult for the capitalists than it is for the proletariat, however, to recognize the self-alienation and objectification that capitalism produces. After all, it is wage-workers – chicken deboners, Walmart shelf-stockers, hotel housekeepers – who experience the dehumanization of the production process most immediately and on a daily basis. By contrast, the bourgeoisie, "the possessing class" (e.g., corporate executives), experiences the profit production process and its results, that is, private property, as affirming their own abilities and power. Consequently, they misrecognize the alienation that capitalism produces for capitalists and wage-workers alike. Further, unlike wage workers, they "experience alienation as a sign of their own [bourgeois] power" (ASC 133). Such misrecognition propels their domination of the proletariat, their exploitation of wage-workers' surplus value in the accumulation of profit. Partly for this reason, according to Marx, the overthrow of capitalism will originate with the workers (discussed previously), or from within what the Hungarian Marxist theorist Georg Lukács (1968: 149) refers to as the **standpoint of the proletariat**. Given the bourgeoisie's exploitation of the proletariat, Marx states, "the proletariat … is compelled to abolish itself and thereby its conditioning opposite – [the capitalist structure] – which makes it a proletariat" (ASC, 133).

ECONOMIC INEQUALITY

The different positions that capitalists and workers objectively occupy in relation to capital – that is, what is surplus value for the capitalist is the worker's surplus labor – produce the oppositional standpoints and polarized class structure that Marx saw as inherent in capitalism. Politicians may celebrate worker productivity and job creation as signs of a strong economy, but Marx offers a different view. He argues that as industry prospers and as the mass of workers grows, "the domination of capital extends over a greater number of individuals" (WLC 34). For Marx, increased employment and increased productivity – even if accompanied by an increase in wages – mean that more surplus labor is being extracted from more workers to provide more wealth for the bourgeoisie. Thus the economic and social gulf between capitalists and workers widens (WLC 34–35).

Marx argues that an increase in wages does nothing to change the structural inequality inherent in capitalism (between capitalists and workers), nor does it diminish the capitalists' privileged access to capital, a privilege seen in corporate executive pay. This inequality inheres in the fact that "the existence of a class which possesses nothing but its capacity to labor is a necessary prerequisite of capital" (WLC 31). Accordingly,

> to say that the most favorable condition for wage labor is the most rapid possible growth of productive capital is only to say that the more rapidly the working-class increases and enlarges the power that is hostile to it, the wealth that does not belong to it and that rules over it, the more favorable will be the conditions under which it is allowed to labor anew at increasing bourgeois wealth, at enlarging the power of capital, content with forging for itself the golden chains by which the bourgeoisie drags it in its train. (WLC 41)

The chains in which workers are enmeshed were more vividly apparent during Marx's day. He was writing when factory conditions were unsafe and unhygienic, child labor was the norm, and extreme poverty was visible on the streets and in the housing tenements of the increasingly populous cities. During the twentieth century, working conditions changed for the better in most sectors of the economy notwithstanding the dangerous conditions that still exist in many workplaces (e.g., meat factories, mines) and especially in the factories and construction sites of expanding capitalist countries

Figure 1.2 Financial crises and evidence of economic inequality motivated the Occupy Wall Street movement in New York City in 2011. Similar Occupy protests occurred in over 200 cities across the world. Source: Paul Davey Creative Photography © PAUL DAVEY. Reproduced with permission of Paul Davey.

(e.g., China). However, despite economic growth and the many changes that have occurred in recent decades – that is, a substantial increase in the number of college graduates, advances in computer technology, and the shift from private to publicly traded companies – economic assets are increasingly concentrated among fewer households. Marx's claim of the relational inequality between wage-workers and capitalists continues to find strong empirical support: In 2016, 12.7 percent of Americans (40.6 million people) were living in poverty; and the top 20 percent of households accounted for 51.5 percent of total US household income (Leubsdorf 2017).

MAINTAINING THE STATUS QUO

Why are wage-workers seemingly content to accept the status quo? Why do workers work as hard as they do (e.g., Burawoy 1979)? And why, notwithstanding the Occupy movement, do we not see much evidence today of the class antagonism that Marx regarded as integral to capitalism? Many reasons are likely. First, the huge post-World War II expansion in education, the expansion of service occupations, occupational mobility, and a growing middle class (largely composed of professional, service, and sales workers) have made a relatively affluent consumer lifestyle available to a large sector of the population in Western societies and especially in the US (Fischer and Hout 2006). Second, even among the working class (composed largely of skilled, semiskilled, and unskilled workers), an increasing proportion of wage-worker households do not rely solely on wages for their livelihood. A half of all American households and about a quarter of British households own investment stock (Halle and Weyher 2005: 209). The transformation in capitalism away from family or individual company ownership toward the shareholder society ushered in by the public selling of company shares on the stock exchange is highly significant. This trend has been accelerated by the rise of the Internet and the digital economy. Facebook, Google, Apple, Microsoft, and Amazon are all public companies. This means that many wage-workers today, regardless of their occupation or where they work, have a direct economic interest in specific corporations, through either personal or work-related pension investments. And although workers own fewer shares than company executives, their shares can constitute a significant proportion of wage-workers' overall economic assets. Despite inequality, therefore, wage-workers have a compelling incentive to support corporate interests and the profit objectives of local and global capitalism.

Accordingly, the line between capitalists and wage-workers is not as clear cut as it was in Marx's time and for much of the twentieth century, when owners' and workers' relations to property and capital were more straightforward. Stock investment gives workers a particular stake in the production (and reproduction) of capital. This is so notwithstanding the empirical truth in Marx's point that the expansion of the economy does not alter the inequality between the capitalists (the industrial and media tycoons and the corporate executive elite) and the proletariat (all those who rely primarily, if not solely, on wages for their livelihoods).

A third reason why class antagonism is relatively muted is due to the role of the state. Governments intervene to dampen some of the most severe effects of capitalist crises by propping up financial institutions and markets (e.g., government bailouts of banks and insurance companies during the 2007–2008 Great Recession). They also buffer individuals against some of the excesses of the profit logic of capitalism (e.g., by giving payments to the unemployed). The state, therefore, has a more active role in softening inequality in capitalist society than envisioned by Marx. The neoliberal turn in Western democracies has seen a decline in welfare benefits, even in countries where the welfare state was strongly embedded, such as the UK and Sweden. Austerity policies stoke political disaffection (e.g., in Ireland, and Greece). Nonetheless, enough welfare benefits remain in place that governments can still claim their policies help hard-working ordinary individuals, even as those same policies reinforce inequality and the capitalism system.

Fourth, worker unionization and the legal right of unionized workers to go on strike also help to quell workers' concerns that they are being exploited by employers. Many employers resist unionization and in some instances prohibit workers from joining unions. Some workers vote against unionization, as did nearly two-to-one employees at a Nissan plant in Mississippi in 2017; others believe, nonetheless, that union membership protects them from employer mistreatment. Increasingly, however, this is a minority view. In the 1950s, 35 percent of employees in the US were union members; this proportion declined to 20 percent in 1983, and to 11.1 percent in 2015. Workers in government and the public sector are far more likely than those in the private sector to be union members; and in the private sector, construction workers are more likely to be unionized than retail or sales employees (Dunn and Walker 2016). European countries and Australia, New Zealand, and Canada have a stronger labor movement tradition, and labor unions are still relatively strong in these places. The Nordic countries have the highest rates of unionization (ranging from 74 percent in Finland to 52 percent in Norway). But just over a quarter of workers in Ireland (29 percent) and the UK (26 percent) are unionized, and fewer in Germany (18 percent) (see European Trade Union Institute; www.etui.org). Nevertheless, in some European countries (e.g., Ireland), unions are part of the institutionalized policymaking process; they are considered "social partners" along with the government and employers' organizations, and participate in joint discussions establishing pay scales, benefits, etc.

All of these adaptations of capitalism (e.g., expanding middle class, changes in capital ownership, an activist state, unionization) contribute to workers' acceptance of economic and social inequality. Another, and perhaps the strongest, reason why workers accept the status quo is their immersion in an ideological and cultural system that masks inequality and, when visible, makes it seem fair and justified. This is the topic to which I now turn.

IDEOLOGY AND POWER

To talk of **ideology** is basically to refer to the ordinary, everyday ideas that permeate society. These ideas organically derive from our lived, material-social existence. Lived experience – everyday practical reality – is what determines our ideas about what is normal. Marx emphasizes that:

> Consciousness can never be anything else than conscious existence, and the existence of men in their actual life-process … [i.e.] developing their material production … Life [social/economic existence] is not determined by consciousness, but consciousness by life [by material-social existence]. (GI 14, 15)

The everyday activities and experiences in capitalist societies make it seem normal that wage-workers and owners and executives should work as hard as they do. Although the financial rewards differ, most people consent to produce the surplus labor and surplus value that create the profit needed to sustain capitalism.

EVERYDAY EXISTENCE AND NORMAL IDEAS

More generally, the ideas we have about what is normal, and about what's inane and what's cool, and whether, for example, to go to college and what to do afterwards, do not just pop into our heads out of nowhere. *What* we think about, and *how* we think about those things come from our everyday existence. They derive from what we already know and have already seen and experience in our families and neighborhoods, at school, and on the Internet and in magazines, etc. Many young people don't apply to university. This is not because they are not interested in education but because their material/social existence essentially rules out the normality of this idea and the feasibility and affordability of this option.

FREEDOM TO SHOP

Individuals' social experiences vary in all kinds of intersecting ways from place to place and by gender, race, socioeconomic class, sexuality, religion, etc. But, across today's globalizing economy (see chapter 15), the common cultural denominator is the primacy of consumption in everyday life (notwithstanding the persistence of poverty). Consumption is not only encouraged; it is required by the commodity production that is critical to capital and profit accumulation. A snapshot of any city in the world will testify to the prominence of consumer culture, highlighted by the well-known brand names on shop fronts, billboards, buses, and other public advertisements. We live, as we are frequently reminded, in a consuming society and many partake directly and vicariously of the great range of commodities available. Marx predicted the globalization of consumerism: "The bourgeoisie has through its exploitation of the world-market given a cosmopolitan character to production and consumption in every country … In place of the old wants, satisfied by the productions of the country, we find new wants, requiring for their satisfaction the products of distant lands" (CM 83).

As I have noted, freedom and capitalism tend to go together, though for Marx "free" labor is coerced (addressed previously). Democratic societies are almost always capitalistic societies. In nondemocratic countries such as China and Russia, however, a growing capitalist economy coincides with and requires the freedom of consumer choice, but not the freedom of the press, the freedom to vote, to criticize the government, or to publicly assemble, etc., that is, freedoms institutionalized in the everyday culture of Western societies. Each semester when I ask students to list what it means to be American, they invariably name all of these political freedoms without much prompting. These are the freedoms that democratic societies take for granted.

Additionally in capitalist societies, one of the most ingrained freedoms is the freedom of choice, and its twin, the freedom to shop. Yet it is rare for students to mention these freedoms in an initial listing of American values. Because the freedom to shop and to make choices every day at the vending machine and in the supermarket and on our favorite merchandise websites is so ingrained in our social existence, we don't think of it as something special; it is simply what we do. It is an everyday, easy freedom in contrast to one we might deploy more occasionally by voting, going to a place of religious worship, or attending a political rally.

IDEOLOGY OF CONSUMPTION

Consumption pervades our existence – which is why so many people work as hard as they do: They endure the burdens of work so that they can buy the things they covet. We work to live, Marx tells us, and many define their life by what they own. The power of money to buy all of the things we do not ourselves possess – for example, beauty, popularity, friends, status – Marx argues, lures us into reproducing capitalism through consumption. "All the things which you cannot do, your money can do. It can eat and drink, go to the dance hall and the theater; it can travel, it can appropriate art, learning, the treasures of the past, political power – all this it can appropriate for you – it can buy all this for you" (EPM 119). Hence many affluent men buy "trophy wives" and trophy ranches or vineyards, and billionaires buy trophy football teams. It is so "natural" for us to shop, to consume, and to own things, we don't consider this a special freedom or privilege. It is our existence. This is the power of ideology in everyday existence: Consumption, and ideas about consumption, structure who we are and what we do and how we evaluate others.

We rarely wonder, moreover, where the impulse to buy comes from, or how things get produced; we don't usually contemplate the labor invested in making commodities, or the heavy lifting housekeepers must do in moving the super-thick mattresses in a hotel's "heavenly" beds (see Introduction). It is only when a favorite brand is missing from the shelf that we wonder what unnatural thing might have happened to account for its mysterious absence. The expected and coveted presence of commodities in our lives, in defining and anchoring our everyday social existence, is what makes capitalism so alluring. It also makes the critique of capitalism difficult, even at an intellectual level (i.e., while studying Marx). We are enchanted with consumption because that is what is real to us; we are more likely to shop than to vote, or assemble for a religious, political, or civic event. Public holidays – for example, Labor Day/May Day, Thanksgiving, Veterans Day – days on which we might well ponder the value of labor, are instead occasions for shopping, promoted by the additional allure of heavily marketed "super sales events."

THE MYSTICAL VALUE OF COMMODITIES

We relish being consumers and by extension living in a capitalist society, but because freedom of choice is so routinized in daily life, we remain blissfully unaware of the social relations that underlie our freedom to shop. Marx reminds us that the unequal relations of workers and capitalists to capital and profit underpin commodity production and consumption. He refers to the obfuscation of the production process as the **fetishism of commodities**. We are so fixated with the commodity as an object in itself, we don't recognize what it really is: raw materials transformed by (exploited) human labor (increasingly outsourced to unsafe factories in underdeveloped economies such as Bangladesh) for someone else's profit. As with other aspects of capitalism, we idealize commodities as if they are things that have a life of their own, as if they are mysteriously independent of the social organization of production (and consumption). But as Marx emphasizes, production is "always production … by social individuals … Production mediates consumption; it creates [consumption's] material; without it, consumption would lack an object" (Gru 85, 91). He elaborates,

> A commodity appears at first sight, a very trivial thing, and easily understood … So far as it has a value in use, there is nothing mysterious about it, … it is capable of satisfying human wants, … [and is] the product of human labour. It is as clear as noon-day, that man, by his industry, changes the … materials furnished by Nature, in such a way as to make them useful to him. The form of wood, for instance, is altered by making a table out of it. Yet, for all that, the table continues to be that common, every-day thing, wood. But, so soon as it steps forth as a commodity, it is changed into something transcendent … The mystical character of commodities does not originate, therefore, in their use-value … A commodity is … a mysterious thing, simply because in it the social character of men's labour appears to them as an objective character stamped upon the product of that labour … the products of labour become commodities, social things whose qualities are at the same time perceptible and imperceptible by the senses … There is a physical relation between physical things. But it is different with commodities. There, the existence of the things qua commodities, and the value-relation between the products of labor which stamps them as commodities, have absolutely no connection with their physical properties and with the material relations arising therefrom … the definite social relation between men [as producers of the products of labor] … assumes … the fantastic form of a relation between things. (Cap 81–83)

Marx is not opposed to consumption. His writings fully acknowledge that needs are not just physical but social, and that each mode of existence produces new needs. Thus, college students today need an iPhone. But what Marx critiques is how we let our idealization of commodities obscure the unequal relations that underpin commodity production (and consumption), and how in this process we objectify the workers as well as ourselves. "You are known by what you own" was a tag line used a few years ago by Zebo, an Internet and advertising technology company. This is not simply a cliché. It is the ideology – the dominating idea – that infuses capitalist societies. The class that owns the means of production (e.g., land, oil, financial capital) also owns more things and has more wealth than the working class. We are reduced to what we own. We own our labor power but are coerced to sell it for wages (in order to live); but we can consume the (other) commodities we possess. We ourselves are active promoters of consumer ideology in our own everyday habits and relationships. And we are heavily encouraged by the advertising industry to do so. Advertising celebrates consumption and in doing so celebrates capitalism as a system of commodity production: It "glorifies the pleasures and freedoms of consumer choice" (Schudson 1984: 218). Every advertisement – on the highway, in the subway, at the bus stop, in the football stadium, on television and the Internet, in magazines and church bulletins – is celebrating the everyday capitalist freedom to shop – even if it is not showcasing a product that we ourselves want. We might not be persuaded to buy a given advertised item, but each advertisement reminds us of what we can own and, importantly too, what we should aspire to own (e.g., Marchand 1985).

Our social existence and our consciousness are determined by capitalism. And though we make our own history, as Marx tells us, it is not under conditions of our own choosing: "Men make their own

Figure 1.3   The freedom to shop is at the heart of everyday life in capitalist society. Source: © Maciej Gowin/ iStockphoto.

history, but they do not make it just as they please; they do not make it under circumstances chosen by themselves, but under circumstances directly found, given, and transmitted from the past" (Bru 595). We freely consume, but in ways and under conditions not chosen by us but by the capitalist class and by the advertising industry, which is one of its core channels of power.

The allure of consumption further dampens the development of class consciousness. The freedom to shop means we can all go to the mall and enjoy the commodities produced by capitalism (some more, some less). False consciousness keeps us from perceiving that we are cheaper than the commodities our labor power produces and cheaper than the commodities we buy (see the section on Wage-Labor and Surplus Value). Additionally, we deceive ourselves into thinking we will be worth more if we buy more. Marx presumed that in pushing through a revolution against capitalism, "The proletarians have nothing to lose but their chains" (CM 121). The failure of Marx's prediction, however, is itself a testament, in part, to the insightfulness of his analysis of the power of money and of consumer ideology within capitalism. Commodity consumption is such an integral part of lived existence in economically developed societies that it makes a vision of society in which "we are *not* what we own" beyond the imagination of most of us (though some individuals and families experiment with living a simpler life). Consumption, and the ideology of consumption, bind us to capitalism; they are the mark of global civilization. (See the section on Global Consumer Culture in chapter 15.)

THE CAPITALIST SUPERSTRUCTURE

The advertising industry is just one, albeit a very powerful, element in the larger ideological system that governs our everyday existence. Marx highlights that other institutions in society, those not tied directly to economic markets, also promote capitalist ideology. He argues that because the social institutions in a capitalist society evolved in ways that are compatible with capitalism, they serve the economic interests of the bourgeoisie. The ideology of "free competition [is] accompanied by a social and political constitution adapted to it, and by the economic and political sway of the bourgeois class" (CM 85). In this view, the political, legal, educational, family, religious, and cultural institutions – all those spheres of social existence whose (apparent) purpose is not economic/capital production – promote ideas and practices that support and reinforce capitalism. And they suppress those ideas that might in any way challenge the capitalist status quo (EPM 102–103; CM 100).

Marx refers to these institutions as the **superstructure**; their existence and activities bolster the foundational, **economic base** of capitalism, and the structural inequality of capitalists and wage-workers.

> In the social production of their life, men enter into definite relations that are indispensable and independent of their will, relations of production which correspond to a definite stage of development of their material productive forces. The sum total of these relations of production constitutes the economic structure of society, the real foundation, on which rises a legal and political superstructure and to which correspond definite forms of social consciousness. The mode of production of material life conditions the social, political and intellectual life process in general. It is not the consciousness of men that determines their being, but, on the contrary, their social being [everyday existence/experiences] that determines their consciousness [ideas]. (Preface 5)

The everyday institutional practices of the state, the media, education, the church, the family, the courts, and the parliament, in executing their specialized activities and constraining individuals' social experiences, are, at the same time, practices that support profit accumulation and the ideology of capitalism that underpins and justifies it. Thus, Marx argues, the organization of the bourgeois family and the gender inequality and exploitation it institutionalizes is "based on capital, on private gain … the bourgeois [man] sees in his wife a mere instrument of production" (CM 100–101; see also Engels 1844/1978): She produces the next generation of wage-workers and capitalists and her (unpaid) labor in the home (as well as her paid labor if she is employed) contributes to the surplus value required and appropriated by the capitalist class.[5]

When we look at education, we see that schools and colleges (and parents) emphasize daily practices affirming disciplined work habits, focus, and productivity; and you are required to major in a specialized field of study rather than dabble in several of your intellectual and creative interests. Colleges verbalize the intellectual value of an allegedly wide-ranging "liberal arts" education. Yet, this must be balanced with training graduates who are able to meet the economy's demand for specialized workers and entrepreneurs. In the legal domain, the courts protect individuals' property rights. In politics, there is a lot of hand-wringing about big business and corporate donations having too much influence on the political process. Yet, the right of business leaders and political lobbyists to make large campaign donations is defended as part of their constitutional rights, that is, their (political-economic) freedom of expression. See Topic 1.7.

In a capitalist society, the rights of capital are more strongly protected than the rights of workers and of the poor. As Marx emphasizes, you "cannot give to one class without taking from another" (Bru 616). Hence when politicians approve legislation (e.g., freezing the minimum wage), or universities are revising the curriculum, or the courts are evaluating particular laws (e.g., workplace discrimination), we are prompted to ask: "Who benefits?" The answer in most instances can be traced to the capitalist class. And even when workers appear to be benefitting, it's likely also that capitalism too is being propped up (as with welfare payments). What the poor do have, Marx argued, is religion. For Marx, religion is yet another institution that upholds capitalist ideology and the status quo; it distracts workers from consciousness of their exploitation. Just as wage-labor (coerced by capitalism) produces alienation (see the preceding section on Alienated Labor), so too Marx argues, does religious faith; "The more man puts into God, the less he retains in himself" (EPM 72). Thus religion becomes an alien power over the individual. The core ideas in Christianity, for example, can be seen as promoting the interests of the capitalist class: It is meekness and nonmaterial values that Christian scripture affirms: "Blessed are the meek, for they will inherit the land; blessed are the poor for theirs is the

---

Topic 1.7   The uberization of corporate political influence

The Internet is expanding opportunities for ordinary individuals to engage in political communication and activism, and it is also changing how wealthy individuals and corporations influence the political process. The sociologist Edward Walker (2017) highlights how Internet corporations mobilize "protest on demand" movements to resist government regulation of their company practices. The "uber-ization of activism" refers to how "companies and interest groups galvanize their own users as unpaid campaigners, and do so all with the tap of an app." Walker discusses Uber's mobilization of grassroots activists in its intensive (and mostly successful) efforts in the US and elsewhere to resist government regulations. In 2015, when New York City's Mayor Bill de Blasio attempted to restrict the number of Uber cars in NYC, Uber "added a 'de Blasio's Uber' feature (NO CARS – SEE WHY), so that every time New Yorkers logged on to order a car, they were reminded of the mayor's threat and were sent directly to a petition opposing the new rules." Uber also offered them free rides to a rally against the measure at City Hall.

In the San Francisco Bay Area, where housing is both scarce and highly expensive, Airbnb provided funding for the "Fair to Share" short-term housing rentals campaign against government efforts to prevent properties being primarily used for Airbnb rentals. And e-mails from eBay to its users nudged them to fight online sales tax legislation. As Walker notes, these companies also use traditional political campaign tools (e.g., television ads, robo calls, mass mailings, celebrity endorsements, and public relations and lobbyist firms). Uber, for example, has a third more state lobbyists than Walmart. He argues that given companies' leveraging of their own social media and Internet tools and users, we need to differentiate between "corporate populism" that benefits a wealthy patron, and genuine grassroots activism that uses social media, such as #blacklivesmatter or Bill McKibben's climate change activist organization "350. org" (Walker 2017; see also Walker 2014).

Other corporations curry political favor using television advertisements, but with a twist. Rather than targeting customers, they are trying to catch Donald Trump's attention. Trump's success in winning the US presidency was partly driven by his insistence that he would bring manufacturing jobs back to America. This may or may not happen. But non-American, global corporate giants like the German car manufacturer Volkswagen and Japan's Toyota are buying advertisements on US morning television news shows Trump is known to watch. They are specifically targeting him with information about their extensive manufacturing footprint in the US (*Wall Street Journal*, June 8 2017). Perhaps, they want to avoid being publicly berated – like Apple, Ford, Carrier, and other companies – for not doing enough to protect American jobs. And the American corrugated box-making company, Pratt, placed a full-page advertisement in the *Wall Street Journal* (on July 24, 2017) touting its pledged $2 billion to create 5,000 high-paying manufacturing jobs in the US. Alongside its amplified tag, "Standing up for American jobs," it featured a photo of Donald Trump watching television and applauding Anthony Pratt's announcement.

Kingdom of God." And although activists in disadvantaged neighborhoods frequently use religion to challenge economic and social inequality (e.g., Wood and Fulton 2015), for the most part, religion has a stabilizing rather than a revolutionary impact in society.

Across various social institutions, therefore, we see that the ideas routinely articulated are ideas that serve the interests of the capitalist class – that is, the **ruling class** – and of capitalism as a system (of inequality). Marx explains:

> The ideas of the ruling class are in every epoch the **ruling ideas**, i.e., the class which is the ruling material force of society, is at the same time its ruling intellectual force. The class which has the means of material production at its disposal, has control at the same time over the means of mental production, so that thereby, generally speaking, the ideas of those who lack the means of mental production are subject to it. (GI 39)

As I have highlighted, the interests and ideas of the ruling class are affirmed and protected across noneconomic social institutions (e.g., education, law, politics, etc.). Additionally, the ruling class has the capital to purchase media and other opportunities to directly disseminate advertisements and political and economic messages that serve its interests. The class that owns or controls access to capital gets to define literally what we are reading or watching. And by extension, it also controls the sorts of things and issues we are prompted to think about and how to think about them (e.g., Gitlin 1987). Even with the democratizing opportunities provided by YouTube, Facebook, Twitter, and blogs, corporations and wealthy business owners and executives tend to have greater resources to publicize their ideas than ordinary individuals. It is hard to compete, for example, against the American beverage and restaurant industry (represented by the American Beverage Association), which placed full-page advertisements in large circulation news media opposing in-car breathalyzers (ignition interlocks). Such devices would not just mean fewer drunk drivers, it argued, but the end of "moderate responsible drinking prior to driving" and thus "no more champagne toasts at weddings … no more beer at ballgames" (*New York Times*, May 20, 2008). It also ran a successful campaign against a New York City initiative to restrict the size of soda containers that can be sold in the city to 16 oz. The Beverage Association sponsored a humorous – and ideologically powerful – one-page color advertisement in the *New York Times* (June 2, 2012, p. A5) that stated, "The Nanny: *You only* thought *you lived in the land of the free*" – thus explicitly linking political freedom with consumer freedom, the freedom to buy whatever one pleases. In short, it is easy for the capitalist class to pay for and widely disseminate ideas that protect their economic interests, a point amplified by the "Nanny" advertisement's note that readers can find out more about the issue at the aptly named website: consumerfreedom.com.

THE RULING POWER OF MONEY IN POLITICS

The ideas of the ruling class also get directly transmitted into the halls of political power as a result of the ruling class's political spending. Once again, we can refer to Marx's analysis of the power of money in a capitalist society. Just as the capitalist can buy bravery, culture, glamour, love, a "trophy wife," so too can he buy political power. Money is crucial in determining who runs for and gets elected to political office. Although Donald Trump may be an exceptionally wealthy businessman, others who competed in the 2016 US presidential election (including Hillary Clinton, and Jeb Bush and Ted Cruz) reported multimillion dollar personal assets; similarly, the US Senate is aptly referred to as a "millionaires' club." In the UK, David Cameron's personal assets while he was prime minister were reported to be over $4 million, and many in his elite inner circle of cabinet members and advisers were similarly wealthy.

Additionally, money can buy access to politicians in multiple ways. Company owners and corporate executives move in much the same social circles as politicians, making it easy for them to press their economic concerns at all sorts of informal and formal gatherings – whether at dinner parties or Davos (at the World Economic Forum). But corporations do not have to wait for dinner parties, fundraisers, golf tournaments, and other events to communicate with politicians. The extensive lobbying system in politics provides a well-organized, routinized way for corporations, industries (e.g., the American Beverage Association), and other groups to advance their economic and legislative interests. And many paid lobbyists have themselves been political officeholders (or intimately related to legislators). In short, networks matter (see chapter 7), and in a capitalist society money buys network connections. Corporate interests readily receive greater priority from politicians than the everyday issues that matter to ordinary wage-workers and their families. This is so despite the opportunity ordinary people have to e-mail politicians or to meet with their local political representatives during public constituency meetings.

Further, as underscored by the routine eruption of political corruption scandals, some politicians sell their political (labor) power (as either legislators or lobbyists) in exchange for free dinners, golf trips, and cash. And, as is true of all wage-labor, politicians' use-value to the capitalist extends beyond their exchange value. The use-value continues with the politicians' ongoing policy interventions aiding capitalist profit accumulation, long after they have consumed free meals, vacations, and other gifts.

In sum, the power of money in the political process and in determining the political agenda illustrates Marx's thesis that the ruling ideas in society are, and always will be, those that accord with the interests of those who are the ruling economic force in society. Think here, for example, of "free trade" as a ruling idea, or of the elevation of economic priorities over human rights in US and European relations with China. And these ideas serve not simply the individual interests of a given entrepreneur but, more important, the interests, practices, and ideology of capitalism as a whole.

SUMMARY

Marx argued that each mode of production (e.g., imperial Rome, feudal Europe, capitalism) contains the seeds of its own destruction. His thesis assumes that the form of economic and social organization that was once an improvement over its predecessor will eventually suffer its own demise, and be replaced with a system that improves on it. In this framing, history will end with the destruction of capitalism and its replacement by communism. This latter stage has (so far) not emerged. To the contrary, capitalism continues its global expansion, and has shown itself to be remarkably adaptive to integrating the crises and contradictions that inhere in it. Moreover, its basic structure (e.g., division of labor, unequal class relations), and processes (e.g., commodification, production of surplus value/ profit), are highly resilient. Indeed, with the increasingly global reach of capitalism and consumer culture, Marx's analysis remains highly relevant to understanding contemporary society.

POINTS TO REMEMBER

Marx focused on the structure of capitalist society

- Marx saw history as a progression in material forces and conditions:
  - Slave society
  - Feudal society

- Capitalism
- Communism
- Marx emphasized that capitalism and all existing societies are characterized by inequality Characteristics of capitalism emphasized by Marx:
- The objective of capitalism is the production of capital/profit
- Capitalism is a system of structured class inequality based on unequal relations to capital
- There are two dichotomously opposed classes:
  - The bourgeoisie (capitalists/owners)
  - The proletariat (wage-workers who produce capital/profit)
- Capitalism is a system of commodity production
- Labor power is itself a commodity
- Wage-labor is exploited labor; labor power is used by the capitalist to produce profit for the capitalist
- Surplus value produced by wage-workers becomes the capitalist's profit
- Surplus value derives from the gap between workers' exchange-value and their use-value to the capitalist
- The division of labor produces estranged or alienated labor:
  - Alienation from the product produced
  - Alienation in the production process
  - Alienation from our own species being
  - Alienation from other workers
- Economic power determines political and social power
- Everyday economic and social existence determine our consciousness of society; how we live determines what we know and think
- Economic relations determine ideology; the ideas of the ruling (capitalist) class are the ruling ideas in society
- Economic/profit logic (the base of society) determines the logic/practices of all social institutions (superstructure)

GLOSSARY

alienated labor the objective result of the economic and social organization of capitalist production (e.g., division of labor):

(a) alienation from products produced Wage-workers are alienated from the product of their labor; a worker's labor power is owned by the capitalist, and consequently the products of the worker's labor belong not to the worker but to the capitalist who profits from them.

(b) alienation within the production process Wage-workers are actively alienated by the production process; labor is not for the worker an end in itself, freely chosen, but coerced by and performed for the capitalist; the worker is an object in the production process.

(c) alienation of workers from their species being By being reduced to their use-value (capitalist profit), workers are estranged from the creativity and higher consciousness that distinguish humans from animals.

(d) alienation of individuals from one another The competitive production process and workplace demands alienate individuals from others.

bourgeoisie the capitalist class; owners of capital and of the means of production, who stand in a position of domination over the proletariat (the wage-workers).

capital money and other (large-scale) privately owned resources (oil wells, land, software) used in the production of commodities whose sale accumulates profit for the capitalist.

capitalism a historically specific way of organizing commodity production; produces profit for the owners of the means of production (e.g., factories, land, oil wells, financial capital); based on structured inequality between capitalists and wage-laborers whose exploited labor power produces capitalist profit.

class consciousness the group consciousness necessary if wage-workers (the proletariat) are to recognize that their individual exploitation is part and parcel of capitalism, which requires the exploitation of the labor power of all wage-workers (as a class) by the capitalist class in the production of profit.

class relations unequal relations of capitalists and wage-workers to capital (and each other). Capitalists (who own the means of production used to produce capital/profit) are in a position of domination over wage-workers, who, in order to live, must sell their labor power to the capitalists.

commodification of labor power the process by which, like manufactured commodities, wage-workers' labor power is exchanged and traded on the market for a price (wages).

communism envisioned by Marx as the final phase in the evolution of history, whereby capitalism would be overthrown by proletarian class revolution, resulting in a society wherein the division of labor, private property, and profit would no longer exist.

dialectical materialism the idea that historical change (i.e., material/economic change) is the result of conscious human activity emerging from and acting on the socially experienced inequalities and contradictions in historically conditioned (i.e., human-made) economic forces and relations.

division of labor the separation of occupational sectors and workers into specialized spheres of activity; produces for Marx, alienated labor.

economic base the economic structure or the mode of production of material life in capitalist society. Economic relations (relations of production) are determined by ownership of the means of production and rest on inequality between private-property-owning capitalists (bourgeoisie) and propertyless wage-workers. Economic relations determine social relations and social institutional practices (i.e., the superstructure).

exchange-value the price (wages) wage-workers get on the market for the (coerced) sale of their labor power to the capitalist; determined by how much the capitalist needs to pay the wage-workers in order to maintain their labor power, so that the workers can subsist and maintain their use-value in producing profit for the capitalist. The workers' exchange-value is of less value to the worker than their use-value is to the capitalist.

exploitation the capitalist class caring about wage-workers only to the extent that wage-workers have "use-value," that is, can be used to produce surplus value/profit.

false consciousness the embrace of the illusionary promises of capitalism.

fetishism of commodities the mystification of capitalist production whereby we inject commodities with special properties beyond what they really are (e.g., elevating an Abercrombie & Fitch shirt to something other than what is really is, that is, cotton converted into a commodity), while remaining ignorant of the exploited labor and unequal class relations that determine production and consumption processes.

historical materialism history as the progressive expansion in the economic-material-productive forces in society.

ideology ideas in everyday circulation; determined by the ruling economic class such that they make our current social existence seem normal and desirable.

inequality structured into the profit objectives and organization of capitalism whereby the exploited labor power of wage-workers produces surplus value (profit) for the capitalist class.

means of production resources (e.g., land, oil wells, factories, corporations, financial capital) owned by the bourgeoisie and used for the production of commodities/profit as a result of the labor power of wage-workers.

mode of production how a society organizes its material-social existence (e.g., capitalism rather than feudalism or socialism).

objectification the dehumanization of wage-workers as machine-like objects, whose maintenance (with subsistence wages) is necessary to the production of commodities (objects) necessary to capital accumulation/profit. The term is interchangeable with "alienation."

private property the source and result of the profit accumulated by capitalists; and a source and consequence of the inequality between capitalists and wage-workers.

profit capitalists' accumulation of capital as a result of the surplus value generated by wage-workers' (exploited) labor power.

proletariat wage-workers who, in order to live, must sell their labor power to the capitalist class, which uses it to produce surplus value/profit.

ruling class the class that is the ruling material force in society (capitalists/bourgeoisie) is also the ruling intellectual/ ideological force, ensuring the protection and expansion of capitalist economic interests.

ruling ideas ideas disseminated by the ruling (capitalist) class, invariably bolstering capitalism.

species being what is distinctive of the human species (e.g., mindful creativity).

standpoint of the proletariat the positioning of the proletariat vis-à-vis the production process, from within which they perceive the dehumanization and self-alienation structured into capitalism, unlike the bourgeoisie, who experience capitalism (erroneously) as self-affirming.

subsistence wage minimum needed to sustain workers' existence (livelihood) so that their labor power is maintained and reproduced for the capitalist class.

superstructure noneconomic social institutions (legal, political, educational, cultural, religious, family) whose routine institutional practices and activities promote the beliefs, ideas, and practices that are necessary to maintaining and reproducing capitalism.

surplus value capitalist profit from the difference between a worker's exchange-value (wages) and use-value; the extra value over and above the costs of commodity production (i.e., raw materials, infrastructure, workers' wages) created by the labor power of wage-workers.

use-value the usefulness of wage-workers' labor power in the production of profit.

QUESTIONS FOR REVIEW

1   What specific characteristics of capitalism contribute to the inequality that is inherent in capitalism as an economic and social system?
2   How does the organization of production under capitalism contribute to dehumanizing the individual?
3   What is ideology, and how does it work in everyday life?
4   What are the structural and cultural (ideological) factors in contemporary society that seem to militate against the development of class consciousness?
5   How do the state and other social institutions (e.g., universities) prop up capitalism?

NOTES

1   In citing Marx's writings (and subsequently Durkheim's, chapter 2, and Weber's, chapter 3), I reference the book initials rather than the date of publication. Thus in this first quote, "CM" refers to Marx's *Communist Manifesto*. I do this to help students keep in mind the classical theorists' main books, which comprise the core foundation of sociological theory. A list of the theorist's writings, their dates, and the book title initials for referencing them appears after the biographical note in the chapter.
2   The influential Hungarian Marxist theorist Georg Lukács (1885–1971), elaborates the centrality of the concept of reification in Marx's writing (1968: 83–222). See also chapter 5 on Critical Theory in this textbook.
3   Marx argues that we misunderstand history because we do not perceive the real conditions of everyday life, instead preferring to talk in general terms of some universal spirit or universal idea (e.g., freedom). Under capitalism and the division of labor to which we must consent, individuals' material activities become divorced from their real interests and hence their economic activities "become an alien power opposed" to them (GI 22), a power that makes us desensitized to the real, unequal, material forces in society (GI 20–24). See section in this chapter on historical materialism.
4   Lukács (1968: 48–55) elaborates on Marx's theory of class consciousness. He emphasizes that Marx's collaborator Friedrich Engels pointed out that although humans make history and do so consciously, this consciousness is false insofar as it is part of "the historical totality" of class-conditioned social relations of inequality that exist under capitalism, and which can only be transcended by the class-conscious revolutionary political action of the proletariat.
5   There are times when superstructural institutions critique capitalism – for example, the critique by the Catholic church of consumerism and of the extremes of economic inequality within the West and between the so-called first and third worlds; or the fledging discussion among university economists of the limits of free market ideology. These critiques, however, tend to be of specific capitalistic practices and ideas, rather than of the system of capitalism as a whole.

REFERENCES

Abrams, Rachel. 2017. "Walmart is Accused of Punishing Workers for Sick Days." *New York Times* (June 1).

Bunge, Jacob. 2017. "Chicken Processors Seek Speedup." *Wall Street Journal* (September 12), pp. A1, B2.

Burawoy, Michael. 1979. *Manufacturing Consent.* Chicago: University of Chicago Press.

Dunn, Megan, and James Walker. 2016. *Union Membership in the United States.* Washington, DC: U.S. Bureau of Labor Statistics.

Economist. 2017a. "The Marxist Moment." (May 13), p. 52.

Economist. 2017b. "Workers Disunited." (August 19), p. 37.

Engels, Friedrich. 1844/1978. "The Origin of the Family, Private Property, and the State." Pp. 734–759 in Robert Tucker, ed. *The Marx–Engels Reader.* 2nd edition. New York: Norton.

Engels, Friedrich. 1878/1978. "Socialism: Utopian and Scientific." Pp. 683–717 in Robert Tucker, ed. *The Marx–Engels Reader.* 2nd edition. New York: Norton.

Fan, Jiayang. 2016. "The Golden Generation." *New Yorker* (February 22), pp. 30–35.

Fischer, Claude, and Michael Hout. 2006. *Century of Difference: How America Changed in the Last One Hundred Years.* New York: Russell Sage Foundation.

Gitlin, Todd. 1987. *The Sixties: Years of Hope, Days of Rage.* New York: Bantam Books.

Grabell, Michael. 2017. "Cut to the Bone: How a Poultry Company Exploits Immigration Laws." *New Yorker* (May 8), pp. 46–53.

Greenhouse, Steven. 2012. "At Caterpillar, Pressing Labor while Business Booms." *New York Times* (July 22), pp. A1, 3.

Greenhouse, Steven, and Michael Barbaro. 2006. "Wal-Mart to Add More Part-timers and Wage Caps." *New York Times* (October 2), p. A1.

Halle, David, and L. Frank Weyher. 2005. "New Developments in Class and Culture." Pp. 207–219 in Mark Jacobs and Nancy Hanrahan, eds. *The Blackwell Companion to the Sociology of Culture.* Oxford: Blackwell.

Heller, Nathan. 2017. "The Gig is Up." *New Yorker* (May 15), pp. 52–63.

Kimmel, Michael. 2007. *Classical Sociological Theory.* New York: Oxford University Press.

Kurmanaev, Anatoly, and Siranush Sharoyan. 2017. "Where Do Cuban Tourists Go To Splurge? Moscow's Flea markets." *Wall Street Journal* (June 8), pp. A1, 10.

Leubsdorf, Ben. 2017. "New Record for Household Incomes." *Wall Street Journal* (September 13), p. A2.

Lin, Liza. 2017a. "China's Expanding Web of Riches." *Wall Street Journal* (June 9), pp. B1, 4.

Lin, Liza. 2017b. "Alibaba-Marriott Deal Pursues Chinese Travelers." *Wall Street Journal* (August 18), p. B3.

Lukacs, Georg. 1968. *History and Class Consciousness: Studies in Marxist Dialectics.* Cambridge, MA: MIT Press.

Marchand, Roland. 1985. *Advertising the American Dream.* Berkeley: University of California Press.

Marx, Karl. 1844a/1978. "Alienation and Social Classes." Pp. 133–135 in Robert Tucker, ed. *The Marx–Engels Reader.* 2nd edition. New York: Norton.

Marx, Karl. 1844b/1988. *Economic and Philosophical Manuscripts.* Amherst, NY: Prometheus Books.

Marx, Karl. 1847/1978. *Wage Labour and Capital.* Peking: Foreign Language Press.

Marx, Karl. 1858/1973. *Grundrisse. Foundations of the Critique of Political Economy.* New York: Random House.

Marx, Karl. 1859/1978. "Preface to 'A Contribution to the Critique of Political Economy.'" Pp. 3–6 in Robert Tucker, ed. *The Marx–Engels Reader.* 2nd edition. New York: Norton.

Marx, Karl. 1852/1978. "The Eighteenth Brumaire of Louis Bonaparte." Pp. 594–617 in Robert Tucker, ed. *The Marx–Engels Reader.* 2nd edition. New York: Norton.

Marx, Karl. 1867/1906. *Capital: A Critique of Political Economy.* New York: Modern Library.

Marx, Karl, and Friedrich Engels. 1846/1947. *The German Ideology.* New York: International Publishers.

Marx, Karl, and Friedrich Engels. 1848/1967. *The Communist Manifesto.* Introduction by A.J.P. Taylor. London: Penguin.

McMillan, Douglas, and Newley Purnell. 2017. "Uber Knowingly Leased Unsafe Cars to Drivers." *Wall Street Journal* (August 4), pp. A1, 9.

Miraftab, Faranak. 2017. *Global Heartland: Displaced Labor, Transnational Lives and Local Placemaking.* Bloomington, IN: Indiana University Press.

Packer, David. 2007. "A Job Interview Where Each Second Makes a Difference," *New York Times* (February 8), p. C16.

Patterson, Orlando. 1982. *Slavery and Social Death: A Comparative Study.* Cambridge, MA: Harvard University Press.

Schudson, Michael. 1984. *Advertising: The Uneasy Persuasion.* Berkeley: University of California Press.

Simmel, Georg. 1903/1950. *The Sociology of Georg Simmel.* Glencoe, IL: Free Press. Translated, edited, and with an introduction by Kurt Wolff.

Simmel, Georg. 1907/1971. *On Individuality and Social Forms.* Chicago: University of Chicago Press. Edited and with an introduction by Donald Levine.

Tucker, Robert, ed. (1978) *The Marx–Engels Reader.* 2nd edition. New York: Norton.

Walker, Edward. 2014. *Grassroots for Hire.* New York: Cambridge University Press.

Walker, Edward. 2017. "The Uber-ization of activism." *New York Times* (August 7).

Wall Street Journal. 2017. "Overheard." (June 8).

Wong, Edward. 2013. "Survey in China Shows a Wide Gap in Income." *New York Times* (July 20), p. A9.

Wood, Richard, and Brad Fulton. 2015. *A Shared Future: Faith-Based Organizing for Racial Equity and Ethical Democracy.* Chicago: University of Chicago Press.

CHAPTER TWO

EMILE DURKHEIM (1858–1917)

CHAPTER MENU

Introduction to Sociological Theory: Theorists, Concepts, and Their Applicability to the Twenty-First Century,
Third Edition. Michele Dillon.
© 2020 John Wiley & Sons Ltd. Published 2020 by John Wiley & Sons Ltd.
Companion website: www.wiley.com/go/dillon

Timeline 2.1	Major events spanning Durkheim's lifetime (1858–1917)
1861	Telegraph line across the US completed
1863	Football Association (soccer) established in Britain
1864	Red Cross established
1867	US purchases Alaska from Russia
1872	Friendly (charity) Societies in Britain report four million members
1873	Herbert Spencer, *The Study of Sociology*
1879	Church of Christ Scientist (Christian Science) established in Boston
1883	Statue of Liberty presented by France to the US
1889	Compulsory old-age and incapacity pensions introduced in Germany

1896	First modern Olympic Games held in Athens
1900	10-hour working day mandated in France
1902	Public Health Act in France leads to better living conditions for the working class
1903	Formation of the Women's Social and Political Union in Britain by Emmeline Pankhurst, demanding votes for women
1906	Alfred Dreyfus, French Jewish army captain (and Durkheim's brother-in-law), cleared of treason, having been wrongly accused due to anti-Semitism
1908	Separate courts established for juveniles in Britain
1909	National Association for the Advancement of Colored People (NAACP) founded in the US
1910	A ratio of one car to every 44 households in the US
1914	Outbreak of World War I; Germany declares war on Russia and France
1915	Einstein, General Theory of Relativity
1917	US declares war on Germany; Proletarian Revolution in Russia – abdication of the tsar, triumph of Lenin
1918	End of World War I

Emile Durkheim (1858-1917) lived in Europe – in France – during much the same era as Karl Marx (1818–1883), though his life extended into the twentieth century and World War I (1914–1918), in which his only son, André, was killed. Living through a time of social, economic, and political upheaval, he too focused on social change and industrial society. But unlike Marx, who focused on the structural contradictions in capitalism (e.g., class inequality), Durkheim was preoccupied with the question of social order. Like Saint-Simon, Comte, and Rousseau (see Introduction), he was interested in probing how social order is achieved and maintained amidst social progress (Bellah 1973: xviii). He gave particular attention to how, in the evolution from traditional to modern society, the forms of social organization and social relationships adapt so that society, social life, continues to function effectively.

Durkheim conceptualized society as a complex system whose component parts or structures (e.g., economic activity, law, science, family, religion, etc.) are interrelated but whose independent functioning is necessary to the functioning of the whole society. For this reason, his sociology is often referred to as **functionalism** or structural functionalism. Social structures, Durkheim argues, necessitate "a certain mode of acting" (DL 272–273), a particular way of organizing social life whose effects, in turn, function to maintain society, and which make other modes of being "almost impossible" (DL 273, 276).[1] Durkheim, therefore, offers a very different perspective on the organization of society and social relations than does Marx. In fact, among the theorists discussed in this book, the greatest theoretical divide is between Marx and Durkheim. Durkheim's contributions to sociology are both methodological and substantive. Although these intertwine in his writings, I first discuss his methodology and then focus on his substantive topics.

BIOGRAPHICAL NOTE

Emile Durkheim was born in April 1858 into a middle-class orthodox Jewish family in northeastern France. His father, grandfather, and great-grandfather were rabbis, and his mother ran a successful embroidery business. Emile was the youngest of four children; his family emphasized hard work, morality, and duty – habits maintained by Durkheim throughout his life. He married Louise Dreyfus in 1887, and with their two children, Marie and André, enjoyed an idyllic family life despite his serious personality. Louise helped with Durkheim's writing: "she copied manuscripts, corrected proofs and shared in the administrative editorial work of the *Année sociologique*" (Lukes 1973: 99), a prestigious multivolume journal that Durkheim founded, edited, and wrote for, using it to establish what he considered sociology's specialized content. The end of Durkheim's life coincided with the ravages and disorder produced by World War I, and the death of his son in military action in 1915 was "a blow from which he would never recover" (Lukes 1973: 554). He continued to lecture and write, though with a marked social and emotional detachment, and he died two years later, in 1917, at age 59 (Lukes 1973: 39–40, 99–100, 554–559).

Durkheim's Writings
1893: *The Division of Labour in Society*, DL
1895: *The Rules of Sociological Method*, RSM
1897: *Suicide*, Su
1912: *The Elementary Forms of Religious Life*, EFRL
1914: "The Dualism of Human Nature and Its Social Conditions," HN

DURKHEIM'S METHODOLOGICAL RULES

SCIENTIFIC SOCIOLOGY: THE STUDY OF SOCIAL FACTS

Although Durkheim is less well known than Marx among the general public, his enduring influence on the everyday practice of sociology is greater. This is particularly true of American sociology. Although many sociologists today might not acknowledge any debt to Durkheim, the major way sociologists go about studying the world owes much to his methodological approach. He outlined scientific sociological methodology in *The Rules of Sociological Method* (first published in 1895). And in a pioneering study of suicide rates in nineteenth-century Europe (published in *Suicide*, 1897), he demonstrated the scientific method that has influenced what sociologists do when they conduct quantitative research. This includes the definition and measurement of social variables and the statistical study of the correlation of independent and dependent variables.

For Durkheim, sociology was the "science of civilization" (HN 149), in line with the view of scientific sociology elaborated by Saint-Simon, Comte, and Martineau (see Introduction). He thus embarked on the analysis of what he called **social facts**, that is, all those *external* and *collective* ways in which society shapes, structures, and constrains our behavior. Durkheim states: "A social fact is any way of acting … [that is] capable of exerting over the individual an external constraint; or which is general over the whole of a given society, whilst having an existence of its own, independent of its individual manifestations" (RSM 59). Social facts – "the beliefs, tendencies, and practices of the group taken collectively" (RSM 54) – are what sociologists study; we do not study individual psychological facts or physical or biological facts, though these may impinge on social facts.

For Durkheim, society is not simply a collection of individuals. It is a collectivity with features and characteristics of its own. Society is thus more than the sum of the individuals that comprise it. It includes social relationships (e.g., family, friends, community), social patterns (e.g., demographic trends), and forms of social organization (e.g., occupational divisions, bureaucracy, marriage, church), and these collective forces independently regulate individual, group, and institutional behavior.

Although marriage, for example, is contracted by two individuals, marriage as a social fact predates and outlives the lifetime of any couple. Moreover, the propensity of individuals to marry is itself constrained not alone by sexual attraction (itself a social fact), but by many other social facts including economic conditions, religious expectations and prohibitions, divorce legislation, and cultural expectations (e.g., of age of marriage/cohabitation, etc.). Thus, Durkheim argues, society has its own reality, what he calls a ***sui generis* reality**, meaning that it is a collective reality that exerts its own force *independent* of individuals (*genus* is the Latin for group; *sui generis* translates to "of the group in and of itself").

Society, therefore, through its various social structures and everyday customs and norms, constrains how we think, feel, and act; and how groups, institutions (e.g. universities), and whole countries, too, act. These external constraints exist outside of the self; they have an independent existence in society and cannot be willed out of existence by the individual. A 19-year-old who doesn't go to college does not internalize society's expectations of how college students should act, and college graduates may forget these expectations soon after they leave college and have a full-time job. But these expectations still exist nonetheless in society. As social facts, they have an objective, external existence independent of any given individual; moreover, the *collective* expression of a social phenomenon can vary from its expression in any particular person's life.

The collective incidence of something in society – of divorce, immigration, or economic inequality, etc. – is separate from any one individual's experience of divorce. Yet that individual's divorce contributes to the collective (social) phenomenon of divorce. By the same token, the incidence of divorce in a particular community, and public opinion about divorce are social facts external to the individual. And as such, they shape individual attitudes toward divorce in general and individuals' decisions about marriage and divorce (RSM 55).

Social facts should *not* be equated with "statistical facts," such as the percentage of young adults who go to college or the divorce or birth rates. These statistical facts are social facts insofar as they contribute to shaping social behavior, including social policies, cultural expectations, and decisions made by individuals, families, and institutions about various things. Social facts encompass much more than statistical facts: They include all social phenomena, that is, all the ways in which social structures, social norms, and collective expectations constrain social behavior.

Topic 2.1   Born on the Bayou and barely feeling any urge to roam

The constraining power of society on individual and group behavior is evident in Vacherie, Louisiana. Here we see how the social forces of population mobility, immigration history, the occupational structure, family and gender structures, and collective expectations of everyday food, leisure, and gender roles impact daily life.–Vacherie is one of the most settled places in the US. Almost all (98 percent) of its residents were born in Louisiana, compared to an average of 60 percent for other American states. In this bayou town on the Mississippi River less than 30 miles west of New Orleans, families stay put over several generations and there are strong cultural and family expectations that they will do so. In the Reulet family, for example, whose descendants settled in Vacherie from France in the 1820s, all eight adult children live within a five-mile radius of their parents' home; middle-aged sons drop by for coffee and hot chocolate at the start of the workday before heading to nearby manufacturing plants and oil refineries; and Sunday brings the obligatory extended-family dinner of Cajun pork and potatoes prepared every week by the Reulet adult daughters. Alongside Cajun food and culture, fishing and hunting are the main leisure activities in Vacherie, not surfing the Internet (see Harden 2002a).[2]

How, as sociologists, should we scientifically study social facts? According to Durkheim, "the first and most basic rule is to consider social facts as things" (RSM 60) – as things that objectively exist in society. Such things have a reality external to individuals and can be studied with **objectivity** (as Comte too believed). The command to investigate "social facts as things" is not as straightforward as it may seem. We cannot, for example, simply look around and automatically see friendship or social ties – we cannot put them under a microscope in the same way that biologists study cells or microbes. And yet, social relationships are a core part of social life. Durkheim acknowledges the difficulty in measuring social phenomena – the fact that in and of themselves they are "not amenable to exact observation and especially not to measurement" (DL 24).

What then are we to do? How can we be scientists of social life if we cannot measure what constitutes social life? The answer, Durkheim states, is that although we cannot observe social processes directly we can study them scientifically by defining (or operationalizing) the things we study in terms of directly observable manifestations or indicators of the topic in question: "We must … substitute for [a particular social phenomenon] … an external [measure] which symbolizes it, and then study the former through the latter" (DL 24). Definition is critical, because otherwise we don't know what we are looking for, or how to categorize and differentiate among things; "moreover, since this initial definition determines the subject matter itself … that subject matter will either consist of a thing or not, according to how this definition is formulated" (RSM 75).

This is precisely what sociologists do. If you look at the "Methods" section of any quantitative research article you will see that sociologists outline in detail how they define and measure the particular variables of interest. Thus, for example, the authors of a study of older adults' social connectedness *defined* social connectedness as interpersonal ties and community participation. They *measured* the respondents' interpersonal social ties by the frequency of their interaction with, and subjective emotional closeness to, individuals in their circle (or network); and they measured the respondents' community participation (or integration) by the frequency of their neighborly socializing, religious participation, volunteering, and organized group involvement (Cornwell et al. 2008).

Sociological objectivity

By treating social facts as things that objectively exist outside of us and that can be objectively measured using specific indicators, we can study social phenomena irrespective of our own views or feelings on the topic. Consider religion. Religion is about a lot of unknowns. Does God exist? Does God answer prayers? Is there an afterlife? These are questions that no researcher, and not even the most devout faith believer, can verify empirically. Nonetheless, many sociologists, following Durkheim, study religion as a social fact, as an objective thing in society – using indicators of its thing-ness, such as how often individuals attend a place of worship. Sociologists then investigate how frequency of religious attendance relates to other social things, e.g., how it constrains and is constrained by other forms of social behavior, such as gender, volunteering in the community, and voting.

Sociologists similarly study crime, homelessness, stress, income inequality, etc. These are all social facts that have an external, independent existence in society. Each of these "social phenomena … must be considered in themselves detached from the conscious beings who form their own mental representations of them" (RSM 70). We "cannot live among things without forming ideas about them according to which" we regulate our behavior" (RSM 60). But as social scientists, we must leave aside our preconceived ideas about society and how it works – ideas that necessarily derive from our own immersion in society – and instead focus on what comprises the (objective) social reality (social facts).

As such, sociologists' empirical findings and conclusions about religion, crime, or any social fact are independent of their own personal beliefs about God, crime, etc. Further, because, as Durkheim argues, all social facts are produced by other social facts, we should see all social facts in terms of their social context. Therefore, we should study the social conditions and circumstances that give rise to crime and to particular types of crime, and not psychologically, in terms of a particular criminal's individual psyche (RSM 134).

Data-centered sociology

The relationship between the sociologist and the things we study is more complicated than Durkheim acknowledged. This is a very important point highlighted by Harriet Martineau (see Introduction), developed by Max Weber (chapter 3), and further elaborated by contemporary feminist theorists (chapter 10). Nonetheless, Durkheim's scientific method still informs much of what comprises empirical sociology. Research proceeds from things (data) to ideas, and not the reverse (RSM 60); "to treat phenomena as things is to treat them as data and this constitutes the starting point for science" (RSM 69). In this scientific process, the whole of social reality is open to empirical investigation, wherein "the conventional character of a practice or an institution should never be assumed in advance" (RSM 70). Although we study things that may seem obvious or that we think we already know (such as pop culture, crime, and families), by studying these topics scientifically (i.e., using data and making inferences based on data), we will likely discover or clarify characteristics about the phenomenon.[3]

SOCIAL FACTS AND SOCIAL PROBLEMS

An emphasis on social facts as objective things also means that crime, homelessness, and other things we might consider "social problems" are in fact sociologically "normal." They are things that exist in society; they are part of collective life. As such, we can measure and compare the occurrence and prevalence of these things (social facts), and their relation to other things (social facts) across different cities or countries that share a similar level of socioeconomic development (RSM 92).

Durkheim argues, for example, that crime, which he defines as any action that is punished, "is normal because it is completely impossible for any society entirely free of it to exist" (RSM 99). Further, he notes that the criminal "plays a normal role in social life" (RSM 102), as do judges, laws, criminologists, prisons, etc., and all are functionally interrelated. All "social problems" raise important political and policymaking questions, as underscored by the opioid crisis (see Topic 2.2). But for the sociologist, they are first and foremost social facts worthy of investigation. Such investigation will show how they vary in different social contexts, and variously relate to other social facts (e.g., unemployment). A normal social phenomenon (e.g., unemployment, drug addiction) becomes a problem – or for Durkheim, "pathological" – only when its incidence becomes abnormally high compared to its established or regular incidence in that society or in other similarly developed countries. In the US, for example, a 4 percent unemployment rate is considered normal in times of economic prosperity, but an 8 percent unemployment rate is an indicator of recession, that is, of an abnormality in the economy/society. Politicians and policymakers thus make great efforts to dampen the negative effects of recession (e.g., factory and bank closures, home foreclosures); they want to limit its disruptive impact on the normal functioning and cohesiveness of particular communities and of society as a whole. The maintenance of social cohesion was Durkheim's main substantive focus, to which I now turn.

Topic 2.2   Opioid addiction

Deaths from drug addiction, alcohol, and suicide have been on the rise in the US. The suicide rate in 2016 was the highest it has been for 30 years; drug-overdose deaths have tripled since 2000; and alcohol-induced deaths continue to add to the toll. Though individual acts, these are all, as Durkheim emphasizes, *social* phenomena, and thus grounded in societal conditions and related to various other social phenomena. A Durkheimian framework sheds light on their explanation.

Most basically there is the *definition* and *measurement* of the phenomena in question. This entails identifying whether death is caused by a disease or injury unrelated to drugs, alcohol, or suicide. If alcohol or drugs are a contributing but not a direct or underlying cause of death, such deaths are not counted as drug or alcohol induced. If drugs or alcohol are used intentionally to cause self-poisoning, they are categorized as deaths from suicide. The determination of an individual's cause of death is made – or certified - by a local coroner; and death certificates issued by local coroners are collated and analyzed by the Centers for Disease Control and Prevention (CDC). The CDC uses these data to document the mortality *rate* in the US for any given year, to itemize or differentiate among and categorize the various causes of mortality, and to track the overall mortality rate and the categorized causes over time (usually on an annual basis going back several decades). The actual absolute number of deaths and the number per each cause are converted into statistical rates per 100,000 of the US population; rates rather than raw numbers are more accurate and meaningful because they adjust for changes (increases or decreases) in overall population.

Mortality rates are sociologically interesting *in and of themselves* because they tell us significant things about a given society; whether, for example, life expectancy is long or short, and what social habits are revealed by the leading causes of death (e.g., whether drug use, cancer, or heart disease). Demonstrating that all social forces (social facts) are *interrelated* with other social phenomena, opioid death rates are related to several other socially relevant forces. These include age, gender, race, region, marital status, education, and employment. Currently, opioid deaths are most prevalent among middle aged whites, especially so among 25-to 34-year-old white men who are high school graduates, unemployed, and unmarried; and though geographically dispersed, more apparent in rural areas in the northeast. In short, opioid addiction is related to several other social phenomena.

Similarly, in Durkheimian terms, opioid addiction is a *normal* part of society and functions in relation to and is interdependent with other social things, including medical doctors, prescription writing norms/practices, pharmaceutical companies, drug rehabilitation programs, drug counselors, unemployment, politicians, election campaigns, health insurance, financial strain, poverty, and racism (e.g., the view that as a "white" problem it is a "public" health crisis, unlike the "black" crack epidemic attributed to black culture).

The social and demographic profile of those dying from opioids has led some analysts to refer to them as "deaths of despair." In Durkheimian language, they are dying from a lack of social *integration*, that is, they are not sufficiently constrained by and into society. Work, and marriage, are constraining forces; in their absence, the individual has fewer ties. And, individual despair is exacerbated by community despair or *anomie*, brought on by social forces such as economic decline (e.g., due to the loss of manufacturing jobs), and community depletion due to aging, the outmigration of young people, and lower aggregate rates of marriage and fertility. Some too suggest that the decline of church is a related cause, as well as a weak "welfare state." Thus in the absence of the *mediating institutions* that tie individuals to one another and to the community and society at large, *disintegration* produces addiction and death.

Durkheim's methodological guidelines also help us to assess whether opioid addiction is a normal or a *pathological* phenomenon. Three empirical patterns point to its pathological dimensions: (1) The *unexpected reversal* of what had been a settled pattern, that is, an increase in the mortality rate of middle-aged whites (men and women), a group for whom mortality had been in a long-term decline; (2) Its *comparative* uniqueness. Although the US rate has increased, a similar trend has not occurred in Canada, Britain, Germany, France, Sweden, or Australia, all countries with a relatively similar level of development to the US. In these countries, middle-aged white mortality continues to decrease; and (3) the fact that the spike in white mortality is due to conditions (e.g., drugs) that previously had a comparatively higher incidence among blacks; in 2000, for example, black men had a higher rate than white men of drug- and alcohol-induced deaths (Case and Deaton 2017; Kolhatkar 2017; Monnat 2017; Tavernise 2016; *The Economist* 2017a, 2017b). The social pathology indicated by opioid mortality reflects broader, underlying social conditions (e.g., a gap between the skills of the white working class and the skills/education functional to a digital economy), whose remediation can contribute to reducing social pathology. At the same time, there is evidence that opioid addiction is becoming normalized, that is, society is adjusting to its reality and finding ways to deal with it, including instituting changes in medical prescription practices that seek to restrict (and constrain) the availability of opioids.

THE NATURE OF SOCIETY

Durkheim emphasized the collective nature of social life; that is, social facts have an external existence independent of individuals and they constrain behavior. Yet it is individuals who live in society. How then do individuals whose individual nature is different from the collective nature of society manage to live in society? This for Durkheim is the core task of sociology: analyzing social **morality** (Bellah 1973: xv). Durkheim uses the word "morality" broadly: it refers to everything that forces individuals to take account of other people (DL 398) and is reflected in the formal and informal social rules that permeate and regulate individuals' behavior vis-à-vis one another in society. It is a morality that is derived not from a religious or philosophical belief system but from socially prescribed or structured "rules of conduct" that reflect and reinforce the *reciprocal* nature of social life. The individual does not exist alone in society; we coexist with and live among other individuals. Social coexistence is contingent on our individual and collective ability to regulate our individual desires vis-à-vis each other and to recognize our mutual, reciprocal dependence. **Social solidarity** emerges from social rules and other social structures (social institutions) because these structures bind individuals to other individuals and to the larger society; thus "morality consists in solidarity with the group, and varies according to that solidarity" (DL 331). Durkheim argues that society could not exist – it could not hold together in a relatively ordered and cohesive fashion – if individuals were to simply pursue their own sensation-seeking desires, impulses, and appetites. We certainly act on those impulses, but we do so while simultaneously orienting ourselves to, cooperating with, and being regulated by, others, that is, society. Durkheim explains:

> Our sensory appetites are necessarily egoistic: they have our individuality and it alone as their object. When we satisfy our hunger, our thirst and so on, without bringing any other tendency into play, it is ourselves, and ourselves alone that we satisfy … moral activity … on the contrary, [is] distinguished by the fact the rules of conduct to which they conform can be universalized [beyond the individual]. Morality begins with [individual] disinterest, with attachment to something other than ourselves [i.e., to the group, society]. (HN 151)

In other words, humans have certain basic biological drives that, according to Durkheim, are necessarily selfish. But as a social species we need to take account of other individuals. This requires a socially learned capacity to transcend self-centered appetites so that, as Durkheim argues, we are able to cooperate with others and become attached to "something other than ourselves" (HN 151) – the external society of family, neighborhood, school, work, nation, etc. The functioning of these group structures and of society as a whole is contingent on our socially learned ability to conform (more or less) to the respective norms and expectations within each of these multiple communities. This is why socialization is so important. From early infancy, we are taught how to interact and behave as social beings; to sacrifice a certain amount of self-interest to the interest of the collectivity – the family, community, society – that is external to us but of which we are a part. Socialization

> consists of a continual effort to impose upon the child ways of seeing, thinking and acting which he himself would not have arrived at spontaneously. From his earliest years we oblige him to eat, drink and sleep at regular hours, and to observe cleanliness, calm and obedience; later we force him to learn how to be mindful of others, to respect customs and conventions, and to work, etc. If this constraint in time ceases to be felt it is because it gradually gives rise to habits, to inner tendencies which render it superfluous; but they supplant the constraint only because they are derived from it. (RSM 53–54)

COOPERATION AS THE KEY TO SOCIAL LIFE

Through socialization, we learn to maintain society by cooperatively coexisting as friends, family members, workmates, housemates, teammates, citizens. – It teaches us that social life necessarily requires reciprocity and consideration of (and engagement with) others, rather than the competitive assertion of my specific individual needs over (or at the expense of) others' needs. The relation of the individual to society is one that necessitates regulation and constraint precisely because of the collective (*sui generis*) nature of society. As Durkheim states,

> society has its own nature, and consequently, its requirements are quite different from those of our nature as individuals: the interests of the whole are not necessarily those of the part. Therefore, society cannot be formed or maintained without our being required to make perpetual and costly sacrifices. Because society surpasses us, it obliges us to surpass ourselves; and to surpass itself, a being must, to some degree, depart from its nature – a departure that does not take place without causing more or less painful tensions … we must … do violence to certain of our strongest inclinations. (HN 163)

You and your roommates probably know well what Durkheim means about tension emanating from competing inclinations – when the nature of community/society and the impulses of individuals are at odds. Your dorm or apartment mimics the tension that confronts society as a whole. This tension may be especially pronounced when you first come to college and share a room with someone you had not previously known. One likes to go to sleep relatively early and another likes to socialize late into the night with friends invited to your room. The resolution of these conflicting impulses necessitates a reciprocal compromise whereby both roommates rein in their individual desires to preserve the effective functioning of both your specific dorm room relationship and, by extension, of college society (i.e., dorm cohabitation). And this scene wherein different individuals and groups must necessarily curb their selfish or self-oriented impulses occurs daily across diverse locales – in families, at work, in the supermarket, and in the conduct of national and global politics. Reciprocity is at the core of social life and hence of all forms of social interaction. It is, as Durkheim's contemporary, the German social theorist Georg Simmel (1858–1918), would say, a "sociologically oriented … feeling" (1903/1950: 384).[4]

THE CONSTRAINT OF SOCIETAL EXPECTATIONS

The multiple expectations associated with being a friend or daughter or student, and the rules of neighborhood and workplace culture, are institutionalized and exert an external constraint on our behavior. These are not our rules but society's rules, most of which were in place long before we were born and will still matter long after we have died. Moreover, even when we create what we think are our own individualized rules for certain things, these too come from society. Even though we may not subjectively feel any social pressure to conform to being a certain kind of friend, daughter, etc., and even when it seems natural for us to behave in certain ways toward others, that behavior is, nonetheless, socially inherited. It is externally given to us from society and it exists independent of us. Durkheim elaborates:

> When I perform my duties as a brother, a husband or a citizen and carry out the commitments I have entered into, I fulfill obligations which are defined in law and custom and which are external to myself and my actions. Even when they conform to my own sentiments and when I feel their reality within me, that reality does not cease to be objective, for it is not I who have prescribed these duties; I have received them through education [socialization]. Moreover, how often does it happen that we are ignorant of the details of the obligations that we must assume, and that, to know them, we must consult the legal code and its authorized interpreters! Similarly, the [religious] believer has discovered from birth, ready fashioned, the beliefs and practices of his religious life; if they existed before he did, it follows that they exist outside him. The system of signs that I employ to express my thoughts, the monetary system I use to pay my debts, the credit instruments I utilise in my commercial relationships, the practices I follow in my profession, etc. all function independently of the use I make of them … Thus there are ways of acting, thinking and feeling which possess the remarkable property of existing outside the consciousness of the individual. Not only are these types of behavior and thinking external to the individual, but they are endued with a compelling and coercive power by virtue of which, whether he wishes it or not, they impose themselves upon him. Undoubtedly, when I conform to them of my own free will, this coercion is not felt or felt hardly at all, since it is unnecessary. None the less, it is intrinsically a characteristic of these facts; the proof of this is that it asserts itself as soon as I try to resist. If I attempt to violate the rules of law they react against me so as to forestall my action, if there is still time … If I do not conform to ordinary conventions, if in my mode of dress I pay no heed to what is customary in my country and in my social class, the laughter I provoke, the social distance at which I am kept, produce, although in a more mitigated form, the same results as any real [legal] penalty. In other cases, although it may be indirect, constraint is no less effective. I am not forced to speak French with my compatriots, nor to use the legal currency, but it is impossible for me to do otherwise. If I try to escape the necessity, my attempt would fail miserably. (RSM 50–51)

AN ARMY OF ONE

Some of you, understandably, may be surprised by Durkheim's emphasis on the necessarily constraining force of society. His view may seem especially jarring in America, which has a strong emphasis on individualism, self-reliance, and the rights and aspirations of the individual (e.g., Bellah et al. 1985).

This ethos is deeply present. Recruitment advertisements for the American army, an institution that necessarily demands cooperative teamwork and a strong sense of group bonding, advertises itself as "An army of one." This conveys that the lone individual soldier is equal to the entire army – as if the parts are greater than the whole, rather than the inverse. Or perhaps, it means the inverse: that the army is so disciplined and so tightly bonded that all its members act in unison as one collective unit.

In emphasizing the external and constraining force that society exerts on the individual, Durkheim is not discounting the role of individual reason and free will in a person's actions. Nor is he dismissing the nuances of personality in how individuals may respond to social customs and conventions (RSM 52). He is simply highlighting that society exists independent of the individual and that it necessarily constrains individual and group behavior. Durkheim argues that rather than being diminished by the awareness that we are not dependent on ourselves alone, we are in fact enriched by our social dependence; "it is indisputable today that most of our ideas and tendencies are not developed by ourselves, but come to us from outside, they can only penetrate us by imposing themselves upon us" (RSM 52). And they impose themselves through society, through socialization and social interaction. Durkheim's main thesis is that individuals are socially interdependent. Social cohesion comes from individuals' ties to others; our sense of social belonging comes from our ties to other people and to the groups of which we are a part.

CHANGE AND RESISTANCE

Although Durkheim's emphasis on society's existence prior to and beyond individual existence might seem to imply that social change never occurs, this, of course, is not the case. Social change happens, as Durkheim was well aware. Political and social upheaval was normal in France immediately prior to and during his early years: France had seen "three monarchies, two empires, and two republics in the period between 1789 and 1870" (Bellah 1973: xvi). But social change, whether large scale (e.g., the legalization of same-sex marriage) or local (e.g., change in the structure of the campus cafeteria), does not occur without a struggle; most change is initially resisted as a result of the collective force of existing social facts. Social forces, the patterns and structures already in place, cast a long shadow on people's expectations of what is "normal," and what functions effectively. As things external to us, social facts are "principally recognizable by virtue of not being capable of modification through a mere act of the will. This is not because it is intractable to all modification. But to effect change the will is not sufficient; it needs a degree of arduous effort because of the strength of the resistance it offers, which even then cannot always be overcome" (RSM 70).

Just think for a moment of marriage. It is a social fact that constrains collective expectations, as well as the actuality, of who can marry whom, and it dims our ability to recognize alternative possibilities. It was only in 1967, for example, that the US Supreme Court struck down state laws banning interracial marriage. And, of course, it is even more recently that same-sex couples can marry in the US, Canada, the Republic of Ireland, England, Wales, Scotland, and in many other Western European and South American countries, as well as in New Zealand and Australia. At the same time, nevertheless, traditional gender expectations persist in multiple arenas. And as highlighted in the movie *Meet the Parents* (starring Ben Stiller), although it is not against the law, there is still a strong cultural expectation that women should marry men who have traditional male occupations – that women, not men, are nurses, though more men today are entering nursing and other service occupations that have traditionally been dominated by women. It is hard to escape the constraining power of society. Although social change occurs, it is not simply willed by individuals. It has to be accomplished collectively and in tune with collective forces (e.g., public opinion, economic transformation). Durkheim comments:

"As an industrialist, nothing prevents me from working with the processes and methods of the previous century, but if I do I will most certainly ruin myself. Even when, in fact, I can struggle free from these rules or successfully break them, it is never without being forced to fight against them" (RSM 51). Similar challenges confront any individual or group who tries to defy any social convention.

SOCIETAL TRANSFORMATION AND SOCIAL COHESION

Today, there is a lot of talk about the immensity of social changes occurring because of economic and cultural globalization (see chapters 14 and 15). There was also a lot of economic, social, and technological change happening in the latter part of the nineteenth century when Durkheim and Marx (and Max Weber) were writing. Like Marx, Durkheim was preoccupied with the large-scale changes around him: industrialization, urbanization, immigration, and population growth – changes that sociologists typically see as differentiating modern from traditional societies. From the 1840s to the end of the nineteenth century, the US, for example, experienced a massive increase in immigration (e.g., Fischer and Hout 2006,: 23–56). Thousands of Irish, Italians, Germans, Swedes, and Poles, among others, made their way to America and found jobs in its rapidly expanding manufacturing industries. In Great Britain, first, and then America, the invention of the power loom moved textile production from a household-based craft to cloth-making by a highly specialized workforce producing standardized output in highly regulated factories in newly expanding urban areas (Smelser 1959; Williams 1990: 94–95). The convergence of these changes transformed society, speeding its transition from traditional to modern forms of social organization. This transformative process was highlighted during the televised opening ceremony at the London 2012 Olympics: One scene showed Britain's transition from lush green pastures full of grazing sheep to dark industrial factories whose large chimneys dominated the urban skyline.

Durkheim was particularly interested in how such large-scale social change affects social relations and the overall order and cohesion of society. In times of change and upheaval, what holds society together? Can we assume that society will more or less coalesce regardless of the changes it undergoes? These are the same questions publicly debated in several countries today as people grapple with the globalizing impact of economic change and of migration trends that are changing the ethnic and racial composition of relatively homogenized countries. Ferdinand Tonnies (1855–1936) distinguished between small-scale local community (*Gemeinschaft*) and large-scale, urban society characterized by relatively impersonal social relations (*Gesellschaft*). Similarly, Durkheim makes a clear analytical distinction between traditional and modern societies. He does so to elaborate how differences in social structure produce different mechanisms that function to create social cohesion or solidarity.

TRADITIONAL SOCIETY

Traditional (preindustrial or agricultural) societies and communities tend to be characterized by *sameness*, by the similarities that exist among people. Anyone who spends time in a rural community knows this. In farming communities today, for example, farmers do a similar kind of farming (e.g., wheat, or cattle) using similar methods and tools (e.g., same-brand tractors, combine harvesters, pickup trucks, etc.), and each one is able to do the breadth of farm-related chores (e.g., harvesting, fixing tractors) required on any neighboring farm. Rather than specializing in one very specific aspect of one very specific farm chore (the specialization seen in the division of labor in modern factory production; see chapter 1), these farmers have a breadth of competence, and one farmer's

Figure 2.1   Small towns and rural communities have different characteristics, different constraints, and different types of social relations than those found in urban or metropolitan areas. Source: Author.

breadth of competence is similar to that of the next. Each farmer lives, moreover, in a relatively homogeneous community composed of more or less similar-looking farms, farmers, and farm families. This is the sort of sameness that captures the social organization seen in traditional societies and communities.

In traditional societies, social ties and relationships – the bonds of social solidarity – are relatively easy to maintain because people share a lot in common. The same individuals and families tend to live in the same place and engage in similar occupations over several generations. And similarly, there is a sameness of ancestry, ethnicity, religious and political beliefs, and culture.

The organization and structure of everyday life in traditional communities are such that people meet each other in all kinds of overlapping contexts over the course of their daily or weekly routines; they meet at the same one or two churches, the same diner, the same post office, the same stores, and their children go to the same school, play on the same football team, etc. It's the type of society or community in which everyone basically knows everyone else; and even if they do not know them personally, they know who they are, who their mother or brother is. Family, school, work, and leisure are all intersecting domains of activity and of social ties. In traditional communities characterized by overlapping ties, the maintenance of social solidarity does not require much effort, because as Durkheim states: "The more closely knit the members of a society, the more they maintain various relationships either with one another or with the group collectively. For if they met together rarely, they would not be mutually dependent, except sporadically and somewhat weakly" (DL 25). There are many places in the US, the UK, Ireland, Norway, Italy, and in other modern societies where overlapping social ties are the norm. This is especially true of rural locales but tight-knit communities exist within major cities and in large metropolitan areas too.

THE SOCIETAL ABSORPTION OF THE INDIVIDUAL

We expect small towns and rural communities to have a robust **collective conscience**. Durkheim uses this term (translated from the French *conscience collective*) to refer to a society's or community's collectively shared feelings, values, and ideals (DL 43). He explains:

> The totality of beliefs and sentiments common to the average members of a society forms a determinate system with a life of its own. It can be termed the collective or common consciousness [conscience] … By definition it is diffused over society as a whole … it is independent of the particular conditions in which individuals find themselves. Individuals pass on, but it abides … [and] links successive generations to one another. (DL 38–39)

Durkheim gives a lot of emphasis in his writings to the strong hold of the collective conscience and of society's "collective feelings" (RSM 99; DL 39) on a community's beliefs and practices. But as feminist theorists like Dorothy Smith would point out, the allegedly objective "collective feeling" frequently excludes those who are not part of the dominant (white male heterosexual) group in society (see chapter 10).

The collective conscience, nevertheless, exerts a strong authority over the whole community, maintaining social order and cohesiveness by tightly regulating the expectations and behavior of individuals. In Vacherie, Louisiana, for example, it would be hard for a woman to defy the expectation of helping to prepare the extended family's Sunday dinner (see Topic 2.1). In traditional communities there is little individualism, little personal freedom and anonymity; the individual, rather, "is absorbed into the collective" (DL 242). This brings a strong feeling of social belonging but it also means that the individual has little freedom to stray from the norms and authority of the community. Anyone who has grown up in a small town knows this feeling well. It's hard to escape your neighbor's watchful eyes, and particularly as you move through your teenage years looking for excitement, you might find the community's "social horizon" (DL 242) too limiting, too constraining and overpowering of your individual desires.

The authority of the collective conscience is keenly felt if you don't toe the line; and the repressive, punishing power of gossip, shame, and ostracism is felt not only by the individual deviant, but by their family and friends too in the loss of honor imposed on them (DL 47).[5] More generally, a community's informal sanctions and conventions function to affirm the collective conscience by outlining particular expectations as well as variously punishing those who offend against strongly held collective feelings. "Punishment constitutes an emotional reaction" (DL 44) aimed at avenging and pouring scorn on the deviant act – the violation of the collective conscience – and defending the community against further challenges to the authority of its collective beliefs (DL 44). Through punishment, therefore, we "stir up [and reaffirm] the social sentiments that have been offended" (DL 47–48). In short, punishment functions to repress the threat to societal cohesion the deviance represents.

MECHANICAL SOLIDARITY

The structural and cultural sameness that characterizes the beliefs and social relationships in traditional societies produces what Durkheim calls **mechanical solidarity**: The creation and maintenance of social ties are fairly mechanical because they are built into the very structure of the community. When people in a community have relatively similar occupations, family histories, experiences and beliefs, and overlapping social relationships, these similarities make it relatively easy to produce social cohesion. The similarity in what people do (e.g., farming, fishing, mill work, etc.), and in who and what they know, means that no one individual or family is necessary to the functioning of the whole community because each individual/family basically replicates the next (like segments in an orange). Hence the absence of any one individual/family from the community (due to death or ostracism, for example) does not affect the overall functioning of the community.

Vacherie, Louisiana, the most rooted town in the most rooted state in America, is a good illustration of the mechanical solidarity that Durkheim attributes to traditional communities (see Topic 2.1). Its tightly bounded and overlapping family and neighborhood relationships, the force of its collective expectations on social habits (e.g., Sunday dinner with the extended family), and long-established shared occupational histories and leisure routines ensure a fairly mechanical maintenance of the community's social ties, order, and cohesion.

MODERN SOCIETY

Even in Vacherie, however, there are emerging threats to the maintenance of tight social solidarity. Well-paid blue-collar work is on the decline, thus pushing Vacherie's young people to continue education beyond high school. Those who leave Vacherie to go away to college are less likely to return and settle there, and as more young people avail of economic opportunities outside of Vacherie, the strong family and community bonds that have characterized Vacherie for several generations may weaken. Such mobility (a social fact) is precisely one of the defining characteristics of modern society. Is it possible then for solidarity (social cohesion) to characterize modern societies that, by definition, do not have the structured overlapping social relationships seen in traditional societies?

Modern societies, after all, look almost exactly the opposite of traditional societies (see Box 2.1). They are characterized by population density, urbanization, geographical and social mobility, and a diversity of occupational, religious, political, ethnic, and cultural groups. Diversity brings a lot of personal freedom, anonymity, and impersonal relations; individual difference rather than sameness is the norm (see Box 2.2). If we think of any densely populated city, such as Chicago, Toronto, Birmingham, or Mumbai (Bombay), we have a snapshot of modern society. Durkheim argues that in

---

Box 2.1   Georg Simmel: Urbanism as a way of acting, thinking, and feeling

Georg Simmel (1858–1918) also emphasized the contrasting ways of life in urban and rural society. Like Durkheim, he recognized "functional specialization" as the hallmark of urban society and how it forges interdependence among individuals. "This specialization makes one individual incomparable to another, and each of them indispensable … However, this specialization makes each man the more directly dependent upon the supplementary activities of all others" (1903/1950: 409). This interdependence is more cool headed than the emotional investment found in rural society, and Simmel suggests it is in fact a necessary accommodation to the constant nervous stimulation of the city. The diversity and intensity of the urban metropolis, Simmel wrote, produces an "intensification of nervous stimulation … With each crossing of the street, with the tempo and multiplicity of economic, occupational and social life, the city sets up a deep contrast with small town and rural life … [where] the rhythm of life … flows more slowly, more habitually, and more evenly" (1903/1950: 410). Amid such stimulation, it is easier to maintain psychological equilibrium by reacting with one's "head instead of [one's] heart," and maintaining a "matter-of-fact attitude" (1903/1950: 410, 411). This more rational and impersonal response is also required, Simmel argues, by the dominance of the money economy in the metropolis, which for Simmel, as we saw (see Box 1.1), requires the calculating attitude that penetrates the whole structure and culture of urbanism as a way of life. "Through the calculative nature of money a new precision, a certainty in the definition of identities and differences, an unambiguousness in agreements and arrangements has been brought about in the relations of life-elements – just as externally this precision has been effected by the universal diffusion of pocket watches. However, the conditions of metropolitan life are at once cause and effect of this trait. The relationships and affairs of the typical metropolitan are usually so varied and complex that without the strictest punctuality in promises and services the whole structure would break down into an inextricable chaos. Above all, this necessity is brought about by the aggregation of so many people with such differentiated interests, who must integrate their relations and activities into a highly complex organism. If all clocks and watches in Berlin would suddenly go wrong in different ways, even if only by one hour, all economic life and communication of the city would be disrupted for a long time … Thus, the technique of metropolitan life is unimaginable without the most punctual integration of all activities and mutual relations into a stable and impersonal time schedule … Punctuality, calculability, exactness are forced upon life by the complexity and extension of metropolitan existence … these traits must color the contents of life and favor the exclusion of … irrational impulses" (Simmel 1903/1950: 412–413).

modern, urban societies (unlike in traditional societies), the collective conscience is less forceful and less encompassing, and less controlling of the individual:

> As society spreads out and becomes denser, it envelops the individual less tightly, and in consequence can restrain less efficiently the diverging tendencies that appear … in large towns the individual is much more liberated from the yoke of the collectivity … the pressure of opinion is felt with less force in large population centers. It is because the attention of each individual is distracted in too many different directions. Moreover we do not know one another so well. Even neighbors and members of the same family are in contact less often and less regularly, separated as they are at every moment by a host of matters and other people who come between them. (DL 238–239)

Thus the solidarity that derives from shared experiences, beliefs, and sentiments is harder to find in modern societies, notwithstanding the existence of many relatively homogenized, traditional communities within the urban metropolis (e.g., Boston's Italian North End, Brixton's "Little Jamaica" in London) and in modern societies more generally (e.g., Vacherie, Louisiana).

SPECIALIZED DIVISION OF LABOR

Yet, despite the individual freedom and the mobility, diversity, and weaker collective feelings that characterize modern society, there is still social cohesion. How is this possible? The reason, Durkheim argues, lies in the highly specialized **division of labor** that characterizes modern societies. The crucial variable differentiating modern from traditional societies is the extent to which there is specialization across and within various sectors of society. Durkheim wrote about these processes in a book of this very title, *The Division of Labor in Society* (DL). Sounding a lot like Karl Marx (see chapter 1, The Division of Labor and Alienation), Durkheim emphasized the structural importance of an increasingly specialized division of labor that coincides with the expansion of modern industrialization. It

> involves increasingly powerful mechanisms, large-scale groupings of power and capital, and consequently an extreme division of labor. Inside factories, not only are jobs demarcated, becoming extremely specialized, but each product is itself a specialty entailing the existence of others … the division of labor is not peculiar to economic life. We can observe its increasing influence in the most diverse sectors of society. Functions, whether political, administrative, or judicial, are becoming more and more specialized. The same is true in the arts and sciences. (DL 1–2)

Modern societies, in short, are characterized by specialization. There is a division of labor not only in the economy (e.g., factory production) and in the functions of government but also in the responsibility for child socialization, for example, whereby socialization functions are dispersed across institutions – with the family, the church, and the education system all having discrete and specific institutional roles. And within the university, for example, education is divided across specialized colleges and schools (of business, law, liberal arts) and further specialized departments and disciplines (sociology, economics, history, English, etc.). Similarly, the government has its specialized divisions and departments, as does the judicial system. Traditional societies, by contrast, have a limited division of labor (as we discussed; see the previous section on Societal Transformation and Social Cohesion).

SOCIAL INTERDEPENDENCE

Population growth and concentration *necessitate* a division of labor. Durkheim states, "The division of labour varies in direct proportion to the volume and density of societies and if it progresses in a continuous manner over the course of social development it is because societies become regularly more dense and generally more voluminous" (DL 205). The increasingly specialized division of labor that characterizes modern society, Durkheim argues, affects "profoundly our moral constitution" (DL 3); it heightens our reciprocal dependence on and ties to one another. Thus Durkheim, unlike Marx, did not see the division of labor as producing alienation (cf. chapter 1), but as reinforcing social **interdependence**. This is because occupational specialization *requires* individual specialization, and each individual's specialty contributes to the functioning of the whole.

Thus the division of labor produces "a moral effect" (DL 17): cooperation among individuals. Durkheim notes, "The division of labor can only occur within the framework of an already existing society. By this we do not just simply mean that individuals must cling materially to one another, but moral ties must also exist between them" (DL 218). Accordingly, for Durkheim, individual interdependence creates and regulates social solidarity because of the social-moral ties that underlie interdependence, ties that exist outside the division of labor (but that are also encompassed within it) (DL 219). He states: the division of labor "creates between men a whole system of rights and duties joining them in a lasting way to one another" (DL 337–338). Thus, contrary to Marx (cf. chapter 1), Durkheim argues that there is "nothing antisocial" or alienating about the division of labor. It is not antisocial "because it is a product of society" (DL 221), and it organically connects and integrates individuals. Moreover, contrary to the utilitarian view of unregulated individual self-interest advocated by Adam Smith and John Locke (see Introduction), it enables and requires reciprocity and cooperation among individuals in modern society; thus "moral life permeates all the relationships that go to make up co-operation" (DL 220–221).

For Durkheim, therefore, the division of labor produces interdependence and social cohesion. It is a functional accommodation to the increase in population growth and the concentrated population density (urbanization) associated with the development of modern societies. He explains: "the number of social relationships increases generally with the number of individuals ... [who] must be in fairly intimate contact so as to act and react upon one another"; they cannot be separated by "mutually impenetrable" environments (DL 205). With more and more people moving within an increasingly concentrated or dense space, there is, by default, increased social interaction and dependence. The division of labor not only makes it possible for, but requires, increasing numbers of individuals to act and interact with one another – "for functions to specialize even more, there must be additional cooperating elements, which must be grouped close enough together to be able to co-operate" (DL 205).

THE DENSITY OF SOCIAL INTERACTION

We generally do not have the same regularity of contact with family and relatives as would occur in a traditional society, but we are in contact with many others who literally cross our path every day. As we go about our daily business (getting coffee; going to work, school, or the gym; attending a ball game), many of the people we meet are different from us in some way – different family background, ethnicity, occupation, or even different political and religious beliefs. These many individuals comprise and contribute to the **physical density** of our environment; literally, the number of people we encounter during the day. (Census reports use *population density*, i.e., the number of people per specified area, to differentiate among places; cities have high, and rural areas low, population density.) What is significant about physical density for Durkheim is the social or **moral density** that it gives rise to; the more people we meet, the more social interacting we must do, however fleetingly, and therefore the more densely we are constrained by social-moral norms of reciprocity and cooperation. Thus walking down a busy city street we continuously monitor and adjust our path to make sure we don't bump into others, and most others act in a similarly considerate manner (though the habit of checking text messages while walking impedes such cooperation!).

The division of specialized labor brings us into contact with more and more people not like us (occupationally, economically, culturally, etc.) and makes us dependent on one another. As Durkheim asserts, "Each one of us depends more intimately upon society the more labour is divided up ... Society becomes more effective in moving in concert, at the same time as each of its elements has more movements that are peculiarly its own" (DL 85).

ORGANIC SOLIDARITY

The interdependence that is required by and results from the highly specialized division of labor produces what Durkheim calls **organic solidarity**: "This solidarity resembles that observed in the higher animals. In fact each organ has its own special characteristics and autonomy, yet the greater the unity of the organism, the more marked the individualization of the parts. Using this analogy, we propose to call 'organic' the solidarity that is due to the division of labor" (DL 85). We recognize that although each organ in the body (e.g., lungs, kidneys, stomach) performs a very specialized function, a healthy body is dependent on the effective simultaneous functioning of each independent (and interdependent) organ. So too with modern society: Social cohesion (social health) results from the interdependence of individuals each with their own specialty. Modern society not only affirms but requires individualism. Such individualism, however, produces interindividual dependence rather than individual isolation.

THE MORAL-SOCIAL BASIS OF CONTRACT

Durkheim points out that the interdependence in modern society is not determined solely by contractual exchange (even though laws proliferate in modern society). **Contract** certainly matters; it formally regulates social relationships and behavior in all sorts of ways (e.g., marriage, club membership, housing leases, almost all financial transactions). And when contracts get broken, modern societies have laws in place that seek to restore the order that the laws were intended to protect (see note 5). But, as Durkheim argues, "if a contract has binding force, it is society which confers that force" (DL 71). Contracts have legitimacy only because they institutionalize (or legalize) the expectations and customs that we in society believe are necessary to maintaining and enforcing the norms of human reciprocity necessary to social life. Contracts formalize collective moral expectations of how we should treat one another in society.

Durkheim argues that contracts are an expression not of utilitarian exchange based on individual self-interests (as Adam Smith or John Locke would argue; see Introduction), but of social morality (DL 221). Like all social

Figure 2.2 The specialized division of labor makes individuals dependent on one another; interdependence creates social ties or solidarity. Source: © Joe Howell/AP/Press Association.

facts, contracts originate within society and it is society that gives them and all rules of conduct their obligatory (moral) force. They simply represent the interindividual cooperativeness that society considers moral in the first place; they do not have an existence or a power independent of society. Hence "the contract is not sufficient by itself, but is only possible because of the regulation of contracts, which is of social origin" (DL 162). Contracts emerge from society (social morality) in order to protect social relationships and social order.

All contractual relationships therefore also have at the same time a precontractual, moral (social) element over and above the protection of the individual interests at stake. In this view, contracts are not simply formal legal rules established to restrain individuals' avaricious appetites (cf. Hobbes) or even a social mechanism to protect individual rights (as in Rousseau's *social contract*). Rather, for Durkheim, contracts are thoroughly social: They originate in and function to protect *society*, that is, contracts protect the interdependent social relationships that form a functioning society. They are collective forces that reflect and impact the moral (socially constraining) ties among individuals.

When we do things that go beyond the requirements stipulated by contract, we vividly demonstrate the moral-social basis of society that Durkheim emphasizes. Volunteers who travel miles to help others whose homes and livelihoods have been destroyed by hurricanes, floods, or earthquakes epitomize the moral force toward cooperation exerted by society. Such behavior underscores the attachment of individuals to something other than themselves (i.e., to others, to society). It demonstrates awareness of the reciprocity and interdependence that underpins and builds society.

Thus although we have self-interests (and appetites), self-interest alone is a fragile source of community; it does not foster social solidarity:

> if mutual interest draws men closer, it is never more than for a few moments. It can only create between them an external bond. In the fact of exchange the various agents involved remain apart from one another, and once the operation is over, each one finds himself again "reassuming his self" in its entirety. The different consciousnesses are only superficially in contact: they neither interpenetrate nor do they cleave closely to one another … For where interests alone reign, as nothing arises to check the egoisms confronting one another, each self finds itself in relation to the other on a war footing … Self-interest is, in fact, the least constant thing in the world. Today it is useful for me to unite with you; tomorrow the same reason will make me your enemy. (DL 152)

The individualism of modern society, therefore, does not preclude a felt responsibility toward others; it is, for Durkheim, a **moral individualism** that goes beyond our contractual obligations (while also shaping them). Society is possible only because individuals transcend the self and attach themselves to something other than themselves: They recognize the necessity of cooperative interdependence

---

Box 2.2   Analytical contrasts between traditional and modern society

Traditional society	Modern society
Preindustrial/rural society	Industrialized, urban society
Sameness	Diversity
Strong collective conscience	Weaker collective conscience
Limited division of labor	Highly specialized division of labor
Repressive, punitive law	Contract-type law stipulating reciprocal rights
> Produces mechanical solidarity	> Produces organic solidarity

with others, an interdependence demanded by the ever-increasing complexity in the organization of modern society. Whereas the solidarity in traditional societies derives from the sameness of the community, in modern societies the cooperation required by the specialized division of labor produces a solidarity based on social interdependence. In sum, both traditional and modern societies are socially cohesive, but the source and nature of the solidarity varies because of differences in the social structures and forms of organization in these different types of society.

SOCIAL CONDITIONS OF SUICIDE

As part of his focus on the social structures (e.g., the division of labor) that create social solidarity and integrate individuals into society, Durkheim wrote extensively about the social conditions that are both conducive to, and weakening of, **social integration**. He did so primarily in *Suicide* (1897), a major empirical study of suicide rates in nineteenth-century Europe (and the first to demonstrate the methodology of scientific sociology that he advocated; see the beginning of the chapter). He examines how various independent (predictor) variables (e.g., marital status) produce varying amounts of social regulation that either increase or decrease the likelihood of suicide (the dependent variable). In addition to its methodological importance, Durkheim's *Suicide* is important theoretically. It further elaborates his core emphasis on social interdependence and shows how social structures function to regulate the individual's attachment to society. Further, his highlighting of particular categories or types of suicide allows him to show how different social conditions or circumstances and different social relationships can produce different social consequences.

SUICIDE: A SOCIAL PHENOMENON

Although suicide is an individual act, it is also a social phenomenon. And although we might think of suicide as a "social problem," it is "normal" in the Durkheimian sense (discussed previously) because every society has a certain level of suicide. Already in the early nineteenth century, Harriet Martineau had defined suicide as "the voluntary surrender of life from any cause" (1838: 103).As Durkheim would too, she recognized it as a normal social fact, and one indicative of varying levels of social regulation and integration. Martineau stated: "Every society has its suicides, and much may be learned from their character and number, both as to the notions on morals which prevail and the religious sentiment which ... controls the act" (1838: 105).

From a sociological perspective, therefore, notwithstanding the personal circumstances in which individuals commit suicide, suicide can (and should, according to Martineau and Durkheim) be studied in terms of its antecedent social context, specifically, its relation to social integration. Durkheim's analysis of suicide rates in Western Europe led him to conclude that "suicide varies inversely with the degree of integration of the social groups of which the individual forms a part" (Su 209). Social groups, and the extent to which those groups are tightly integrated, exert a constraining hold on the individual, because, Durkheim explains,

> a collective force is one of the obstacles best calculated to restrain suicide, its weakening involves a development of suicide. When society is strongly integrated, it holds individuals under its control, considers them at its service and thus forbids them to dispose willfully of themselves. Accordingly, it opposes their evading their duties to it through death ... they cling to life more resolutely when belonging to a group they love, so as not to betray interests they put before their own. The bond that unites them with the common cause attaches them to life. (Su 209–210)

So although many people think of suicide in psychological terms (e.g., related to depression), Durkheim sees it and studies it as a social phenomenon, a social fact, related to the social circumstances and group relationships whose constraints variously regulate the social cohesion that is critical to the maintenance of society (DL xxxv).

Durkheim argues that different societal contexts produce different conditions of social integration. When community/society is either too tightly or too loosely integrated, suicide results. He identified *egoistic* and *anomic* suicide as more characteristic of modern society and *altruistic suicide* as more likely to be found in the premodern era or in specific, tightly bonded social circumstances in contemporary times.[6]

ALTRUISTIC SUICIDE

In traditional societies or communities, suicide can occur as result of individuals' excessively tight relation to, or absorption by, the community. In these circumstances of high social integration, individuals are so closely oriented to fulfilling the expectations of the community or group that suicide becomes the obligatory honorable option when they fail to meet those expectations (Su 221). Durkheim calls this **altruistic suicide** (altruism conveys a strong selfless commitment to others). Japan, for example, has a long history of high rates of suicide attributed to individuals' loss of honor in the community, whether due, historically, to defeat in military battles, or in current times, to economic failure. Altruistic suicide can emerge in any tightly-bonded community where social pressure from the "yoke of the collectivity" is strong. Two miners, whose job included watching for safety hazards, committed suicide shortly after 12 of their coworkers were killed in a blast at the Sago mine in West Virginia. Their action might be considered an instance of altruistic suicide. Although they were not blamed for the disaster – the blast was caused by lightning – they may have felt responsible for their workmates' loss and been unable to imagine continuing to work and live in the close-knit rural mining community in their absence.

EGOISTIC SUICIDE

Egoistic suicide, as the label suggests, refers to suicide under social conditions in which individuals are excessively self-oriented, and hence loosely bound to other individuals and social groups. In modern Western society individualism is highly valued; the advanced division of labor associated with industrialization requires, as Durkheim emphasized, individual specialization. The collective conscience does not rein in the individual's egoistic appetites, but instead encourages individual freedom and ambition. Thus geographical and occupational mobility – and emotional mobility too (e.g., divorce) – are normative features of modern society. It is not surprising, then, that individuals become detached from others; they may have fewer opportunities for ongoing family, friendship, and community relationships.

Young graduates who aspire to successful corporate careers in law and finance work long hours, often spending weekends in the office rather than with friends and in social activities. Although they are well compensated financially, the demands of work do not end once they get a coveted promotion. The egoistic "cutthroat" culture of the corporate world is not conducive to individuals developing supportive social ties. When something goes wrong, as happened with the $6 billion loss on a risky bet by JPMorgan Chase bankers in May 2012, the backstory exposes the edgy risk practices of advanced capitalism (see chapter 14). It also reveals the clash of unbridled egos among individuals who, though working in the same unit, compete against one another for power. Further, when high-flying executives are fired or forced to resign, their overinvestment in work may mean that they are not as cushioned from its stress as someone who has managed to maintain close family, friendship, and other bonds. In sum, the egoistic individual, the personality type favored in the corporate world as well as in modern society more generally, may lack the social constraints and socioemotional attachments that can protect against suicide.

Social structures and social relationships

Relationships are constraining forces; they tie us into social commitments. Durkheim found that single people were more likely to commit suicide than married people. Marriage is a constraining condition; it literally binds you to someone else and thus has a regulatory and socially integrating force in the individual's life (Su 196–198). Similarly, Durkheim noted that suicide varied inversely with the number of children per marital household. Marriage is a constraint, but having children is even more constraining: The every day/every night demands that its responsibilities impose are not easily set aside. They tie parents down, and as such the structure of the parent–child relationship has both an integrating and a regulatory force on the parent.

Accordingly, Durkheim emphasizes that it is not just social relationships in general but differences in the structure of social relationships that also matter. Some social structures (e.g., marriage, parenthood) are more likely than others to regulate and integrate individuals into society. This structural point is well exemplified for Durkheim (Su 152–154) by the lower incidence of suicide in predominantly Catholic (e.g., Spain, Portugal, Italy) than in predominantly Protestant countries (e.g., Germany, Denmark). This statistical difference seems initially puzzling. If participation in a social group is functional to social integration, and churches are social groups that have a regulatory force in individuals' lives (as Martineau too observed),[7] then why would Catholics and Protestants vary in the propensity to commit suicide? You might reasonably suggest that perhaps the doctrines of the two churches differ on suicide; if Catholicism were more opposed than Protestantism to suicide, we might expect fewer Catholic suicides. In the nineteenth century, however, both churches were equally disapproving of suicide. What, then, explains their different suicide rates? Durkheim argues that it is not doctrine but variation in the structure or social organization of the churches that accounts for variation in religious adherents' suicide rates.

Structurally, the Catholic Church is much more constraining of the individual than is Protestantism. Protestants emphasize the individual's responsibility to interpret the Bible, whereas Catholics are expected to defer to the interpretive authority of the church hierarchy (pope, bishops, etc.). Indeed, Protestantism is strongly associated with the individualism (the egoism) of modern capitalist society (cf. Weber; see chapter 3). Catholicism, by contrast, embeds the individual Catholic in layered church relationships and practices (e.g., weekly Mass, confession). These require the individual's integration (communion) with the Catholic collectivity, and by extension, provide the social integration that more strongly buffers against suicide. Durkheim elaborates:

> All *variation* is abhorrent to Catholic thought. The Protestant is far more the author of his faith. The Bible is put in his hands and no interpretation is imposed upon him … The proclivity of Protestantism for suicide must relate to the spirit of free inquiry that animates this religion … Free inquiry itself is only the effect of another cause … if Protestantism concedes a greater freedom to individual thought than Catholicism, it is because it has fewer common beliefs and practices. Now a religious society [a church/ religious denomination or community] cannot exist without a collective credo, and the more extensive the credo the more unified and strong is the society … It socializes men only by attaching them completely to an identical body of doctrine and socializes them in proportion as this body of doctrine is extensive and

firm. The more numerous the manners of action and thought of a religious character are, which are accordingly removed from free inquiry, the more the idea of God presents itself in all details of existence, and makes individual wills converge to one identical goal. Inversely, the greater concessions a confessional group [a specific religious denomination/church] makes to individual judgment the less it dominates lives, the less its cohesion and vitality. We thus reach the conclusion that the superiority [higher incidence] of Protestantism with respect to suicide results from its being a less strongly integrated church than the Catholic church. (Su 158–159)

In short, we learn from Durkheim's discussion of suicide that different forms of social organization, different ways of structuring or organizing social and community life, have different social consequences and effects.

ANOMIC SUICIDE

Although the egoistic individualism of modern society can weaken our ties to others, social upheaval produces anomic conditions that can also disrupt the individual's bond with society, producing what Durkheim calls **anomic suicide**. *Anomie* is a French word meaning the absence of norms or of established standards; it refers to circumstances when the normal patterns of social life are suddenly uprooted. Many people today live in communities that are aptly characterized as "places without roots." These are places that attract people on the move for various economic and personal reasons. As such it is difficult for these communities to exert the collective regulatory force that can socially integrate

Figure 2.3   Hurricanes, earthquakes, and other natural disasters create social anomie; they unexpectedly rupture the normalcy of everyday routines for individuals, families, and whole communities. Source: © Mike Groll/ AP/Press Association.

individuals and families. In these anomic places, we would expect suicide rates to be high. Nevada, home to Las Vegas, is the most rootless place in America, and it has the nation's highest suicide rates for teenagers, adults, and the elderly. It also has high rates of alcoholism, high school dropouts, child abuse deaths, teenage pregnancy, smoking, and compulsive gambling (see Harden 2002b).

But anomie can also strike communities and places that have deep roots. This happens during times of rapid social change or cultural turmoil and crisis – when those ways of acting, thinking, and feeling that we take for granted as normal, get uprooted and overturned. Anomic suicide results from social conditions in which

> the scale is upset; but a new scale cannot be immediately improvised. Time is required for the public conscience to reclassify men and things. So long as the social forces thus freed have not regained equilibrium, their respective values are unknown and so all regulation is lacking for a time. The limits are unknown between the possible and the impossible, what is just and unjust, legitimate claims and hopes and those which are immoderate. Consequently there is no restraint upon aspirations ... Appetites, not being controlled by a public opinion, become disoriented, no longer recognize the limits proper to them. (Su 253)

During times of social and political upheaval, the force of society, of collective opinion, weakens precisely because what the collectivity thinks is itself in turmoil; it is unable to make sense of what it is experiencing. The terrorist events of September 11, 2001, in New York City exemplify a crisis that caused anomic societal conditions. In addition to the severed ties it caused for the thousands of families and coworkers directly affected by the deaths on that day, 9/11 also upended people's expectations about many things: their everyday security, their trust in airlines and airports, their trust in technology, their belief in America as an open and welcoming immigrant society, and their trust in government and its various agencies. In short, 9/11 ruptured individual lives, families and communities, as well as much of what had long rooted and anchored American society as a whole. And subsequent terrorist attacks – in Paris, Brussels, London, and Manchester – though less disruptive than 9/11 – similarly disrupt the taken-for-granted normality of daily life: sitting in a café with friends, browsing at a food market, attending a concert or a football game.

The dislocating impact of natural disasters
Natural disasters also create anomic social conditions. Tsunamis, hurricanes, earthquakes, floods, and fires literally uproot whole communities to varying degrees and in the process uproot people from the structures and the social groups and relationships that regulate their daily lives and integrate them into society. In the US, and in several Caribbean countries, for example, hurricanes regularly displace tens of thousands of individuals and families from their homes, schools, neighborhoods and workplaces – from all their familiar anchors (see Topic 2.3).

In the aftermath of Hurricane Katrina, medical sociologists documented a twofold increase in the incidence of mental illness (e.g., depression, anxiety, and posttraumatic stress) among individuals in the New Orleans area (a population that had also been studied prior to Katrina). These studies underscore the negative social impact of disruptive events. Yet, despite the increased prevalence of mental illness, the prevalence of suicide and of suicide plans was lower among those diagnosed with mental illness after Katrina than it was in the New Orleans mentally ill population prior to Katrina. This finding might seem contrary to Durkheim's argument about the relation between anomie and suicide. However, Durkheim's larger point that social relationships integrate individuals into society and buffer against suicide is also supported by the data. The researchers attributed the lower incidence of suicide to, among other factors, the increased social support given to individuals in Katrina's aftermath

(Kessler et al. 2006). Beyond natural disasters, people who serve in the military also experience dislocation. In particular, the disruptive and traumatizing effects of military combat on soldiers' lives and their families increase the incidence of suicide and suicide-like symptoms. The military is responding to this with initiatives increasing the social support (e.g., marital counseling) and family-oriented social activities available to them. By strengthening their ties to others it aims to buffer against the traumatic consequences of war (see also chapter 9). More generally, medical researchers, aware of the empirical links between loneliness and heart disease and stroke, are urging preventative measures that get isolated individuals connected to others prior to developing these illnesses, rather than waiting to do so after they are diagnosed (Valtorta et al. 2016).

Topic 2.3   Resilience and change

Individuals respond to stress in different ways and so too do cities and communities. David Remnick (2015: 38) describes New Orleans as "a city of both persistent suffering and persistent renewal." It has seen many changes since Katrina, including a revamped school system, new playgrounds and community centers, and a new state-of-the-art medical complex. But it has nearly fewer 100,000 black residents than it did in 2000, and these declines have occurred across all income levels. The white population has also decreased (by about 11,000) but it is wealthier than before. Child poverty and overall poverty rates are basically unchanged since 2000, and longstanding disparities of race and class also continue. Variation in the character of the city's diverse neighborhoods also continues. The Lower Ninth Ward, the neighborhood worst hit by Katrina, is now one of only four city neighborhoods that has less than half of its pre-Katrina population. Treme, whose everyday culture was vividly portrayed in the HBO television drama series, is the birthplace of jazz and one of the country's oldest African-American neighborhoods, is almost back to its pre-Katrina population size. Though the flooding was not so bad there, many residents, mostly renters, left. Now rents have spiked, and the white population (at 36 percent) is more than twice what it was in 2000; and with most of them born outside of Louisiana (Robertson and Fausset 2015).

Economic transformation

Economic events too can cause anomie, whether due to recession, the crash of a staple food crop, or the closing of a large factory in a midsize town. Social disruption may also result from the transformative effect that new money can have on a community (and individuals') way of being. The "Boomtown blues" phenomenon, for example, captures this negative effect, as we see in places like mineral-rich Wyoming cowboy country (e.g., Fuller 2007) or in high-tech Bangalore, India's suicide capital. In sum, as Durkheim states, "when society is disturbed by some painful crisis or by beneficent but abrupt transitions, it is momentarily incapable of exercising [a restraining] influence; thence come the sudden rises in the curve of suicides" (Su 252). See Topic 2.4.

ABNORMALITIES THAT THREATEN SOCIAL COHESION

Although suicide is a normal social phenomenon, if suicide or, for example, crime, homelessness, or unemployment rates are abnormally high in any given society, this can be considered a social pathology; it suggests a rupture in social ties. Durkheim argued that this can occur in modern societies as a result of "abnormalities" or crises in the division of labor. These emerge if functional interdependence is displaced by

Topic 2.4 The anomie of economic globalization

Globalizing economic forces can create the sorts of anomic conditions that contribute to an increase in suicide rates. Even in societies that have supportive labor protection policies, the uncertainties associated with increased competition within various economic sectors, shifts in the geographical location of industries, and the impact of production outsourcing and downsizing can add to worker stress. In France, for example, despite good working conditions (e.g., a 35-hour week, paid vacation time), legal guarantees of job security and the image of a pampered workforce, a spate of suicides in 2009 at France Telecom, a large, partially privatized and partially state-subsidized telephone company, was attributed by mental health experts to job-related stress prompted by restructuring due to increased competition in the global telephone market. "From 2006 through 2008, the company cut more than 22,000 jobs through voluntary departures, and it is estimated that between 2004 and 2009, half of all its employees had either changed jobs internally, changed work locations, or both [and this] has created a sense of constant upheaval and insecurity" (Jolly and Saltmarsh 2009: B3).

At Foxconn Technology in Shenzhen/Guangdong, China, by contrast, the increased demand for workers and products contributed to anomic conditions and a surge in suicides. Owned by one of the richest men in Asia, Foxconn is the world's biggest electronics maker, a major supplier to Apple, Dell, and Hewlett-Packard. It has 800,000 Chinese employees, approximate annual revenue of $60 billion, and is known for its "military-style efficiency." "Foxconn's production line system is designed so well that no worker will rest even one second during work; they make sure you're always busy for every second" according to the executive director of China Labor Watch, a New York based labor rights group (Barboza 2010a: B1). The pressure on workers to meet high production quotas (see Marx, chapter 1) to fulfill the high demand for iPhones and other products means that workers have little time for socializing with their coworkers or for leisure time outside of work, thus adding to their stress. Additionally, because the demand for unskilled workers is so great, many of the workers at Foxconn are young migrants from rural areas in China unaccustomed to factory conditions. In the city, they live in cramped housing and with no family or other social support networks, anomie is exacerbated. The company responded to the spate of suicides by increasing salaries and improving working conditions; it built new dormitories, swimming pools, and other recreational facilities for employees. It also put enormous safety nets up on factory buildings to deter suicides (Barboza 2010b: B3). Working conditions have improved at Foxconn. The suicide nets remain but wages are better, the dormitories are pleasant, and workers have access to a range of food courts. Company executives, moreover, are limiting overtime demands and are now requiring workers to take a day off every week (*The Economist*, 2012, pp. 63–64).

a situation in which one social group "seeks to live at the expense" of another (DL 291). Sounding here like Marx, Durkheim suggests that increased industrial development, market expansion and "the hostility between labour and capital" can produce conflict and anomic conditions rather than solidarity:

As industrial functions specialize more the struggle becomes more fierce, far from solidarity increasing. In the Middle Ages the workman everywhere lived side by side with his master, sharing in his work "in the same shop, on the same bench." … Both were almost equal to one another … conflicts were completely exceptional. From the fifteenth century onwards things began to change. (DL 292)

Unlike Marx, however, who argued that inequality and conflict between workers and capitalists would lead to the overthrow of capitalism (chapter 1), Durkheim saw such conflict as an abnormality in the functioning of society that could be remedied; he did not see it as leading to the demise of industrial society.

Another abnormality for Durkheim occurs if the individualism required by the division of labor becomes excessive, so that individuals isolate themselves from others, believing that their specialized activity – including feverish consumption in the pursuit of novelty (Su) – is superior to that of others (DL 294). In these circumstances, the moral, socially anchored individualism that Durkheim saw as necessary to modern society gets displaced by a narcissistic, self-seeking, and self-satisfied individualism (e.g., Bellah et al. 1985). In sum, abnormalities in the functioning of society that weaken either interindividual or intergroup ties threaten social interdependence and social cohesion.

ANOMIE THAT FOSTERS SOCIAL COHESION

Anomie produces conditions that increase suicide: detachment from society. But it is also the case, Durkheim argues, that societal crises can have a socially unifying effect. He cites war as an example of a social disturbance that can strengthen rather than weaken social cohesion. Observing that the incidence of suicides decreased in urban but not in rural areas in France in 1870–1871 (during the Franco-Prussian War), Durkheim sought to identify the larger societal circumstances that accounted for this (having ruled out errors in recordkeeping). He concluded:

> The war produced its full moral [socially integrating] effect only on the urban population, more sensitive, impressionable and also better informed on current events than the rural population. These facts are therefore susceptible of only one interpretation; namely that great social disturbances and great popular wars rouse collective sentiments, stimulate partisan spirit and patriotism, political and national faith, alike, and concentrating activity toward a single end, at least temporarily cause a stronger integration of society. The salutary influence which we have just shown to exist is due not to the crisis but to the struggles it occasions. As they force men to close ranks and confront the common danger, the individual thinks less of himself and more of the common cause. (Su 208)

Thus, some disruptive events can have a socially binding effect, leading individuals to affirm their solidarity with one another. 9/11, as I've noted, certainly caused anomie. But it also prompted collective gatherings across the US, at memorial services and in informal public spaces. These gatherings, many of which were spontaneous, produced and strengthened individuals' sense of connection to, or solidarity with, others. A similar pattern of strangers coming together is evident in response to tragedies and disruptive events elsewhere, and as such highlight Durkheim's insight that the individual needs to attach to something other than the self – that is, to others, to society. See Topic 2.5.

RELIGION AND THE SACRED

As part of his focus on the social circumstances that impact social cohesion, Durkheim also wrote extensively about the social nature and functions of religion. We already know from *Suicide* that religion acts as an integrating social force. This is still the case today, even though religion is frequently associated with divisive conflicts in local, national, and world politics. Durkheim recognized religion

Topic 2.5 When tragedy brings strangers together

In the week after the 9/11 (September 11, 2001) New York City terrorist attacks, crowds of people spontaneously gathered in Union Square in Manhattan to express grief, anger, and loss, or simply "just to be around other people," during that unsettling time. Thousands of people brought flowers, photographs, and candles to makeshift shrines near the square's George Washington statue. What happened at Union Square was the coming together of strangers, causing a "sense of unity," as one person who had visited the park several nights in a row since 9/11 said. She further commented: "We all feel differently about what to do … but everybody seems to agree that we've got to be together no matter what happens. So you get a little bit of hope in togetherness" (Kimmelman 2001: E5). A similar collective affirmation of strangers coming together occurred in the streets of London following Princess Diana's tragic death.

Similarly in Paris there was "consolation in community" following the November 2015 terrorist attacks that killed 129 people: "When [residents] were cautioned to avoid public squares, they gathered. When they were asked to stay at home, they convened in cafes and lined up in droves to donate blood….[People] sought solace in the close-knit community of regulars at [the local] café….It's here among Parisians and foreigners embracing, sipping coffee and sharing stories, that I could breathe again" (Tramuta 2015: 9). Solidarity was also seen on the football (soccer) field: At a match between England and France in London "four days after the Paris attacks…and an hour after the threat of an attack had cancelled another high-profile game in Europe, 44 players walked out of the tunnel and onto the field just before kickoff. Normally, it would only be each team's starting lineup; on this night, every player draped an arm around the one next to him….after the teams' coaches joined Prince William in laying flowers on the sideline in memory of the victims… the national anthems were played. Normally, the visiting team's anthem would be played first; on this night, 'La Marseillaise' was played last and the fans – nearly all of them, not just the French contingent tucked in the corner of the upper deck – stood and sang together…. [one fan said] We came because we care….We came because we wanted to be together" (Borden 2015: B11).

as a social fact, and as such, something that can be studied objectively, and in relation to other social facts (see the section Scientific Sociology: The Study of Social Facts).

Durkheim's definition of religion, or more precisely, the sacred, is remarkably broad. He argued that all societies, from the most "primitive," such as Australian Aboriginal society, to the most modern, invariably categorize all things into two mutually exclusive categories: the **sacred** and the **profane**. We generally tend to think of religion as institutionalized churches and established religious traditions, and we might readily call to mind well-known sacred sites, religious prayers, and collectively recognized religious **symbols** such as the Cross (Christianity), the Star of David (Judaism), and the Crescent (Islam). Durkheim argues that the sacred includes all of these; yet, importantly, it also includes many other things so defined as sacred by any given community or society.

SACRED THINGS

The sacred is all things "set apart" (sanctified), and whose devaluing is prohibited (EFRL 46). The collectivity, society, requires us to have a certain reverential attitude toward sacred things. Consequently, if some individuals do not partake in worshipping the sacred things in a particular community, this detaches the individual from the community in which those sacred things are worshipped. The sacred refers to any and all of those things that have a special symbolic significance in a specific, bounded community. The community isolates and protects sacred things from being violated or contaminated by the profane, that is, the ordinary mundane things in which we have not invested symbolic significance.

Durkheim argues, "What makes a thing holy is … the collective feeling attached to it" (EFRL 308). Every **religion**, and hence every community or society, recognizes a "plurality of sacred things" (EFRL 40). Sacred things are not divinely ordained or historically predetermined but are defined as sacred by the particular society. Durkheim states, "Since neither man nor nature is inherently sacred, this quality of sacredness must come from another source" (EFRL 76). That source is society – the many different groups and communities to which we belong and which comprise the larger society. Hence the sacred is highly variable; different communities categorize some things as sacred and other things as profane, and these categorizations may change with time. Regardless, the scared comes from society. Thus, "it is the unity and the diversity of social life that creates both the unity and the diversity of sacred beings and things" (EFRL 309).

In the US, for example, the nation's flag is sacred – it is a symbolic, **collective representation** of Americans' shared national identity, a shared sacred history of freedom, democracy, patriotism. The flag's sacredness is visible in its prominent public presence in people's yards and especially in the nation's collective civic life, at official events and in official places such as the White House. Many other countries also give prominence to their national flag. It is a sacred symbol that functions to unify society amid the varied sources of its diversity. The UK flag, for example, composed of four crosscutting lines, signifies the political-cultural unity of the peoples of England, Wales, Scotland, and Northern Ireland notwithstanding each country's own unique history and culture. As a unifying symbol, the flag reminds British people today that despite the rupturing of their shared understanding of what it means to be British (evident in the Brexit vote in 2016 to leave the European Union (EU), of which the UK has been a member since 1973), their collectively shared identity is (or may be) greater than their differences. See Topic 2.6.

Topic 2.6   Flags and anthems

Flags and anthems are sacred symbols of collective identity. They convey **imagined community** (Anderson 1983), the collective sense of a shared togetherness based on a certain cultural-geographical or political-historical uniqueness of a people bounded together in counterdistinction to Others. The sacredness of these symbols is illuminated in various places today:

- In the UK: Although "God Save the Queen" became the national anthem at the beginning of the nineteenth century, some English sports fans want their own English-specific anthem played. Each UK country has its own flag, but not its own country-specific anthem. It's not that they are opposed to the monarch (or to God), but because when "God Save the Queen" is played at international matches, it suggests that being English is synonymous with being British. England, Scotland, and Wales each field their own rugby team and there is a lot of competitive rivalry between them in the Six Nations Cup international championship (which also includes Ireland, France, and Italy). Wales has its own anthem, "Land of My Fathers" first sung in 1905 in response to the New Zealand rugby team's traditional haka, a Maori war chant), and Scotland has "The Flower of Scotland" (see Castle 2016). Waving the English flag proudly signifies Englishness, but having their own anthem would add to the collective effervescence and group solidarity produced by and at sacred events (see Castle 2016).

- In the US, there is political controversy because some football players protest against racism and social injustice by kneeling (rather than standing) while the anthem is played before a game; they argue that American policing and criminal justice practices deviate from the values of equality and fairness represented by the flag and the anthem.
- New Zealand has frequently debated changing its flag. It currently features the Union Jack (because it is still a member of the British Commonwealth and thus a constitutional monarchy under the Queen) and the Southern Cross, which is a symbol also featured on neighboring Australia's flag. Those who favor a new design argue that "any new flag must be mistakenly from New Zealand….We must be able to recognize ourselves in it" (Innis 2015). Not surprisingly, some variation of the symbol of the fern used by the New Zealand rugby team – one well recognized as distinctive by both New Zealanders and non-New Zealanders alike, is a popular contender (see Innis 2015).
- In Poland, even though a large majority of Poles have a favorable view of the EU (72 percent according to the Pew Research Center), a resurgent nationalism – with appeals to "Let Poland be Poland" – is evident in the conservative Law and Justice government's decision removing the joint display of Polish and EU flags from government press briefings and government settings, instead displaying only the Polish flag.
- In Quebec, Canada, one is more likely to see public displays of the "Fleur de lis" symbol, representing the province's cultural identity ties to France, than the equally distinctive (and geographically more encompassing) Canadian flag with its red maple leaf.
- In Melbourne, municipal buildings fly both the Australian flag and the flag of indigenous Aboriginal Australians.
- And in many places in the US and elsewhere, the rainbow flag outside a church indicates that it is a gay-friendly (LGBT-inclusive) congregation.

As Durkheim emphasizes, collective symbols vary by social contexts but in all cases reinforce and demarcate particular solidarities.

SACRED BELIEFS AND RITUALS

We know what things and ideas a society or religion deems sacred by the beliefs and **rituals** (rites) that they classify as, and attach to, the sacred: "Religious phenomena fall quite naturally into two basic categories: beliefs and rites. The first are states of opinion and consist of representations [symbols]; the second are fixed modes of actions [specific practices]" (EFRL 36). Thus, what we believe or worship and how we worship comprise religion. And not surprisingly, given Durkheim's emphasis on the thoroughly *social* and *collective* nature of social facts, religious beliefs and rituals are not unique to the individual but are, and must necessarily be, shared collectively.

Religious beliefs proper are always held by a defined collectivity that professes them and practices the rites that go with them. These beliefs are not only embraced by all the members of this collectivity as individuals, they belong to the group and unite it. The individuals who make up this group are bound to one another by their common beliefs. A society [or community] whose members are united because they share a common conception of the sacred world and its relation to the profane world, and who translate this common conception into identical practices, is what we call a **church**. (EFRL 42–43)

Figure 2.4   Sports arenas can function as sacred space. Source: © Gordon Bell/iStockphoto.

Church, then, is the collective coming together of people with similar beliefs and rituals, the practice of which further unites and solidifies the group and the solidarity of its members. It is in, and through, and around sacred things that individuals collectively unite as a **moral community** affirming a shared solidarity: "A religion is this unified system of beliefs and practices relative to sacred things, that is to say, things set apart and surrounded by prohibitions – beliefs and practices that unite its adherents in a single moral community called a church" (EFRL 46).

Importantly, because Durkheim's definition of the sacred includes all things that a community collectively holds sacred, religion/church can take many forms. In many societies, sports, for example, are sacred: for example, football (soccer) in England, Italy, Mexico, and Brazil; football and baseball in the US; Gaelic football in Ireland; ice hockey in Canada; table tennis in South Korea and China; or cricket in Australia, India, and Pakistan. In these specific communities, sport functions as the equivalent of (church) religion. In looking at sport through the lens of the sacred we see: the collective awe and reverence that collectivities (fans, local communities, nations) have toward particular sports teams; the sacred space in which the teams play and fans congregate (worship); and the presence of various sacred symbols (logos, clothing), icons (stars, heroes), hymns (e.g., songs such as Liverpool Football Club's "You'll never walk alone"), and rituals (e.g., seventh inning stretch in baseball). Thus, for Red Sox baseball fans, church is Fenway Park; for Manchester United fans, it is Old Trafford; for cricket fans in Australia, it is the Melbourne Cricket Ground: These are the sacred sites at which people collectively worship and unify around all that they experience as sacred in sport and around which they come together on a regular basis.

THE ASSEMBLING OF COMMUNITY

As social beings, we worship something other than ourselves; and what we worship is, in essence, our shared collective life. Coming together as one, whether at a family event, at church, mosque or temple worship, at a sports event, or at other public gatherings, we affirm a shared solidarity. The gathering affirms the fact that we belong to this particular community, and the process of interacting together itself strengthens our shared bonds (see Topic 2.5). Robert Bellah (1967) uses the term **civil religion** to refer to the civic-political ceremonies and rituals (e.g., presidential inaugurations, State of the Union addresses) that characterize the public life of American society. These ceremonies function to affirm and maintain the (political) unity of the (indivisible) nation, notwithstanding partisan political affiliations. Special ritualized events – whether with family and friends or at larger community or national gatherings – remind us of the interdependent communal bonds we have with one another and with society as a whole.

The regulatory significance of communal gatherings on social integration is well illustrated by funeral rituals and memorials. They affirm the bonds of the living to the deceased person, to one another, and to society (see Topic 2.5). Durkheim states:

> When an individual dies, the family group to which he belongs feels diminished, and in order to react against this diminishment, it assembles. A common misfortune has the same effects as the arrival of a happy event: it awakens collective feelings that impel individuals to seek each other out and come together.

We have even seen this need affirmed with special energy – people kiss, embrace, and press against one another as much as possible. But the emotional state in which the group finds itself reflects the immediate circumstances. Not only do the relatives most directly affected bring their personal pain to the gathering, but society exerts a moral pressure on its members to put their feelings in harmony with the situation. To allow them to remain indifferent to the blow that strikes and diminishes them would be to proclaim that society does not hold its rightful place in their hearts, and this would be to deny itself. A family that tolerates a death among its members without weeping bears witness that it lacks moral unity and cohesion. It abdicates, it renounces its being. (EFRL 296–297)

The assembling family's response to the death of one of its members extends more generally to any community/society which suffers a loss. Thus the public response to tragedies, for example (see Topic 2.5), is both the collective mourning of the society's particular loss and, simultaneously, the collective affirmation of the bonds that unite those remaining and which regenerate society.

When we as individuals remain aloof from such rituals, including joyous events (e.g., a family wedding, graduation, a celebration of a sports team's accomplishments, a local community festival), our indifference both reflects and further debilitates our weakened ties to the collectivity. Moreover, it dampens the collective effervescence (emotional vitality) of those gathered. Durkheim argues:

For his part, when the individual is firmly attached to the society to which he belongs he feels morally compelled to share its joys and sorrows; to remain a disinterested observer would be to break the ties that bind him to the collectivity, to give up wanting the collectivity, and to contradict himself … We know from other sources how human feelings are intensified when they are affirmed collectively. Sadness, like joy, is exalted and amplified by its reverberation from [individual] consciousness to [individual] consciousness … Each person is led along by all the others … [individuals] weep together because they value one another and because the collectivity, despite this blow [e.g., death], is not damaged. Of course, in this instance they share only sad emotions; but to commune in sadness is still to commune, and every communion of consciousness, of whatever kind [sadness or joy], increases the social vitality … [and makes] society even more vigorous and active than ever. (EFRL 297, 299)

Because religion – the sacred – compels us to assemble, to act in unison together, it thereby bends our individual impulses to the force of our shared collective life. Assemblies and ceremonies, therefore, strengthen us in our individual and collective ability to regulate and cope with life's joys and sorrows (EFRL 311, 313, 309). Durkheim thus regarded religion as eternally necessary because of its social force and social function:

There is something eternal in religion … that is destined to survive all the particular symbols in which religious thought has successfully cloaked itself. No society can exist that does not feel the need at regular intervals to sustain and reaffirm the collective feelings and ideas that constitute its unity … this moral [social] remaking can be achieved only by means of meetings, assemblies, or congregations in which individuals, brought into close contact, reaffirm in common their common feelings: hence those ceremonies whose goals, results, and methods do not differ in kind from properly religious ceremonies. (EFRL 322)

In sum, the sacred is present in each and every collective assembly.

RELIGION AND SCIENCE

Durkheim recognized that with the rise of modern society – in particular, the increase in individualism (required by the specialized division of labor) and the expansion of scientific reasoning – the hold of traditional religious systems would wane (EFRL 325). Nevertheless, he also recognized that scientific knowledge alone is not sufficient to tie people together. He did not see science and religion in conflict with one another, but as having interdependent functions. Science provides knowledge, but religion (and its functional equivalents such as football, etc.) provides action, the action that comes from the "moral remaking," the social bonding, that exists around its rituals. Hence, "science could not possibly take religion's place. For if science expresses life, it does not create it" (EFRL 325). It does not revitalize social ties. Thus, Durkheim argued, religion would maintain itself as an eternal social fact; it would adapt and transform rather than disappear (EFRL 324–326). As we see today, although traditional religion is a significant source of social integration in many societies (and especially in the US), there are also many other sacred things (e.g., sports events, knitting groups, book clubs) that draw people together and invigorate social cohesion and solidarity.[8]

SUMMARY

Durkheim's writings demonstrate the rules of scientific sociology and its substantive content. In particular, his discussion of social facts; his differentiation between traditional and modern society and of the different forms of social organization that produce different types of solidarity; his analysis of suicide as a function of social integration; and his study of religion as the collective representation of the sacred in society, show the breadth of Durkheim's focus and the range of topics that sociologists study.

POINTS TO REMEMBER

For Durkheim
- Sociology is the science of moral life, that is, it studies the social structures, social ties, and social forces that bind the individual to society
- Society is greater than the sum of its individuals; it has its own collective force and exerts as a regulatory and external constraint on individual impulses
- Society exists independently of the individuals who comprise it; the basic rule of sociological method is to "Treat social facts as things"
- Social facts are objective, collective forces that constrain the ways of acting, thinking, and feeling in society; they can, and should be, studied objectively and with objectivity
- Traditional society is characterized by a mechanical solidarity derived from the overlapping social relationships and bonds that exist among relatively homogeneous individuals
- Organic solidarity refers to the social interdependence characteristic of modern, heterogeneous societies
- The collective conscience is a powerful social force; it refers to the beliefs and sentiments shared in common in a given community/society
- Social integration is a function of social regulation and attachments
- Suicide is a social fact; it varies across societal conditions and is a function of social integration
    - Altruistic suicide is characteristic of social contexts where the yoke of the collectivity is strong
    - Egoistic suicide is characteristic of social contexts where excessive individualism dominates and social attachments are weak
    - Anomic suicide emerges in conditions of societal upheaval, normlessness, rootlessness

- Religion is a social fact, a social phenomenon; it is defined by what society considers sacred
- All societies classify things/ideas into two mutually exclusive categories
  - Sacred things/ideas
  - Profane (mundane, ordinary) things/ideas
- Symbols are collective representations; they represent collective life, values, and beliefs
- Rituals are collective celebrations that reaffirm and strengthen social solidarity
- Church is any moral (social) community united by shared beliefs and rituals pertaining to the sacred

GLOSSARY

altruistic suicide results from tightly regulated social conditions in which the loss of close comrades, or an individual's loss of honor in the community, makes suicide obligatory.

anomic suicide results when society experiences a major disruption that uproots the established norms.

church any community unified by sacred beliefs and ritual practices.

civil religion the civic-political symbols, ceremonies, and rituals that characterize society's public life and reaffirm its shared values.

collective conscience a society's collectively shared beliefs and sentiments; has authority over social conduct.

collective representation the symbols and categories a society uses to denote its commonly shared, collective beliefs, values, interpretations, and meanings.

contract society's legal regulation of the obligations it expects of individuals in their relations with one another; its regulatory force comes from society.

division of labor the separation of occupational sectors, workers, and institutions into specialized spheres of activity; produces, for Durkheim, social interdependence.

egoistic suicide results from modern societal conditions in which individuals are excessively self-oriented and insufficiently integrated into social groups/society.

functionalism term used (often interchangeably with "structural functionalism") to refer to the theorizing of Durkheim (and successor sociologists, e.g., Parsons) because of a focus on how social structures determine and are effective in, or functional to, maintaining social cohesion/the social order.

imagined community concept introduced by Benedict Anderson (1983) elaborating how the nation as a political community is imagined in the sense that the felt affinities toward diverse others with whom one shares a given legal-geographical national territory are imagined rather than based on personal ties to them. Although the nation is a significant communal unit, one may think of oneself as belonging to several different, imagined communities – for example, the Catholic community, the LGBTQ community.

interdependence ties among individuals (and groups and institutions); for Durkheim, the individualism required by the specialized division of labor creates functional and social interdependence.

mechanical solidarity social bonds and cohesion resulting from the overlapping social ties that characterize traditional societies/communities.

moral community any group or collectivity unified by common beliefs and practices and a shared solidarity.

moral density the density of social interaction associated with encountering and interacting with a multiplicity of diverse others in modern society.

moral individualism individuals (as social beings) interacting with others for purposes other than simply serving their own selfish or material interests.

morality social life; the ties to group life that regulate individual appetites and attach individuals to something other than themselves, that is, to other individuals, groups, society; sociology's subject matter; can be studied with scientific objectivity.

objectivity the idea that sociology as a science can provide an objective or unbiased description and analysis of any observable and measurable social phenomenon/social fact.

organic solidarity social ties and cohesion produced by the functional and social interdependence of individuals, groups, and institutions in modern society.

physical density the number of people encountered in the conduct of everyday life.

profane ordinary, mundane, nonsacred things in society.

religion a social phenomenon, collectively defined by the things, ideas, beliefs, and practices a society or community holds sacred; a socially integrating force.

rituals collectively shared, sacred rites and practices that affirm and strengthen social ties, and maintain social order.

sacred all things a society collectively sets apart as special, and requiring reverence.

social facts external and collective social forces (structures, practices, norms, beliefs) regulating and constraining the ways of acting, thinking, and feeling in society.

social integration degree to which individuals and groups are attached to society. Individuals are interlinked and constrained by their ties to others.

social solidarity social cohesion resulting from shared social ties/bonds/interdependence.

sociology of knowledge demonstrates how the organization and content of knowledge is a social activity contingent on the particular sociohistorical circumstances in which it is produced.

***sui generis* reality** the idea that society has its own nature or reality – its own collective characteristics or properties that emerge and exist as a constraining force independent of the characteristics of the individuals in society.

symbol any signs/images whose interpretation and meaning are socially shared; collective representation of a community's/society's collectively shared beliefs and values.

QUESTIONS FOR REVIEW

1 What are the many things about a social role that make it a social fact?
2 Why for Durkheim should we think of drug addiction, poverty, or crime, for example as "social facts" rather than as "social problems"?
3 How is solidarity organized or achieved in modern society? How does it differ from the ways in which cohesion is produced in traditional societies?
4 Compare and contrast how societal conditions of anomie and of egoism may manifest in contemporary society and discuss the consequences of each for individual and societal well-being.
5 Describe one thing that is sacred in your neighborhood/locality/region. Explain the characteristics that make it sacred, and identify how its manifestation and consequences regenerate religion/the sacred.

NOTES

1 In citing Durkheim's writings, I reference the book's initials rather than the date of publication. A list of Durkheim's core writings, their date of publication, and the book title initials I use to reference them follows the biographical note.
2 Vacherie is located in St. James Parish in Louisiana, a parish/Census unit that borders the New Orleans parishes that were hardest hit by Hurricane Katrina in September 2005.
3 Durkheim's emphasis on empirical data as the starting point for social science is referred to as *induction*; we induce or infer from data an explanation about how the social world works. This approach contrasts with *deduction*, which uses theoretical and nonempirical statements about a particular phenomenon as the starting point for making generalizable claims about the class of phenomena more broadly;

deduction proceeds by logically deducing from one idea other similar or parallel processes in the logic of the social world. Most sociologists today tend to be inductive in their approach to describing and explaining society.
4 For a detailed introduction to Simmel, see Frisby (1994).
5 Durkheim differentiates between the *repressive* penal laws that characterize traditional societies – stripping individuals and groups of honor (and social rights) – and the *restitutive* laws that tend to characterize modern societies – laws that seek to restore the status quo to what it was before the deviant act; e.g., individuals pay damages to an injured or third party to offset their culpability (DL 68–70).
6 Durkheim (Su 276) also briefly noted a fourth category: "*fatalistic* suicide," typical of social circumstances which are

characterized by "excessive regulation" wherein individuals (e.g., slaves; those in arranged marriages in tradition-bound cultures today – such as in Sinjar, Iraq) see no alternatives to their current situation. Martineau highlighted suicides due to duty or loss of honor in the community – for example, "the defeated warrior," "the injured woman," and situations "when men and women destroyed themselves to avoid disgrace" (1838: 103), as well as the suicides of "those who have devoted themselves to others." According to Martineau's biographer (Hoecker-Drysdale 1992), Durkheim had read but did not acknowledge Martineau.

7   Martineau noted the regulatory impact of religion on suicide, which she inferred from the higher rates of suicide in relatively nonreligious France compared to the more religiously devout Ireland (1838: 106–107).

8   Durkheim's emphasis on the social origins of the sacred is an important contribution to the **sociology of knowledge**. Durkheim argued that all categories, and hence all ideas or concepts, are collective representations; they provide members of a society with a common, shared system of communication and interpretation. Just as members of a given nation recognize the national flag, so too the members of a given society use a language that derives from and can be used to describe and categorize their particular societal characteristics and experiences. In other words, there is no conceptual logic – no language or concepts – independent of, or prior to, society. Rather, concepts and language are "eminently social" (EFRL 11); they "express collective realities" (EFRL 11). Durkheim's emphasis on the social origins and functions of concepts (as collective representations) is regarded as a "crucial first step" in the sociology of knowledge (Lukes 1973: 448). It helps us see that particular concepts, knowledge, and understandings of the world emerge out of particular socio-historical and generational contexts (cf. Mannheim 1936/1968).

REFERENCES

Anderson, Benedict. 1983. *Imagined Communities: Reflections on the Origins and Spread of Nationalism*. London: Verso.

Barboza, David. 2010a. "Deaths Shake A Titan in China: A Global Tech Supplier Grapples with a Spate of Worker Suicides." *New York Times* (May 27), pp. B1, 3.

Barboza, David. 2010b. "After Spate of Suicides, Technology Firm in China Raises Workers' Salaries." *New York Times* (June 3), B3.

Bellah, Robert. 1967. "Civil Religion in America." *Daedalus* 96: 1–21.

Bellah, Robert. 1973. "Introduction." Pp. ix–lv in Robert Bellah, ed. *Emile Durkheim: On Morality and Society*. Chicago: University of Chicago Press.

Bellah, Robert, Richard Madsen, William Sullivan, Ann Swidler, and Steven Tipton. 1985. *Habits of the Heart: Individualism and Commitment in American Life*. Berkeley: University of California Press.

Borden, Sam. 2015. "A Friendly in Every Sense of the Word." *New York Times* (November 18), p. B11.

Case, Anne, and Angus Deaton. 2017. "Mortality and Morbidity in the 21st Century." Washington, DC: Brookings Institution.

Castle, Stephen. 2016. "God Save the Queen, but the Anthem? England is Split." *New York Times* (January 14).

Cornwell, Benjamin, Edward Laumann, and L. Philip Schumm. 2008. "The Social Connectedness of Older Adults: A National Profile." *American Sociological Review* 73: 185–203.

Durkheim, Emile. 1893/1984. *The Division of Labour in Society*. Introduction by Lewis Coser. Translated by W.D. Halls. New York: Free Press.

Durkheim, Emile. 1895/1982 *The Rules of Sociological Method*. Edited and with an introduction by Steven Lukes. Translated by W.D. Halls. New York: Free Press.

Durkheim, Emile. 1897/1951. *Suicide: A Study in Sociology*. Introduction by George Simpson. Translated by John Spaulding and George Simpson. New York: Free Press.

Durkheim, Emile. 1912/2001. *The Elementary Forms of Religious Life*. Translated by Carol Cosman. Oxford: Oxford University Press.

Durkheim, Emile. 1914/1973. "The Dualism of Human Nature and Its Social Conditions." Pp. 149–163 in Robert Bellah, ed. *Emile Durkheim: On Morality and Society*. Chicago: University of Chicago Press.

Economist. 2012. "When Workers Dream of a Life Beyond the Factory Gates." (December 15), pp. 63–64.

Economist. 2017a. "Deaths of Despair." (March 25), p. 67.

Economist. 2017b. "What Would Hippocrates Do?" (July 15), p. 24.

Epstein, Cynthia Fuchs, Bonnie Oglensky, Robert Saute, and Carroll Seron. 1999. *The Part Time Paradox: Time Norms, Professional Lives, Family and Gender*. New York: Routledge.

Fischer, Claude, and Michael Hout. 2006. *Century of Difference: How America Changed in the Last One Hundred Years*. New York: Russell Sage Foundation.

Frisby, David, ed. 1994. *Georg Simmel: Critical Assessments*, volume 1. London: Routledge.

Fuller, Alexandra. 2007. "Boomtown Blues: How Natural Gas Changed the Way of Life in Sublette County." *New Yorker* (February 5), pp. 38–44.

Harden, Blaine. 2002a. "Born on the Bayou and Barely Feeling Any Urge to Roam." *New York Times* (September 30), p. A16.

Harden, Blaine. 2002b. "A Place Without Roots That Some Call Home." *New York Times* (September 30), p. A16.

Hoecker-Drysdale, Susan. 1992. *Harriet Martineau: First Woman Sociologist*. Oxford: Berg.

Innis, Michelle. 2015. "New Zealand debates replacing Union Jack flag, but with what?" *New York Times* (October 28).

Jolly, David, and Matthew Saltmarsh. 2009. "After Suicides, France Wrestles with Worker Stress." *New York Times* (October 1), p. B3.

Kessler, Ronald, Sandro Galea, Russell Jones, and Holly Parker. 2006. "Mental Illness and Suicidality after Hurricane Katrina." *Bulletin of the World Health Organization*. www.who.int/bulletin/volumes/84/10/06-03319.pdf

Kimmelman, Michael. 2001. "In a Square, a Sense of Unity." *New York Times* (September 19), pp. E1, 5.

Kolhatkar, Sheelah. 2017. "National Disaster." *New Yorker* (September 18), p. 21.

Lukes, Steven. 1973. *Emile Durkheim: His Life and Work*. New York: Penguin.

Mannheim, Karl. 1936/1968. *Ideology and Utopia: An Introduction to the Sociology of Knowledge*. New York: Harcourt, Brace, and World.

Martineau, Harriet. 1838. *How to Observe Morals and Manners*. London: Charles Knight.

Monnat, Shannon. 2017. *Drugs, Alcohol, and Suicide Represent Growing Share of US Mortality*. National Issue Brief #112. Durham, NH: Carsey School of Public Policy.

Remnick, David. 2015. "City of Water," *New Yorker* (August 24), p. 38.

Robertson, Campbell, and Richard Fausset. 2015. "New Orleans Remade, for Better and Worse." *New York Times* (August 27), pp. A1, 12–14.

Simmel, Georg. 1903/1950. *The Sociology of Georg Simmel*. Translated, edited, and with an introduction by Kurt Wolff. Glencoe, IL: Free Press.

Smelser, Neil. 1959. *Social Change in the Industrial Revolution*. Chicago: University of Chicago Press.

Tavernise, Sabrina. 2016. "Sweeping Pain as Suicides Hit a 30-Year High." New York Times (April 22), pp. A1, 16.

Tramuta, Lindsey. 2015. "Consolation in Community." *New York Times* (November 29), p. A9.

Valtorta, NK., et al. 2016. "Loneliness and Social Isolation as Risk Factors for Coronary Heart Disease and Stroke." *Heart* 102: 1009–1016.

Williams, Richard. 1990. *Hierarchical Structures and Social Value: The Creation of Black and Irish Identities in the United States*. New York: Cambridge University Press.

CHAPTER THREE
MAX WEBER (1864–1920)

KEY CONCEPTS

subjectively meaningful
   action
interpretive understanding
Verstehen
this-worldly
other-worldly
asceticism
calling
rationality
Calvinism
predestination
Puritan ethic

individualism
ideal type
rational action
value-rational action
instrumental rational action
nonrational action
emotional action
traditional action
power
domination
legal authority
traditional authority

nation-state
bureaucracy
charisma
charismatic community
routinization of charisma
stratification
class
status
parties
values
value neutrality
objectivity

CHAPTER MENU

Introduction to Sociological Theory: Theorists, Concepts, and Their Applicability to the Twenty-First Century,
Third Edition. Michele Dillon.
© 2020 John Wiley & Sons Ltd. Published 2020 by John Wiley & Sons Ltd.
Companion website: www.wiley.com/go/dillon

Timeline 3.1	Major events spanning Weber's lifetime (1864–1920)
1864	Pope Pius IX criticizes liberalism, socialism, and rationalism in the *Syllabus of Errors*
1865	US President Lincoln assassinated
1865	John D. Rockefeller, Sr., establishes Standard Oil
1866	Mary Baker Eddy introduces Christian Science
1867	Karl Marx, *Capital* (*Das Kapital*)
1870	First Vatican Council: Declaration of Papal Infallibility
1870	Diamonds discovered in South Africa
1873	Design of the first commercially successful typewriter
1876	Alexander Graham Bell invents the telephone
1877	Thomas Edison patents his phonograph
1883	Standardization of Greenwich Mean Time (GMT)

1883	Completion of the Brooklyn Bridge linking Manhattan and Brooklyn
1887	German domination of the chemical industry
1889	T.H. Huxley, *Agnosticism*
1890	Fall of Bismarck in Germany
1892	Gold discovered in Western Australia
1895	Gillette invents the safety razor
1900	Expansion of the German navy
1903	Henry Ford sets up the Motor Company
1904	Separation of church and state accomplished in France
1907	Pope Pius IX denounces Modernism
1909	Women admitted to German universities
1911	Standard Oil Trust split up into 33 companies; Rockefellers retain a major interest in Exxon, Mobil, Amoco, and Standard Oil of California
1914	Outbreak of World War I; Germany declares war on Russia, and France and invades Belgium
1918	Republic declared in Germany; Germany agrees to Armistice; end of World War I
1920	Prohibition in effect throughout the US

Like his fellow-German Karl Marx, **Max Weber** had much to say about the structure of capitalism and inequality. But unlike Marx, he paid a lot of attention to the cultural and noneconomic motivations underlying social action. Like Durkheim, Weber wrote extensively about religion. In contrast to Durkheim, who focused on the social functions of religion, Weber was concerned with its substantive content – the subjective meanings and worldviews that particular religions give rise to at a given point in history – and how they get translated into institutional practices. In analyzing religious content, Weber discussed and compared Christianity, ancient Judaism, and Islam – the world's major God-centered religions; and Confucianism, Hinduism, and Buddhism, religions that affirm an impersonal, cosmocentric force.

BIOGRAPHICAL NOTE

Max Weber was born in Germany in 1864. His father came from a business family and was active in industry and politics; his mother was a devout and well-educated Protestant. Weber grew up in a suburb of Berlin and his neighborhood included several important intellectual and political figures who socialized with his parents. Even as a child, Weber had expansive intellectual interests. Subsequently, he studied law, economics, history, and philosophy at Heidelberg University and, though studious, he also actively participated in the university's robust social life; he joined a dueling fraternity and was also a regular afternoon card-player. At age 19, while enrolled at Heidelberg, Weber moved to Strasbourg to complete a mandatory year of army training; he had a hard time adjusting to military discipline and mechanical drills but became a commissioned officer, highly respected by his peers and superiors.

After Heidelberg, Weber returned to Berlin, where he practiced law and completed his PhD on the history of trading companies during the Middle Ages. In 1893, he married Marianne Schnitger, following a remorseful breakup with another woman with whom he had been in love for six years, and he assumed the career of a hardworking and successful academic with positions at prestigious German universities. As time went on, Weber suffered recurring episodes of severe depression and fatigue; nonetheless, he managed to lecture and write prodigiously. He and Marianne had no children, and they traveled extensively in Europe for rest and respite (including to Ireland, Scotland, Spain, and Italy). In 1904, Weber visited the United States. He presented a paper at a congress in St. Louis organized as part of the Universal Exposition that year, and he also visited New York, other east coast cities (Boston, Baltimore, Washington, DC, Philadelphia), Chicago, and several southern states. Weber was mesmerized by what he saw of life in America – by both the "good" and the "bad" of capitalism – and was enthralled by the tenor of American life. He was "fascinated by the rush hour in lower Manhattan, which he liked to view from the middle of the Brooklyn Bridge as a panorama of mass transportation and noisy motion" (Gerth and Mills 1946: 15). Following his return to Germany, Weber finished writing *The Protestant Ethic and the Spirit of Capitalism*. At the beginning of World War I (1914), he was a captain in the reserve corps and for a year had responsibility for running nine hospitals in the Heidelberg area, an experience that gave him first-hand knowledge of the workings of bureaucracy. Although energized by the politics surrounding the war, Weber did not live long enough to see the aftermath of its resolution. He died in 1920, at age 56, from pneumonia (Gerth and Mills 1946: 3–31).

Weber's Writings

1904–1905: The Protestant Ethic and the Spirit of Capitalism, PE

1909–1920: Economy and Society, ES (Several of its sections are reprinted in condensed form in FMW).

1915: "The Social Psychology of the World Religions," in From Max Weber: Essays in Sociology, FMW

1919: "Politics as a Vocation," in From Max Weber: Essays in Sociology, FMW

"Science as a Vocation," in From Max Weber: Essays in Sociology, FMW

1903–1917: The Methodology of the Social Sciences, MSS

SOCIOLOGY: UNDERSTANDING SOCIAL ACTION

For Weber, the domain of sociology is **subjectively meaningful action**:

> Sociology … is a science concerning itself with the **interpretive understanding** of social action and thereby with a causal explanation of its course and consequence. We shall speak of "action" insofar as the acting individual attaches a subjective meaning to his behavior … Action is "social" insofar as its subjective meaning takes account of the behavior of others and is thereby oriented in its course. (ES 4)[1]

It is the sociologist's task to make sense of all the varying motivations that propel social action, and to do so by reaching an understanding – *Verstehen* (see this book's Introduction) – of why individuals and institutions and whole societies behave in certain ways: why they attach meaning to some goals and not others, and why certain behavioral patterns and consequences emerge in a given sociohistorical context. Unlike Durkheim, therefore, who focused on the external manifestations of social phenomena or social facts (e.g., marriage) and how they regulate and constrain social behavior (see chapter 2), Weber probed the historical and cultural origins of social phenomena (e.g., capitalism) and the particular institutional practices they produced (e.g., bureaucracy).

Following Weber, sociologists aim to achieve either an emotional-empathic or a rational-logical understanding of motivation "by placing the observed act in an intelligible and more inclusive context of meaning" (ES 8). In order to get an interpretive grasp or a deep understanding of social action, therefore, we have to immerse ourselves in the world and the worldviews of those we are studying. As Harriet Martineau (1838: 25, 52) advised, we must adopt a nonjudgmental attitude, and sympathetically, "find our way to the hearts and minds" of those whom we are studying (see Introduction).[2]

We do not have to be Caesar to understand Caesar (ES 5), Weber tells us, but we do have to commit to research that aims to understand the meaning of social action. Thus sociologists seek to explain the context in which particular social patterns and meanings emerge. This is why we conduct qualitative, in-depth interviews with individuals to understand the meanings that they, and their peers who are involved in a particular activity, inject into that activity. Similarly, we conduct ethnographic observation studies and historical and comparative research to understand why some communities, organizations, and societies do things in one particular way whereas others do things differently. This rich research legacy comes from Weber; an interpretive-hermeneutic, qualitative methodology that complements sociology's quantitative survey methods (see Introduction).

CULTURE AND ECONOMIC ACTIVITY

Weber's best-known book, and one that demonstrates what is entailed in the task of interpretive understanding, is *The Protestant Ethic and the Spirit of Capitalism*, published in 1904–1905. As is evident from the title, Weber illuminates the links between two domains of activity, *religion* and *economics*, that are generally thought of as separate, or, as in Marx's analysis of base–superstructure, reducible to one another (see chapter 1). Weber probes the relation between the **this-worldly** concerns that orient economic activity, material acquisition, and wealth; and the **other-worldly** concerns (e.g., afterlife, salvation) of religious belief. The impetus for Weber's study came from his empirical observation that, historically in modern capitalism (approximately from the seventeenth through the mid-nineteenth century), Protestants rather than Catholics predominated in business: "A glance at the occupational statistics of any country of mixed religious composition brings to light with remarkable frequency … the fact that business leaders and owners of capital, as well as the higher grades of skilled labour, and even more the higher technically and commercially trained personnel of modern enterprises, are overwhelmingly Protestant" (PE 35). Weber acknowledged that the overrepresentation of Protestants in industry and business may have been due to historical circumstances favoring them (e.g., English penal laws in Ireland from the seventeenth to the early nineteenth century prohibited Catholics from owning property and going to college). Nevertheless, Weber observed that even in those countries where Catholics were unrestricted, they, unlike Protestants, tended to opt for nonbusiness occupations, and among skilled workers, tended to remain in crafts rather than pursue clerical or skilled employment in the newly established factories (PE 38).[3]

THE PROTESTANT-CAPITALIST PUZZLE

Weber, therefore, starts with what for Durkheim would be an objective social fact (i.e., denominational differences in occupational specialization), explainable by other social facts, namely, the different social integrating structures of Catholicism and Protestantism, and their varying constraints on individual ambition (cf. *Suicide*; see chapter 2). For Weber, however, these social phenomena in and of themselves beg for further understanding. Thus, in accord with his own definition of sociology, he proceeded to investigate what underlying religious-doctrinal or cultural beliefs gave rise to different religious and social structures (institutions) in the first place, and specifically, what was culturally peculiar to Protestantism that would account for the discrepancy between Catholics and Protestants in their affinity for business and industry.

A second puzzle noted by Weber was the extent to which the character or spirit of modern capitalism was marked by **asceticism** – the disciplined imposition of a frugality and sobriety regarding the wealth accumulated through hard work. This contrasted with material acquisition in preindustrial eras, which was driven by individuals' basic survival needs, and it also differed from the greed of adventurers and pirates.

THE PROTESTANT ETHIC

Weber was intrigued that the ascetic attitude was cogently summarized in the pithy phrase "Time is money," a maxim made famous by Benjamin Franklin (1706–1790), one of America's founding fathers who was also a prolific writer and inventor (PE 48-50). This saying clearly has a utilitarian thrust, that is, the more time you spend doing useful things, the more productive you are and the more money you make (PE 48-50). It also has a larger meaning, one grounded in a religious ethic. Weber states that although Franklin was not religiously devout, he was nonetheless heavily influenced by his strict Protestant upbringing and his father's endless sermonizing about the virtues of work. Franklin knew these virtues well, and as Weber notes, he readily quoted from the Bible's Book of Proverbs, "Seest thou a man diligent in his business? He shall stand before kings" (PE 53). Not being diligent, therefore, takes on a religious meaning: Wasting time is an offense against God.

Accordingly, Weber argues, "the earning of money within the modern economic order is, so long as it is done legally, the result and the expression of virtue and proficiency in a **calling** [selfless, diligent commitment to a vocation/work] … [the idea of] duty in a calling, is what is most characteristic of the social ethic of capitalistic culture. It is an obligation which the individual is supposed to feel and does feel towards the content of his professional activity" (PE 53–54). This ethic – embracing work as a duty with its own intrinsic reward of giving glory to God and thus working hard irrespective of the job, or its fit with one's talents, or its material reward – preceded the expansion of capitalism. Medieval monks, for example, lived a life of simplicity and asceticism (disciplined frugality), laboring in the monastery fields cultivating crops to meet their own needs and those of the local beggars.

Weber notes that capitalism harnessed this work ethic, transforming it into a disciplined, methodical **rationality** that justified the pursuit of profit. Economic success, not simple subsistence, became the objective. The accumulation of money/profit resulting from diligent work and a frugal lifestyle led to the investment and reinvestment of the capital necessary to building the factories and plants and general infrastructure (e.g., railroads) essential to the expansion of capitalism (PE 17).

THE REFORMATION

Timeline 3.2	The emergence of Protestantism and the expansion of capitalism
1495–1498	Leonardo da Vinci paints *The Last Supper*
1504	Michelangelo's statue of *David* installed in Florence
1517	Martin Luther nails his theses denouncing the Catholic Church to the doors of Wittenberg cathedral
1527	Sweden becomes Lutheran

1531	In England, Henry VIII forces the (Catholic) clergy to recognize him as head of the (Protestant) Church of England
1539	First printing of the English (Protestant) Bible
1545	The Council of Trent: the beginning of the Catholic Counter-Reformation
1546	Martin Luther dies
1553	Queen Mary returns England to Catholicism
1558	Queen Elizabeth I reestablishes Protestantism in England
1564	John Calvin dies
1583	Jesuit missionaries settle in China
1584	Potato introduced to Europe
1607	Tea introduced to Europe
1607	English found Jamestown, Virginia
1611	Publication of the authorized King James (Protestant) Bible
1620	English pilgrims land at Plymouth, Massachusetts
1626	Dutch found New Amsterdam on Manhattan Island (New York)
1630	John Winthrop founds Boston, Massachusetts
1683	First German immigrants arrive in North America
1701	Founding of Yale College, New Haven, Connecticut, as a Protestant Congregational seminary
1706	Benjamin Franklin born
1730	John and Charles Wesley found the Methodist Society at Oxford University, England
1746	Princeton University (College of New Jersey) founded as a Presbyterian seminary
1760	Expansion of British cotton production
1776	Declaration of Independence by American colonies
1790	Beginnings of multistory factory blocks bigger than mills

In the *Protestant Ethic*, Weber traces how the idea of work as a duty or calling got entwined with profit-oriented, everyday economic activity. To understand its evolution, we first need to review the Protestant Reformation, whose 500th anniversary was widely commemorated in 2017. The Reformation is a critical event in shaping Western modernity, and especially American culture and society. In 1517, when Martin Luther (1483–1546), a German monk and theology professor, nailed 95 theses to the doors of Wittenberg cathedral, protesting the abuses and excesses in the Catholic church, his break with the church established Protestantism (derived from the word *protest*).

Luther disagreed with many aspects of Catholicism. Foremost was his rejection of the church's emphasis that the individual believer needed the intervention of the church hierarchy (the pope, bishops, and priests) to interpret scripture and God's intentions, and that the sacraments were necessary to confer the divine grace necessary for salvation. Luther also strongly objected to the church's use of special indulgences (e.g., forgiveness of sins) given in exchange for good works, pilgrimages, or financial donations to the church. Instead, Luther maintained, the individual believer was directly given grace and salvation by God, and hence did not need indulgences and sacraments, and nor, by extension, any intermediaries (such as the pope).

Luther is important because he did the groundwork for the emergence of Protestantism (and specifically Lutheranism), and it quickly evolved into an array of separate denominations (e.g., Presbyterians, Congregationalists, Methodists, Quakers, Baptists). The history of Protestantism, especially in the sixteenth and seventeenth centuries in England and northern Europe, and in the seventeenth and eighteenth centuries in North America, was characterized by various theological disputes as different groups argued over core doctrines and beliefs and established new denominations affirming the purity of their particular beliefs.

SALVATION AND PREDESTINATION

Among the early Protestant strands, **Calvinism**, named for John Calvin (1509–1564), the French-Swiss reformer who developed its doctrine, has particular significance for Weber's thesis. Although Calvin was one of Luther's successors and disciples, his beliefs departed in important ways from Luther's. Calvin disagreed with Luther about God directly giving grace to the lowly individual. He instead postulated the doctrine of **predestination** – the belief that the individual's salvation was already predetermined, predestined, by God. In other words, at birth, your salvation – whether you are going to heaven or hell – is already known to God and no matter how you live your life, no matter how many good works you do or how much you seek God's grace, you can do nothing to affect your after-life destiny. This dogma was expressed in the "authoritative Westminster Confession," which Weber quotes: "By the decree of God, for the manifestation of His glory, some men and angels are predestined unto everlasting life, and others foreordained to everlasting death" (PE 99–100).

While busy with your college life, you may not give much thought to the afterlife. But the question of eternal salvation was *very* important to many people in the sixteenth and seventeenth centuries. Indeed, it is important for many people today; 72 percent of Americans believe in heaven, and over half (58 percent) in hell (Pew Research Center 2015). For Calvin and his followers who believed in predestination, the dilemma of what to do about salvation became an enormous psychological challenge. If you believe in an all-powerful and glorious God, and you believe that God has already sealed your fate, and you know that you cannot know God's plans, what are you to do? Unlike the Lutherans, who could believe in God reaching down to give them grace and, ultimately, salvation, and unlike the Catholics, who could earn grace and salvation through the church (e.g., by confession), the Calvinist could turn to no one for hints or assurance about salvation.

Weber writes:

> In its extreme inhumanity this doctrine [predestination] must above all have had one consequence for the life of a generation which surrendered to its magnificent consistency. That was a feeling of unprecedented inner loneliness of the single individual. In what was for the man of the age of the Reformation the most important thing in life, his eternal salvation, he was forced to follow his path alone to meet a destiny which had been decreed for him from eternity. No one could help him. No priest, for the chosen one can understand the word of God only in his own heart. No sacraments, for though the sacraments had been ordained by God for the increase of His glory, and hence must be scrupulously observed, they are not a means to the attainment of grace … No church … Finally, even no God. For even Christ had died only for the elect, for whose benefit God had decreed His martyrdom for eternity. (PE 104)

The Calvinist's inner loneliness, his "deep spiritual isolation" (PE 107), did not lead, however, to either self-indulgent hedonism or melancholic fatalism. It did not make the Calvinist feel that one should live life as one pleases and throw caution to the wind given that there was nothing one could do to change one's predestined fate. That attitude would have contravened the Calvinist and general Puritan belief in asceticism, and the related view that self-indulgence, emotional spontaneity, and sociability were to be avoided. These were all seen as unholy distractions, tempting the individual from the purpose of diligently glorifying God (PE 105–106). For Calvinists, Weber argues,

> The world exists to serve the glorification of God and for that purpose alone. The elected [saved] Christian is in the world only to increase this glory of God by fulfilling His commandments to the best of his ability … The social activity of the Christian in the world is solely activity [for the glory of God]. This character is hence shared by labour in a calling which serves the mundane [ordinary] life of the community. (PE 108)

PROVING YOUR SALVATION

As God-fearing believers faced with the nagging question "Am I one of the elect?" Calvinists had to convince themselves of their salvation. And they justified or rationalized this conviction through intense activity in the world – by glorifying God in everyday activity, specifically, as the Biblical proverb instructs, through diligence in business (PE123). Hence success, resulting from hard work in the everyday world, would be a *sign* of one's salvation – but not a *means* to salvation; it would signify or prove one's membership among the elect, as one of the saved. Taking the pragmatic view that "God helps those who help themselves" (PE 115), the Calvinists took it as their duty to demonstrate (prove) their salvation to themselves and to others through evidence of material success. Weber states that unlike Catholics who achieve salvation through the gradual accumulation of credit (from indulgences, the sacraments, etc.), the Calvinist "creates his own salvation, or, as would be more correct, the conviction of it" through "systematic self-control which at every moment stands before the inexorable alternative, chosen or damned" (PE 115). Faith in the conviction that you are one of the chosen was demonstrated not by emotional feelings of closeness to God, but by the objective *proof* provided by the visible material results of your morally disciplined and methodical worldly activity, the fruits of your labor. As Weber noted, "The God of Calvinism demanded of his believers not single good works, but a life of good works" (PE 117), a life that allowed for no failures or lapses in glorifying God through disciplined, everyday activity.

RATIONAL SELF-REGULATION AND SELF-CONTROL

The sermons of Richard Baxter (1615–1691), an influential English Puritan, repeatedly emphasized the ethical importance of "hard, continuous bodily or mental labour" (PE 158), because "every hour lost is lost to labour for the glory of God" (PE 158). Moreover, the impulse not to work, regardless of one's wealth, is itself "symptomatic of the lack of grace" (PE 159). Thus, the **Puritan ethic** not only affirmed the idea of work as a calling; it also denounced time spent not in work but in leisure as sinful because it departs from the command to glorify God through work. Weber's interpretive analysis of the sermons and writings of several Puritan church leaders showed that the asceticism of the Calvinist ethic "turned with all its force against one thing: the spontaneous enjoyment of life and all it had to offer" (PE 166). The Puritans had an aversion to sport, for example, accepting it only if it

> served a rational purpose, that of recreation necessary for physical efficiency [in work]. But as a means for the spontaneous expression of undisciplined impulses, it was under suspicion; and in so far as it became

purely a means of enjoyment, or awakened pride, raw instincts or the irrational gambling instinct, it was of course strictly condemned. Impulsive enjoyment of life, which leads away both from work in a calling and from religion, was as such the enemy of rational asceticism. (PE 167)

The Calvinists, therefore, infused rationality – a deliberate, planful, methodical focus – into everyday life; their cultural legacy was "the rationalization of conduct within this world ... [penetrating] the daily routine of life with methodicalness" (PE 154). The regulation and control of the Catholic Church that Martin Luther protested was thus replaced with the *self*-regulation of the individual over all aspects of daily life; it required the individual "to bring his actions under constant self-control with a careful consideration of their ethical considerations [to serve God]" (PE 119).

In turn, individual self-regulation and self-discipline animated the expansion of capitalism. Calvinist religious beliefs – in particular, predestination – and the rationalization of those beliefs through activity in *this* world, led to the harnessing of a disciplined work ethic. Proof of salvation required the objective attainment of economic success; and economic success combined with ascetic frugality fed the accumulation of capital. Protestantism did not create capitalism; but as evidenced from history, it accelerated its development. Capitalist industrialization expanded in the eighteenth and nineteenth centuries in countries where rational, ascetic Protestantism predominated (e.g., England, Germany, America). Thus, an *unintended* consequence of Calvinism was the expansion of capitalism.

PROTESTANT-WESTERN INDIVIDUALISM

Calvinism also sowed the seeds of **individualism**. If the individual stands alone before God in a state of spiritual isolation and inner loneliness, and is alone responsible for establishing proof of their salvation, this requires the cultivation of individual independence, self-reliance, self-regulation, and personal responsibility (PE 105–106). These are habits and values that many parents and teachers today seek to instill in children. Their cultural relevance is further underscored by their centrality to public policy debates in the US – and increasingly in Europe – on government versus individual responsibility regarding poverty, health, and welfare. Thus, Weber argued, there is a fit, an "elective affinity," between a particular culture or a particular religious belief-system, and the particular personality type that it fosters; the associated personality traits get instilled into the national character and a country's social institutions (PE 105–106). Protestantism produces individualism, "respect for quiet self-control ... [and] the destruction of spontaneous, impulsive enjoyment" (PE 119), traits that are conducive to individual (and cultural) achievement and economic productivity. By contrast, world-rejecting Buddhism, for example, fosters a personality type of "concentrated contemplation ... regarding the solidarity of all living, and hence transitory, beings" (ES 627–628), an ethic that may help account, in part, for the "slower" economic development of Vietnam a country with a strong Buddhist history and culture.

Weber's discussion of the links between culture (e.g., religious beliefs) and the expansion of capitalism is important for social theory because it illuminates how capitalist society can be understood in ways that are independent of a purely economic framing. Karl Marx accentuated the economic logic of capitalism (property relations, profit) and saw culture and beliefs as not independent of, but serving, capitalist ideology/practices (see chapter 1). Weber, by contrast, emphasizes that cultural beliefs and values matter in and of themselves. Moreover, they shape social institutions including the economy. Calvinists did not set out to influence the development of capitalism. But, as a result of their particular religious beliefs and their this-worldly rationalization, they chose a course of action – rational methodical asceticism in work and in all aspects of everyday activity – whose consequences produced profit and capitalist investment. Importantly, too, they institutionalized the cultural values of hard work and self-reliant individualism.

IDEAL TYPES

Weber's analysis of the methodical individualism associated with Protestantism (and its contrast with the Buddhist mystical contemplative) is illustrative of a crucial aspect of his methodology, namely, his use of **ideal types**. He uses ideal types to describe and highlight the unique expected characteristics of a particular social phenomenon (e.g., Protestantism) and to compare its ideal typical representation with the ideal typical representations of other religions. Thus Protestantism, in its ideal typical expression, has characteristics that are different to Buddhism or Islam; and each has different social origins and different consequences for everyday social action (FMW 323–359; ES 576–634). If we were to conduct a comparative study, for example, of social attitudes in the US, Vietnam, and Morocco, we would expect our findings (e.g., on gender equality) to map onto (or have an affinity with) ideas in the culturally dominant religious tradition in each society. Although there would be individual variation within each country, nonetheless we would expect (in ideal-typical fashion) that the within-country variation would be less than the between-country variation.

Ideal types are thus helpful in orienting sociological research. They anchor our inquiry as we go about understanding and explaining diverse forms of social action and social relationships (ES 26). They are basically yardsticks that we can use to measure and compare how social actors measure up to the standard set by other individuals (e.g., in academic achievement), groups (e.g., sports leagues), organizations (e.g., a company's hiring and promotion practices), or nation states (e.g., economic development). Weber explains,

> The ideal typical concept will help to develop our skill in imputation in *research*: it *is* no "hypothesis" but it offers guidance to the construction of hypotheses. It is not a *description* of reality but it aims to give unambiguous means of expression to such a description … An ideal type is formed by the one sided *accentuation* of one or more points of view and by the synthesis of a great many diffuse, discrete, more or less present and occasionally absent *concrete individual* phenomena, which are arranged according to those one-sidedly emphasized viewpoints into a unified *analytical* construct. In its conceptual purity, this mental construct cannot be found empirically anywhere in reality … Historical research faces the task of determining in each individual case, the extent to which this ideal-construct approximates to or diverges from reality … When carefully applied, those concepts are particularly useful in research and exposition. (MSS 90; italics in original)

Weber regarded the characteristics he outlined as distinctive of a certain type of social action or social organization as the set of standardized characteristics that we should expect to see if the construct being studied empirically were to approximate the "pure" or "ideal" type (the yardstick) of the construct as theorized or defined. For him, the usefulness of any ideal-type categorization was to be judged in terms of the empirical results it yielded in a particular sociohistorical context (ES 26). He emphasized that precisely because his ideal types are (theoretically) pure, "it would be very unusual to find concrete cases of social action which were oriented *only* in one or another of these ways" (ES 26). This becomes especially clear when we study the different types of social action that Weber identified, the topic to which we now turn.

SOCIAL ACTION

VALUE-RATIONAL ACTION

Weber's *Protestant Ethic* showed that values are a well-spring or motivator of social action. We might be inclined to think of values as being nonrational – it is, after all, hard to argue in favor of the objective superiority of one value over another. The important point for Weber, however, is that values, irrespective of their content or substance (e.g., equality, multicultural diversity, beauty), not only motivate action but can motivate **rational action**, that is, motivate individuals, groups, and organizations to act in a highly deliberate, planful, methodical way in the actualization of those values. For him, this is one (ideal) type of social action, what he calls **value-rational action**. Value-rational action occurs when an individual or a group, organization, or whole society values a particular principle such that they decide to rationally act on that value, to demonstrate their commitment to that value, regardless of the expected or unexpected costs of that action to them. "For my country, right or wrong!" is the cry of the soldier heading to war. "Here I stand, I can do no other" (FMW 127) is the voice of a principled person explaining their decision about a particular course of action, whether demonstrating a commitment to family, friendship, social justice, or environmental sustainability, etc. Value-rational action is "determined by a conscious belief in the value for its own sake of some ethical, aesthetic, religious, or other form of behavior, independently of its prospects for success" (ES 24–25).

When our siblings or friends choose to enlist in the military and, by extension, choose to put themselves in the face of great personal danger, many do so because of their commitment to the value of patriotism (and independent of the social and economic benefits and costs of enlistment). Once committed to that value, they then methodically proceed to act on that value: Their enrollment in military training and their personal sacrifices are rational actions in the service of their values. Similarly, many childless couples go to great lengths to have a child; they invest a lot of time and money and endure a lot of heartache (expectation and disappointment) as they experiment with various fertility programs or go through the arduous process of trying to successfully adopt a child. These are all rational, well-thought-out options they deliberately pursue because of their commitment to the value of children.

When you help a friend or neighbor even though doing so involves a great personal cost to you in terms of time, energy, money, or other opportunities lost, your conduct is rational vis-à-vis your values – your valuing of friendship, loyalty, etc. By the same token, a university's commitment to the value of multicultural diversity can lead it to rationally implement recruitment and admission policies and changes in curriculum offerings and faculty hiring plans that, though economically (and perhaps politically) costly to the university, produce a more diverse student body and a more diverse learning environment for all its students. The rationally deliberate, planful steps the university makes toward accomplishing its goal (despite its costs) make sense given the value it places on diversity.

In sum, many different values (e.g., inclusivity, duty, loyalty, beauty, equality) can motivate rational action; as Weber notes, "value-rational action always involves 'commands' or 'demands' which, in the actor's opinion, are binding on him" (ES 25). Anytime, therefore, that we are puzzled by the actions of individuals, organizations, religious or political groups, or whole countries, – we should probe whether the behavior is being driven by commitment to a particular value. We might not personally hold that particular value, but from Weber we learn to recognize that values can motivate highly rational, deliberative action (as we saw with Calvinism).

INSTRUMENTAL RATIONAL ACTION

Another type of rational behavior, and one Weber sees as dominating modern capitalist society, is what he calls **instrumental rational action**. In contrast to value-rational action, which is driven by commitment to a particular value (irrespective of the costs imposed), instrumental rational action is strategic, cost–benefit action. According to Weber, when a given actor is interested in achieving a particular, rationally calculated goal or end (e.g., economic wealth), they assesses the most effective means to achieve that end among the options available: "Action is instrumentally rational when the end [goal], the means, and the secondary results are all rationally taken into account and weighed" (ES 26).

Instrumental rational action thus captures the calculating means–end behavior that individuals, organizations, and societies engage in when they make cost–benefit decisions about a course of action (e.g., college education) whose planned outcome (high postcollege income) is intended to benefit the actor making the decision. We make instrumentally rational decisions about all sorts of things on the basis of their perceived costs to us – what college to attend, which highway route to take when going to visit a friend who has moved to a different city, etc. Instrumental rational action is, according to Weber, "determined by expectations as to the behavior of objects in the environment [e.g., the housing market] and of other human beings; these expectations are used as 'conditions' or 'means' for the attainment of the actor's own rationally pursued and calculated end" (ES 24). In capitalist society, cost–benefit rationality predominates; profit-and-loss is the ledger used, with net profit or net gain being the decisive criterion in determining behavior.

The world of work and economic relations provides much evidence illustrating the pervasiveness of instrumental rational action in contemporary society. Topic 1.5, on poultry workers, used to highlight Marx's ideas about surplus value, exploitation, and alienated labor, also illustrates Weber's concept of instrumental rational action. Notably, Weber's construct applies equally to the factory owners and to the workers seeking unionization. Both groups are trying to maximize their benefits: for the owners, profit resulting, for example, from the speed of the line-production process; and for the workers, the economic and health and safety benefits that would result from better working conditions. Similarly, when the American car manufacturing company General Motors (GM) made sweeping cost cuts to bolster its tenuous economic situation, these cuts eliminated the health benefits of its older white-collar retirees. Although GM is renowned for its value commitment to workers' health, it acted in an instrumental rather than in a value-rational way: maintaining its cash reserves has greater strategic value for GM than does preserving its retirees' health benefits.

The iron cage of contemporary capitalism

When Weber writes about the dominance of instrumental rationality in modern society he sounds a lot like Marx (chapter 1). Although Weber highlighted the historical role of religious values in capitalist expansion (see *Protestant Ethic*), his conclusion about modern-day capitalism (at the beginning of the twentieth century) was that it had *lost* its religious, ethical foundations. He believed it was no longer driven by nonmaterial (e.g., religious) values but, as Marx argued, by economic interests. Rather than making work our calling (our vocation), the demands of capitalist society have become so all-pervasive and controlling that we are coerced into fulfilling the rational cost–benefit expectations of the capitalist marketplace. Thus:

> The Puritan wanted to work in a calling; we are forced to do so. For when asceticism was carried out of monastic cells into everyday life, and began to dominate worldly morality, it did its part in building the tremendous cosmos of the modern economic order. This order is now bound to the technical and economic

conditions of machine production which to-day determine the lives of all individuals who are born into this mechanism, not only those directly concerned with economic acquisition, with irresistible force. Perhaps it will so determine them until the last ton of fossilized coal is burnt. In [Richard] Baxter's view the care for external goods should only lie on the shoulders of the "saint like a light cloak, which can be thrown aside at any moment." But fate decreed that the cloak should become an iron cage ... material goods have gained an increasing and finally an inexorable power over the lives of men as at no previous period in history. (PE 181)

The ethos of instrumental rationality pervades many aspects of modern life and culture, constituting an "iron cage" of economic and technological determinism. Indeed, we routinely make decisions based on 'marginal utility' a calculating, methodical assessment of the opportunities and alternatives available (e.g., whether to buy the latest iPhone or Samsung Galaxy). We opt (and are expected to opt) for the course of action whose consequences are most likely to best serve our strategic interests.

NONRATIONAL ACTION

Value-rational and instrumental rational action are examples of the meaningful social action that, for Weber, is the focus of sociology. Not all meaningful action, however, is rational action. We know from our own everyday lives that emotion, for example, underlies many of the things we do. Emotion is at the root of a lot of social interaction even in places where we might think that emotion and **nonrational action** in general don't belong – in Congress and parliament, for example, where, following Enlightenment ideals, we would expect to find only well-argued rational debate (see Introduction), not angry outbursts; or on Wall Street, where we might expect that trading decisions would not be driven by fear and panic but by calculated plans designed to ensure long-term financial gains. Yet just a cursory eye on the day's news reminds us that emotion permeates politics and economics.

Weber recognized the socially meaningful significance of emotion. He categorized affectual or **emotional action** as a third type of social action, that which is determined by the actor's specific feeling states: "Action is affectual [emotional] if it satisfies a need for revenge, sensual gratification, devotion, contemplative bliss, or for working off emotional tensions" (ES 25). A second type of nonrational action (and Weber's fourth type of social action) is **traditional action**. Many families have particular holiday (e.g., Christmas, Thanksgiving) and other traditions, habits, and customs they follow simply because they have always done things that way. Family and religious, cultural, and institutional traditions matter; they are powerful motivators of social action. (See Topic 3.1.)

Topic 3.1   Explaining Brexit with Weber: Rational and Nonrational Action

On June 23, 2016, a majority of people in the UK (52 percent) voted in favor of Britain's exit (Brexit) from the European Union (EU). Britain has been a member of the EU, or what used to be called the European Economic Community (EEC) since January 1, 1973, when it, along with the Republic of Ireland and Denmark, joined the original members (France, Germany, Belgium, the Netherlands, Italy, and Luxembourg). It has long been "a reluctant European"; it chose to maintain its own currency rather than use the Euro (like most member states), and opinion polls going back to the 1970s report a lack of enthusiasm about the benefits of membership. Nevertheless, the Brexit result took many by surprise, and the UK is currently in the throes of negotiating the terms of exit. This is a complicated task given the array of treaties in place over more than 40 years, as well as the everyday realities of its economic, political and cultural relationships with other member countries. Notwithstanding the increased significance of global trade, the UK exports more to Ireland (its close, historically complicated, neighbor) than to Brazil, India, Japan, and South Africa combined. Overall, 52 percent of exports of British goods go to the EU and 7 percent of EU exports go to Britain.

The polarized Brexit vote unveiled key divisions within the UK: Whereas a slim majority in England (53 percent) and Wales (52 percent) voted to exit, a larger majority in Scotland (62 percent) and Northern Ireland (56 percent) voted to remain. The vote also revealed a gulf in support between London and the rest of England, between young and old, and between the better and less well educated. In some sense, the vote captures a divide between a cosmopolitan and a more traditional worldview. A Weberian analysis helps illuminate the multilayered complexity of the various reasons and motivations in play.

Instrumental rational action: Economic interests motivate both sides. Each side appreciates the benefits of free trade and a single market and the fact that there is, for example, a cost cap on mobile phones (due to an EU regulation). And both sides agree that Britain should not provide (economically costly) social welfare payments to EU migrants. Many on each side also favor restrictions on the free movement of people from other EU countries to the UK. From a *value-rational* perspective, this might be seen as evidence of the value of commitment to state sovereignty and a nation's right to control its own borders (i.e., its own territory and laws). The free movement of people, however, is directly entangled with the (economic) benefits of free trade. Britain's economic productivity over the past 15 years is due in part to the influx of workers from other EU countries; in 2017, there were more than 2.3 million workers from other parts of the EU employed in the UK, two-and-a-half times as many as a decade earlier. As *The Economist* notes, current migration flows work in Britain's favor: Most of its migrants are young, healthy and taxpaying. We see tension, therefore, between instrumental and value rationality, between the economic benefits of free trade and the cultural affirmation of border/territorial sovereignty. This tension is reflected among voters: Those who favor remaining in the EU prioritize free movement over free trade, whereas those who favor exiting favor free trade over free movement.

Emotion is also relevant: Pride and prejudice. For some, there is hurt pride that Britain's influence in the EU has diminished over time. This is partly due to its absence from the Euro. But it is also simply due numerically to the expansion of the EU itself. In 1973, the UK had 2 of the 13 EU commissioner spots; 20 percent of voting members in the European Parliament; and 17 percent of the Council of Ministers. In 2017, it has 1 of 28 commissioners; 9.5 percent of the votes in Parliament, and 8 percent on the council. Emotion is also conveyed by the anti-immigration sentiments voiced during the Brexit campaign and in public discourse for some time. In 2010, David Cameron pledged to reduce net migration to 100,000. The British government's continuing goal to cut immigration is partly a reflection of the prejudice some British people feel toward the increased visibility of "nonnationals" over the past 15 years (especially since 2004 when the EU expanded to include Poland, Hungary, Lithuania and other eastern and central European countries). Anti-immigrant sentiment is complicated, however. Immigrants from Southeast Asia voted in large numbers in favor of Brexit with the hope that restrictions on EU migrants would open up more space for more Asian immigrants (thus reflecting, perhaps, emotion and instrumental rationality). *Tradition* also matters. Most notably, some in the Conservative party who advocated for Brexit want to retrieve the glory of Britain's imperial past. They argue that the old symbols of the British Empire should be reinstated, including the iconic royal yacht, *Britannia* (Data sources: *The Economist*, "The Future of the European Union," March 25, 2017, p. 50; and May 20, 2017, p. 49; and Taub 2016: A6).

THE INTERPLAY OF RATIONAL AND NONRATIONAL ACTION

The authority of tradition frequently collides with modern lifestyles, as some young French Muslim women know well. But Muslim women also demonstrate that the force of tradition can in turn spur rational strategic decisions (e.g., hymen-restoration surgery) (see Topic 3.2). As Weber elaborated, social action does not necessarily correspond to any one "ideal type"; rather, various types of action can coexist in any given context. This will become more apparent in the next section as we consider additional examples of social action and assess them in terms of Weber's four types (Box 3.1).

Box 3.1	Types of meaningful social action: Meaningful action can be driven by multiple and diverse motivating forces

Rational or purposive action	Nonrational action
1 Instrumental rational action	3 Emotional action
2 Value-rational action	4 Traditional action

VALUES AND EMOTIONS IN THE CORPORATE WORLD

Although we can predict that almost any story about corporate hiring and investment practices will highlight the pervasiveness of instrumental rationality, Weber's fourfold classification of social action helps us notice how different types of action coexist. Value-rational and emotional action can occur even in corporate boardrooms typically dominated by instrumental rational action. This mix of motivating forces is seen in the response of Sandler O'Neill, a small investment-banking firm that lost many employees in the 9/11 terrorist attacks in Manhattan. In the immediate aftermath of the attacks, the firm not only set up a foundation to pay for the education of the 71 children of its deceased employees, it also made an eight-year commitment to pay the bereaved families the full health benefits that its employees receive. Further, it paid bonus and stock money to the deceased employees' families. One senior partner explained that the firm had so many close-knit, family-like ties with the (deceased) employees and their families that it couldn't imagine *not* making a systematic effort to care for them in tangible ways. We thus see that on Wall Street, despite the constant pressure of a profit-oriented strategic rationality, firms occasionally reject instrumental criteria (e.g., self-profit and company profit) in favor of noneconomic considerations. Similarly when the pharmaceutical company Pfizer laid off thousands of workers in Brooklyn, New York, it acted in an instrumental way; nonetheless Pfizer also continued subsidizing housing and schools in the community, thereby acting on its values, that is, its commitment to neighborhood well-being. It was also motivated by tradition – Brooklyn is Pfizer's birthplace – and by emotion, that is, its sentimental attachment to the place.

WANTING A CHILD: EMOTION, VALUES, AND INSTRUMENTAL RATIONALITY

Clearly, value-rational and nonrational (emotional and traditional) action can penetrate corporate behavior, notwithstanding the larger instrumental, strategic context in which businesses operate. By the same token, instrumental rationality can penetrate areas of life that we generally regard as motivated primarily by emotion or values. Take, for example, the decision to have a child. When a person

Topic 3.2   Muslim women and virginity: Two worlds collide

In private clinics in fashionable neighborhoods in Paris, hymen-restoration surgery is increasingly sought by young Muslim women who, despite the freedoms they enjoy in France, are under intense family pressure to provide certificates of virginity prior to their wedding night. These certificates are demanded by their own fathers and brothers as well as by their future in-laws. Thus hymenoplasties are on the rise: short cosmetic surgical procedures "involving one semicircular cut, 10 dissolving stitches and a discounted fee of $2,900" allow Muslim women to avoid becoming targets of the anger and degradation that is invariably directed toward them once it is publicly announced that they had lost their virginity prior to marriage. One young Muslim female student explained: "In my culture, not to be a virgin is to be dirt." The hymen-replacement surgery is nondetectable and provides the necessary proof of vaginal bleeding on the wedding night (Sciolino and Mekhennet 2008).

or couple decide they want a child, we generally assume that this is driven by emotional fulfillment, as well as by commitment to the value of family. But we also see evidence that couples' decisions to have children are not entirely lacking instrumental motivation. The classified personal advertisements for egg donors seen in college newspapers indicate that some couples have very specific requirements about the kinds of children they want.

The requirements outlined in Topic 3.3 suggest the calculated presumption that egg donors who can meet the criteria will most likely produce emotionally, cognitively, and physically high-functioning children. These donor-seeking couples, therefore, do not seem to want children solely because they value children. Rather, they seem to value a particular type of child – one who starts out with a higher than average probability of being strategically poised to have a successful life.

There are also couples who seek to have children *with* specific disabilities. Some prospective parents intentionally choose to undergo invasive genetic diagnoses and fertility implants by which they choose "malfunctioning genes that produce disabilities like deafness or dwarfness … painful and expensive fertility procedure for the express purpose of having children with a defective gene" (Sanghavi 2006, D5). From a Weberian perspective, these parents are acting in a highly rational, methodical, and calculating manner; they are choosing defective genes in order to realize their commitment to the value of deafness, for example. These parents have a concern that amid societal expectations that prospective parents should screen out for disability, those with a disability will become increasingly marginalized. In this context, intentionally choosing to have embryonic implants that will ensure deafness can be considered a value-rational act. There is also an element of tradition; interest in maintaining the culture and traditions of deaf people (although not elevating deafness as an overarching identity). And there is an emotional component: Deaf people may feel especially close emotionally to a deaf child.

In sum, as Weber's analysis of social action demonstrates, social behavior is complex. Although it can frequently be characterized as illustrating one type of social action more so than another, in many instances, the social action we observe variously combines instrumental rational and value-rational motivations as well as elements of emotion and tradition (see Topics 3.1 and 3.4). More generally, Weber's analysis of social action demonstrates his commitment to understanding the broad gamut of social behavior. Unlike Marx, he does not see social behavior as reducible to economic or property relations, and unlike Durkheim, he is not concerned primarily with analyzing social solidarity.

Topic 3.3   Egg donors wanted

"Help loving couples who want to have a baby. 20–29 years of age, physically/emotionally healthy, college-educated, no anti-depressant use or history of mental illness, non-smoking or smoke-free for at least one year, height/weight proportionate, no drug use or alcohol abuse … $5–10 K compensation." (*Wellesley College News*, September 20, 2006)

Topic 3.4   "Why is she wearing that?" Ski-masks as beach fashion in China

Beach-going is becoming more popular in China, and new beach-going practices attest to the diverse motivations underpinning social behavior. It is increasingly common for Chinese women to wear brightly-colored, stretch-fabric ski masks covering their face and neck while at the beach (Levin 2012). Despite the stares this invites, Chinese women are behaving very rationally in choosing to wear these rather intimidating and out-of-place masks. The masks serve a straight-forward instrumental purpose: They are the most effective way to enjoy being on the beach and swimming in the sea while simultaneously keeping one's skin color fair. Feminine beauty in China (and across Asia more generally) is equated with a pallid complexion; hence mask wearing on the beach can be considered an example of value rational action: It demonstrates women's commitment to the value of beauty and the methodical and strategic purposefulness they bring to serving that value, regardless of discomfort and embarrassment. Chinese women are not alone in worrying about their faces; South Korea has the highest rate of plastic surgery per capita in the world, and Americans are sixth (Marx 2015; see also chapter 8, Topic 8.3).

Mask-wearing also has an instrumental rational purpose. The continued salience of the traditional Chinese proverb, "Fair skin conceals a thousand flaws," makes the masks an efficient way to present a strategically youthful and unblemished visage, and further, to uphold a middle-class status. One mask-wearing woman declared: "A woman should always have fair skin. Otherwise people will think you're a peasant" (Levin 2012: A3). With China's rapidly expanding economic entrepreneurialism, there is a brisk market for masks and for sun-gloves and special cosmetic creams with names such as "White Swan and Snow White, promising a natural-looking aristocratic hue" (Levin 2012: A1, 3). As in other settings, Weber's typology of action helps us appreciate the varied motivations that can illuminate the meaningfulness of behavior that might otherwise seem puzzling. Ironically, in the case of Chinese beach-practices, it is rational commitment to the value of beauty that drives some women to sacrifice beauty temporarily (while on the beach).

POWER, AUTHORITY, AND DOMINATION

Social action and social relationships do not occur in a vacuum, but in societal and institutional contexts characterized by different forms of power and authority, and different sources of legitimation. This is a subject extensively discussed by Weber, who tended to use the terms power, authority, domination, and legitimation interchangeably. For Weber, **power** is "the probability that one actor within a social relationship will be in a position to carry out his own will despite resistance" (ES 53). More precisely, **domination** or authority is:

> the probability that certain specific commands (or all commands) will be obeyed by a given group of persons … Domination may be based on the most diverse motives of compliance: all the way from simple habituation to the most purely rational calculation of advantage. Hence every genuine form of domination implies a minimum of voluntary compliance, that is, an interest (based on ulterior motives or genuine acceptance) in obedience. (ES 212)

Weber gave particular attention to distinguishing between the (ideal) types of

Figure 3.1 Traditions and symbols of tradition still matter and exert authority in modern society. Source: © Arthur Edwards/AP/ Press Association.

domination in modern society compared to earlier times. He noted that authority in modern society is typically **legal authority**, that is, based on norms and rules grounded in a society's collective and intentionally established, impersonal force of law (ES 954). It is imposed by "ruling organizations" (ES 53) such as the state and other bureaucracies (ES 217–220). By contrast, feudal society and other traditional societies and communities are characterized by **traditional authority**. In these contexts, it is personal loyalty to an estate lord or master or to a community elder or religious leader – and loyalty to the community's traditions – which secure individual obedience and compliance (ES 226–241). Thus, "Authority will be called traditional if legitimacy is claimed for it and believed in by virtue of the sanctity of age-old rules and powers. The masters are designated according to traditional rules and are obeyed because of their traditional status" (ES 226).[4]

We see evidence of the legitimacy of traditional authority today in countries that still have a monarchy (e.g., Queen Elizabeth II and the royal family in the UK), and in the global presence of the Catholic Church and Pope Francis. As Weber emphasizes, regarding all ideal typical classifications, "The forms of domination occurring in historical reality constitute combinations, mixtures, adaptations, or modification of these 'pure' [or ideal] types" (ES 954). Highlighting the blurred lines that exist between traditional and rational-legal authority, the Catholic Church, for example, establishes legitimacy through its many age-old traditions, symbols, and rules. But it also relies on a highly rational (and periodically updated) set of modern laws (i.e., canon law) defining specific institutional procedures as well as its property and other rights vis-à-vis its own members and relative to other institutions (e.g., the state). Notably, the Catholic Church has relied more heavily on its legal than its traditional authority in its institutional response to public outrage over priests' sexual abuse of children, though it was traditional authority (e.g., the sacred authority of priests and bishops as perceived by church members as well as by national governments) that largely enabled priests to engage in child sexual abuse and bishops to suppress it.

THE LEGAL AUTHORITY OF THE STATE

In general, however, the state has much greater power and authority than the church in modern society. The state's ability to impose its will despite resistance comes from its unique power: The **nation-state** is legally entitled to engage in violence against other states, and against individuals and groups within its borders.

> A state is a human community that (successfully) claims the monopoly of the legitimate use of physical force within a given territory. Note that "territory" is one of the characteristics of the state ... the right to use physical force is ascribed to other institutions or to individuals only to the extent to which the state permits it. The state is considered the sole source of the "right" to use violence. (FMW 78)

There are two important points to emphasize regarding Weber's definition of the state. First, he defines the nation-state primarily in terms of its legal-political territory and structure; thus, shared ethnic roots, language, or cultural sentiments are not sufficient to constitute a nation (FMW 172–173). Second, he underscores the specific means or instruments that are peculiar to the state, namely legal violence. The state uses physical violence to defend itself (and society) against threats to its security that come both from within the state and from other states and other entities. "The state is valued as the agency that guarantees security, and this is above all the case in times of external danger, when sentiments of national solidarity flare up, at least intermittently" (FMW 177). The terrorist events of 9/11 dramatically violated the physical and cultural security of the US, and the government's response demonstrates the power of the state to strike with physical-military force against the ongoing security threat posed by terrorism. Current world events underscore that the state (acting alone or jointly with other nation-states) engages in physical violence (i.e., warfare) within nation-states (e.g., Afghanistan, Iraq) and against terrorist individuals and groups (e.g., ISIS, Al-Qaeda, Hezbollah) who may or may not be supported financially or logistically by a given state (e.g., Iran, Qatar, Saudi Arabia) or by a formal or informal alliance among a few states.

Again, highlighting the blurred lines between legal and traditional authority, we see, for example, that when the US president – who has extensive legal authority – makes important speeches announcing military action or outlining a new domestic policy program, he does so amidst some of the nation's most powerful symbols of tradition – customarily speaking from the Oval Office in the White House, a space embodying the historical authority that inheres in the tradition of American democracy. Further underscoring the power of tradition that surrounds presidential authority, whenever the president makes a speech there is, typically, an American flag draped in the background.

Marx would emphasize the economic motivation underlying state violence against other states; some neo-Marxists claim, for example, that US military action in the Middle East is "all about oil" (Harvey 2003: 25; see chapter 14). By contrast, Weber notes that political expansion is not always motivated by economic objectives (FMW 164). The glory of power and national prestige for its own sake drives competition between nation-states. Similarly, a nation's interest either in maintaining a historical tradition of geopolitical dominance or in asserting a newly found national pride can also motivate state action vis-à-vis other states. Political expansion, moreover, does not always involve the use of coercion and violence. States seek to dominate other states and to ensure their own prestige and their military, economic, and cultural security through diplomatic initiatives and alliances. Weber argues, "The prestige of power, as such, means in practice the glory of power over other communities; it means the expansion of power, though not always by way of incorporation or subjection. The big political communities are the natural exponents of such pretensions to prestige. Every political structure naturally prefers to have weak rather than strong neighbors" (FMW 160). As witnessed following the collapse of the Soviet Union in 1989, when weak states (e.g., Poland) have strong neighbors (e.g., Russia), they build economic, defensive, and cultural bridges with other strong states (e.g., becoming a member of the European Union) that can, in principle, buffer against their strong neighbor. However, as Poland's resurgent nationalism and government attempts to roll back democratic norms show (e.g., legislation in 2017 curbing the independence of the supreme court), a comparatively weak state can exert power in ways that complicate both its internal and external political relationships. Polish events also illuminate weaknesses in the authority of the stronger state alliance, that is, the ability of the EU to "punish" Poland for its deviation from principles of European democracy.

The state's response to internal threats

The modern state also uses coercion and violence in policing behavior as it responds to criminal activity and other perceived threats to social order within its borders, including those posed by public protests. Specifically, the police force is the institutionalized, legal-rational, bureaucratic structure that monitors behavior within the state. The police are sanctioned and obliged by the state to use physical force to restrain individuals and groups; for example, the state-sanctioned use of force was evident when police in riot gear forced the removal of Occupy protesters in London, Frankfurt, and New York. Most people in society accept the police's use of physical violence as a routinized form of social control. Generally, it is only when the police act with what is perceived as *excessive* physical force that individuals are collectively mobilized to comment on what are, essentially, state-enforced, rational-legal procedures. Notwithstanding the public controversies occasioned by "police brutality" (e.g., Blauner 2001: 193–196), these instances tend to be seen as aberrations rather than the consequence of routine police procedures enacting their legal right to use violence.

In sum, the state has a monopoly on the use of violence. Violence alone, however, is not necessarily the first, and typically not the only, action engaged in by the state in protecting security. The state's use of violence and the degree to which it uses it are themselves determined by a given nation's regard for human rights and political values (e.g., the right to a fair trial). Weighing competing values is a challenging task, and state policies that favor one (e.g., security) over another (e.g., individual freedom) ignite heated public debate. Weber argued, "All political structures use force, but they differ in the manner in which and the extent to which they use or threaten to use it against other political organizations. These differences play a specific role in determining the form and destiny of political communities" (FMW 159).

This point applies well to political debates in democratic countries about the use of torture in interrogating terrorists. A key argument is that democratic states should not engage in the kinds of physical force (suppressing constitutionally protected individual rights) typically associated with nondemocratic, authoritarian regimes. Thus the state's use of physical force, though guaranteed by state law, is constrained by value-rational, cultural norms. Indeed, admission to the club of high-status (economically, socially, and politically) modern nations is contingent on members' demonstrated commitment to human rights (this is an obstacle blocking Turkey's admission to the European Union even though it is a democracy). In short, as Weber would affirm, the political destiny of countries rests on the degree to which their respective states use physical violence and to what ends they use it.

BUREAUCRACY

The state's legal authority is typically institutionalized and exercised through **bureaucracy** (e.g., the Pentagon, the Department of Justice, federal regulatory agencies, the military, etc.). In contemporary society, bureaucratic organization is also evident across many other domains of daily life – economic corporations; television networks (e.g., ESPN, CNN, BBC, Fox); churches, universities, and nonprofit organizations; dentists', doctors', and lawyers' offices; and professional sports teams. The bureaucracies that many of us might encounter on a given day include, most immediately, the university, as well as the federal government (when you apply for financial aid), your local bank (when you apply for a supplementary student loan), the Registry of Motor Vehicles (when you renew your driver's license), your car insurance company, your health clinic. The list is long. Common to all these organizations are legally recognized technical or procedural rules, and official policies and regulations that guide their specific activities and the social relationships in which they are engaged, whether these relationships are with individuals, government departments, corporations, or other bureaucratic organizations.

Bureaucratic authority

Bureaucracies, Weber states, are legitimate structures of domination in modern society. They are formal organizations exerting legal authority over us, making us behave in specific, required ways. Most of the time, we may have little awareness of the multiple ways in which bureaucratic authority pervades daily life. Yet we are readily reminded of bureaucratic authority any time we try to bypass official rules. Any student who has "petitioned" the dean's office for a waiver of some rule is well aware of what bureaucratic authority can entail: if the right form is not completed, if we get in the "wrong" line to speak to the official in charge of these (and not other) specific petitions, if we fail to meet the specified deadline, if we fail to submit all of the required supporting documents, if we forget to secure all the required signatures from other various officials, etc. We are often frustrated by what we see as the inefficiency of bureaucracy, and Weber recognized that it can produce inefficiencies. But he also saw it as the most rational, that is, the most efficient and methodical way of accomplishing tasks in modern society. See Topic 3.5.

Impersonal criteria

Bureaucratic rationality is institutionalized through the application of specific practices and procedures designed to ensure that impersonal (rational) criteria rather than personal or other considerations (of values, emotion, or tradition) determine the outcome of the exchange. For example, when you request a waiver from the dean's office on some college graduation requirement, the person you talk to does not determine your fate on the basis of personal like or dislike, or whether you are related to a prominent person in the community. If college administrators were to be swayed by such considerations, they would not be acting in accord with the (legally enforced) rules of bureaucratic rationality. In traditional (patrimonial) societies, personal criteria (e.g., knowing you or your family) might well play a large part in determining the outcome of your interaction with officials (e.g., college administrators, police officers, school principals); these officials, in turn, likely owe their position to family connections. In modern society, by contrast, impersonal rationality (i.e., based on merit, not personal connections) informs the behavior of, and within, social organizations. And this rationality is institutionalized and routinized through the hierarchical division of labor and the corresponding rules and authority structure that characterize bureaucracies. For example, you cannot walk directly into the dean's office (even if you have an appointment); you will first have to speak to the office receptionist, then perhaps an associate dean, and then the dean. Similarly, under the triage system in medical offices you are first screened by a receptionist, then by the nursing assistant, then by the nurse practitioner, then (if you are *really* sick) by the doctor, and perhaps subsequently by an even more specialized doctor.

Thus, Weber states,

> The purest type of exercise of legal authority is that which employs a bureaucratic administrative staff. Only the supreme chief of the organization occupies his position of dominance by virtue of appropriation, of election, or of having been designated for the succession. But even *his* authority consists in a separate sphere of legal "competence." The whole administrative staff under the supreme authority then consists, in

the purest type, of individual officials … who are appointed and function according to the following criteria: (i) They are personally free and subject to authority only with respect to their impersonal official obligations. (ii) They are organized in a clearly defined hierarchy of offices. (iii) Each office has a clearly defined sphere of competence in the legal sense. (iv) The office is filled by a free contractual relationship. Thus, in principle, there is free selection. (v) Candidates are selected on the basis of technical qualifications. In the most rational case, this is tested by examination or guaranteed by diplomas certifying technical training, or both. They are *appointed* not elected. (vi) They are remunerated by fixed salaries in money, for the most part with a right to pensions. Only under certain circumstances does the employing authority, especially in private organizations, have a right to terminate the appointment, but the official is always free to resign. The salary scale is graded according to rank in the hierarchy; but in addition to this criterion, the responsibility of the position and the requirements of the incumbent's social status may be taken into account. (vii) The office is treated as the sole, or at least the primary, occupation of the incumbent. (viii) It constitutes a career. There is a system of "promotion" according to seniority or to achievement or both. Promotion is dependent on the judgment of superiors. (ix) The official works entirely separated from ownership of the means of administration and without appropriation of his position. (x) He is subject to strict and systematic discipline and control in the conduct of the office. (ES 220–221)

Bureaucratic rules and procedures thus minimize the interference of nonrational forces (e.g., emotional likes and dislikes, tradition) in work and other organizational relationships. Similarly, with a premium on efficiency and competence, the hierarchical organization of expertise and responsibilities ensures that you seek assistance from those most qualified. This expertise is certified or credentialed by an external, objective authority based on rational evaluative criteria of competence. With the rise of the sharing economy (see Topic 1.2), workers are evaluated by service users deploying both emotional (one can like or dislike the Uber driver's attitude) and rational (the punctuality and efficiency of the driver) criteria, thus making the ratings somewhat arbitrary.

Certified expertise

We still see much public evidence of bureaucratic certification (itself a rational process to help us avoid wasting time seeking unqualified help or faulty services/products). Certificates on the walls of various establishments attest to individuals' qualifications (e.g., doctors, dentists, beauticians, garage mechanics). On construction vans, we see that plumbers, carpenters, and electricians are licensed to do the work they advertise. Certification shadows everyday experiences: In restaurants, we see certificates of the restaurant's hygiene standards, in car sales showrooms, we see certificates clarifying the technical and sales information about the car, and, as noted earlier, some Muslim women need certificates of virginity (see Topic 3.2). Specialized Internet websites (e.g., Angie's List, TripAdvisor) and social media (e.g., gossip apps) offer additional or alternative sources of certified authority.

Topic 3.5   Bureaucratic rationality: Bringing order to chaos at the White House

Bureaucratic rules sometimes get in the way of things. After the Brazilian footballer Neymar transferred from Barcelona (for a record-breaking 322 million Euros or $263 million) to Paris Saint Germain (PSG) in August 2017, PSG failed to submit the required international transfer *certificate* to the French League. Neymar, therefore, had to sit out his first game for the club (though fans got to see him in the stadium at least). Bureaucratic organization is the most effective way to get things done, however. It imposes discipline, impersonal norms, and hierarchical authority. When John Kelly, a retired four-star general, was appointed as President Trump's Chief of Staff in July 2017, he quickly went about imposing order on what many reporters had described as a highly chaotic, factionalized and feuding White House. His goal, in his own words, was to "rationalize the chaos" (Thrush and Haberman 2017: A1). Prior to Kelly's arrival, "the president's senior aides enjoyed wide discretion on whom they could meet, what issues they could tackle and when they could bring their thoughts to the president" (Bender and Ballhaus 2017: A10). Among other new rules, Mr. Kelly:

- Instituted a formal process for meetings with the president. This requires President Trump's official advisers, including his daughter Ivanka and son-in-law Jared Kushner (and their respective staff) to report directly to Kelly (and not directly to the president). As a result of the new rules, "Staffers no longer loiter outside an open Oval Office door, hoping to catch the president's eye to be waved in for a chat or a chance to pitch a new idea. The door is now closed. Aides can't linger outside the chief of staff's office either….they are asked to wait in the lobby."
- Laid down "clear lines of authority and ordered aides to stick to their assigned areas." This means that discussions with senators and other elected officials and their staff should be reported to the White House legislative affairs director, and that all discussions with diplomats should be reported to the Secretary of State.
- Required that all paper submissions to the president be screened by Mr. Kelly's office, including unsolicited policy proposals and news articles, "in part to reduce the risk of erroneous material appearing on the presidential Twitter feed."
- Formalized senior staff meetings. Unlike his predecessor who held staff meetings in his office, "where the television was often turned on and where the staff could often redirect the discussion away from the agenda," he holds them in the elegant Roosevelt Room around a long mahogany table.
- Barred senior aides from conducting conflict-ridden, side-debates during Oval Office meetings, ordering them instead to resolve their differences beforehand (Bender and Ballhaus 2017: A4, 10).

CHARISMATIC AUTHORITY

Alongside legal and traditional authority, Weber discusses the significance of a third (ideal) type of legitimation or domination in society: the nonrational authority that derives from **charisma**, that special charm that gives an individual power over others. When charismatic authority is present, it always (and only) resides in a particular *individual*. Groups and organizations do not have charisma (although their leaders may, and hence may be able to expand or consolidate the organization's power). Charismatic authority is an attribute of an individual's personality; we acknowledge this anytime we comment that someone is a "natural" or "born" leader. Weber tells us,

> The term "charisma" will be applied to a certain quality of an individual personality by virtue of which he is considered extraordinary and treated as endowed with supernatural, superhuman, or at least exceptional powers or qualities. These are such as are not accessible to the ordinary person, but are regarded as of divine origin or as exemplary, and on the basis of them the individual concerned is treated as a "leader." (ES 241)

Figure 3.2   In modern society, even those not working in bureaucratic organizations are subject to rational legal authority; mobile food vendors must be licensed to sell food. Source: © Jeff Whyte/iStockphoto.

You may have a friend or family member who you would describe as charismatic, that person who has the extra spark and energy, the one who always seems to manage to persuade you to do something or other. And in the public world we can think of individuals who many people would likely describe as charismatic – who have shown remarkable ability in persuading people to act in particular positive or negative ways. Across history, those who have had charismatic authority include Jesus Christ, John F. Kennedy, Nelson Mandela, the Dalai Lama, Pope John Paul II, Princess Diana, Bill Clinton, Bono, and Oprah Winfrey, among others.

Anticipating Weber's construal of charisma, Harriet Martineau observed that

> Man-worship is as universal a practice as that of the higher sort of religion … Every community has its saints, its heroes, its sages, – whose tombs are visited, whose deeds are celebrated, whose words have become the rules by which men live … Now the moral taste of a people is nowhere more clearly shown than in its choice of idols. (1838: 126)

Today, pop cultural idols Bono and Willie Nelson use their celebrity status and charismatic power to persuade world political leaders and ordinary people to work to redress poverty and hunger. In the corporate world, some chief executive officers (CEOs) have a charisma that gives an extra edge to their business reputation, allowing them (even in retirement) to command financial rewards and acclaim (even when their actual track record may not fully support their gilded reputation).

The perception of charisma

Individuals who follow and defer to a charismatic leader comprise a **charismatic community**. They accept the leader's authority not because this is required by the leader's official authority or credentials, or because of the person's traditional status in the community. They do so rather as "disciples" involved in "an emotional form of communal relationship" (ES 243) and because they *perceive* the charismatic figure as "qualified" to lead them (ES 242). Charismatic leaders are perceived, essentially, as "prophets" or "messiahs," or at least as approximating someone with messianic promise. Charismatic figures, in turn, comport themselves in ways that befit a messiah, projecting the self-confident conviction that they truly are uniquely able to lead their followers to achieve whatever the designated goal may be (ES 631).

Charismatic leaders preserve charismatic authority by showing indifference to the material cares and concerns of the everyday world; like Jesus, they cannot be perceived as personally benefiting from their charisma (ES 633). This can be challenging especially for corporate and celebrity charismatic leaders whose affluent lifestyle may be further enriched by the "charismatic" (and commercial) appeal of their "brand." The Dalai Lama, on the other hand, though he writes best-selling books that earn a lot of money, maintains simplicity in his public demeanor: He dresses in plain, unadorned robes, and his lack of ostentation likely strengthens his followers' convictions about his lofty mission.

The temporality and routinization of charisma

Because charisma inheres in a person (and not in bureaucratic office), when the person dies (or loses credibility), the charisma dies too. This poses a problem: How can the mission or agenda of the charismatic leader continue after their death? Weber argues that the mission can continue only if it is rationalized, that is, if it is converted into an organizational goal. In other words, the charismatic leader's (nonrational) personal (emotional) power must be converted into the rational, impersonal, administrative power of official authority (ES 246–251). This can happen if the goals of the charismatic leader are taken over and routinized through the establishment of a bureaucratic organization rationally equipped to execute those goals. For example, Oprah Winfrey does not rely solely on her own personal charisma but has also established a business corporation (Harpo Productions Inc.) to ensure the (long-term) success of her goals.

The Catholic Church exemplifies the successful **routinization of charisma** (ES 246–249) – the translation of Jesus's personal charismatic authority into enduring symbolic traditions and into bureaucratic organizational hierarchies, rules, and procedures. Weber states:

> In its pure form charismatic authority has a character specifically foreign to everyday routine structures. The social relationships directly involved are strictly personal, based on the validity and practice of charismatic personal qualities. If this is not to remain a purely transitory phenomenon, but to take on the character of a permanent relationship, a community of disciples or followers or a party organization or any sort of [formal] organization, it is necessary for the character of charismatic authority to become radically changed … It cannot remain stable but becomes either traditionalized or rationalized, or a combination of both. (ES 246)

In sum, charismatic authority, though highly effective, is always temporary: It inheres in an individual and ceases with the death (or disgrace, or lack of mission success) of that individual. Charismatic power, therefore, is unstable. It is very different to the institutionalized permanence of both bureaucratic and traditional forms of authority. An organization's goals and routines outlive the individuals who work in and lead the organization, and organizations do not typically rely on the creative energy of any one particular individual in ensuring organizational success and continuity.

Despite the creative energy charismatic leaders contribute to an organization's success – think of the late Steve Jobs at Apple – the organization's structure is highly rationalized (bureaucratized) so that the demise of the leader will be accommodated relatively smoothly by the organizational practices and decision-making structure already methodically in place. Nonetheless, with the death of a charismatic CEO, the company may experience some hiccups in its operations, as occurred when Apple released the iPhone 5 and its map app did not work, thus causing frustration among its loyal customer base.

SOCIAL STRATIFICATION

Like Marx, Weber wrote about inequality or **stratification**, that is, the structures and processes in society which determine individuals' objective location in a hierarchical system of social classes or strata. The stratified location of individuals and groups is based on their differential access to resources and the various forms of authority they can exercise in society. Unlike Marx, however, Weber focused not just on economic resources, but also on how noneconomic resources, specifically social status and political power, create and maintain social inequality. As Weber notes, "Man does not strive for power only in order to enrich himself economically. Power, including economic power, may be valued for its own sake. Very frequently the striving for power is also conditioned by the social honor it entails … 'classes,' 'status groups,' and 'parties' are phenomena of the distribution of power within a community" (ES 926–927).

GRADIENTS OF ECONOMIC INEQUALITY

Weber uses the word **class** to denote individuals' shared economic situation: individuals who have similar economic interests and assets and who have similar life chances as a result of property, income, and labor market opportunity (ES 927). In particular, he distinguishes between property and the lack of property as a major factor differentiating classes, and further, among property owners, its scale and purpose (e.g., entrepreneurial or commercial) (ES 302–304).

Whereas Marx posited two dichotomously opposed classes – capital owners (bourgeoisie) and wage-workers (proletariat) – Weber outlined a more differentiated class structure. He argued that the "middle classes" exist between the "positively privileged property classes" (typically including large-scale owners who receive income from land, mines, factories, ships, creditors, and securities), and the "negatively privileged property classes" (i.e., debtors and paupers). The middle classes broadly encompass individuals variously dependent on income earned from property or acquired skills. They include the "positively privileged" commercial classes (e.g., entrepreneurs and bankers), and professionals with sought-after expertise or training (e.g., lawyers, doctors, artists), and the "negatively privileged" commercial classes (composed of "laborers with varying qualifications; skilled, semiskilled, and unskilled"). Weber summarized four different classes: (1) the working class (laborers); (2) the petty bourgeoisie (self-employed farmers, grocers, and craftsmen); (3) the property-less intelligentsia and specialists (e.g., white-collar employees, civil servants); and (4) the classes privileged through property and education (ES 303).

Given the complexities in today's economy – the extent to which many people work in corporate finance and in upper-managerial and professional strata within corporations – Weber's differentiated class model is more applicable than Marx's to analyzing the specific characteristics of the occupational and class structure. As Weber recognized, investment managers and professional and expert employees occupy a "positively privileged" location vis-à-vis corporate capitalism (without necessarily owning the corporation). They have access to highly rewarding economic opportunities typically less accessible to clerical, skilled, and unskilled workers. Nonetheless, Marx's emphasis on the profit logic and economic inequality structured into capitalist society (chapter 1) continues to make sense in analyzing the organization of work and other social phenomena (e.g., sports), as well as highlighting the economic interests that underpin social relations.

SOCIAL STATUS

Independent of sharing a common economic class, individuals can share a similar social status. **Status** is "an effective claim to social esteem in terms of positive or negative privileges," which typically, according to Weber, are founded on style of life, education, and hereditary or occupational prestige (ES 305–306). In American society, for example, the highest status group historically was composed of white Protestant males, from the upper socioeconomic echelons, and educated at elite private schools and universities (e.g., Harvard, Yale, and Princeton) whose admissions policies excluded those whose profile did not match these criteria of privilege (Karabel 2005: 22–23). This relatively closed system of privilege and inequality began to crack somewhat in the late 1960s when elite universities expanded the admission of women, blacks, Jews, and Catholics (Karabel 2005). In the UK, Oxford and Cambridge universities remain as the premier destinations for the children of the British elite as well as for those from highly privileged families in ex-British colonial countries (e.g., India, Pakistan). Despite an overall increase in access to university, race and gender continue to be major sources of status (and economic) inequality, as underscored by the exclusion of women and racial minorities from full membership in some elite golf and country clubs.

Status and class

Weber emphasizes that status and prestige are not solely determined by economic class, even though the costly fees entailed in admission to exclusive housing developments and prestigious colleges and country clubs highlight the close relation between economic class and social status. Nevertheless, a person might have a lot of wealth but little prestige or honor in the community. This may be because the individual's family "pedigree" is less "pure" than that of others: Their wealth might be "new" (e.g., the *nouveau riche*) rather than accumulated over many family generations. As Weber notes, "Mere economic power, and especially 'naked' money power, is by no means a recognized basis of social honor" (ES 926). Money, nonetheless, makes it easier for families to send their children to elite colleges, which, in turn, confer prestige of their own as well as enhancing the occupational, lifestyle, and related status opportunities available to those graduates. Similarly, some country clubs are more elitist (and more costly) than others. Gaining access to the more prestigious club readily confers status on a given individual and establishes additional opportunities for consolidating one's status in the community, through sponsorship of charity or philanthropic causes, hosting political events, etc.

Membership of a particular status group confers prestige, but it also obliges a certain "style of life" (ES 932–933): Group members must maintain particular lifestyle visibly shared with others of similar status (e.g., what neighborhoods or towns to live in; whom to marry; what restaurants to dine at). Thus, "a specific style of life is expected from all those who wish to belong to the [status] circle" (ES 932). These expectations may account for why there is high demand today from newly super-rich Russian, Chinese, and Middle

Figure 3.3 In many societies, success in sports is rewarded with social prestige and economic rewards, including for the Norwegian women's soccer team (pictured here) who since 2018 have pay parity with their male counterparts. Source: © Lars Baron – FIFA/Getty Images.

Eastern business magnates for British-trained butlers, a core vestige of Britain's landed aristocracy (as seen in the popular television series *Downton Abbey*). In their new elite economic status, they seek to acquire a traditional marker of "old money" prestige.

Weber presciently recognized the consumption-driven status lifestyles prevalent today: "Every status society lives by conventions, which regulate the style of life, and hence creates economically irrational consumption patterns" (ES 307). "Keeping up with the Joneses" in order to signal social status (or status aspirations) can be economically costly, leading to the (nonrational) impulsive embrace of particular consumption fads. At the same time, such behavior has a rational dimension insofar as purchases are instrumentally used to achieve a rationally calculated social end (status). Importantly, too, independent of consumption, laws determine status behavior; all formally organized clubs and associations are bound by legally enforced rules regulating members' behavior (a point highlighted on HBO's television comedy show *Curb Your Enthusiasm*, when the show's main protagonist, Larry David, is expelled from his golf club for his persistent [and never subtle!] rudeness to other members). One final point on the class–status relation: Weber notes that in times of economic and technological transformation, it is typically class situation (economic power) that comes to the fore as the primary source of stratification, whereas in economically settled or stable contexts, it is status that tends to have primacy (ES 938). This insight helps to illuminate the apparent primacy of "naked money power" (ES 926) in stratifying individuals today amid the wealth gains generated by the Internet-digital economy. Historically in India, for example, status-honor (e.g., related to family caste) was somewhat independent of economic assets. Today, however, the transformative expansion of capitalism makes the pursuit of economic capital and what it can buy the more salient status marker. (See also chapter 14.)

POLITICAL POWER

Economic class and social status, though analytically independent sources of stratification and authority, can influence and overlap one another. An additional source of stratification is differential access to political or social power. Political groups and associations, or **parties**, engage in action "oriented toward the acquisition of social power, that is to say, toward influencing social action no matter what its content may be. In principle, parties may exist in a social club as well as in a state" (ES 938). Thus, politics is "the striving to influence the distribution of power, either among states or among groups within a state" (FMW 78). Within any given club, community, or society, we all engage to varying degrees in political behavior, seeking to influence the distribution of power.

The goals toward which parties plan their actions may be issue oriented or ideological (e.g., workers' safety, gender and racial equality, environmental protection, LGBTQ rights). Or the goals may be personal like seeking prestige and honor for a party leader and/or for specific party members (ES 938). Typically, political power aims toward the achievement of both ideological/issue and personal goals. Weber notes, "*all* party struggles are struggles for the patronage of office, as well as struggles for objective goals" (FMW 87). Indeed, at times, it is hard to differentiate between these goals insofar as an individual's reputation/political clout and the ideological issues they fight for get entwined.

Power can be attained in several ways. Voting and campaign behavior certainly matter but so too do other means (ES 938). Weber points out that political power can be achieved through the influence of money (as also emphasized by Marx; see chapter 1), by social status and through coercive, illegal, and sometimes even violent means. Democracies emphasize the procedural (e.g., one person, one vote) and substantive (e.g., equality) values that inhere in the legally rational, democratic electoral process. Yet, these principles are not always observed in practice. In fledgling democratic societies (e.g., Kenya, Iraq,

Lebanon), moreover, violence by one party against another is a frequent occurrence, though violence between political parties within the same democratic state tends to be rare and illegal; as discussed previously, violence is the legal right of the state, and can only be legitimately approved by the state.

MODERNITY AND COMPETING VALUES

Another subject that Weber addressed and that has much salience today is the tension among conflicting values and their negotiation. The unfettered march of progress, propelled by advances in science and technology, means that modern societies have the capability to accomplish many goals. The triumph of reason and science over mythical and magical thinking, first celebrated by Enlightenment thinkers (see Introduction), has not freed us, however, from confronting the question: "What is the value of science?" (FMW 140). What **values**, what ends, should science serve? The ongoing discoveries of science – regarding cancer, stem cells, genetic engineering, climate change – do not resolve for us how we as a society should deal with these issues.

SCIENCE AND VALUES

Science does not, and cannot, tell us how to use science and its findings. This is a point strongly emphasized by Weber. Scientific tools and data do not help us rank priorities regarding what topics merit scientific investigation, or which projects should be funded with federal money, and who should benefit from scientific discovery. These are all questions about values. And the tensions that invariably emerge between competing values and value stances are glaringly obvious in public debates about global warming, abortion, end of life care, DNA testing, etc. Weber quotes the great Russian novelist Leo Tolstoy to underscore the enormous challenge that modern societies encounter in deciding among diverse values: "Science is meaningless because it gives no answer to our question, the only question important for us: 'What shall we do and how shall we live?'" (FMW 143).

Many in society fully embrace the intrinsic and practical value of scientific knowledge and its relevance to advancing economic and social progress. But as Weber highlights, it cannot "be proved that the existence of the world which these sciences describe is worth while, that it has any 'meaning,' or that it makes sense to live in such a world. Science does not ask for the answers to such questions" (FMW 144). And we should not expect it to. Scientists, no matter how well qualified and distinguished, cannot use their scientific expertise to answer society's questions about what is meaningful, worthwhile, or morally right. And neither can sociologists, nor experts in any field of study (FMW 145). What shall we do? And how shall we arrange our lives (FMW 152–153)? These are questions that transcend science. Scientific data certainly inform our public debates, as we see on climate change, for example (though contested; see Introduction Topic I.2). But scientific data alone can never determine how we use scientific data nor how we decide among competing values (see also chapter 4, Box 4.3). These ultimately are collective, political decisions about what sort of society we want to create and maintain.

THE VALUE NEUTRALITY OF SCIENCE

It is our duty as scientists and sociologists, Weber argues, to present all the data pertaining to a given topic, and not simply to document that which agrees with our personal opinions. We are not politicians or demagogues. They are obliged to take a political stand; it is legitimate for them to be partisan and to strongly canvass and defend their stance against opposing views. But politics, Weber emphasizes, does not "belong in the lecture room"; the "prophet and the demagogue do not belong on the academic platform" (FMW 145–146); each has its own distinct sphere. Moreover, "'scientific' pleading is meaningless in principle because the various value spheres [e.g., economic development, environmental preservation] ... stand in irreconcilable conflict with each other ... different gods struggle with one another, now and for all times to come" (FMW 147–148). Our fate is to decide which of the warring gods to serve. Only prophets or saviors (e.g., political and religious leaders), Weber argues, can help us with this, not bureaucrats or scientists whose credentialed, professional expertise requires them to maintain **value neutrality**.

The principle of value neutrality or **objectivity** is the professional ethic of the scientist (see also chapter 4, Box 4.3). We as individuals have our own values and passions. But, we should not, Weber argues, let them impose on the conduct of our research or on our sociological interpretations. We should be passionate about our work – as Weber states, "nothing is worthy of man as man unless he can pursue it with passionate devotion" (FMW 135). Regardless of our own opinions and values, however, we must be open to the findings we uncover in our data gathering and analysis. Sociologists (and all scientists) must be open, and teach students to be open, to recognizing "inconvenient facts" (FMW 147). In other words, as Durkheim also outlines (chapter 2), we need to be open to any and all ideas, data, and occurrences that contravene our personal beliefs and opinions about how the world works.

Objectivity in cultural context

Whereas Durkheim also emphasized sociological objectivity (see chapter 2), Weber's understanding is much more contextual. Recall that Weber defined sociology as a science concerning itself with the interpretive understanding of subjectively meaningful social action (ES 4). The objectivity Weber proposes, therefore, requires the sociologist to investigate and understand (i.e., interpret) the subjective meanings that social actors inject into behavior. Such understanding is impossible without appreciation of the cultural and historical context in which meaningful behavior occurs (as Weber himself showed in the *Protestant Ethic*). Therefore, whereas Durkheim's command to "treat social facts as things" (chapter 2) suggests that social facts can be objectively studied independent of the societal context (i.e., independent of both the facts and the sociologist), for Weber, the objective analysis of social phenomena (e.g., work, family, religion, capitalism, bureaucracy) is always historically and culturally grounded. Thus Weber emphasized that knowledge, including what we study and how, is shaped by cultural context:

> All knowledge of cultural reality ... is always knowledge from *particular points of view*. When we require [researchers to] ... distinguish the important from the trivial ... we mean that they must understand how to relate the events of the real world ... to universal "cultural values" and to select out those relationships which are significant for us. If the notion that those standpoints can be derived from the "facts themselves" continually recurs, it is due to the naïve self-deception of the specialist who is unaware that it is due to the evaluative ideas with which he unconsciously approaches his subject matter ... Cultural science ... involves subjective presuppositions insofar as it concerns itself only with those components of reality which have some relationships, however indirect, to events to which we attach cultural significance. Nonetheless, it is entirely causal knowledge exactly in the same sense as the knowledge of significant concrete natural events which have a qualitative character. (MSS 82–83)

For Weber, then, the attainment of objectivity in sociological understanding and explanation is not at the expense of either scientific rigor or the historical and cultural context in which science, and social life as a whole, occur. Recognition of how different contexts inform everyday experiences and social relations, and disrupt notions of an allegedly pure objectivity, is a critical theme elaborated by contemporary feminist theorists (see chapter 10).

SUMMARY

Weber's theorizing engages with a remarkable breadth of topics: How culture and ideas, not just material interests, matter in shaping social and institutional behavior; the many ways in which rational and nonrational motivations permeate everyday individual, group, and institutional practices; the varied sources of authority and legitimation in society; the multiple sources of social stratification; values dilemmas; and contextual objectivity in science.

POINTS TO REMEMBER

- Weber defined sociology as the interpretive understanding of subjectively meaningful social action in its historical and cultural context
- Weber uses ideal types – descriptions of the standardized and accentuated characteristics of a particular social phenomenon – to assist in comparative analysis of social structures/social action

Weber analyzed the relation between ideas and economic structures and modern capitalist culture in his study of the Protestant/Calvinist ethic.

- This entails historical understanding of the Reformation, its leader, Martin Luther, and Luther's disciple, John Calvin
- Calvinist tenets:
  - The purpose of this-worldly activities is to serve an all-powerful God
  - The individual stands alone before God (no mediating structures/relationships)
  - God's will cannot be known
  - Predestination: one's fate (heaven/hell) already decided by God
    - Deal with uncertainty about salvation through this-worldly rationalization
    - Work as a calling; hard work for the glorification of God
    - Time not spent in work is sinful, that is, not glorifying God
    - Ascetic conduct in this world; sobriety, frugality
    - Doctrine of proof: this-worldly success (based on disciplined, methodical hard work) is a *sign* of other-worldly salvation
- The Protestant ethic:
  - Accelerated the expansion of capitalism: economic profits from work invested (not spent on nonwork activities)
  - Contributed to advancing an ethos of individualism (e.g., self-reliance; "God helps those who help themselves")

Weber identified four (ideal) types of social action:

- Instrumental rational action: strategic, means–end, cost–benefit analysis
- Value-rational action: values (e.g., equality, loyalty) set the ends/goals pursued irrespective of costs
- Emotional action
- Traditional action; habit, custom

Weber identified three (ideal) types of authority/domination:
- Traditional authority
- Rational legal authority:
  - The state
  - Bureaucratic, hierarchical organization
- Charismatic authority; individual; unstable, needs to be routinized to ensure the continuation of goals

Stratification
- Class; economic
- Status; prestige, lifestyle
- Party; political power

Science and values
- Science cannot tell us what goals to pursue or what values to cherish
- Scientific inquiry requires value neutrality or objectivity; personal and political values have no place in the conduct of research and academic analysis
- Objectivity does not preclude attentiveness to the relevance of historical and cultural context

GLOSSARY

asceticism avoidance of emotion and spontaneous enjoyment as demonstrated by the disciplined, methodical frugality and sobriety of the early Calvinists.

bureaucracy formal organizational structure characterized by rationality legal authority, hierarchy, credentialed and certified expertise, and impersonal rules and procedures.

calling intrinsically felt obligation toward work; work valued as its own reward, an opportunity to glorify God.

Calvinism theology derived from John Calvin; emphasis on the lone individual whose afterlife is already predestined at birth by God.

charisma nonrational authority held by an individual who is perceived by others to have a special personal gift for leadership.

charismatic community group of individuals (disciples) who follow and defer to a charismatic individual's personal leadership authority.

class individuals who share an objectively similar economic situation determined by property, income, and occupational resources.

domination authority/legitimacy; the probability that individuals and groups will be persuaded/obliged to comply with a given command.

emotional action subjectively meaningful, nonrational social action motivated by feelings.

ideal type an exhaustive description of the characteristics distinctive to, and expected of, a given phenomenon (e.g. of a bureaucracy).

individualism cultural ethos of individual independence, responsibility, and self-reliance.

instrumental rational action behavioral decisions or actions (of individuals, groups, organizations, etc.) based on calculating, strategic, cost–benefit analysis of goals and means.

interpretive understanding *Verstehen*; task of the sociologist in making sense of the varied motivations that underlie meaningful action; because sociology studies human lived experience (as opposed to physical phenomena), sociologists need a methodology enabling them to empathically understand human-social behavior.

legal authority based on rational, impersonal norms and rules; imposed by the state and other bureaucratic organizations; dominant in modern societies.

nation-state rational, legal, bureaucratic actor; has specific territorial interests; entitled to use physical force to protect and defend its internal and external security.

nonrational action behavior motivated by emotion and/or tradition rather than by reasoned judgment.

objectivity the professional obligation of scientists, researchers, and teachers to report and discuss "inconvenient facts," that is, facts that disagree with or contradict their personal feelings and opinions.

other-worldly nonmaterial motivations; e.g., after-death salvation; the opposite of this-worldly.

parties political groups or associations that seek to influence the distribution of power in society.

power the probability that a social actor (e.g., the state, an organization, an individual) can impose its will despite resistance.

predestination Calvinist belief that an individual's salvation is already determined at birth by God.

Puritan ethic emphasis on disciplined and methodical work, sober frugality, and the avoidance of spontaneous emotion.

rational action behavior motivated by a deliberate, analytical (reasoned) evaluation of a social actor's (e.g. an individual, a group, an organization) goals/ends and the means by which to pursue them.

rationality emphasis on the objective and impersonal authority of reason in deliberating about, and evaluating explanations of, social behavior/social phenomena.

routinization of charisma the rational translation of individual charisma into organizational goals and procedures.

status social esteem or prestige associated with style of life, education, and hereditary or occupational prestige.

stratification inequality between groups (strata) in society based on differences in economic resources, social status and prestige, and political power.

subjectively meaningful action individuals/groups engage in behavior that is subjectively meaningful (or important) to them and that takes account of, and is oriented to, the behavior of others.

this-worldly the material reality of the everyday world in which we live and work.

traditional action nonrational, subjectively meaningful social action motivated by custom and habit.

traditional authority derived from long-established traditions or customs; dominant in traditional societies but coexists in modern society with legal-bureaucratic and charismatic authority.

value neutrality the idea that scientists and researchers do not inject their personal beliefs and values into the conduct, evaluation, and presentation of their research.

value-rational action rational, purposeful behavior (of individuals, groups, organizations, etc.) motivated by commitment to a particular value (e.g., loyalty, environmental sustainability, education) and independent of the probability of its successful outcome.

values what a social actor (e.g., an individual, a group, an organization) values (such as equality, or environmental preservation); raises questions concerning the goals or ends that individuals, organizations, institutions, and societies should purposefully embrace and pursue.

Verstehen German for "understanding"; refers to the process by which sociologists seek interpretive understanding of the subjective meanings that individuals and collectivities give to their behavior/social action.

QUESTIONS FOR REVIEW

1   How is it possible for social action to be meaningful without it being rational?
2   Why does Weber argue that we need to pay attention to, and understand the beliefs or worldviews of individuals and groups? How can we do this as sociologists?
3   How does Weber's analysis of stratification differ from that of Marx?
4   What are the various forms of authority in contemporary society? Which ones are the most imposing?
5   Why are ongoing debates about climate change, for example, or abortion, not resolvable by making recourse to the available scientific information pertaining to these topics?

NOTES

1   In citing Weber's writings, I reference the book's initials rather than the date of publication. A list of Weber's core writings, their date of publication, and the book title initials I use to reference them follows the biographical note.

Some everyday personal routines, for example, brushing teeth, can be considered *social* action insofar as we are keenly aware that not brushing our teeth would diminish our status among friends; action is social action if it is meaningfully oriented to, and takes account of, the reactions of others (cf. ES 23–24).

2 There is no apparent evidence that Weber was familiar with Martineau's ideas (see Hoecker-Drysdale 1992).

3 Weber is criticized for exaggerating the occupational and economic differences between Catholics and Protestants (e.g., Giddens 1976: 12). Nonetheless, whatever the historical-empirical accuracy of Weber's claims, the thesis he outlines in *The Protestant Ethic* is still highly relevant in helping us understand the cultural origins of Western (and today's globalizing capitalist) economy and society.

4 Weber tends to refer to feudal relationships and to other similarly traditional social arrangements as representing a *patrimonial* system of authority; this refers essentially to a system of personal loyalty to, and dependence on, a lord or master (e.g., ES 231–236; 1070–1073). In contemporary society, we might think of the relationships depicted in *The Godfather* and *The Sopranos* as approximating patrimonial relationships – the preeminent criterion determining the behavior of the Godfather's associates, subordinates, and bodyguards (and the privileges they receive) is loyalty or fidelity to the Godfather.

REFERENCES

Bender, Michael, and Rebecca Ballhaus. 2017. "The West Wing's New Sheriff." *Wall Street Journal* (August 5–6), pp. A1, 10.

Blauner, Robert. 2001. *Still the Big News: Racial Oppression in America*. Philadelphia: Temple University Press.

Gerth, H.H., and C. Wright Mills. 1946. "Introduction: A Biographical View." Pp. 1–31 in Max Weber, *From Max Weber: Essays in Sociology*. Translated, edited, and with an introduction by H.H. Gerth and C. Wright Mills. New York: Oxford University Press.

Giddens, Anthony. 1976. "Introduction." Pp. 1–12b in Max Weber, 1904–1905/1958. *The Protestant Ethic and the Spirit of Capitalism*. Translated by Talcott Parsons. New York: Scribner's and Sons.

Harvey, David. 2003. *The New Imperialism*. Oxford: Oxford University Press.

Hoecker-Drysdale, Susan. 1992. *Harriet Martineau: First Woman Sociologist*. Oxford: Berg

Karabel, Jerome. 2005. *The Chosen: The Hidden History of Admission and Exclusion at Harvard, Yale, and Princeton*. Boston: Houghton Mifflin.

Levin, Dan. 2012. "Beach Essentials in China: Flip-Flops, a Towel and a Ski Mask." *New York Times* (August 6), pp. A1, 3.

Martineau, Harriet. 1838. *How to Observe Morals and Manners*. London: Charles Knight.

Marx, Patricia. 2015. "About Face: Why is South Korea the World's Plastic Surgery Capital?" *New Yorker* (March 23), pp. 50–55.

Pew Research Center. 2015. *US Public Becoming Less Religious*. Washington, DC: Pew Research Center.

Sanghavi, Darshak. 2006. "Wanting Babies Like Themselves, Some Parents Choose Genetic Defects." *New York Times* (December 5), pp. D5, 8.

Sciolino, Elaine, and Souad Mekhennet. 2008. "Muslim Women and Virginity: Two Worlds Collide." *New York Times* (June 11), pp. A1, 13.

Taub, Amanda. 2016. "Behind the Gathering Turmoil, a Crisis of White Identity." *New York Times* (November 2).

Thrush, Glenn, and Maggie Haberman. 2017. "Forceful Chief of Staff Grates on Trump, and the Feeling is Mutual." *New York Times* (September 1), p. A1.

Weber, Max. 1904–1905/1958. *The Protestant Ethic and the Spirit of Capitalism*. Translated by Talcott Parsons. Introduction by Anthony Giddens. New York: Scribner's and Sons [1976].

Weber, Max. 1946. *From Max Weber: Essays in Sociology*. Translated, edited, and with an introduction by H.H. Gerth and C. Wright Mills. New York: Oxford University Press.

Weber, Max. 1949. *The Methodology of the Social Sciences*. Translated and edited by Edward A. Shils and Henry A. Finch. New York: Free Press.

Weber, Max. 1978. *Economy and Society*, volume 1. Edited by Guenther Roth and Claus Wittich. Berkeley: University of California Press.

CHAPTER FOUR

AMERICAN CLASSICS: THE CHICAGO SCHOOL, TALCOTT PARSONS, AND ROBERT MERTON

KEY CONCEPTS

public sociology
pragmatism
working concepts
self-fulfilling prophecy
human ecology
social disorganization
cultural lag
marginal man
grand theory
social system
functions
structural-functionalist
subsystems
adaptation
goal attainment
integration
latency (pattern maintenance)

unit act
voluntaristic action
cultural system
value system
personality system
secularization
Christianizing of secular society
pattern variables
universalistic versus particularistic
specificity versus diffuseness
achievement versus ascription
neutrality versus affectivity
self versus collectivity
modernization theory
status differentials

uneven modernization
middle-range theory
functional analysis
manifest functions
latent functions
deviance
institutionalized means
cultural goals
conformist
innovator
ritualist
retreatist
rebel
neofunctionalism
autopoiesis
civil sphere
noncivil sphere

Introduction to Sociological Theory: Theorists, Concepts, and Their Applicability to the Twenty-First Century, Third Edition. Michele Dillon.
© 2020 John Wiley & Sons Ltd. Published 2020 by John Wiley & Sons Ltd.
Companion website: www.wiley.com/go/dillon

CHAPTER MENU

THE CHICAGO SCHOOL OF SOCIOLOGY

The first sociology department in the US was established at the University of Chicago in 1892, and a couple of years later its faculty founded the *American Journal of Sociology* (1895). The Chicago School of Sociology (1915–1935) is the label given to the intellectually diverse group of Chicago scholars whose work decisively elevated the development of sociology. Its main focus was qualitative empirical studies of urban communities, a legacy that vastly expanded the rich ethnographic tradition pioneered by W.E.B. Du Bois's study of *The Philadelphia Negro* (1899) (Anderson and Massey 2001: 3–4). The research and writing of the Chicago School showed that sociology was a discipline particularly well-suited to studying and making sense of modern industrial society and the forces of social change. In the late-nineteenth and early twentieth century, Chicago was a rapidly growing, bustling, industrial city, home to many of the thousands of European immigrants who headed to America, to many rural migrants from its farming hinterlands, and to a steadily growing black population (Bulmer 1984: 12-13). The city became a natural laboratory for the Chicago sociologists. They studied its spatial organization, its social structure, and its ethnically diverse populations and their everyday habits.

LOCAL PRAGMATIC KNOWLEDGE

Amid larger political debates over social problems and social reforms (e.g., the Progressive Movement), the Chicago sociologists focused on the practical life contexts of individuals, families, and communities and the social relations, social processes and problems that arise with urbanism and social change. Their landmark studies exemplified the breadth of qualitative empirical resources relevant to sociological inquiry. They variously combined fieldwork, including firsthand observation of events, oral life histories, personal letters and diaries, newspapers, church records and parish histories, social-geographical mapping, and ecological analysis. Distinctive to the Chicago School was the "blending of firsthand inquiry with general ideas, the integration of research and theory as part of an organized program" (Bulmer 1984: 3). Their theorizing was not about abstract generalization but about delving into the local empirical world and drawing out findings and conclusions that they advanced as typical or prototypical of a given social phenomenon (e.g., Chicago as exemplary of the modern industrial city) or of a social process more generally (e.g., urbanization, immigration, social change). In this endeavor, some Chicago researchers engaged with local on-the-ground activists thus setting an example for what in recent years has come to be known as a strand of **public sociology** (Burawoy 2005). Most notably, the social activist Jane Addams (1860–1935) spearheaded conversations among academics, politicians, and reformers about both the measurement and the implications of social problems (Bulmer 1984: 23–25).

The Chicago School's practical, Chicago-anchored research reflected a philosophical strand dominant in American intellectual circles at the time, namely **pragmatism**, associated in particular with Charles Peirce (1839–1914). It emphasized the practical conditions for and consequences of social interaction. Peirce's fellow pragmatists include the psychologist William James (1842–1910) and the philosopher John Dewey (1859–1952), popularly known for inventing the Dewey decimal system used in libraries as an efficient way to categorize books by subject and author. Of particular significance to sociological theory, pragmatism influenced George Herbert Mead (1863–1961) who spent most of his career at the University of Chicago. Mead's insights on the centrality of symbolic exchange in the development of the self are foundational to symbolic interactionism (discussed in chapter 8). The phenomenological theorizing of Alfred Schutz is also influenced by pragmatism, and his conceptualization of typifications and everyday sense-making was translated and elaborated into the influential social constructionism of Peter Berger and Thomas Luckmann (discussed in chapter 9).

The Chicago School was interested in **working concepts**. As Robert Park (1864–1944), one of its foremost figures explained: Sociology "could not have anything like scientific research unless we had a system of classification and a frame of reference into which we could sort out and describe in general terms the things we were attempting to investigate" (see http://www.asanet.org/about-asa/asa-story/asa-history/past-asa-officers/presidents). Based on their wide-ranging empirical investigations,

Chicago sociologists made several important theoretical contributions. Among the most renowned, W.I. Thomas and Florian Znaniecki's (1927) *The Polish Peasant in Europe and America* is exemplary of sociology's distinctive way of framing the structural and cultural analysis of social life. It established immigration, migration, and community as topics of sociological inquiry and among its many rich findings, drew attention to the significance of local group associations and economic institutions in the adaptation of individuals and families to social change. It "was a landmark because it attempted to integrate theory and data in a way no American study had done before" (Bulmer 1984: 45), and resulted in the prominence of such concepts as adaptation, adjustment, and assimilation.

A prolific scholar, Thomas (1864–1947) also developed what Robert Merton (1948/1996: 183) admiringly called the Thomas theorem: If people define situations as real, they are real in their consequences. The *definition of the situation* (1923) is central to symbolic interactionism (see chapter 8). More generally, as a **self-fulfilling prophecy** it can be a crucial mechanism of institutional and social change, that is, people's (possibly false) perceptions of a given situation lead them to behave in ways that result in bringing about an objectively changed reality).

HUMAN ECOLOGY

Park (1936) innovatively construed social life in terms of **human ecology**. Influenced by Charles Darwin's focus on "the struggle for life" among different plants and animals, Park argued that the social life of human populations could be construed as "a process of competitive cooperation." In his ecological conceptualization, "the essential characteristics of a community [are] (1) a population territorially organized, (2) more or less completely rooted in the soil it occupies, (3), its individual units living in a relationship of mutual interdependence that is symbiotic [i.e., organically interrelated in a complex relationship of interdependence]" (Park 1936: 4).

Park's focus on the ecology of the city and the correlation between spatial and social relations is foundational to urban sociology and the sociology of community. He and his colleagues, including Ernest Burgess (e.g., Park et al. 1925) and Louis Wirth (1938), mapped the city's spatial organization around different population groups and interdependent functions (e.g., various types of business and of residential areas). They documented how spatial relations give rise to various place-attachment patterns and ethnic group solidarities, as well as institutional and intergroup competition. They also highlighted **social disorganization** (e.g., the ecological concentration of social problems such as poverty, tenement housing, and crime). Another colleague, William Ogburn (1927–1951), using survey and social indicator data, highlighted variation in patterns of community adjustment to social change. He introduced the concept of **cultural lag** (1957/1964) to capture how social problems arise when some aspects of a community's norms (e.g., attachment to family or neighborhood) are at odds with other aspects (e.g., economic aspirations), a construct also influential in modernization theory (discussed later). Scholars in the 1970s showed a revived interest in ecological principles, applying them to the organizational ecology of firms.

Beyond urban and community sociology and the study of social change, other important Chicago School theoretical contributions include Park's differentiation of "the public" from "the crowd," influential in the understanding of collective behavior (subsequently refined by social movement researchers). And like Mead, his insights on the self and self-conception shaped the sociological analysis of social roles. His construal of the **marginal man** (1928) who moves between different, possibly conflicting, racial/cultural contexts, takes on renewed significance today amid debates about cultural diversity and the multiple mobilities and dislocations of contemporary global society (see chapters

12–15). Notwithstanding the Chicago School's multifaceted theoretical contributions, the recognition of its significance to the development of sociological theory was eclipsed by Talcott Parsons.

TALCOTT PARSONS

Talcott Parsons is a towering figure in sociology. Although his name is less frequently invoked in sociology classrooms today compared to a few decades ago (the 1940s–1980s), his impact on the development of sociology is immense. His theorizing provides both a bridge to the classical tradition and the stimulus that led many of his peers and successors to enrich contemporary theory with empirically based reconceptualizations in conversation with his highly generalizing **grand theory**. Though Parsons was criticized for his tendency toward abstraction and social conservatism, recent years have seen a revival of interest in his ideas (see, e.g., Alexander 1985; Moss and Savchenko 2006).

BIOGRAPHICAL NOTE

Talcott Parsons was born in Colorado in 1902. His father was a (Protestant) Congregational minister who served on the faculty and as dean at Colorado College; the family emphasized a modest and disciplined lifestyle. Parsons completed his undergraduate education at Amherst College (in Massachusetts), and subsequently studied at the London School of Economics (LSE), and the University of Heidelberg (Germany), where he received his PhD, based on his analysis of capitalism in German thought (including Weber's). In 1927, Parsons became an instructor in the Department of Economics at Harvard University; he transferred in 1930 to the newly created Sociology Department, where he received tenure, and subsequently was a founding member of Harvard's interdisciplinary Department of Social Relations, which combined sociology, cultural anthropology, and social psychology. Parsons married Helen Walker, whom he had met while at the LSE, and they had three children. He remained at Harvard until his death in 1979. During his lifetime, Parsons received many national and international awards and honors, and served as president of the American Sociological Association (1949–1950) (Lidz 2000: 389–398).

DEVELOPING SOCIOLOGICAL THEORY

In the 1930s, when Parsons returned to the US having completed his PhD at the University of Heidelberg (where Max Weber had been professor until his death in 1920), American sociology was primarily defined by the Chicago School. In contrast to its emphasis on "working concepts," Parsons (1949/1954: 212–213) was determined to provide a systematic, abstract, and generalizable theory of social action. He wanted sociology to be a theoretically informed science whose analytical laws would be applicable to any society, and he saw the development of theory as essential to sociology's growth and maturation. Despite Parsons's commitment to developing a broad, general, and integrated theory about how society, the **social system**, works, he was not interested in theory for the sake of theory. He wanted a generalizable theory of society that other sociologists would apply in specific societal contexts and use to make sense of the empirical data they gathered. In turn, he believed that the empirical puzzles sociologists encountered on the ground would propel him and others to rework and modify theories to take account of such realities. Therefore, although Parsons repudiated an empiricism that "blindly rejects the help of theoretical tools" (1949/1954: 220), he strongly argued for the blending of theory and data (1949/1954: 220, 364, 366).

PARSONS'S INTELLECTUAL DEBT TO WEBER AND DURKHEIM

The Structure of Social Action (Parsons 1937) provides a densely argued analysis of the writings of Weber and Durkheim (and of the Italian economist Alfred Pareto). It became the gateway to sociological theory for American and other English-speaking students. Additionally, Parsons played a critical role in making Weber's work accessible, having translated *The Protestant Ethic* (in 1930). Parsons's theorizing is influenced by Weber, but it also integrates distinct elements from Durkheim. For Parsons, as for Weber and Durkheim, individual behavior cannot be understood in terms of individuals' internal processes (what psychologists study), but in the context of the social structures and the cultural values that invariably constrain the individual and determine all social action.

THE SOCIAL SYSTEM

Parsons regarded all social units, whether groups, institutions or whole societies as self-contained social systems (1949/1954: 13) or social action systems; each could be studied and analyzed in its own right. Like Durkheim, who underscored the **functions** of specific social structures (e.g., division of labor, crime, religion), Parsons is regarded as a **structural-functionalist**, because he focused on analyzing the structure of the social system (society) and its subsystems (social institutions and structures), and their consequences for, or functional relevance in, maintaining society, social order, or system equilibrium (Parsons 1951: 21–22).

Society, for Parsons, is an action system "analytically divisible into four primary subsystems" of action (Parsons 1971: 10) – economy, politics, law, and culture. These four **subsystems** are the core institutional structure of modern societies established to accomplish the economic, political, societal integration, and cultural socialization functions necessary for societies to maintain themselves and adapt to change. These core functions are (1) **adaptation** to the environment (e.g., economic production); (2) **goal attainment** (the political system with, in democratic societies, the goals of equality and universal rights); (3) **integration** into the societal community by articulating and enforcing society's collective norms (e.g., the legal system); and (4) **latency** or **pattern maintenance**, that is, the intergenerational transmission of society's generally shared values through socialization (e.g., the family, education) so that the value or normative orientations of society effectively regulate individual behavior and social action (Parsons 1971: 10–15). See Box 4.1.

Box 4.1	The functional requirements (A, G, I, L) of society as an action system composed of four subsystems of action

Adaptation (A)	**Goal attainment (G)**
Economic subsystem	Political subsystem
Integration (I)	**Latency (L)**
Legal subsystem	Cultural subsystem

(Adapted from Parsons 1971, Table 2, p. 11)

A functionalist analysis of the education system, for example, would show that in the mid-nineteenth century, high school education was not necessary (or adaptive) to the basic functioning of the economy: Industrial and factory production did not need young people to have skills beyond basic math and literacy (e.g., Smelser 1959). Moreover, it was working side by side with adults, not high school courses, which socialized children into the work ethic and skills necessary to being a productive worker. Today, by contrast, college education in science and math is required for the effective functioning of the high-tech economy, and internships function to socialize students into corporate work habits. See also Topic 4.1.

Topic 4.1   Contemporary China in systemic action

According to Parsons, society can be construed as a dynamic action system. Every society (any social system) has to meet the functional requirements of its four subsystems (A, G, I, L; see Box 4.1). Although each subsystem is highly differentiated, and relatively autonomous from the other subsystems, they are also interdependent because the effective functioning of the system requires the effective functioning of all its subsystems. The differentiation between the subsystems produces tension and strain, as it would be very difficult for the functional requirements of each subsystem to be met simultaneously. China today provides a good illustrative example of the tension and strain that can emerge between the functional requirements of a societal system's subsystems. China's rapid economic growth (economic adaptation) is producing tensions with and between its other subsystems.

- Tension between **A**daptation and **G**oal Attainment functions: There is tension between the individualism and entrepreneurialism required for business expansion and continued economic growth and the political goals of the state in instituting new programs since 2017 that seek to instill "cultural confidence" by reviving China's traditional emphasis on deference to family and government authority.
- Tension between **A**daptation and **I**ntegration functions: Some of the adaptive strategies of the economic subsystem (e.g., hiring migrant workers, imposing large production quotas and overtime on workers) are in tension with the functions of the integrative (legal) subsystem. They are producing social strain indicated, for example, by a surge in worker protests and in suicides (see Topics 1.1. and 2.4, and an increase in white-collar crimes (e.g., bribery, smuggling) committed by Chinese business tycoons and political leaders.
- Tension between **A**daptation and **L**atency (cultural maintenance): The consequences of economic adaption (e.g., increased productivity, profits, consumerism, pollution) are in tension with the cultural maintenance requirements of a society that seeks to maintain the confidence of a growing professional middle class despite suppression of individual freedoms (e.g., Internet and media bans) and the privileges enjoyed by the political elite and their children, China's "princelings," who flaunt a visibly ostentatious consumerism (e.g., Fan 2016; see also Topic 1.1 and Topic 15.1).
- Tension between **I**ntegration functional requirements (e.g., the legal system's lack of protection of human rights) and the **G**oal attainment functions of the political subsystem (e.g., global status as a respected member of the G20 group of nations).

SOCIAL ACTION

Central to Parsons's theory of action is the construct of the **unit act**. A unit act is composed, at a minimum, of (1) a social actor (e.g., a person, a family, an occupational group); (2) an end (a goal or objective), a concrete future state of affairs toward which the action is directed; (3) a concrete situation in which the act must be initiated and in which certain social and physical conditions will apply; and (4) a normative (value) orientation that regulates the relationship between these elements (Parsons 1937: 43–45). In other words, in a given societal context, social actors choose (among culturally bounded) goals and the (culturally and structurally available) means toward achieving those goals.

The conditions of the situation (e.g., social class) determine some of the social actor's options, but, as Parsons emphasized, the social actor has freedom to choose among various goals and means. Hence, Parsons called his a theory of **voluntaristic action** (1937: 11); choices are voluntary rather than coerced or predetermined. This freedom, nonetheless, is always culturally bounded; social action is restrained by the societal norms and values that predominate in a given sociohistorical context (1937: 75). For example, although Americans have a lot of freedom regarding occupational choices, their choices are ultimately constrained by the strong cultural expectation that individuals will be economically self-reliant (and career oriented) in adulthood, and not dependent on parents or on the state for economic support. Similarly, Muslim women in France who have sex before marriage make choices that are influenced by French cultural norms (i.e., that sex before marriage is acceptable). And, by the same token, when some of these women subsequently choose to have restorative surgery to demonstrate that they are virgins to their future Muslim husbands (and their families), this action is also culturally constrained – by the social and gender expectations in Muslim communities (see chapter 3, Topic 3.2).

NORMATIVE REGULATION

Parsons builds on Max Weber (see chapter 3) in emphasizing the importance of culture or values in shaping social action: All social action is systemically contingent on a normative or values orientation. Weber concluded *The Protestant Ethic* (1904–1905) with the assertion that values were becoming less salient in motivating social action in modern society; they were being displaced by the increasing domination of instrumental rational action. Yet, writing in 1937, Parsons was very clear: social action is produced by, and needs to be regulated by, a normative orientation. Social disorder would likely result if social actors were to follow utilitarian or instrumental ends. Indeed Parsons argued that when utilitarianism (or instrumental rationality) dominates social action, there is a "precariousness of order" (1937: 95), an argument echoing Durkheim's emphasis on the instability of purely contractual social ties (chapter 2). Parsons states: "A purely utilitarian society is chaotic and unstable, because in the absence of limitations on the use of means, particularly force and fraud, it must … resolve itself into an unlimited struggle for power; and in the struggle for the immediate end, power, all prospect of attainment of the ultimate [end, social order] is irreparably lost" (1937: 93–94).

For Parsons, a consensual value-orientation necessarily imposes a discipline on conduct; it restrains people's immediate "satisfaction of the appetites, the pursuit of wealth and power" (1937: 284–285). The **cultural system**, specifically, "a common **value system**, manifested in the legitimacy of institutional norms" (1937: 768), is seen as being so central to societal order that he defines the study of this domain of social action as the core of sociology: sociology is the "science which attempts to develop an analytical theory of social action in so far as these systems can be understood in terms of the property of common-value integration" (1937: 768). Thus, for Parsons, as for Weber, culture has a *causal* role (along with social structures) in social action. Today, the sociology of culture is a vibrant area of inquiry. It has moved beyond Parsons's emphasis on consensual values to instead focus on the diverse cultural scripts, repertoires and tool-kits that dynamically produce social action (e.g., Swidler 2001). Its development, nonetheless, owes much to the earlier theorizing of Parsons (and Weber).[1]

SOCIALIZATION AND SOCIETAL INTEGRATION

For Parsons (1951), social action emerges from the interdependence of social, cultural, and **personality systems**. It is the outcome of the interaction of a plurality of social actors whose expectations and behavior are oriented to a situation and for which there is "a commonly understood system of cultural symbols" (1951: 5). As Parsons emphasized, "even the most elementary communication is not possible without some degree of conformity to the 'conventions' of the symbolic system" (1951: 11). It is through the socialization of the individual personality that culture – symbols, meanings, norms, and expectations held in common – is transmitted, learned and shared (1951: 13). Socialization into the norms and behavior required across the varied social roles and relationships in which the individual participates is thus a core functional requirement of society:

> Since a social system is a system of processes of interaction between actors, it is the structure of the relations between the actors … involved in the interactive process which is essentially the structure of the social system. The system is a network of such relationships … Without the requisite cultural resources to be assimilated through internalization it is not possible for a human level of personality to emerge and hence for a human type of social system to develop. (Parsons 1951: 25, 34)

Socialization is necessary because individuals have to be adequately motivated to fulfill the functional requirements of the social system; individual needs must be more or less in synchrony with the functional needs of the social system. Using Parsons's language, we can say that the smooth functioning of the economy (economic subsystem) requires and rewards (through the stratification subsystem) well-trained (educated) and "goal-directed" individuals with the analytical skills to be productive in today's economy, and hence requires that children be socialized into developing both the good work habits necessary for educational and economic success *and* the desire or motivation for achievement (e.g., Parsons 1949/1954: 72). If there is too much slippage between the social system's requirements and individual personality, this produces strain and tension in the social system which can result in dysfunctional consequences (e.g., high school drop-out rates which in turn impact the economy, juvenile crime, the socialization of the next generation, etc.). The social system relies on mechanisms of social control or integration (e.g., laws mandating school attendance and levels of performance) as a way to ensure that tendencies toward deviant behavior can be regulated to the extent that deviance does not result in producing dysfunctional consequences (Parsons 1951: 35). The objective, in short, is to integrate the social, personality-motivational, and cultural elements so that "they are brought together in an ordered system" (1951: 36).

VALUES CONSENSUS

The idea that a common value system is necessary to society may strike people today as out-of-step with our affirmation of multiculturalism. And this was also the case in the 1960s and 1970s when advocates of women's rights, civil rights, and gay rights – were actively challenging the values and institutional practices of the (white male) Establishment. Understandably, Parsons's theorizing came to be seen as socially conservative. If institutions must maintain the consensual norms already in place, how is social change possible? How can change occur when the newly proposed norms (e.g., greater equality for women and minority racial and sexual groups) are at odds with the norms already institutionalized? The perception of Parsons's conservatism was further fueled by his thesis that religion provides an integrating value system.

SOCIAL CHANGE AND THE SECULARIZATION OF PROTESTANTISM

Following Weber (see chapter 3), Parsons argued that religion is a significant cultural determinant of social action. He also argued that as modern society evolves, and becomes more complex in its structure and institutions (and has a more differentiated division of labor, as elaborated by Durkheim; see chapter 2), so too does religion. With industrialization, social institutions (e.g., economy, family, religion, the legal system) become more differentiated both internally and with respect to one another; they become more specialized in the functions they perform.

Religion, therefore, is differentiated from other social institutions and has its own (relatively narrow) functional specialization (e.g., worship, transmission of religious doctrine). Thus there is a separation of church and state, and each has its own autonomous and bounded functions. Modernization accelerates **secularization**—the decline in the authority and scope of religious institutions (e.g., Chaves 1994). However, this does not mean the disappearance of religion as a normative or cultural system. Although the church has a narrower and more specific institutional function in individual lives, Christianity, for example, as a value system (in the US) continues to have an integrating role in society as a whole (1967: 396). It provides, Parsons argues,

Figure 4.1 Institutional differentiation and specialization characterize modern society. The tasks of economic productivity (e.g., corporate offices) and values transmission (e.g., church) have their own particular spaces, amicably coexisting side by side. Source: © FernandoAH/iStockphoto.

a common matrix of value-commitment [values] … broadly shared between denominations, and which forms the basis of the sense in which the society as a whole forms a religiously based moral community. This has, in the American case, been extended to cover a very wide range. Its core certainly lies in the institutionalized Protestant denominations, but with certain strains and only partial institutionalizations, it extends to … the Catholic Church, the various branches of Judaism, and not least important, those who prefer to remain aloof from any formal denominational affiliation. (Parsons 1967: 414)

As such, religion can be described as being functionally necessary "to the maintenance of the main patterns of the society" (Parsons 1967: 418). Protestantism provides the underlying values orienting social action in the US, values like individualism, achievement, and pluralism or respect for difference. The respect for difference institutionalized in America's long history of denominational pluralism and its affirmation of religious freedom is similarly embodied in acceptance of church-state and other forms of institutional differentiation. Parsons refers to this as the **Christianizing of secular society**, that is, the translation of Christian/Protestant ideas into secular culture and institutions even as the specifically religious hold of Protestantism itself declines.

THE VALUE OF TOLERANCE AMID GLOBAL SOCIAL CHANGE

Parsons argues that precisely because of the complex technical and moral problems that confront modern society, there is all the more need of values, of "moral orientations toward the problems of life in this world" (1967: 420). He was careful to note, however, that Christianity as a religion per se is not necessarily the answer to contemporary problems. Moreover, he presciently commented on the emergence of what we today call globalization (discussed in chapters 14 and 15), and notably too, its cultural divisions: "For the first time in history something approaching a world society is in process of emerging. For the first time in its history Christianity is now involved in a deep confrontation with the major religious traditions of the Orient" (Parsons 1967: 420–421).

Parsons did not greet this new historical situation with dismay but as an opportunity for the further adaptation of religion and of other societal structures. He argued:

any relative success in the institutionalization of Christian values cannot be taken as final, but rather as a point of departure for new religious stock-taking … We are deeply committed to our own great traditions. These have tended to emphasize the exclusive possession of the truth. Yet we have also institutionalized the values of tolerance and equality of rights for all. (Parsons 1967: 421)

Thus, Parsons concluded that just as Christianity had adapted historically to changes in the evolving structure of society, it could also adapt to new societal challenges and draw on its values of tolerance to embrace the increasing religious and cultural pluralism of society. In this, we see a hint that Parsons is both less parochial and more open to the adaptive requirements of societal change than some of his critics acknowledge.

PATTERN VARIABLES

The maintenance of a society's main cultural patterns—that is, the norms and values that underlie social action—is accomplished through institutionalization. Parsons argued that there are many different kinds of value-orientation patterns, and systems of patterns, and "many different ways in which role-expectations may be structured relative to them" (1951: 43). He identified five contrasting value

Box 4.2   Parsons's patterned value-orientations (pattern variables)

- Universalistic versus Particularistic
- Specificity versus Diffuseness
- Achievement versus Ascription
- Neutrality versus Affectivity
- Self versus Collective

orientations **pattern variables** – that shape social behavior and in terms of which it can be analyzed (Box 4.2). This schema can be applied anywhere social action occurs, to characterize whole societies or the structures within a given society (or across several societies). Unlike earlier models of society (e.g., Durkheim's distinction between mechanical and organic solidarity; see chapter 2), Parsons's schema, by using five dichotomous dimensions rather than just one, offers a more precise and richly layered analytical tool. This means that, as Parsons emphasized, we can be attentive to the ways in which different combinations of elements or normative orientations characterize social processes., and with what functional or dysfunctional consequences.

THE DOCTOR–PATIENT RELATIONSHIP

We can see the application of Parsons's pattern variables (and their possible multiple combinations) in how, for example, a society's occupational system is structured (Parsons 1949/1954: 34–37). Parsons (1951: 428) focused on the medical system and the doctor–patient relationship to illustrate "the major structural outlines of the social system". And, in support of his insistence that both theory and data are necessary to the development of sociology, his theoretical analysis of the medical system derived in part from time he had spent earlier in his career doing fieldwork in Boston-area hospitals (1951: 428, n2). Accordingly, his analysis of the medical system, though abstracted from particular situations, is empirically informed.

Parsons defines illness as a "state of disturbance in the 'normal' functioning of the total human individual," and medical practice as a "mechanism in the social system for coping with the illnesses of its members" (1951: 431–432). When people get sick, their functional contribution to the family, at work, and to society as a whole is diminished; that is, they are not fully functioning. Society, therefore, needs to ensure that illness does not threaten the functioning of society and its subsystems. Health, illness, and medicine are social (and systemic) phenomena and are institutionalized as systems of social action. In other words, there are patterned or institutionalized ways in which the medical and insurance systems work, in how sick people behave, and in how doctors and patients behave toward one another. And there are similarly institutionalized, patterned ways characterizing how society and all of its subsystems (the economy, the family, the university, etc.) function.

The doctor–patient relationship (and any professional relationship, including the professor–student or the lawyer–client relationship), in contrast, for example, to the parent–child relationship, is based on **universalistic** criteria. This means that whereas a parent responds to their child based on a very **particularistic** and personal sense of who the child is (my very special child), the doctor treats any one patient in ways that are guided by objective, impersonal criteria applicable to all their patients (Parsons 1951: 438). The doctor uses a process of technical (medical) judgment and classification about sickness and treatment that extends beyond the symptoms of any particular individual to encompass illness and patients in general. The code of ethics of the American or British Medical Association (or of any professional association) institutionalizes these universal criteria, that is, the judgment and classificatory criteria that all doctors should use in treating all patients.

Doctors and patients have very **specific** functions vis-à-vis one another; their role expectations are well defined and their domains of interaction very specific. We go to the doctor because we have a specific ailment. We do not go to the doctor to seek financial or gardening advice or to get advice about whether we should split up with a boyfriend. By the same token, the doctor is not expected to ask the patient about these aspects of their patient's life and can ethically do so only insofar as this information might cast some light on the patient's health (e.g., stress, allergies, partner violence). In contrast, our family and friend relationships generally have a **diffuse** orientation. We talk about all sorts of things and the expectations of reciprocity are much broader and more encompassing than in a professional or business setting. When you borrow money from your mother, for example, expectations about repayment may be vague about (i.e., whether and when you have to pay it back). In fact, other expectations may be involved (i.e., promises to quit smoking or to visit more frequently). The boundaries defining expectations and behavior are much more narrowly and clearly drawn in the public world of occupational relationships than in the private sphere of family and friendship.

Related to the doctor's specific expertise is the very specific training doctors receive to ensure proficiency in treating patients. The doctor's professional status is **achieved** rather than **ascribed** (or inherited); doctors have to pass several examinations and demonstrate competence to perform the certified role of doctor. The professional role of doctor cannot simply be claimed as a person's birthright; by contrast, family roles are ascribed. We are born into or adopted by a particular family, and we inherit particular, that is, socially institutionalized sex and racial statuses upon birth, a social inheritance that circumscribes the individual's status – the "institutionally defined position of an individual in the social structure" (Parsons 1949/1954: 76) – and hence their social experiences, life chances, and outcomes. Thus regardless of achieved competence, women and men are expected in some quarters still today, by virtue of their socially ascribed sex, to do (and only do) certain things (see Topic 4.3). Additionally, the smooth functioning of professional roles and relationships requires emotional **neutrality** rather than **affectivity** or emotional engagement. The doctor is expected to behave as "an applied scientist," to "treat an objective problem in objective, scientifically justifiable terms," irrespective of whether they like the patient (Parsons 1951: 435). By contrast, the parent–child relationship is built on and maintained by affective or emotional ties. Thus, medical doctors typically avoid performing the role of doctor in their own family; close emotional ties would likely impair the doctor's medical judgment, and the consequences of misdiagnosis are not only detrimental to the patient but dysfunctional for society's subsystems (e.g., role functioning in the family, at work, etc.).

Finally, Parsons argues that professional roles are structured such that doctors, for example, are expected to put the welfare of patients before their own welfare. This altruistic prioritization of others – a **collective** orientation – contrasts with the **self**-orientation of the business person, who is expected to advance personal interests over other considerations. In short, the institutional and cultural (normative) expectation is for business executives to be motivated by profit, but not so the physician (Parsons 1951: 435), or for that matter family members (that is, in their interactions with each other).

THE CORPORATIZATION OF MEDICINE

Following Parsons's emphasis that pattern variables are useful not only in analyzing social structures and relationships, but also in assessing social change, let us consider the extent to which the present-day doctor–patient relationship demonstrates the norms Parsons outlined. Medicine has certainly changed since the 1950s (e.g., Starr 1982). Indeed, Parsons recognized its emerging transformation already in the late 1940s, noting that "an increasing proportion of medical practice is now taking place in the context of organization" (1951: 436). He argued that this was primarily "necessitated by the technological development of medicine itself" (1951: 436), making it difficult for doctors to practice without access to a medical-technological complex.

Hence, today, the traditional practice of the local family doctor making home visits to patients is no longer adaptive to the changes that have occurred in society. The increased technological sophistication of medicine in the diagnosis, treatment, and tracking of patients has contributed to the development of HMOs (health maintenance organizations). HMOs are corporate bureaucratic organizations that own a network of individual clinics and are affiliated with specific hospitals. They are characterized by impersonality, a hierarchical division of specialized expertise, efficiency (including economic efficiency as determined by the HMO's medical insurance professionals rather than its doctors), and routines and other features common to bureaucracies (as outlined by Weber; see chapter 3). This organizational shift fundamentally alters the structure of the doctor–patient relationship, that is, the value orientations determining the behavior of both patients and doctors. Despite the personal trust we may have with our doctor, the doctor–patient relationship is shifting more toward self-interested (business-like) considerations. Because small-scale clinics are no longer economically viable, doctors in small private practices are selling their practices to HMOs and hospitals. Large HMOs and hospitals, therefore, tend to have a near monopoly on the medical services business in a given region. They encourage their doctor employees to recommend only their own consultants and medical services to patients, even if a medical consultant working for a different HMO/hospital might be more appropriate given a particular patient's medical needs. Doctors may profit when they sell their practice but many subsequently are frustrated by the restrictions on their professional autonomy in diagnosing and making recommendations to patients once they become corporate employees working for the large HMOs and hospitals who maintain a close eye of the costs of medical care (see Creswell and Abelson 2012). Doctors' decisions are closely monitored by supervisors, and financial bonuses and salary cuts act as motivating forces influencing doctors' diagnostic and referral decisions.

Today, therefore, medicine and the medical profession are increasingly intertwined with economic corporate interests (see Topic 4.2). From a functionalist perspective, this might be explained as a necessary adaptation by the medical profession and hospitals to the high financial costs imposed on the practice of medicine as a result of technological-organizational change and the general increase in the competitive character of the health-care sector. The intermixing of medicine and corporate finance, whatever adaptive functions it may serve, also threatens the professional status of the medicine being delivered. It raises questions as to whether a given medical diagnosis and treatment are influenced by a doctor's or a hospital's economic interests, rather than by the impartiality, neutrality, and expertise necessary to ensure effectively functioning doctor–patient relationships (and by extension, a smoothly functioning society). Indeed, the American Medical Association is so concerned about the impact of economic considerations on medical treatment that in December 2012 it issued guidelines reminding doctors that "a physician's paramount responsibility is to [the] patients" (i.e., a "collective" rather than self-interested orientation). It acknowledged that doctors owe loyalty to their employers but cautioned that this divided loyalty can create conflicts of interest that may lead doctors to either under- or overtreat patients (Pear 2012: 16).

MODERNIZATION THEORY

The commercialization of the doctor–patient relationship depicts the analytical usefulness of Parsons's pattern variables in describing (and identifying changes in) institutions and social processes. Parsons (1971) also used pattern variables to conceptualize the characteristics of modern society, outlined in what sociologists refer to as **modernization theory**.

Topic 4.2   Blurring the lines between medical diagnoses and economic profit

The commercialization of medicine is seen in the ties forged between hospitals and professional sports teams. Seeking to capitalize on the promotional advantage of being affiliated with a sports franchise, some hospitals pay teams over one million dollars annually for the right to treat their high-salaried players. In addition to this fee, sports franchises get the services of the provider's physicians either without charge or at deeply discounted rates. In return, the hospital is granted the exclusive right to market itself as the team's "official" hospital or medical provider. Among those who have million-dollar team–hospital contracts are the New York Mets, with New York University Hospital for Joint Diseases; the Boston Celtics, with New England Baptist Hospital; and the Houston Astros, with Texas Methodist Hospital. Hospitals and medical groups aren't the only organizations teaming up with professional sports franchises —manufacturing companies are sponsoring medical services, as well. For example, Clinique, the global cosmetics company, made a $4.75-million donation to the Weil Medical College of Cornell University (Manhattan, New York) to finance a new "Clinique Skin Wellness Center." The Clinique Center, which includes examination rooms where doctors conduct skin examinations, focuses on educating patients in how to prevent skin cancer and maintain skin health. Not coincidentally, patients at the center may also make "on-site appointments with Clinique representatives to learn about makeup that can cover skin redness or facial scars" (Singer 2007).

Taking the US as the "lead society" in the latest phase of modernization (Parsons 1971: 114), Parsons argued that the system of modern societies is characterized by its positioning along each of the five pattern variables. In his analysis, the US and other Western societies with a high degree of modernization, that is, that have undergone democratization, industrialization, urbanization, and the expansion of education, literacy, and mass media (see also Smelser 1959, and Smelser 1968: 125–146), can be described as favoring or institutionalizing in their societal structures the following norms:

1 Criteria of achievement over ascription: Modern societies are democratic rather than aristocratic or monarchic; hence political, occupational, and social status is achieved rather than inherited or ascribed at birth. Modern societies are stratified societies, but the system of stratification is based on differential rankings related to individually achieved competence and merit rather than characteristics and outcomes determined by family or ethnic background.

2 Universalistic over particularistic criteria: Modern societies are pluralistic and diverse; hence no one group in society is favored. Instead, individuals are socialized into being citizens of the nation (or the world) rather than primarily associating with a particularistic ethnic, tribal, social class, or religious community. Societal structures and values affirm generalized rather than particularistic values; laws and public policies, for example, respect religion in general rather than a particularistic, denominational affiliation. In sum, there is an emphasis on cosmopolitanism rather than localism.

3 Specific over diffuse criteria: Modern societies require individuals to master certain bodies of basic knowledge and an ability to specialize in specific competencies. The occupational structure requires specific qualifications; in modern politics, there is a tendency toward role specialization rather than the diffuse obligations associated with traditional patronage. Additionally,

the system of stratification in modern society is, *in principle*, according to Parsons, based on the acquisition of specific competencies; because of the specific "competence gap" between doctors and patients, for example, there is a social **status differential** between them. Thus lingering inequalities based on membership of a generalized or diffuse group (e.g., a racial, ethnic, gender, or religious group) is evidence of the vestige of less modernized or more traditional expectations (Parsons 1971: 110).

4   Emotional neutrality over affectivity: In modern societies, there is a differentiation between public (e.g., work occupations) and private (e.g., family) spheres and their respective normative orientations to emotion. Unlike in traditional societies, where family and work tasks commingle (e.g., "the family farm"), modern societies maintain a clear functional separation between work (the office) and family (the home). The public sphere is based on an emotionally neutral, impersonal instrumentality (expressed in the execution of specific functions) whereas the private sphere is oriented by expressivity and emotion (in dealing with family relational diffuseness).

5   Modern societies are characterized by self-orientation rather than collective or other-orientation. Individuals are expected to follow their desires in choosing an occupation, a marriage partner, etc., unlike in more traditional societies, where family, ethnicity, and religious affiliation constrain these choices. "Following in father's footsteps" is the hallmark of occupational histories in traditional societies (e.g., Hout 1989), whereas in modern societies, the individual is free (indeed required) to be an entrepreneurial trailblazer. Individual self-determination is reflected in the stratification system. With status achieved as a result of individual choices rather than family ascription, some people experience upward mobility, and others downward mobility, relative to the socioeconomic status of their family of origin.

AMERICAN SOCIETY AS THE PROTOTYPE OF MODERNIZATION

Parsons maintained that American society, as the most developed and advanced modern society, is characterized by the orientations listed previously; that is, its generalized value orientations are achievement, universalism, specificity, emotional neutrality, and self-orientation. Its economic and social progress is driven by these patterns; thus "American society has gone farther than any comparable large-scale society in its dissociation from the older ascriptive inequalities and the institutionalization of a basically egalitarian pattern" (Parsons 1971: 114). This imperative, according to Parsons, must permeate all modern and modernizing societies.

Parsons's modernization theory stimulated a large body of macro-societal empirical research, as sociologists including his student Neil Smelser (1968) and other scholars (e.g., Black 1966; Gerschenkron 1962; Inkeles and Smith 1974) investigated the extent to which various societies could be described as modernized, modernizing, or economically and culturally "backward." Many neo-Marxist critics (e.g., Gunder Frank 1967; Cardoso and Faletto 1979) contended that modernization theory was essentially ethnocentric because it regarded American society as the prototype and any deviations from it as inferior. Parsons's conceptualization, these scholars pointed out, ignored the different histories (e.g., of colonialism; see chapter 12) and political cultures of different countries, and the impact of these differences on how different societies modernize or evolve over time (these theories are discussed in chapter 6). Notwithstanding the validity of these criticisms, modernization research provided a richly informative series of country case studies that illuminated the diverse social processes within countries, and differences among them. These studies (inadvertently) highlighted the process of **uneven modernization**, that is, variation in the extent to which a country embraces economic, social, and cultural change simultaneously. They also illuminated the societal conditions in which they overcome cultural lag (Ogburn 1957/1964), that is, the gap between their achieved economic modernization and the vestiges of cultural traditionalism (e.g., Ireland in the 1970s and 1980s; cf. Dillon 1993).

STRATIFICATION AND INEQUALITY

Parsons's modernization theory was also criticized for its inattentiveness to the unevenness of modernization *within* American society. In particular, ongoing gender and racial inequalities in America challenged his argument that modernized societies affirmed individual achievement rather than the status inherited (or ascribed) at birth on the basis of sex and race. Parsons acknowledged these sources of societal strain. He nonetheless argued that "equality of opportunity" and the ethos of "accountability" (objective performance) institutionalized in America meant that social status "cannot be determined primarily by birth or membership in kinship units" (Parsons 1971: 118; 1949/1954: 79). Parsons regarded status differentials – individual differences in income and occupational prestige – as functionally necessary to reward individuals for their comparatively greater technical/professional achievement and competence in contributing to the specialized functioning of society (1949/1954: 83–84). This thesis is further explicated by Davis and Moore (1945) in their functionalist explanation of social inequality. These status differentials, Parsons contended, derived largely from individual achievement within the occupational system rather than from any ascribed privilege (notwithstanding inherited wealth): "We determine status very largely on the basis of achievement within an occupational system which is in turn organized primarily in terms of criteria of performance and status within functionally specialized fields" (Parsons 1949/1954: 78–79).

For Parsons (1949/1954: 79), the occupational system, which is crucial to the functional imperatives of the economy (adaptation), necessarily "coexists in our society with a strong institutional emphasis on membership in kinship [family] units," befitting the family's socialization function (cultural/values maintenance; latency). The functioning of the family system, and the maintenance of solidarity within it, is based on emotion, relationship quality, particularism, diffuseness, and collective orientation. These orientations are, however, incompatible with the achievement and other normative orientations of the occupational system. The societal strain that could emerge from this incompatibility is partially resolved by the institutionalization of children's role in society: "Dependent children are not involved in competition [with parents] for status in the occupational system, and hence their achievements or lack of them are not likely to be of primary importance to the status of the family group as a whole" (1949/1954: 79).

SEX ROLES AND SOCIAL CHANGE

But what about the strain on society that would come from status competition between parents? Parsons argued that strain is avoided by having a clear sex-role separation, whereby men compete in the occupational structure and women occupy the home-based roles of wife and mother. He explained:

> If both [parents] were equally in competition for occupational status, there might indeed be a very serious strain on the solidarity of the family unit, for there is no general reason why they would be likely to come out very nearly equally, while, in their capacity of husband and wife, it is very important that they should be treated as equals. One mechanism which can serve to prevent the kind of "invidious comparison" between husband and wife which might be disruptive of family solidarity is a clear separation of the sex roles such as to insure that they do not come into competition with each other. (Parsons 1949/1954: 79–80)

Aware that even in the 1940s (when he first published this essay), many married women were working outside the home, Parsons observed that it is "for the great majority, in occupations which are not in direct competition for status with men of their own class" (1949/1954: 80). Moreover, Parsons claimed:

> Women's interests and the standards of judgment applied to them, run in our society, far more in the direction of personal adornment and the related qualities of personal charm than is the case with men. Men's dress is practically a uniform … This serves to concentrate the judgment and valuation of men on their occupational achievements, while the valuation of women is diverted into realms outside the occupationally relevant sphere. (Parsons 1949/1954: 80)

In short, for Parsons, sex-role segregation is functionally necessary to maintaining societal equilibrium. Clearly defined sex-role boundaries, norms, and expectations maintain social order and avoid the dysfunctional consequences that would arise from status competition between women and men.

Not surprisingly, Parsons's sex-role thesis was criticized by the then-emerging women's movement. Betty Friedan's best-selling book *The Feminine Mystique*, published in 1963, ignited public debate about the alleged emptiness of the lives of stay-at-home wives and mothers. Although Parsons's theoretical interest was in explaining how various social structures (e.g., gender roles, occupations) function to maintain a particular social order, his sex-role theory was seen as undermining women's equality and stalling the fledgling efforts to grant women greater equality in the public sphere (of work, mass media, and politics) as well as in the home. He further annoyed advocates of women's equality with his claim that because sex-role segregation is structurally necessary to the effective functioning of society, "the feminist movement has had such difficulty in breaking it down" (1949/1954: 80).

Time, of course, would prove Parsons partially wrong. Sex-role segregation is, at least officially and legally, largely a thing of the past in Western societies. Nevertheless, in line with his emphasis on the relative resistance of social systems and institutionalized patterns against efforts to change them (e.g., the women's movement), there are still many structural and cultural obstacles impeding women's full equality. Their increased participation in the labor force and the prominence of mothers as the primary breadwinner in families (e.g., Smith 2012; Wang et al. 2013), has, as Parsons might suggest, given rise to certain "disequilibrating" effects. These include wage differentials that penalize women (especially mothers), the prevalence of sexual harassment, and the overburdening of women with the time-management and emotional challenges associated with maintaining career and family aspirations as well as caregiving obligations (both toward children and aging parents/parents-in-law; e.g., Bianchi et al. 2006; Jacobs and Gerson 2004; Stone 2007). We explore contemporary theorizing on gender equality in chapter 10. But from a functionalist perspective one can argue that the "disequilibrium" resulting from advances in women's equality requires new institutional adaptations, like those outlined in Topic 4.3.

> **Topic 4.3**   Creating an inclusive workplace: Achievement versus ascription at Google
>
> The increased recognition of the economic value of women's labor force participation as well as a commitment to the value of gender equality has nudged many companies and universities to make "institutional adaptations," that is, systematic efforts to develop more gender-inclusive environments and to educate, hire and retain women workers, especially in the financial, scientific, and technology fields that have relatively few women. "Women in the workplace" events are spearheaded by well-known senior female executives, like Sheryl Sandberg, the chief operating officer at Facebook (and the author of *Lean In*), whose 2017 report takes an in-depth look at the gender-inclusive practices of over 200 companies (womenintheworkplace.com). New antidiscrimination laws and workplace policies that are both more woman friendly and more family friendly – such as parental and caregiving leave for women *and* men – can foster greater gender equality (and life satisfaction) both at work and at home.
>
> An incident at Google in the summer of 2017 illuminates how new institutional policies about what women (and men) can *achieve* are in tension with cultural beliefs that still see women and men in terms of *ascribed* qualities and characteristics. A male engineer employee wrote an internal memo (that went viral) criticizing Google's gender-inclusive programs; he argued that there are fewer women engineers because men are better suited to the job. The memo, and the response to it was controversial (for a number of reasons, including the right of employees to exercise free speech at work.) From an institutional perspective what is interesting is that the memo was criticized by Google's vice president for diversity, itself a recently created occupational position in large organizations (including universities), and the memo writer was fired. Google's CEO said that the writer had violated company policy and that portions of the memo "cross the line by advancing harmful gender stereotypes in our workplace" (Nicas 2017). Parsons would probably not have anticipated this. But today, companies that are leaders in our dynamically changing economy (Adaptation), are also at the forefront of socialization: They are actively engaged in socializing their workers into a values orientation (e.g., equality), a function that in the past was seen as the domain primarily of families and the church (Cultural maintenance/Latency). And perhaps some of the tension regarding workplace inclusivity is due to a cultural lag between Google's and other organizations' institutionalized commitment to the value of achievement (and equality) and the remnants of family socialization habits that (implicitly or explicitly) emphasize sex/gender role ascription.

ROBERT MERTON

Among many influential sociologists who studied and worked closely with Parsons, **Robert Merton** (1910–2003) argued against the generalized theorizing Parsons favored. He instead emphasized **middle-range theory** whose purpose is to guide empirical inquiry:

> sociological theory refers to logically interconnected conceptions which are limited and modest in scope, rather than all embracing and grandiose [or "grand"] … I focus attention on what might be called theories of the middle range: theories intermediate to the minor working hypotheses evolved in abundance during the day-to-day routines of research, and the all-inclusive speculations comprising a master conceptual scheme from which it is hoped to derive a very large number of empirically observed uniformities of social behavior. (Merton 1949/1968: 39)

Middle-range theories are those closely tied to a society's empirical realities, articulating the relationships that exist among particular variables, as exemplified by Weber's *Protestant Ethic* and Durkheim's *Suicide* (Merton 1949/1968: 63). Merton rejected Parsons's presumption that data had to be fitted into a general theoretical system applicable to all societies, which would explain all intersocietal structures and subsystems. Instead, he emphasized (1949/1968: 45) the development of sociological theories applicable to limited ranges of empirical data (e.g., regarding institutions, social organization, social class, group conflict, social change, etc.).

BIOGRAPHICAL NOTE

Robert Merton was born in 1910, in Philadelphia, to a working-class Jewish immigrant family. From childhood he was a voracious reader; after graduating from Temple University he won a scholarship to Harvard, where he studied under Parsons. Merton spent most of his career at Columbia University (New York), where he collaborated with Paul Lazarsfeld in pioneering studies of mass media and public opinion.

Merton wrote about an extensive range of topics and is most renowned for middle-range theory and his contributions to the sociology of deviance as well as to the sociology of science. He was active in national and international professional associations, and, like Parsons, served as president of the American Sociological Association (1956–1957). He died in 2003 at age 92.

MANIFEST AND LATENT FUNCTIONS

Nonetheless, showing his intellectual debt to Parsons, Merton too emphasized a **functional analysis** of society, and one that depended on the interplay of theory, method, and research data (1949/1968: 73). He argued that,

> the entire range of sociological data can be…subjected to functional analysis. The basic requirement is that the object of analysis represents a standardized (i.e., patterned and repetitive) item such as social roles, institutional patterns, social processes, cultural patterns, culturally patterned emotions, social norms, group organization, social structure, mechanisms of social control, etc." (Merton 1949/1968: 104)

He maintained, moreover, that "*the clues to the imputed functions* [of a given societal pattern – conspicuous consumption, for example; or the scientific profession, see Box 4.3] *are provided almost wholly by the description of the pattern itself*" (1949/1968: 112, emphasis in original). He made an important distinction between the motives for, and the consequences of, action (1949/1968: 113). Additionally, he distinguished between two types of functions: **manifest functions**, "those objective consequences contributing to the adjustment or adaptation of the system which are intended and recognized by participants in the system," and **latent functions**, those objective consequences that "are neither intended nor recognized" (1949/1968: 105). In Merton's framing (and following Durkheim; see chapter 2), the punishment of crime, for example, has both manifest and latent functions. The manifest function of sending a criminal to prison is to punish the criminal for wrongdoing, and its latent function is the affirmation of the behavioral norms institutionalized for the community as a whole. In short, structures and functions have a mutual impact on one another. And Merton argued, "*the discovery of latent functions represents important advances in sociological knowledge* (1949/1968:122, emphasis in original). This is partly because such discoveries typically highlight the interdependence of the various elements of a given social structure (1949/1968: 106–107) and the interdependence of various structures in society (e.g., family, education, and the stratification system).

Box 4.3   Robert Merton: The sociology of science amid social disorder

Although Durkheim and Weber wrote about the importance of science in modern society (and in, and for, sociology), Robert Merton's essays on the social structure of science were critical to establishing the sociology of science as a specialized subfield. He drew attention to the "cultural structure of science," that is, to the norms and values that it institutionalizes and that affect science, the conduct of scientists, and the public reception of science (Merton 1942/1996: 267). Drawing on Parsons's pattern variables (see Box 4.2), Merton argued that the ethos of science includes, the principle of universalism. This means that "truth-claims, whatever their source, are to be subjected to *preestablished impersonal criteria*: consonant with observation and with previously confirmed knowledge. The acceptance or rejection of claims entering the lists of science is not to depend on the personal or social attributes of their protagonists" (1942/1996: 269, italics in original). This insight takes on added significance today in light of the so-called "post-truth" society (see Introduction, Topic I.2). As Merton (ibid.) also elaborated, because "the institution of science is part of a larger social structure with which it is not always integrated....when the larger culture [or elements of it] opposes universalism, the ethos of science is subjected to serious strain." Ethnocentrism, cultural polarization, ideological biases, and political conflict (e.g., regarding climate change and government regulation) are among the social forces affecting variation in the development, functions, and consequences of science.

Merton (1957/1996) also discussed the reward structure institutionalized within the scientific community (e.g., the status and prestige associated with research grants, publications and citations). These rewards function to motivate scientists to work hard and to persevere in their pursuit of knowledge. Somewhat unintendedly, this institutionalized reward system also effects what particular authors and topics get priority; and it may also motivate deviance (e.g., scientific fraud and plagiarism). Such effects may be dysfunctional insofar as they contribute to hostility toward science in general.

In light of contemporary controversies regarding both the truth and the value of scientific data (e.g., Topic I.2), Merton's (1938/1996: 285) prescient words are worth remembering: "Precisely because scientific research is not conducted in a social vacuum, its effects ramify into other spheres of value and interest. Insofar as these effects are deemed socially undesirable, science is charged with responsibility. The goods of science are no longer considered an unqualified blessing....There is a tendency for scientists to assume that the social effects of science *must* be beneficial in the long run. This article of faith performs the function of providing a rationale for scientific research, but it is manifestly not a statement of fact. It involves the confusion of truth and social utility which is characteristically found in the nonlogical penumbra [shadow] of science..."

SOCIAL CONSEQUENCES

All social actions can have multiple consequences, either for the whole society or for just some individuals and subgroups. Some of these consequences may be unanticipated insofar as they were not intended to occur, and though unintended, can be (1) functional, (2) dysfunctional, or (3) irrelevant in a given societal context (Merton 1949/1968: 105).

Dysfunctional consequences, or social strains and tensions in the social system in its existing form (e.g., regarding immigration, see Topic 4.4; or science; see Box 4.3), can, however, have a positive function. As Merton notes, they can be instrumental in leading to changes in that system (1949/1968: 107). Whether and how this occurs are questions for empirical investigation.

Topic 4.4   Apple orchards and immigration restrictions: A case of anticipated and dysfunctional consequences

York Springs in rural Pennsylvania is part of the South Mountain Fruit Belt, with an abundance of apple orchards that help make it the fourth-highest apple producing region in the US. Like a lot of rural places, many young people leave once they finish high school, and the orchard owners and fruit-canning plants rely on Mexican immigrants: "Many people came…as seasonal apple pickers, and orchards need tending so they stayed year round. Some became orchard managers, and some started businesses: hair salons and restaurants, grocery stores and landscaping companies….in 2012, the town was aging and dying, though Mexican newcomers were already bringing green shoots….There has been a little tension, but York Springs in recent years has developed a vibrant, intersectional culture, insofar as that's possible in a sparsely populated place….There was until recently, even street life of sorts popping up: a Mexican food truck, children playing *futbol*, the occasional inter-ethnic teen couple holding hands at Griest Park." Now however, anti-immigration policies of the Trump administration are being sharply felt. Immigrant arrests and detentions are separating families, spreading fear, and silencing community life: "The "stringent enforcement of immigration law is destroying a rich, new rural culture. It's likely to destroy the economy, too. The orchards generate over $500 million a year, and one way or another, most of the jobs. But the local growers, many of whom have been operating the family orchards for generations" worry that they won't have enough workers to harvest this year's crop. Two-thirds of the county voted for Trump, even though some at the time had reservations about his promised restrictions on immigration. But whether anticipated or unanticipated, the immigration crackdown has dysfunctional consequences: A newly thriving rural community is spiraling "into a local depression that is personal, cultural, and economic" (Sartwell 2017).

STRAIN BETWEEN CULTURE AND SOCIAL STRUCTURE

One of Merton's significant contributions is his explanation of the links between social structural and cultural determinants of **deviance**. Although indebted to Parsons's emphasis on the relevance of cultural values and institutional structures in determining social action, Merton highlighted the variation in cultural values or goals, and he showed that the interrelation between goals and their realization was more open ended than Parsons acknowledged. Thus, he argued that deviance is not simply due to the faulty transmission of cultural values or an individual's faulty socialization (as a Parsonian analysis would suggest). Rather, Merton argued:

> some *social structures exert a definite pressure upon certain persons in the society to engage in nonconforming rather than conforming conduct.* If we can locate groups primarily subject to such pressures, we should expect to find fairly high rates of deviant behavior in these groups, not because the human beings comprising them are compounded of distinctive biological tendencies but because they are responding normally to the social situations in which they find themselves. (Merton 1949/1968: 186, emphasis in original)

Thus for Merton, socially deviant behavior, just like socially conforming behavior, is a product of particular social structural circumstances.

Merton distinguished between the goals, purposes, and interests that a given society defines as culturally acceptable and the acceptable norms and **institutionalized means** for attaining those goals. Individuals have freedom in choosing the means used to attain desired **cultural goals**. For example, the money to support the culturally valued goal of a consumer lifestyle can be attained through a variety of means: family inheritance, winning the lottery, working in a financially rewarding occupation, stock market investment, theft, or embezzlement.

Merton's framework highlights outcomes that are likely when individuals' social circumstances prevent them from being able to attain desired cultural goals (e.g., prestige, success). He argues that when a gap or discrepancy exists between the goals affirmed in society and access to the institutional means to attain them, individuals adapt their behavior. They either reject the culturally acceptable goals, or they reject the institutional means for attaining them. These options lead to various socially patterned ways by which individuals respond to the goals/means dilemmas encountered, adaptations which Merton outlined (1949/1968: 194); see Box 4.4.

Merton's typology thus introduces the **conformist**, who accepts cultural goals and society's approved means for their attainment; the **innovator**, who accepts the goals but finds new ways to achieve them; the **ritualist**, who, though rejecting the culturally sanctioned goals, nonetheless passively goes along with the behavior necessary to achieve those goals; the **retreatist**, who opts out of both the goals and the goal behavior; and finally, the **rebel**, who rejects the cultural goals and the institutionalized means but substitutes new goals and means of their own. The conformist accepts the cultural goal of academic success and conforms to professors' expectations of coursework requirements toward excellence; the innovator accepts the goal of academic success but finds ways to circumvent the work required by the assignments; the ritualist rejects academic ambition but dutifully goes along with all of the required coursework; the retreatist disavows any interest in academic work and makes no effort to do well in class; the rebel rejects offers of college admission and instead goes off to the mountains, spending time perfecting their skiing technique but with no interest in enhancing their status or prestige (culturally acceptable goals) by participating in ski competitions (Merton 1949/1968: 193–211).

Because Merton's typology highlights "individual" adaptation, this may obscure how the access of whole groups in society to the institutional opportunities necessary for the achievement of cultural goals gets blocked by poverty, racism, sexism, LGBTQ discrimination, etc. His typology is useful, nonetheless, because it highlights how a functional analysis can be helpful in explaining "social problems," and more generally, in highlighting the conjoint institutional and cultural conditions that can variously produce and predict deviance. It also illuminates the several possible sources of strain toward deviance (or anomie) that can exist in society, given that so many different goals can characterize any individual's social context. Different forms of success (e.g., economic, academic, athletic, artistic, military) receive greater affirmation in some families, groups, or communities than in others; and, in addition to success and prestige, society also emphasizes the values of civic duty, loyalty, neighborhood spirit, etc. There are, therefore, many opportunities for discrepancies to arise between cultural goals and the institutionalized means toward achieving them, depending on the individual's social situation.

NEOFUNCTIONALISM

Parsons's influence on contemporary theorizing is apparent in the work of Niklas Luhmann and Jeffrey Alexander, two very different scholars representative of **neofunctionalism**, that is, an approach that embraces but also substantially reworks Parsons's functionalism.

Box 4.4   Modes of individual adaptation to societal conditions

Modes of adaptation	Cultural goals	Institutionalized means
I Conformity	+	+
II Innovation	+	−
III Ritualism	−	+
IV Retreatism	−	−
V Rebellion	+/−	+/−

Key: + = acceptance; − = rejection; +/− = rejection of prevailing goals and means and substitution by new goals and means. Source: Merton (1949/1968: 140).

NIKLAS LUHMANN: SYSTEMS THEORY

Niklas Luhmann (1927–1998) a German social theorist, was another of Parsons's students at Harvard. His systems theoretic approach offers a very sharp contrast both to Parsons's understanding of society as a social system (see Box 4.1) and to Merton's middle-range functional analysis. For Luhmann (2002), society has to be construed and analyzed as a highly abstract, self-contained, self-regulating, and self-referential system. His systems approach is highly technical and a radical departure from the ways sociologists in general think about society and social action. Unlike Weber and Parsons, Luhmann is not interested in what motivates and structures social action. He argues instead that modern society is so highly differentiated and complex that it must necessarily rely on its own, internally autonomous, systemic properties and processes of system self-regulation and reproduction (similar to the **autopoiesis** process in biology whereby living systems self-regulate).

For Luhmann, the systems complexity of modern society transcends individual and collective agency and interaction; it is beyond socio-logic. Instead, it self-perpetuates as a result of some machine-like systemic logic (almost as if a Google algorithm today were to drive and regulate social life). It functions largely independent of institutional processes, values, and human-social agency. Systemic communication, not institutional action, is what matters. The system's self-contained, self-referencing structure uses narrowly drawn communication codes that are internal to and specific to each discrete system, and that, unlike how we customarily think of communication and the use of symbols/language, cannot extend or translate to other systems. Luhmann states, for example, that

> society is an operationally closed, autonomous system of communication. Consequently everything it observes and describes (everything that is communicated about) is self-referentially observed and described. That holds for the description of the societal system itself, and it also holds with the same necessity for the description of the environment of the societal system … It is as though the distinction between a map and a territory – a territory in which the map has to be made – itself has to be inscribed on the map. (Luhmann 2002: 125)

Luhmann's highly abstract and technical theorizing makes it very difficult to translate into testable, sociological research questions.

JEFFREY ALEXANDER: THE CIVIL SPHERE

Jeffrey Alexander (born in 1947), is an American sociologist (currently at Yale University). He did his doctoral dissertation at the University of California at Berkeley under the two renowned and Parsonian-trained sociologists, Robert Bellah and Neil Smelser. Following in the tradition of Durkheim and Parsons, Alexander is interested in the question of societal integration, but unlike them he does not assume that different institutional spheres coexist and function in harmonious interchange

(Alexander 2006: 33–34). He instead probes how societal community (i.e., solidarity) is carved amidst institutionalized forces that may threaten it in a given sociohistorical context. These forces include various institutional practices (e.g., exploitative economic markets, raw political power) and cultural or symbolic codes that, for example, designate some groups as inferior, as "polluted others".

Alexander differentiates between the civil sphere and what he calls the noncivil sphere. The **civil sphere** is "a world of values and institutions that generates the capacity for social criticism and democratic integration at the same time. Such a sphere relies on solidarity, on feelings for others whom we do not know but whom we respect out of principle" (Alexander 2006: 4). It includes the many public discourses in society (e.g., public opinion, law, civic ethics and principles, the content of popular culture, protest and advocacy) and the various institutions that facilitate and encourage such communication (e.g., news media; movies; social movements; and civil associations, such as Mothers Against Drunk Driving). The civil sphere is bounded by the **noncivil sphere**: "by such worlds as the state, economy, religion, family and community." Alexander emphasizes that, like the civil sphere, the noncivil domains too are core to the quality of life and the pluralism in society. Moreover, the civil and the noncivil are interdependent. This is so even though the goals, interests, and forms of organization of the noncivil are frequently at odds with the crafting of an inclusive, nonhierarchical solidarity that seeks justice for all society's members.

Alexander is realistic about the impediments to solidarity. He is fully cognizant, for example, of the inequalities (e.g., of the market economy, gender, race, etc.), symbolic codes (e.g., popular stereotypes), and partisan interests and values that militate against universal community solidarity. But he is at the same time optimistic about its realization. He argues that it is often necessary for the civil to "invade" the noncivil in order to bring about reforms that maintain democracy and achieve justice (Alexander 2006: 34). And he draws on extensive case-study evidence to show how American society at various points in its history has been able not only to articulate ideals that transcend economic, political, and cultural divisiveness but also to achieve civil repair. He discusses, for example, the processes by which the civil rights and feminist movements succeeded in reconstructing a solidarity beyond their own particular group interests, and how the integration of Jewish otherness into mainstream American literature and popular culture was achieved (e.g., the movie *Annie Hall*). Thus Alexander concludes, "civil society is a project," an ongoing and restless project toward a just and universal solidarity that cannot be fully achieved or sustained, but also one that can never be completely suppressed (2006: 9; 549–553).

SUMMARY

The Chicago School's research and theoretical insights demonstrated the relevance of sociology as a discipline for studying the dynamics of modern society and social change. Talcott Parsons highlighted the value in large-scale theoretical analysis. His model of society as an action system is fruitful to understanding the interdependence of social institutions, as well as the significance of culture in determining action. His pattern variables provide conceptual dimensions that are useful in the descriptive and comparative analysis of social processes (e.g., social change, social roles), and his attention to values and societal integration has stimulated new thinking about civil society, as exemplified by Alexander.

Merton's functionalist analysis is central to mainstream sociology in, for example, conceptualizing the institutionalization of scientific practices and of science as a profession, and in identifying the social mechanisms that help explain differential outcomes in crime and inequality.

POINTS TO REMEMBER

The Chicago School:
- Had a primary focus on urban community life and social change
- Most of its research used qualitative methods, including ethnographic fieldwork, social mapping, personal interviews, and wide-ranging documentary sources
- Its extensive empirical studies yielded numerous important theoretical insights, influential across a range of theoretical perspectives (e.g., symbolic interactionism), and subfields (e.g., urban and community sociology, deviance, immigration)

Talcott Parsons:
- Sought to develop an abstract, generalizable sociological theory that would be universally applicable
- Adopted a systems approach to society
- Each societal system has four primary subsystems of action
  - Adaptation; for example, the economy
  - Goal attainment; for example, politics
  - Integration; for example, legal/regulatory functions
  - Latency or pattern maintenance; cultural socialization, transmission of values and norms
- Social action is voluntaristic; actors choose among various, culturally bounded, goals and means
- Structural functionalism: focus on the functional relevance of societal structures (e.g., occupational structure; stratification) in maintaining system equilibrium or social order
- Pattern variables: patterned value orientations determining how society and its subsystems are structured and function
  - Universalistic – Particularistic
  - Specificity – Diffuseness
  - Achievement – Ascription
  - Neutrality – Affectivity
  - Self – Collective orientation

Robert Merton:
- Outlined a "middle-range" approach to sociological theory. Middle-range theory seeks close ties between conceptual hypotheses and empirical realities; it seeks to guide empirical inquiry
- Functional analysis is applicable to all social phenomena
- Manifest functions: intended and recognized consequences of a given social phenomenon
- Latent functions: unintended and unrecognized consequences of a given social phenomenon
- Deviance is a function of strain between cultural goals and institutionalized means toward their attainment
- There are different types of individual adaptation to cultural/institutional strain

Neofunctionalists include Niklas Luhmann and Jeffrey Alexander

GLOSSARY: CHICAGO SCHOOL

cultural lag when communities or societies experience an adjustment gap between different norms and values (e.g., a delay in adjusting their traditional values to accommodate social change).

human ecology geographical spaces (e.g., cities) can be understood in terms of cooperative competition among diverse population groups, the outcomes of which produce social change; there is a correlation between spatial relations and social relations.

marginal man a person who lives in and moves between two diverse (and possibly conflicting) cultural groups (Park).

pragmatism strand in American philosophy emphasizing the practicalities that characterize, and the practical consequences of, social action and interaction.

public sociology research addressing questions relevant to social activists and other audiences outside of academia and with the goal of critiquing existing knowledge and practices.

self-fulfilling prophecy individuals' (possibly false) perceptions of a given situation lead them to behave in ways that result in bringing about an objectively changed reality; known as the Thomas theorem.

social disorganization the result of the co-presence of numerous interrelated social problems (e.g., unemployment and crime).

working concepts general definitions or fames of reference that seek to specify what a particular social phenomenon is before empirically investigating it (e.g., specifying what "a gang" is).

GLOSSARY: PARSONS

achievement versus ascription one of Parsons's five patterned value orientations whereby, for example, modern society emphasizes achievement rather than ascriptive (e.g., inherited status) criteria.

adaptation economic function (or institutional subsystem) necessary in all societies and societal subunits.

Christianizing of secular society the thesis that Christian-derived values (e.g., Protestant individualism, pluralism) penetrate the everyday culture and nonreligious institutional spheres of modern secular society.

cultural system institutionalized norms, values, motivations, symbols, and beliefs (cultural resources).

functions necessary tasks accomplished by specific social institutions (e.g., family, economy, law, occupational structure) ensuring the smooth functioning of society.

goal attainment – political function (or institutional subsystem) necessary in all societies and societal subunits.

grand theory elaborate, highly abstract theory that seeks to have universal application.

integration regulatory (e.g., legal) function (or institutional subsystem) necessary in all societies (and societal subunits).

latency (or pattern maintenance); cultural socialization function (or institutional subsystem) necessary in all societies and societal subunits.

modernization theory the thesis that all societies will inevitably and invariably follow the same linear path of economic (e.g., industrialization), social (e.g., urbanization, education), and cultural (e.g., democracy; self-orientation) progress achieved by American society.

neofunctionalism refers to the approach of contemporary sociologists who embrace Parsons's theoretical perspective but who amend some of its claims.

neutrality versus affectivity one of Parsons's five patterned value-orientations whereby, for example, modern societies differentiate between institutional spheres and relationships based on impersonality (e.g., work) rather than emotion (e.g., family).

pattern maintenance latency; socialization function (or institutional subsystem) necessary in all societies and societal subunits.

pattern variables Parsons's schema of five separate, dichotomously opposed value orientations determining social action.

personality system the individual's inculcation of the values and habits necessary to effective functioning in a given society (e.g., ambitious, hardworking, and conscientious personality types favored in the US).

secularization the thesis that religious institutions and religious authority decline with the increased modernization of, and institutional differentiation in, society.

self- versus collectivity orientation one of Parsons's five patterned value orientations whereby, for example, modern society emphasizes individual over communal interests.

social system(s) interconnected institutional subsystems and relationships that comprise society and all of its subunits.

specificity versus diffuseness one of Parsons's five patterned value orientations whereby, for example, modern society emphasizes role specialization rather than general competence.

status differentials comprise social inequality (stratification); gap in achievement and rewards based on differences in individuals' achieved competence (doctor/patient) and ascribed social roles (male/female).

structural-functionalism term used to refer to the theorizing of Durkheim and Parsons because of their focus on how social structures determine, and are effective in (or functional to) maintaining, the social order, society (social equilibrium).

subsystems spheres of social (or institutional) action required for the functioning and maintenance of the social system (society) and its subunits (institutions, small groups, etc.).

uneven modernization when societies experience modernization more quickly in one sphere of society (e.g., the economy) than in another (e.g., in education, the failure to develop the educated workforce necessary to the changed economy).

unit act analytically, the core of social action; comprised of a social actor, a goal, specific circumstances, and a normative or value orientation.

universalistic versus particularistic one of Parsons's five patterned value orientations whereby, for example, modern society emphasizes impersonal rules and general principles rather than personal relationships.

value system shared value orientation (culture) that functions to maintain societal cohesion/integration.

voluntaristic action social actors are free to choose among culturally constrained goals and the means to accomplish those goals.

GLOSSARY: MERTON

conformist individual who accepts cultural goals and institutionalized means toward their achievement.

cultural goals objectives and values affirmed in a given society; for example, economic success.

deviance the result of discrepancies between society's culturally approved goals and the institutional means toward their realization.

functional analysis the combination of theory, method, and data to provide a detailed account of a given social phenomenon such that the description illuminates the phenomenon's particular social functions.

innovator individual who accepts cultural goals but substitutes new means toward their attainment.

institutionalized means approved practices in society toward the achievement of specific goals (e.g., a college education as the means toward achieving a good career or economic success).

latent functions unanticipated and unrecognized (functional or dysfunctional) consequences of an intended course of action.

manifest functions intended and recognized consequences of a particular course of action.

middle-range theory generates theoretical explanations grounded in and extending beyond specific empirical realities.

rebel individual who rejects cultural goals and institutionalized means and who substitutes alternative goals and alternative means toward attaining those goals.

retreatist individual who rejects cultural goals and institutionalized means, and who, by and large, withdraws from active participation in society.

ritualist individual who rejects cultural goals but who accepts and goes along with the institutional means toward their achievement.

GLOSSARY: LUHMANN

autopoiesis process in biology whereby living systems self-regulate; so, too, society is a self-regulating system.

GLOSSARY: ALEXANDER

civil sphere a sphere of activity with its own values (e.g., democracy, justice) and institutions (e.g., civic associations, social movements, popular media) focused on ongoing efforts to create an inclusive, just, and universally integrating solidarity in society.

noncivil sphere the domains of state, economy, family, community, religion; each with particularized goals, interests, and structures.

QUESTIONS FOR REVIEW

1   What are the societal subsystems and what is the function of each? Identify how Parsons's model might be applied to understanding the social structure of the city or country in which you live.

2   Outline how you would apply Parsons's "pattern variables" to describing the professor–student relationship. What things might complicate or strain the maintenance of its patterned boundaries?

3   Assess the strengths and weaknesses of Parsons's modernization theory in helping to explain the nature of contemporary society.

4   Identify a policy change or experience in your local community that would be a good illustration of (1) anticipated and functional social consequences; (2) unanticipated and functional social consequences; and (3) unanticipated and dysfunctional social consequences.

5   How, as identified by Merton, is it possible for the same cultural goals to lead individuals to different outcomes?

NOTE

1   Contrary to Parsons's view of the endurance of particular values in shaping individual and social action, Ann Swidler (2001: 80), a leading sociologist of culture, argues that people change their goals (and values) depending on changed circumstances; thus an immigrant in an economically developed country is motivated to pursue wealth whereas in his or her home country he or she might have sought the preservation of family ties.

REFERENCES

Alexander, Jeffrey, ed. 1985. *Neofunctionalism*. Beverly Hills, CA: Sage.

Alexander, Jeffrey. 2006. *The Civil Sphere*. New York: Oxford University Press.

Anderson, Elijah, and Douglas Massey. 2001. "The Sociology of Race in the United States." Pp. 3–12 in Elijah Anderson and Douglas Massey, eds. *Problem of the Century: Racial Stratification in the United States*. New York: Russell Sage Foundation.

Bianchi, Suzanne, John Robinson, and Melissa Milkie. 2006. *Changing Rhythms of American Family Life*. New York: Russell Sage Foundation.

Black, C.E. 1966. *The Dynamics of Modernization: A Study in Comparative History*. New York: Harper and Row.

Bulmer, Martin. 1984. *The Chicago School of Sociology*. Chicago: University of Chicago Press.

Burawoy, Michael. 2005. "For Public Sociology." *American Sociological Review* 70: 4–28.

Cardoso, Fernando, and Enzo Faletto. 1979. *Dependency and Development in Latin America*. Berkeley: University of California Press.

Chaves, Mark. 1994. "Secularization as Declining Religious Authority." *Social Forces* 72: 749–774.

Creswell, Julie, and Reed Abelson. 2012. "A Hospital War Reflects a Bind for US Doctors." *New York Times* (December 1), A1, 17.

Davis, Kingsley, and Wilbert Moore. 1945. "Some Principles of Stratification." *American Sociological Review* 10: 242–249.

Dillon, Michele. 1993. *Debating Divorce: Moral Conflict in Ireland*. Lexington: University Press of Kentucky.

Fan, Jiayang. 2016. "The Golden Generation." *New Yorker* (February 22), p. 30–35.

Friedan, Betty. 1963. *The Feminine Mystique*. New York: Norton

Gerschenkron, Alexander. 1962. *Economic Backwardness in Historical Perspective*. Cambridge, MA: Harvard University Press.

Gunder Frank, Andre. 1967. *Capitalism and Underdevelopment in Latin America*. New York: Monthly Review Press.

Hout, Michael. 1989. *Following in Father's Footsteps: Social Mobility in Ireland*. Cambridge, MA: Harvard University Press.

Inkeles, Alex, and David Smith. 1974. *Becoming Modern: Individual Change in Six Developing Countries*. Cambridge, MA: Harvard University Press.

Jacobs, Jerry, and Kathleen Gerson. 2004. *The Time Divide: Work, Family, and Gender Inequality*. Cambridge, MA: Harvard University Press.

Lidz, Victor. 2000. "Talcott Parsons." Pp. 388–431 in George Ritzer, ed. *The Blackwell Companion to Major Social Theorists.* Oxford: Blackwell.

Luhmann, Niklas. 2002. *Theories of Distinction: Redescribing the Descriptions of Modernity.* Stanford, CA: Stanford University Press.

Merton, Robert. 1938/1996. "Science and the Social Order." Pp. 277–285 in Piotr Sztompka, ed. *Robert Merton: On Social Structure and Science.* Chicago: University of Chicago Press.

Merton, Robert. 1942/1996. "The Ethos of Science." Pp. 267–276 in Piotr Sztompka, ed. *Robert Merton: On Social Structure and Science.* Chicago: University of Chicago Press.

Merton, Robert. 1948/1996. "The Self-Fulfilling Prophecy." Pp. 183–201 in Piotr Sztompka, ed. *Robert Merton: On Social Structure and Science.* Chicago: University of Chicago Press.

Merton, Robert K. 1949/1968. *Social Theory and Social Structure.* Enlarged edition. New York: The Free Press.

Merton, Robert. 1957/1996. "The Reward System of Science." Pp. 286–304 in Piotr Sztompka, ed. *Robert Merton: On Social Structure and Science.* Chicago: University of Chicago Press.

Moss, Laurence, and Andrew Savchenko. 2006. *Talcott Parsons: Economic Sociologist of the Twentieth Century.* Oxford: Blackwell.

Nicas, Jack. 2017. "Google Employee Fired for Memo." *Wall Street Journal* (August 8), p. B1.

Ogburn, Walter. 1957/1964. *On Culture and Social Change.* Chicago: University of Chicago Press.

Park, Robert, Ernest Burgess, and Roderick McKenzie. 1925. *The City.* Chicago: University of Chicago Press.

Park, Robert Ezra. 1928. "Human Migration and the Marginal Man." *American Journal of Sociology* 33: 881–893.

Park, Robert E. 1936. "Human Ecology." *American Journal of Sociology* 42: 1–15.

Parsons, Talcott. 1937. *The Structure of Social Action.* New York: Free Press.

Parsons, Talcott. 1949/1954. *Essays in Sociological Theory.* Glencoe, IL: Free Press.

Parsons, Talcott. 1951. *The Social System.* Glencoe, IL. Free Press.

Parsons, Talcott. 1967. "Christianity and Modern Industrial Society." Pp. 385–421 in Talcott Parsons. *Sociological Theory and Modern Society.* New York: Free Press.

Parsons, Talcott. 1971. *The System of Modern Societies.* Englewood Cliffs, NJ: Prentice Hall.

Pear, Robert. 2012. "Doctors Warned on 'Divided Loyalty.'" *New York Times* (December 27): p. A12.

Sartwell, Crispin. 2017. "Fiestas and Apple Orchards: Small-Town Life Before Trump." *Wall Street Journal* (June 10–11), p. A13.

Singer, Natasha. 2007. "A Word from our Sponsor." *New York Times* (January 25), pp. E1, 3.

Smelser, Neil. 1959. *Social Change in the Industrial Revolution.* Chicago: University of Chicago Press.

Smelser, Neil. 1968. *Essays in Sociological Explanation.* Englewood Cliffs, NJ: Prentice Hall.

Smith, Kristin. 2012. *Recessions Accelerate Trend of Wives as Breadwinners.* Issue Brief 56. Durham, NH: Carsey Institute, University of New Hampshire.

Starr, Paul. 1982. *The Social Transformation of American Medicine.* New York: Basic Books.

Stone, Pamela. 2007. *Opting Out? Why Women Really Quit Careers and Head Home.* Berkeley: University of California Press.

Thomas, W.I., and Florian Znaniecki. 1927. *The Polish Peasant in Europe and America.* 2 volumes. New York: Knopf.

Swidler, Ann. 2001. *Talk of Love: How Culture Matters.* Chicago: University of Chicago Press.

Wang, Wendy, Kim Parker, and Paul Taylor. 2013. *Breadwinner Moms.* Washington, DC: Pew Research Center.

Wirth, Louis. 1938. "Urbanism as a Way of Life." *American Journal of Sociology* 44: 1–24.

CHAPTER FIVE

CRITICAL THEORY
TECHNOLOGY, CULTURE, AND POLITICS

KEY CONCEPTS

critical theory	standardization	political dependency
emancipated society	technological determinism	lifeworld
Enlightenment	reification	legitimation crisis
technical rationality	hegemony	public sphere
instrumental domination	promotional culture	civil society
normative rationality	one-dimensionality	colonization of the lifeworld
mystique of science	false needs	communicative action
dialectic of Enlightenment	celebrity	systems of domination
social control	cultural totalitarianism	ideal speech situation
scientific management	administered world	communicative rationality
mass culture	steering problems	distorted communication
culture industry	crisis	
homogenization	class depoliticization	

CHAPTER MENU

Introduction to Sociological Theory: Theorists, Concepts, and Their Applicability to the Twenty-First Century,
Third Edition. Michele Dillon.
© 2020 John Wiley & Sons Ltd. Published 2020 by John Wiley & Sons Ltd.
Companion website: www.wiley.com/go/dillon

Timeline 5.1	Major events from the end of World War I to the present
1918	End of World War I
1919	Jazz arrives in Europe
1920	First radio broadcasting station opens in Pittsburgh (US)
1922	BBC (British Broadcasting Company) established as state broadcaster in Great Britain
1923	Hitler attempts to overthrow Bavarian government in Munich
1923	Mussolini begins to turn Italy into a Fascist state
1923	Collapse of German currency due to inflation
1924	Italian elections: Fascist majority win
1924	Establishment of Chrysler (car) Corporation
1926	Kodak produces first 16 mm movie film
1927	Introduction of sound into movies
1928	Discovery of penicillin
1929	Wall Street crash: economic Depression
1929	Pope recognizes Mussolini's Fascist government in exchange for establishment of Catholicism as Italian state religion
1929	Museum of Modern Art, New York, founded
1931	Empire State Building in New York completed

1932	Aldous Huxley, *Brave New World*
1933	Hitler appointed chancellor of Germany with dictatorial powers
1933	President Roosevelt launches New Deal in US
1936	Hitler and Mussolini establish Berlin–Rome Axis
1936	BBC announces a television service
1936	Charlie Chaplin stars in *Modern Times*
1937	Movies become fourteenth largest business in US
1938	Germany invades and annexes Austria
1938	Munich Pact made, with Britain agreeing to Hitler's takeover of German-speaking region of Czechoslovakia
1938	Anti-Semitic legislation passed in Italy
1938	Disney, *Snow White and the Seven Dwarfs*
1938	Principle of paid vacations established in Britain
1939	Germany invades Poland; the start of World War II
1940	30 million homes in US have radios
1941	Japan attacks US fleet at Pearl Harbor, Hawaii; US declares war on Japan
1941	First Jewish extermination camps set up in Poland and Russia
1941	Manhattan Project of intense nuclear research gets underway in the US to develop atomic bomb
1941	Orson Welles, *Citizen Kane*
1942	First nuclear reactor established at University of Chicago
1942	First automatic computer developed in US
1942	Magnetic recording tape invented
1943	Allied forces begin round-the-clock bombing of Germany; Allies invade Italy
1944	Allied forces land at Normandy beaches (France); liberate Paris and Belgium
1945	Hitler kills himself (April 30)
1945	US drops atomic bombs on Hiroshima and Nagasaki
1947	Christian Dior opens fashion salon in Paris
1948	United Nations Declaration of Human Rights
1948	Long-playing (LP) record invented
1948	USSR withdraws from coalition with war allies
1949	USSR explodes its first atomic bomb; escalation of arms race with US
1951	First peaceful use of atomic energy in producing electric power in US

1952	Britain explodes its first atomic bomb
1952	First commercial jet airline service launched
1953	Discovery of DNA structure
1954	29 million homes in US have television
1955	Bill Haley, "Rock Around the Clock"
1958	Stereophonic records come into use
1962	First American (John Glenn) to orbit space
1966	Wide adoption of color television in US
1967	Marshall McLuhan, *The Medium Is the Message*
1967	100 million telephones in use in US
1968	Student anti-Vietnam War and civil rights protests in US and Europe
1969	American astronauts land on the moon
1973	World Trade Center Twin Towers, New York, completed; 411.5 meters high
1977	Research indicates smoking is unhealthy
1977	Introduction of personal computers (Apple)
1978	Birth of the world's first test-tube baby
1980	CNN (Cable News Network) established
1988	US B-2 "Stealth Bomber" unveiled
1991	Introduction of mobile phones
1993	World's first human embryo cloned
2001	The iPod and iTunes introduced
2004	Indian Ocean earthquake, one of the deadliest in history, causing devastation in Indonesia, Sri Lanka, Thailand, and India
2005	Hurricane Katrina causes widespread devastation and loss of life in New Orleans, US
2008	135 million Internet users watch videos on YouTube and other websites
2008	Major earthquake in the Sichuan region of China killing over 900,000 people
2010	Introduction of the iPad
February 2011	Mass political uprising in Tahrir Square, Cairo (Egypt) brings about the collapse of the authoritarian Mubarak regime
March 2011	Major nuclear accident in Fukushima, Japan, triggered by an earthquake and tsunami
May 2011	Osama bin Laden killed by US forces near Islamabad, in Pakistan
July 2011	Rupert Murdoch, owner/chief executive of News Corporation closes down the tabloid newspaper *News of the World* following a phone-hacking scandal (involving its journalists intercepting the cell phone of a missing/murdered English teenager)

October 2011	Libyan leader Moammar Gaddafi captured and killed by armed protesters
September 2011	Occupy Wall Street in New York City spawns similar Occupy protest movements in many other cities in the US and around the world (e.g., London, Frankfurt, Singapore)
2012	Facebook has 1 billion registered users Twitter has 500 million registered users
June 2012	Muhammad Morsi democratically elected as President of Egypt
October 2012	Hurricane Sandy lashes the coasts of New Jersey and New York causing the death of over 100 people, and thousands of dollars in damage to homeowners and communities
June 2013	President Morsi of Egypt ousted by military leaders, a move widely supported by large numbers of Egyptians, giving rise to violent mass protests between them and Morsi's Muslim Brotherhood supporters
2013	Twitter has 200 million monthly visitors
2014	ISIS (the Islamic State) terrorist group comes to prominence
June 2015	Pope Francis release his encyclical on climate change, *Laudato Si'* (On care for our common home)
April 2016	Beyonce releases her *Lemonade* visual album, using live streaming; in 2017 it is listed as the sixth greatest female album of all time
June 2016	A majority of people in the UK vote to leave the European Union (EU); a decision known as Brexit
November 2016	Donald Trump, elected President of the US (inaugurated January 2017)
August 2017	Hurricane Harvey devastates Texas and the US Gulf Coast
September 2017	Hurricane Irma devastates several Caribbean islands and causes widespread evacuations and flooding in Florida; Two earthquakes devastate Mexico City
2019	126 million people use Twitter every day; 1.59 billion people use Facebook daily

THE SOCIETAL CRITIQUE OF HORKHEIMER, ADORNO, AND MARCUSE

The body of writing discussed in this chapter is referred to as **critical theory**, so called because it emphasizes the critical, reflective use of reason in assessing and advancing society's implementation of Enlightenment values (e.g., reason, equality, individual and collective self-determination; see Introduction). Critical theory is most closely associated with theorists who were part of the Frankfurt School – so named because of its founding as an independent Institute for Social Research (ISR) in Frankfurt, Germany, in 1923. Its core members include **Theodor Adorno**, **Max Horkheimer**, and **Herbert Marcuse**, whose lives spanned much of the twentieth century. Today, its societal critique is pushed in new directions by **Jürgen Habermas**, currently a retired sociology professor at the University of Frankfurt. Marxism was the ISR's "ruling principle," and soon after the Nazis came to power in 1933, Adolf Hitler shut it down for "tendencies hostile to the state"; its vast library was seized by the government but not its financial endowment, which Horkheimer, its director, had earlier transferred to Holland. Exiled from Germany, Horkheimer and his colleagues settled in the US (initially at Columbia University, New York City) and after the war traveled back and forth to Europe (Jay 1973: 8–9, 29, 26, 40; see biographical notes). They continued to write in German, thus restricting their accessibility to English-speaking audiences; Horkheimer and Adorno's (1972/2002) important book *Dialectic of Enlightenment* (DE), for example, was not translated into English until 1972, though its first German edition was published in 1944.

Critical theorists argue that critical thought is suppressed in society by the mass media and other institutions including economic corporations, schools and universities, and the political sphere, all of which seek to control and strategically dominate what individuals think and do. The elimination of critical thought and the suppression of meaningful dissent, whether in political opinions, social values, or fashion choices, strip individuals and society of their potential to craft a more equal and fully participative, democratic society. Critical theorists argue that it is only through a critical theory of society – by using reason to critique how society works – that we can collectively create an **emancipated society** in which we are not beholden to, but are free to act against, the controlling, manipulative ways in which capitalism uses a calculating reason to strategically penetrates every aspect of everyday life, including our inner desires. As Marcuse (1964: 227) notes, "Critical thought strives to define the irrational character of the established rationality." Accordingly, critical theorists argue that individuals should engage in systematic critique of how society is organized, the goals and interests served, and their consequences (e.g., economic inequality, global warming).

BIOGRAPHICAL NOTE

Theodor Adorno was born in 1903 in Frankfurt, Germany, to prosperous Jewish-Catholic parents. He studied music composition in Vienna, Austria, and also philosophy, writing his doctorate on Edmund Husserl. Adorno joined the Institute for Social Research in Frankfurt in 1938. He subsequently spent four years at Oxford University in England before moving to America to join his exiled colleagues until the reopening of the ISR in Frankfurt after the war. With a strong personal and intellectual interest in classical and contemporary music, he worked at the renowned Columbia University Institute of Radio Research (which pioneered survey research of radio audiences) before moving to Pacific Palisades, near Los Angeles. He continued to write prolifically on wide-ranging topics, including a cultural analysis of jazz and its liberating (though ultimately repressed) potential to break the individual free of the constraints of the status quo. He also conducted content analyses of television shows and newspaper astrology columns, and contributed to pioneering survey research on authoritarianism and prejudice (Adorno et al. 1950). Adorno, who became an American citizen, died in 1969 (Jay 1973: 22, 172, 188, 196–197).

BIOGRAPHICAL NOTE

Max Horkheimer was born in 1895 in Stuttgart, Germany; his father was a prominent Jewish manufacturer who encouraged him to travel throughout Europe. Horkheimer worked for a few years in his father's business but then pursued academic studies. After completing his military service, he wrote his doctoral thesis on Immanuel Kant and subsequently became director (in 1930) of the Institute for Social Research. In the US, in exile as a result of the rise of German Nazism, Horkheimer suffered from heart disease and at his doctor's urging moved to Pacific Palisades in Southern California, where he and Adorno wrote *Dialectic of Enlightenment*. He traveled back and forth between Frankfurt and the US in the years after the war, and he died, an American citizen, in Germany in 1973 (Jay 1973: 6–7, 234, 254).

BIOGRAPHICAL NOTE

Herbert Marcuse was born in 1898 in Berlin, Germany; he too had prosperous Jewish parents, and also completed military service. Subsequently, he studied philosophy and received his doctorate from the University of Freiburg. While in the US, he worked with the State Department (until 1950) and subsequently at Columbia University, Brandeis University, and the University of California, San Diego. Marcuse became associated with the New Left and the student and antiwar protest movements of the 1960s and 1970s. He died in 1979 (Jay 1973: 28, 71, 80, 284).

TECHNOLOGY AND SOCIAL PROGRESS

Notwithstanding the very different – pre-Internet – society in which Horkheimer and Adorno (whose names I shorten to H & A in this chapter) wrote, their analysis of technology and culture is highly applicable today given the pervasiveness of digital technology in our lives. They recognize that technology is crucial to ensuring efficiency in goal accomplishment; clearly, most of the technological devices we use every day make our lives more efficient and give us more control over our activities. Just think about how much time and trouble we save by using e-mail, cell phones, and texting, or how Internet access gives us so much information about so many things (books, politics, restaurants), and how we, in turn, actively use technology to personally add to the flow of images, information, and opinion (through Facebook, Instagram, Twitter, blogs, YouTube, etc.).

Critical theorists fully appreciate the many positive ways that technological advances can enhance social institutions and everyday life. In fact, they remind us of the great promise of social progress instilled by the **Enlightenment** affirmation of scientific reasoning as the way forward from the nonrational myths and traditions that legitimated social inequality (e.g., the unquestioned divine rights of monarchies; see Introduction). H & A state, "Enlightenment, understood in the widest sense as the advance of thought, has always aimed at liberating human beings from fear and installing them as masters … Enlightenment's program was the disenchantment of the world. It wanted to dispel myths, to overthrow fantasy with knowledge" (DE 1).

Normative evaluation of technological and social progress
The emancipatory progress promised by advances in knowledge has not come to fruition, according to H & A. Instead, following Weber (see chapter 3), they argue that it is stalled by an instrumental or a **technical rationality** that focuses on the efficiency of the method used to accomplish goals, without any thought given to the ethics of the goals being pursued and the values they serve. H & A are not opposed to rationality and how it is used to advance science and technology, but they want us to evaluate the purposes to which science and technology – these "gifts of fortune" (DE xviii) – are applied. Take, for example, politicians' use of robocalls during election campaigns. Technology makes it possible for thousands of preselected phone numbers to be dialed and targeted with a standardized taped message. In principle, robocall technology can be used for many purposes that serve the common good (e.g., to alert a whole community of a fast-moving tornado). But when political advocates use this technology it is simply to bolster their own candidate and to denigrate the opposition. This may be strategically efficient and effective from a given candidate's perspective. But critical theorists would ask whether the use of this technique bolsters the quality of democracy and political

Figure 5.1   Technology companies are among the world's most recognizable and successful brands today. Source: © Erik Khalitov/ iStockphoto.

accountability. Does it enhance the dissemination of high-quality information that is necessary if voters are to fully engage in the political process and to make rational and deliberative decisions? Does it enhance or dilute democratic values of civility, fairness, and justice? For H & A, the use of science and technology in the **instrumental domination** of individuals, groups, social processes (e.g., political campaigns) and of the natural environment, is evidence of a technical rationality that is divorced from the Enlightenment vision of the use of reason as a force emancipating society from domination. This is a broad theoretical and values-based or normative claim. Its core thesis, however, can be empirically tested across an array of institutional and societal contexts.

Not coincidentally, H & A outlined their thesis in the wake of World War II – a war precipitated by the instrumentally planned and rationally executed destruction of human life crystallized by the Holocaust. World War II (1939-1945), an event of our Enlightened modern epoch, demonstrates "one of the most vexing aspects of advanced industrial civilization: the rational character of its irrationality" (Marcuse 1964: 9). In other words, rational humans engage in the rational pursuit of the irrational destruction of humanity. Similarly, advances in scientific and technological knowledge have made nuclear energy possible; a knowledge that is used in a highly rational way not only for energy-efficiency purposes, but also for militaristic goals (e.g., atomic bombs) thereby fueling an ongoing global nuclear arms race and the threat of nuclear destruction.

Max Weber argued that science cannot provide answers to ethical questions about how society should use scientific knowledge – science cannot tell us how we should live or what values should guide us (see chapter 3). Going beyond Weber, H & A argue that we need to inject ethics and normative expectations in evaluating how societies use scientific and technological knowledge. And those expectations, they argue, should accord with the Enlightenment's understanding of reason and progress as an emancipatory force. We should thus employ a **normative rationality**, that is, use reason in the pursuit of goals that advance Enlightenment norms or values of social equality, democratic participation, and human flourishing, as opposed to using reason only for purposes of instrumental, strategic, or technical control and domination.

In other words, we should not be deceived by the **mystique of science**: the unquestioned presumption that the accumulation, application, and everyday use of scientific data and scientific advances are inherently good and that they should be automatically welcomed as evidence of social progress. Because we live in a time of great scientific and technological progress, we believe that we are in control of our lives, of our economic, lifestyle, and political choices, and of nature. But in actual fact, H & A argue, we are dominated and controlled, and stand powerless against an array of corporate, political, and bureaucratic actors. Thus, although the advances in scientific and technological knowledge give us the means to eliminate many social ills (e.g., poverty, illiteracy, hunger) and to create a society in which all members can fully participate and flourish, we instead, H & A argue, collectively use technological knowledge for strategic purposes that serve the interests of those individuals, groups, and corporations who are already economically and politically powerful (DE 30–31, xvii).

DIALECTIC OF ENLIGHTENMENT

H & A (1972/2002) call this general state of affairs – that is, the strategic use of technological and economic rationality for domination rather than emancipation – the **dialectic of Enlightenment**. Don't be intimidated by this phrase. It basically means that the Enlightenment has become the contradictory opposite, or the antithesis, of what it promised. Our one-sided implementation of its promises, by focusing on technical at the expense of normative rationality, has resulted in our being less free, less autonomous, and less enlightened than we believe ourselves to be. Instead of social progress and greater equality, our technologically advanced society is characterized by regression; instead of freedom, it is characterized by domination.

The social, political, and economic use of technology today is more complicated than Horkheimer and Adorno envisioned. Cell phones and the Internet, especially text-messaging, Facebook, and YouTube, clearly increase the everyday autonomy of individuals and groups, and in many instances, allow them to bypass the gatekeeping power of political, mass media, and other authorities (including parents and teachers). Large public protests against authoritarian (or incompetent) rulers – first in Tunisia and Egypt in the spring of 2011, then again in Egypt, and in Turkey in the summer of 2013 – provide a good example of the grassroots, democratic ends to which Internet technology can be used. Instant messaging and cell phone photographs taken by protesters and onlookers were critical to motivating others to join the protests as well as in gaining Western support for them. But although the Internet can be used to advance freedom and equality, it is also the object of strategic control by powerful actors, especially states and corporations (see Topics 5.1 and 5.5).

Topic 5.1   Social media: Political empowerment and government control

As a testament to the powerful role that online technology and social media in particular (i.e., Facebook, YouTube, Twitter) are playing in mobilizing political protest and democratic rights around the world, it was symbolically fitting that a Google executive in Egypt – Wael Ghonim, the person in charge of Google marketing in the Middle East and North Africa – was among those in Cairo who were arrested and imprisoned for their role in spearheading mass protests in January 2011 against Hosni Mubarak's repressive authoritarian rule (Kirkpatrick and Preston 2011: A10). Ghonim was behind the anonymous postings on Facebook and YouTube that are widely credited with instigating and expanding support for the mass public demonstrations that began in late January 2011 in Tahrir Square in Cairo. It was a bloody time, and many protesters were killed by government forces. Nonetheless, the mass political revolt contributed to the overthrow of the repressive Mubarak regime, giving rise to the emergence of democratic processes (e.g., elections), however temporary and fragile, before the elected Islamist President, Muhammad Morsi, was toppled by the military under General Abdel-Fattah al-Sisi.

Although social media are powerful in mobilizing grassroots campaigns and protests in authoritarian as well as in democratic societies (e.g., the Occupy Movement; Black Lives Matter), we are also frequently reminded that control of the Internet resides in the hands of governments. In Egypt, the Mubarak government imposed an Internet blackout. It did not last long (five days) and nor did it prevent the regime from toppling and the emergence of a new democratic order (however fragile). Nevertheless, the fact that the Egyptian government managed literally "switch off" the Internet in a highly wired, tech-savvy country gives pause to the assumption that the

Internet spells freedom. Egyptian engineers subsequently identified how it was possible for a blackout to be imposed: "The government commanded powerful instruments of control: it owns the pipelines that carry information across the country and out into the world" (Glanz and Markoff 2011: A10). A similar Internet control structure operates in several other authoritarian countries including Syria, Jordan, Saudi Arabia, Bahrain, and Iran, giving those governments the power to hit their country's Internet "off" switch – or to slow its speed – in the face of democratic challenges. North African countries, including Tunisia, which also saw a powerful role for social media in stoking political protests there during the same spring, are also vulnerable to Internet blackouts because most of them "rely on only a small number of fiber-optic lines for most of their international traffic" (Glanz and Markoff 2011: A10).

Similarly, although we find much fun and many other benefits in using Facebook and Google, their corporate owners have technologically sophisticated ways to mine the information, including photos, on users' personal pages. These accumulated data can be used to develop individually targeted advertising that translates into increased corporate profits. H & A emphasize that the strategic use of technology has a clear economic logic; following Marx, they contend that technology is used to extend the economic interests of capitalism and of capitalist institutions (e.g., the state, the university, the media). Thus, critical theorists merge Weber's focus on instrumental rationality with Marx's emphasis on the profit logic of capitalism. Analytically, then, the dialectic of Enlightenment is driven by capitalist forces, whose ethically unrestrained, strategic economic use of technology directly penetrates all spheres of society. Technological knowledge

serves all the purposes of the bourgeois economy both in factories and on the battlefield, it is at the disposal of entrepreneurs regardless of their origins … [Technology] is as democratic as the economic system with which it evolved. Technology is the essence of this knowledge. It aims to produce neither concepts nor images, nor the joy of understanding, but method [technique; technical knowledge], exploitation of the labor of others, capital … What human beings seek to learn from nature is how to use it to dominate wholly both it and human beings. Nothing else counts. (DE 2)

TECHNOLOGY AS SOCIAL CONTROL

A couple of examples help illustrate the idea that technology is an instrument of domination or **social control**. We can begin right on campus. Most colleges today use electronic swipe-card systems to provide students with access to various campus facilities. These systems are generally seen as efficient and secure, and they are also effective tracking devices (see Topic 5.2).

And similarly, electronic tolls and digital sensors on major roads and bridges can be used to track our movements. GPS tracking systems are so effective that some parents use such devices to control their teenagers' movements (and lives), so that they can always know their precise whereabouts. Other devices (e.g., car ignition locks, electronic bands) are programmed by parents and others (e.g., police) to prohibit certain activities (e.g., driving after drinking alcohol, exceeding the speed limit, or roaming beyond a specified location), and by adult children who monitor their ailing parents' daily habits from afar. Electronic forensic evidence (e.g., taken from e-mail and text messages) is becoming a staple of divorce, sexual harassment, and political and corporate corruption cases, and the pervasiveness of digitalized access cards at universities, workplaces, hotels, train stations, etc. provides officials with a vast amount of detailed, time- and space-specific information about individuals' everyday movements.

Topic 5.2   Technology and the changing contours of control in everyday life

- Smartphones' automatically loaded health and fitness apps track the minutiae of our daily activities – steps taken, flights climbed, miles run or walked, hours slept, etc.
- There are more than 200 menstruation tracking apps, providing users not only with dates and reminders about their periods but related data – about their emotions, their eating habits, and their sexual activity – as well as reminders about tampons and birth control.
- NEST, a digitally controlled indoor security camera subtly placed in a family's living room allows parents to see what's happening in their home while they are away.
- Louis van Gaal, known for a time as the "best coach in the world," and for a short time Manchester United's coach, was alleged to use e-mail tracking apps so he could check that individual players opened his postmatch e-mails detailing the aspects of their performance that needed improvement.
- Moveon.org, a progressive advocacy organization in the US, tracks whether its 8 million members read the messages it sends.
- Equinox gives its members the option of using an app that sends them reminders nudging them to set fitness goals (and to go to the gym!). New members who use the app visited the club 40 percent more than those who opted out of the app; and those who work out more often are also more likely to maintain their gym membership despite the expense.
- "Active wellness" in California is testing face recognition technology that will likely replace swipe cards…and when you go to the gym will not only automatically admit you but when you step on the treadmill will recognize you and automatically load all your favorite settings and accumulated data.
- Sensors on tennis racquets feed data to your smartphone telling you how you can improve your serve.
- In Boston, one-third of the city's garbage/waste bins have sensors for tracking when a bin is full, thus making garbage collection more efficient; and Street Bump, an app that collects vibration data from moving cars is used to pinpoint potholes (and eventually fix them!).
- Sensors on bridges report information about traffic congestion, the physical state of the road (e.g., whether icy, and salted), and the quality of the water and sea life below.
- Norway is pioneering the development of crewless ships; *The Yara Birkeland*, scheduled for launch in 2020, will use GPS radar, cameras and sensors to maneuver itself around other vessels and to dock on its own. In addition to reducing fuel and labor costs, it is also expected to cut carbon emissions; it is expected to replace 40,000 truck journeys a year through urban areas in southern Norway.
- Google Maps have physically recorded eye-level imagery of some of the most remote parts of the world, include Ayers Rock/Uluru in the Australian Outback, a 1,700 mile drive from Sydney; as a result of Street View, you can now take a virtual walk around much of it (just as you can see from afar a friend's backyard and what's happening there).
- A Facebook feature allows users to flag messages that convey suicidal or other self-harming intentions, and after review by a specially trained Facebook team, a supportive message and various menu options (e.g., talk with a friend, contact a helpline) are sent via Facebook to the person who posted the flagged message.

Clearly, although the use of apps and various digital devices have multiple benefits, their pervasiveness also underscores the penetration of technology as a means of control into domains of life that in the past were unburdened by constant surveillance (by either ourselves or others). They thus illuminate a core critical theory claim: "Technology serves to institute new, more effective, and more pleasant forms of social control and social cohesion ... the traditional notion of the 'neutrality' of technology can no longer be maintained. Technology as such cannot be isolated from the use to which it is put; the technological society is a system of domination" (Marcuse 1964: 158, xv–xvi).

Figure 5.2   Smartphones allow us to keep a track on our own and others' movements. Source: © FatCamera/ iStockphoto.

Rational, scientific management

Long before GPS technology, **scientific management** became a catch-phrase in the world of business. Inspired by the early twentieth-century experiments of Frederick Taylor (1911) on managerial control of work processes and workers' tasks, this method focused on making workers' physical movements as automated as the machines they were working on. Hence, "time and motion" studies emerged as a popular way of finding the most efficient use of workers' hand and body movements in executing their assigned tasks; the method was exemplified by workers on the automated assembly lines of Henry Ford's then-fledgling car industry plant in Detroit (and thus is often called Fordism). Today, Walmart uses standardized, automated temperature controls set at its headquarters (in Bentonville, Arkansas, in the US) and imposes them at all of its approx. 3,500 stores worldwide, irrespective of the physical climate of the place where a Walmart store is located. Thus the controlling reach of scientific-technological management is extensive.

THE IRRATIONALITY OF SOCIETY'S RATIONAL CONTROL OF NATURE

Critical theorists emphasize that society has long used technology not only to advance economic interests but also to control the physical environment, nature. Today the pervasive extent of our manipulation and control of nature is such that Dubai, for example, a city in the middle of the desert, boasts the world's third largest indoor ski slope. Although increasing our freedoms in some ways (e.g., where and when we ski), our control over nature also exacts a high economic and environmental cost. The expense of buying and maintaining snow-making machines has driven many small ski-resort operators out of business in favor of large resorts confined to a few elite locations. And, as a result of the global warming that snow-making and other machines have contributed to, there is less natural snow because of the buildup of greenhouse gases that are warming the climate.

It is not just snow that we try to control. When homes are destroyed as a result of earthquakes and floods, we are reminded that we rational humans choose time and again to build against the irrational force of nature. We do so even though we are well aware that nature has its own logic, a force that we irrationally believe we can control. The devastating impact of hurricanes highlights the nonrationality of the historically long, economically driven desire to rationally control nature: many cities are built on what once were swamps and thus still prone to severe flooding. When Hurricane Harvey, for example, overwhelmed Houston in August 2017, its third so-called "500-year storm" since 1979, many impartial commentators noted that Houston has minimal restrictions on land use. Since 2010, it has allowed the construction of more than 8,600 buildings inside a land area with a high probability of flooding and without taking the measures that would help alleviate surplus water (*The Economist*, 2017c, p. 9)

In sum, H & A would emphasize that the domination of nature, rationally (strategically) executed in the pursuit of economic profit, fails to control nature and (frequently too) fails to be (rationally) cost effective: "In the mastery of nature … enslavement to nature persists" (DE 31). Such is the dialectic of Enlightenment; the mastery of nature (thesis) becomes its antithesis (domination by or enslavement to nature). We literally sink money into houses and other buildings that are destined to collapse (from floods, earthquakes, etc.) and to destroy lives and local economies, and nature itself.

Caring for nature, humanity, and society

Notwithstanding critical theorists' insights about the (irrational) rational exploitation of nature, there is some evidence today that amidst growing environmental awareness, corporations are exploring ways to use technological knowledge to help alleviate the negative effects of global warming and other societal ills (e.g., poverty, disease, discrimination). One Silicon Valley entrepreneur, for example, founded Change.org, an Internet site that allows its 140 million users to start online petitions to promote social change; the Gates Foundation (funded by Microsoft founder Bill Gates) commits millions of dollars every year to fighting global poverty and infectious diseases; Coca Cola funds drinking water projects in Africa; and Texas-based billionaire Michael Dell (of Dell computers) pledged $36 million to help the victims of Hurricane Harvey. These initiatives suggest that, as critical theorists would maintain, *normative* rational action, that is, action that seeks to fulfill Enlightenment hopes for a more inclusive and flourishing society, recognizes our ethical obligations to one another and to our physical and social environment. Such actions may ensure that "the gifts of fortune themselves [will not] become elements of misfortune" (DE xviii). Rather, we can use the gifts of nature – human potential, reasoned insight, scientific knowledge, environmental beauty – for constructive rather than destructive outcomes.

MASS CULTURE AND CONSUMPTION

Critical theory also focuses on **mass culture**, the media content produced by the technologically sophisticated, profit-driven **culture industry**. The early decades of television saw a corporate commitment (e.g., by NBC, CBS, and ABC in the US and the BBC in the UK) to educating the public, to keeping viewers well informed about politics and current events, and providing them with entertainment that would stimulate their intellectual and cultural curiosity and enhance their understanding of the human condition. This aim is increasingly displaced, however, by a concern with corporate profit margins. Thus, for example, today, television networks are *entertainment* businesses (see DE 108–109). News programs are entertainment, and are increasingly driven by economic and political partisan interests (e.g., Fox News/Sky Television, owned by Rupert Murdoch). Additionally, many large media businesses are part of even bigger global media and economic conglomerates (e.g., General Electric owns NBC).

The mass media, therefore, are an industry, and as such the production, packaging, marketing, and distribution of media products (news and other entertainment shows) are driven by the same profit criteria as in any other industry. Long before the media industry became as profit oriented as it is today, H & A emphasized the capitalist economic structure of the culture industry and the mass production and mass **homogenization** (sameness) and **standardization** of the (cultural) goods produced.

> Culture today is infecting everything with sameness. Film, radio, and magazines … no longer need to present themselves as art. The truth that they are nothing but business is used as an ideology to legitimize the trash they intentionally produce. They call themselves industries, and the published figures for their directors' incomes quell any doubts about the social necessity of their finished products. (DE 94–95)

TECHNOLOGY AND PROFIT

Some might argue that television and film, for example, because they are visual media, must necessarily use content that appeals to our visual senses – and hence the tendency for action images and adventure stunts to be given greater emphasis than the narrative plot itself; with special effects, we don't need much plot (DE 132). This argument is referred to as **technological determinism**, and it can be applied to any instance where technology is used as the logic (or excuse) for why something is the way it is. In this view, "technology has become the great vehicle of **reification** – reification in its most mature and effective form. The social position of the individual and his relation to others appear … as calculable manifestations of (scientific) rationality. The world tends to become the stuff of total administration, which absorbs even the administrators" (Marcuse 1964: 168–169). Reification means that technology is seen as having a self-regulating life of its own; technological tools are treated as if they themselves have an inherent rationality (and a political neutrality) such that decisions about their use in society are beyond human control. Hence, it is claimed, we must do what the technology allows us to do irrespective of whether we want to, and without consideration of the values at stake.

Critical theorists reject technological determinism; instead they emphasize that economic interests determine how technology is used. In the case of mass media, economic interests determine the content used to make profit and, by extension, these interests control audiences (for profit):

> Interested parties like to explain the culture industry in technological terms. Its millions of participants, they argue, demand reproduction processes which inevitably lead to the use of standard products to meet the same needs at countless locations … What is not mentioned is that the basis on which technology is gaining power over society is the power of those whose economic position in society is strongest. (DE 95)

Figure 5.3   Customers wait patiently in line to buy the latest iPhone, even though the differences between it and earlier iPhone models and other smartphone brands are relatively small. Source: © Carterdayne/iStockphoto.

Because the culture industry is so tied into economic profit, it produces entertainment standardized to have mass appeal to audiences who will watch (buy) that content and, importantly, buy the products advertised around it – and as part of it. The most efficient way for television and other media businesses to make money is through selling their own products (shows), and the products other businesses produce, to the people who are most likely to buy those products. In short, advertising is the real business of the culture industry. And the best way to ensure that the largest possible audience of consumers sees the paid advertising and product placement on television – and in/at the movies and on Internet sites – is to produce content standardized to fit targeted consumer demographic segments. According to H & A, the media industry manipulates us into watching only that which it predicts will sell. A similar manipulative logic is used by politicians: messages are tailored to themes that focus-group research indicates will sell (i.e., will convert into money or votes). Moreover, even with this targeted slicing or squeezing of the audience into different groups, the content produced remains standardized; the differences are not of substance but of packaging. A homogenized culture of sameness is what is being sold, whether in media entertainment or in politics. H & A elaborate:

> The dependence of the most powerful broadcasting company on the electrical industry, or of film on the banks, characterizes the whole sphere [the whole culture industry], the individual sectors of which [film, television, music production, etc.] are themselves economically intertwined. Everything is so tightly clustered that the concentration of intellect reaches a level where it overflows the demarcations between company names and technical sectors. The relentless unity of the culture industry bears witness to the emergent unity of politics. Sharp distinctions like those between [allegedly different] films … do not so much reflect real differences as assist in the classification, organization, and identification of consumers. Something is provided for everyone so that no one can escape; … Everyone is supposed to behave spontaneously according to a "level" determined by indices and to select the category of mass

product manufactured for their type. On the charts of research organizations, indistinguishable from those of political propaganda, consumers are divided up as statistical material into red, green, and blue areas according to income group …

That the difference between the models of Chrysler and General Motors is fundamentally illusory is known by any child who is fascinated by that very difference. The advantages and disadvantages debated by enthusiasts serve only to perpetuate the appearance of competition and choice. It is no different with the offerings of Warner Brothers and Metro-Goldwyn-Mayer. But the differences, even between the more expensive and cheaper products from the same firm, are shrinking – in cars to the different number of cylinders, engine capacity, and details of the gadgets, and in films to the different number of stars, the expense lavished on technology, labor and costumes, or the use of the latest psychological formulae … The budgeted differences of value in the culture industry have nothing to do with actual differences, with the meaning of the product itself. (DE 96–97)

Box 5.1   Antonio Gramsci and the concept of hegemony

Critical theory's emphasis on the importance of cultural processes in perpetuating the status quo and thus impeding the emancipatory progress promised by the Enlightenment (e.g., equality and reasoned democratic participation), reflected a more general cultural turn by influential Marxist theorists in the early part of the twentieth century. Among these was Antonio Gramsci (1891–1937), an Italian journalist and political activist who became general secretary of the Italian Communist Party in the 1920s. Imprisoned in 1926 by Benito Mussolini's Fascist dictatorship, his *Selections from the Prison Notebooks* (not translated into English until 1971) provide a fruitful analytical resource for thinking about the relation between political ideas and practical political action.

Gramsci opened up discussion of how the ruling ideology (and inequality) gets produced in everyday life. Whereas Marx argued that the ideas of the ruling class are the ruling ideas (see chapter 1), Gramsci (1971) argued that the notion of "ideological unity" either within a social class or a political bloc (political group/party), is somewhat misguided. In his framing, the reproduction of inequality is a much more dynamic process. Rather than a unified ruling ideology, he instead argued that many diverse currents of thought coexist in any historical period. And what needs to be explained is "how these currents are born, how they are diffused, and why in the process of diffusion they fracture along certain lines and in certain directions" (1971: 327). Various fragments, including dissenting or contrary ideas, get taken up in various ways across multiple domains of activity; they produce a "conception of the world" that is "implicitly manifest in art, in law, in economic activity and in all manifestations of individual and collective life" (ibid.). Importantly, there is enough space for "a progressive forward movement" that allows contrary ideas and demands to get satisfied to some extent, but in a way that does not disturb the equilibrium. Ideology, then, becomes essentially the common sense that "serves to cement and unify" separately stratified individuals and groups in consenting to the existing social order (ibid.). In this cementing, it is not the ruling class who imposes ruling ideas and coerces others into their acceptance. Rather, it is a more organic process whereby the lower strata ("the ruled") come to spontaneously believe in, or consent to, the common sense reasonableness of the very ideas that in practice serve the interests of the ruling class. This is hegemony: It is spontaneous, but implicitly orchestrated, consent to the status quo. The concept is highly influential in the sociology of culture, political sociology, cultural and literary studies, and in postcolonial and Southern theory (see chapter 12).

CULTURE OF ADVERTISING

The culture industry advertises (sells) consumption and keeps our attention focused on consumption, thus illuminating what Antonio Gramsci (see Box 5.1) would call the **hegemony** of consumption. The concept of hegemony captures the authoritative way in which certain cultural assumptions and practices appear so normal and natural that we freely *consent* to them (even though we are not legally required to accept them and, in principle, we can resist and contest them). The hegemony of consumption refers to the many intersecting and overlapping ways by which consumption (and the ideology of consumption) is organized and promoted such that consumption appears as the most attractive and natural thing to do. Whether surfing the Internet or riding the subway, we are flooded with information. And much of this is a very particular kind of information: It is promotional information about products to buy. We are thus entangled in a **promotional culture**. We are continuously reminded of various things that we should buy – what to eat, drink, wear, drive, own. The judges on *American Idol* sip from Coca-Cola cups and the *X Factor* judges sip Pepsi. Despite the appearance of consumer choice and competition, both shows are owned by Fox and both promote consumption and yield profit. Our promotional culture smoothly reproduces the capitalist status quo. And it is a never-ending stream. If we try to escape by going out to lunch to a popular restaurant – The Cheesecake Factory, for example – we encounter large attractive ads for several luxury products (diamond jewelry, cruise vacations, leather bags) as we flip through the menu (see Topic 5.3).

Topic 5.3   Advertising, advertising everywhere

So pervasive is advertising in contemporary society that "Anywhere the eye can see, it's now likely to see an ad" (Story 2007). Supermarket eggs advertise television shows, subway turnstiles promote Geico insurance, art museum buildings hang large supersized banners advertising expensive watches, Continental Airlines is promoted on Chinese food takeout cartons, and US Airways sells its air-sickness bags as advertising space. Digitalized advertising screens dominate not only in Piccadilly and Times Square but also along the highway, on the sides of buildings, at bus stops, and in elevators in department stores, hotels, and dental offices. In short, "in blank spaces in public places, advertisers see branding opportunities" (Story 2007: A14).

With ongoing advances in technology – and its harnessing to economic profit – Internet and consumer brand companies continuously seek and develop new ways to target us. As noted earlier in this chapter, Facebook uses new technology programmed to scan the information on users' personal pages and summon targeted ads; Google scans e-mail users' in-boxes to deliver ads related to those messages; and other companies listen in on Internet phone users' conversations so that they can deliver same-time ads related to the phone message content. Most of us don't give this constant scanning of our lives a second thought; that's the way it is. While at the beach or at a ballgame we are accustomed to seeing messages in the air, and now while in the air we expect to see some ads. A company called "Ad-Air" has created what it calls the "first global aerial advertising network" – giant, billboard-like ads that will be visible from the air as planes approach runways (Pfanner 2007: C10).

CONTROLLED CONSUMPTION

Although the advertising industry appeals to our individual vanity, it essentially promotes a culture of sameness – a **one-dimensionality** that suppresses individuality and variation (Marcuse 1964: 1) in favor of standardized sameness in how we look, feel, and think, and in what we think about. Thus, critical theorists argue, the culture industry does not promote political critique and participation but its opposite: the paralysis of criticism (Marcuse 1964: ix). Moreover, it does not respond to our real needs but to fabricated or **false needs** that it controls; fabricated, because rather than trying to establish what our real needs might be, the media industry determines our needs, as evidenced by what we buy in relation to what is made available to us:

> False needs are those which are superimposed upon the individual by particular social interests in his repression: the needs which perpetuate toil, aggressiveness, misery and injustice. Their satisfaction might be most gratifying to the individual but this happiness is not a condition which has to be maintained and protected if it serves to arrest the development of this ability (his own and others) to recognize the disease of the whole and grasp the chances of curing that disease … Most of the prevailing needs to relax, to have fun, to behave and consume in accordance with the advertisements, to love and hate what others love and hate, belong to this category of false needs. (Marcuse 1964: 4–5)

What we "need" or buy is controlled by the culture industry that manipulates us into buying from among the artificial choices it makes available to us; we cannot buy what is not offered. However, it is also apparent, contrary to this exaggerated view of the controlling power of mass media and advertising, that individuals find ways to make their needs known to manufacturers, and companies respond accordingly; this is seen, for example, in the decreased popularity of soda drinks and the expanded availability of more health-conscious (albeit manufactured) water and energy drinks. Similarly, when television audiences indicate their pleasure with a particular show, the media industry responds to audience interests (needs) with new similarly-themed shows (e.g., the popularity of *American Idol*-like contests, and reality shows).

In any case, the media and other consumer conglomerates use technology to track both what we buy and what we are likely to buy. Walmart, for example, closely tracks its customers' preferences from purchases made, and uses that detailed information to confidently predict the kind of things its customers will likely want in the future. And, reflecting the "insatiable uniformity" (DE 97) that characterizes choice in a capitalist society, it strategically divides its millions of customers into just three types of shoppers (see Topic 5.4).

Topic 5.4   Walmart shoppers

1 *Brand aspirationals*, people with low incomes who are obsessed with brand names like KitchenAid.
2 *Price-sensitive affluents*, wealthier shoppers who love deals.
3 *Value-price shoppers*, who like low prices and cannot afford much more (Barbaro 2007).

The sociological power of fashion imitation, as first noted by Georg Simmel – with whom Adorno studied – "gives to the individual the satisfaction of not standing alone in his actions. Whenever we imitate, we transfer not only the demand for creative activity, but also the responsibility for the action from ourselves to others. Thus the individual is freed from the worry of choosing and appears simply as a creature of the group." Though we proclaim our individual uniqueness, we are content with similarity and uniformity (Simmel 1904/1971: 295). In this framing, there seems to be only one way to be a 20-something today: You must look like you stepped out of an advertisement for Abercrombie & Fitch.

Through the language they speak, the customers make their own contribution to culture as advertising … the language and gestures of listeners and spectators are more deeply permeated by the patterns of the culture industry than ever before … All are free to dance and amuse themselves … But freedom to choose an ideology, which

Figure 5.4 According to critical theorists, the sameness or homogenization that characterizes mass media content also extends to a sameness in individual appearance and personality. Source: Author.

always reflects economic coercion, everywhere proves to be freedom to be the same. The way in which the young girl accepts and performs the obligatory date, the tone of voice used on the telephone and in the most intimate situations, the choice of words in conversation, indeed the whole inner life compartmentalized according to the categories of vulgarized depth psychology, bears witness to the attempt to turn oneself into an apparatus meeting the requirements of success, an apparatus which, even in its unconscious impulses, conforms to the model presented by the culture industry. The most intimate reactions of human beings have become so entirely reified, even to themselves, that the idea of anything peculiar to them survives only in extreme abstraction: personality means hardly more than dazzling white teeth and freedom from body odor and emotions. That is the triumph of advertising in the culture industry: the compulsive imitation by consumers of cultural commodities which, at the same time, they recognize as false. (DE 133, 135–136)

MEDIA REALITY AS THE LEGITIMATE REALITY

Whatever the content, all media – whether billed as fact (e.g., news, interviews) or fiction (drama) – is advertising, according to H & A, aimed at making us buy more media and other products. Thus, "Every film is a preview of the next, which promises yet again to unite the same heroic couple under the same exotic sun. Anyone arriving late cannot tell whether he is watching the trailer or the real thing" (DE 132). And we see promotional advertising not just in the movie theater, but across all media sectors. *ABC World News Tonight* will have a segment on an issue that is also being featured on one of ABC's sitcoms or dramas; the commentators on *Monday Night Football* will interrupt their play-by-play analysis of the live action on the field to take a few minutes to chat with the **celebrity** star of a soon-to-be-released movie owned by their parent company or of a new show starting on its network.

The mass mediated reality and the real reality frequently blur. This is especially evident in the so-called "reality" shows – which we eventually discover are not really reality shows but fictionalized and stylized enactments of a reality scripted by the TV producers. Celebrities further blur TV reality and real reality. Thus Richard Gere, who played a man who fell in love with a high-end prostitute (played by Julia Roberts) in the movie *Pretty Woman*, has the legitimacy to encourage thousands of Indian prostitutes to refuse sex without condoms to prevent the spread of HIV/AIDS. Harrison Ford is inducted into the Archaeology Hall of Fame, not because he is an archaeologist but because he is Indiana Jones (a popular movie character). And a pregnant Kim Kardashian, enthusiastically told her millions of social media followers that her morning sickness was much better since she started taking "Diclegis" a prescription morning sickness medicine; her post included a photo of her holding the branded Diclegis pill bottle. The legitimacy of celebrities persuading us to behave in particular ways might be explained from a Weberian perspective as being due to charismatic authority (see chapter 3). Nonetheless, most of us don't think it unusual to see celebrities engaging in public health, environmental, or other forms of advocacy. Nor is it unusual for the celebrity host of *The Apprentice*, Donald Trump, to become president of the US despite having no prior experience of any elected office. It seems natural to us that media reality is the reality. We (more or less) accept its definitions of the world as if they are, and should be, the only ones that count.

CULTURAL TOTALITARIANISM

Critical theorists thus conclude that mass consumer society produces a new form of totalitarianism, a **cultural totalitarianism** crystallized by the creation of false needs and the attendant suppression of ideas and needs that contravene those marketed in the perpetuation of capitalism. Marcuse elaborates:

> By virtue of the way it has organized its technological base, contemporary industrial society tends to be totalitarian. For "totalitarian" is not only a terroristic political coordination of society, but also a non-terroristic economic-technical coordination which operates through the manipulation of needs by vested interests … All liberation depends on the consciousness of servitude, and the emergence of this consciousness is always hampered by the predominance of needs and satisfactions which, to a great extent, have become the individual's own … the optimal goal is the replacement of false needs by true ones … The range of choice open to the individual is not the decisive factor in determining the degree of human freedom but *what* can be chosen and what *is* chosen by the individual. The criterion for free choice can never be an absolute one, but neither is it entirely relative. Free election of masters does not abolish the masters or the slaves. Free choice among a wide variety of goods and services does not signify freedom if these goods and services sustain social controls over a life of toil and fear, that is, if they sustain alienation. And the spontaneous reproduction of superimposed needs by the individual does not establish autonomy; it only testifies to the efficacy of the controls. (Marcuse 1964: 3, 7–8)

ACTIVE CONSUMERS AND AUDIENCES

Although these arguments about consumer culture accurately capture much of what surrounds us today, they tend to exaggerate the extent to which individuals passively embrace mass media and consumer culture. Several influential studies from as early as the mid-1970s (e.g., Hall and Jefferson 1976; McRobbie 1991) show that many viewers/readers of television dramas, soap operas, and romance and fashion magazines, draw on their own everyday experiences in interpreting media content. And although many people enjoy seeing the glamorous lifestyles celebrated in several television shows, this does not prevent them from actively comparing the television reality with the more burdensome and economically strained circumstances in their own lives and from criticizing the economic structures that produce stark inequalities (e.g., Ang 1985).

The current popularity of interactive-audience shows (such as *American Idol* with its phone/text audience votes), and the participatory culture required by Internet blogging and YouTube (e.g., Burgess and Green 2009), further challenge the claim that audiences are passive. Additionally, many Internet users actively protest against the tracking devices and advertising that clutter their favorite websites, as underscored by controversies in response to Facebook's policies regarding its ownership of users' personal information and other Internet advertising initiatives. The political success of ordinary people in getting technology and media companies to change their policies suggests a slightly greater democracy in technology-media control than acknowledged by critical theorists.

POLITICS: UNIFORMITY AND CONTROL

As noted previously, the sameness or homogeneity characterizing consumer culture also extends to politics. Politicians are packaged and advised by well-paid media handlers, and their "off-message" spontaneity is further curbed by their entangled ties to lobbyists and the media industry, which suppress any ideologically subversive views that politicians might be tempted to voice. In branding – and rebranding – their candidate-clients, the handlers also brand (and seek to control) the electorate, composed of (controllable) homogenized groups: soccer moms, NASCAR (competitive car-racing) dads, angry white men, and Walmart women (voters with lower incomes and lower education, who tend to be conservative and to have experienced economic difficulties). These homogenized groups are assumed to think alike. This makes it easier for political candidates and their consultants to target voters with clichéd policy messages that will feed into their perceived (short-term) needs, rather than opening up a discussion of the many pressing issues that voters, irrespective of demographics, are concerned about (e.g., health care). Thus, "One dimensional thought is systematically promoted by the makers of politics and their purveyors of mass information. Their universe of discourse is populated by self-validating hypotheses which, incessantly and monopolistically repeated, become hypnotic definitions or dictations" (Marcuse 1964: 14).

Topic 5.5 Social media in populist politics

Donald Trump's presidency and presidential campaign highlights the power of Twitter and social media as tools to rally supporters and denigrate perceived enemies (including cabinet members such as his hand-picked attorney general, Jeff Sessions). President Trump has 35 million followers on Twitter and he uses it several times a day to comment on all kinds of everything. The use of social media tends to reinforce partisanship and zealotry rather than expose people to reasonable differences of opinion. This dilution of the rationality of the public sphere is exacerbated by the increasing influence of partisan news organizations. Fox News, for example, tends to eschew the principles of evidence-based, impartial and objective reporting and tends instead to amplify "alternative facts" and "Trump truths" about, for example, climate change, President Trump's popularity (and President Obama's nationality and religion). Among Republicans, 70 percent say they trust Donald Trump more than the highly reputable *New York Times* and the *Washington Post*; and they also trust Trump more than the intellectually conservative magazines, the *Weekly Standard* and the *National Review*. Their trust in these outlets (always relatively low), declined further after Trump's election, reflective perhaps of the impact of his tweets that frequently praise Fox News and attack mainstream media as "fake news" (*The Economist*, 2017b, p. 22)

In Europe, populist parties were early adopters of social media. France's Marine le Pen's National Front coordinates hashtags, memes and animated videos across social media platforms. In Germany, the Pegida anti-Muslim movement began with a Facebook group, and the far right Alternative for Germany has more Facebook likes than any other German party (*The Economist*, 2017a, p. 41). It made notable gains in the German election in September 2017 and cast a shadow on Angela Merkel's victory. Similarly in the US, white nationalists are amplifying their numbers through social media and the Internet and coordinating what used to be several disparate factions into a more unified and visible movement (Frosch, McWhirter, and Kesling 2017).

TECHNOLOGY AS POLITICAL CONTROL

Like the media industry (and universities, stores, governments, parents), political consultants too use new technologies to control people. Brain-scanning MRI technology (like other new technologies) has many benefits; it can be used to help people as a result of the early detection and treatment of brain tumors. But, apparently, MRI technology can also detect political partisanship. We are accustomed to researchers conducting focus groups and surveys to control voters by finding out in advance what issues motivate them and what kinds of campaign advertising strategies they are likely to favor or frown upon. Now, technology can circumvent this kind of social research by allowing researchers to conduct experimental MRI assessments of voters' brains. As one of its sponsors (a former campaign strategist and aide to President Clinton) stated: "These new tools could help us someday … put a bit more science in political science" (Tierney 2004: A17). Science, as critical theorists emphasize, offers the promise of social and political progress. But what will this extra political science accomplish? It will likely be used, as critical theory would predict, to further assist campaign strategists and the advertising and media industry in their ceaseless efforts to gain strategic advantage over the competition, whether they are trying to sell a political candidate, a movie, or any other product.

It is unlikely that MRI or many other new technologies will be used to implement more egalitarian public policies (in health care, education, etc.), but as Marcuse predicted, to further sustain the status quo:

> Today political power asserts itself through its power over the machine process and over the technical organization of the apparatus. The government of advanced and advancing industrial societies can secure and maintain itself only when it succeeds in mobilizing, organizing, and exploiting the technical, scientific, and mechanical productivity available to industrial civilization … the machine [is] the most effective political instrument in any society whose basic organization is that of the machine process. (Marcuse 1964: 3)

As Jews who had to flee Nazi Germany, Horkheimer, Adorno, and Marcuse saw firsthand the prejudice and horror (e.g., the Holocaust) that are unleashed when passivity is the response to totalitarian control (e.g., Hitler). For this reason, they urge the rejection of the uniformity and standardization (sameness) that pervade contemporary culture, whether in political debate, advertising and media content, or consumer lifestyles. They instead advocate our engagement in a reasoned and values-oriented (normative) critique of the economic, political, and cultural forces that seek to control us – though it is, of course, hard to do, immersed as we are in this everyday reality. Nevertheless, the many geopolitical conflicts in the world today, and the accelerating expansion of global consumerism, make the remarks of H & A, written in the aftermath of World War II, a useful reminder that the thoughtful use of reason is ever-more necessary to stem the assault of manipulation and domination on so many aspects of everyday life:

> In a period of political division into immense blocs driven by an objective tendency to collide, horror has been prolonged. The conflicts in the third world and the renewed growth of [political, economic, and cultural] totalitarianism are not mere historical interludes any more than … fascism was … [in the 1930s and 1940s]. Critical thought … requires us to take up the cause of the remnants of freedom, of tendencies toward real humanity, even though they seem powerless in face of the great historical trend … What matters today is to preserve and disseminate freedom, rather than to accelerate, however indirectly, the advance toward the **administered world** [of government/state- regulation and corporate-bureaucratic control]. (DE xi–xii)

JÜRGEN HABERMAS: THE STATE AND THE PUBLIC SPHERE

For many years, **Jürgen Habermas** has drawn attention to the systemic problems in the economic and political spheres in late capitalist society. He highlights how the government needs to intervene more and more in trying to administer or control various crises in society (e.g., the collapse of the mortgage industry in the US in 2007–2008), crises that frequently result from a narrow, strategic rationality in the first place. Writing in the 1970s, Habermas argued that "in liberal capitalist societies … crises become endemic because temporarily unresolved **steering problems** which the process of economic growth produces at more or less regular intervals, *as such* endanger social integration" (1975: 25). Steering problems are prevalent, and frequently result from the routine profit-driven practices of the financial sector. When the losses from banks' risky bets – such as the $6 billion loss on a hedging decision by a banker at JP Morgan – become so large that they threaten the bank's viability and thus the financial assets of other institutions and individuals who have large deposits in the bank, the government is expected to step in to the rescue. Yet, many people wonder whether some banks should be saved, especially when there is a consistent pattern of profit-driven, risky behavior. These are the sorts of scenarios Habermas has in mind when he talks of societal crisis due to economic steering problems. He does not use the term **crisis** lightly. To the contrary, he states: "only when members of a society experience structural [institutional] alterations as critical for continued existence and feel their social identity threatened can we speak of crises" (1975: 3). The banks are essential to the local, national and global economy, and individuals and families have traditionally looked to the banking sector as a safe haven in assuring their pursuit of economic security and upward mobility. Banks' ongoing risky lending and money management practices, however, and the failures of banking executives, business leaders, and government regulators to correct these problems, weaken our trust in banking and by extension our feelings of economic security.

The perception of crisis is not driven, as Marx envisioned, by economic inequality and the revolution of the proletariat (see chapter 1). The likelihood of class consciousness developing has been diminished by the media industry and its promotion of consumption-driven lifestyles, as well as by the vast improvements in the standard of living of most people across the globe, notwithstanding persistent inequality (see Giddens 2003). Habermas argues that in Western capitalist societies, where citizens (more or less) have access to the same consumer goods, social class becomes "depoliticized" (1975: 25) – ordinary individuals lose their motivation to actively participate in the political process. Although the Occupy Wall Street movement is an important counterexample (see chapter 14), many who are not part of the highly affluent "1 percent" nonetheless believe that they should not make a political issue of economic inequality when we can all (more or less) go to the mall and when we can all (more or less) achieve a consumer lifestyle (see also chapter 15).

ECONOMIC AND POLITICAL STEERING PROBLEMS

Despite **class depoliticization** and the general public acceptance of the idea that the market's "invisible hand" works to produce both economic growth and social integration, ongoing tensions and crises within society (e.g., recession) indicate otherwise. There are, as Habermas states, steering problems in the circulation of money that make it periodically veer off track. Stock markets experience sudden declines, banks and corporations go bankrupt as a result of market forces (loss of profit) and/or financial corruption (e.g., embezzlement; manipulation of trading markets), and other corporations encounter severe financial shortfalls due, in large part, to cost and product mismanagement and the lack of prudent planning such that they request (and receive) multibillion dollar loan guarantees (bailouts) from the government, as occurred in the US, the UK, Ireland, and elsewhere during the 2008–2009 recession.

These problems might appear to us as narrow economic problems whose discussion should be confined to economists and business executives. But they are, in fact, not just economic but social and political problems. As Habermas notes, "In liberal capitalism, crises appear *in the form* of unresolved economic steering problems" (1975: 24). The economic system is not just responsible for economic productivity but plays a major role in the task of societal integration, that is, through its direct impact on employment, education, and opportunities for upward mobility; and on perpetuating the values (or ideology) of consumption, equality, and the depoliticized notion that "we are all middle class." Accordingly, economic problems threaten the whole structure of society. This is a direct result of the system interdependency (see Parsons, chapter 4) within modern society. Although there is institutional specialization, all institutions and spheres of activity are interdependent; thus, for example, the financial losses of Citibank, JP Morgan, and other banks in the US in 2007 led, among other consequences, to the severe curtailment of loans to community-college students, a sector of the population for whom access to affordable education is an urgent priority if they are to improve on their highly disadvantaged economic background. Therefore, precisely because the economic system has its own economically unresolvable steering problems, and because these problems can cause other problems in society and threaten its integration, the state (i.e., the government) needs to step in to prop up the economy, to steer it on a different course. This is why the US government launched its historically unprecedented rescue of several financial companies in 2008 and why the EU continues to come to the rescue of Greece, for example, despite the fact that Greece has not altered the structural organization of (and the problems that inhere in) its business, financial, and taxation systems.

LEGITIMATION CRISES

Among other consequences, government bailouts of banks and financial institutions underscored the **political dependency** of economic and financial markets; the economic steering mechanism is neither invisible – as some economists would argue – nor a self-contained system. Political dependency becomes apparent when ongoing, systemic problems in the economy and in interrelated systems (housing mortgages, health care, welfare, education, etc.) come to the fore. In such circumstances, we as citizens – no longer thinking of ourselves in terms of Marx's categories of wage-workers and capitalists – look to the state to manage or administer the crises and problems in society. Specifically, these problems pertain to what Habermas calls the **lifeworld** (following Alfred Schutz's conceptualization; see chapter 9): Our everyday world, and the normative (values) and institutional (workplace, school, family, etc.) context in which we organize and live our everyday lives (Habermas 1984: 70). We look to the state to fix the systems that break down or threaten to break down and to compensate for the dysfunctional consequences of capitalism (Habermas 1975: 54).

The state frequently fails to respond adequately to systemic problems. It is not clear even now (in 2019) whether government financial bailouts (back in 2008–2009) have been effective in steering either the local or the global economy back onto paths of sustained economic growth. Moreover, in administering to societal problems, government frequently falls short; this is evident for example in its failure to provide adequate low-income housing; to ensure the safety of people in public housing – as highlighted by the tragic Grenfell Tower fire in London; or in dealing with public health threats posed by Ebola and other infectious diseases. In other instances, the state may overreach into individuals' lives, regulating complex personal decisions (e.g., relating to abortion or to assisted suicide) or monitoring private e-mail and text-messaging conversations. The tension between individual freedom and government control came to the fore in 2013 with the public disclosure by Edward Snowden, an employee of the US National Security Agency (NSA), that the US government is widely engaged in logging information based on Americans' personal e-mails, phone calls, and other digital traffic. This major breach in US intelligence, in addition to subsequent disclosures about US intelligence gathering alliances with other governments (e.g., Britain), has stoked public and legislative debate in many countries regarding the balance between individuals' private data and the interests of national and international security.

When individuals perceive the state as either having failed to intervene sufficiently or having overreached into the lifeworld, then we have what Habermas calls a **legitimation crisis**. This occurs when "the legitimizing system does not succeed in maintaining the requisite level of mass loyalty while the steering imperatives taken over from the economic system are carried through" (Habermas 1975: 46). In other words, it constitutes a sort of "identity crisis" (1975: 46) among the citizenry, because "the people," the governed, feel that they can no longer consent to the tasks the government sets for itself (and for the nation), and nor to the methods it uses in attempting to manage those tasks. Such crises typically mobilize individuals and groups to engage in political action – whether mass protest (e.g., favoring immigration reform, or Wikileaks), social movement participation advocating specific reforms (e.g., Occupy groups, the women's movement, the civil rights movement, the green movement), or simply voting.

BIOGRAPHICAL NOTE

Jürgen Habermas was born near Cologne, Germany, in 1929. He studied philosophy, history, psychology, and German literature and received his doctorate from Bonn University in 1954. Soon thereafter, he became Adorno's research assistant at the ISR, then reestablished back in Frankfurt. Habermas has held important sociology professorships at a number of German universities as well as delivering public lectures in the US. In addition to writing his many scholarly works, he is a frequent commentator on German and Western politics (Outhwaite 2000: 659–661).

COMMUNICATION IN THE PUBLIC SPHERE

Political protest, and political discussion in general, is core to democracy. It can also be a significant engine of change in nondemocratic societies (e.g., Poland's Solidarity Movement in undermining the Soviet Union). Habermas has long emphasized the centrality of communication and of communicative freedom as among the requisite norms of democratic society. In particular, he has focused on the historical significance of the emergence of a vibrant **public sphere** or **civil society**, composed of citizens/individuals coming together in, and as, a public to freely and openly debate the issues of the day (Habermas 1989: 27). Historically (e.g., in late seventeenth-/eighteenth-century Europe), this sphere of public discussion was relatively autonomous of government, church, and economic control; and the rise of mass distributed newspapers expanded the range of topics and issues discussed. Today, however, Habermas argues, a democratic public sphere wherein individuals come together in groups and in informal public settings to talk with each other about political and economic issues is increasingly colonized or infiltrated by corporate economic and self-interested political actors. The polarization of political discourse (e.g., on climate change) and the dissemination of falsehoods on social and online media make reason a casualty of the so-called post-truth society (see Introduction, Topic I.2, and chapter 5, Topic 5.5).

Aside from the ubiquity of heavily commercialized media content, even informal conversation at Starbucks occurs against the preselected background music that it advertises to customers for instant iPod downloading. Moreover, casual conversation itself – while waiting for a bus or for class to begin and even at the dinner table – is impeded by our habit of checking our smartphone's constant stream of activity (much of it advertising). Habermas argues that this **colonization of the lifeworld** needs to be resisted and supplanted by the reactivation of engaged, reasoned conversation.

For him, reasoned communication with others with whom we disagree (whether individuals, groups, organizations, or governments) is the only way forward toward the retrieval of a rational democratic society. This is the core idea of Habermas's (1984; 1987) theory of **communicative action** (TCA). His intent in TCA is to retrieve reason from its distorted, one-sided association with instrumental rationality evident in the various forces of strategic domination in society (discussed previously) and to reattach it to its Enlightenment association as a resource in advancing social and political equality (see McCarthy 1984). Habermas focuses on how communicative reason can be used to resist and move beyond the colonization of the lifeworld (the domination of everyday life) by **systems of domination** (the state, commercialized mass media, corporations). He emphasizes that reason can be used, not just to dominate and control, but to emancipate (as Enlightenment thinkers envisioned), to secure our freedom from the iron cage imposed by instrumental, technical rationality. We can use language, he argues, reasoned arguments, to critique domination and find ways out of it.

Habermas introduces the construct of an **ideal speech situation** – a theoretically imagined context in which participants use reason not to dominate or bully one another but to seek to reach a common understanding of the question at issue and of plans for mutually agreed, future action. The ideal speech situation, therefore, is characterized by **communicative rationality** and not by strategic or instrumental rationality. Communicative rationality requires participants (interlocutors) to use reasoned arguments to query or to raise validity claims about (1) the propositional (objective) truth, (2) the normative or values rightness, and (3) the sincerity of statements made by one another (Habermas 1984: 86, 75). The purpose of reciprocal, reasoned deliberation is to find a reasoned consensus that, in turn, becomes the basis for action. Communicative action is thus a cooperative (and not a strategic) process of reasoned interpretive negotiation "in which no participant has a monopoly on correct interpretation" (1984: 100).

We can see, therefore, that the creation of an ideal speech situation for communicative exchange might help to move us beyond the stalemates that characterize everyday culture and politics. Whatever the issue (e.g., Israeli–Palestinian conflict, abortion, physician-assisted suicide, immigration reform) and whether it is local or global in scope,

> Communicatively achieved agreement must be based in the end on reasons. And the rationality of those who participate in this communicative practice is determined by whether, if necessary, they could under suitable circumstances provide reasons for their expressions … The "strength" of an argument is measured in a given context by the soundness of the reasons; that can be seen in, among other things, whether or not an argument is able to convince the participants in a discourse, that is, to motivate them to accept the validity claim in question. (Habermas 1984: 17–18)

In other words, individuals (or political parties, or trade unions, or nation-states) cannot enter communication situations with a preset, stubborn notion of acceptable outcomes. Instead, there has to be sincere openness to the reasoned arguments of others, and we must be able to reason in response to the claims they put forward and offer counterarguments until we reach a consensus. Similarly, our communication partners must be open to our arguments and prepared to counterargue. Such reflexively reasoned communication facilitates cooperation in reaching a decision on which there is a consensus toward some future action.

DISTORTED COMMUNICATION

Although Habermas's ideal speech situation offers a hopeful way of thinking about the resolution of conflict, it can be difficult to realize in practice. Even when negotiating a restaurant choice with our friends, it is difficult to transcend our own individual assumptions and preferences, to not act in a calculating and strategic fashion, no matter what surface appearance we may present. We are so accustomed to the principle of exchange in social life (see chapter 7), we tend to think of compromise as something we do today with the expectation that someone will do something for us later. Compromise, however, is not the same as reaching consensus. A rationally achieved *consensus* requires the crafting of what may be a totally new action outcome, one not initially intended (or strategically manipulated) by any of the participants. Compromise, by contrast, tends to be a solution that honors, however partially, the initial agendas/interests of the participants and typically does not require the participants to reexamine the assumptions informing their preferences, interests, or values. Compromise often works well, whether in politics or among friends, but it may not do much to remedy inequality and other pressing social problems.

At the societal level, there are many institutional blocks to communicative rationality. Habermas acknowledges that the steering mechanisms within capitalist society, that is, money and power and the range of economic, social, and ecological problems they exacerbate (1996: xlii), produce **distorted communication**; they distort and dilute the possibilities for (nonstrategic) communicative rationality. The resolution of the health-care crisis in the US, for example, would necessarily require an examination of the fundamental ways in which health-care distribution is managed and organized. This would inevitably raise basic questions about the economics of health care, and by extension, spotlight the fundamental assumptions built into capitalism, not least of which is its structurally inherent, economic and social inequality. No matter how well intentioned any player in the health sector may be, the many varied economic and political interests at stake among the participants – hospitals, insurance companies, pharmaceutical drug companies, doctors' and nurses' professional organizations, corporate and small business employers, federal and state government, patients' groups, and medical malpractice lawyers – diminish the possibility that all of the players would be willing to reflexively examine how their particular strategic interests may be getting in the way of creating a more equitable, more efficient, and more effective health-care system. This distortion – deeply grounded in the very structure of our society and its forms of institutional and social organization – thus impedes the likelihood of communicative rational action regarding health care.

REASON IN THE CONTEXT OF EVERYDAY LIFE

In general, given everyday lived realities, the application of Habermas's concept of an ideal speech situation ruled by communicative reason may seem unrealistic, notwithstanding the hope it stimulates for realizing a more communicatively open and participative democracy. Habermas has been criticized for marginalizing the impact of the power inequalities in social interaction and the different interests, experiences, traditions, language capabilities, and informal narrative storytelling styles that participants variously bring to a particular communicative context (e.g., Calhoun 1995; Collins 1990: 212; Frazer and Lacey 1993: 19–21, 144–147). Further, he tends to exclude the relevance of emotions despite their obvious centrality to communication and social interaction, as highlighted by feminist theorists such as Arlie Hochschild (see chapter 10). Moreover, notwithstanding the ways in which religious ideas can facilitate reasoned communication and institutional critique (e.g., Dillon 1999), Habermas has expressed a skeptical view of religion in the public sphere, seeing it as a distorting influence due to its nonrational elements (Habermas 1987: 77). He has, however recently revised his understanding (e.g., Habermas 2008) and does so in the context of a broader reassessment by sociologists of the nature of modernity and its problems and possibilities, a topic to which we turn in chapter 15.

SUMMARY

Critical theorists offer an insightful critique of contemporary culture, society, and politics. They argue that while we use reason to produce new scientific knowledge and sophisticated technologies that enhance our lives, at the same time we use much of this knowledge for social control, and to advance capitalist economic, political, and cultural domination. This is the "dialectic of Enlightenment," seen, for example, in the one-dimensional content (the sameness) that characterizes the (false) choices celebrated in advertising and consumption and in the polarized shrillness of political discourse. Jürgen Habermas glimpses a way out of this domination. He argues that we need to retrieve an emancipatory, communicative rationality such that through reasoned discourse and engagement with others we can recommit to the Enlightenment values of equality and human flourishing, and thus reject the colonization of the lifeworld – the domination of everyday life – by economic, political, and other self-serving instrumental forces. There is much evidence to support the pessimistic view of mass culture, politics, and technological colonization articulated by critical theorists. But, importantly, there are many empirical instances that challenge or nuance their theoretical claims.

POINTS TO REMEMBER

Enlightenment values affirm:
- Reason
- Equality
- Emancipation

The Dialectic of Enlightenment (Horkheimer and Adorno):

Critiques the selective implementation of Enlightenment values/ideals. It highlights that:

- Reason has become equated with instrumental, strategic, or technical reason
- Technical rationality trumps normative (or values) rationality

This one-sided use of reason results in domination and subjugation, not emancipation or social progress. It produces repression, not illumination, and a society in which culture and politics are characterized by homogenization, standardization, uniformity, and conformity

Habermas:

Focuses on rational domination and the steering of an administered society by money and power interests, resulting in the colonization of the lifeworld

Highlights the depoliticization of class, and the sources and consequences of legitimation crises

His theory of communicative action aims to:

- Rescue reason from its one-sided association with instrumental rationality/domination
- Retrieve reasoned communication; emphasize communicative rationality, not instrumental rationality
    - This is possible through the ideal speech situation in which participants make validity claims and counterclaims regarding assumptions and goals
- Communicative action aims to build a reasoned consensus, and to avoid domination
    - It is impeded by structures and power interests within capitalism that produce distorted communication

GLOSSARY

administered world bureaucratic-state regulation and control diminishing the political autonomy of individuals and the public sphere.

celebrity mass media celebration of the public legitimacy and influence of actors and other media personalities irrespective of their credentials.

civil society sphere of society mediating between individuals and the state, for example, informal groups, social movements, mass media.

class depoliticization growth in working-class affluence and consumerism reduces the (Marxist-assumed) class-based motivation to use the political process to protest against economic inequality.

colonization of the lifeworld the idea that the state and economic corporations (including advertising and mass media) increasingly penetrate and dominate all aspects of everyday life.

communicative action the idea that social action should be determined by a rationally argued consensus driven by empirically grounded claims and rationally argued ethical norms rather than strategic partisan interests.

communicative rationality back-and-forth reasoning and reflexive examination of the claims made in a given communicative exchange. The reasonableness of the arguments articulated rather than the power or status of the communication partners determines the communicative outcome.

critical theory critique of the one-sided, instrumental, strategic, or technical use of reason in democratic capitalist societies to advance economic, political, and cultural power and suppress critique of social institutions and social processes, rather than to increase freedom, social equality, and democratic participation. Critical theory highlights the irrational character of what society presents as rational; this perspective is most closely associated with Frankfurt School theorists.

cultural totalitarianism the repression of diversity in the expression of individual needs and opinions; accomplished by the restricted sameness of content and choices available in the economic, political, and cultural marketplace.

culture industry corporate economic control of the mass media and its emphasis on advertising and business rather than providing cultural content (e.g., ideas, story plots) that would challenge rather than bolster the status quo.

dialectic of Enlightenment the thesis that the ideas affirmed by the Enlightenment (e.g., the use of reason in the advancement of freedom, knowledge, and democracy) have been turned into their opposite (reason in the service of control, inequality, political passivity) by the instrumentally rational domination exerted by capitalist institutions (e.g., the state and financial, technological, and media companies).

distorted communication ways in which current social, economic and political arrangements and cultural assumptions (e.g., free markets; hierarchical authority; individual self-reliance) impede communicative rationality.

emancipated society when previously marginalized individuals and groups are free to fully participate across all spheres of society; one in which freedom rather than domination is evident in social and institutional practices.

Enlightenment eighteenth-century philosophical movement emphasizing the centrality of individual reason, human equality, and scientific rationality over nonrational beliefs and forms of social organization (e.g., monarchy).

false needs the fabrication or imposition of consumer wants (needs) as determined by mass media, advertising, and economic corporations in the promotion of particular consumer lifestyles; and which consumers (falsely) feel as authentically theirs.

hegemony the everyday, authoritative ways in which certain cultural assumptions appear so normal and natural that we freely consent to them; for example, advertising and media culture orchestrate our consent to consumerism and more generally to the status quo and the dominant ideology (Gramsci).

homogenization standardization of products, content, and choices in consumption and politics driven by the mass orientation (sameness) most profitable or advantageous to the culture industry, and other corporate and political actors.

ideal speech situation when communication partners use reason (communicative rationality) to seek a common understanding of a question at issue and to embark on rationally justified, mutually agreed, future action.

instrumental domination strategic use of reason (knowledge, science, technology) to control others.

legitimation crisis when national or other collectivities lose trust in the ability of the state (or other institutions) to adequately respond to systemic disruptions in the execution of institutional tasks (e.g., the effective functioning of the banking system).

lifeworld from the German word *Lebenswelt*; the world of everyday life and its taken-for-granted routines, customs, habits, and knowledge.

mass culture advertising and other mass mediated content delivered by a technologically sophisticated, profit-driven, corporate culture industry.

mystique of science unquestioned presumption that the accumulation, application, and everyday use of scientific data and scientific advances are invariably good and that they should be automatically welcomed as evidence of social progress.

normative rationality evaluative use of reason to advance values (or prescriptive norms) of equality and freedom.

one-dimensionality sameness, homogenization, or standardization; lack of meaningful alternatives in mass culture and politics.

political dependency dependence of citizens and economic and other institutions on the state to resolve problems and crises created, by and large, by the state and economic institutions.

promotional culture constant stream of consumer advertising dominating mass media content and public space (e.g., highways).

public sphere public, relatively informal spaces (e.g., coffee shops, public squares) and non-state-controlled institutional settings (e.g., mass media, voluntary and nonprofit organizations) where individuals and groups freely assemble and discuss political and social issues; produces "public opinion." *See also* civil society.

reification from the Latin word *res*, "thing"; process whereby we think of social structures (e.g., capitalism), social institutions and other socially created things (e.g., language, technology, "Wall Street," "The City") as things independent of human construction rather than as social creations that can be modified and changed to meet a society's changing needs and interests and to accomplish particular normative or strategic goals.

scientific management industrial method introduced in the early twentieth century by Frederick Taylor to increase worker efficiency and productivity by controlling workers' physical movements/techniques.

social control methodical regulation curtailing the freedom of individuals, groups, and society as a whole.

standardization imposition of sameness or homogenization in culture and politics.

steering problems emerge when economic and political institutions do not work as functionally intended and as ideologically assumed (e.g., the market's "invisible hand" working to produce economic growth and social integration), thus causing problems (e.g., recession) whose resolution demands state intervention in the system (e.g., federal monetary policy).

systems of domination penetration of the regulatory control of the state and other bureaucratic and corporate entities into everyday life.

technical rationality calculated procedures and techniques used in the strategic implementation of instrumental goals typically in the service of economic profit and/or social control.

technological determinism the assumption that the use of a particular technology is determined by features of the technology itself rather than by the dominant economic, political, and cultural interests in society.

QUESTIONS FOR REVIEW

1   What does it mean to say that the Enlightenment has turned into the opposite of what it promised? What factors have contributed to this societal condition?
2   How are contemporary forms of technology used as instruments of control? And by whom? And with what consequences?
3   How is rationality used irrationally? And can society's response to its consequences be considered rational or irrational? Explain, using a local example.
4   How is one-dimensionality manifested today in entertainment, and in politics?
5   How does Habermas's framework and, in particular, his response to the dominance of instrumental or strategic rationality, differ from that of his older colleagues?

REFERENCES

Adorno, Theodor, E. Frenkel-Brunswik, D.J. Levinson, and R.N. Sanford. 1950. *The Authoritarian Personality*. New York: Harper and Row.

Ang, Ien. 1985. *Watching Dallas: Soap Opera and the Melodramatic Imagination*. New York: Routledge.

Barbaro, Michael. 2007. "It's Not Only about Price at Wal-Mart." *New York Times* (March 2), pp. C1, 6.

Burgess, Jean, and Joshua Green. 2009. *YouTube: Online Video and the Politics of Participatory Culture*. Oxford: John Wiley & Sons/Polity.

Calhoun, Craig. 1995. *Critical Social Theory: Culture, History, and the Challenge of Difference*. Oxford: Blackwell.

Collins, Patricia Hill. 1990. *Black Feminist Thought: Knowledge, Consciousness, and the Politics of Empowerment*. New York: Routledge. 2nd edition 2000.

Dillon, Michele. 1999. "The Authority of the Holy Revisited: Habermas, Religion, and Emancipatory Possibilities." *Sociological Theory* 17: 290–306.

Economist. 2017a. "Twitter Harvest." (March 4), p. 41.

Economist. 2017b. "Fox Populi." (August 5), p. 22.

Economist. 2017c. "How to Cope with Floods." (September 2), p. 9.

Frazer, Elizabeth, and Nicola Lacey. 1993. *The Politics of Community: A Feminist Critique of the Liberal-Communitarian Debate*. Toronto: University of Toronto Press.

Frosch, Dan, Cameron McWhirter, and Ben Kesling. 2017. "The New Extremism: Unified, Tech-Savvy." *Wall Street Journal* (August 17), p. A1.

Giddens, Anthony. 2003. *Runaway World: How Globalization is Reshaping our Lives*. New York: Routledge.

Glanz, James, and John Markoff. 2011. "Egypt's Autocracy Found Internet's 'Off' Switch." *New York Times* (February 6), pp. A1, 10.

Gramsci, Antonio. 1971. *Selections from the Prison Notebooks of Antonio Gramsci*. Edited and translated by Quentin Hoare and Geoffrey Nowell-Smith. New York: International Publishers.

Habermas, Jürgen. 1975. *Legitimation Crisis*. Boston: Beacon Press.

Habermas, Jürgen. 1984. *The Theory of Communicative Action*, volume 1. Boston: Beacon Press.

Habermas, Jürgen. 1987. *The Theory of Communicative Action*, volume 2. Boston: Beacon Press.

Habermas, Jürgen. 1989. *The Structural Transformation of the Public Sphere*. Cambridge, MA: MIT Press.

Habermas, Jürgen. 1996. *Between Facts and Norms: Contributions to a Discourse Theory of Law and Democracy*. Cambridge, MA: MIT Press.

Habermas, Jürgen. 2008. "Notes on a Post-Secular Society." *New Perspectives Quarterly* 25: 4.

Hall, Stuart, and Tony Jefferson, eds. 1976. *Resistance through Rituals: Youth Subcultures in Post-War Britain*. London: Hutchinson.

Horkheimer Max, and Theodor Adorno. 1972/2002. *The Dialectic of Enlightenment*. Edited by Gunzelin Schmid Noerr. Translated by Edmund Jephcott. Stanford, CA: Stanford University Press.

Jay, Martin. 1973. *The Dialectical Imagination: A History of the Frankfurt School and the Institute of Social Research 1923–1950*. London: Heinemann.

Kirkpatrick, David D., and Jennifer Preston. 2011. "Google Executive Who Was Jailed Said He Was Part of an Online Campaign in Egypt." *New York Times* (February 8), p. A10.

Marcuse, Herbert. 1964. *One-Dimensional Man: Studies in the Ideology of Advanced Industrial Society*. Boston: Beacon Press.

McCarthy, Thomas. 1984. "Translator's Introduction." Pp. v–xlii in Jürgen Habermas, *The Theory of Communicative Action*, volume 1. Boston: Beacon Press.

McRobbie, Angela. 1991. *Feminism and Youth Culture: From Jackie to Just Seventeen*. Boston: Unwin Hyman.

Outhwaite, William. 2000. "Jürgen Habermas." Pp. 651–669 in George Ritzer, ed. *The Blackwell Companion to Major Social Theorists*. Oxford: Blackwell.

Pfanner, Eric. 2007. "The View from Your Airplane Window Was Brought to You by …" *New York Times* (September 25), p. C10.

Simmel, Georg. 1904/1971. *On Individuality and Social Forms*. Chicago: University of Chicago Press. Edited and with an introduction by Donald Levine.

Story, Louise. 2007. "Anywhere the Eye Can See, It's Now Likely to See an Ad." *New York Times* (January 15), pp. A1, 14.

Taylor, Frederick. 1911. *The Principles of Scientific Management*. New York: Harper.

Tierney, John. 2004. "Politics on the Brain? Resorting to MRIs for Partisan Signals." *New York Times* (April 4), pp. A1, 17.

CHAPTER SIX

CONFLICT, POWER, AND DEPENDENCY IN MACRO-SOCIETAL PROCESSES

KEY CONCEPTS

group conflict

power

dialectic of power and
    resistance

interest group

manifest interests

latent interests

democratization of conflict

functions of social conflict

postcapitalist society

conflict groups

authority structures

new middle class

postindustrial society

power elite

triangle of power

mass society thesis

neo-Marxist

development

underdevelopment

world system

center–satellite

dependence

situations of dependency

CHAPTER MENU

Introduction to Sociological Theory: Theorists, Concepts, and Their Applicability to the Twenty-First Century,
Third Edition. Michele Dillon.
© 2020 John Wiley & Sons Ltd. Published 2020 by John Wiley & Sons Ltd.
Companion website: www.wiley.com/go/dillon

Given Talcott Parsons's influence on American and much of European sociology from the 1940s to the 1980s (see chapter 4), students might have had little familiarity with the ideas of other theorists writing at that time. Critical theory had a small readership in the English-speaking world until the 1970s (see chapter 5), and other European theorists of that generation, most notably Louis Althusser (1969), Georg Lukács(1968), and Antonio Gramsci (1929/1971) – all intellectually indebted to Karl Marx – remained similarly inaccessible to English-speaking audiences. Nevertheless, these same decades saw important challenges to Parsons's core ideas. While Parsons was emphasizing the importance of shared values in orienting social action, Ralf Dahrendorf was emphasizing the centrality of conflict. While Parsons was emphasizing the smooth functioning of institutional structures, C. Wright Mills was highlighting the matrix of power within the institutional system. And while Parsons was elaborating an allegedly universal, American-centered modernization theory, Latin American-based scholars such as Andre Gunder Frank and Fernando Cardoso were emphasizing the structurally dependent, economic relations between countries and geographical regions. This chapter traces these diverse perspectives to highlight how they conceptualize macro-societal processes in ways that build on classical theory (especially that of Marx and Weber; see chapters 1 and 3), while also moving beyond Parsons's framework. Although the theorists in this chapter do not share a coherent intellectual perspective, their joint relevance lies in their contributions articulating alternative ideas to Parsons's about how macro-societal processes work. And each in his own right also advances sociological thinking about specific phenomena: conflict, power, and economic change and development.

RALF DAHRENDORF'S THEORY OF GROUP CONFLICT

Ralf Dahrendorf was a German-born sociologist who spent most of his career in England. He is most associated with underscoring the normalcy of **group conflict** in society, a thesis he counterposed against Parsons's emphasis on values consensus. For Dahrendorf, society is composed of unequal power and competing group interests and should thus be understood in terms of coercion and constraint rather than voluntary obedience or consensus. **Power**, he argues, "is unequally divided, and therefore a lasting source of friction" (Dahrendorf 1968: 138). Thus, Dahrendorf claims, any given sociopolitical context can be described in terms of the antagonism between power and resistance (1968: 145). He explains:

> Power always implies non-power and therefore resistance. The **dialectic of power and resistance** is the motive force of history. From the interests of those in power at a given time we can infer the interests of the

powerless, and with them the direction of change ... Power produces conflict, and conflict between antagonistic interests gives lasting expression to the fundamental uncertainty of human existence, by ever giving rise to new solutions and ever casting doubt on them as soon as they take form. (Dahrendorf 1968: 227)

Justice, then, in this view, is "the permanently changing outcome of the dialectic of power and resistance" (1968: 150).

BIOGRAPHICAL NOTE

Ralf Dahrendorf was born in Hamburg, Germany, in 1929. He received his PhD from the London School of Economics (LSE) and subsequently had a distinguished academic and political career, holding professorships of sociology at several German universities and serving as director of the LSE. He retired as warden of St. Anthony's College in Oxford in 1997. In the early 1970s, he served in the German parliament and was Germany's European Commissioner in Brussels. Dahrendorf became a British citizen in 1988. Among many honors, he was granted a peerage by the queen in 1993, thus privileging him with a seat in the British Parliament's upper House of Lords. He contributed frequently to scholarly and political debates until his death in 2009.

Dahrendorf does not see conflict as a threat to society, though some conflicts produce violence that undermines the fabric of a given community (e.g., gang violence) or country (such as election violence in Kenya despite its embrace of multiparty democracy). Nonviolent conflict, however, is what mostly characterizes democratic societies. It inheres in social life, a result of the unequal distribution of power and authority, and does not necessarily produce disorder or chaos. Dahrendorf explains:

Institutions have to be set up in such a way as to accommodate change, conflict, and the interplay of power and resistance. There is no foolproof recipe for creating such institutions, and someday we may well conclude that parliaments, elections, and the other traditional democratic political machinery are only one of many arrangements of roughly equal effectiveness. In any case, such institutions should allow for conflict; they should be designed to control power rather than to camouflage it behind an ideology of consensus, and they should permit change even in the unwieldy structure of a complex modern society. (Dahrendorf 1968: 149)

The establishment of democratic institutions, however, is difficult – as highlighted by the ongoing obstacles encountered in efforts to establish civic structures in Iraq, for example, that would be fair to all competing groups (and be perceived as fair). We see similar hurdles in the various community-policing initiatives that aim to build trust among competing gangs in inner-city neighborhoods. Nonetheless, Dahrendorf emphasizes that conflict is part and parcel of social life and that society, rather than ignoring conflict, deals with its normalcy by institutionally regulating it. Bureaucratic division within organizations is one relatively effective way to regulate different groups' differential access to power and authority (e.g., between engineers and accountants in a large construction or computer-software firm).

CONFLICT GROUPS

Formally organized interest groups such as labor unions, other employee and professional groups, and employer/management associations are all part of the institutionalization of conflicting interest groups and of class conflict in democratic industrial societies (Dahrendorf 1959: 257). An **interest group** is

Box 6.1   Donald Black: Conflict in social space

Donald Black (a distinguished professor of sociology at the University of Virginia) has written extensively on the sociology of conflict, law, and justice. He offers a stimulating framework for thinking about social conflict in his book *Moral Time* (2011). Black views social life in geometrical-spatial terms. He construes a multidimensional structure of social space, composed of relational, vertical, and cultural dimensions to predict and explain conflict. Relational distance is a degree of *intimacy* (relational closeness – e.g., in friendship, marriage, at work); vertical distance is a degree of *inequality*, such as differences in wealth or authority; and cultural distance is a degree of *diversity*, such as differences that emerge from religion, ethnicity, traditions, creative ideas, scientific discoveries, or innovative practices. Black argues that "Social space fluctuates and thus the movement of social time – the ceaseless motion of the social universe – is the cause of all conflict" (2011: 5). Specifically, the ceaseless movement of social time produces either an increase or a decrease of intimacy, inequality, or diversity, and changes in these events produce conflict. Because social space is never frozen but always marked by the movement of social time (i.e., ongoing social activity), conflict is pervasive, ubiquitous, inevitable, and ongoing. Every conflict is an event, either positive or negative, and has a history; and because conflict itself is an event, it causes more conflict. By contrast, "If social space were frozen forever, conflict would never occur" (2011: 5). We can use Black's innovative analysis to predict any kind of social conflict: cultural conflict (e.g., due to the lifestyle differences between American-born young Koreans and their Korean-born immigrant parents in the US; intra-institutional conflict (e.g., as a result of the relational, vertical, and cultural distance between Catholic bishops and Catholic laity); interinstitutional conflict (e.g., as a result of the vertical distance between the banking industry and government regulators); and international conflict (e.g., as a result of the relational, cultural, and vertical distance between the US and Pakistan). See also Topic 6.1.

any "organized collectivity of individuals sharing **manifest interests**," that is, interests that the collectivity is consciously aware of and articulates as being their interests. Groups, by virtue of their organizational position vis-à-vis other groups, also have interests of which they may be unaware; such objective (though perhaps unacknowledged) interests are referred to as **latent interests**. For Dahrendorf, the **democratization of conflict** represents structural change to society, "which is due to no small extent to the effects of industrial conflict" (1959: 257). Society has adapted to conflict with the establishment of diverse interest groups and organizations and of conflict-mediating/negotiating bodies (such as labor courts for the mediation of employee–management disputes, especially prominent in Western Europe).

Class antagonisms between factory workers and owners, vividly apparent as a result of unsafe working conditions in late nineteenth-century factories and mills, gave rise to political solutions establishing new norms (e.g., legislation regulating work-hours) and new structures and opportunities (e.g., legalization of employee unions) for the airing and negotiation of grievances. Dahrendorf argues that the establishment of trade unions reduces the intensity of conflict between workers and owners. With the democratization of conflict, "Organized groups stand in open, and therefore in controllable, conflict" (1959: 259). This process is exemplified in the US in the relations between the car manufacturing companies (e.g., GM, Ford, Chrysler) and the car workers' union, the United Auto Workers (UAW). Though they frequently have tense relations, both sides ultimately resolve their disputed issues (at least temporarily). Perhaps for this same reason, Walmart is rethinking its negative attitude toward unionization, recognizing that conflict is more easily controlled when it is institutionalized rather than suppressed.

Although Dahrendorf positions himself as a critic of functionalism, it is more accurate to say that he is a critic not of functionalism but of Parsons's emphasis on the functionalism of generalized, consensual values in society. Instead, Dahrendorf emphasizes the **functions of social conflict**. Social conflict has an integrative function insofar as it is an essential feature built into the structures of social life, allowing for the coexistence and interdependence of numerous groups with diverse, overlapping, and conflicting interests (Dahrendorf 1959: 206–207). At the same time, social conflict also functions as a mechanism of social change (1959: 206–207).Conflicts can result in structural changes (e.g., workplace antidiscrimination laws) instituted to resolve other conflicts, which, in turn, will likely give rise to new conflicts (see Coser 1956).

CLASS CONFLICT IN INDUSTRIAL SOCIETY

Dahrendorf's emphasis on the normalcy of interest-group conflict; his language discussing the "dialectic of power and resistance as the motive force of history" (1968: 227); and his rejection of equilibrium (social order) models in favor of what he contends is the superior, more plausible and informative, coercion theory of society (as opposed to the *integration* theory of society) (1968: 150) might suggest that he is a theorist in the tradition of Marx. But although Dahrendorf engages with Marx's theory, he is very critical of its core assumptions and their applicability to contemporary society.

In his influential book *Class and Class Conflict in Industrial Society* (1959), Dahrendorf subjects Marx's theory of capitalism to a detailed critical reassessment in light of the changes in capitalism

Figure 6.1   Conflict and protest are a normal part of democratic society. Source: © vichinterlang/iStockphoto.

in the first half of the twentieth century. He argues that the dichotomized property and class relations assumed by Marx no longer characterize capitalism (Dahrendorf 1959: 244–245). Instead, echoing Weber, he argues that the economic structure is more differentiated (e.g., multiple economic or occupational groups/classes) and that other forms of differentiation matter such as those derived from bureaucratic authority and political power. Hence Dahrendorf argues it is more appropriate to refer to contemporary capitalist economies as advanced or **postcapitalist society.** In other words, though capitalism is still the form of economic and social organization dominating Western and increasingly, global society (see chapter 14), it has evolved significantly and has moved beyond its earlier industrialized form; basically, it is *post*industrial as other theorists suggest.

THE CHANGING CHARACTER OF CLASS CONFLICT

Dahrendorf highlights several structural changes in capitalism. Among these is the decomposition of the capitalist class, that is, the capitalist class is no longer simply the owners of capital, factories, etc., but is differentiated between ownership and management (Dahrendorf 1959: 44–45). Thus, as Weber outlined (see chapter 3), a stratum of business executives and professionals manage, but don't own, capital; and the ownership of capital itself has become even more differentiated with the emergence of public shareholder companies. Similarly, there is the decomposition of the working class: "the working class of today, far from being a homogeneous group of equally unskilled and impoverished people, is in fact a stratum differentiated by numerous subtle and not-so-subtle distinctions" (1959: 48). As Weber also outlined, there are numerous categories of semiskilled and highly skilled workers whose skills require hefty economic compensation in the market. Dahrendorf argues, therefore, that although the "increasing uniformity of the working class was an indispensable condition" – in Marx's view – for the intensification of class conflict and the anticipated proletarian revolution, the changing conditions of capitalism make that presumption implausible (1959: 51). Additionally, he argues, the structural opportunities provided by occupational and social mobility and the rise of the salaried middle class (1959: 51–61) further complicate any discussion of the working class and class conflict.

There is, by extension, no one ruling class, because the decomposition of the capitalist class means that no one class controls the means of production (capital ownership). Instead, Dahrendorf argues, there is a plurality of ruling groups or ruling elites:

> Ruling groups are … no more than ruling groups within defined associations. In theory, there can be as many competing, conflicting, or coexisting dominating **conflict groups** in a society as there are [industrial, social, political] associations … it is analytically necessary and empirically fruitful to retain the possibility of a competition or even conflict between the ruling groups of different associations. In this sense, the expression "ruling class" is, in the singular, quite misleading. (Dahrendorf 1959: 197–198)

In short, contemporary capitalism has a plurality of (economic) classes and non-economic interest groups, thus diffusing class relations and the conflicting interests between various class and noneconomic interest groups. Thus Dahrendorf maintains that although there is inequality between classes, "to conclude merely that we are still living in a class society is as insufficient as it is unsatisfactory" (1959: 247). Instead, again echoing Weber (chapter 3), he argues that there are different **authority structures**, variously based on diverse economic, political, social status, and bureaucratic resources and interests (1959: 248, 256–257).

THE MULTIPLICITY OF CONFLICT GROUPS

Given these multiple authority structures, Dahrendorf argues that we should think of economic classes as conflict groups. As conflict groups, classes coexist and compete with other (conflict) groups and quasi-groups (i.e., the array of organized and semiformal groups and associations that have social, political, cultural, or religious interests). Dahrendorf defines *group conflict* as "Any antagonistic relationship between organized collectivities of individuals that can be explained in terms of patterns of social structure (and is not, therefore, sociologically random)" (1959: 238). In sum, Dahrendorf sees society as composed of diverse interest groups whose structural interests vary (e.g., based on gender, ethnicity, occupation, etc.) and that operate – and compete for available resources – in an open but regulated social and political environment. Intergroup conflict emerges when one group becomes aware of the threat posed to its interests by the legitimate existence and behavior of some other group.

Topic 6.1   Ethnic conflict in India ... amplified by social media

Intergroup conflict is normal (see Dahrendorf) and as Donald Black emphasizes (see Box 6.1) because social space (i.e., society) is never frozen, conflict is an ongoing social phenomenon. India is a society that has undergone a lot of economic development and change over the last few years. Its computer engineering sector is particularly strong as numerous global high-tech outsourcing companies (e.g., Infosys, Tata, Wipro) are based in India. As in China, thousands of rural Indian migrants come from distant hinterlands to work in cities like Bangalore, Siruseri, and Chennai. Although stories of conflict in India tend to focus on Hindu–Muslim divisions, the country has many different ethnic groups and ethnic tension tends to be contained to specific regions in which particular groups are concentrated. The changing economy, urban migration, and the accelerated expansion of Internet and social media, however, are shifting the dynamics and consequences of ethnic tensions.

   In the summer of 2012, mass panic ensued in several Indian cities when rumors spread that Bengali Muslims intended to kill migrants and students from the indigenous Indian Bodo tribe. Located in the remote northeast of the country (in Assam), the region has long been characterized by local Bodo–Muslim conflict over land and property rights, and political control (Yardley 2012). Tens of thousands of panicked migrants and students boarded trains in Bangalore and other cities to head back to their native region as the rumors and fabricated photos of alleged killings mostly disseminated by text messages and other social media caused mass contagion. Violence erupted amidst the panic at a Muslim protest in Mumbai, for example, and it took several days before the rumors were squelched, in part because the Indian government was slow to respond, though it sought a blanket blocking of websites and text messages, a move that Google, Twitter, and Facebook argued was too sweeping and intrusive (Bajaj 2012).

C. WRIGHT MILLS: CLASS AND POWER

While Dahrendorf was challenging Parsons's emphasis on societal consensus, the influential American sociologist **C. Wright Mills** was critiquing the conceptual abstraction in Parsons's writing, referring to it sarcastically as "grand theory" (Mills 1959: 33–59). He argued that because sociology is (or should be) concerned with "all the social worlds in which men have lived, are living, and might live" (1959: 147), it must necessarily be attentive to the empirical realities in individual lives, and their intersection with history and social structures: "Biography, history, society … are the coordinate points" (1959: 159) of sociological inquiry, a theme Mills elaborated in his widely read book *The Sociological Imagination* (1959).

BIOGRAPHICAL NOTE

C. Wright Mills was born in Waco, Texas, in 1916. He completed his undergraduate education at the University of Texas, Austin, and received his PhD from the University of Wisconsin. He was subsequently professor of sociology at Columbia University. As well as writing many influential books and articles, Mills also edited and translated several of Weber's essays in *From Max Weber* (with H. H. Gerth). Mills died in 1962, at age 46.

THE NEW MIDDLE CLASS

Mills wrote about many social issues, but most especially, he documented the changing composition of the class structure that began to emerge in the US in the 1940s. Mills (1951) highlighted, for example, the transition from the "old middle class" composed of farmers, business people, and independent professionals (e.g., family doctors) to the "**new middle class**," composed of managers, salaried professionals, sales people, and office workers. This shift was driven by the changing post-World War II American consumer economy and the expansion of government, corporate, professional, and service and sales bureaucracies, including the expansion of media, advertising, and public relations companies. Some scholars, such as Daniel Bell (1973) and Alain Touraine (1971) refer to these changes as producing a **postindustrial society**, a term that, comparable to Dahrendorf's notion of postcapitalist society, recognizes the declining importance (especially since the 1970s) of industrial manufacturing and manual labor to the economy, and the growing importance of information exchange and of service and professional workers.

Mills underscores the domineering control exerted by economic markets and bureaucratic organization (its emphasis on rationality, impersonality, hierarchy, etc.; cf. Weber; see chapter 3). He argues that the bureaucratization of work has produced a "personality market"; employees have standardized, self-alienated personalities molded by "the market mentality" that dominates bureaucratic society (Mills 1951: 182). He identified the emergence of the "managerial type" (1951: 77): the standardized, managerial-entrepreneurial personality who, essentially, bends and blends their own personality and interests to fit with the strategic interests of the organization they serve (1951: 77–111). The control institutionalized in bureaucratic organization extends to self-control; self-control over the employee's own feelings and desires, as exemplified by "the salesgirl," who must maintain a "friendly" personality – "a commercial mask" – to impress customers, remembering that she represents the organization, and not herself (1951: 182–184). (We return to the theme of personality control at and *as* work and as self-alienation when we discuss Arlie Hochschild's sociology of emotions; see chapter 10.) Mills argues that the new middle class has succumbed to the demands of the bureaucratic and consumer society, and to the desire for status and prestige (e.g., Mills 1951: 240–241), rather than political or civic commitment; it is a "politically indifferent" class (1951: 327).

THE POWER ELITE

Most notably, Mills highlights the lack of power of the salaried middle class and of blue-collar workers (the working class) against what he calls the **power elite**: the decision makers in the upper echelons of the political, economic, and military institutions. Of his several books, *The Power Elite* (1956) is still especially relevant to highlighting the overlapping composition of the institutional power structure in contemporary society. Contrary to Dahrendorf's intergroup conflict theory of society, Mills emphasizes the unilateral and far-reaching, consolidated power of the ruling institutional elite. He discusses the expansion of the state's bureaucratic, administrative authority and the extending reach of economic and technical rationality (first highlighted by Weber, see chapter 3; and elaborated by critical theorists, see chapter 5). He argues: "there is an ever-increasing interlocking of economic, military, and political structures" that constitutes a "**triangle of power** … In each of these institutional areas, the means of power at the disposal of decision makers have increased enormously; their central executive powers have been enhanced … As each of these domains become enlarged and centralized, the consequences of its activities become greater, and its traffic with the other increases" (1956: 8, 7).

The power elite possess power, wealth, and celebrity; they present themselves, and are perceived by those beneath them, as being of superior moral and psychological character (Mills 1956: 13). Arguing against the view that Fate, Chance, or some Unseen Hand determines history, Mills instead emphasizes that "The course of events in our time depends more on a series of human decisions than on any inevitable fate … in our time the pivotal moment does arise, and at that moment, small circles do decide or fail to decide. In either case, they are an elite of power" (1956: 21, 22). And they control an ever-expanding, sophisticated technological arsenal in ensuring the organizational effectiveness of their decisions (1956: 23).

SHIFTS IN THE COMPOSITION OF THE POWER ELITE

Mills noted that the institutional composition of the power elite is not set in stone: "No matter how we might define the elite, the extent of its members' power is subject to historical variation" (Mills 1956: 20). He thus recognized that the institutional domains comprising the power structure can vary over time, though he also argued that such changes were usually a matter of relative degree rather than challenging the power elite's basic authority (1956: 269). The continuing interlocking power of corporate economic and political decision makers is readily apparent today, as documented by Domhoff (2006a). What is new today, however, is the ascendancy (since the 1970s) of a media elite to prominence and power far beyond Hollywood and media circles. This is underscored by the narrow concentration of media owners (e.g., Rupert Murdoch) and executives who control a greatly expanded and globalizing media industry and whose power commands the attention and friendship of political and economic elites. As highlighted by the public inquiries in the UK into the phone-hacking abuses of journalists working for Murdoch's tabloid newspapers, the Murdoch family and its corporation's senior executives were/are close friends with prime ministers (David Cameron and Tony Blair) and cabinet members, attending each other's family birthday parties, weddings, and other social events. The composition of the power elite is also been dramatically reshaped by the rise of an economic-technological elite composed of the founders and owners of Uber, Google, Facebook, Apple, Microsoft, Amazon, etc., and the executives and creative professionals working in/for these companies. Increasingly, this elite is consolidating the reach of its expansive local and global power.

The defense industry continues to be a major corporate-political force (e.g., General Electric, Halliburton, Lockheed Martin, Boeing), and military-defense industry executives, as is true of all corporate executives, have a network of cross-cutting ties with several diverse corporations (banks, food manufacturers, etc.; Domhoff 2006a: 27–28, 35). Unlike defense industry executives, however, military commanders have limited political influence. As underscored in military and other accounts of the Iraq war, the assessments and judgments of senior military commanders are frequently ignored if they do not fit the agenda established by political elites (e.g., decision makers in the White House, nonmilitary Pentagon officials, etc.). Major General Taguba, a distinguished two-star army general who was assigned by the Army to investigate the Abu Ghraib prisoner abuse scandal in Iraq in late 2003, reported to his superiors that "Numerous incidents of sadistic, blatant, and wanton criminal abuses were inflicted on several detainees … [indicating] systemic and illegal abuse." Subsequently told by his superiors to retire earlier than he had planned, Taguba commented, "They always shoot the messenger … I was being ostracized for doing what I was asked to do" (Hersh 2007). Military decision makers today thus seem to have less autonomy than argued by Mills, and it is likely that back in the 1950s too, they had less power than their economic and political counterparts (Domhoff 2006b).

WOMEN IN THE POWER ELITE

One aspect of the power elite that has not changed very much since the 1950s is its gendered character. In the 1950s, the exclusion of women from the halls of power was so taken for granted that Mills, "an outspoken radical but a product of his times on matters of gender … did not even mention [women's] absence among corporate and military leaders" (Karabel 2005: 410). Today, although there are more women in the upper echelons of government, and more women corporate executives, judges, and military generals, they still comprise a small minority among elite decision makers (e.g., see Topic 6.2). I elaborate on the institutional and cultural barriers to women's equality and power in chapter 10.

Topic 6.2   Women in the economic power elite

Despite significant advances in women's equality, women continue to be under-represented on corporate boards and executive committees. McKinsey and Company, the well-known management consultancy firm, argues that it makes good business sense for companies to increase the number of women at all levels of the managerial hierarchy. Yet, despite the visibility of women CEOs at such high-profile companies as IBM, Yahoo, Xerox, Hewlett-Packard, and eBay, there are very few women in corporate boardrooms. In 2017, women were in charge of 27 of the S&P 500 companies (just 5 percent), and of 32 of the Fortune 500 companies (just 6 percent). Additionally, in the US, the UK, and Australia women account for approximately 25 percent of board members The probusiness *Wall Street Journal*, and a sponsor of Women in the Workplace events, suggests that "gender parity in corporate life is at a virtual standstill, despite companies' ever more vocal commitments to diversity" (Lublin 2017). In Asia (excluding Australia), women have even lower representation rates. They comprise 8 percent of board members in China and Taiwan and slightly fewer in Singapore, Malaysia, Indonesia, and India. In Japan and South Korea, only 1 to 2 percent of board members are women (Süssmuth-Dyckerhoff et al. 2012).

The paucity as well as variation in women's representation in top management is not due to their lack of educational qualifications or relevant work experience. Approximately half of all college graduates in Asian countries are women (with the exception of India where women's basic literacy is much lower than that of men and thus curtails their access to higher education). In China, Singapore, and Hong Kong, for example, a half of all entry-level corporate professional positions are occupied by women; but their numbers progressively dwindle at mid- to senior level management, and precipitously so at CEO/board level (Süssmuth-Dyckerhoff et al. 2012). Similarly in the US, although women comprise over a half of the Wall Street workforce, they account for only 7 percent of investment managers, for example, down from 10 percent in 2009 (Silver-Greenberg 2013; Rogow 2017).

Gender stereotyping, a self-promotional corporate culture, strong cultural expectations against married women in the workforce (e.g., especially in Japan, South Korea), sexual harassment, and lingering ambivalence toward gender diversity in the workplace affect women's opportunities and their promotional and managerial paths. In countries attentive to gender equality and the economic value of women's human capital, a range of strategies are in place. Government quotas are used in some European countries (e.g., France, Norway) to ensure greater female representation on public sector and private corporate boards, and private sector initiatives are also popular. In Australia, the Male Champions of Change group lobbies for women's representation on boards and the Australian Institute of Company Directors has a mentoring program for women who are prospective board members. In the UK, the "30% Club," championed by Helen Alexander (who served as chief executive of *The Economist* publishing group for many years) has been influential in increasing the number of women on financially strong corporate boards (the 100 listed on the London-based Financial Times Stock Exchange) from 12.5 percent when the initiative started in 2010 to 27 percent in 2017. In the US, several top-tier investment banks have programs specifically targeting women college students with internships and mentoring programs cultivating them for future employment and management opportunities. Another approach is that of State Street Global Advisors, a major investment fund; in 2017, it voted against the reelection of directors at 400 companies on grounds that they failed to make efforts to add women to their boards (Rogow 2017).

THE PASSIVE, MASS SOCIETY

Unlike Dahrendorf, who noted the differentiation within the upper class between owners and executives and thus the possibility for intergroup conflict within that stratum, Mills highlighted what he saw as the overall unity of the ruling elite, notwithstanding differences among them based on family wealth (Mills 1956: 62–65). He also contrasted elite unity with what he saw as the powerlessness and fragmentation of other classes and groups. Thus, contrary to Marx's view that revolutionary social change would inevitably emerge from class antagonism between capitalists and workers, and contrary to Dahrendorf's construal of intergroup conflict and social change, Mills regarded those outside the power elite, including the new middle class, as incapable of effecting social change: they stand powerless in the face of the ruling elite's decisive and consequential power.

Thus Mills (1956: 302–303) articulated a **mass society thesis**, namely, the idea that the vast majority of people outside the corporate power structure are both helpless and uninterested in influencing the ruling decisions determining their fate; as critical theorists also argued, they are manipulated and controlled by the mass media into passivity (see chapter 5). Mills argued that "mass education" fulfills a

Figure 6.2   Although changes have occurred in recent years in the gender composition of the power elite, the hierarchy of the Catholic Church remains a bastion of male power. Source: © Erich Vandeville/ABACA/Press Association.

similar function. Education is not a prerequisite for "political alertness," a point supported by the active political interest and involvement of earlier uneducated generations (Mills 1951: 338). "Mass education" – criticized by Mills for its narrow, unimaginative and boring content – trivializes politics and, he maintains, contributes to the masses' greater fascination with media entertainment than with politics (1951: 338–339).

Political indifference and passivity stand in sharp contrast to the democratic ethos and its affirmation of the participation of citizens and voluntary groups and associations in shaping society (Mills 1956: 28–29). Consequently, for Mills, social change is contingent not on political activism but on changes in the institutional landscape (1956: 280), depending on which institutional sectors become more prominent than others. He did not recognize the protest-mobilizing impact of Martin Luther King, Jr, in the mid-1950s (e.g., Halberstam 1993: 423–424). Nor did he anticipate the subsequent expansion in grassroots civil rights activism in the 1960s and 1970s, which succeeded in gains in equality for blacks, women, gays and lesbians, and physically disabled individuals (Domhoff 2006b). Despite these omissions, Mills's (1951) attentiveness to "managerial culture," and to the consequential significance of an interlocked network of powerful political, economic, and military figures in shaping the history of the present, finds considerable empirical support today.

DEPENDENCY THEORY: GUNDER FRANK'S AND CARDOSO'S NEO-MARXIST CRITIQUES OF ECONOMIC DEVELOPMENT

Despite their different analytical approaches to conflict and power, Dahrendorf and Mills, like Parsons, had a US/Western focus, reflective of the assumption that all countries would eventually take on the same patterns of modernization as the US (see chapter 4). The unevenness, however, and the costs of

Western modernization were on display in the 1960s and 70s. In the US, for example, despite an expanding middle class, there were still large numbers living in poverty; and social protest movements highlighted the unevenness in the equality of blacks, women, and gays and lesbians. At the same time, the then-fledgling environmental movement highlighted the negative impact of unregulated economic growth on local communities and on the natural environment. Thus the modernization narrative of a progressive expansion in economic and social prosperity had many vocal detractors in the US, among both the elite and those on the margins (cf. Gitlin 1980).

CAPITALIST DEVELOPMENT OF UNDERDEVELOPMENT

The theoretical challenge to the modernization paradigm, however, came primarily from scholars who, in the 1970s, took a more global perspective on economic development and social change, and extended the lens beyond the US and Europe. Scholars associated with the Economic Commission for Latin America (ECLA), an organization sponsored by the United Nations, directly challenged its assumptions. Notable among these, **Andre Gunder Frank**, a European-born scholar who worked for many years in Chile, outlined a **neo-Marxist** framework for thinking about **development**. Against the backdrop of heated political debate in the US and Europe (the so-called "first world," which also includes Canada, Japan, Australia, and New Zealand) about how to deal with economic **underdevelopment** in the so-called "third world" (South and Central America, Africa, and much of Asia), the self-avowedly "political" Gunder Frank (1967: xiv) argued that the historical analysis of underdevelopment in Chile and Brazil provided clear evidence of the *capitalist* development of underdevelopment. He stated: "I believe… it is capitalism, both world and national, which produced underdevelopment in the past and which still generates underdevelopment in the present" (1967: vii).

BIOGRAPHICAL NOTE

Andre Gunder Frank was born in Germany in 1929, but his family fled the country with the rise of Hitler and eventually settled in the US. He received his PhD in economics from the University of Chicago (in 1957) and soon thereafter moved to Latin America, where he completed several country case studies of development. As professor of sociology and economics at the University of Chile in Santiago, Gunder Frank was involved in implementing the democratic reforms of the Allende government, but after its military overthrow in 1973, he moved back to Europe. He retired from the University of Amsterdam in 1994 and died in 2005.

Gunder Frank highlighted the significance of capitalism in producing and deepening underdevelopment in poor countries, thereby countering the common view of modernization and development, a view he too accepted until he went to live and do research in Latin America. The assumed view was that underdevelopment was due to the "backward" country's own internal problems – to "largely domestic problems of capital scarcity, feudal and traditional institutions which impede saving and investment, concentration of political power in the hands of rural oligarchies" (Gunder Frank 1967: vii), and many other domestic obstacles to economic development. Instead, he maintained, underdevelopment was generated and persisted in Latin America because of the innate contradictions in the capitalist production of capital/profit, that is, the inherent structure of capitalism such that profit must always, and can only, be generated at the expense of workers' labor and the surplus value (profit) it produces for factory owners and landowners (and corporations, etc.). This is the core Marxist point about the inequality and exploitation structured into capitalist relations of production (see chapter 1). Gunder Frank insightfully extended this analysis to the unequal relations of production not just within one country but the entire **world system**. He argued that capitalism requires structural inequality between developed and underdeveloped economies in the pursuit of its core goal: profit accumulation.

Center–satellite relations in global capitalism

Specifically, Gunder Frank argued that to understand underdevelopment in Chile or Brazil or any other Latin American country, we "must locate it in the economic structure of the world system as a whole," and in particular, in the concentrated monopolization of capital accumulation in the metropolitan center, [based on] profit accumulated from the expropriation of value and wealth produced in peripheral satellite locations (Gunder Frank 1967: 8). This analysis of **center–satellite** polarization in access to surplus capital (money/profit) was applicable, Gunder Frank argued, not only externally (i.e., in Chile's relations to foreign capital) but also to economic relations within the country. Within Chile, the center takes the economic surplus (profit) produced in its satellite regions and localities; but in turn, the (internal) center is converted into a satellite country in the world system, "its surplus being appropriated by others before [Chile] can firmly launch its own development" (1967: 10).

Gunder Frank contends that this center–satellite (or core–periphery) dynamic, explains the ongoing generation and appropriation of capital such that capitalism produces *underdevelopment* rather than development at the periphery. In short, the periphery lacks access to its own surplus capital, to its own wealth, which becomes profit for the core (Gunder Frank 1967: 9). As Marx argued, wage-laborers do not have access to the surplus value their work produces; rather, it is profit for the capitalist. Similarly, core economies profit by exploiting peripheral economies. Thus Gunder Frank (1967: 9) argued:

> Economic development and underdevelopment are the opposite faces of the same coin. Both are the necessary result and contemporary manifestation of internal contradictions in the world capitalist system. Economic development and underdevelopment are not just relative and quantitative, in that one represents more economic development than the other; economic development and underdevelopment are relational and qualitative, in that each is structurally different from, yet caused by its relation with, the other. Yet development and underdevelopment are the same in that they are the product of a single but dialectically contradictory, economic structure and process of capitalism.

Consequently, he maintained, underdeveloped countries are condemned to underdevelopment, unless capitalism dissolves or they abandon the capitalist world system and opt for a "rapid passage to socialism" (1967: 9, 277).

The development today of what economists and sociologists call newly industrializing countries (NICs) challenges the empirical validity of Gunder Frank's prediction. Some neo-Marxists concede that enclaves of economic prosperity and social development are possible in the underdeveloped or third world even if such enclaves ultimately reproduce "First World–Third World exploitation within Third World cities and rural areas" (Sklair 2002: 32–33). Gunder Frank, however, unequivocally rejects the idea "that capitalism could ever develop the Third World" (Sklair 2002: 32). His view, therefore, is at odds with what has happened since the early 1990s in some third world countries (e.g., Vietnam, Bangladesh). It also counters the traditional Marxist idea that countries go through various evolutionary stages of economic development (see chapter 1).

In sum, Gunder Frank's thesis of the capitalist development of underdevelopment is theoretically interesting, especially his insight pointing to the determining relevance of a country's colonial-economic history. However, though it may have empirical application in some sociohistorical contexts, it is insufficiently nuanced to explain the economic and social development that is occurring as a result of economic globalization on societies previously deemed underdeveloped (see chapters 14 and 15). Other neo-Marxist scholars who focus on the historical world context in which economic development occurs, such as the American sociologist Immanuel Wallerstein, also take a skeptical view of economic globalization, as is discussed in chapter 14.

DEPENDENCY RELATIONS IN ECONOMIC UNDERDEVELOPMENT

Other Latin American scholars associated with ECLA also elaborated strands in the neo-Marxist sociology of development. Among these, **Fernando Cardoso** is the best-known, having been president of Brazil (1995–2002), though notably, in that role, his economic policies were more aligned with the "Washington consensus" (e.g., US political-economic agendas, World Bank policies, etc.) promulgating global capitalist development (see Held 2004). In *Dependency and Development in Latin America*, Cardoso and Faletto (1979: ix) clearly stated their theoretical goal:

> We seek a global and dynamic understanding of social structures instead of looking only at specific dimensions of the social process … we stress the socio-politico nature of the economic relations of production … This methodological approach, which found its highest expression in Marx, assumes that the hierarchy that exists in society is the result of established ways of organizing the production of material … life. This hierarchy also serves to assure the unequal appropriation of nature and of the results of human work by social classes and groups. So we attempt to analyze domination in its connection with economic expansion.

BIOGRAPHICAL NOTE

Fernando Cardoso was born in Rio de Janeiro, Brazil, in 1931. Trained as a sociologist, for many years he was professor of political science and sociology at the University of São Paulo, prior to becoming president of Brazil (1995–2002). Over the years, Cardoso has lectured at many American and European universities, and received numerous academic and international public policy awards. He continues to write about economic development and globalization and is currently a professor-at-large at Brown University in Providence, Rhode Island. In 2012, he was awarded the US Library of Congress $1 million Kluge Prize in recognition for lifetime intellectual achievement in the humanities and social sciences.

Societal context and economic development

Like Gunder Frank, Cardoso was interested in the inequalities that inhere in societal development. But he was also committed to outlining how economic development is interdependent with noneconomic, social and political processes; that is, how a given country's specific patterns of social change or continuity are related to the specific sociohistorical and structural contexts in which they emerge. Cardoso noted that any given developing country's historical and structural context is impacted by *external* forces: Western empires or superpowers, multinational corporations, foreign technology, international financial systems and policies (e.g., the International Monetary Fund [IMF]), and foreign embassies and armies (Cardoso and Faletto 1979: xvi). Additionally, he highlighted the *internal* societal forces that matter: the cultural (e.g., religious ties, political ideologies) and structural (e.g., class structure; church–state links) factors that affect political mobilization, specific ideologies, and patterns of class inequality within the society at any given historical moment.

For Cardoso, the interplay of internal and external forces means that any analysis of political and economic domination necessarily involves the analysis of class inequality and class conflict (manifest or latent) within the developing country (e.g., Chile, Bolivia, etc.), and of the structural inequality of that country as a geopolitical-economic unit vis-à-vis other developing and developed countries. He thus recognized that some underdeveloped countries undergo economic development, but that their development is contingent on dependency relations. He places his analysis squarely in terms of the unequal (economic and political) **dependence** of peripheral economies on those at the center. And, in contrast to what Talcott Parsons and others might more benignly call functional "interdependence" (Cardoso and Faletto 1979: xxi), he underscores the exploitative nature of dependence, as highlighted, for example, by the US intervention against neo-Marxist socialist governments in South and Central America (e.g., Guatemala, 1954; Chile, 1973; Panama, 1989), and the close ties maintained by the US government with military dictatorships in the 1980s (e.g., Brazil, Argentina).

Complicated character of dependency

For Cardoso, the dynamic interplay between external and internal forces produces complicated relations and **situations of dependency** that invalidate the assumption "that *all* forms of dependency had common features" (Cardoso and Faletto 1979: xxiii, xiii). Rather, dependence produces (or at least can produce) multiple sets of dependency relations. This conceptualization deviates from the colonial model whereby the developing country is dependent solely on the capital, technology, and expertise of the richer and more powerful country. It also deviates from the neocolonial model whereby the newly decolonized country remains unilaterally dependent for resources on the colonizer, and thus remains backward (in the modernization paradigm) because, by itself, it is unable to modernize its own country's economic, social, and cultural processes.

One of the key points Cardoso emphasizes is that there are "coincidences of interests between local dominant classes and international ones," and these interests "are challenged by local dominated groups and classes" (Cardoso and Faletto 1979: xvi). Thus there are not simply "external forms of exploitation and coercion," but more complex "networks of coincident or reconciled interests" between and among specific groups or classes within the developing country, and between these and dominant interests in the external country (1979: xvi). Further, these varying interests get advanced and/or contested by the active mobilization of groups pursuing particular goals. Thus political mobilization and social movements matter in shaping the structural contours of developing (and developed) societies. Cardoso states:

> Social structures impose limits on social processes and reiterate established forms of behavior. However, they also generate contradictions and social tensions, opening the possibilities for social movements and ideologies of change … In this process, subordinated social groups and classes, as well as dominated countries, try to counterattack dominant interests that sustain structures of domination … social structures are the product of man's collective behavior. Therefore, although enduring, social structures can be and in fact are continuously transformed by social movements. (Cardoso and Faletto 1979: xi, x)

Although Cardoso affirms the significance of social movements in bringing about change, he is also realistic about the extent to which they can resist structures of domination. The interests of (select) local groups can coincide with foreign interests. He notes, however, that the system of domination represented by external domination (imperialism) can also mean that external foreign interests co-opt local interests in the pursuit of their own (foreign) interests (Cardoso and Faletto 1979).

In any event, how various local and international interests intersect within the specific political and economic context in a given developing country is what determines the particular ways in which capitalism evolves in that country. Moreover, as Cardoso underscores, not all developing economies are in a similar situation of dependency. For example, economic growth and social and economic inequality in Latin America vary from country to country as a result of internal industrialization and the local structures in place to expand capital. But in all situations of dependency (and in all capitalist countries), it is not the logic of capital accumulation alone, but its interpenetration with a number of other historical and societal factors that matters, and this includes the political implications of particular alliances between local and foreign interests (Cardoso and Faletto 1979: xvii). It is important that Cardoso highlights the varied ways in which countries develop and their varied situations of dependency. However, because he does not specify how particular internal and external factors would likely interact, it is difficult to generate empirically testable hypotheses from the dependency thesis. Nonetheless, it is still a useful framework with which to think about how crosscutting forces affect variation among Latin American countries today. For example, economic growth is relatively strong in Bolivia and Central America, but not in Peru; internal political instability is a significant factor in Brazil (due to high-level corruption scandals) but not in Chile; and external political uncertainty such as President Trump's proposed renegotiation of NAFTA affects Mexico.

CHALLENGES TO MODERNIZATION THEORY

Despite the shortcomings in both Gunder Frank's and Cardoso's elaboration of underdevelopment/ dependency, we can appreciate how their arguments prompt sociologists to rethink the applicability of Talcott Parsons's modernization thesis that all societies would follow a uniform, linear path toward economic and social development (see chapter 4). Cardoso's move slightly away from Gunder Frank's generalized emphasis on economic exploitation, to spotlight the internal social and political forces (e.g., social movements) that contribute to the evolution of change in developing societies is important. It provided sociologists with a more thorough sociological view of development, and one that simultaneously challenged modernization theory.

In sum, dependency theory underscored three major, interrelated points challenging modernization. One, development is not an automatic process driven by industrialization or economic modernization alone. Rather, it is driven by an intermix of economic, social, historical, and cultural factors, including the developing country's unequal relations with already-developed countries. Two, development is not a universal process with each developing country progressing in the same unilinear and inevitable fashion. Rather, different societies have different patterns of development (due to factors cited in the first point), notwithstanding commonalities of history, culture, etc. Three, by highlighting the political significance of class alliances and the mobilization of elite and/ or grassroots efforts to implement particular ideologies, dependency theory redressed Parsons's emphasis that values, though central to the consensus legitimating social structure, are relatively static and in the background. Dependency theory recognized a more dynamic relation between culture and structure, whereby ideologies and values are actively articulated and contested by social movements and political alliances and used to prod and reshape existing economic and political structures.

SUMMARY

This chapter has highlighted a variety of important theoretical contributions. We discussed Dahrendorf's delineation of the normalcy of intergroup conflict in society, and his critique of the applicability of Marx's analysis of capitalism and class polarization to contemporary, postcapitalist or postindustrial society. We then reviewed Mills's challenge to both the consensus/power-equilibrium view of society (Parsons) and the group-conflict model (Dahrendorf), as explicated in his construal of the relatively unchecked and unified power wielded by the power elite, the decision makers in the triangle of economic, political, and military institutions. Shifting focus from Western society, we discussed the challenge posed to modernization theory by the Latin American-based, dependency relation theory of economic development elaborated by Gunder Frank and Cardoso.

POINTS TO REMEMBER

Ralf Dahrendorf
- Focused on the normalcy of intergroup conflict in society in response to unequal distribution of power and authority
- Argued that group conflict arises when the manifest interests of one group are at odds with those of another
- Highlighted that intergroup conflict is institutionally regulated in democratic, industrial societies and hence typically does not lead to violence
- Noted that group conflict can function to produce social change resulting from its institutional resolution
- Critiqued the applicability of Marx's understanding of polarized class conflict to contemporary society given occupational mobility and the existence of many occupational groups and economic classes
- Argued that economic classes should be considered as conflict groups similar to other interest groups

C. Wright Mills
- Focused on post-World War II, American society, specifically the expansion of the new middle class, bureaucratization, and consumerism
- Highlighted the interlocking, elite concentration of power among decision makers in political, economic, and military institutions
- Disregarded the role of social movements in challenging the institutional power structure

Dependency development theory
- Analyzes of economic development in Latin American countries
- Has an explicitly Marxist/neo-Marxist framework
- Highlights the structural existence of center–satellite inequality between capitalist and developing economies (Gunder Frank)
- Emphasizes the coinciding economic and political interests of particular local and foreign interests in developing countries (Cardoso)
- Highlights the significance of social movements and alternative ideologies in resisting capitalism (Cardoso)
- Emphasizes that situations of dependency vary between and within Latin American countries

GLOSSARY

authority structures varied sources of legitimation, authority, or power in modern society; possible sources of ongoing normal conflict.

center–satellite the idea that some states/regions are dominant in (core to) world economic production whereas others are marginal or peripheral (e.g., the North–South divide).

conflict groups competing interest groups in society.

democratization of conflict establishment of formally organized interest groups and of institutional mechanisms (e.g., labor courts, mediation panels) to regulate group conflicts.

dependence an underdeveloped or peripheral country's relation to a developed country due to the historical economic and structural inequalities between them.

development economic growth and related societal changes in previously undeveloped countries.

dialectic of power and resistance ongoing conflicts (and changes) in society produced by group power inequalities and group resistance to those inequalities.

functions of social conflict social integration due to the interdependent coexistence of conflict groups and social change resulting from institutional resolution of group conflict.

group conflict emerges when the manifest interests of one group conflict with those of another.

interest group any group whose members consciously share and express similar interests.

latent interests unspoken, tacit interests of one group vis-à-vis another.

manifest interests explicitly stated objectives.

mass society thesis idea that individuals in society are passive, unaware of and uninvolved in politics.

neo-Marxist ideas derived from Marx's theory of capitalism but reworked in new ways and/or with new applications to take account of the transformations in capitalism; (*neo* derives from the Greek word for new).

new middle class the expanding sector of educated (but politically indifferent) salaried managers, professionals, and sales and office workers that resulted from the post-World War II expansion of bureaucracy and the consumer economy.

postcapitalist society Dahrendorf's term; the result of transformations in the economy and in the occupational and class structures since the mid-twentieth century that make contemporary capitalist society structurally different from its late nineteenth-century incarnation (when Marx was writing about the capitalist structure and class relations).

postindustrial society changes in economy and society resulting from the decline of manufacturing industry and the increased and growing importance of services and information as economic engines/sources of employment (basically refers to the same processes highlighted by Dahrendorf in his notion of postcapitalist society).

power an unequally divided, perpetual source of conflict and resistance.

power elite upper echelon in the interlocking network of economic, political, and military decision makers; holders of power, prestige, and wealth in society.

situations of dependency term used to highlight the social, historical, and economic variation that exists among developing economies.

triangle of power the intersection of economic, political, and military institutions.

underdevelopment economies in the third world whose development is hindered by their relational dependence on, and exploitation by, the economically developed first world.

world system the world as a relational system composed of structurally unequal, developed and underdeveloped economies.

QUESTIONS FOR REVIEW

1   What does it mean to say that group conflict is normal in society? How does it show its normalcy? What are its sources and consequences?
2   Who or what is the power elite? Is it stable? How does an elite view of power pose tension for a democratic society? Is conflict between elite groups normal?

3   How do power inequalities between countries manifest at the macro level? What are relations of economic dependency? And how might they change over time?

4   Outline how variation along three different social dimensions might be used to predict conflict within and between groups, and within and between countries.

REFERENCES

Althusser, Louis. 1969. *For Marx*. New York: Pantheon.

Bajaj, Vikas. 2012. "Internet Moves by India to Stem Rumors and Panic Raise Questions." *New York Times* (August 22), p. B4.

Bell, Daniel. 1973. *The Coming of Post-Industrial Society*. New York: Basic Books.

Black, Donald. 2011. *Moral Time*. New York: Oxford University Press.

Cardoso, Fernando, and Enzo Faletto. 1979. *Dependency and Development in Latin America*. Berkeley: University of California Press.

Coser, Lewis. 1956. *The Functions of Social Conflict*. Glencoe, IL: Free Press.

Dahrendorf, Ralf. 1959. *Class and Class Conflict in Industrial Society*. Stanford, CA: Stanford University Press.

Dahrendorf, Ralf. 1968. *Essays in the Theory of Society*. Stanford, CA: Stanford University Press.

Domhoff, G. William. 2006a. *Who Rules America? Power, Politics and Social Change*. New York: McGraw-Hill.

Domhoff, G. William. 2006b. "Mills's *The Power Elite* 50 Years Later." *Contemporary Sociology* 35: 547–550.

Gitlin, Todd. 1980. *The Whole World is Watching: Mass Media in the Making and Unmaking of the New Left*. Berkeley: University of California Press.

Gramsci, Antonio. 1929/1971. *Selections from the Prison Notebooks*. London: Lawrence and Wishart. Edited and translated by Quentin Hoare and Geoffrey Nowell Smith.

Gunder Frank, Andre. 1967. *Capitalism and Underdevelopment in Latin America*. New York: Monthly Review Press.

Halberstam, David. 1993. *The Fifties*. New York: Ballantine Books.

Held, David. 2004. *Global Covenant: The Social Democratic Alternative to the Washington Consensus*. Cambridge: Polity.

Hersh, Seymour. 2007. "The General's Report." *New Yorker* (June 25).

Karabel, Jerome. 2005. *The Chosen: The Hidden History of Admission and Exclusion at Harvard, Yale, and Princeton*. Boston: Houghton Mifflin.

Lublin, Joann. 2017. "Ranks of Women CEOs Get Slimmer." *Wall Street Journal* (August 3), p. B2.

Lukács, Georg. 1968. *History and Class Consciousness: Studies in Marxist Dialectics*. Cambridge, MA: MIT Press.

Mills, C. Wright. 1951. *White Collar: The American Middle Classes*. New York: Oxford University Press.

Mills, C. Wright. 1956. *The Power Elite*. New York: Oxford University Press.

Mills, C. Wright. 1959. *The Sociological Imagination*. New York: Oxford University Press.

Rogow, Geoffrey. 2017. "Group Seeks to Close Wall Street's Gender Gap." *Wall Street Journal* (July 29-30), B10.

Silver-Greenberg, Jennifer. 2013. "A Suite of Their Own." *New York Times* (April 3), p. F6.

Sklair, Leslie. 2002. *Globalization: Capitalism and Its Alternatives*. Oxford: Oxford University Press.

Süssmuth-Dyckerhoff, Claudia, Jin Wang, and Josephine Chen. 2012. *Women Matter: An Asian Perspective*. Boston: McKinsey & Company.

Touraine, Alain. 1971. *The Post-Industrial Society*. New York: Random House.

Yardley, Jim. 2012. "Panic Seizes India as a Region's Strife Radiates." *New York Times* (August 18), pp. A1, 7.

CHAPTER SEVEN

EXCHANGE, EXCHANGE NETWORK, AND RATIONAL CHOICE THEORIES

KEY CONCEPTS

social exchange

behavior conditioning

action–reward/punishment
  orientation

power imbalances

scarcity value

trust

diffuseness of expectations

exchange network

power dependence

encapsulated interest

social capital

strong ties

weak ties

actants

microeconomic model

economic efficiency

maximization of utility

marginal utility

systems of trust

human capital

net gain

analytical Marxism

game theory

organization assets

contradictory class locations

CHAPTER MENU

Introduction to Sociological Theory: Theorists, Concepts, and Their Applicability to the Twenty-First Century,
Third Edition. Michele Dillon.
© 2020 John Wiley & Sons Ltd. Published 2020 by John Wiley & Sons Ltd.
Companion website: www.wiley.com/go/dillon

Although exchange, exchange network, and rational choice theories comprise discrete perspectives on social life, I group them together in this chapter because they variously focus on the processes whereby individual or collective actors (e.g., couples, work teams, etc.) seek and exchange resources (money, status, power, influence, information). To think of social relations in terms of exchange is not new. Enlightenment philosophers conceptualized the social contract as a form of political exchange (see Introduction); classical anthropology highlighted the centrality of gift exchange in everyday life (e.g., Mauss 1967); classical economics underscored the productive efficiency and utility of exchange in human relations (e.g., John Stuart Mill, Adam Smith; see Introduction); and of course, among classical sociologists, Karl Marx stressed the unequal exchange that is structured into capitalist relations (see chapter 1).

EXCHANGE THEORY: GEORGE HOMANS AND PETER BLAU

Whereas Marx focused on economic exchange relations at a macro level, subsequent theorists shifted attention to encompass the many noneconomic forms of social exchange characterizing interpersonal and group relations. Georg Simmel observed: "Most relationships… can be considered under the category of exchange. Exchange is the purest and most concentrated form of all human interactions in which serious interests are at stake … every conversation, every love (even when requited unfavorably), every game, every act of looking one another over" (1907/1971: 43, 33). Whether in the marketplace, politics, the classroom, or at home, **social exchange** is the core social process underlying relations between individuals and within and between groups (cf. Blau 1964: 4). As Peter Blau (1964: 5) noted, "Two conditions must be met for behavior to lead to social exchange. It must be oriented toward ends [goals] that can only be achieved through interaction with other persons, and it must seek to adapt means to further the achievement of these ends."

GEORGE HOMANS: INDIVIDUAL ACTORS IN SOCIAL EXCHANGE

One of the leading theorists associated with social exchange was the Boston-born Harvard sociologist **George Homans.** In the post-World War II era dominated by a focus on impersonal social systems and subsystems (following Parsons; see chapter 4), Homans brought attention back to individual and small-group behavior and away from the macro structures, organizations, and processes that sociologists tended to emphasize. He argued that all elementary forms of social behavior can be explained in terms of the psychological motives of the individual (Homans 1961/1974: 12). In his framing, individual motives explain why institutions exist; they exist only because they enlist and coordinate the motives of individuals in support (or in spite) of the institution's aims (1961/1974: 372–373).

Thus, whereas Durkheim insisted that the behavior of individuals (e.g., marriage) could and must only be explained sociologically, that is, as a social force related to other social forces (e.g., migration, education; see chapter 2), Homans took the opposite view. For him, essentially, sociology was a corollary of psychology – of individuals in interaction with other psychologically motivated individuals, whether in small groups or in organizations. Weber affirmed the significance of individual actors engaged in subjectively meaningful action (see chapter 3), but he also highlighted the specific sociological characteristics of groups and organizations (e.g., bureaucracy). By contrast, Homans argued that organizations do not have a sociological character of their own; organizations are simply "shorthand for the persistent, concerted activities of a number of persons" (1961/1974: 357). For him, all social behavior is a manifestation of *individually* motivated behavior and, further contrary to Weber, is independent of the historical, cultural, and organizational context in which individuals act.

BIOGRAPHICAL NOTE

George Homans was born into a well-established upper-class Boston family in 1910. He spent most of his life at Harvard University, first as a student – concentrating on English and American literature as an undergraduate, and sociology and economics for his PhD – and subsequently as a professor. He married Nancy Parshall, whom he credits (Homans 1950: xxvi) for drawing the various charts he used to illustrate relations among individuals in dyads and groups. Homans was president of the American Sociological Association in 1964; he died in Cambridge, Massachusetts, in 1989.

Exchange behavior

The elementary basis of all individual/social behavior, Homans argued, has to do with the fact that the individual's behavior "is a function of its payoffs, of its outcomes, whether rewarding or punishing, and they hold good whether or not the payoffs are provided by the non-human environment or by other human beings" (Homans 1961/1974: 12). In other words, we can begin to understand human behavior, that is, human interaction, only if we consider it exchange behavior (1961/1974: 56). The exchange that occurs in interpersonal interaction is extensive. We exchange opinions, advice, friendship, clothes, favors, etc. In any exchange, Homans argues, "There are two kinds of dimensions along which a person and others who observe him assess his status. He is ranked on what he does himself – that is, on what he gives in social exchange – and on what he gets from others" (1961/1974: 225).

Following the **behavior conditioning** thesis popularized in psychology by B.F. Skinner (1938), Homans outlined a set of deductive propositions emphasizing a basic **action–reward/punishment orientation** to social behavior. Among other propositions, he argued,

> For all actions taken by persons, the more often a particular action of a person is rewarded, the more likely the person is to perform that action … If in the past the occurrence of a particular stimulus, or set of

stimuli, has been the occasion on which a person's action has been rewarded, then the more similar the present stimuli are to the past ones, the more likely the person is to perform the action, or some similar action, now ... the more valuable to a person is the result of his action, the more likely he is to perform the action. (Homans 1961/1974: 16, 22–23, 25)

Power in social exchange

Social action and interaction, therefore, are driven by the individual's experience and learned anticipation of rewards and punishment. This is not, however, a simple calculation. Because social exchange is characterized by **power imbalances** such that one person within the interaction gets more out of the exchange than the other person (Homans 1961/1974: 70–71), the value of the exchange has to be weighed in relatively subtle ways. Further, the power dynamics shift once a third person is involved in the interaction – a situation typifying small-group interaction. Homans notes: "A difference between [individuals] in their capacity to change the behavior of others and to change it in their favor is what we mean by a difference in power" (1961/1974: 73); "what a person ... gives in social exchange ... determines [their] power" (1961/1974: 223). Because of imbalances in power, in what people give and are able to give, individuals make choices among alternative courses of action on the basis of their projected assumptions as to which course of action will yield greater rewards.

For example, three of four roommates sharing an apartment may do all of the cleaning chores because they want their apartment to look tidy when other friends visit (the reward of both a tidy apartment and their guests' approval); they thus invest in this activity even though the fourth roommate gets to similarly enjoy the rewards of the others' efforts. There is a clear exchange imbalance in the group's relationship. But this chore imbalance might be offset by other resources the fourth roommate contributes; that person may be a good cook who happily prepares a tasty meal for all the roommates once a week. In all one-to-one or group relationships, Homans argues, "Power ... depends on an ability to provide rewards that are valuable because they are scarce ... What determines the **scarcity value** of a reward is the relation between the supply of it and the demand for it" (Homans 1967: 55). Thus, the fourth roommate will retain the power not to be nudged out of the apartment by the others only so long as the meals continue to satisfy the roommates and/or they cannot get or afford such good meals elsewhere. If, by contrast, a roommate or friend continues to disappoint, to violate your expectations of how they should behave, and to give "nothing" in exchange – not even affirmation of your efforts – you will likely engage in deprivation or punishment behavior by withholding your approval or other symbolic rewards (e.g., your company). But you will engage in such behavior only to the extent that it does not simultaneously deprive you of rewards. Therefore, although you might in frustration refuse to tidy the apartment, you too, and not just your roommate, will be deprived of the rewards of your (time and effort) investment in chores. Despite power imbalances, "One never gets [or gives] something for nothing" (1967: 73). But why some rewards are given priority and others dismissed and in what circumstances are unaddressed by Homans. He does not acknowledge the larger societal context and how, for example, it shapes relationships (e.g., marriage) and individuals' expectations of and within relationships. Individuals have different expectations of friends than of work colleagues and of teammates than of roommates. These varied expectations are also contingent on and mediated by intersecting differences in individuals' gender, class, sexuality, and racial and other social locations. Therefore, although an exchange–rewards logic characterizes social relations, how it unfolds and plays out in interpersonal and group relationships is more complicated than the individual-motives logic outlined by Homans.

PETER BLAU: SOCIAL EXCHANGE IN ORGANIZATIONS

Homans's perspective is also of limited use in explaining the behavior of organizations, a challenge taken up by **Peter Blau**. In his influential book *Exchange and Power in Social Life* (1964), Blau stated,

> The core of a theory of society has to explain the complex interdependence between substructures of numerous kinds … The foundation required for a systematic theory of social structure is a thorough knowledge of the processes of social association, from the simplest that characterize the interpersonal relations between individuals to the most complex that pertain to the relations in and among large collectivities. (Blau 1964: 2)

Blau studied how social exchange (defined previously) operates in organizations by investigating workers' behavior in several different bureaucratic settings. His research findings showed how the characteristics of organizations, such as occupational rank and status among workers, lead to social exchanges that (contrary to Homans) are not reducible to workers' individual psychological motives. Blau noted that employees in any organization are typically required to defer to a hierarchical order of authority (e.g., to consult about a work-task problem with their supervisor rather than with coworkers) and to follow highly specified impersonal rules and procedures for accomplishing tasks (cf. Weber on bureaucracy, chapter 3). But he also discovered that employees' work is dependent too on social exchange and the **trust** it implies. For example, when work colleagues informally seek advice from one another about a task, this builds esteem among colleagues (flattered that their colleagues recognize their competence) and contributes to the effective completion of the work-task at hand (Blau 1974: 6–8, 157–169).

BIOGRAPHICAL NOTE

Peter Blau was born in Vienna, Austria, in 1918; his parents were secular Jews who were imprisoned with the rise of Nazism and subsequently executed in Auschwitz (in 1942). Blau managed to escape from Europe and settled in New York, where he completed his PhD in sociology under the guidance of Robert Merton. He held distinguished faculty appointments at the University of Chicago, Columbia University, and after his retirement (in 1988), at the University of North Carolina, Chapel Hill. Blau was president of the American Sociological Association. He married Judith Blau, also a sociologist (at the University of North Carolina), and they had two daughters. He died in 2002, at age 84.

Trust relationships

Blau's insights into social exchange and trust relationships in organizations are supported in today's corporate workplace. There is much recognition that the effectiveness of teamwork in task accomplishment is dependent not just on everyone following the correct technical procedures, but on worker-team cohesiveness, a point underscored in many corporate advertisements and in the prevalence of company-financed, team-building activities (e.g., Outward Bound weekend camps, treasure hunts, etc.) and social clubs for their employees.

Beyond the workplace, politicians have long known the value of developing personal relations of reciprocity and trust that encompass but extend beyond strategic interests. Especially in the international political arena, the development of personal trust between potential allies and adversaries is seen as important to building and maintaining intercountry ties. This accounts for the frequency with which political leaders visit each other not just at their official residences and offices but also at their personal or family vacation homes; such social exchange creates both the structure and the expectation for future interpersonal and strategic exchanges.

However, unlike economic exchange relationships, wherein we typically pay a specified amount of money in return for a specified product or service, the sociological significance (and intrigue) of social exchange lies largely in its **diffuseness of expectations:**

> Social exchange … entails supplying benefits that create diffuse future obligations. The nature of the return is invariably not stipulated in advance, cannot be bargained about, and must be left to the discretion of the one who makes it … Generally, a [person] expects some expressions of gratitude and appreciation for favors he/she has done for others, but he/she can neither bargain with them over how to reciprocate nor force them to reciprocate at all … The distinctive significance of social obligations requires that they remain unspecific and the fact that social, as distinguished from economic, commodities have no exact price facilitates meeting this requirement. Since the recipient is the one who decides when and how to reciprocate for a favor, or whether to reciprocate at all, social exchange requires trusting others, whereas the immediate transfer of goods or the formal contract that can be enforced obviates such trust in economic exchange. Typically, however, social exchange relations evolve in a slow process, starting with minor transactions in which little trust is required because little risk is involved and in which both partners can prove their trustworthiness, enabling them to expand the relation and engage in major transactions. (Blau 1974: 209)

Balancing the imbalances in social exchange

Moreover, Blau notes, "A paradox of social exchange is that it serves not only to establish bonds of friendship between peers but also to create status differences between persons" (Blau 1974: 210; see also 1964: 88–114), differences that invariably revolve around differences in power and rank. Thus "there is a strain toward imbalance as well as toward reciprocity in social associations," including friendship and marriage (Blau 1964: 26–27). We give birthday presents to our friends with the (unspoken) expectation (or trust) that they will reciprocate and not only give us a present on our birthday but give us one of comparable value to the gift we gave them. This seems like a fairly balanced social exchange. A "strain toward imbalance" emerges, however, when Friend A has more friends than Friend B. This gives Friend A more power in the A–B relationship because A has more alternative friends to hang out with (and more birthday presents to buy), and hence may not feel constrained to give B a gift of comparable value to the one received from B. Giving a less expensive (or no) gift may have negative consequences (e.g., losing a friend), but these consequences will be greater for B than for A. Unlike B, A does not have a scarcity of friends. The (less expensive) gift A gives B, therefore, affirms the friendship, but it simultaneously affirms the power imbalance in the friendship. In short, friendship (and cohabitation/marriage) are exchange relationships, and they tend toward imbalance, given the variation in the resources (of money, skills, emotional investment, popularity, beauty, etc.) that individuals bring to and take from the relationship.

Figure 7.1   In giving we expect to receive … something in return … sometime in the future. Source: Andrew Wink.

The differentiation of power, however, does not necessarily lead to change in the structure of social relationships. Change occurs only in circumstances where those involved in the (imbalanced power) exchange perceive that change might enhance their net access to greater rewards (e.g., nicer friends, a promotion, votes). In many relationships – between spouses, family members, and friends; in bureaucratic work settings; or in politics – the perceived downside is neutralized by the perceived advantages. This occurs because of a general overall reciprocity (rather than a unilateral dependence) in the exchange relationship such that the exchange more or less balances power (Blau 1964: 29; as discussed in the roommate example earlier).

Topic 7.1   Depleted trust: Drunken abuse of the police in South Korea

Trust is important in maintaining interpersonal and community relationships, in building team effectiveness in the workplace, and in ensuring cooperation across organizations whose interests may overlap (e.g., among local and state police and national security bureaus such as FBI, CIA, MI5). Trust is also important in ensuring respect for, and the effective functioning of, civic institutions (including mass media) that serve to maintain the public good. In any social context, trust takes a while to build. And if there is a legacy of mistrust, cultivating trust can be especially challenging. Attitudes toward the police in South Korea exemplify this.

South Korea has one of the highest rates of alcohol consumption in the world; it is ranked by the World Health Organization (WHO) as number 13 overall and number 1 in hard liquor consumption. Not only is public drunkenness by young people in jeans and well-dressed men in business suits quite common but so too is abusive behavior by drunks toward the police. "Almost every night in almost every police station in Seoul, drunken men – and sometimes women – can be found abusing officers verbally and even physically, as an accepted way of banishing anger. They are usually allowed to sleep it off and go home, their punishment no more than a small fine" (Sang-Hun 2012: A4). Although the Seoul Metropolitan Police Agency recently decided on a crack-down against serial offenders, one of the reasons why the police themselves are a target of drunken violence is that many Koreans today have a distrustful attitude toward the police – a cultural remnant of Japan's colonial rule over Korea from 1910 to 1945. The police had worked for the Japanese authorities and subsequently after Korea's liberation in 1945, they successfully opposed the pro-democracy movement, instead favoring authoritarian rule by the South Korean military. Then, once democratization became successful (in 1987), South Koreans assumed a view of citizenship that basically regarded the police as subservient to citizens' needs. Generational and political change has not increased respect for or trust in the police, and police officers, therefore, are the object of drunken vitriol by South Korea's hard-working but heavy drinking population.

EXCHANGE NETWORK THEORY: RICHARD EMERSON, KAREN COOK, MARK GRANOVETTER

The impact of power imbalances on the development of trust is one of the questions explored by contemporary sociologists who use a social psychological approach to the study of social exchange networks. The study of exchange networks is heavily indebted to the social exchange theory of **Richard Emerson**, who is widely recognized for developing Homans's individual exchange model to make it applicable not just to dyads (two-person units) and small groups but to larger social units. The now-common idea that organizations, corporations, and states are actors involved in networks of unequal exchange relationships owes much to Emerson's theorizing (see Cook and Whitmeyer 2000).

BIOGRAPHICAL NOTE

Richard Emerson was born in Utah in 1925. He majored in sociology at the University of Utah and received his PhD in sociology and psychology from the University of Minnesota. He spent most of his career at the University of Washington. During World War II, he served in an elite mountaineering army division, and in 1963 participated in the first successful US mountain-eering expedition to climb Mount Everest, during which he also conducted prize-winning sociological fieldwork on communication networks. Emerson was also an accomplished mountain photographer. He and his wife, Pat, had two children. Emerson, who suffered from cancer, died unexpectedly in 1982 (Cook and Whitmeyer 2000: 486–488).

For Emerson, an **exchange network** "is a set of actors linked together directly or indirectly through exchange relations. An actor is then conceived as a point where many exchange relations connect" (Emerson 1972: 57; also quoted in Cook and Whitmeyer 2000: 495). Importantly then, as Cook and Whitmeyer elaborate, "a connection exists not between actors but between exchange relations. A connection between two exchange relations is either *positive* or *negative* … use of power in an exchange relation entails obtaining terms of exchange more favorable to oneself. Therefore, the more powerful actor in an exchange relation should obtain more favorable terms of exchange" (2000: 495–496, 497–498).

Emerson's focus on exchange relations has been useful in studying organizations, marriage and family dynamics, marketing, and geopolitics (Cook and Whitmeyer 2000: 501). And as world politics and economics result in more intricately intertwined networks, we can assume that the usefulness of network analysis will expand. For example, international efforts to dissuade Kim Jong Un against expanding North Korea's nuclear aspirations require cooperation among a network of states that includes the US, China, Russia, and South Korea, despite various tensions among these four powers. Similarly, after the British voted to exit the EU (Brexit, June 2016), some analysts criticized David Cameron for his lack of prior networking with other European leaders. Apparently, he tended to focus on Angela Merkel, given that she is the leader of the EU's strongest economy (Germany), but failed to recognize that networking with other EU leaders might have strengthened his ability to win conces-sions from the EU that, in turn, might have dampened the tensions within the UK Conservative Party that led to a referendum on EU membership.

POWER AND MISTRUST IN SOCIAL EXCHANGE NETWORKS

Karen Cook and her coauthors (e.g., Cook et al. 2005) use Emerson's (1962) conceptualization of **power dependence** to assess how power differences militate against the development of trust across different types of relationships. They explain,

The main power-dependence proposition is that *dependence is the basis of power in an exchange relation …* That is, the power of actor A over actor B in the A–B relation is a function of B's dependence on A. This general proposition relating power and dependence has been demonstrated to apply in many types of relations, including employer–employee relationships, marital relationships, friendship and dating relationships, and other social exchange relations involving mutual dependence that can be defined as relations of **encapsulated interest** [the idea that we trust someone because we believe that they take our interests to heart and encapsulate or merge our interests in/with their interests] … In addition, the power-dependence proposition applies to other types of social units, including relations between groups, organizations and even nation-states. (Cook et al. 2005: 42–43)

They note that although trust may emerge in unequal power relationships, it tends to be fragile, because the relative power of individuals (and of groups or nations) has an impact on how they perceive the relationship (Cook et al. 2005: 43). (See also Topic 7.1.)

BIOGRAPHICAL NOTE

Karen Cook received her undergraduate and graduate education at Stanford University, and after many years on the faculty at the University of Washington, where she collaborated with Richard Emerson, returned to Stanford, where she is currently a distinguished professor of sociology. She has published widely and has received many awards, including election to the National Academy of Sciences, and to the American Academy of Arts and Sciences. Cook served as vice president of the American Sociological Association in 1994–1995.

THE INSTITUTIONAL REGULATION OF TRUST

Because power inequalities weaken trust, and because trust is seen as an important element in smooth interpersonal and societal functioning, there are institutional mechanisms designed to supervise and enforce trust (a development that has parallels with Dahrendorf's democratization of conflict; see chapter 6). For example, the expectation of trust in professional relationships (e.g., doctor–patient, banker–client) is strengthened by external agencies and associations that impose detailed codes of ethics. Additionally, the mistrust that may characterize bankers and their clients is attenuated by the guarantees of financial security (e.g., Federal Deposit Insurance Corporation [FDIC]) and oversight (e.g., the Securities and Exchange Commission [SEC]) provided by government agencies.

Belief in trust both as a civic value and as a remedy against crime is so strong in law enforcement that many police departments invest resources in developing personal relationships with residents in disadvantaged neighborhoods. In the wake of a series of highly controversial incidents of police violence in the US, many police departments intensified their community outreach efforts. For example, in the summer of 2017, police in several cities used refitted ice-cream trucks and, with the revised motto "To Protect and Serve Ice Cream," drove around serving free ice cream (Bauerlein 2017). In other contexts, independent mediating agents are frequently appointed to help cultivate feelings of trust between marriage or business partners and in trade disputes between countries. Similarly, impartial monitors are dispatched from the US and the EU to oversee the fairness of elections in fledgling democracies (e.g., Ghana, Kenya), and working with local watchdogs, their presence on the ground helps increase the trust of individuals and political parties in their country's voting procedures and election outcomes.

Clearly, trust-nurturing agents or organizations are not always successful in maintaining trust in the relationships in question. And indeed, as Cook et al. note, in circumstances of declining trust, "reliance on interpersonal mechanisms for maintaining trust gives way to organizational mechanisms that ensure trustworthiness through increased monitoring and sanctioning [with penalties], ironically reducing the possibility for ongoing trust relations" (2005: 47).

NETWORKS AND SOCIAL CAPITAL

One reason why networks are sociologically important is because they function effectively even in the absence of trust relations (Cook et al. 2005: 103). Trust can play a role in initiating your social contacts and acquaintances, but it does not have to. People can do things for you even if they don't trust you and similarly do things to help their neighborhood or community even if they don't like their neighbors. Such behavior is assured by factors other than trust, such as legal requirements, professional duty, an individual's concern about their own and their community's reputation, or for financial (Cook et al. 2005: 86–87; Cook et al. 2009), or altruistic and compassionate reasons (e.g., Dillon and Wink 2007: 158–179). From a network perspective, the important thing is to have (direct or indirect) connections to people who are willing and able to commit to do things on your behalf. This is **social capital**. For network scholars, "Social capital enables us to get things done by people with whom we do not have a substantial trust relationship – indeed, people whom we need not even know" (Cook et al. 2005: 87). In drug rehabilitation, addiction-companion network programs, for example, paid "sober compan- ions," whom alcohol and drug addicts may or may not trust, nonetheless help the addicts-in-recovery maintain an alcohol- and drug-free daily routine. In general, closed networks tend to have both higher levels of trust and greater expected rewards among members (e.g., Burt and Burzynska 2017). However, as Ronald Burt (2010), emphasizes, individuals need to actively *use* their networks to gain, for example, a competitive career advantage; they cannot passively rely on a given network to act for them. (See also Bourdieu, chapter 13.)

THE STRENGTH OF WEAK TIES

Sociologists who study social networks are interested not so much in who we trust or like but who we spend time with (irrespective of whether we trust or like them).[1] As underscored by Mark Granovetter (1973, 1974), overlapping interpersonal ties among individuals are effective in enhancing their life chances (e.g., economic success) as well as community well-being, even, or *especially*, when the ties are weak rather than tightly knit. Granovetter shows that **strong ties** among a small group of individuals (e.g., cliques) may reduce their ties to others outside the group and thus close off their access to information and opportunities that might be effective for them as individ- uals or collectively (e.g., in achieving community goals). When individuals have **weak ties** to several different people (e.g., an old high school acquaintance, a former workmate) who themselves have weak ties to many others, this expands the individual's access to new information and opportunities (which may include high-paying jobs in the financial sector or in some other tightly networked business or occupational culture).

Granovetter notes that although it might intuitively seem that "those with whom one has strong ties are more motivated to help with job information … those to whom we are weakly tied are more likely to move in circles different from our own and will thus have access to information different from that which we receive [from our close friends]" (1973: 1371). In short, word-of-mouth information or rec- ommendations shared across several weakly connected people can create a large domino effect. This, for example, is how the use of steroids among professional baseball players in the US seems to have expanded, as documented by the Mitchell Report (see Topic 7.2).

Topic 7.2   Steroid report depicts a two-player domino effect

The Mitchell Report on steroid abuse in US professional baseball identified a former clubhouse attendant for the New York Mets, Kirk Radomski, as a major supplier of steroids. Among those whom he supplied, David Segui, a Mets player, subsequently went on to play for seven other teams, and he introduced Radomski to players on each of these teams. One of his contacts, in turn, was a trainer on one of those teams, and that trainer became a supplier to Roger Clemens and two other players. As the *New York Times* reported, "The use of steroids and human growth hormone seemed to multiply and stretch after the most ordinary interactions. Introductions were made over lunch or advice was doled out in the locker room, one place that players congregated every day" (Pennington 2007).

Trust certainly matters in social relationships, and closed sanctuaries such as locker rooms are conducive to the development of social solidarity (see Durkheim, chapter 2) and tight-knit relationships. From a social network perspective, however, what is more crucial is the existence of multiple connections across several different contexts – in the case of steroids, across several different teams.

Beyond the relatively confined network of steroid users, weak ties also affect macro-level processes; in the steroids case, congressional investigations and public debate led to changes in drug policy for both professional and amateur baseball players (and for other athletes too). Weak ties can also facilitate the development of bridges to several other individuals when there is a need for community activism. Bridging ties between loosely connected individuals and groups in the larger society, therefore, can produce social cohesion rather than alienation or fragmentation (Granovetter 1973: 1378).

In short, weak ties can create numerous connections among loosely tied individuals and groups. Members of tightly bonded, closed cliques, by contrast, are strongly tied to one another but may have few ties to individuals outside the group. Thus cliques can contribute to community fragmentation; a society of similarly minded cliques who do not communicate with others. Accordingly, the analysis of networks and of micro-level interpersonal ties illuminates how "the personal experience of individuals is closely bound up with larger-scale aspects of social structure, well beyond the purview of particular individuals" (Granovetter 1973: 1377). In sum, interpersonal ties (i.e., whom you talk to) are important; they are a core component of the social or network capital you (and your community) can use to accumulate additional resources. (See also Topic 7.3.)

Topic 7.3   Birds of a feather flock together

Although weak ties with an array of people can be highly beneficial at both a personal and communal level (Granovetter 1973), research shows that like-minded people tend to live near one another and to be friends with one another. Not surprisingly, social insularity is driven by variables such as education, income, and race (Darlin 2016). For example, 29 percent of Americans with a college degree say that all five of their closest friends have a college degree; similarly, 31 percent of those who either never attended or graduated from college say that none of their friends have a college degree. Insularity is even more common among those with a postgraduate education such as doctors, lawyers, professors, and MBA graduates, 57 percent of whom say that their five closest friends are similarly educated. Race is even more isolating: 48 percent of whites say all of their five closest friends are white; 36 percent of blacks say all of their five closest friends are black and 31 percent say none of their closest friends are white. Similar patterns of insularity are evident among people of the same income level and party affiliation (Darlin 2016). Not surprisingly, because people tend to hang out with people who share their views on hot-button issues (e.g., abortion, climate change), they are sometimes surprised upon realizing that so many others (not like them) have a contrary opinion (e.g., same-sex marriage, President Trump's victory, Brexit, etc.).

ACTOR–NETWORK THEORY (ANT): BRUNO LATOUR

Actor–network theory (ANT) has nothing to do with the notion of networks used by the theorists discussed in this chapter or elsewhere in this book (e.g., Castells, chapter 14). Bruno Latour, a French theorist who is most closely associated with ANT, says that ANT is named in an "awkward," "confusing," and "meaningless" way, but because it is now so widely known as ANT, the name cannot simply be discarded (Latour 2005: 9). ANT is proposed by Latour as an alternative social theory, a very different way of thinking about what constitutes the social world and social action than is provided by the typical micro or macro sociological framework. For ANT, the domain of the social includes humans and non-human objects and things, including microbes, scallops, ships, kettles, soap, monkeys, speed bumps, legal precedents. Such objects are actors in their own right whose movement, transformation, translation, and reassembling makes a difference; they do something that impacts social action. Latour argues that "any thing that … modifies a state of affairs by making a difference is an actor" (2005: 71). He sometimes uses the more technical word, **actant**, to refer to actors (2005: 54, 71); an actant is basically an actor, an object or entity that makes a difference or modifies an existing state of affairs and that is thus in interaction and networked with other actors/actants. In essence, as Latour emphasizes, "if an actor [human or non-human] makes no difference, it's not an actor" (Latour 2005: 130).

ANT's approach is contrary to the dominant frameworks in sociological analysis. Weber (see chapter 3), for example, sees social actors as engaging in intentional and subjectively meaningful social behavior. Durkheim emphasizes the ways in which social behavior is ordered and constrained by shared norms and rules of reciprocity (see chapter 2); social behavior is also constrained by a society's generalized values system as elaborated by Parsons (see chapter 4). By contrast, ANT's emphasis on the action and relevance of nonhuman entities and objects challenges sociologists to foreground "humble, mundane, and ubiquitous activities" such as kettles boiling water. Such objects as actors are of analytical relevance to social scientists because they modify and "make a difference in the course of some other agent's action" (Latour 2005: 71).

ANT does not treat material objects as background infrastructure or as objects or props of human-social meaning (as used, for example, in the symbolic interactionist tradition; see chapter 8). Rather, it treats them as actors in their own right and within a network of diverse elements that can include other material objects as well as individual and institutional actors, and economic and political processes. ANT has a slight parallel with ethnomethodology (see chapter 9), because it problematizes the nature and permanence of reality, that is, how reality is created, accounted for, and sustained. ANT does so, however, in a more expansive and far more open-ended way (Latour 2005: 54). In ANT, an account of social reality would have to trace each of the many things that provide context and background to any given set of relations and thus bring to the fore, rather than take for granted, the structures and norms or, in ANT terminology, the many objects and acting elements and entities that matter and make certain things happen. ANT had its origins in the study of science and is influential among scholars in science and technology studies who trace the specific connections and mediations among things in the production of specific associations, controversies, and outcomes. Latour (1987) argues that scientific facts are not just social constructions, that is, principles and laws that are produced (not spontaneously discovered out of the blue) and given legitimation and made "real" in a particular institutional, sociohistorical and cultural context (as a social constructionist perspective would argue; see chapter 9). He argues, rather, that scientific facts should be seen as actors/actants, that is, as acting objects that make a difference in causing, mediating, and setting in motion other independent action. They are "immutable mobiles," meaning that they are simultaneously established as settled or immutable things (established facts/discoveries), and as things that are in motion (mobile), and thus moving agents or entities capable of causing action.

Because objects as actors are moving agents (immutable mobiles), this requires, Latour (2005: 132) argues, that their movements and the "flows of translations" affected by them be traced. The network in ANT is not composed of individuals or organizations as is the case for exchange network theories, for example, and nor does it refer to electronic networks such as the Internet and the World Wide Web (Latour 2005: 143). A network, in ANT, is not made "of any durable substance"; rather, "it is the trace left behind by some moving agent" (2005: 132). It is the tracing of all of the circulating entities and connections that are relevant in the assembling of any flow of action. Such tracing has to be done anew time and again, given the multiple ways in which any actor either directly or as an intermediary makes a difference, that is, modifies an existing state of affairs, whether cooking methods, scientific knowledge, or political revolution. The actor–network thus needs to be traced and accounted for in its multiple and minute specific details and connections. An ANT approach in addiction research, for example, shows that the objects to which individuals are addicted are not simply props (as symbolic interactionists might argue; see chapter 8) but are equally important actors within the network of addiction action as the addicted individuals (e.g., Gomart and Hennion 1999).

ANT, with its emphasis on the tracing of networked actors and elements, is a method or a tool more than a theory; it is, as Latour states, "about *how* to study things, or rather how *not* to study things [as typical sociologists do] – or rather how to let the actors [objects/things/entities] have some room to express themselves" (2005: 142). As a tool, ANT, like other tools and objects for ANT, acts and thus "can modify the goals" the researcher has in mind, and "produce some *effects* that you would not have obtained by some other social theory (2005: 143, emphasis in original). Scholars using ANT adopt an empirical case study, descriptive approach and apply it to many topics. John Law, a British sociologist, has applied an ANT framework to, among other questions, why Portugal was successful in navigating a route to India in the late fifteenth century. He summarizes his contribution as exemplary of ANT:

> How did the Portuguese reach India? How did they maintain their imperial control? Conventional his-tories talk of spices, trade, wealth, military power, and Christianity. With some exceptions, they treat tech-nology as an essential but ultimately uninteresting infrastructure. Maritime history talks of innovations in shipping and navigation, but is usually little concerned with the politics or economics of imperialism … [Law's inquiry] brought the two narratives together. He asked how the Portuguese generated a network that allowed them to control half the world. His answer was that ships, sails, mariners, navigators, stores, spices, winds, currents, astrolabes [ancient astronomical computers], stars, guns, ephemeredes [astronomical ta-bles locating the position of heavenly bodies], gifts, merchants' drafts were all translated into a web. That web, precarious though it was, gave each component a particular shape or form that was to hold together for 150 years … Lisbon became an obligatory point of passage for a whole set of tributaries … the ships became "immutable mobiles" circulating to and fro whilst holding their form and shape constant. This … was crucial to the success of the system. (Law 2009: 146)

ANT, unlike mainstream sociology, can be described as taking a posthuman or postsocial or postcultural approach to social analysis. It is intriguing, but also controversial, in part, because it emphasizes the agency of things/objects and thus of nonhuman actors. By elevating the proactive significance of objects, ANT decenters the human-rational cognitive and moral agency and authority of (human) actors (emphasized since the Enlightenment). It also marginalizes the embodiment of social action, the fact that social action and social processes are contingent on and influenced by embodied individual and collective actors whose embodiment shapes and is shaped by social, institutional, and cultural processes. Many iPhone users, for example, interact with Apple's voice-activated digital assistant Siri, sometimes with appreciation and other times with frustration and impatience; thus as an object, it insinuates itself into users' lives. A social exchange rather than an ANT perspective, however, would argue that Siri and its user are not coequal actors in the exchange network. No matter how polite Siri is, it can always be switched off and redeployed in various ways by its human user and cannot switch itself on or implore the user to switch it on. Moreover, even if Siri succeeds in getting our attention, its "social action" is not and cannot be subjectively meaningful to, or culturally motivated by, Siri itself.

RATIONAL CHOICE THEORY AND ITS CRITIQUE: JAMES COLEMAN, GARY BECKER, PAULA ENGLAND

All theories that focus on exchange convey a certain utilitarian or self-interested understanding of the individual and of social relationships. It is rational choice theory (RCT), however, that makes utilitarianism (see Introduction, p. 15) – the utility of a course of action to the self – a core axis of explanation. **James Coleman**, influenced by Homans's exchange theory (Marsden 2005: 12), and impressed by how economists link micro- and macroeconomic behavior (e.g., the translation of micro, individual demands onto macro supply processes), became a leading proponent of RCT for sociology. Coleman embraced the **microeconomic model** of the self-interested individual in his efforts to understand the mechanisms that link individual behavior to larger, macro processes.

BIOGRAPHICAL NOTE

James Coleman was born in Bedford, Indiana, in 1926. He received his BA in chemical engineering from Purdue University and later studied for his PhD in sociology at Columbia University, where he was deeply influenced by Robert Merton, to whom he dedicated his American Sociological Association (ASA) award-winning book *Foundations of Social Theory* (1990). Coleman spent much of his early academic career as a sociology professor at Johns Hopkins University and then moved to the University of Chicago. His research on race, inequality, and education (Coleman et al. 1966) was highly influential in public policy debates. Coleman was elected president of the ASA in 1991 and was also an elected member of the National Academy of Sciences. He married Zdzislawa Walaszek, and they had four sons. He died in 1995, at age 68 (Marsden 2005).

Although you might be inclined to equate self-interest with selfishness, this is not entirely accurate. Acting on self-interest, as John Stuart Mill (1806–1873) noted long ago, does not necessarily prevent one from serving the interests of others. For example, although we might think of altruism – selfless concern for others – as the opposite of selfishness, altruistic behavior is driven by many different motives, including self-interest (see Dillon and Wink 2007). In any case, the behavior of the self-interested individual reverberates far beyond the individual alone and affects macro processes across multiple domains (e.g., the economy, family relations, health care, politics, religion).

Coleman (1961) first highlighted micro–macro connections when he studied how American adolescents' choices or values – whether they emphasize peer popularity over academic achievement – feed into aggregate, nationwide patterns of educational and occupational success/failure. It was in his later theoretical work, however, that he developed his ideas about the **economic efficiency** or rationality of human behavior, and its implications for social processes that would seem to have little to do with economics. Coleman offers a social theory based on the "purposive action of individuals" (1990: 17). We know from Weber (see chapter 3) that purposive action can have several different motivational sources. Coleman, however, narrowly defines it as the **maximization of utility** – the usefulness of action to advancing the actor's own interests. He frames it this way, in part, he states, because he wants to minimize psychological complexity so as not to complicate his theory of the linkages between individual actions and their manifestation in social organizational processes (Coleman 1990: 19).

MAXIMIZATION OF INDIVIDUAL INTEREST

For Coleman, an individual's rational, cost–benefit evaluations in deciding whom to trust, whom to marry, whether and when to have children and how many, whether to pursue a college education, what church to attend, etc., can predict aggregate societal processes and trends (e.g., 1990: 21–22; 177–196). Given the individual's (economic and noneconomic) resources, the **marginal utility** of one course of action as opposed to another is what determines human behavior. Thus:

> The types of action available to the actor are severely limited. All are carried out with a single purpose – to increase the actor's realization of interests … Actors are connected to resources (and thus indirectly to one another) through only two relations: their control over resources and their interest in resources. Actors have a single principle of action, that of acting so as to maximize their realization of interests. (Coleman 1990: 32, 37)

The purposive maximization of interests is bolstered in modern societies, Coleman argues, by the development of **systems of trust** (or institutionalized trust mechanisms; see the section "The Institutional Regulation of Trust") that contribute to modifying "the decisions of individual actors to place trust and to be trustworthy" (Coleman 1990: 175). According to RCT, trust in individual and collective others, including those "intermediaries in trust" (e.g., brokers, lobbyists) who act on behalf of "interested parties" (1990: 180–183), is a function of the likely future benefits to the (trusting) actor as a result of the negotiated deal. "The expansion of trust leads to increased potential for social action on the part of those who are trusted … and the contraction [diminishment] of trust has the opposite effect" (1990: 196).

HUMAN CAPITAL AND SOCIAL CAPITAL

It was Coleman's colleague Gary Becker (1976), a Nobel award-winning economist, who introduced "the economic approach to human behavior." He argued that the rate of return on investments in human capital (by individuals themselves and by others such as parents, employers and governments) determines not only individual behavior but how couples, organizations, institutions, and societies behave. **Human capital** refers to the "resources in people," such as education, health, job training, and other nonmonetary assets, that "influence future monetary and psychic income" (Becker 1964: 1). Just as we create physical capital by transforming raw materials (e.g., wood) "so as to form tools that facilitate production, human capital is created by changing persons so as to give them skills and capabilities that make them able to act in new ways" (Coleman 1990: 304). Today, when we hear business and university executives and politicians talking about investing in human capital, this is what they mean – training and retraining, retooling, and reeducating individuals so they can be productive in a changing high-tech economy. Human capital, moreover, is something that can be replenished over the life course as individuals acquire new skills and transition to new careers.

NEGOTIATING SCARCE RESOURCES

Individuals need to maximize human capital, economists argue, because there is a scarcity of resources in society: There is a market squeeze in, and hence increased competition for, job opportunities, houses, classroom seats, specialty restaurants, ski slopes, eligible marriage partners. Those who get to maximize utility in these markets will be those who are best able to use their human capital, and their social capital. Human capital can complement social capital if we use it (i.e., our abilities, health, skills, beauty, friendliness, etc.) to develop connections with others (social capital; Coleman 1990: 304–305). As Coleman emphasizes – following the sociologist Pierre Bourdieu (whom he cites, 1990: 300; see chapter 13) – social capital, unlike human capital, is not lodged in individuals but "inheres in the structure of relations between and among persons … it is embodied in the relations among persons" (1990: 302, 304). And, like other forms of capital, "social capital is productive, making possible the achievement of certain ends [goals] that would be unattainable in its absence" (1990: 302). By the same token, "social capital that is valuable in facilitating certain actions may be useless or even harmful for others" (1990: 302).

The people we hang out with, therefore, may facilitate or be functional to our access to certain opportunities that enhance the achievement of our academic and occupational goals. And some of our friends may hinder our prospects for success by distracting us with less productive activities or getting us into trouble with the police, etc. This line of argument captures the significance that Coleman (1961) and other sociologists attach to the role of peers and peer culture in influencing adolescents' study and leisure habits. For Coleman, "effective *norms* can constitute a powerful form of social capital … This social capital not only facilitates certain actions but also constrains others" (1990: 311; emphasis mine). He, then, unlike Bourdieu (see chapter 13), subsumes culture within social capital. He sees culture, like Parsons (see chapter 4; and Becker 1996: 16) in terms of the individual's internalization of the culturally affirmed norms and values that are conducive, for example, to achievement. He does not see it as a separate capital resource that can be actively drawn on to pursue various goals (unlike Bourdieu 1984; see chapter 13; see also Swidler 2001).

Economic theory, according to its proponents, provides a "unified framework for all behavior involving scarce resources, nonmarket as well as market, monetary as well as non-monetary, small group as well as competitive" (Becker 1976: 205). Thinking of marriage, for example, as a "productive" household unit, the prediction would be that "marriage occurs if, and only if, both [Person A and Person B] … are made better off – that is, increase their utility [or expect to increase their utility]" (1976: 207) (see Topic 7.4). Marriage makes sense (i.e., has utility), if, by pooling their resources, marriage partners are more productive and efficient as a household unit than either would be acting alone (as consumers and producers of goods and services such as meals, leisure, etc.). In Becker's view, the division of labor between spouses, for example, would be based on evaluating the **net gain** in efficiency and resources for the family unit as a whole that would result from considering various alternative arrangements; whether one spouse should work for pay and one stay at home minding the children and doing housework; or, if it is efficient for both to work, who should work more and/or do more household chores (so that the family will have more money, more leisure time, etc.).

MARRIAGE: STRUCTURAL AND CULTURAL CONSTRAINTS ON SELF-INTEREST

Paula England is a leading feminist sociologist who has written extensively on gender inequality, work and family (e.g., England 2005, 2006, 2010; England and Farkas 1986), and specifically on exchange relations in marriage. She accepts that optimizing individuals are self-interested actors (as RCT assumes). But she argues, along with exchange theorists (Homans, Blau), that self-interest is not confined to economic rewards. She also points out that Becker and others in the RCT tradition do not consider power imbalances or power dependence relations in their calculations. England probes beyond both RCT and exchange theory, offering a more sociologically rich and nuanced understanding of individual and household behavior. In particular, she underscores the structural (e.g., wage and occupational structures) and cultural constraints (e.g., gender-role expectations in marriage and at work) that actively impinge on optimizing individuals pursuing their self-interests (England and Farkas 1986: 20–21).

England's research with colleagues, using time-management data from the US and Australia (Bittman et al. 2003), lends support to exchange theory (e.g., Homans, Blau; see the first section of the chapter), namely, that "power flows from bringing resources to a relationship and that a spouse can use economically based bargaining power to get the other partner to do housework" (2003: 187).

Exchange-bargaining works such that women decrease their housework when they increase their earnings; in short, "money talks in marriage" (Bittman et al. 2003: 209). But that is not the whole story. Wives' increased income does not seem to push husbands to do more housework; rather, they pay for outside help and services (2003: 209). England and her colleagues also find that exchange-bargaining and the marital division of household labor are not simply a function of financial resources; indeed, their research underscores the larger significance of gender in determining social patterns. For example, not only do women do a larger baseline amount of housework than men, but even in the minority of households where women earn 51 percent or more of the household's total income, "gender trumps money" – meaning that women do more, not less, housework. They do so to compensate for the "gender deviance" of husbands earning less than wives in a society that still expects men not to be economically dependent on women (Bittman et al. 2003: 192, 210; England and Farkas 1986: 96). This is a cultural expectation internalized by high-earning single women whose impression management strategies (see chapter 8) include keeping their lower-earning boyfriends from seeing their affluent apartments.

England and other sociologists thus challenge RCT's narrow, microeconomic, efficiency-maximization approach, and its disregard of the interpersonal, institutional, and cultural contexts in which actors make decisions. More generally, RCT fails to account for the many instances in which individuals and collectivities apparently act against their own utilitarian self-interests. Research suggests that cultural expectations (e.g., of gender roles; Bittman et al. 2003), institutional arrangements (e.g., the split between work and family domains; e.g., Damaske 2011; Jacobs and Gerson 2004), political ideology, religious beliefs, and/or love, loyalty, and other emotions also need to be fully acknowledged as factors determining interpersonal and social behavior.

Topic 7.4   Heterosexual romance and the marriage market in China

In China's blossoming economy (see Topic 1.1, chapter 1), heterosexual romance is also blossoming (and gay life too; see chapter 11). Arranged marriages have been banned in China since 1950 when they were outlawed by Chairman Mao as part of sweeping cultural reforms that also established a woman's right to divorce. However, the tradition of parental oversight – and of oversight by Communist Party officials – over individuals' marriage choices continued, especially in rural areas. The modernization changes of the 1980s brought people greater freedom to act on their own desires (the rise of individualization; e.g., Yan 2003, 2010; see chapter 15 in this book), though the unlawful status of premarital sex remained in place until 1997. Today, reflecting the Chinese experience of increased personal freedom, one-third of couples report cohabiting before marriage, compared to 2 percent who did so in 1970, during the era of the Cultural Revolution (Wong 2013: A9). And in 2017, the divorce rate was more than double what it was a decade earlier (Fan 2017). Finding a romantic partner is not easy. Although there are many single people, there are few bars or other venues for meeting possible dates. The gap is being filled by Internet dating sites. "China's No.1 Matchmaker" is Gong Haiyan, who started an Internet dating company in her dorm room in 2003; the company currently trades on the NASDAQ – its tagline: "The serious dating website." According to Gong, "Our membership has a very clear goal: to get married" (Osnos 2012: 76).

Finding a spouse is serious business and the freedom to act on love does not exclude rational, material considerations. In such a populous country as China, online dating is used not to expand the searchable population (as people in the West like to do) but to narrow it. With such a potentially large marriage market of available dates/prospective spouses, date searchers in China frequently use a combination of very specific filter criteria such as face shape, height, blood type, and zodiac sign to narrow the pool of worthwhile dates. Money (including dowries) has always been explicitly linked to marriage in China (as elsewhere), and currently private property is too. In China today, "A man without a house, a car, and a nest egg is a 'triple-without' [not a good catch]. If he gets married, it's a 'naked wedding'" (Osnos 2012: 81).

The Chinese marriage market is also affected by an oversupply of young single men (as a result of parents opting to abort female fetuses). Thus by 2020, "China is expected to have twenty-four million men of marrying age who are unable to find a spouse." Women, meanwhile, face their own pressures: the cultural pressure not to become a "leftover woman," as single women over 30 are labeled. As in the West, women too feel pressure to downplay their educational achievements so as not to intimidate men. As Gong summarizes, "In China's marriage market, there are three species trying to survive: Men, women, and women with graduate degrees" (Osnos 2012: 81). And for women who want to stay married even as their husbands have love affairs or long-term mistresses, there is increasing recourse to "marriage dispellers," that is, men or women who are hired by wives and who use various creative strategies to keep the straying husband from divorcing his wife (Fan 2017).

ANALYTICAL MARXISM

Although RCT is far removed from Marxist theory (see chapter 1), some of its microeconomic principles are used by some contemporary scholars working within the Marxist tradition. Known as **analytical Marxism**, this empirically oriented approach emerged in the late 1970s as various neo-Marxist sociologists and economists sought to reconceptualize some of Marx's core assumptions (e.g., historical materialism) in the context of late twentieth-century capitalist society (Roemer 1994: ix). Analytical Marxists seek to explain how, for example, occupational mobility and the emergence of an economically strong middle class – characteristics of contemporary capitalism that undermine Marx's stress on class polarization (between the proletariat and the bourgeoisie) – can be nonetheless understood in Marxist terms (e.g., Wright 1997).

Scholars associated with analytical Marxism vary in (1) the arguments they elaborate; (2) their chosen unit of analysis – individuals (e.g., Roemer 1982), social classes (e.g., Wright 1984), or the state (e.g., Block 1987; Przeworski 1985); and (3) their research methods. John Roemer, one its founding theorists, probes whether workers in modern capitalist societies should be considered economically "exploited" (as Marx would aver). An economist, he draws on **game theory** models of interindividual cooperation and competition to hypothesize a general theory of exploitation (Roemer 1982). He conceptualizes the actors in an economy as "a set of agents, each of whom is characterized as having preferences over goods and leisure, and … an initial endowment of goods which can be used as inputs in the production process" (1994: xi). Using experiments that impose varying degrees of difference in individuals' assets and preferences (on hypothetical "labor market island"), Roemer argues, for example, that individuals basically select their own class position as a result of the asset-allocation decisions they make. In this view, it is individuals and not the capitalist class structure (as it is for Marx and for Weber too) that lock individuals into unequal relations. Roemer states: "People are not born into classes, so to speak, but choose their own class positions as a rational (i.e., preference maximizing) response to their wealth constraints. Thus capitalism induces [produces] a class structure in which those who are poor systematically work for those who are rich and are exploited by them in the classical Marxian sense" (1994: xi; see also 1982: 259–263).

CLASS LOCATIONS

Taking a different tack, the prolific American sociologist **Erik Olin Wright** focuses on the changing composition and dynamics of the class structure in contemporary capitalist societies. Using aggregate data from a large-scale, cross-national survey of class structure and class consciousness, Wright argues that "There are class locations that are neither exploiters nor exploited" (1984: 399). This is evidenced by the large sector of self-employed owners/workers, and by professionals and managers who occupy the senior ranks of corporate and noneconomic bureaucratic organizations. These employees have access to **organization assets**, that is, technical knowledge and expertise which they effectively control, as opposed to privately owning the means of production (i.e., property, capital), and which may be used by them to exploit others (Wright 1984: 399). Wright refers to these workers as occupying **contradictory class locations**; they are simultaneously in more than one class. Thus, "Managers, for example, should be viewed as simultaneously in the working class (in so far as they are wage laborers dominated by capitalists) and in the capitalist class (in so far as they control the operation of production and the labor of workers)" (1984: 384).

The interests, therefore, of those who occupy contradictory class locations do not correspond *a priori* to any one class. This, Wright notes, is especially characteristic of state and noneconomic managerial bureaucrats: "state managers … unlike corporate managers, are less likely to have their careers tightly integrated with the interests of the capitalist class" (1984: 402). But as Block (1987) would emphasize, the capitalist context in which the state operates means that it will most likely bolster rather than undermine business interests over the long term even if, at times, it acts against specific interests of the capitalist class (e.g., taxation policy that redistributes wealth from the rich to the less well off).

Wright's identification of a contradictory class location upends the traditional Marxist conceptualization of a "one-to-one correspondence between structural locations filled by individuals and classes" (Wright 1984: 384). This reconceptualization of class illuminates the complex nature of class exploitation and of the interrelation between class location and individual interests, a complexity that highlights the open-endedness of class conflict and class alliances. Wright argues that

> Individuals in contradictory locations within class relations face three broad strategies in their relationship to class struggle: they can try to use their position as an exploiter to gain entry as individuals into the dominant exploiting class; they can attempt to forge an alliance with the dominant exploiting class; or they can form some kind of alliance with the principal exploited class. (Wright 1984: 405)

In sum, class alliances in contemporary society are somewhat open ended, contingent as they are on the interests and interest-maximization strategies of those occupying a contradictory location in the system of class relationships.

SUMMARY

Exchange, exchange network, and rational choice theorists variously underscore that social life can only be understood by recognizing that the exchange of resources underlies and characterizes the range of interpersonal, group, and organizational relationships that constitute society. There are different emphases among the various exchange theories. But, taken as a whole, they alert us to (1) the relevance of utilitarian motivational principles in shaping cooperative behavior; (2) the relevance of power imbalances in exchange relationships; (3) the centrality of trust in social life, and of institutional mechanisms that build and regulate trust; (4) the productive significance of social ties even in the absence of trust; (5) the application of a cost–benefit, economic efficiency assessment to areas of social life that may seem at odds with economic maximization criteria (e.g., marriage); and (6) how asset-maximization strategies produce exploitation, and shape and alter the composition of the class structure. This chapter also introduced actor–network theory (ANT), an approach that highlights and traces the significance of nonhuman actors (e.g., watches, kettles, scientific discoveries) in the process of social action and exchange.

POINTS TO REMEMBER

Exchange theory
- George Homans: interpersonal exchange based on reward/punishment is the basis of all sociological action

- Social exchange refers to what we give to, and get from, others
- Social exchange is characterized by power imbalances
- Peter Blau: extended the analysis of social exchange to organizational behavior
  - Power imbalances get neutralized in social exchange relations of interdependence
  - Social exchange generates trust and diffuse expectations of reciprocity

Exchange network theory
- Exchange networks (Emerson, Cook):
- Exchange networks are composed of sets of exchange relations
- Dependence is the basis of power in exchange relations
- Trust may emerge in unequal power relationships, but tends to be fragile
- Trust relations are institutionally regulated
- Networks are effective independent of relations of trust
- Social networks (e.g., Granovetter):
  - Significance of overlapping weak ties in developing social connections among diverse individuals and groups

Actor–network theory (ANT) (e.g., Latour, Law)
- Offers a very different perspective on the world of "the social" and of social action than found in mainstream sociology
- Regards human actors and a broad mix of non-human objects and things (e.g., a speed bump) as well as scientific discoveries and philosophical ideas as independent agents and entities of social action

Rational choice theory (e.g., Coleman)
- An emphasis on the self-interested, utility-maximizing individual
- Focuses on the economic efficiency of human capital/behavior in noneconomic markets (marriage, etc.)
- Systems of trust facilitate self-interested decision making and gain-maximization behavior
- Emphasizes complementary links between human capital and social capital
- Criticized (e.g., by Paula England) for its inattentiveness to power dependence and the interpersonal, institutional, and cultural contexts shaping social behavior

Analytical Marxism (e.g., Roemer, Wright)
- Uses an empirically grounded, economistic, rational actor perspective to reconceptualize the class structure of contemporary capitalist societies
- Exploitation remains a central construct, though its dynamic in class formation and class relations is more complex than originally theorized by Marx
- Highlights the significance of contradictory class locations in determining individuals' interests (e.g., Wright)

GLOSSARY: EXCHANGE THEORY

action–reward/punishment orientation behavior as motivated by the individual's perception of its likely rewards and punishments.

behavior conditioning human behavior as determined (conditioned) as a function of previous experience of, and/or perceived future, rewards and punishments.

diffuseness of expectations unspecified expectations characterize noneconomic and noncontractual social relationships (e.g., friendships).

power imbalances in any social exchange relation, interaction is contingent on differentiation between and among the actors in terms of who gets more out of the relationship.

scarcity value determines power imbalances in any exchange relationship; a function of the relation between the supply of, and demand for, rewards.

social exchange all forms of social behavior wherein individuals exchange resources with others in order to attain desired ends.

trust confidence in the reciprocity and sincerity of economic, professional, and other social relationships.

GLOSSARY: EXCHANGE NETWORK THEORY

encapsulated interest in exchange relations of mutual dependence, we trust individual, group, and institutional actors, believing that they sincerely appreciate our interests and merge (encapsulate) our interests with theirs.

exchange network sets of actors linked together directly or indirectly through exchange relations.

power dependence basis of power in an exchange relation; the power of actor A over actor B in the A–B relation is a function of B's dependence on A.

social capital individuals' ties or connections to others; can be converted into economic capital.

strong ties exist when people are closely bonded to others (e.g., cliques); can reduce interaction or sharing of information with individuals or groups outside the group; can be a source of community fragmentation.

weak ties when people have loose ties to acquaintances across several different social contexts. Weak ties expand individuals' access to information and opportunities and can facilitate community-oriented action.

GLOSSARY: ACTOR–NETWORK THEORY (ANT)

actant the understanding in ANT that all human actors and nonhuman things (e.g., animals, avatars, physical objects and entities, scientific discoveries) are coequal, agential social entities.

GLOSSARY: RATIONAL CHOICE THEORY

economic efficiency purposive utility and resource rationality of a given course of action.

human capital skills, education, health, and other competences/resources that individuals possess; influences their future economic and social-psychological functioning.

marginal utility extent to which one course of action rather than another proportionally increases an individual's resources or advances their interests.

maximization of utility behavior motivated by principles advancing self-interest.

microeconomic model presumes that individuals act to maximize their own self-interests and self-satisfaction.

net gain when the benefits of a course of action outweigh its costs.

systems of trust establishment of organizations and groups to mediate transactions between social actors. These systems influence the decisions of self-interested actors to place trust and to be trustworthy in order to maximize gains.

GLOSSARY: ANALYTICAL MARXISM

analytical Marxism use of social scientific methods to highlight how the interest maximization strategies of individual and collective rational actors affect class formation, exploitation, and class alliances.

contradictory class locations employees, such as professionals, managers, and bureaucrats, whose objective location in the class-occupational structure as members neither of the capitalist

nor of the proletarian class means that their economic interests are not *a priori* allied with any one particular class.

game theory a scientific experimental method used mostly by economists to predict interest maximization decisions.

organization assets specific skills and resources controlled by the class of professionals/bureaucrats/managers who have technical knowledge and expertise.

QUESTIONS FOR REVIEW

1 How do power imbalances affect cost–benefit assessments in interpersonal and within-group exchange?
2 Is trust between people always necessary for functionally effective (net gain) relationships? How is an absence of trust buffered by institutional practices?
3 Are strong ties between people necessary for functionally effective (net gain) relationships? When, and why, might strong ties be an impediment to social action?
4 How can women optimize the utilitarian value of marriage to them as individuals in a society that unequally rewards women's work relative to men's?

NOTE

1 Early studies of networks, such as the sociometry used by Parsons and Bales (1955) in analyzing friendship patterns in small groups, focused on personal likes and dislikes rather than ties or connections per se. Granovetter (1973: 1376) points out that his network "model differs from sociometric models in that most sociometric tests ask people whom they *like* best or would *prefer* to do something with, rather than with whom they actually spend time."

REFERENCES

Bauerlein, Valerie. 2017. "A Cold Case: New Tactic to Restore Trust." *Wall Street Journal* (August 5–6), p. A3.

Becker, Gary. 1964. *Human Capital*. New York: Columbia University Press.

Becker, Gary. 1976. *The Economic Approach to Human Behavior*. Chicago: University of Chicago Press.

Becker, Gary. 1996. *Accounting for Tastes*. Cambridge, MA: Harvard University Press.

Bittman, Michael, Paula England, Liana Sayer, Nancy Folbre, and George Matheson. 2003. "When Does Gender Trump Money? Bargaining and Time in Household Work." *American Journal of Sociology* 109: 186–214.

Blau, Peter. 1964. *Exchange and Power in Social Life*. New York: John Wiley & Sons.

Blau, Peter. 1974. *On the Nature of Organizations*. New York: John Wiley & Sons.

Block, Fred. 1987. *Revising State Theory: Essays in Politics and Postindustrialism*. Philadelphia: Temple University Press.

Bourdieu, Pierre. 1984. *Distinction: A Social Critique of the Judgment of Taste*. Cambridge, MA: Harvard University Press.

Burt, Ronald. 2010. *Neighbor Networks*. New York: Oxford University Press.

Burt, Ronald, and Katarzyna Burzynska. 2017. "Chinese Entrepreneurs, Social Networks, and Guanxi." *Management Organization Review* 13: 221–260.

Coleman, James. 1961. *The Adolescent Society*. Glencoe, IL: Free Press.

Coleman, James. 1990. *Foundations of Social Theory*. Cambridge, MA: Harvard University Press.

Coleman, James, with E. Campbell, C. Hobson, J. McPartland, A. Mood, F. Weinfeld, and R. York. 1966. *Equality of Educational Opportunity*. Washington, DC: US Government Printing Office.

Cook, Karen, and Joseph Whitmeyer. 2000. "Richard Emerson." Pp. 486–512 in George Ritzer, ed. *The Blackwell Companion to Modern Social Theory*. Oxford: Blackwell.

Cook, Karen, Russell Hardin, and Margaret Levi. 2005. *Cooperation Without Trust?* New York: Russell Sage Foundation.

Cook, Karen, Margaret Levi, and Russell Hardin. 2009. *Whom Can We Trust? How Groups, Networks, and Institutions Make Trust Possible*. New York: Russell Sage Foundation.

Damaske, Sarah. 2011. *For the Family? How Class and Gender Shape Women's Work*. New York: Oxford University Press.

Darlin, Damon. 2016. "A Question About Friends Reveals a Lot About Class." *New York Times* (September 1), p. A3.

Dillon, Michele, and Paul Wink. 2007. *In the Course of a Lifetime: Tracing Religious Belief, Practice, and Change*. Berkeley: University of California Press.

Emerson, Richard. 1962. "Power Dependence Relations." *American Sociological Review* 27: 31–41.

Emerson, Richard. 1972. "Exchange Theory, Part I. A Psychological Basis for Social Exchange. Exchange Theory, Part II. Exchange Relations and Network Structures." Pp. 38–87 in Joseph Berger, Morris Zelditch, and Bo Anderson, eds.

Sociological Theories in Progress, volume 2. Boston: Houghton Mifflin.

England, Paula. 2005. "Gender Inequality in Labor Markets: The Role of Motherhood and Segregation." *Social Politics* 12: 264–288.

England, Paula. 2006. "Devaluation and the Pay of Comparable Male and Female Occupations." Pp. 352–356 in David Grusky and Szonja Szelenyi, eds. *The Inequality Reader: Contemporary and Foundational Readings in Race, Class, and Gender*. Boulder, CO: Westview Press.

England, Paula. 2010. "The Gender Revolution: Uneven and Stalled." *Gender and Society* 24: 149–167.

England, Paula, and George Farkas. 1986. *Households, Employment, and Gender*. New York: Aldine.

Fan, Jiayang. 2017. "The Third Person: China's Marriage Crisis Gives Rise to a New Job: The Marriage Dispeller." *New Yorker* (June 26), pp. 22–28.

Gomart, E, and A. Hennion. 1999. "A Sociology of Attachment: Music Amateurs, Drug Users." Pp. 220–247 in John Law and J. Hassard, eds. *Actor Network Theory and After*. Oxford Blackwell.

Granovetter, Mark. 1973. "The Strength of Weak Ties." *American Journal of Sociology* 78: 1360–1380.

Granovetter, Mark. 1974. *Getting a Job: A Study of Contacts and Careers*. New York: Cambridge University Press.

Homans, George Caspar. 1950. *The Human Group*. New York: Harcourt, Brace.

Homans, George Caspar. 1961/1974. *Social Behavior: Its Elementary Forms*. New York: Harcourt Brace Jovanovich.

Homans, George Caspar. 1967. "Fundamental Social Processes." Pp. 27–78 in Neil Smelser, ed. *Sociology: An Introduction*. New York: John Wiley & Sons.

Jacobs, Jerry, and Kathleen Gerson. 2004. *The Time Divide: Work, Family, and Gender Inequality*. Cambridge, MA: Harvard University Press.

Latour, Bruno. 1987. *Science in Action: How to Follow Scientists and Engineers through Society*. Cambridge, MA: Harvard University Press.

Latour, Bruno. 2005. *Reassembling the Social: An Introduction to Actor–Network Theory*. Oxford: Oxford University Press.

Law, John. 2009. "Actor Network Theory and Material Semiotics." Pp. 141–158 in Bryan Turner, ed. *The Blackwell Companion to Social Theory*. Oxford; Wiley-Blackwell.

Marsden, Peter. 2005. "The Sociology of James Coleman." *Annual Review of Sociology* 31: 1–24.

Mauss, Marcel. 1967. *The Gift: Forms and Functions of Exchange in Archaic Societies*. New York: Norton.

Osnos, Evan. 2012. "The Love Business." *New Yorker* (May 14), pp. 76–82.

Parsons, Talcott, and Robert Bales. 1955. *Family Socialization and Interaction Process*. New York: Free Press.

Pennington, Bill. 2007. "Steroid Report Depicts a Two-Player Domino Effect." *New York Times*, (December 16), pp. A1, 29.

Przeworski, Adam. 1985. *Capitalism and Social Democracy*. New York: Cambridge University Press.

Roemer, John. 1982. "New Directions in the Marxian Theory of Exploitation and Class." *Politics and Society* 11: 253–287.

Roemer, John. 1994. "Introduction." Pp. ix–xvi in John Roemer, ed. *Foundations of Analytical Marxism*, volume 1. Brookfield, VT: Edward Elgar.

Sang-Hun, Choe. 2012. "Korean Police Tire of Abuse by Drunks." *New York Times* (July 25), pp. A4, 8.

Simmel, Georg. 1907/1971. *On Individuality and Social Forms*. Edited and with an introduction by Donald Levine. Chicago: University of Chicago Press.

Skinner, B.F. 1938. *The Behavior of Organisms*. New York: Appleton Century.

Swidler, Ann. 2001. *Talk of Love: How Culture Matters*. Chicago: University of Chicago Press.

Wong, Edward. 2013. "Survey in China Shows a Wide Gap in Income." *New York Times* (July 20), p. A9.

Wright, Erik Olin. 1984. "A General Framework for the Analysis of Class Structure." *Politics and Society* 13: 383–424.

Wright, Erik Olin. 1997. *Class Counts: Comparative Studies in Class Analysis*. New York: Cambridge University Press.

Yan, Yunxiang. 2003. *Private Life under Socialism: Love, Intimacy, and Family Change in a Chinese Village, 1949-1999*. Stanford, CA: Stanford University Press

Yan, Yunxiang. 2010. "The Chinese Path to Individualization." *British Journal of Sociology* 61(3): 489–512.

CHAPTER EIGHT

SYMBOLIC INTERACTIONISM

KEY CONCEPTS

self	social roles	encounters
symbolic interactionism	presentation of self	rituals of subordination
"I"	performance	body idiom
"Me"	actors	impression management
looking-glass self	parts	team
socialization	routines	backstage
primary group	stage	front-stage
generalized other	setting	region
definition of the situation	props	total institutions
behaviorism	audience	segregated audiences
meaning	dramaturgical	stigma
symbols	front	passing
conversation of gestures	appearance	frame
language	manner	on-the-ground observation
interpretive processes	interaction rituals	
cues	ritual	

Introduction to Sociological Theory: Theorists, Concepts, and Their Applicability to the Twenty-First Century,
Third Edition. Michele Dillon.
© 2020 John Wiley & Sons Ltd. Published 2020 by John Wiley & Sons Ltd.
Companion website: www.wiley.com/go/dillon

CHAPTER MENU

Although studying the **self** is generally seen as the domain of psychologists and psychotherapists, there is an important strand in sociological theory that focuses on the self, and, in particular, on the interpretive work of the self in social interaction. This theoretical perspective is **symbolic interactionism** (SI). SI is indebted to the insights of **George Herbert Mead**, who was associated with a school of American philosophy called pragmatism, an approach emphasizing the practical conditions under which action occurs and its practical consequences (noted in chapter 4). Mead's core thesis was that we are not born with an already-made self. Rather, the self emerges out of, and in turn influences, the practical conduct of social interaction.

DEVELOPMENT OF THE SELF THROUGH SOCIAL INTERACTION: G. H. MEAD AND C. H. COOLEY

Mead (1934: 137) argued that the self is active; it is always reflexively processing what's going on. We are engaged, if you will, in an ongoing internal conversation with ourselves, and in this process we monitor and evaluate the self. Even when we are alone we are thinking back on some experience – how

BIOGRAPHICAL NOTE

George Herbert Mead was born in South Hadley, Massachusetts, in 1863 into a strongly Protestant family. Mead, who was "shy, studious, and deferential to his parents" (Shalin 2000: 303), attended Oberlin College, then a Congregationalist institution, where he studied classics and moral philosophy. Although he thought about becoming a pastor, he eventually opted to pursue academic study at Harvard, where his professors included the philosopher Josiah Royce and the psychologist William James. Mead secured an academic position at the University of Michigan, where he became a close friend of his colleague, the philosopher John Dewey; both subsequently moved to the University of Chicago. Mead, who married Helen Castle, an heiress to the Dole Pineapple fortune, had a strong sense of social justice and was keenly interested in politics. He suffered, however, from "writer's block," a condition exaggerated by his anxiety about the originality and importance of his highly original approach to social interaction. Fortunately, his students (including Herbert Blumer) transcribed his lectures, thus making Mead's thinking publicly accessible. Mead died in 1931 (Shalin 2000).

we looked, how we came across to others at last night's social gathering – or thinking about something that someone said to us, or anticipating what we might say to someone when we next meet them. We simultaneously process what others are saying or communicating to us, what we should think about the said thing and what it means, and how we should respond to and act on what they have communicated. This, in essence, is what it means to have a self.

We are simultaneously both subjects, and objects to, ourselves. Mead's insight becomes clear if we consider what happens when we look in the mirror. When I check my look in the mirror (to quote a Bruce Springsteen song), I am a subject (Michele) looking in the mirror, and the object I see in the mirror is Me (Michele). When I (as subject) see Me (as object), I ask: "How do I look?" I might give different answers (depending on the day), but Mead argues that all of these responses originate with my cognitive interpretation of the responses of others to me; for example, how my mother, sister, or friend would say that I look, for example. This is how we develop a sense of Me (my self as an object). It is socially created as part of ongoing interpersonal contact or interaction. The Me that I see is a Me that I have learned to see and evaluate from what others have told me about looking good in general and about how I look, in particular.

This for Mead is the dynamic interaction of the "**I**" and the "**Me**," an ongoing interaction that is critical to the emergence and development of the self. "The essence of the self is … cognitive," that is, the individual takes on or internalizes the attitudes of others shown toward them, and responds or reacts to those attitudes (Mead 1934: 173, 174–175). The self can exist only because you as an "I" have internalized the "Me," that is, the attitude/response toward you expressed by others. The "I," the (subjective) acting self, is able to act only because it (as the "I") has internalized the attitudes toward "Me" (as an object) received from others' behavior toward me. I know who I am and I know how to respond and behave in a given situation because I have learned from others' attitudes toward me (the self that I am aware of) and from how they behave (as selves) in a similar situation or in a common social activity or undertaking (1934: 155). Thus Mead states, "The 'I' reacts to the self which arises through the taking of the attitudes of others. Through taking those attitudes we have introduced the 'Me' and we react to it as an 'I'" (1934: 174); I see "Me" (as an object) through how others see me as indicated by their attitudes toward me. The "I" "is the response of the organism to the attitudes of others" (1934: 175).

The individual, therefore, develops a self and a sense of self out of social interaction and social experience. The self can't be developed any other way. It is social interaction that enables the self to become an object to itself (Mead 1934: 138, 142). Accordingly, "Selves can only exist in definite relationships to other selves" (1934: 164), interacting selves whose behavior is shaped by the family, community, and society in which the individual lives (1934: 155).

THE LOOKING-GLASS SELF

The ongoing subject–object (I–Me), self–other conversation in which the individual is engaged is illuminated by Charles Horton Cooley. He uses the metaphor of the **looking-glass self** to vividly illustrate the self's dynamic interpretive processes. When we look at ourselves in the mirror, Cooley reminds us:

> As we see our face, figure, and dress in the glass, and are interested in them because they are ours, and pleased or otherwise with them according as they do or do not answer to what we should like them to be; so in imagination we perceive in another's mind some thought of our appearance, manners, aims, deeds, character, friends, and so on, and are variously affected by it. A self-idea [self-image] of this sort seems to have three principal elements: the imagination of our appearance to the other person; the imagination of [that person's] judgment of that appearance; and some sort of self-feeling, such as pride or mortification … The thing that moves us to pride or shame is not the mere mechanical reflection of ourselves, *but an imputed sentiment, the imagined effect of this reflection upon another's mind.* This is evident from the fact that the character and weight of that other, in whose mind we see ourselves, makes all the difference with our [self]-feeling. We are ashamed to seem evasive in the presence of a straight-forward [person], cowardly in the presence of a brave one, gross in the eyes of a refined one, and so on. We always imagine, and in imagining share, the judgment of the other mind. (Cooley 1902/1998: 164–165; emphasis mine)

Thus the self is formed and maintained through ongoing interaction (and imagined interaction) with others. See Topic 8.1.

SOCIALIZATION

Because the self can only emerge out of social interaction, this means that we are not born with an already-made self. This is what **socialization** accomplishes: it teaches us how to be social, how to use and interpret symbols and language, and how to interact with others. Socialization is both the means of teaching us to internalize and adopt the perspective of others, and at the same time it is the means of our individualization, our development of particular individual selves (Schubert 1998: 22). Mead tells us: "The self is something which has a development; it is not initially there, at birth, but arises in the process of social experience and activity, that is, develops in the given individual as a result of [their] relations to that process as a whole and to other individuals in that process" (1934: 135).

The family is the primary, most important agent of socialization. Sociologists think of the family as a **primary group** – primary in the sense that it is typically the first source of children's socialization, and because its influence tends to endure over a long period (Cooley 1909: 23–31; Thomas 1923: 43). Socialization teaches us how we should perceive and interpret all of the things in our social environment. It orients us to the expected behavior in our particular families, as well as to that expected by the **generalized other** – the community and society in which we live (Cooley 1902/1998: 157, 163; Mead 1934: 154).

Topic 8.1   Talking mirrors and style assistant robotic cameras

Cooley emphasizes that your distinct self, your self-feelings of pride, joy, embarrassment, shame, etc., are always felt and interpreted in relation to others. This is an insight well understood by the fashion industry and finds a new reality in today's Internet-wired age. At upscale fashion stores such as Bloomingdale's in Manhattan, New York, and John Lewis on Oxford Street in London, there are digitalized interactive mirrors positioned amidst the many high-end dresses and suits that customers try on. The full-length mirror (e.g., StyleME), wired to the Internet, allows customers to send live video images of how they look in a particular dress or when they mix and match various items of clothing to online viewers – their off-site Facebook friends and family members – who can instant-message their immediate feedback to the mirror's screen, telling the person how they look and whether the clothes suit them. Online viewers can also import from the store and from the store's online catalog various clothing items and accessories that might work well with what the customer is trying on; these suggestions get translated into video holograms that appear on the customer alongside or over whatever else the persona is actually wearing. And now at home as you agonize over which blouse goes best with your jeans before heading to class or to a party, you can use Amazon's new Echo Look Hands Free Camera and Style Assistant. You can ask its robot Alexa to take a photo each time you swap one blouse or pants for another, and (based on some current Amazon algorithm) it will render a judgment on which outfit looks best on you. Consequently, as it promises, you can "Love your look. Every day."

As William I. Thomas explained, socialization teaches us the generalized definitions of social conduct that society imposes on the individual:

> Preliminary to any self-determined act of behavior there is always a stage of examination and deliberation which we may call *the **definition of the situation*** … the child is always born into a group of people among whom all the general types of situation which may arise have already been defined and corresponding rules of conduct developed, and where [the child] has not the slightest chance of making [their own] definitions and following [the child's own] wishes without interference. (Thomas 1923: 42)

Thus, echoing Durkheim's emphasis on the social regulation of individual appetites (see chapter 2), "There is therefore always a rivalry between the spontaneous definitions of the situation made by the member of an organized society and the definitions which [their] society has provided for [them]" (Thomas 1923: 42).

Mead, Cooley, and Thomas took it for granted (like Parsons; see chapter 4) that the generalized other represents the collectively shared consensual meanings in society, for example, the valuing in the US of individual achievement and economic success. Today, however, we are much more aware that the generalized other, especially in culturally diverse modern societies, comprises a lot of variation in terms of individuals' and groups' everyday experiences. These differences, in turn, shape the attitudes and expectations of these individuals and groups (and their children), making it difficult for poor inner-city children, for example, to internalize the view that they can do well in school (e.g., MacLeod 2008; Willis 1977). We should also keep in mind that the generalized other encountered by many individuals, especially if they are outside of the dominant gender, class, racial, and sexual-orientation categories in society, will be composed of several, often conflicting, socialization influences (e.g., Collins 2004). In general, different family structures and differences in the individual's social environment relating to gender, race, sexuality, social class, etc., provide different influences on, and contexts for, the development of the self.

BEYOND THE SELF: THE CONVERSATION OF GESTURES

In the early decades of the twentieth century when Mead was writing, **behaviorism** was prominent in intellectual thought, associated with psychologists such as the American John Watson (1930) and the Russian Ivan Pavlov (1927). Behaviorism assumed that, like animals, humans can be conditioned to respond in predictable ways to external stimuli in their environment and that this conditioned behavior can be explained without reference to the fact that individuals have selves. Just as the infamous dogs in Pavlov's experiments predictably salivated when stimulated by the sound of a bell (the cue for dinner), so the presumption was that human behavior is also governed or conditioned by external forces in the environment. Contrary to the behaviorists, Mead argued that because humans have a cognitively reflexive self, that is, they are able to see and think about themselves as objects (as discussed previously). Consequently, human interaction is qualitatively different to animal behavior.

Today, our view of animal (and human) behavior is more complex. Biologists and primatologists document the intelligence and sociability of animals and show that some (e.g., monkeys, elephants, whales), like humans, have sophisticated social networks and structures (e.g., hierarchical or more communal), and engage in social and strategic behavior (e.g., finding a mate, avoiding predators). Scientists are uncertain, however, whether animals are self-consciously aware of why they behave in particular ways. Although there are fascinating similarities between animal and human behavior, there are nonetheless degrees of difference between animals and humans. One of these differences pertains to the relevance of **meaning**.

Mead argued that humans give significance (i.e., give meaning), to what they are communicating or intending to communicate, and these meanings derive from our consciousness of and ability to manipulate, interpret, and use shared **symbols**, language, gestures, etc. Mead explains:

> Self-consciousness … lies in the internalized **conversation of gestures** which constitutes thinking … the origin and foundations of the self, like those of thinking, are social … In the conversation of gestures what we say [or signal] calls out a certain response in another and that in turn changes our own action, so that we shift from what we started to do because of the reply [or signal] the other makes. The conversation of gestures is the beginning of communication. The individual comes to carry on a conversation of gestures with himself. He says something, and that calls out a certain reply in himself which makes him change what he was going to say. (Mead 1934: 173, 140–141)

In other words, we learn to think about and anticipate the consequences of our everyday interactions, of our words and gestures, on creating a response in the other. When I am in a restaurant with a friend, as soon as I pick up the menu to start examining it, my friend interprets this gesture as a signal to stop talking and to also browse the menu; this is the generally accepted "definition of the situation" into which we have both been socialized – we know how to interpret the communication of the other (though we may at times try to impose an alternative definition, and ignore our friend's gesture). Gestures become "significant symbols" when their meaning is shared by the interacting individuals. Indeed, as Mead explains, **language** is a system of significant symbols that signify certain meanings:

Gestures become significant symbols when they implicitly arouse in an individual making them the same responses which they explicitly arouse, or are supposed to arouse, in other individuals, the individuals to whom they are addressed; and in all conversations of gestures ... the individual's consciousness of the content and flow of meaning involved depends on his thus taking the attitude of the other toward his own gestures. (Mead 1934: 46, 47)

Communication can occur only because "through gestures responses are called out on our own attitudes, and as soon as they are called out, they evoke, in turn, other attitudes" (Mead 1934: 181).

In short, communication is impossible without symbols and language whose meanings are shared among those in a given social setting. The universality of symbols means that they produce shared responses and understandings; "A symbol is nothing but the stimulus whose [interpreted] response is given in advance" (Mead 1934: 181). Symbols require and produce shared meanings; they have "the same meanings for all individual members of the given society or social group" (1934: 47), whether among roommates greeting each other, for a whole country (national flag), or globally (McDonald's golden arches). We should also recognize, however, that, as feminist (e.g., Collins 1990; Smith 1987; see chapter 10) and race and cultural theorists (e.g., Gilroy 1987; Hall 1990; see chapter 12) would emphasize, symbols and meanings are often contested, especially by minority racial and cultural groups and others in society whose everyday experiences make them feel excluded by the dominant symbol and meaning systems.

THE PREMISES OF SYMBOLIC INTERACTIONISM: HERBERT BLUMER

Symbolic interactionists build on Mead's and Cooley's insights on the centrality of symbolic exchange to human-social life and the development of the self. They focus on the exchange of symbols that inheres in the ongoing, self–other **interpretive processes** of social interaction. "Symbolic interactionism" is thus an apt description for this perspective. **Herbert Blumer** coined the term, initially using it "in an offhand way" (in 1937), but it caught on and quickly came into general use in sociology to describe "a relatively distinctive approach to the study of human group life and human conduct" (Blumer 1969: 1).

BIOGRAPHICAL NOTE

Herbert Blumer, born in 1900, was a member of the sociology faculty at the University of Chicago during the heyday of the Chicago School of Sociology, when Robert Park and other colleagues produced several community studies of urban life. Blumer studied under and was heavily influenced by Mead, whose ideas he elaborated. Blumer left Chicago in 1952 to help found the sociology department at the University of California, Berkeley, where he maintained a large presence as a much-loved and sought-after figure until his death in 1987. Among many honors, Blumer served as president of the American Sociological Association in 1956.

SI emphasizes that society is human group life, that is, human beings engaging in social (symbolic) interaction (Blumer 1969: 7). Symbolic interactionists view society as an ongoing process of symbolic interaction wherein we continuously interpret and respond to **cues**, that is, signals or messages, in our social environment. Thus, SI sees institutions not in terms of organizational structure (of hierarchically organized, impersonal offices and duties) and norms of bureaucratic rationality, but, according to Blumer, as "arrangements of people who are interlinked in their respective actions," and who act and interact as they handle "situations at their respective positions in the organization" (1969: 58). Therefore, unlike Marx, Durkheim, Weber, and other theorists whose writings are concerned with macro-level, large-scale social structures and processes (capitalism, the division of labor, the state, bureaucracy, inequality, the occupational structure, the culture industry), SI focuses primarily on the micro-level processes and outcomes of everyday, face-to-face interaction. Micro-level interactions occur, nonetheless, in socially structured interaction contexts (Goffman 1959, 1971), and moreover, they have broad, macro-level consequences (e.g., maintaining social inequality).

According to Blumer, SI rests on three basic premises:

> [a] Human beings act toward things on the basis of the meanings that the things have for them [including other human beings and physical objects in the person's environment, social institutions] ... [b] The meaning of such things is derived from, or arises out of, the social interaction that one has with one's fellows ... [c] These meanings are handled in, and modified through, an interpretive process used by the person in dealing with the things he encounters. (Blumer 1969: 2)

Because meaning arises out of (interpretive) social interaction, it is not something that is pregiven independent of language. It does not inhere in things themselves but in the linguistic and social meanings in a given societal context (meanings that, though social in origin, are nonetheless well established and highly constraining).

By the same token, we cannot take the meaning of things (of other individuals, social institutions, physical things) for granted; meaning is neither marginal to social interaction nor set in stone, inscribed once and for all time (Blumer 1969: 3). Rather, because meaning derives from social interaction, from social actors' ongoing definition and redefinition of situations, the meanings we give to symbols and other things can vary across time and from one social context to another (e.g., the meaning of hard work; see Weber, chapter 3).

THE SOCIAL CONTEXT OF HUMAN INTERACTION

Precisely because people act on the basis of the meanings that objects (cars, clothes, wrinkles, other things, people, social institutions) have in their social environment (i.e., their "world of objects"), "the life and action of people necessarily change in line with the changes taking place in their world of objects" (Blumer 1969: 12). We interact with ourselves and others differently in different social environments because of the different meanings and expectations characterizing those contexts. After you graduate from college and secure a job at an insurance company where you receive a commission for every new customer you enroll, you will interpret your world of objects differently. At college, when you look in the mirror (Cooley's looking-glass), you are imagining how your friends would respond to how you look, your clothes and your hair (to continue with Springsteen's song): "Am I cool?" you wonder and evaluate your appearance accordingly. But in your new job, you will look in the mirror and respond to what you imagine will sway your potential customer: "Do I look like I have a solid grasp of car insurance costs and coverage?" You judge yourself accordingly and make adjustments. Importantly, too, these evaluations (of you and by you) will also be influenced by your gender, race, and age, among other considerations. Particular others – airline passengers (Hochschild 1983) and corporate male professionals (Pierce 1995), for example – and the generalized other (society) impose different expectations on women than men (see chapter 10) and on blacks, Arabs, Asians, and Latinx than whites (see chapter 12).

ERVING GOFFMAN: SOCIETY AS RITUALIZED SOCIAL INTERACTION

Although many social theorists discuss social roles (e.g., Parsons; see chapter 4), it is the elements of symbolic exchange in the face-to-face performance of **social roles** that is of most interest to SI. **Erving Goffman** uses the metaphor of a theatrical performance to elaborate the many elements that go into face-to-face interaction in everyday life. For Goffman (1959), social life, the **presentation of self** in everyday life, is the **performance** by social **actors** of different roles, **parts**, and **routines** on various **stages** with different **settings** and **props**. And, as in the theater, the success of any role performance is contingent, in part, on the particular **audience** that is present and that responds to the cues and miscues (mistaken signals) actors convey. Goffman, therefore, offers a **dramaturgical** approach to social life.

Goffman's concepts provide a rich vocabulary for describing face-to-face interaction across the broad range of everyday social settings. He highlights the socially structured expectations imposed on the performance of social roles. In doing so, he provides a "social anthropology" (Collins 1986: 109) of the rituals of everyday social interaction (ordering coffee at a cafe; waiting for and riding the elevator, the bus, etc.). Not surprisingly, many researchers draw on Goffman's concepts in making sense of social life and its many multilayered elements.

BIOGRAPHICAL NOTE

Erving Goffman was born in Alberta, Canada, in 1922, to immigrant Ukrainian Jewish parents. After receiving his undergraduate sociology degree at the University of Toronto, he pursued graduate studies at the University of Chicago. His dissertation research, based on observing everyday life on one of the small Shetland Islands (off the coast of Scotland), formed the basis of his theory of face-to-face interaction. He spent many years at the University of California, Berkeley, invited there by Herbert Blumer, and later moved to the University of Pennsylvania. Goffman was not only a prolific and accessible writer (writing 11 major books), but an enthusiastic gambler and a successful stock-market strategist. On a darker note, his wife, Angelica Choate, experienced severe mental health problems and committed suicide in 1964, leaving Goffman alone with their young son. Almost 20 years later, Goffman remarried but within a few months of having a daughter, Alice, he died of stomach cancer, in 1982, the same year he was president of the American Sociological Association (Fine and Manning 2000). His daughter, Alice Goffman, is also a sociologist and an ethnographer studying urban life.

SOCIAL ROLES

We all perform multiple social roles as we enact the expected behavior associated with "the rights and duties attached to a given status" (Goffman 1959: 16) – the roles of student, daughter or son, friend, roommate, girlfriend or boyfriend, sister or brother, waitress, teammate, football fan, political activist, church member, etc. The content of these and myriad other social roles is preestablished or scripted for us by society, and we learn how to perform the scripts through socialization.

Although social roles and their various parts or routines are scripted, this does not mean that our role-playing is fake or artificial. Although we certainly might enjoy or readily identify with some roles more than others, all social behavior is necessarily role-playing behavior. For SI, social life, society, would be impossible without social roles. Predefined social roles provide the structure for the social interaction required in everyday life (in classrooms, dorms, offices, stores, courts, subways, parliament, etc.). Roles provide the "pattern of appropriate conduct … that must be enacted, portrayed … and realized" (Goffman 1959: 75).

Here, Goffman, like Mead discussing the generalized other (see the section on Socialization), does not question what might be entailed in "appropriate conduct." He takes it for granted that what is appropriate is the role patterns and expectations already in place and established toward "maintaining the normative social order" (Collins 1986: 107). Thus, "When an individual presents himself before others, his performance will tend to incorporate and exemplify the officially accredited values of the society" (Goffman 1959: 35). Goffman (1959: 188–189) acknowledges that performers can disrupt social roles by not playing the part their audience expects, or indeed exaggerating it (as if in parody). However, he does not probe how, or the settings in which, "accredited values," role scripts, and traditional role boundaries get contested, as occurs when, for example, individuals cross over traditional gender-occupational role boundaries such as male nurses (Williams 1993) or women coal miners (Tallichet 2006).

In any case, if you were to list all of your social roles, three things would be apparent. One, it would be hard to imagine having a self, an identity, that is independent of the several roles you play. Two, you are always acting in reciprocal relation to someone else, to others who are playing their roles (e.g., you are a daughter to your mother and father). And, even when we are not in others' company, our self-interaction means that we rehearse or imagine our performance of a particular role for some imaginary other (remember the looking-glass self). Social roles thus exemplify the Mead–Cooley–Blumer emphasis that the self is always a relational self; we cannot have a self without other selves. Three, although we tend to be aware of playing certain roles (e.g., the good student, or the slacker), Goffman would remind us that we are always playing some role; we are never not performing a role. In addition to the roles already listed, we frequently perform many other roles: disgruntled customer, cafeteria diner, house guest, airline passenger, dental patient, marathon runner, etc. Moreover, we are always an audience in interaction with and responding to someone else's role performance. In sum, social life is the ongoing and continuous enactment of role performances, and these performances give rise to and structure our social relationships. Thus, "when an individual or performer plays the same part to the same audience on different occasions, a social relationship is likely to arise" (Goffman 1959: 16).

Topic 8.2   Directions for performing the role of the (considerate) airline passenger

As passengers on an airplane we are simultaneously performing the role of airline passenger and of audience to the role performances of other passengers and of flight attendants, and all of this ongoing symbolic exchange happens in a highly specific and highly structured setting (the airline cabin). American Airlines, whose tagline is "The world's greatest flyers fly American," recently outlined what (from its perspective) it means to be "a great flyer." The campaign ran in 2016, a year before several airlines had to deal with public relations fiascos resulting from their inhospitable treatment of passengers (e.g., prohibiting two teenage girls from boarding until they changed out of their yoga-like fashion pants; physically dragging a male passenger from the plane because it had overbooked the seats and did not have space for an airline employee). According to the American Airlines glossy, double-page insert in the *New York Times* (August 30, 2016), being a "great flyer" "is a skill and an attitude, a philosophy and a behavior. It's the ability to sleep anywhere, their head against a pillow or a much-loved, wadded-up jacket….

[Great flyers] love babies, but always bring noise-canceling headphones….Always upbeat, great flyers make the best of their situation no matter where they're sitting…there's not a friendly greeting from a flight attendant they haven't returned. They love the view, but they always ask before opening or closing the window shade. Just like they always relinquish the armrest to the person in the middle seat…"

PERFORMANCE PRESSURE

Goffman emphasizes that the presentation of self in everyday life – the individual's execution of multiple social roles – is an ongoing task of symbolic exchange, inference, and interaction; we control (or try to control) the cues we emit to others so that we can manage our audiences' impressions of us. Just as an actor in a play does not want to be booed off the stage for a lousy performance, we too want to convey a good impression and hence put on a successful performance. We don't want our supervisors to think we are lazy; our parents to think we are ungrateful; our friends to think we are disloyal, etc.

As Goffman argues (1959: 3–4), in face-to-face interaction it is in everyone's interest to control the conduct of others through their own performance and the response it elicits:

> When an individual plays a part he implicitly requests his observers to take seriously the impression that is fostered before them. They are asked to believe that the character they see actually possesses the attributes he appears to possess, that the task he performs will have the consequences that are implicitly claimed for it, and that in general, matters are what they appear to be. (Goffman 1959: 17)

Goffman's emphasis on social life as role performance is criticized for its relative lack of attention to the relevance of individuals' feelings and emotions. Arlie Hochschild, a sociologist whose research and theorizing draw on Goffman, argues, "Goffman gave us actors without psyches … the characters in Goffman's books actively manage outer impressions but they do not actively manage inner feelings, a habit itself distributed variously across time, age, class, and locale" (Hochschild 2003: 7, 91). The marginalization of emotion by Goffman and in sociological theory in general is redressed by Hochschild, and we discuss her sociology of emotions in chapter 10.

ESTABLISHING THE DEFINITION OF THE SITUATION

Goffman (1959) argues that the most effective way to ensure a convincing role performance is to influence the definition of the situation that others come to have of a given interaction. How things (a setting or a situation) get defined matters enormously to what can subsequently occur in the situation and what is subsequently evaluated as appropriate or convincing behavior. How we initially define the situation will determine how we behave (perform) in that situation: does it require formal dress? joviality? deference toward others? And if we misidentify the situation, however slightly, we will suffer at least embarrassment, and perhaps ostracism. Therefore, the initial defining information we convey to our audience is crucial because, as many advertisements warn, first impressions last. The consequences of our failure to define the situation in ways that foster a good impression of the performance we want to pull off can seriously affect our life chances; if we fail to make a good impression at a coveted job interview, our long-term chances of carving out a particular career may be jeopardized.

According to Goffman, we create a particular definition of a situation by the **front** we maintain: "that part of the individual's performance which regularly functions in a general and fixed fashion to define the situation for those who observe the performance" (Goffman 1959: 22). Thus, the sales associate helping a customer has a different front than that same individual when she is at home with her children, or at church, or at the doctor's office. See also Topic 8.2.

The "fronts" actors present and maintain in interacting with others are made possible because all social interaction occurs in particular settings supported by various props, and the setting and its props signal the kind of role performance expected. A particular setting and its customary props implicitly authenticate the validity of our face-to-face interactions and define the expectations of the performances that are to be enacted. When the setting has somehow been tampered with or when the customary props are not present, we are confused about how we should interpret the situation and define what's really going on. It is easy to perform in a deferential manner toward the airport security screener because we are alerted to do so by the message communicated by the security agent's federal badge, the presence of beeping screens being reviewed by other security agents in our presence, and the visible holding-area for those passengers who are deemed worthy of further personal screening.

Similarly, the doctor's office is a setting that readily establishes that they have the expertise to assist us: its furniture and sterile decor, the range of medical equipment and paraphernalia, and the certificates of qualification and specialization hanging on the wall. In all settings and among all social actors, **appearance** and **manner** are critical to the symbolic work of imposing and sustaining the definition of the situation (Goffman 1959: 24–26). Goffman refers to an individual's appearance as those signals that indicate their social statuses and their "temporary ritual state," as indicated by whether they are dressed for work, formal social activity, or informal recreation (1959: 24). Thus when the doctor makes an appearance you know it is the doctor because of the white coat, the stethoscope around the neck, and the name or status badge on the coat lapel (1959: 22–24); all of these things (props) convey the message that this really is a medical doctor you can trust. As research confirms, patients overwhelmingly prefer and are more likely to confide in doctors who are dressed in white coats than in surgical scrubs, or in business or casual attire. See Topic 8.3.

In some social settings, the presence of certain props can hinder social interaction. High-earning women in New York fear that if they invite their dates – who usually earn less – back to their apartments, the dates will be put off, intimidated by the evidence of the high-class apartment and lifestyle the woman can afford. Because more women than men are currently graduating from college, women increasingly are poised, on average, to earn more money than men (notwithstanding gender wage inequities). Yet cultural and heteronormative expectations of behavior are such that men (and many women too) still expect that male dates and potential future husbands should be the higher-earning partners.

Topic 8.3   Body appearance and body surgery

The soaring increase in dieting programs and in elective plastic surgery and cosmetic dermatology attests to Goffman's insight that appearance and body display are crucial elements in the presentation of self and in creating and maintaining a good impression among one's audiences. Noninvasive medical cosmetic procedures increased by more than 700 percent in the last 15 years. South Korea is "the world's plastic-surgery capital" (Marx 2015), and the US, Brazil, and China are close behind. In the US in 2016, for example, 17.1 million cosmetic surgical procedures were conducted. According to the International Society of Aesthetic Plastic Surgery, eyelid surgery is the most common procedure globally (accounting for 15 percent of all procedures), followed by liposuction and breast augmentation (see www.isaps.org). Body makeovers are no longer the province of the rich and famous; a survey by the American Society of Plastic Surgeons found that a third of people considering plastic surgery reported average household incomes below $30,000. Older women who want to reenter the workforce or change jobs increasingly contemplate the possibility of Botox and cosmetic surgery because a strong résumé alone may not be sufficient for them to secure a job (see Singer 2008). Similarly, politicians, both male and female, are increasingly availing themselves of the services of cosmetologists to remove spots, broken capillaries, wrinkles, and other blemishes. And there has been a rapid increase in the number of trans individuals who are undergoing gender surgery in childhood and early adolescence (Talbot 2013). In sum, appearance matters in role performance and the presentation of self.

INTERACTION RITUALS

For Goffman, everyday life is composed of **interaction rituals**, and the ritual is "accomplished through doings – through making appearances … performing gestures" (Goffman 1979: 10). Goffman does not use the term **ritual** in quite the same way as Durkheim (i.e., regular collective gatherings [rites] that affirm shared beliefs and social ties and, by extension, social order). What interests Goffman is ritualized self-presentation behavior and how such everyday interaction behavior maintains social order. For Goffman, ritual refers to all those simplified, exaggerated, stereotyped behaviors that signal or display particular emotions or social statuses in various interaction situations. Such ritualized display behavior signals to those present something about the individual's "social identity … mood, intent, and expectations, and about the state of his relation to them" (1979: 1). His interest in ritual is largely in its micro-level expression: the signaling role of ritualized expression in face-to-face interaction and its function in establishing the definition of the situation. These micro-situational definitions, however, maintain the larger social order.

Figure 8.1   Prince William and the Duchess of York juggle ritualized work and family roles. Source: © Michael Dunlea/N&S Syndication/EXNEW/AP Images.

Interaction rituals are the institutionalized, though frequently unspoken, ways of behaving in society – whether with friends, or with strangers in the elevator. They are "found in all peopled places, whether public, semi-public or private, and whether under the auspices of an organized social occasion or the flatter constraints of merely a routinized setting" (Goffman 1967: 2). For example, we have many ritualized ways of greeting and bidding farewell in social interaction, and depending on the nature of the relationship and the cultural context, we perform interaction rituals: handshakes, hugs, kisses, head bows, or high-fives, each of which signals varying degrees of friendship or intimacy. When we mistake the greeting rules governing a given relationship, this causes fumbling and embarrassment (Goffman 1971: 74–77).

The interaction rituals of public behavior range from fleeting gestures and facial movements that may initiate a social encounter with a stranger to the enactment of formalized ceremonial rules for terminating a social gathering. Symbolic exchange is so central to everyday behavior that, though we may not always be consciously aware of its demands, it necessarily impinges even on seemingly trivial and minor encounters. As Goffman elaborates, everyday "**encounters** are organized by means of a special set of acts and gestures comprising communication about communicating" (1963b: 99). Thus:

> An encounter is initiated by someone making an opening move, typically by means of a special expression of the eyes but sometimes by a statement or a special tone of voice at the beginning of a statement. The engagement proper begins when this overture is acknowledged by the other, who signals back with his eyes, voice, or stance that he has placed himself at the disposal of the other for purposes of mutual eye-to-eye activity – even if only to ask the initiator to postpone his request for an audience. (Goffman 1963b: 91–92)

All of us have initiated such overtures and have tactfully (or nontactfully) disengaged from similar overtures made by others toward us.

Rituals of subordination

Although interaction rituals occur and are observed in face-to-face interaction, they reflect the norms of the larger social order and, in turn, function to impose that order on and across micro-level interactions. Goffman wrote extensively about **rituals of subordination**: all those behavioral displays by which we indicate and recognize the difference in rank or hierarchy between individuals of different social statuses, and especially the differential status attendant on gender, race, and socioeconomic location. Goffman observes: "A classic stereotype of deference is that of lowering oneself physically in some form or other of prostration. Correspondingly, holding the body erect and the head high is stereotypically a mark of unashamedness, superiority, and disdain" (Goffman 1979: 40). In analyzing advertisements, Goffman noted, for example, that the interaction rituals between women and men typically signal women's subordinate status to men, as indicated by their deferential physical posture toward the man (1979: 42–45) and/or by their emotional display: "in cross-sexed encounters in American society, women smile more, and more expansively, than men" (1979: 48) (see also chapter 10).

NONVERBAL RITUALIZED INTERACTION

Whether in the classroom, the cafeteria, or on the street, and regardless of whether we want to communicate or not, we never stop communicating. We may cease talking but our **body idiom** (body language and display) continues to communicate with those around us. It cannot say nothing (Goffman 1963b: 35). Indeed, so long as there is even one person co-present, there is an

> obligation to convey certain information and not to convey other impressions, just as others present must too ... When individuals come into one another's immediate presence in circumstances where no spoken communication is called for, they none the less inevitably engage one another in communication of a sort [through] ... bodily appearance ... dress, bearing, movement and position, sound level, physical gestures such as waving or saluting, facial decorations, and broad emotional expression. In every society, these communication possibilities are institutionalized ... Half aware that a certain aspect of his activity is available for all present to perceive, the individual tends to modify this activity, employing it with its public character in mind ... a body symbolism, an idiom of individual appearance and gestures that tends to call forth in the actor what it calls forth in the others ... immediately present. (Gofffman 1963b: 35, 33–34)

We can stare at someone (because we are annoyed that they are speaking so loudly on their cell phone) or we can look away (because we are embarrassed to overhear the intimate details of their relationship). In either case, we are communicating a message, and it will always be a message that requires them to respond to our response, to our performance in presenting our selves (as they too must present their selves). The meanings of "the stare" are institutionalized such that it is a mechanism of social control; we stare in disapproval, and when someone stares at us we tend to alter or cover up our behavior, and even literally cover our selves. As Goffman notes, "Given the pain of being stared at, it is understandable that staring itself is widely used as a means of negative sanction, socially controlling all kinds of improper public conduct. Indeed it often constitutes the first warning an individual receives that he is 'out of line' and the last warning that it is necessary to give him" (1963b: 88).

IMPRESSION MANAGEMENT

Across all social encounters, we engage in **impression management**, symbolic work we strategically do to orchestrate a good performance in our various roles.[1] Performance strategies and situational definitions are better institutionalized in some settings than others (e.g., occupational roles are more clearly defined than leisure roles though there are clear routines and expectations of self-presentation in how, for example, joggers or skiers behave in their respective leisure settings). And in some settings, it is a team performance that needs to be managed. For Goffman, a performance **team**

> refers to any set of individuals who co-operate in staging a single routine … While a team-performance is in progress, any member of the team has the power to give the show away or to disrupt it by inappropriate conduct. Each teammate is forced to rely on the good conduct and behavior of his fellows, and they, in turn, are forced to rely on him. There is then … a bond of reciprocal dependence linking teammates to one another. (Goffman 1959: 79, 82)

A team can be a couple; for example, a husband and wife may put on a front of amicability in front of their guests (or for the media if they are a political couple); the dentist and receptionist put on a front of office efficiency and professionalism for the waiting patient. Teams can also include groups of three or more, as, for example, in a restaurant with the waitresses colluding with the manager to convey the impression that it's the friendliest restaurant in town. Such teamwork, though easily disrupted, is generally effective, notwithstanding the fact that, as Marx (chapter 1) would underscore, the waitresses' labor, including their friendliness (e.g., Hochschild; see chapter 10), is being exploited by the restaurant owner for profit.

Politicians, more than other role-performing professionals in society, have to incessantly maintain a front, especially given the widespread use of instant social media and the speed with which politicians' (and celebrities') miscued performances are widely disseminated. Typically, even when politicians are allegedly **backstage**, relaxing and engaged in leisure activities, they are actually engaged in **front-stage** behavior. In the presence of press photographers, for example, male politicians frequently project the impression of cool masculinity – sailing, hunting, golfing, biking, clearing brush, playing basketball, or any other activity involving athleticism and/or strength.

Goffman distinguished between front and back region (or front- and backstage) to emphasize that role performance is contingent on the presence of an actor's primary audience. A **region** is "any place that is bounded to some degree by barriers to perception" (Goffman 1959: 106). Such barriers are most visibly marked by the walls dividing a restaurant's kitchen from its dining area, a family's living rooms from its bedrooms, the company executive's office from the pool of administrative assistants, the football team's dressing rooms from the pitch area, and so on. The "front region" refers to the place where

---

Topic 8.4   Disruptive team performances at the White House and Downing Street

Cohesive team performances in government are necessary to projecting the impression that the president or prime minister has things under control and can be trusted to run the country well. Typically, although personality clashes and policy disagreements are common among a president's staff and cabinet members, they put on a front of cooperation and amicability, despite backstage conflicts; this is the impression management that an effective team performance requires. It is only *after* there has been a change in government that its members give tell-all interviews or write memoirs with the backstage story (usually an *account* that paints a positive portrait of themselves; see chapter 9 on accounts). The Trump administration, by contrast, exemplifies disruptive team performance and does so, moreover, as front-stage behavior. It not only leaks its renowned in-fighting (something apparently encouraged by the president) to the media in real time, but performs its in-fighting in public, that is, the president and several of his staff frequently use both social media and high-brow magazine interviews (e.g., the *New Yorker* interview with Anthony Scaramucci) to publicly denigrate cabinet members and other senior staff advisors (and frequently in vulgar terms). Similarly in the UK, Boris Johnson, as foreign secretary, frequently expressed opinions in public that directly deviated from Prime Minister Theresa May's stated policy positions (e.g., on Brexit negotiations), thus stoking confusion among the government's overlapping audiences as to its specific intentions or plans.

---

the performance is given (e.g., waitresses perform for guests in the restaurant's dining area), and the "back region" is literally the staging area for the front-region behavior; it is where actors do the preparatory work to ensure a successful performance. See Topic 8.4.

As in the theater, actors can be more relaxed backstage; there is less performance pressure. Goffman notes, "One of the most interesting times to observe impression management is the moment when a performer leaves the back region and enters the place where the audience is to be found, or when he returns therefrom, for at these moments one can detect a wonderful putting on and taking off of character" (Goffman 1959: 121). However, as Goffman elaborates, the backstage also has its own audience and performance expectations. When waiters return to the kitchen they are still performing, but for a different audience: for the chefs and other kitchen workers and for the other waiters and waitresses as they come and go. Waiters and waitresses behave differently in the restaurant dining area than in the kitchen; front-stage and backstage, they are performing different roles to different audiences. And similarly doctors, teachers, sales assistants, etc., all perform roles for varied audiences.

TOTAL INSTITUTIONS

Although politicians choose their role and thus voluntarily accept (and reinforce) the blurring between back- and front-stage behavior that society imposes on politicians, not all individuals have such freedom. Inmates in mental health hospitals, prisons, and other institutions to which individuals are confined because of their inability to function in, or because of the threat they pose to, society do not have this option. These types of settings, what Goffman calls **total institutions**, remove the barriers that typically separate individuals' everyday functions (e.g., sleeping, therapy, or work). Instead, all activities are performed in the presence of similarly regulated co-participants (e.g., inmates) and their

Figure 8.2   World leaders dress down, appearing in informal attire, in the more relaxed backstage setting of Camp David, the US president's mountain retreat. This orchestrated self-presentation, however, is still audience(s)-driven and expected role-playing behavior: the performance of the relaxed politician (notwithstanding the serious economic and geopolitical issues that dominate the G8 leaders' meetings). Source: © Charles Dharapak/AP/Press Association.

supervisors (Goffman 1961: 5–6). This principle also applies in institutional settings in which particular work-like tasks are assumed to be best accomplished, such as army barracks, boarding schools, and monasteries (1961: 5).

Goffman argues that all these highly structured, highly regulated settings require highly specified role performances of inmates and of supervisory staff (e.g., wardens, headmasters, etc.), that, although they may seem punishing, serve "good functional reasons" (Goffman 1961: 124). Total institutions use various strategies (e.g., mortification, denial of privileges) to produce a stripped-down self, rid of any autonomous signs of individuality (hence the required wearing of uniforms, short hair, etc.) (1961: 12–29, 71). This self is defined primarily (if not solely) in terms of a role performance that conforms to the institution's regimented authority structure (1961: 41–42) and for which there is no backstage respite (not even temporary or transitional).

In recent decades there has been a trend toward the de-institutionalization of mental health services and a shift away from asylums toward community-based care. Nevertheless, many of the same self-stripping strategies identified by Goffman can be observed today in settings that care for the elderly and other special populations (e.g., those with a severe mental or physical disability). When doctors, nurses, and care assistants talk to an elderly person in the third person as if they are in fact an object rather than someone with a subjective intact self – e.g., "How is Joan today?" rather than "Hi Joan. How are you?" – they strip the person of their individuality and weaken the person's sense of self (and self-esteem).

MANAGING OUR AUDIENCES

Outside of total institutions, everyday life is structured such that individuals' various social roles are typically witnessed by **segregated audiences**; that is, individuals who are audience to one of our roles will not see us perform in other roles (Goffman 1959: 137). Typically, your parents are not present when you are socializing with friends or in class. The advantage of playing to segregated or compartmentalized audiences is that it decreases the likelihood that inconsistent or contradictory role information will enter and confuse the definition of the situation. Playing one role to one audience at a time generally means that we have less "covering up" to do (e.g., managing information flow to our parents).

Politicians, by contrast, encounter diverse overlapping audiences, a performance dilemma crystallized during election campaigns when politicians typically have to simultaneously self-present in public to such diverse audiences as skilled factory workers, corporate executives, and country-club retirees. Because of the complicated symbolic work associated with role performance to overlapping audiences, and given the gaps that may exist between politicians' front- and back-region behavior, it is not surprising that politicians pay a lot of money to media-savvy public relations consultants in order to influence (or manipulate) voters' knowledge and impression of them (see chapter 5).

MISREPRESENTATION

A certain amount of misrepresentation is structured, however, into all face-to-face interaction. Tact, when we mask honesty with politeness or obfuscation, is critical, according to Georg Simmel (1917/1950: 45), to regulating and maintaining the sociability of human relations. This is as true of friendship as of politics, corporate relations, and international diplomacy. The management of politeness – an art accentuated at Disneyworld – is especially required across all service industries, from restaurants and airlines to banks and customer sales departments.

Politeness and good manners (i.e., social etiquette) are expected in civilized society, and thus society has institutionalized several ways of orchestrating good impression management in everyday behavior. Notwithstanding the profit logic underlying these practices (see Marx, chapter 1), brides-to-be spend large sums of money on specialized bridal magazines and wedding planners who will help them to put on a successful wedding-day performance. And corporations send new recruits to workshops on table manners; because the self-presentation of employees conveys the impression of the company as a whole, if the investment advisor eats in a messy manner, it may also convey that the company itself is less than professional in its accounting practices.

STIGMA

Impression management is all the more challenging for those individuals in society who are stigmatized because they carry some "undesired differentness" from what we consider "normal" (Goffman 1963a: 5). One of Goffman's most famous books, *Stigma: Notes on the Management of Spoiled Identity*, analyzes the sociological bases of **stigma**. Goffman differentiates among three sources of stigma:

> [i] abominations of the body – the various physical deformities … [ii] blemishes of character perceived as weak will, domineering or unnatural passions, treacherous and rigid beliefs, and dishonesty, these being inferred from a known record of, for example, mental disorder, imprisonment, addiction, alcoholism, homosexuality, unemployment, suicidal attempts, and radical political behavior … [iii] the tribal stigma of race, nation, and religion, these being stigma that can be transmitted through lineages and equally contaminate all members of a family. (Goffman 1963a: 4)

Although Goffman compiled his list in the early 1960s, the kinds of people and attributes that society stigmatizes have not changed very much since that era despite advances in social tolerance and legal equality (e.g., protecting the rights of the disabled). Stigma – who or what is labeled "abnormal" – is socially defined. Hence it can vary across different societal contexts, and as societal expectations and understandings change, vary with time. Thus, for example, in 1974, as a result of pressure from gay rights organizations and also driven by a more complex understanding of gay sexuality, the American Psychiatric Association's influential *Diagnostic and Statistical Manual of Mental Disorders* removed homosexuality from its list of mental illnesses. Many LGBTQ individuals, however, despite significant advances in sexual equality (see chapter 11), still tend to experience stigma on account of their sexuality. Trans individuals too, despite a shift in medical terminology that currently labels them as having gender dysphoria (i.e., extreme distress with their biological sex) rather than a gender identity "disorder," also experience stigma (see Talbot 2013).

Goffman observes that in everyday discourse, body language, and behavior "we exercise varieties of discrimination, through which we effectively, if often unthinkingly, reduce [the stigmatized person's] life chances" (Goffman 1963a: 5). In essence, "we believe the person with a stigma is not quite human," and treat them accordingly (1963a: 5). Moreover, stigmatized or discredited individuals know that they fall short of "normal." Given that selves, as Mead (1934) argued, can only develop from interaction with other selves, stigmatized individuals come to internalize the negative attitude others have toward them. Stigma, therefore, is socially defined; it derives from and is reinforced in and through social interaction.

PASSING

The stigmatized necessarily engage in impression-management behavior toward gaining acceptance and respect among "the normals." Hence they work at presenting an uncontaminated or "unspoiled" identity when in the co-presence of others from whom they must hide their stigma. Goffman (1963a: 73) notes, for example, that although prostitutes have to present as prostitutes when dealing with their clients, they must hide this role-identity in the presence of others (e.g., the police, family members, etc.). Taking their cues from socially accepted identities and performances, stigmatized individuals learn to develop ways to correct for their stigma. The cancer patient/survivor works at continuing to excel at sports, as exemplified by cyclist Lance Armstrong, the seven-time Tour de France winner (subsequently stripped of his titles in 2012 due to steroid use charges), and the disabled veteran learns to perform a new athletic activity and excels in it at the Paralympics. If the stigmatized condition cannot be physically or otherwise corrected, the stigmatized individual can learn to cover it up and to pass as normal. **Passing** is always learned behavior. Like all social interaction, it is about controlling the information, the "definition of the situation," and the impression that others come to have in interacting with you. Lance Armstrong, no longer stigmatized as a cancer patient but as a steroid user, now works to control the documented information about his steroid use and his cover-up of it. Within a week after the detailed evidence against him was made public, he focused on the impression management task of passing as a steroid nonuser. Speaking at a public event celebrating the fifteenth anniversary of Livestrong, his cancer foundation, he defiantly attempted to redefine the situation by presenting himself as a victim of untrue accusations (though he chose not to officially contest the evidence). Three months later (January 2013), he sought to convey a new definition of the situation when he admitted on television to Oprah Winfrey that he had used performance enhancing drugs during his cycling career. We see with Armstrong, therefore, the ongoing role performance work required as an individual moves sequentially from passing in one role to another (from cancer survivor-star athlete to steroid nonuser to admitted steroid user).

Passing strategies, however, can accomplish only so much. In Armstrong's case, many remain skeptical of his apparent contrition. Beyond specific individual cases, the persistence of racism, for example, means that some individuals have a far higher bar to cross than others in making – and getting rewarded for making – a good impression. Skin tone matters. Research indicates that light-skinned immigrants in the US make more money on average than those with darker complexions, even after controlling for English-language proficiency, education, occupation and country of origin. Skin tone also matters in Asia. As discussed in Topic 3.4 (see chapter 3), middle-class women in China go to great lengths to avoid getting tanned and thus "looking like peasants." Goffman's perceptive analysis of the various role-performance strategies required in the presentation of self encourages us to see the many "fronts" individuals put on as they interact with someone of a different race (or some other stigmatized status). These insights then need to be harnessed to a broader level of analysis, one that incorporates the underlying systemic ways in which social inequality – racism (see chapter 12) and sexism (see chapter 10), for example – are structured into everyday life irrespective of the individuals interacting in any given face-to-face setting.

INSTITUTIONAL FRAME ANALYSIS

SI's focus on face-to-face interaction has direct implications for macro societal structures and processes; as noted, the smooth functioning of families, universities, service industries, corporations, and politics depends, in part, on the role performances of individuals. Moreover, it is not just individuals who have to impose definitions of the situation on everyday activities; so too do organizations, institutions, and social movements. Goffman argues that individuals make sense of the multiple simultaneous activities surrounding them by selecting from the reality and imposing some kind of **frame**, a "unitary exposition and simplicity" on the situation (Goffman 1974: 8–9). Building on Goffman's frame analysis, sociologists have examined how large-scale social actors such as mass media organizations frame or package organizationally defined "newsworthy" events for readers/audiences. Just as individuals interpret or frame select cues in their reality to manage and respond to that reality, the organizational news-gathering routines and divisions (e.g., crime, lifestyle, business) developed by media organizations allow them to manage, select, and predefine "the news." All of the many events in our local and global world on a given day are thus reduced to fit with the media frames that then serve as our (mass mediated) "definition of the situation."

The sociologist Todd Gitlin, following Goffman, argues that

> Media frames, largely unspoken and unacknowledged, organize the world both for journalists who report it and, in some important degree, for us who rely on their reports. Media frames are persistent patterns of cognition, interpretation, and presentation, of selection, emphasis, and exclusion by which symbol-handlers routinely organize discourse, whether verbal or visual. Frames enable journalists to process large amounts of information quickly and routinely: to recognize it as information, to assign it to cognitive categories, and to package it for efficient relay to their audiences. Thus, for organizational reasons alone, frames are unavoidable, and journalism is organized to regulate their production. (Gitlin 1980: 7)

How the media frames a given event – an Occupy protest in London or Los Angeles, for example, or ongoing processes such as income inequality – can have important consequences for how readers/audiences come to interpret and act on that event or issue (e.g., Gitlin 1980; Gamson 1992).

SYMBOLIC INTERACTIONISM AND ETHNOGRAPHIC RESEARCH

SI's focus on face-to-face interaction and the practical implications of role performances in localized settings has been very influential in advancing qualitative, observation research. As Blumer argued (1969: 38), when we are interested in everyday interaction, we need to study through first-hand observation what is actually happening in a given area of social life. In this view, the dynamics of social interaction can be understood not by relying on survey responses or census data, but by looking carefully and closely and seeing how humans engage with and respond to one another. It is only through such firsthand, **on-the-ground observation** that we can "expand and deepen our perception of group life" (Blumer 1969: 39), and get a more accurate awareness of what is taking place as individuals interact with one another in a given setting. Thus Blumer states:

> The metaphor that I like is that of lifting the veils that obscure or hide what is going on. The task of scientific study is to lift the veils that cover the area of group life that one proposes to study … The veils are lifted by getting close to the area and by digging deep into it through careful study … SI is a down-to-earth approach to the scientific study of group life and human conduct. Its empirical world is the natural world of such group life and conduct. (Blumer 1969: 39, 47)

Many sociologists use on-the-ground methodology to systematically observe social behavior, conducting ethnographies of social interaction in varied family (e.g., Lareau 2003; Moore 2011), work (Tallichet 2006), and organizational settings (e.g., Pierce 1995), in the boxing gym (Wacquant 2004), and on the streets in urban neighborhoods (e.g., Anderson 1999; Goffman 2014; Small 2009). These researchers invariably draw on insights from Goffman in making sense of some of the observation data they gather.

SUMMARY

Symbolic interactionism provides a conceptual framework for analyzing the process of symbolic exchange that underpins all incidences of face-to-face interaction occurring across multiple micro settings, and that comprises social life. It builds on the insight that individuals' self-conception comes from the (verbal and nonverbal) symbolic information received in interaction with primary others (e.g., parents/family) and the generalized other (e.g., society). Symbolic exchange underlies, and is critical to, the performance of social roles, and it is an ongoing process. Social life requires individuals to perform a broad array of socially structured and socially patterned social roles across multiple and diverse settings to multiple and diverse audiences (and *as* audience to others' performing specific roles in a given setting/situation). Symbolic exchange and impression management are facilitated by socialization and, in any particular micro-setting, by the definition of the situation conveyed by the setting structure (including props) as well as by the interpretive activity (cues and miscues) of performers (including teams) and audiences.

POINTS TO REMEMBER

George H. Mead (1863–1931) emphasized that:
- The self is a reflective, thinking self
- The self is an object to itself (I can see/imagine myself)
- The self is composed of the interaction of the "I" and the "Me"

- The "I" is the response of the self to the attitudes of others
  - The "Me" is the self taking on the attitudes of others toward me
  - The self develops in and through social interaction
  - Individuals communicate through symbols, language, and gestures
  - Symbols are universally shared (though sometimes contested)

Charles H. Cooley (1864–1929)
- Looking-glass self; we see ourselves through how (imagined) particular others see us

Herbert Blumer (1900–1987)
- Social interaction is the interpretation of symbols, gestures, and language
- Society: is an ongoing process of symbolic interaction
- We respond to the meanings that objects or things (e.g., cues, people, institutions, processes) have in our social environment (i.e., our "world of objects")
- Sociologists deepen their understanding of group life through on-the-ground, systematic observation of individuals in interaction in specific settings

Erving Goffman (1922–1982)
- Dramaturgical perspective
- Face-to-face interaction: reciprocal influence of individuals upon one another's actions when in one another's immediate physical presence
- Role: enactment of rights and duties attached to a given status (student, daughter) and performed on a series of occasions in defined settings to the same kinds of audience
- Performance: activity of a given individual on a given occasion in a specific setting that serves to influence in any way any of the other participants
- Audience: performance observers and co-participants
- Front: that part of the individual's appearance in performance that regularly functions in a general and fixed fashion to define the situation for those who observe the performance
- Setting: stage, scenery, props, and audience informing a specific role-performance execution
- Props: contribute to defining the situation; (e.g., office insignia, personal effects, clothing)
- Definition of the situation: how we convey and infer the type of socially expected behavior required in a given situation; process by which we control the conduct of others
- Impression management: strategies that foster successful role performance; helps establish the definition of the situation
- Front-stage behavior: role behavior in the setting where the performance is given (e.g., waitresses perform for guests in restaurant dining area)
- Backstage behavior: preparatory behavior in the staging area for front-region behavior
- Individuals and organizations impose particular frames on everyday life to selectively negotiate among simultaneously occurring cues and activities

GLOSSARY

actors dramaturgical – individuals performing roles.

appearance signals indicating the individual's social statuses and "temporary ritual state" (e.g., a nurse dressed for work).

audience individuals who witness our role performance and for whom we perform.

backstage staging area for front-region behavior, where actors do the preparatory work to ensure a successful performance.

behaviorism strand in psychology emphasizing that humans behave in predictable ways in particular situations.

body idiom information conveyed through body language/display.

conversation of gestures process by which our signals or gestures bring forth a meaningful response in another.

cues verbal and nonverbal signs, signals, gestures, messages.

definition of the situation socialization of individuals into a society's generalized expectations of behavior across an array of social settings (Thomas); crucial to how actors interpret and perform in a particular role-performance setting (Goffman).

dramaturgical perspective of SI (Goffman) using the metaphor of drama to describe social life.

encounter acts and gestures comprising communication about communicating (e.g., how we respond when we encounter a stranger on an elevator or unexpectedly meet an acquaintance on the street).

frame simplifies reality by selectively interpreting and categorizing (and prioritizing) simultaneously occurring activities.

front the self-presentation maintained by the individual to project an intended definition of the situation in executing a particular role performance.

front-stage area where role performances are given.

generalized other community or society as a whole.

"I" part of the self; the "I" is the (subjective) acting self, and is able to act only because it internalizes the attitudes toward the "Me" (as an object) received from others' behavior/responses toward the acting "I" (Mead).

impression management symbolic and strategic communicative work toward orchestrating a particular definition of the situation and a successful role performance.

interaction rituals routinized ways of self-presenting/behaving in the co-presence of others (e.g., greeting rituals).

interpretive process interpretation of the meaning of individuals' verbal and nonverbal communication and of the meanings of other objects/things in our environment is an ongoing activity.

language a socially shared symbol and meaning system.

looking-glass self self-perception and behavior contingent on our knowing (or imagining) how others (would) respond toward us.

manner signals which function to indicate the tone in the interaction role a performer expects to play in an oncoming situation (e.g., the sympathetic grief counselor).

"Me" part of the self; the self as object ("Me"); the internalization of the expectations and attitudes of others toward "Me" and to which "I" (as the acting subject) respond (Mead).

meaning significance given to particular symbols and objects/things in our environment.

on-the-ground observation systematic data gathering in the everyday social contexts or settings in which individuals interact; ethnography.

part aspect of a social role.

passing the impression management and self-presentation symbolic work an individual must do in order to cover up or secretly maintain a stigmatized identity.

performance the idea that social life, society, is based on the socially structured, acting out (performance) of particular social roles.

presentation of self ongoing symbolic work the role-performing actor does to project an intended definition of a situation.

primary group has a crucially formative and enduring significance in child socialization (e.g., the primacy of the family).

props objects/things in a setting that bolster (prop up) the actor's intended definition of the situation.

region any role-performance setting bounded to some extent by barriers to perception (e.g., walls divide a restaurant's kitchen from its dining area).

rituals routinized ways of face-to-face acting and interacting that reflect status differences and maintain social order (Goffman).

rituals of subordination signals in self-presentation (e.g., body posture of one actor vis-à-vis another) symbolizing or indicating status differences or social inequality.

routines socially prescribed, ordered ways of accomplishing particular tasks or establishing particular situational definitions and meanings in executing a role performance.

segregated audiences when role-performing actors are able to keep the audiences to their different roles separate from one another; facilitates the impression management required in a particular setting.

self reflexively active interpreter of symbols and meanings in the individual's environment; composed of the "I" and the "Me" (Mead).

setting the bounded social situation/context in which a social role is performed.

social roles socially scripted role-performance behavior required of a person occupying a particular status and/or in a particular setting; individuals perform multiple social roles.

socialization process by which individuals learn how to be social – how to participate in society – and thus how to use and interpret symbols and language, and interact with others.

stage specific setting or place where the role-performing actor performs a particular social role.

stigma society's categorization or differentiation of its members as inferior based on the social evaluation and labeling of various attributes of undesired difference.

symbol any sign whose interpretation and meaning are socially shared.

symbolic interactionism sociological perspective emphasizing society/social life as an ongoing process wherein individuals continuously exchange and interpret symbols.

team when role performers cooperate to stage a single routine or performance, and project a shared definition of the situation.

total institutions highly regimented settings (e.g., prisons) in which the barriers that customarily divide individuals' everyday functions (sleeping, eating, and working) are removed.

QUESTIONS FOR REVIEW

1 Explain why it makes sense to call Goffman's framework for analyzing social life a "dramaturgical" perspective?

2 What elements need to be in place for the successful enactment of a role performance?

3 If a friend of yours was to describe a situation where they said they were "playing out of role," what would you say in response that would offer a different perspective on what they described?

4 What does it mean to say that social life entails ongoing symbolic interpretive work?

5 What is stigma? Where does it come from? How might it be negotiated? Can a stigmatized behavior or identity change over the course of an individual's lifetime?

NOTE

1 Goffman (1969) occasionally called his approach "strategic interaction." He elaborated: "Strategic interaction is, of course, close to Meadian social psychology and to what has come to be called 'symbolic interaction' – since nowhere more than in game analysis does one see the actor as putting himself in the place of the other and seeing things, temporarily at least, from his point of view … Strategic interaction appears to advance the symbolic interactionist approach in two ways. [i] the strategic approach, by insisting on full interdependence of outcomes, on mutual awareness of this fact, and on the capacity to make use of this knowledge, provides a natural means for excluding from consideration merely any kind of interdependence … [ii] strategic interaction addresses itself directly to the dynamics of interdependence involving mutual awareness; it seeks out basic moves and inquires into natural stopping points in the potentially infinite cycle of two players taking into consideration their consideration of each other's consideration, and so forth" (1969: 136–137). Goffman frequently used the example of a poker game to illustrate the interdependent awareness of individuals engaged in strategic interaction. This point is exemplified by James Bond in the movie *Casino Royale*. About to embark on a high-stakes game of poker, Bond says: "You never play your hand. You play the man across from you." And presumably (supporting the notion of symbolic interaction and strategic interdependence) that is what the person across from him would say too.

REFERENCES

Anderson, Elijah. 1999. *Code of the Street*. New York: Norton.

Blumer, Herbert. 1969. *Symbolic Interactionism: Perspective and Method*. Englewood Cliffs, NJ: Prentice Hall.

Collins, Patricia Hill. 1990. *Black Feminist Thought: Knowledge, Consciousness, and the Politics of Empowerment*. New York: Routledge. 2nd edition 2000.

Collins, Patricia Hill. 2004. *Black Sexual Politics*. New York: Routledge.

Collins, Randall. 1986. "The Passing of Intellectual Generations: Reflections on the Death of Erving Goffman." *Sociological Theory* 4: 106–113.

Cooley, Charles Horton. 1902/1998. *On Self and Social Organization*. Edited and with an introduction by Hans-Joachim Schubert. Chicago: University of Chicago Press.

Cooley, Charles Horton. 1909. *Social Organization: A Study of the Larger Mind*. New York: Charles Scribner's Sons.

Fine, Gary Alan, and Philip Manning. 2000. "Erving Goffman." Pp. 457–485 in George Ritzer, ed. *The Blackwell Companion to Major Social Theorists*. Oxford: Blackwell.

Gamson, William. 1992. *Talking Politics*. New York: Cambridge University Press.

Gilroy, Paul. 1987. *"There Ain't No Black in the Union Jack": The Cultural Politics of Race and Nation*. London: Hutchinson.

Gitlin, Todd. 1980. *The Whole World Is Watching: Mass Media in the Making and Unmaking of the New Left*. Berkeley: University of California Press.

Goffman, Alice. 2014. *On the Run*. Chicago: University of Chicago Press

Goffman, Erving. 1959. *The Presentation of Self in Everyday Life*. New York: Doubleday.

Goffman, Erving. 1961. *Asylums: Essays on the Social Situation of Mental Patients and Other Inmates*. Chicago: Aldine.

Goffman, Erving. 1963a. *Stigma: Notes on the Management of Spoiled Identity*. New York: Simon & Schuster.

Goffman, Erving. 1963b. *Behavior in Public Places: Notes on the Social Organization of Gatherings*. Glencoe, IL: Free Press.

Goffman, Erving. 1967. *Interaction Ritual: Essays in Face-to-Face Behavior*. Chicago: Aldine.

Goffman, Erving. 1969. *Strategic Interaction*. Philadelphia: University of Pennsylvania Press.

Goffman, Erving. 1971. *Relations in Public*. New York: Basic Books.

Goffman, Erving. 1974. *Frame Analysis: An Essay on the Organization of Experience*. Cambridge, MA: Harvard University Press.

Goffman, Erving. 1979. *Gender Advertisements*. Cambridge, MA: Harvard University Press.

Hall, Stuart. 1990. "Cultural Identity and Diaspora." Pp. 222–237 in Jonathan Rutherford, ed. *Identity: Community, Culture, Difference*. London: Lawrence & Wishart.

Hochschild, Arlie. 1983. *The Managed Heart: Commercialization of Human Feeling*. Berkeley: University of California Press.

Hochschild, Arlie. 2003. *The Commercialization of Intimate Life: Notes from Home and Work*. Berkeley: University of California Press.

Lareau, Annette. 2003. *Unequal Childhoods: Class, Race, and Family Life*. Berkeley: University of California Press.

MacLeod, Jay. 2008. *Ain't No Makin' It: Aspirations and Attainment in a Low-Income Neighborhood*. 3rd edition. Boulder, CO: Westview Press.

Marx, Patricia. 2015. "About Face: Why Is South Korea the World's Plastic Surgery Capital?" *New Yorker* (March 23), 50–55.

Mead, George Herbert. 1934. *Mind, Self, and Society*. Chicago: University of Chicago Press.

Moore, Mignon. 2011. *Invisible Families: Gay Identities, Relationships, and Motherhood among Black Women*. Berkeley: University of California Press.

Pavlov, Ivan. 1927. *Conditioned Reflexes*. New York: Oxford University Press.

Pierce, Jennifer. 1995. *Gender Trials: Emotional Lives in Contemporary Law Firms*. Berkeley: University of California Press.

Schubert, Hans-Joachim. 1998. "Introduction." Pp. 1–31 in Charles Horton Cooley. 1902/1998. *On Self and Social Organization*. Chicago: University of Chicago Press.

Shalin, Dmitri. 2000. "George Herbert Mead." Pp. 302–344 in George Ritzer, ed. *The Blackwell Companion to Major Social Theorists*. Oxford: Blackwell.

Simmel, Georg. 1917/1950. *The Sociology of Georg Simmel*. Translated, edited, and with an introduction by Kurt Wolff. Glencoe, IL: Free Press.

Singer, Natasha. 2008. "Nice Resume: Have You Considered Botox?" *New York Times* (January 24), p. E3.

Small, Mario. 2009. *Unanticipated Gains: Origins of Network Inequality in Everyday Life*. New York: Oxford University Press.

Smith, Dorothy. 1987. *The Everyday World as Problematic: A Feminist Sociology*. Boston: Northeastern University Press.

Talbot, Margaret. 2013. "About a Boy: Transgender Surgery at Sixteen." *New Yorker* (March 18), pp. 56–65.

Tallichet, Suzanne. 2006. *Daughters of the Mountains: Women Coal Miners in Central Appalachia*. University Park: Pennsylvania State University Press.

Thomas, William I. 1923. *The Unadjusted Girl*. Boston: Little, Brown.

Wacquant, Loic. 2004. *Body and Soul: Notebooks of an Apprentice Boxer*. New York: Oxford University Press.

Watson, John B. 1930. *Behaviorism*. Chicago: University of Chicago Press.

Williams, Christine. 1993. *Doing "Women's Work": Men in Nontraditional Occupations*. Newbury Park, CA: Sage.

Willis, Paul. 1977. *Learning to Labour: How Working Class Kids Get Working Class Jobs*. Farnborough, UK: Saxon House.

CHAPTER NINE

PHENOMENOLOGY AND ETHNOMETHODOLOGY

KEY CONCEPTS

phenomenology
natural attitude
wide-awake attention
here-and-now
practical knowledge
scheme of reference
lifeworld
stock of preconstituted
  knowledge
typifications
common-sense knowledge

recipe knowledge
social construction of reality
objective reality
externalization
internalization
subjective reality
Reification
in-group
out-group
symbolic universe
subuniverse of meaning

plausibility structures
ethnomethodology
accomplishment of social
  reality
members
accounts
background knowledge
breaching experiments
conversation analysis
glossing practices

CHAPTER MENU

There has been a lot of talk over the last few years about the adjustment problems faced by soldiers returning home from the wars in Iraq and Afghanistan. Consider for a moment that soldiers have to accept long periods of deployment in a war zone where they must constantly be alert to the threat of insurgent sniper attacks and roadside bombs, witness the death and paralyzing injuries of fellow combatants, and are so constantly and anxiously alert that when they "sleep," they sleep in combat gear with their rifle to the ready. You might think, then, that for these soldiers, coming home could only be a relief. Yet returning to the everyday reality of home presents soldiers and their families with readjustment challenges. This is because the practical, everyday realities of life in any one particular social context and what is "natural" and relevant in that context are very different from those in a different everyday context. Perhaps you had a similar experience when you returned home from college for the first time.

PHENOMENOLOGY: ALFRED SCHUTZ, PETER BERGER, AND THOMAS LUCKMANN

Phenomenology focuses on the significance of everyday reality and everyday experiences on how individuals construct knowledge of their social world and the practical implications of such knowledge. In contrast to the focus on macro societal structures and large-scale social processes (e.g., inequality) that characterizes many sociological theorists (e.g., Marx, Durkheim, Weber, critical theorists, Parsons), phenomenologists analyze "the world of everyday life" (Schutz 1970: 72). Phenomenology is attentive to how individuals recognize and make sense of the experiences that characterize their everyday reality. This approach is called "phenomenology" because it probes how particular experiences or *phenomena* (things as perceived by us) are selected and given attention from the ongoing, flowing stream of experiences that exist.

EXPERIENCE, MEANING, AND SOCIAL ACTION

Phenomenological sociology has its roots in twentieth-century philosophy, in the ideas elaborated by the German philosopher Edmund Husserl (1859–1938). Husserl argued that the consciousness of human beings is *intentional* – it is intentionally directed toward objects in individuals' sociocultural environment. It is, therefore, a consciousness of particular experiences rather than of a general reality beyond individual experience. Husserl's student **Alfred Schutz**, an Austrian who emigrated to New York in the 1930s, applied this idea to highlight the relevance of everyday life, that is, ordinary everyday experiences, in how individuals construe, and act in and upon, a particular social reality. Schutz explained:

> The world of everyday life is the scene and also the object of our actions and interactions. We have to dominate it and we have to change it in order to realize the purposes which we pursue within it among our fellow-men. Thus we operate not only within but upon the world … a pragmatic motive governs our **natural attitude** toward the world of daily life. (Schutz 1970: 72–73)

BIOGRAPHICAL NOTE

Alfred Schutz was born in Vienna, Austria, in 1899. He served in the Austrian-Hungarian army during World War I and studied law and social sciences in Vienna. In 1938, with the rise of Hitler and Nazism in Germany, he, with his wife, Ilse, and their two children, emigrated to Paris and then to New York, where he was affiliated with the New School for Social Research (along with many other war-exile intellectuals). Schutz founded the International Phenomenological Society in 1941. He died in New York in 1959.

Individuals live in the everyday world as subjectively engaged social actors, as emphasized by Max Weber, who defined sociology as the study of "subjectively meaningful action" (see chapter 3). His theorizing influenced Schutz (Luckmann 1978: 10). But Weber was more interested in how different historical and cultural-interpretive contexts (e.g., Calvinism) and social structures (e.g., bureaucracy) shape social action than in individuals' experiences of everyday reality and their interpretation of that reality – the focus of phenomenology. Similarly, although symbolic interactionists (SI) highlight the processes of meaning exchange and interpretation that occur in face-to-face interaction (see chapter 8), they are interested in the socially structured and ritualized nature of interaction, meaning (symbols, language), and role performance and not the individual's experiences of their roles. It is precisely the individual's experience of everyday reality that preoccupies phenomenologists.

HERE-AND-NOW, EVERYDAY REALITY

Phenomenology emphasizes that we don't simply see the social world as detached observers (though many sociologists adopt a detached approach as social scientists conducting "objective" research on social life). The practical tasks of getting on with everyday life demand our **wide-awake attention** to the **here-and-now** of everyday reality. Wide-awakeness is the concept Schutz uses to capture what consciousness entails, that is, "full attention to life and its requirements" (Schutz 1970: 69; see also 1970: 129).

The reality to which individuals are most wide awake is their here-and-now, everyday reality, a reality that is highly pragmatic. Amidst all the big and small things going on in society, on campus, in the classroom, it is your particular "here-and-now" that is of most relevance to you. Irrespective of any big existential questions we might ask about life and irrespective of the political debates in Washington, DC, Westminster, the European Parliament, or the United Nations, we are most alert to the practical tasks, the "natural" routines, in our particular here-and-now. Making breakfast, finding a seat on the train, getting an assignment submitted on time, picking up your child from day-care – these are just a few of the many ordinary (but consequential) things we do routinely. We typically don't pause to reflect on these daily tasks because they are so familiar and so apparently natural. We know how to do these things because we inherit a way of doing them: We mimic behavior considered normal or natural by those with whom we live. It is only when the car doesn't start that we begin to wonder, and to do so rather urgently, "How does this car work?" "What do I need to do to get it moving?" This is an everyday knowledge I really don't need to know, because most of the time my car works fine and because it works, I don't need to know how and why it works; I can trust in, or suspend disbelief about, the mechanics of car engines. (Of course, self-driving cars will require me to suspend disbelief about many things!) But at least now I still need to know how to drive, and how to scan documents and send attachments and use my coffee machine. This is my everyday world and I have a great deal of the **practical knowledge** necessary to smoothly negotiate its routine tasks. By contrast, the everyday world of the car mechanic down the road, the everyday knowledge they have, is very different.

What is deemed relevant knowledge – engine mechanics, the bus or train timetable, or what to eat for dinner and how to cook it, and when and how to eat it – is variously shaped by the family, community, and society in which we live. It is from the practical context of our daily lives that we learn to identify and to compartmentalize the salience of relevant experiences (e.g., whether we need to know how to cook pasta but not how to make sushi). Our interpretation of everyday reality "is based upon a stock of previous experiences of it, our own experiences and those handed down to us by our parents and teachers, which in the form of 'knowledge at hand' function as a **scheme of reference**" (Schutz 1970: 72) that anchors and orients us.

The paramount nature of any particular individual's here-and-now reality – the fact that you have to file a study-abroad petition with the dean's office while your roommate has to rush to a medical appointment or to a job shift – means that although you both share a common reality as college students, the specific pragmatic tasks that inhere in your respective here-and-now realities vary. Each individual necessarily inhabits a unique "biographically determined situation" (Schutz 1970: 163); for example, two brothers, though close in age and interests, will have different memories and experiences of growing up in their shared family world. Similarly, no two students in a particular theory class on a particular day will have the same subjective experience of that shared classroom reality. Each person's consciousness of, attentiveness to, and feelings about their particular, subjective here-and-now reality will vary (Schutz 1970: 165).

SHARED, INTERSUBJECTIVE REALITY

Nevertheless, although any individual's specific here-and-now reality differs from a sibling's or a classmate's, this does not mean that individuals create their own reality or that reality can be whatever we deem it to be. Quite the contrary. Despite the uniqueness of subjective experiences, it is the *intersubjectivity* of human life that demarcates human consciousness and human society:

the world of my daily life is by no means my private world but is from the outset an intersubjective one, shared with, … experienced and interpreted by others … The unique biographical situation in which I find myself within the world at any moment of my existence is only to a very small extent of my own making. I find myself always within an historically given world which, as a world of nature as well as a sociocultural world, had existed before my birth and which will continue to exist after my death. This means that the world is not only mine but also [others'] environment; moreover, these [other individuals] are elements of my own situation, as I am of theirs. (Schutz 1970: 163–164)

In other words, our reality is always social, always shared with others. As Mead emphasized (see chapter 8), the self can only emerge out of social interaction. Similarly, the world of everyday life, what Schutz calls the **lifeworld** (1970: 72), is a world shared with other selves. My (personally) subjective reality is tied to and contingent on the intersubjective (self–others) shared reality that is society, and society structures and organizes my (and others') everyday reality. As individuals we

bring into each concrete situation a **stock of preconstituted knowledge** [experience] which includes a network of **typifications** of human individuals in general, of typical human motivations, goals, and action patterns. It also includes knowledge of expressive and interpretive schemes, of objective sign-systems and in particular, of the vernacular [local] language. In addition to such general knowledge I have more specific information about particular kinds and groups of [people], of their motivations and actions. (Schutz 1962: 29–30)

Everyday reality is experienced by us through its many typifications: the typical (and stereotypical) ways we expect individuals of varying statuses (e.g., celebrities, working class people), roles (e.g., police officers), identities (e.g., Americans, French people), and institutions (e.g., the state, the media, the economy, the church) in our social world to act. Typifications provide the individual with "appropriate tools for coming to terms with things and [people], accepted as such by the group into which [the person] was born" (Schutz 1970: 119).

EVERYDAY REALITY AS *THE* SOCIAL REALITY

Phenomenologists thus emphasize that we experience and know everyday social reality as a natural reality whose **common-sense knowledge** we take for granted. The everyday ways of doing things in a particular community (or among members of a particular group) are accepted as the *right* way to do things; they work and make sense and have stood the test of time. Hence this **recipe knowledge** is taken for granted; it provides ready-made ways of doing things and these tried-and-true ways don't need to be explained or justified (Schutz 1970: 80–81).

ORDERED REALITY

Peter Berger and **Thomas Luckmann** are sociologists who popularized Schutz's ideas in their well-known book *The Social Construction of Reality* (1966). They emphasize that social reality is human made and human experienced, and it is a highly ordered reality: "Social order is a human product, or more precisely, an ongoing human production" (Berger and Luckmann 1966: 52). More so than Schutz, Berger and Luckmann emphasize the significance of institutions – human-made and human-experienced institutions – in the dynamic, ongoing construction of social reality. The **social construction of reality** means that individuals collectively create an objective social reality whose objects (e.g., things, tools, institutions) they designate and arrange (i.e., order) in ways that make sense to them as they subjectively experience that reality. Social reality is produced as a result of individuals' ongoing negotiation and experience of the external, **objective reality** – of the socially institutionalized processes and practices in a given society. Thus the "institutional world" is "experienced as an objective reality" (1966: 60), that is, it is an objectification of the product of human-social activity and given **externalization** in the institutions and order created by humans in society. Individuals experience this objective, externalized reality through a process of **internalization**: the external reality is based upon *their* social reality, their individual experiences in a particular family-community-social environment (1966: 130–132). The objective social reality (e.g., economic inequality) is thus internalized and interpreted, in part, on the basis of idiosyncrasies that characterize the individual's family reality (e.g., income level, and whether the family mood is one of contentment or dissatisfaction with the status quo).

BIOGRAPHICAL NOTES

Peter Berger was born in Vienna in 1929; he and his wife, Brigitte Berger, also a sociologist, moved to the US after World War II. After many years on the faculty at Rutgers University, New Jersey, the Bergers moved to Boston University, where Peter is currently an emeritus professor and director of the Institute for the Study of Economic Culture. **Thomas Luckmann** was born in Slovenia in 1927 and spent most of his career at the University of Konstanz, in Germany. Along with *The Social Construction of Reality*, he is widely known for his book *The Invisible Religion*; he died in 2016.

The individual's subjective internalization and experience of (the externalized) reality is the reality in and from which they participate in the ongoing creation and maintenance of an external social reality. The individual internalizes an objectified reality, makes it their own **subjective reality**, and in turn acts backs on that reality – the objectified reality can be readily translated into subjective reality and vice versa (Berger and Luckmann 1966: 22, 35, 37, 129–130). In short, there is an ongoing creative, back-and-forth relationship or translation between the individual and society (1966: 61), through the processes of internalization and externalization. Language is the principal vehicle of this ongoing translation (1966: 133). Language names all of the things in our everyday environment – our country, our town, our family, the occupations in our society, the cars people drive, the kitchen utensils we use, the food we eat, etc. – and thus gives them an objective existence. These objects constitute the external reality – one that existed before we were born – an objective reality that we encounter and must negotiate. Thus:

> The reality of everyday life appears already objectified, that is, constituted by an order of objects that have been designated as objects before my appearance on the scene. The language used in everyday life continuously provides me with the necessary objectifications and posits the order within which these make sense and within which everyday life has meaning for me … The reality of everyday life is not only filled with objectifications; it is only possible because of them. (Berger and Luckmann 1966: 22, 35; see also Schutz 1970: 80–81)

We use language to construct and to label and to maintain our reality. And when the language we have no longer works to label our experiences, we devise new words, new ways of labeling those experiences; as such we objectify and legitimate the validity of these experiences as part of everyday reality.

Hence, today, we have new words and new experiences – googling, friending, and ubering. And these words reflect everyday reality—what people do and how they do it, but they also shape and define our (subjective and objective) everyday reality. Language, and all social institutions (e.g., marriage, law, government), are human-created realities. They are social constructions, and hence their definition evolves and changes in tandem with other changes in society, including individuals' experiences of and responses to their changing, lived reality. This does not mean that social institutions are not "real." Clearly, they have an objectified reality. But as human-social products, they are subject to human-social decision making and control; they do not have a reified existence. **Reification**, as Berger and Luckmann explain, is:

> the apprehension of human phenomena as if they were things ... *as if* they were something else than human products – such as facts of nature, results of cosmic laws, or manifestations of divine will. Reification implies that [humans are] capable of forgetting [their] own authorship of the human world ... The reified world is, by definition, a dehumanized world. It is experienced by [people] as a strange facticity ... over which [they have] no control rather than as ... [their] own productive activity ... As soon as an objective social world is established, the possibility of reification is never far away. The objectivity of the social world means that it confronts [people] as something outside of [themselves]. The decisive question is whether [we] still retain the awareness that, however objectified, the social world was made by [people] – and therefore can be remade by them. (Berger and Luckmann 1966: 89)

PHENOMENOLOGICAL DIVERSITY

Because we take the naturalness of our everyday reality for granted, it is easy to think of that reality as a reified rather than a socially constructed reality. The taken-for-grantedness of our everyday world becomes apparent to us generally only after we step out of that reality. This happens when we move from the everyday reality of our (phenomenological) **in-group** – the reality of our family, our neighborhood, our college campus, etc. – to that of someone else's everyday reality, the social world of an **out-group** (those whose everyday typifications and experiences are different to ours). It may seem trivial, but how we set the dinner table and do several other basic everyday things is highly salient to how we experience and make sense of everyday life. This is all part of our natural common-sense knowledge. As such, we feel that this knowledge is of paramount relevance not only to us and others like us, but to all people. It shapes our expectations of what is "normal" behavior. But this common sense may not work as smoothly when in the company of a particular "out-group" (e.g., visiting your boyfriend's family, who has a different way of organizing dinner and other routine tasks), because you and they have different schemes of reference.

Because of the wide-ranging everyday experiences that differently situated individuals have, there are different ways of knowing and different ways of evaluating the knowledge that is handed down as the objective, one, true knowledge. Once we recognize that something as ordinary as having dinner at a friend's home can challenge what we consider to be the common-sense way to do things, we can, by extension, begin to appreciate the diversity in everyday lived experience of individuals and groups who live in social environments very different from ours. Intersecting differences across race, income, gender, ethnicity, occupation, sexuality, region, country, religion, etc., produce lived experiences whose diversity challenge knowledge claims that are presumed to be universal, that is, applicable to everyone's experiences. This phenomenological insight informs the work of feminist theorists such as Dorothy Smith (1987) and Patricia Hill Collins (1990), whose ideas we discuss in chapter 10; they argue against the presumption that there is one (objective) reality and one knowledge.

The stranger

Schutz elaborates on the typifications of the *stranger* and the *homecomer* to highlight the contrasting realities, perceptions, and experiences of everyday life. A *stranger*, by definition, is one for whom the everyday habits in a given community are strange, and whose own habits appear strange to those settled there. Georg Simmel construed the stranger "not as the wanderer who comes today and goes tomorrow, but as the person who comes today and stays tomorrow" (1908/1950: 402). Similarly, for Schutz, a stranger is not simply a tourist, but someone who wants to be a member of, or permanently accepted or tolerated by, a specific group (Schutz 1962: 91).

The immigrant clearly is a stranger but so too is anyone who wants to be a member in a "closed club" – whether this is a family into which you marry, a person from a working-class background who graduates from college and moves into the middle class, an urban cosmopolitan who moves to a rural area, etc. (Schutz 1962: 91). Indeed, we tend to see as strange all those who are in any way culturally different to us, and this is especially true of those who are racially different, as underscored by the phenomenological experience of "the fact of blackness," recounted by Frantz Fanon (1967) (see chapter 12).

The stranger, then, is someone who has a history and a set of habits different to those of the host or dominant cultural group. As such, strangers invariably challenge the typifications and ways of being they necessarily encounter in their new social environment. Thus, as Simmel first wrote, the stranger "is not radically committed to the unique ingredients and peculiar tendencies of the group, and therefore, approaches them with the specific attitude of 'objectivity.' But objectivity does not simply involve passivity and detachment; it is a particular structure composed of distance and nearness, indifference and involvement" (Simmel 1908/1950: 405). Strangers find as strange the everyday, recipe knowledge that those "at home" in the environment take for granted as they go about everyday tasks. They basically question all of the things and all of the everyday ways of doing things, that are taken for granted by the in-group (the community in which they seek acceptance); their ways are not the community's (taken-for-granted) ways (Schutz 1962: 96–97). The stranger will continue to maintain the "natural attitude" that worked in their own home group because that is their history, their way of interpreting reality: "the stranger starts to interpret [their] new social environment in terms of [their] thinking as usual," but this scheme of reference will not work in the new situation (1962: 97). Accordingly, the stranger has to learn new ways of thinking about and doing things, acquiring the in-group's recipe knowledge for interpreting and understanding this new social environment so that the "strange" ways in this newly entered social world can eventually acquire sufficient coherence and make sense (1962: 95).

The homecomer

We expect the stranger to undergo a process of social adjustment – an insight reflected in universities' first-year orientation programs. But Schutz alerts us that the *homecomer* too needs to adjust to "home." The homecomer's experience, perhaps even more than the stranger's, highlights how the experience of everyday life is so thoroughly a subjectively (and intersubjectively) experienced reality. The homecomer is someone who is returning home after an absence and who is returning not simply for a temporary stay, like you for an end-of-semester vacation, but permanently – "who comes for good to his home" (Schutz 1962: 107). The idea of "home" connotes many varied things. As Schutz notes, "Home means different things to different people … home means one thing to the [person] who has never left it, another thing to the [person] who dwells far from it, and still another to [the one] who returns" (1962: 108).

Whatever particular connotation home has for you, Schutz argues, one thing is fairly certain:

> Life at home follows an organized pattern of routine; it has its well-determined goals and well-proved means to bring them about, consisting of a set of traditions, habits, institutions, timetables for activities of all kinds, etc. Most of the problems of daily life can be mastered by following this pattern ... The way of life at home governs as a scheme of expression and interpretation not only my own acts but also those of the other members of the in-group. I may trust that, using this scheme, I shall understand what the Other means and make myself understandable to [them]. (Schutz 1962: 108)

Life at home, therefore, is predictable and familiar; even in a chaotic home, the chaos is fairly predictable. Home interactions and routines follow a rhythm known

Figure 9.1 Coming home means negotiating the transition from one here-and-now reality to a different here-and-now reality, realities that are made different both by our presence and our absence. Source: © Videodet/iStockphoto.

to all who are at home. And when home life is ruptured, as is the experience of immigrants, refugees, and victims of natural disasters, the individual's scheme of reference is thrown into disarray.

But precisely because the homecomer is someone who has left home, they have become familiar with a different set of typifications, a different "system of coordinates" than that used as the scheme of reference for life at home (Schutz 1962: 111). The homecomer, then, is unlike the stranger, in that they return to a social environment they have committed to memory and which they think they already know. While away from home, however, people change – they have had different everyday experiences – and in their absence, the family members left at home have also had different everyday experiences, from which the homecomer is excluded. The homecomer's stock of (remembered) home typifications has not changed, but the remaining family members have devised some new typifications as they go about the everyday reality experienced in the person's absence and, consequently, the old typifications or schemes of reference held by the homecomer may no longer work in their (old) home environment.

THE PHENOMENOLOGY OF THE HOMECOMING VETERAN

The phenomenological dilemma faced by the homecomer is well captured by the returning veteran, an example used by Schutz, and one that is still salient. As noted at the chapter's opening, anyone who spends time in a war zone experiences an everyday reality that is radically different from even the most tumultuous (and violent) home environment in their home-place. Although soldiers at war face a highly threatening enemy, they are equipped to deal with the war zone's chaos and anomie (see Durkheim; chapter 2) by the clearly defined norms of authority and the tight network of social relationships that typify their military in-group. The soldier's in-group knows (more or less) who the out-group is (the enemy) and what (more or less) is required in in-group/out-group encounters.

When the soldier returns home, they encounter a reality that is also characterized by anomie – a shift in norms created largely by the soldier's absence. This home-anomie is different to the anomie of war. Absence matters. Having left home, the soldier thinks of and remembers home differently than if they had never left, and differently than if they had stayed away (see Schutz 1962: 108). The absence has also created a new reality for the family left at home. Families organize and experience things differently when one of their members is absent, producing a shift in the family's scheme of reference. Further, the soldier's war experiences and war typifications do not prepare the veteran for making sense of their home-anomie experiences. At home, unlike at war, the soldier is no longer battling an enemy they know how to respond to but is now battling their in-group, the very family of which the soldier was an integral part prior to going to war.

The gulf in the different experiential realities of the soldier and those of their family is exacerbated by the fact that those remaining at home have an image of the soldier's wartime experience that tends to be distorted by idealized media images of war (Schutz 1962: 118–119). These distortions continue today, notwithstanding the coverage given to the "actual" reality of war by movies, newspapers, and Internet blogs. But even in-depth accounts can never fully convey what it really means to be a soldier at war, even as blockbuster movies such as *Dunkirk* give us a vivid glimpse of the fear and uncertainty that infuses the soldier's subjectively experienced realities. The social and psychological consequences of being a homecoming-veteran-stranger are underscored by the fact that an estimated one-third of US troops returning from Iraq or Afghanistan have either major depression, post-traumatic stress disorder, or traumatic brain injury (see www.rand.org; search "Invisible wounds of war"). Compounding the home-anomie, many homecomer-soldiers have to deal with problems stemming from the military's rejection of their medical insurance claims, financial problems, and constrained educational opportunities (e.g., many veterans are ineligible for government education benefits). The different worlds of everyday experience that the soldier *and* their family experience while the soldier is at war mean that both the returning veteran and their family are, phenomenologically, strangers to one another, at least for a while, and in many instances, for a long time. War experiences and homecoming experiences converge to produce new everyday realities for both the homecomer and the home-family; for many, these are conflicted and confusing realities that translate into high rates of marital strain, separation, divorce, and domestic violence, including murder, among soldiers/veterans and their families.

The gulf that necessarily separates the everyday realities of veterans and of their families prompted Schutz to argue that, just as the military prepares its veterans for their return to their (strange) homeland, it should also prepare veterans' families for the return of their (strange) homecomer. "In the beginning it is not only the homeland that shows to the homecomer an unaccustomed face. The homecomer appears equally strange to those who expect him, and the thick air about him will keep him unknown. Both the homecomer and the welcomer will need the help of a Mentor to 'make them wise to things'" (Schutz 1962: 119).

Topic 9.1   Homecoming strangers: "After war, love can be a battlefield"

At special weekend retreats organized by the US Army for small groups of officers and their spouses, returning veterans squirm uncomfortably as they acknowledge to their own spouse and to the other couples present the emotional difficulties they are encountering in settling back to life at home. Officers talk about their feelings of detachment from their young children, of a general emotional numbness, and of anger and resentment toward their spouse. This emotional sharing, and the opportunity to spend a weekend at a relaxing resort reconnecting with their spouse and hanging out with other couples experiencing similar strains, is seen by the Army as one way to help stem the tide of marital breakdown that appears to be on the increase among its highly valued, highly experienced officer corps. Like the military's foot-soldiers, they too find it difficult to settle back into life at home after harrowing tours of duty in Iraq and Afghanistan (see Kaufman 2008).

The military recognizes the need to organize programs aimed at making veterans and their families wise to one another's realities. Suicide hotlines link veterans to local care and emergency response workers, and as we see from Topic 9.1, marital counseling and other family programs are intended to help the adjustment experience of military families, notwithstanding the gap between the soldier's and the family's experiences and schemes of reference.

Symbolic universes

Although (or because) individuals live in very specific, here-and-now realities, they seek to integrate their everyday realities into a larger system of meaning, a "meaningful totality" or a **symbolic universe** of meaning that helps to explain and even justify the nature of their experiences (Berger and Luckmann 1966: 96). Berger and Luckmann explain, "The symbolic universe provides order for the subjective apprehension of biographical experience. Experiences belonging to different spheres of reality are integrated by incorporation in the same, overarching universe of meaning" (1966: 97). Religion is one such symbolic universe; science is another. These are overarching meaning systems that help the individual make sense of disruptive experiences in their reality – of war, of ostracism, of tragic accidents and natural disasters as well as impose some interpretive order on the disorder that can accompany life-course transitions (e.g., starting college, marriage, childbirth, divorce), including the expected reality of death (1966: 97–102).

We typically come together with others with whom we share a **subuniverse of meaning** when we go to church or participate in various social support (e.g., Alcoholics Anonymous) and other particular groups. These groups objectively legitimate our subjective experiences and the meanings with which we interpret reality – as happens when veterans' spouses have an opportunity to share their marital experiences with one another. Similarly, when an LGBT Catholic participates in organized worship and social activities in a group with other gay Catholics they come to know that they are not the only gay Catholic in the world and that their personal, subjective experiences of being gay *and* Catholic are not so unusual but are in part of an objective and collective reality, demonstrated by the existence of several other LGBT Catholics. Such experiences affirm and reinforce the normalcy of being LGBT *and* Catholic (Dillon 1999). Transgender Latinas in New York City, some of whom are illegal immigrants, find a similar identity-affirming community when they participate in a support group where they freely share their experiences and learn concrete life skills about navigating the many challenges they encounter (Turkewitz and Linderman 2012). Participation in groups with others who have similar experiences and similar interpretive frameworks makes our particular feelings, experiences, and identities plausible (Berger 1967: 50). "Like all social edifices of meaning, the subuniverses must be 'carried' by a particular collectivity, that is, by the group that ongoingly produces the meanings in question and within which these meanings have objective reality" (Berger and Luckmann 1966: 85). Such collectivities or groups thus form part of the **plausibility structure** that affirms and legitimates the facticity, the realness, of individuals' subjectively experienced everyday reality.

In particular, groups whose members experience social marginality (e.g., gays), or a conflict between a subjectively experienced and objective reality, help to facilitate participants' questioning of the objective or institutionally defined reality. This process, in turn, can mobilize activism toward social and institutional change (e.g., the gay rights movement's advocacy of same-sex marriage). And when laws change, both reflecting and ushering in a new reality – e.g., same-sex marriage – this new objective reality further affirms both the subjective and the objective plausibility of collectively shared meanings, typifications, and institutional practices. The significance of this dynamic is captured by the comments of a lesbian woman who married her partner. Recounting her astonishment at the support she received from her straight friends, she learned, she said, the importance of marriage as a rite of passage: "With a real wedding – not a commitment ceremony, not a domestic partnership registry – we were initiated into a crowded circle of people who automatically affirmed our very beings. It was a club we never even knew existed until we joined" (Osborn 2008: S6); see also Topic 9.2.

Topic 9.2   "I am Cait": Naming reality

Renaming Ceremonies have become common for transgender people in recent years. Following Caitlyn Jenner's example (in the season finale of the E! television reality show "I am Cait"), these ceremonies give public affirmation to the person's newly evolved identity and to its new here-and-now realities. In doing so, they strengthen both the subjective (personal) and the objective (social) plausibility of the new identity; that is, it's okay to be transgender. Nevertheless, and underscoring the fact that different people live in different here-and-now realities with different typifications, assumptions, and aspirations, the four girls' names that saw the most dramatic decline in 2016 were Caitlin, Caitlyn, Katelynn, and Kaitlynn (Collins 2017: 25).

ETHNOMETHODOLOGY: HAROLD GARFINKEL

Schutz's focus on everyday reality influenced the development of **ethnomethodology,** a separate field of study founded by the American sociologist **Harold Garfinkel.** *Ethnos* is the Greek word for people—the term "ethnomethodology" simply refers to the methods people use to create an ordered reality. Garfinkel (1967), concerned with what he regarded as sociological theory's general tendency to take social order and social processes for granted, argued instead that these need to be accomplished on an ongoing basis. Specifically targeting Durkheim's assumption of the given-ness (or thing-ness) of "social facts," Garfinkel's focus is on the processes by which social facts get made, and thus on the **accomplishment of social reality**. He explained:

> in contrast to certain versions of Durkheim that teach that the objective reality of social facts is sociology's fundamental principle, the lesson is taken instead … that the objective reality of social facts *as* an ongoing accomplishment of the concerted activities of daily life, with the ordinary, artful ways of that accomplishment being by [society] members known, used, and taken for granted, is for members a fundamental phenomenon. (Garfinkel 1967: vii)

BIOGRAPHICAL NOTE

Harold Garfinkel was born in Newark, New Jersey, in 1917. While taking business courses at the University of Newark, he learned the "theory of accounts," a method that would later have an impact on his sociological thinking. He received his master's degree at the University of North Carolina, and after serving time in the air force during World War II, he completed his PhD at Harvard, studying with Talcott Parsons. He had a long and distinguished career at the University of California at Los Angeles (UCLA), making UCLA the center for ethnomethodological studies. He and his wife, Arlene, whom he married during the war, had two sons (Rawls 2000).

Ethnomethodologists thus concern themselves with documenting in detail how (i.e., the methods by which) individuals in society (what Garfinkel calls **members**) work at creating an ordered or organized social reality. As such, ethnomethodology is not a theory with an explicit set of concepts that can be used to explain social life. It is a way of looking at and describing how people categorize and process everyday experiences so that they can recognize and organize or accomplish a highly ordered, everyday social reality.

THE ACCOMPLISHMENT OF SOCIAL REALITY

Ethnomethodologists emphasize that individuals (societal members) accomplish order as they go about their everyday business, recognizing and making sense of their experiences in ways that fit with the shared norms of order and reasonableness in society. "Ethnomethodological studies analyze everyday activities as members' methods for making those same activities visibly-rational-and-reportable-for-all-practical-purposes, i.e., 'accountable,' as organizations of commonplace everyday activities" (Garfinkel 1967: vii). In other words, the focus is on how individuals use society's expectations of how and why things happen (or are expected to happen) to explain "what really happened" (1967: 15) in a particular setting regarding a particular event or activity.

Garfinkel argues that we can discern how members accomplish social reality by looking at the usual organized practices (what he calls "artful practices") that underlie and shape how individuals negotiate everyday tasks (Garfinkel 1967: 11). These routine tasks invariably demand the organization and categorization of things and experiences on the basis of past experiences and their categorization in everyday family, work, and other settings. In various institutional settings (classrooms, offices, hospitals, courtrooms, science laboratories, etc.), the routines individuals follow are organized in an orderly and sequential manner. This ensures that the sequence adhered to will enable them to produce retrospective reasonable **accounts** (of procedures, actions, etc.) that will hold up under scrutiny were they to be asked to provide a defensible account of some event or decision (e.g., a professor explaining why a student received a specific grade).

All decisions have consequences; reality is consequential. Hence, societal members have to be able to establish a reasonable account of what really happened (e.g., for a student to deserve a B or an A) and of how we know what really happened, when so many reasonable category choices or decisions may be available. Notably, many corporate and public controversies stem from accounts by participants whose evasiveness, inconsistencies, and contradictions make it hard for others to believe what their accounts claim about what *really* happened regarding a particular decision or series of events.

THE CORONER'S OFFICE: ESTABLISHING HOW INDIVIDUALS DIED AND LIVED

How, for example, can workers in a coroner's office "formulate accounts of how a death really-for-all-practical-purposes happened," when they themselves have not witnessed the death firsthand? How do they decide, and account for, whether a particular death is the result of natural causes, a suicide, a homicide, or an accident (Garfinkel 1967: 13–14)? Garfinkel argues that in arriving at a decision, the coroner uses all the "remains" available to make a determination. There are the "physical remains" – how the body appeared upon death: Was the throat slashed? And if so, did it show the "hesitation cuts" of a suicidal death or the less hesitant ones that might accompany a homicide? And of course "cuts that look like hesitation cuts can be produced by other mechanisms [not just a suicidal person's hesitation]" (1967: 17). Because other courses of action are imaginable … one needs to start with the actual display and imagine how different courses of actions could have been organized such that *that* picture would be compatible with it. One might think of the photographed display [of the dead body] as a phase-of-the-action. In any actual display is there a course of action with which that phase is uniquely compatible? *That's* the coroner's question. (Garfinkel 1967: 17–18)

The coroner also has access to what might be called the social "remains":

rumors, passing remarks, and stories – materials in the "repertoires" of whosoever might be consulted via the common work of conversations. These *whatsoever* bits and pieces that a story or a rule or proverb might make intelligible are used to formulate a recognizably coherent, standard, typical, cogent, uniform, planful, i.e., a professionally [and culturally] defensible, and thereby for members, a recognizably rational account of how the society worked to produce those remains. (Garfinkel 1967: 17)

"*Whatsoever* bits" are the rumors about a person (e.g., "He was having financial trouble") and the extent to which proverbs or common sayings are applicable to the dead person's life and the circumstances of the death. The physical and social remains have to be woven into accounts that are seen as credible and defensible; they have to add up. They have to fit with what it is we believe or know to be in keeping with the person's everyday routines, the person's social repertoire. As such the coroner's report does not just tell us how someone died but also how they *lived* (e.g., death from occupational injuries or from a drug overdose).

Gendering of accounts

The coherence of the social remains, of the bits believed about a person, and what is imputed to the physical remains are socially differentiated. If the dead person is black, a woman, or an immigrant, for example, this information makes some presumptions and interpretations more culturally defensible than others. Indeed, some commentators have noted that female celebrities "behaving badly" receive much more negative media coverage than their male peers who also have a reputation for partying. As feminist sociologists have long emphasized, in a patriarchal society wherein women are unequal to men, women, and especially mothers, are expected to behave differently than men (see chapter 10). By the same token, racial Others (Said 1978), that is, those outside the dominant racial group, are expected to behave in certain culturally stereotyped ways – to commit more crime, for example (Gilroy 1987; see chapter 12).

The categorization of reality by the accounts of coroners, and more generally, by lawyers, publicists, police officers, medical personnel, and all those ordinary individuals who just so happened to have gone to school, etc., with the person of note (whether dead or alive), imposes an order on reality that is informed by – and reaffirms – dominant societal expectations regarding what kinds of people do and should be doing what kinds of things. Thus, for example, when the actor Heath Ledger died from an apparent but *accidental* drug overdose in 2008, media commentators expressed surprise at the circumstances of his death notwithstanding the "bits and pieces" indicating personal turmoil due to his separation from his wife, as well as a party-going reputation. By contrast, in 2011, when Amy Winehouse was found dead in her home surrounded by empty vodka bottles, there was much less surprise. And the coroner subsequently confirmed what everyone "knew" or assumed, namely, that she died of alcohol poisoning. Similarly, when the famed pop singer and music innovator Prince died suddenly in April 2016, there were many rumors about what he might have died from. Bits and pieces from his life (and from his edgy song lyrics) led some to suggest AIDS or HI, and others a drug overdose or suicide; the coroner subsequently confirmed an opioid overdose.

JURORS ACCOMPLISHING REALITY

Jury deliberations also illuminate how an ordered social reality gets accomplished. Removed from their own everyday settings, jurors enter a courtroom trial setting and deliberate among many possible alternative accounts and alternative outcomes in order to render a verdict as to what *really* happened, as opposed to what *allegedly* happened, in a given criminal case (Garfinkel 1967: 104–115). The ambiguity in finding out what really happened (the real sequence and circumstances of the alleged wrongdoing) is exacerbated because what seems credible is, as with coroners' accounts, socially differentiated. The gender, race, social class, and other social locations of the individual(s) being charged with a crime, of the person(s) bringing the charge, and of the jurors all matter in determining the accounts and the outcome of the case, patterns that are well documented by sociologists of law who emphasize the social distance in equality between the victim and the perpetrator (e.g., Black 1976; 2011).

PRODUCING AN ORDERED REALITY

What jurors do in arriving at a credible account of an event is what we as individuals do in deciding among possible alternative scenarios and accounts of our reality (and this includes sociologists doing research about the social world). We make inferential judgments about our daily experiences. We actively categorize – and know how to categorize – what we are doing or experiencing in the present from our already experienced, culturally learned everyday knowledge of social reality.

Garfinkel elaborates:

> jurors decide between what is fact and what is fancy; between what actually happened and what "merely appeared" to happen; between what is put on and what is truth, regardless of detracting appearances; between what is credible and … what is calculated and said by design; between what is an issue and what is decided; between what is *still* an issue compared with what is irrelevant and will not be brought up again except by a person who has an axe to grind; between what is mere personal opinion and with what any right-thinking person would have to agree to … Jurors come to an agreement amongst themselves as to what actually happened. They decide "the facts," i.e., among alternative claims about speed of travel or extent of injury … They do this by consulting the consistency of alternative claims with common sense models. Those common sense models are models jurors use to depict, for example, what culturally known types of persons drive in what culturally known types of ways at what typical speeds at what types of intersections for what typical motives. The test runs that the matter that is meaningfully consistent may be correctly treated as the thing that actually occurred. If the interpretation makes good sense, then that's what happened. (Garfinkel 1967: 105–106)

Social reality is thus accomplished by individuals referencing the societal rules and norms regarding what will pass as being credible to all those who make it their business to know what *really* happened (Garfinkel 1967: 15). Whatever reality we are accomplishing, our accounts of what really happened (at the party, in causing one to be late for work, etc.) have to demonstrate that a given outcome or course of action was justified by the actions and events preceding it; our accounts have to be "adequately told, sufficiently detailed, clear, etc., for all practical purposes" (1967: 15). Accounts, moreover, can be revised to create an ordered reality in light of the anticipated consequences of the decision (1967: 15). Revising an account, however – calling a death a homicide after first categorizing it as a suicide – does not remove accountability; the coroner must now account for the revised decision and the changed account also needs to be credible. The reordering of reality must make the (revised) inferences and actions look sensible.

In sum, Garfinkel emphasizes, any account of reality has to make practical sense; it has to be believable and recognizably rational by the standards of the society in which the accounts are produced (cf. Garfinkel 1967: 12–13, 16–17). Again, however, what makes practical sense in one particular social context may not necessarily translate to another. This is why, for example, feminist (e.g., Smith 1987; see chapter 10), queer (e.g., Seidman 1997; see chapter 11), and postcolonial (see chapter 12) theorists highlight how particular categorizations that reflect the ruling or dominant norms in society impose particular definitions of credibility that are at odds with the lived experiences and everyday knowledge of outsider individuals and groups (e.g., women, and LGBT, black, and disabled individuals).

GENDER AS AN ACCOMPLISHED REALITY: CANDACE WEST AND DON ZIMMERMAN

The accounts individuals provide of reality are not simply verbal or written but also include actions; how people typically behave (e.g., students, politicians, celebrities such as Lindsay Lohan or Justin Bieber) – how they *live*, what they *do* – is core to establishing the credibility and believability of accounts. Although Garfinkel did not acknowledge the gender and other power inequalities that comprise any social reality, nor indeed how social realities might be contested, he did recognize that gender – like everything else in society – is something that has to be accomplished. It is common for sociologists today to talk about "doing gender" – largely due to an influential essay by Candace West and Don Zimmerman (1987). Their ethnomethodological approach to disentangling sex and gender highlights that gender is something that emerges and gets accomplished in and through everyday social life. Their analysis builds on and considerably extends an insight first elaborated by Garfinkel (1967).

Garfinkel wrote about "Agnes," a person he interviewed and whom he said "was born a boy with normal-appearing male genitals" but who developed "secondary feminine sex characteristics" at puberty, and subsequently had a transsexual surgical operation that made her physically a woman, which Agnes felt was her "natural, normal" self (Garfinkel 1967: 120–121; 119). Garfinkel's account of Agnes and her medical history, and his interpretations of that history are controversial among sociologists (e.g., Denzin 1990, 1991; Hilbert 1991). In part, this is because after completing his study Garfinkel learned that Agnes had lied in her interviews and that in fact, "she was not a biologically defective male" (Garfinkel 1967: 285). Notwithstanding this important revision to Garfinkel's account (ironic, given his concern with account credibility), from the point of view of pushing theoretical understanding of the relation between (biological) sex and (social) gender, his discussion of Agnes is still theoretically useful. His elaboration of Agnes's "abiding practical preoccupation with competent female sexuality" (1967: 121) and efforts to accomplish that reality, to "act in accordance with expected attitudes, appearances, affiliations, dress, style of life, etc." (1967: 119), underscores that what is considered appropriate sex/gender behavior is not natural but socially learned (notwithstanding biological influences). Agnes knew what was expected of women though she also knew that her (biologically male) biographical history and experiences were at odds with what "normally" accompanies being a woman, despite her "convincingly female" appearance (1967: 119). Therefore, she had to pass as a woman; she had, in Goffman's terms (see chapter 8), to perform the expected female roles. And she had to accomplish this knowing that she had access to vitally relevant information about her own experiences that others with whom she was interacting did not have. Moreover, had they had such information, Agnes was aware that it would have led them to seriously question her ("natural") competence as a woman.

For symbolic interactionists (Goffman; chapter 8), Agnes would need to ensure the presentation of an effective gender-role performance that would not be disrupted by an impression-management lapse revealing her (secret) stigma. For Garfinkel, however, an ethnomethodologist, **background knowledge** is not something to be managed or suppressed (in order for the individual to pass as normal). It inheres, rather, in the experiences individuals draw on as they anticipate and demonstrate the credibility of their gendered (and other accomplished) realities. Thus, Garfinkel argues, showing competence as a "natural" female against any anticipated claims that interested parties might make about one's gender competence is not a strategic game (or dramaturgical performance; see Goffman, chapter 8) that one engages in episodically (in performing the role of woman to particular audiences). Rather, it is an ongoing process that has to be continuously accomplished. The "ongoing-ness" of action with which ethnomethodologists are concerned leads Garfinkel to note: "it would be incorrect to say of Agnes that she has passed. The active mode is needed: she is passing" (1967: 167). She is, in short, actively engaged in accomplishing the ongoing social reality of being a "natural" woman. McCloskey's (1999) personal narrative of her journey from being Donald (a 52-year-old man) to being Deirdre (a 55-year-old woman) discusses the routines and role expectations she follows in accomplishing a credible female identity. Her account reflects the perceived need to accentuate (traditional) feminine appearance and actions, something also apparent in Caitlyn Jenner's cover and feature-story photos in *Vanity Fair* (June 2015). The everyday tasks involved in accomplishing gender are also underscored in the accounts of the increasing numbers of individuals today, including young teenagers, who are transitioning from male to female or female to male (see Talbot 2013).

In sum, for ethnomethodologists, social life, society, is not composed of scripted roles (as in symbolic interaction), nor of pregiven social facts (see Durkheim, chapter 2). It is, rather, an ongoing social accomplishment, achieved by accountable (and account-making) individuals actively producing behavioral claims and outcomes that are recognizable, credible, and rationally defensible in terms of established cultural and societal expectations.

RESEARCHING THE DOING OF REALITY-MAKING

Ethnomethodologists draw on a variety of research methods to show the experience-categorization methods individuals use in order-making and accomplishing (like jurors and coroners) particular accounts of reality. The research methods include in-depth interviews, participant and nonparticipant observation (including videotaped observation), and especially "the documentary method of interpretation" (Garfinkel 1967: 78), first outlined by the German theorist Karl Mannheim. Mannheim (1936/1968: 78–81, 184–191, 198–202) stressed that knowledge of, and from, a particular reality is always determined by the concrete sociohistorical context in which that reality is known or experienced. Sociologists who use documentary or historical research methods thus identify the particular patterns of social structure and social order that emerge through their analysis of official reports, institutional records, newspapers, personal letters and diaries, etc. Garfinkel (1967: 40) argues that this is the same method that all individuals basically use "in the conduct of everyday affairs": We impose an accountable order on those occurrences.

BREACHING EXPERIMENTS

Ethnomethodologists' interest in "the routine grounds of everyday activities" (Garfinkel 1967: 35–75) leads them to conduct **breaching experiments** designed to disrupt the routines that comprise particular social realities so as to demonstrate the fragility that underlies everyday social order. These experiments "modify the *objective* structure of the familiar, known-in-common environment by rendering the background expectancies inoperative. Specifically, this modification would consist of subjecting a person to a breach of the background expectancies of everyday life" (1967: 54).

For example, student research assistants are asked to act as strangers or as polite visitors in their own homes (Garfinkel 1967: 44–49), or to have conversations with friends who keep questioning or asking for clarification of mundane and (apparently) self-evident statements – e.g. "What do you mean you had a flat tire?" "What do you mean your boyfriend is feeling fine?" (1967: 42–44). These experiments, the nature and purpose of which are not disclosed to family members or friends, are designed to make familiar details, objects, and scenes unfamiliar and strange. The consequences of these inversions of role behavior (e.g., from daughter to visitor) and of conversational pickiness are far greater than one might expect. They generally cause much bewilderment (1967: 47, 53–65), a point used by Garfinkel to underscore how much work goes into the creation and maintenance of everyday reality, and to highlight "the role that a background of common understandings plays in the production, control and recognition" of reality (1967: 49).

Although effective in accomplishing their goal, it may be hard for breaching experiments to meet the disclosure requirement of university committees on research on human subjects (institutional review boards) that individuals be made aware of and freely consent to the research in which they are participating. It is also uncertain whether the benefits of the research outweigh the possible stress that the experiments can cause (e.g., bewilderment to unsuspecting family members or friends).

CONVERSATION ANALYSIS

Less controversially, ethnomethodologists also engage in **conversation analysis** aimed at detailing the specific, pragmatic steps that establish meaning, i.e., order, in everyday interaction. This method has become popular in fields beyond sociology including linguistics, anthropology, and cognitive science (see Heritage 2009). The classical conversation analysis approach as outlined by Garfinkel and Sacks (1986) is to document how speaking individuals are able to master the natural language and understand one another in conversation so that they appear to each other to be "talking reasonably," as "speaking English (or [Spanish or] French, or whatever)" and using "clear, consistent, cogent speech, i.e., rational speech" (Garfinkel and Sacks 1986: 165). This research shows that individuals are able to have efficient conversations because of **glossing practices**. "Glossing practices exist in empirical multitude. In endless, but particular, analyzable ways, glossing practices are methods for producing observable and reportable understanding, with, in, and of natural language" (1986: 164–165).

When we are interacting with our friends we generally use fewer words than would be grammatically required to say what we need to say in order to be understood. Typically, because there is an already established context for our relationship, we talk in shorthand – we gloss over a lot of specifics – and yet we expect the other person to know what we mean; and indeed the friend with whom we are communicating usually does know what we mean. Thus, "*Whatever*" is said "provides the very materials to be used in *making out*" what is said (Garfinkel and Sacks 1986: 165). The way we gloss over many of the necessary-to-be-known background assumptions and details allows us to order our reality claims to our friend in ways that enhance their quick comprehension of how, for all practical purposes, things really happened.

The comprehension of claims is more complicated than is fully acknowledged by Garfinkel. Because social interaction is *social*, conversational practices, including interruptions, turn-taking, hesitations, pauses, and silences, as well as how language is used, are not independent of social class, gender, sexuality, racial, ethnic, and other differences. These differences matter in translating words and glossing practices across the particular contexts in which individuals must necessarily interact with others (e.g., schools, playgrounds, doctors' offices, corporate offices, parliament). Women and men, for example, use different conversation tactics and strategies, and this in turn leads to and exacerbates female–male miscommunication (e.g., West and Zimmerman 1983).

Micro–macro linkage

These differences are not simply conversation differences, but differences that reproduce gender inequality and inequalities embodied in the intersectionality of gender, race, and class (e.g., DeVault 1991; Fenstermaker and West 2002); see Box 9.1. These differences, moreover, tend to get glossed over in ordinary, everyday conversation as well as in the (male-dominated) halls of power. Therefore, although ethnomethodology maintains a core micro-focus, its insights can be applied beyond the specific micro-contexts in which accounts and conversations are accomplished (e.g., Hilbert 1990).

SUMMARY

Phenomenology focuses on everyday reality and how individuals recognize and organize their everyday experiences. It is a tradition indebted to the writings of Alfred Schutz and elaborated by Berger and Luckmann (1966), who emphasize the social construction of reality and the dynamic dialectical inter-relation between subjective experiences and objective institutional structures. A second strand focusing on everyday reality is ethnomethodology, elaborated by Harold Garfinkel. It is concerned with the socioculturally determined, categorizing methods societal members use to recognize, account for, and accomplish the everyday institutional and social routines that accomplish social order.

Box 9.1   Pardon the interruption: Conversation differences between women and men

- Women use more indirect and euphemistic forms of speech than men (e.g., Tannen 2012).
- Women are more likely to be interrupted than men.
- Men are more likely than women to interrupt.
- Women who interrupt others are viewed more negatively than men who interrupt others.
- Women job candidates (in academic engineering departments) are interrupted more frequently than male candidates (Blair-Loy et al. 2017).
- Male physicians are more likely than female physicians to interrupt their patients.
- Patients in conversation with female doctors interrupt as much as, or more than, their physicians.
- White male physicians are more likely to interrupt white female than male patients.
- White male physicians are even more likely to interrupt black male and female patients (West 1984: 56–58).

"Woman interrupted," a smartphone app (released in March 2017, coinciding with International Women's Day), uses your phone's microphone to analyze your conversations and track how many times women are interrupted by men in a given conversation (it does not track how much interrupting women do of men).

POINTS TO REMEMBER

Phenomenology
- Focuses on the world of everyday life and everyday experiences
- The world of everyday life is a subjectively experienced, and an intersubjectively shared, social world
- The pragmatic demands of our "here-and-now" reality require our full, wide-awake attention
- Though we live in a shared social environment, individuals' unique socio-biographical situations shape what is relevant for them in the here-and-now
- Common-sense knowledge derived from individuals' shared stock of social experience is the knowledge that anchors and orients everyday social reality
- Social reality is the product of human design
- Because humans have created society and its social institutions, culture, etc., humans can change what they have created; that is, social and institutional change is always a possibility
- Symbolic universes integrate individuals into a meaningful, collectively shared social reality that help them to make sense of their experienced reality

Ethnomethodology
- Is a strand of sociological inquiry influenced by Schutz's emphasis on everyday experience and elaborated by Harold Garfinkel who focused on the organization and ordering of experience
- Individuals accomplish social reality in everyday life by categorizing experiences and producing accounts of those experiences so as to produce an ordered social reality that fits with assumptions of how things really happen in a given social and institutional setting
- The accounts produced must be culturally credible such that they provide a defensible and reasonable account of how social life/society works to produce certain outcomes
- For ethnomethodologists, gender, for example, is not a societal process or a social role performance but an ongoing, active, practical accomplishment
- The practical accomplishment of any ordered reality is contingent on the background of common understandings that determines the production, control, and recognition of reality
- The content and structure of everyday conversation play a key role in making accounts and their outcomes and consequences intelligible and credible

GLOSSARY: PHENOMENOLOGY

common-sense knowledge knowledge derived from individuals' everyday practices; what seems "natural" or obvious in their social environment.

externalization an aspect of the dynamic process by which individuals maintain social reality, whereby they act on and in regard to the already existing (human-created and externalized) objective reality (e.g., institutions, everyday practices in society).

here-and-now reality immediate pragmatic salience of individuals' everyday reality.

in-group particular community (or group/society) in which we are immersed, whose habits we have inherited, and with which we are "at home."

internalization an aspect of the dynamic process by which individuals create social reality such that, in experiencing an external, objective reality (e.g., institutional practices, social inequality), they translate (internalize) it into their own particular, subjectively experienced reality.

lifeworld from the German word *Lebenswelt*; the world of everyday life and its taken-for-granted routines, customs, habits, and knowledge.

natural attitude the individual's orientation toward his or her social environment, a reality that seems natural because it is the everyday reality that he or she knows.

objective reality the social reality, including objectively existing social institutions (economic, legal, etc.), language, and social processes (e.g., gender/race inequalities), into which individuals are socialized.

out-group everyday reality of those who have different everyday habits to us and that to us seem "strange."

phenomenology focuses on the reality of everyday life and how individuals make sense of their everyday experiences.

plausibility structure group and institutional settings (e.g., churches) and laws that affirm (make plausible) the objective reality of individuals' subjectively experienced realities.

practical knowledge knowledge needed to accomplish routine everyday tasks in the individual's environment.

recipe knowledge particular ways of doing things in a particular social environment.

reification when we see or treat human/socially created things (e.g., institutions, laws, customs) as if they are things set in stone and that cannot be changed.

scheme of reference stock of accumulated knowledge and experiences we use to interpret and make sense of new experiences.

social construction of reality social reality as the product of humans acting intersubjectively and collectively. Social reality exists as an objective (human-social) reality that individuals subjectively experience, to which they respond and, acting collectively, can change.

stock of preconstituted knowledge cumulative body of everyday knowledge and experiences that individuals have from living in a particular social environment.

subjective reality the individual's subjective experience and interpretation of the external, objective reality.

subuniverses of meaning collectivities that share and objectify (or institutionalize) individuals' similarly meaningful experiences and interpretations of reality.

symbolic universes overarching meaning systems (e.g., religion, science) that integrate and order individuals' everyday realities.

typifications customary (typical) ways in which an individual's intersubjective social environment is organized; how things, individuals (e.g., as role/status types), and institutions are presumed to work/behave.

wide-awakeness the practical consciousness and attentiveness required in attending to the "here-and-now" tasks and realities of everyday life.

GLOSSARY: ETHNOMETHODOLOGY

accomplishment of social reality the idea that social reality does not have a pregiven objective order but needs to be achieved on an ongoing basis by societal members.

accounts how individuals categorize events, experiences, and everyday reality such that their accounts produce an ordered, sequential reality that makes sense and is credible in a given societal context.

background knowledge an individual's stock of previous experiences and knowledge of reality; affects how they categorize and evaluate current experiences.

breaching experiments designed to disrupt a particular micro-social reality in order to illustrate the fragility that underlies the order and routines of everyday reality.

conversation analysis detailed analysis of the specific, pragmatic steps in how language and speech are used in everyday conversation to create order.

ethnomethodology shared methods societal members use to make sense of everyday experiences across different settings.

glossing practices shorthand ways in which language and speech utterances are used to communicate in particular social contexts.

members individuals, that is, societal members; they accomplish social reality.

QUESTIONS FOR REVIEW

1 Why does a phenomenological approach to social life mark a major shift in emphasis in sociological theory?

2 What does it mean to say that individuals' "here-and-now" reality is an ongoing production?

3   Explain the relevance of social institutions in Berger and Luckmann's analysis. Can we subjectively experience an everyday reality that is devoid of institutional constraints?

4   Is social change possible? How is it accomplished? What "here-and-now" realities might facilitate and/or impede change? Discuss, using a local empirical example to support your arguments.

5   What does an ethnomethodological perspective illuminate about social reality, social processes (e.g., inequality), social roles, and the maintenance of social order?

REFERENCES

Berger, Peter, 1967. *The Sacred Canopy: Elements of a Sociological Theory of Religion.* Garden City, NY: Doubleday.

Berger, Peter, and Thomas Luckmann. 1966. *The Social Construction of Reality: A Treatise in the Sociology of Knowledge.* New York: Anchor Books. 1967 edition.

Black, Donald. 1976. *The Behavior of Law.* New York: Academic Press.

Black, Donald. 2011. *Moral Time.* New York: Oxford University Press.

Blair-Loy, Mary, Laura E. Rogers, Daniela Glaser, Y. L. Anne Wong, Danielle Abraham, and Pamela C. Cosman. 2017. "Gender in Engineering Departments: Are There Gender Differences in Interruptions of Academic Job Talks." *Social Sciences* 6: 1–19.

Collins, Lauren. 2017. "Identity Crisis." *New Yorker* (August 7 & 14), pp. 24–28.

Collins, Patricia Hill. 1990. *Black Feminist Thought: Knowledge, Consciousness, and the Politics of Empowerment.* New York: Routledge. 2nd edition 2000.

Denzin, Norman. 1990. "Harold and Agnes: A Feminist Narrative Unfolding." *Sociological Theory* 9: 198–216.

Denzin, Norman. 1991. "Back to Harold and Agnes." *Sociological Theory* 9: 280–285.

DeVault, Marjorie. 1991. *Feeding the Family: The Social Construction of Caring as Gendered Work.* Chicago: University of Chicago Press.

Dillon, Michele. 1999. *Catholic Identity: Balancing Reason, Faith, and Power.* New York: Cambridge University Press.

Fanon, Frantz. 1967. *Black Skin, White Masks.* Translated by Charles Lam Markmann. New York: Grove Press.

Fenstermaker, Sarah, and Candace West, eds. 2002. *Doing Gender, Doing Difference: Inequality, Power, and Institutional Change.* New York: Routledge.

Garfinkel, Harold. 1967. *Studies in Ethnomethodology.* Englewood Cliffs, NJ: Prentice Hall.

Garfinkel, Harold, and Harvey Sacks. 1986. "On Formal Structures of Practical Actions." Pp. 160–192 in Harold Garfinkel, ed. *Ethnomethodological Studies of Work.* London: Routledge and Kegan Paul.

Gilroy, Paul. 1987. *"There Ain't No Black in the Union Jack": The Cultural Politics of Race and Nation.* London: Hutchinson.

Heritage, John. 2009. "Conversation Analysis as Social Theory." Pp. 300–320 in Bryan Turner, ed. *The New Blackwell Companion to Social Theory.* Oxford: Blackwell.

Hilbert, Richard. 1990. "Ethnomethodology and the Micro-Macro Order." *American Sociological Review* 6: 794–808.

Hilbert, Richard. 1991. "Norman and Sigmund: Comment on Denzin's Harold and Agnes." *Sociological Theory* 9: 264–268.

Kaufman, Leslie. 2008. "After War, Love Can Be a Battlefield." *New York Times* (April 6): Styles pp. 1, 10.

Luckmann, Thomas. 1978. "Preface." Pp. 7–13 in Thomas Luckmann, ed. *Phenomenology and Sociology.* New York: Penguin.

Mannheim, Karl. 1936/1968. *Ideology and Utopia: An Introduction to the Sociology of Knowledge.* New York: Harcourt, Brace, and World.

McCloskey, Deirdre. 1999. *Crossing: A Memoir.* Chicago: University of Chicago Press.

Osborn, Torie. 2008. "The Joy of Marriage Was Ours, for a While." *New York Times* (April 20): Styles p. 6.

Rawls, Anne. 2000. "Harold Garfinkel." Pp. 545–576 in George Ritzer, ed., *The Blackwell Companion to Major Social Theorists.* Oxford: Blackwell.

Said, Edward. 1978. *Orientalism.* New York: Random House.

Schutz, Alfred. 1962. *Collected Papers.* Edited and with an introduction by Maurice Natanson. The Hague: M. Nijhoff.

Schutz, Alfred. 1970. *On Phenomenology and Social Relations: Selected Writings.* Edited and with an introduction by Helmut Wagner. Chicago: University of Chicago Press.

Seidman, Steven. 1997. *Difference Troubles: Queering Social Theory and Sexual Politics.* New York: Cambridge University Press.

Simmel, Georg. 1908/1950. *The Sociology of Georg Simmel.* Translated, edited, and with an introduction by Kurt Wolff. Glencoe, IL: Free Press.

Smith, Dorothy. 1987. *The Everyday World as Problematic: A Feminist Sociology*. Boston: Northeastern University Press.

Talbot, Margaret. 2013. "About a Boy: Transgender Surgery at Sixteen." *New Yorker* (March 18), pp. 56–65.

Tannen, Deborah. 2012. "Would You Please Let me Finish …" *New York Times* (October 18), p. A27.

Turkewitz, Julie, and Juliet Linderman. 2012. "Transgender Latinas Find a Refuge." *New York Times* (December 3), p. A21.

West, Candace. 1984. *Routine Complications: Trouble with Talk between Doctors and Patients*. Bloomington: Indiana University Press.

West, Candace, and Don Zimmerman. 1983. "Small Insults: A Study of Interruptions in Conversations between Unacquainted Persons." Pp. 102–117 in Barrie Thorne, C. Kramarae, and N. Nelney, eds. *Language, Gender and Society*. Rowley, MA: Newbury House.

West, Candace, and Don Zimmerman. 1987. "Doing Gender." *Gender and Society* 2: 125–151.

CHAPTER TEN

FEMINIST THEORIES

Introduction to Sociological Theory: Theorists, Concepts, and Their Applicability to the Twenty-First Century,
Third Edition. Michele Dillon.
© 2020 John Wiley & Sons Ltd. Published 2020 by John Wiley & Sons Ltd.
Companion website: www.wiley.com/go/dillon

Timeline 10.1	Major events in the achievement of women's equality (1865–present)
1865	Women admitted to Cornell University (US) at its inception; the only Ivy League university open to women
1869	National Women's Suffrage Association (in US) founded by Susan B. Anthony and Elizabeth Cady Stanton
1893	New Zealand first currently existing country to grant women voting rights
1901	Mixed bathing permitted on British beaches
1903	Formation of Women's Social and Political Union in Britain by Emmeline Pankhurst, demanding votes for women
1903	Marie Curie awarded Nobel Prize in Physics for the discovery of radioactivity
1910	Increased public use of "feminism" as a term to summarize women's demands for equality
1918	Women over age 30 allowed to vote in Ireland and Britain; and over 18 in Canada
1920	American women receive right to vote

1926	Gertrude Ederle becomes the first woman to swim across the English Channel; she beat the record by two hours and her father rewarded her with a red sports car
1944	Women receive right to vote in France (one of last Western countries to grant this right)
1949	Women receive right to vote in China
1950	Women admitted to Harvard Law School
1952	Dorothy Swaine Thomas elected first woman president of the American Sociological Association
1963	Valentina Tereshkova, cosmonaut from the Soviet Union, first woman in space
1966	Bobbe Gibb first woman to complete the Boston marathon (but without an official number)
1969	Yale and Princeton universities admit women students
1972	Title IX US federal regulations prohibiting sex discrimination in education and sports programs
1978	Six women chosen by NASA (US space agency) as astronaut candidates
1979	Margaret Thatcher elected first woman prime minister of UK
1979	Simone Veil, a French woman who as teenager was sent to Auschwitz by the Nazis, becomes the first directly elected president of the European Parliament; she died in 2017
1981	Sandra Day O'Connor first woman confirmed to US Supreme Court
1983	Columbia University admits women students
1983	Sally Ride first American woman astronaut in space
1984	Women allowed for the first time to run a marathon (at the Los Angeles Olympics)
1986	*Oprah Winfrey Show*, produced and presented by Oprah Winfrey, goes into national syndication; currently broadcast in 134 countries
1990	Mary Robinson elected first woman president of Ireland
1992	The General Synod of the Church of England votes to allow women priests
1993	Ruth Bader Ginsburg second woman confirmed to US Supreme Court
1993	Judith Rodin becomes first woman president of an Ivy League university, University of Pennsylvania
1994	Women of all races in South Africa granted voting rights
1997–2001	Madeleine Albright first woman US secretary of state
2000	Vashti McKenzie first woman bishop of African Methodist Episcopal Church
2003	Eileen Collins first woman US space shuttle commander
2005	US Census data; majority of women (51 percent) living without a spouse
2005	16 percent of corporate officers at Fortune 500 companies are women; less than 2 percent are CEOs
2006	Katie Couric first woman to anchor US television evening newscast (CBS)
2006	Katharine Jefferts Schori first woman presiding bishop of Episcopal Church in US
April 2008	Danica Patrick, an American, first woman to win Indy Japan 300 race (in Motegi, Japan)

June 2008	Hillary Rodham Clinton comes close to becoming first woman nominee for president of US (defeated by Barack Obama)
June 2008	Lt. Gen. Ann Dunwoody first woman in US military chosen for promotion to four-star general
2009	Hillary Rodham Clinton appointed US Secretary of State
2009	Sonia Sotomayor, the first Hispanic and the third woman appointed to the US Supreme Court
2009	Angela Merkel becomes chancellor of Germany
2010	Julia Gillard becomes prime minister of Australia, first woman to hold that office and also the first woman to be elected leader of Australia's Labour Party
2011	Women in Saudi Arabia are granted the right to vote (but are not free to drive)
2011	Christine Lagarde, a lawyer and former minister of finance and of commerce in France, becomes the eleventh managing director of the International Monetary Fund (IMF)
2012	Saudi Arabia, Qatar, and Brunei allow women for the first time to compete in the Olympics at London; for the first time, the US Olympics team fielded more women than men
2012	Park Geun-hye becomes the first woman elected president of South Korea
August 2013	Serena Williams wins the US Open Tennis Championship, her seventeenth grand slam title
July 2014	The General Synod of the Church of England votes to allow women bishops
December 2015	Women in Saudi Arabia allowed to vote and to run for office for the first time in the Kingdom's 83-year existence.
July 2016	Hillary Clinton, a Democrat, becomes the first woman nominated as a candidate in the US presidential election
July 2016	Theresa May is elected leader of the Conservative Party in the UK, and assumes the role of prime minister
June 2017	"Wonder Woman" movie released, directed by Patty Jenkins and based on the comic superhero
July 2017	Marion Diamond (born in 1926) dies; a professor at the University of California, Berkeley, her pioneering experimental studies of the anatomy of the brain led her to conclude: "Use it or lose it."
July 2017	Jane Austen's image is incorporated in the new British 10 pound sterling note (2017 is the bicentenary of her death)
July 2017	For the first time in Saudi Arabia, girls are allowed to take physical education (PE) classes
September 2017	Angela Merkel is elected to a fourth term as chancellor of Germany
September 2017	Women in Saudi Arabia are allowed to drive a car and to do so unaccompanied by a man
2018	Women and men soccer players in Norway receive equal pay
January 2019	Sarah Thomas, first woman to umpire a US professional football game (between Patriots and Chargers)

CONSCIOUSNESS OF WOMEN'S INEQUALITY: CHARLOTTE PERKINS GILMAN

In 1985, two prominent feminist sociologists, Judith Stacey and Barrie Thorne, diagnosed the "missing **feminist revolution** in sociology." They argued that sociology was resistant to the theoretical challenges presented by feminism and to rethinking sociological understanding of the permeation of gender inequality in all societal processes. Today, many feminist sociologists voice frustration that gender is still marginalized. Despite the noteworthy increase in empirical studies of gender, there is a lingering sense that feminist theory is not really considered a core part of sociological theory (e.g., Ray 2006), but an add-on, something mentioned among other "alternative" ideas. At the same time, women have achieved significant visibility in society and in sociology. Patricia Hill Collins, one of sociology's leading feminist theorists, was elected president of the American Sociological Association for 2009, joining Parsons, Merton, Goffman, and other influential theorists. Nonetheless, women confront many obstacles in sociology as in society as a whole, in fields as varied as corporate finance, science, architecture, and music.

Feminist theory is composed of several different strands and feminist sociologists research a great variety of topics. At the core of feminist theory, the focus is on women's inequality and how that inequality is structured and experienced at macro and micro levels. As early as the 1830s, feminist sociologists such as Harriet Martineau (see Introduction) were highlighting the contradictions between political ideals of equality and social structures and practices that impede women's ability to participate in the political, educational, occupational, and economic opportunities available to men. The women's movement in the US came to prominence in the late nineteenth century around an agenda focused on establishing voting rights (suffrage) and equal economic opportunities for women. The "most influential mentor" in this effort (Cott 1987: 40–41), was feminist sociologist **Charlotte Perkins Gilman** (1860–1935).

BIOGRAPHICAL NOTE

Charlotte Perkins Gilman was born in 1860 into a well-established Boston family, but her childhood was economically strained as a result of her father deserting the family. She studied at the Rhode Island School of Design and married Charles Stetson, a painter, at age 24. Soon thereafter, she suffered a nervous breakdown, and the couple divorced in 1890. Charlotte subsequently lived and raised her daughter in California, getting married in 1900 to George Houghton Gilman, with whom she seemed happy. By then, despite her fragile mental health and the challenges of being a single mother, she was already a renowned and prolific book-writer and lecturer on women's issues in both the US and Europe. Diagnosed with breast cancer in 1932, she took her own life three years later (O'Neill 1972: vii–xi). Gilman's classic short story, "The Yellow Wallpaper" (1892), based upon her own experiences of mental illness, has become an iconic feminist text.

Gilman (1911) underscored that women and men live in a "man-made world." This is an "**androcentric culture**" in which only one sex – man – is "accepted as the race type," as human, and women are considered a "subspecies." Thus men have "monopolized all human activities, called them man's work, and managed them as such" (1911: 18, 25). In this man-made world, women are restricted to a separate sex-specific sphere, the home:

> To the man, the whole world was his world; his because he was male; and the whole world of women was the home; because she was female. She had her prescribed sphere, strictly limited to her feminine occupations and interests; he had all the rest of life; and not only so, but, having it, insisted on calling it male. (Gilman 1911: 23)

Gilman argued that the exclusion of women from the world of work and the industrial economy was an "abnormal restriction" (Gilman 1911: 38); it contravened the human desire to work and essentially reduced women to the inferior status of "domestic servant" (1911: 39). In Gilman's view, the right to work is core to *human* existence; it is neither male nor female: "Labor is not merely a means of supporting human life – it is human life" (1911: 231). In androcentric society, "Economic Woman" does not exist; hence for women, life is denied.

True progress could be achieved, she argued, only when society transcends its abnormal androcentric divisions and allows women to be both workers and mothers. Ironically, in light of the feminist tendency today to reject natural biological reasons as explanations for the social differences between women and men, Gilman believed that both motherhood and economic labor were *natural* feminine-maternal instincts (Gilman 1911: 233). She stated: "As a matter of fact industry is in its origin feminine; that is maternal. It is the overflowing fountain of mother-love and mother-power which first prompts the human race to labor" (1911: 233). She further maintained that when women are free to work, and thus able to realize their humanity, they will also become more, not less, efficient as mothers – not mothers androcentrically defined as personal servants in the home, but mothers of the next generation of the human race, "motherhood [being] the highest process" in the evolution of humanity (1911: 245), "the noblest and most valuable profession" (Gilman 1903/1972: 122). Bolstering her view that women could (and should) mother *and* work for pay, she envisioned the occupational professionalization of home cooking and home cleaning through the employment of those who are scientifically trained and best able to do such work (1903/1972: 138).

Hence, for Gilman, women's equality rests on the socially institutionalized freedom to act on what she regarded as women's natural feminine instincts: to mother and to work. This state of affairs is attainable, she argued, only if society ruptures the interwoven "concepts of maleness and humanness," that is, the idea that whereas "men are people," women are "only females" and hence not deserving of human equality (Gilman 1911: 237). Thus, it is only "when we learn to differentiate between humanity and masculinity [that] we shall give honor where honor is due" (1911: 6).

The validation of men's ideas and experiences as *the objective* and *legitimate* human experience continues to permeate gender structures and social relations and consequently is a prominent theme among contemporary feminist sociologists. Feminist theory resurged as part of the transformation in the public consciousness of social inequality that came to the fore in many Western countries in the 1960s and 1970s as a result of that era's social and political protest movements. In particular, the women's movement challenged the established view that biological differences between men and women naturally legitimated social role and status inequality. Spurred by the increased political awareness of gender inequality, women sociologists turned their gaze to the discipline of sociology itself. The patterns they saw reflected trends in the larger society. Notably, despite the important writings of Gilman and of Harriet Martineau (see Introduction), the canon was all male, with an exclusive emphasis on the "founding fathers" – Marx, Durkheim, and Weber – and they and their successors (e.g., Parsons, Dahrendorf, Berger, Goffman) comprised a male-centered curriculum bolstered by the dominance of male sociology professors and graduate students. Thus feminist sociologists were prompted to ask, "Where are the women?" (Wallace 1989:7-8). And they focused their efforts, as Jessie Bernard (1998: 6) phrased it, on "what women (and sympathetic men) can do for sociology" – and for society at large – to redress the androcentric biases (see also Laslett and Thorne 1997; Myers et al. 1998). These questions remain at the fore of feminist theorizing and research in sociology.

STANDPOINT THEORY: DOROTHY SMITH AND THE RELATIONS OF RULING

RULING TEXTS IN A PATRIARCHAL SOCIETY

Dorothy Smith elaborates how the practices of sociology crystallize the larger structural and everyday dilemmas of gender in a **patriarchal society**. She argues that what counts for authoritative knowledge in sociology and in society is determined by standards that privilege men and exclude women. It is not that men are intent on sabotaging women, but the structures and expectations institutionalized in society are the historical creation of men. Men, not women, wrote the texts – they literally wrote the rules – that have come to define society and how we think about things.

BIOGRAPHICAL NOTE

Dorothy Smith was born into a middle-class family in Yorkshire, England, in 1926. Thinking that a college degree might land her a good job as a secretary, she applied and was admitted to the prestigious London School of Economics (LSE), where she majored in sociology and social anthropology. She met her husband, William Smith, while at the LSE and together they left England for graduate study at the University of California, Berkeley. Her two children were born while she was completing her doctoral dissertation in sociology, and soon thereafter, she and Bill divorced, leaving her to deal with the challenges of single motherhood

and earning a living. After Berkeley, Smith and her sons returned to England for a few years; she then accepted a faculty position at the University of British Columbia, Vancouver, Canada, where she was influential in establishing the legitimacy of women's studies. In 1997, she accepted a faculty position at the Ontario Institute for Studies in Education. Currently retired, Smith has received several awards in recognition of her trailblazing impact on feminist sociology, including the American Sociological Association's award for a Career of Distinguished Scholarship, and its Jessie Bernard Award for feminist scholarship.

We can readily list some of the **ruling texts** in Western society. The Bible is one. It is a text written by men, for example, the New Testament gospels of Matthew, Mark, Luke, and John and the epistles of Paul. And it is men who through history have been the Bible's primary interpreters. In the Catholic Church, only men can be popes, cardinals, bishops, and priests; the Protestant Reformers were all men (e.g., Martin Luther, John Calvin); and still today in Western society the leaders of the various religious denominations are men (with a couple of notable exceptions; see Timeline 10.1). In the US, another core text is the Declaration of Independence, written by a group of men. So too is the US Constitution, written and signed by George Washington and 38 state representatives, all of whom were men. The many significant Supreme Court cases that define Americans' legal rights have also been written by men, that is, the justices on the Supreme Court, until Sandra Day O'Connor became its first woman member in 1981 (see Timeline 10.1).

Texts have a highly significant role in organizing a society's **ruling practices**. They define who can do what, how it should be done, and how it should be evaluated. And these practices, in turn, determine the kinds of texts and ideas that are produced and validated. Texts are thus the centerpiece of what Smith calls the **relations of ruling**. She explains:

> When I speak here of governing or ruling I mean something more general than the notion of government as political organization. I refer rather to that total complex of activities, differentiated into many spheres, by which our kind of society is ruled, managed, and administered. It includes what the business world calls *management*, it includes the professions, it includes government and the activities of those who are selecting, training, and indoctrinating those who will be its governors. [It] includes those who provide and elaborate the procedures by which it is governed and develop methods for how it is to be done – namely, the business schools, the sociologists, the economists. These are the institutions through which we are ruled and through which we, and I emphasize this *we*, participate in ruling. (Smith 1990a: 14)

The ruling texts are not confined to formal or printed texts (e.g., the Bible, laws, etc.), but are far more encompassing. They include the many visual images in society – found in stores, on television, and in advertising, for example. Ruling texts also include the various discourses that circulate and not only reflect but organize and remind us of the very practices and social relations that govern our **everyday/everynight worlds** (Smith 1990b: 164). As Smith emphasizes, the texts that govern being a woman do not end, as they do for many men, at 5 p.m. (when the regular workday ends), nor do they end when the kids are settled in bed. The texts operate 24/7 for women.

ADVERTISING FEMININITY

Among these ideologically powerful texts are all those (often contradictory) texts that compose a distinctive **discourse of femininity**. The ruling texts of **femininity** structure, and are situated in, the gender relations in society – relations organized around women as objects.

> Texts enter into and order courses of action and relations among individuals ... Texts ... must not be isolated from the practices in which they are embedded and which they organize ... In our time to address femininity is to address, directly or indirectly, a textual discourse vested in women's magazines and television, advertisements, the appearance of cosmetics counters, fashion displays and to a lesser extent books ... Discourse also involves the talk women do in relation to such texts, the work of producing oneself to realize the textual images, the skills involved in going shopping, in making and choosing clothes, in making decisions about colors, styles, makeup, and the ways in which these

become a matter of interest among men … Ideologies and doctrines of femininity are explicit, publicly spoken and written … [they] generate and interpret the visual images of femininity and interpret its embodied correlate in women's appearances. The doctrines … are reproduced, revised, updated in popular philosophy, theology, and psychology, in magazines, in books, and as schemata governing the morality of soap operas, sit-coms, TV game shows, and so forth. Their interpretive paradigms are commercially produced on television, in movies, in advertising in multiple settings, including packaging, and shop-window and counter displays. (Smith 1990b: 162, 163, 170–171, 174)

THE RULES OF SOCIOLOGY AND THE EXCLUSION OF WOMEN'S STANDPOINT

Sociologists participate in the relations of ruling as teachers, researchers, writers, advisers, media commentators, etc. Smith argues that sociology's ruling texts, its conceptual and methodological rules and procedures that organize sociological practice, marginalize women. The ethos of impersonal, scientific objectivity institutionalized in sociology (see Introduction) – the set of scientific procedures that "serve to separate the discipline's body of knowledge from its practitioners" (Smith 1990a: 16) – excludes the everyday/everynight experiences of women and their firsthand knowledge of these experiences (Smith 1990b: 164). This ethos, Smith notes, is itself determined by a conceptual order that demands the exclusion of subjectively embodied, localized and particularized experiences. The preordered concepts, categories, and definitions we use to study society (e.g., bureaucracy, social class, race, family, crime, etc.), and the research methods we use in empirically testing these concepts, are themselves ordered by the relations of ruling, that is, by the (scientific) discipline of sociology itself. Thus as sociologists,

we learn to think sociology as it is thought and to practice it as it is practiced. We learn that some topics are relevant and others are not. We learn to discard our personal experience as a source of reliable information about the character of the world and to confine our focus and insights within the conceptual frameworks and relevances of the discipline. (Smith 1990a: 15)

RULING TEXTS AND THE EXCLUSION OF EVERYDAY EXPERIENCES

Our learned sociological way of thinking, of knowing what is relevant and what isn't, intertwines with other ruling institutions in society. In particular, what sociologists research is contingent on the expectations of the government, industry, and funding organizations that predetermine what topics and issues are worthy of study. And although much of this information has relevance for our lives, Smith argues that it largely excludes the direct experiences of women and other subordinated (e.g., racial or LGBTQ+) groups in society (Smith 1990a: 27). Nevertheless, in its claim to scientific knowledge, sociology presents this knowledge as a universally true, objective account of the world. We do not think of it as being partial, as privileging a particular set of (male) experiences. Rather, we think of it as neutral and not as a "sociology written from the **standpoint** of men located in the relations of ruling our societies" (Smith 1987: 1).

Figure 10.1 Despite advances in women's equality with men, women and men are reminded to see women as objects for men. Starting in 2018, the UK's advertising authority is implementing new restrictions on gender stereotypes in advertisements. On other institutional initiatives to redress gender stereotyping, see Topics 4.3 and 6.2. Source: Author.

> **Box 10.1   Woman as the Other**
>
> The noted French feminist and author Simone de Beauvoir writes: Humanity is male and man defines woman not in herself but as relative to him; she is not regarded as an autonomous being … Man can think of himself without woman. She cannot think of herself without man. And she is simply what man decrees … she appears essentially to the male as a sexual being. For him, she is sex – absolute sex, no less. She is defined and differentiated with reference to man and not he with reference to her; she is the incidental, the inessential as opposed to the essential. He is the subject, he is the Absolute – she is the Other … In men's eyes – and for the legions of women who see through men's eyes – it is not enough to have a woman's body nor to assume the female function as mistress or mother in order to be a "true woman." In sexuality and maternity woman as subject can claim autonomy; but to be a true woman she must accept herself as the Other. The men of today show a certain duplicity which is painfully lacerating to women; they are willing… to accept woman as a fellow being, an equal; but they still require her to remain the inessential. For her these two destinies are incompatible; she hesitates between one and the other without being exactly adapted to either … With man there is no break between public and private life: the more he confirms his grasp on the world in action and in work, the more virile he seems to be; human and vital values are combined in him. Whereas woman's independent successes are in contradiction with her femininity, since the true woman is required to make herself object, to be the Other. (De Beauvoir 1949/1953: 16, 291)

Missing from the sociological and the other texts that comprise our society's objectified knowledge, Smith argues, are the everyday experiences of particular people in particular situated contexts. Sociologists impose the discipline's generalized concepts of objective experience on people's subjective experiences. And we rarely pause to wonder whether in fact there is correspondence between our sociological categories and the categories used by the people, the human subjects, we study. In every sense, these people are governed by our scientific canon, our privileged knowledge, and who, ironically, are stripped of their subjectivity by our privileging of objectivity. Consequently, Smith argues, "Sociological procedures legislate a reality rather than discover one" (1990a: 53).

Rather than setting out to discover and understand how specifically situated people experience everyday reality, we make the reality fit into the (objectified) conceptual order we impose. We suppress individuals' experiences under the objectified concepts we have been trained to use, as if concepts are sufficient to know and understand the gamut of people's everyday experiences. As Smith (1990a: 55) notes, "Living individuals in their actual contexts of action have already been obliterated [by sociological concepts] before their representation reaches the sociologist … Who acts and how [they act] disappears." Thus she (1990a: 24–25) reminds us that although we talk in abstract conceptual terms about various social processes (e.g., stratification, domestic violence, etc.), these processes are not abstracted *from* real people but instead determine and shape the representations sociologists offer of these people in particular social locations (e.g., immigrant women deboning chickens in a poultry factory; see Topic 1.6, chapter 1).

Smith illustrates the divide between the presumed objectivity and objectified knowledge of the sociologist, and our exclusion of the subjective, relational context of those studied:

Riding a train not long ago in Ontario I saw a family of Indians [Native Americans] – woman, man, and three children – standing together on a spur above a river, watching the train go by. I realized that I could tell this incident – the train, those five people seen on the other side of the glass – as it was, but that my description was built on my position and my interpretations. I have called them "Indians" and a family; I have said they were watching the train. My understanding has already subsumed theirs. Everything may have been quite different for them. My description is privileged to stand as what actually happened because theirs is not heard in the contexts in which I may speak. If we begin from the world as we actually experience it, it is at least possible to see that we are indeed located and that what we know of the other is conditional upon that location. There are and must be different experiences of the world and different bases of experience. We must not do away with them by taking advantage of our privileged speaking to construct a sociological version that we then impose upon them as their reality. We may not rewrite the other's world or impose upon it a conceptual framework that extracts from it what fits with ours. Their reality, their varieties of experience, must be an unconditional datum. It is the place from which inquiry begins. (Smith 1990a: 24–25)

KNOWING FROM WITHIN LOCAL EXPERIENCES

The exclusion of the varieties of social experience produces distorted knowledge, one that veils rather than illuminates social processes. There is, for example, a disjuncture between women's *experiences* and the objectified knowledge produced by sociology, notwithstanding its claim to produce knowledge about the world women (and men) live in (Smith 1990a: 27). Smith argues that "The only way of knowing a socially constructed world is knowing it from within. We can never stand outside it" (1990a: 22). **Knowing from within** means that "sociological inquiry is necessarily a social relation" (1990a: 23).

Thus, contrary to the positivist tradition of objectivity (see Comte, in Introduction; Durkheim, chapter 2), sociologists inhabit particular social worlds and the people we study also inhabit particular social worlds; we cannot assume that (as sociologists) we know and understand what is going on in those worlds. We can begin to understand social life only when we begin to see how our social location affects how we see and interpret the experiences of those whose experiences are separate from ours and when we see those people's experiences from within their subjectively embodied location. In short, Smith emphasizes that the standpoint of the researcher and the standpoint of the individuals and groups we seek to know exist in relation to one another. Knowledge emerges from within this relation and cannot be independent of it. Awareness of this relation necessarily tempers the (positivist) view that sociology objectively studies an objectively observable, objective social reality. We cannot talk about social reality as if there is just one reality similarly experienced by all. The existence of different standpoints means we cannot accept as universally true the objectified (male-centered) reality given authority by ruling texts (e.g., sociological studies, news reports, census classifications, medical records, etc.).

WOMEN'S REALITIES

Women's phenomenological reality (see chapter 9), their everyday "here-and-now" experiences, also matter. These are legitimate and discoverable realities. Smith states: "The opening up of women's experience gives sociologists access to social realities previously unavailable, indeed repressed" (Smith 1990a: 12). Women's reality is the **domestic world** – the worlds of household, children, and neighborhood. This domestic world is not just different from men's reality, the **public world**, but, Smith argues, it must defer to men's reality. The male world stands in authority over the domestic world:

The worlds of men have had, and still have, an authority over the worlds that are traditionally women's and still are predominantly women's – the worlds of household, children, and neighborhood. And though women do not inhabit only these worlds, for the vast majority of women they are the primary ground of our lives, shaping the course of our lives and our participation in other relations. Furthermore, objectified knowledges are part of the world from which our kind of society is governed. The domestic world stands in a dependent relation to that other, and its whole character is subordinate to it. (Smith 1990a: 13)

Women experience a reality that not only is different to men's but that they necessarily experience (and have interpreted) through the prism of the images, language, expectations, and laws determined by men and by the overarching (male-constructed) ruling discourse of femininity that structures women's everyday subordination and objectification by men.

Men know that paid work is valued, and women too learn to know that men's work/reality is more valuable than their home-based experiences. When women say "I'm just a housewife," they are not simply being humble about how they spend their time; they are speaking for society. They are speaking the father-tongue that tells men and women that housework and mothering are inferior realities. Yet, at the same time, women know from their embodied experiences in the domestic world that it is different from how men define it to be. Hence there is a disjuncture between what women know and what men tell them they should (objectively) know as the objectified reality. Following a Marxist strand (see chapter 1), Smith argues that women are objectively alienated from their own everyday experiences by the systematic way in which the subordinated domestic world, and their experiences within that world, are deemed irrelevant by the male ruling structure (in politics, industry, academia, medicine, mass media, etc.; see Smith 1990a: 19). In our (patriarchal) society, the "real" world, the dominant and dominating reality, is the public world; that is where the action is, and women's standpoint is marginalized.

Even when, as is increasingly the case, women participate in the public world of academia, law, medicine, corporate management, and politics (see Timeline 10.1), their experiences of that world are necessarily different from men's. The gender divide structured into the separation of the public and the domestic worlds continues to matter such that women's participation in the public world is not structured on their terms but by the terms and conditions laid down by men. We should not be surprised, then, that although women have higher levels of college achievement than men, once employed, they are paid less than male graduates. Women must play by rules and ruling texts, including pay scales and promotion criteria, created by men. And to be successful within this public world, women must suspend their knowledge of their experiences in the domestic world (Smith 1990a: 21). Even though the attitudes of women and men toward family life are increasingly converging, the pressures on women who move within and between family and work spheres remain: At work, women have to behave as if they have no children, that is, they have to be flexibly available for whatever Walmart shift they are assigned on a given day, or show the extensive time commitment required on Wall Street; and at home they have to suppress the body aches and stressors (including harassment) that accompany them from work so as to give their required attention to the double-shift, their work as mothers and wives (e.g., Hochschild and Machung 1990). See Topic 10.1.

Topic 10.1   Gender gaps

Since 2006, the World Economic Forum (WEF) has been tracking gender disparities in access to resources and opportunities in health, education, economy, and politics across 144 countries. It uses reliable databases to measure labor-force participation, wages, and economic opportunity; literacy and access to education; participation in high-level political decision making; and health, nutrition, and life expectancy. The 2016 Global Gender Gap Index shows that although women have almost closed the gap with men in access to education and health, they lag far behind when it comes to economic and political empowerment (see also Topic 6.2, "Women in the economic power elite," chapter 6). The gender gap varies widely across different countries – even in the same geographical region – thus pointing to how, in addition to economic development, a given country's sociopolitical and cultural context affects gender roles and opportunities. The WEF concludes that the slow rate of progress in closing the gender gap (e.g., in wages and in women's significantly greater proportion of unpaid work) is a call to action to policymakers and stakeholders in all countries to accelerate gender equality. The overall rankings in gender equality for select countries are:

Iceland: 1	Slovenia: 8	Denmark: 19	Israel: 49
Finland: 2	New Zealand: 9	UK: 20	Italy: 50
Norway: 3	Nicaragua: 10	Spain: 29	Russia: 75
Sweden: 4	Switzerland: 11	Canada: 35	Brazil: 79
Rwanda: 5	Germany: 13	Poland: 38	India: 87
Ireland: 6	South Africa: 15	United States: 45	China: 99
Philippines: 7	France: 17	Australia: 46	South Korea: 116

Pakistan, Iran, Turkey, Syria, Egypt, Saudi Arabia and other Middle Eastern as well as North African countries received the lowest rankings. For more details and interactive tables, see the full report: http://reports.weforum.org/global-gender-gap-report-2016/rankings/

NEGOTIATING TWO WORLDS SIMULTANEOUSLY

Women who move between these two worlds – the public and the domestic – come to know from direct experience what Smith (1990a: 17) calls a **bifurcation of consciousness**. The notion of bifurcation captures the conflicted realities that all women experience because of the split between objectified knowledge and women's everyday, localized experiences. Consciousness of this bifurcation becomes especially accessible to women who move between the domestic and the public worlds; their everyday experiences as workers (e.g., waitresses, professors, politicians, etc.) and as mothers, for example, expose them directly to the contradictions within and between the two worlds. Traditional gender roles – with men in the public world of work and politics, and women in the domestic world of home and family – "deny the existence of the contradiction; suppression makes it invisible" (Smith 1990a: 19).

Smith's view of gender (and the feminist view as a whole) contrasts sharply with Talcott Parsons's emphasis on the functional complementarity of male and female roles (see chapter 4). Parsons did not see role differentiation in terms of the invisibility or exclusion of women's experiences, or in terms of women's lack of power vis-à-vis men and the "real" world. He saw it rather as a structural arrangement whereby different male and female roles were necessary to avoid status competition within and across family and work spheres.

The structure of work (and the public world in general) is such that it depends on the smooth functioning of the domestic world, the world wherein women do the work to maintain men's participation in the public world. When women enter the public world, however, they still maintain a large responsibility for the domestic world (their second shift; Hochschild with Machung 1990) and hence must negotiate the contradictory demands of the two worlds simultaneously. Moreover, whether in the domestic world, or in the public world, or as they move in and between both worlds, women's relations to men are structured by the ruling discourse of femininity (discussed previously). This is a discourse that exacerbates women's disempowerment rather than helping them deal with questions emerging from the everyday/everynight contradictions they necessarily experience. Smith emphasizes that these are not abstract but highly practical "here-and-now" questions that women confront in their everyday world. Smith – a woman, a mother, and a sociologist – outlines these conflicting practical demands and their implications:

> How are we to manage career and children (including of course negotiating sharing that work with a man)? How is domestic work to get done? How is career time to be coordinated with family caring time? How is the remorseless structure of the children's school schedule to be coordinated with the equally exigent scheduling of professional and managerial work? Rarely are these problems solved by the full sharing of responsibilities between women and men. But for the most part these claims, these calls, these somehow unavoidable demands, are still ongoingly present and pressing for women, particularly, of course, for those with children. Thus the relation between ourselves as practicing sociologists and ourselves as working wwomen is always there for us as a practical matter, an ordinary, unremarked, yet pervasive aspect of our experience of the world. The bifurcation of consciousness becomes for us a daily chasm to be crossed, on the one side of which is this special conceptual activity of thought, research, teaching, and administration, and on the other the world of localized activities oriented toward particular others, keeping things clean, managing somehow the house and household and the children – a world in which the particularities of persons in their full organic immediacy (feeding, cleaning up the vomit, changing the diapers) are inescapable … We have learned, as women in sociology, that the discipline has not been one that we could enter and occupy on the same terms as men. We do not fully appropriate its authority, that is, the right to author and to authorize the acts of knowing and thinking that are the knowing and thinking of the discipline. Feminist theory in sociology is still *feminist* theory and not just plain sociological theory … The frames of reference that ordered the terms upon which inquiry and discussion are conducted have originated with men. (Smith 1990a: 20–21)

A FEMINIST SOCIOLOGY: THE STANDPOINT OF WOMEN

To give validation to the everyday/everynight realities of women's experiences, Smith proposes an alternative way of doing sociology – and of governing society – that would take seriously women's particularized location(s). She advocates a sociology that would *begin* from women's standpoint and which would attempt to deal seriously with that standpoint (1990a: 12). She explains:

> Women's standpoint … discredits sociology's claim to constitute an objective knowledge independent of the sociologist's situation … I am not proposing an immediate and radical transformation of the subject matter and methods of the discipline nor the junking of everything that has gone before. What I am suggesting is more in the nature of a reorganization of the relationship of sociologists to the object of our knowledge and of our problematic. This reorganization involves first placing sociologists where we are actually situated, namely, at the beginning of those acts by which we know or will come to know, and second, making our direct embodied experience of the everyday world the primary ground of our knowledge. (Smith 1990a: 21–22)

In short, "an **alternative sociology**, from the standpoint of women, makes the everyday world [the real, actual world outside the text] its problematic [domain of inquiry]" (Smith 1990a: 27). Smith thus challenges sociology to address Marxist-inspired questions about the relations of domination, questions whose answers will emancipate women and men (Smith 2005: 1). These questions would necessarily focus on women and their subordinate relation to the ruling male world and inquire into women's direct experience of the everyday/everynight world and how those experiences are organized and determined by forces beyond women's direct experience (2005: 27; see also Smith 1987: 47). Marx presumed (see chapter 1) that the standpoint of the proletariat, that is, wage-workers' everyday experiences of their objectification and dehumanization within the capitalist structure, gives them a clearer perception of, and ability to recognize, the alienation that inheres in capitalism (as opposed to the bourgeoisie who tend to equate their interests – accumulating money/profit – with capitalism). Following a similar line of argument, Smith sees women's standpoint, women's experience, as the one from within which the gender contradictions in society can be apprehended and transformed.[1] She elaborates:

> the standpoint of women situates the inquirer in the site of her bodily existence and in the local actualities of her working world. It is a standpoint that positions inquiry but has no specific content [no predefined concepts]. Those who undertake inquiry from this standpoint begin always from women's experience as it is for women [and not as it is predefined by men]. We [women] are the authoritative speakers of our experience … From this standpoint, we know the everyday world through the particularities of our local practices and activities, in the actual places of our work and the actual time it takes. In making the everyday world problematic we also problematize the everyday localized practices of the objectified forms of knowledge organizing our everyday worlds. (Smith 1990a: 28)

Figure 10.2 Theresa May and Nicole Sturgeon: Despite their achievements, women leaders still must contend with sexist expectations. Source: © Solo Syndication.

Standpoint knowledge thus transforms the status of women by recognizing them as people who have experiences that matter. It also transforms the doing of sociology and of "ruling" in general, because by focusing on localized, everyday embodied experiences, it challenges what we take for granted as the (male) canon and how society is/should be organized.

DOING ALTERNATIVE SOCIOLOGY

Doing sociology (and politics, business, etc.) from the standpoint of women entails taking seriously women's experiences and using the knowledge that comes directly from those experiences to restructure social life and social institutions. The knowledge produced from an alternative sociology would produce knowledge that would be empowering for all individuals, both women and men; it would be political knowledge, that is, knowledge that would stimulate "consciousness raising" about inequality (Smith 2005: 1). Smith explains:

> an alternative sociology cannot be confined to a particular category of people. If it is a sociology that explores the social from women's standpoint and aims to be able to spell out for women just how the everyday world of our experience is put together by [institutional] relations that extend vastly beyond the everyday, then it has to work for both women and men. It has to be a sociology for people, as contrasted with the sociology in which I was so properly educated, the sociology in which people were the objects, they whose behavior was to be explained … Though it starts from where we are in our everyday lives, it explores social relations and organization in which our everyday doings participate but which are not fully visible to us … [thus] expanding people's own knowledge. (Smith 2005: 1)

Such knowledge would not be androcentric (Gilman 1911: 6), but human centered, producing a transformation that would rupture the unequal gender structures and relations on which a sociology and a society that privileges the male standpoint rely.

Many ethnographic studies reveal aspects of the mosaic of social and institutional inequality and illuminate the many ways in which inequality affects individuals' everyday lived experiences. Such research, however, does not fully approximate the kind of alternative sociology Smith envisions (2005: 35–38). She argues that an alternative sociology "has no prior interpretive commitment" (2005: 36) – its process of discovery is not driven by theoretical concepts or by political agendas nor does it focus on places (research sites) or on people. Its sole focus, rather, is the standpoint that emerges from talking to one or more individuals, and using the experiences of those people as the starting point for investigating how their experiences (positively or negatively) intermesh with the institutional processes that determine their lives (2005: 36). Smith (2005) calls this approach **institutional ethnography** (IE). She does not mean us to simply conduct ethnographies of specific institutional sites or settings, but to discover women's experiences within these institutional contexts and from those experiences explore and discover how institutions might work better for women and for men too (given that gender equality benefits all in society).

For example, Smith (2005: 205–222) approvingly cites the research of Pence (see Pence and McMahon 2003; Pence and Paymar 1993), who used battered women's experiences of abuse, and of the judicial system's prosecution of their abusive husbands, as a way to explore how the safety of women, from women's standpoint, may be very different to that institutionalized in the judicial system. Pence's research data track the abused women's first moment of contact with the 911 operator, to subsequent contact with the police and court officers, and include the various texts this process creates (e.g., police officers' reports of their initial visits to the abused victim). Using these data, Pence subsequently helped to change police procedures in Minnesota and elsewhere; for example, the adoption of a protocol indicating the degree of violence experienced by the victim, thus producing greater institutional alertness to the range and types of violence that impede women's safety (see Smith 2005: 205–222). This, for Smith, is a sociology *for* people. IE has gained considerable influence not only in documenting processes of gender inequality but additionally in illuminating institutional practices in health care, social services, education, and other organizational sectors and contexts (e.g., DeVault, 2008; Rankin and Campbell 2006; Tuchman 2011). IE research is particularly useful in identifying institutional interventions that can improve the lives of the people (women and men) who are subject to particular organizational routines and procedures. Much of this research is conducted by sociologists active in the IE section of the Society for the Study of Social Problems (SSSP) and in the IE thematic group of the International Sociological Association.

DOROTHY SMITH'S INTEGRATED VISION OF SOCIETAL EQUALITY

In summary, Smith outlines the mechanisms that produce women's subjugation and the varied consequences of that subjugation not just for women, but for society as a whole. Drawing on phenomenology, she argues that we need to be attentive to the particular everyday/everynight experiences of women (and of other excluded groups) and to recognize how those localized voices and experiences are different from what sociologists and other ruling groups in society take as the objective, relevant reality. At the same time, building on Marx's analysis of structural inequality, she underscores how the power structure in society – the institutional arrangements that determine the organization of work, politics, law, family life, education, mass media, etc. – relies on institutional texts (e.g., discourses of femininity) and practices (family/work divide) that are structured so as to maintain women's inequality vis-à-vis men. For Smith, a feminist standpoint is emancipatory for women and men; beginning with women's experiences, it would produce transformative knowledge and social equality.

MASCULINITIES: R. W. CONNELL

Smith's analysis of the ways in which society (and sociology) gives privileged recognition to one standpoint, that is, the male standpoint, opens up new awareness of women's experiences and other marginalized standpoints. As befits its push for a more egalitarian society and more emancipatory practices and knowledges, standpoint theory also has implications for the unpacking of **masculinity**. Paralleling femininity, masculinity is sharply delineated in society and its standards and expectations are a part of, and differently affect, gender relations and gendered institutional and everyday practices. **R.W. Connell**'s writing and research from the early 1980s onward give particular attention to how notions of masculinity have evolved and impact gender and power in society (e.g., Connell 1983, 1987, Connell 1995). Similar to other feminist theorists, Connell rejects the sex role theory that had long dominated sociology (e.g., Talcott Parsons, chapter 4). She thus rejects the notion that biological sex is determinative of the different social roles that women and men occupy, the view phrased (and also rejected) by Simone de Beauvoir (1949/1953) that "biology is destiny" (i.e., that women's natural biological reproductive function also functions to circumscribe women's primary and essential social roles as mothers/housewives, confined to the domestic sphere) (see also Box 10.1).

Rejecting biological determinism, Connell (1995: 71) emphasizes that "gender is a way in which social practice is ordered … Gender is a social practice that constantly refers to bodies and what bodies do, it is not social practice reduced to the body." Across all spheres of society including the economy, the state, law, family, sexuality, culture, etc., social practices construct and structure

BIOGRAPHICAL NOTE

R.W. (Raewyn) Connell was born in 1944 and grew up mainly in Sydney. She went to the University of Melbourne for her undergraduate education and completed her PhD at the University of Sydney. Her pioneering impact on the field of masculinities and gender relations is reflected in her being named the 2017 recipient of the American Sociological Association's Jessie Bernard Award. For many years she taught at the University of California, Santa Cruz and is currently professor emerita at the University of Sydney. She is a self-described transsexual woman. In addition to her impact on gender, she also articulates Southern Theory, focusing attention on the need in sociology and other disciplines to redress the postcolonial legacy in knowledge practices (see chapter 12).

femininity and they also construct and structure masculinity (1995: 65). As such, masculinity marginalizes certain types of male behavior and accentuates others. Masculinity is socially organized; and as with femininity, it varies across and within cultural, historical, and everyday lived contexts. Masculinity differs, too, among men. Recognizing the intersectionality of gender, race, class, and sexuality (see Collins in the next section), Connell argues that there are **multiple masculinities** that vary by class, race, geography, and sexuality. This is not to suggest that there is, for example, an essentialized gay or black masculinity, but to highlight that masculinities are objectively positioned in terms of structural (e.g., legal and economic discrimination) and cultural conditions. Masculinities exist in hierarchical relation to each other and their status is positioned by the dominant and culturally most authoritative definition of masculinity institutionalized and rewarded in any given society.

Connell argues that the dominant or **hegemonic masculinity** in Western society is the dominance of men and the subordination of women. More specifically, it is the dominance of heterosexual men and the subordination of homosexual men, and the marginalization, for example, of black gay men. Hegemonic masculinity, as is true of cultural hegemony in general (following Gramsci, see chapter 5), is always open to contestation. As currently construed, however, it affirms heterosexuality, a strong and fierce physicality, an emphasis on competitive sports, and the suppression of emotional vulnerability. Kimmel (2005: 25–42) observes that the culture of masculinity in the US affirms a macho, though disguised, homophobia and encourages the suppression of any signs of femininity in the male self. And in Australia, the hegemonic masculinity is "outward-turned and plays down all private emotion" (Connell 1995: 64).

Connell is careful to emphasize the cultural power of the authoritative masculinity, irrespective of whether it is visible in individual lives: "The most visible bearers of hegemonic masculinity are [not] always the most powerful people. They may be exemplars, such as film actors." Similarly,

> Individual holders of institutional power or great wealth may be far from the hegemonic pattern in their personal lives … Nevertheless, hegemony is likely to be established only if there is some correspondence between cultural ideal and institutional power, collective if not individual. So, the top levels of business, the military and government provide a fairly convincing corporate display of masculinity, still very little shaken by feminist women or dissenting men. It is the successful claim to authority … that is the mark of hegemony. (Connell 1995: 77)

The power of the culture of hegemonic masculinity (Connell) lies precisely in the fact that it so authoritatively pervades a variety of institutional settings, including schools (e.g., Pascoe 2007) and workplaces (e.g., Hochschild 1983). It also permeates the everyday/everynight practices and ways of being that reproduce gender differences and inequality, and the structures and cultures that maintain these inequalities. Although resistance against the dominating forces of masculinity and femininity is possible – and change does occur – most of the time many of us (irrespective of gender or sexuality, and of our other intersecting social locations) are somewhat complicit in the reproduction of patriarchal, hetero-masculine norms. We return to these themes of power and inequality when we focus on the institutional disciplining of bodies and the construal of sexuality (chapter 11), the cultural commodification of the colored body (chapter 12), and everyday body practices and habits (chapter 13).

BIOGRAPHICAL NOTE

Patricia Hill Collins was born to working-class parents in Philadelphia in 1948. After receiving her undergraduate education at Brandeis University and an MA in teaching from Harvard University, she worked in Boston community schools for many years. She was director of the Tufts University African-American Center before returning to Brandeis for her PhD in sociology. She subsequently received a faculty appointment at the University of Cincinnati, and upon her retirement held its distinguished Taft professorship of sociology and was director of African-American Studies. In 2006, she became a distinguished university professor of sociology at the University of Maryland. A prolific author, Collins has received numerous career awards, including the Jessie Bernard Award from the American Sociological Association and the C. Wright Mills Award from the Society for the Study of Social Problems. In 2009, Collins served as president of the American Sociological Association, and in 2017, she was awarded its W.E.B. DuBois Career of Distinguished Scholarship Award. She is married to Roger Collins, a professor of education at the University of Cincinnati.

PATRICIA HILL COLLINS: BLACK WOMEN'S STANDPOINT

Dorothy Smith recognized that the eclipsing of women's voices from the ruling institutional texts marginalized the experiences of nonwhite women to a greater extent than it did white women (Smith 1987: 43, n. 45). **Patricia Hill Collins**, another major feminist and standpoint theorist, dissects how the absence of black women's voices from the structures of power has both defined black women and exacerbated their oppression.[2] She outlines the core themes constitutive of a **black women's standpoint** in her 1990 book, *Black Feminist Thought* (subsequently revised in 2000). She states:

All African-American women share the common experience of being Black women in a society that denigrates women of African descent. This commonality of experience suggests that certain characteristic themes will be prominent in a Black women's standpoint … one core theme is a legacy of struggle. Katie Cannon observes, "throughout the history of the United States, the interrelationship of white supremacy and male superiority has characterized the Black woman's reality as a situation of struggle – struggle to survive in two contradictory worlds simultaneously, one white, privileged, and oppressive, the other black, exploited, and oppressed" (1985, 30). Black women's vulnerability to assaults in the workplace, on the street, and at home has stimulated Black women's independence and self-reliance. In spite of differences created by historical era, age, social class, sexual orientation or ethnicity, the legacy of struggle against racism and sexism is a common thread binding African-American women. (Collins 1990: 22)

Because Collins recognizes that different black women have different localized experiences (depending on country-of-family origin, social class, sexual orientation, etc.) and thus respond to the black legacy of struggle in varying ways, she argues that this diversity makes it "more accurate to discuss a Black women's standpoint than a Black woman's standpoint" (Collins 1990: 24). She thus avoids making the essentializing claim that all black women think and act alike, while simultaneously recognizing the commonality of black women's shared history.

BLACK WOMEN'S HISTORY: SLAVERY AND COMMUNITY

Black women's shared history of struggle includes the formative experience of slavery. Enslavement, Collins argues, was critical to the development of a different understanding among black women of the relation between family and work. Unlike the split between the domestic and public worlds that defined (middle-class) white women's experiences, slavery prompted a different way of organizing everyday life for black women. During the early nineteenth-century expansion of capitalism, white middle-class urban families adopted nuclear households units, whereas the majority of African-American families "had great difficulty maintaining private households in public spheres controlled by white slave owners." They thus recreated

> African notions of family as extended kin units. … The entire slave community/family stood in opposition to the public sphere of a capitalist political economy controlled by elite white men. For Black women the domestic sphere encompassed a broad range of kin and community relations beyond the nuclear family household. The line separating the Black community from whites served as a more accurate boundary delineating public and private spheres for African-Americans than that separating Black households from the surrounding Black community. (Collins 1990: 48–49)

Therefore, the gender divide institutionalized in the split between the (white) domestic and public sphere did not become a defining part of the black experience. Instead, enslavement pitted blacks (property), regardless of gender, against whites (property owners). Black women combined mothering and work (as slaves for their owners). As workers, they were powerless, but as mothers and as enslaved workers they had the support of an extended black family-community.

The end of slavery expanded the opportunities for black women and men in the workplace. Nevertheless, because of the limited educational, work, and political opportunities available to African-American men in particular, and the resulting negative effects on their earning power, Collins argues that black women continued to combine work and family to help ensure a sufficient family household income (Collins 1990: 52–55). And, despite the many changes entailed in late nineteenth-century migration in the US from the rural South to northern cities, black families continued to live in largely black (neighborhood-segregated) communities, thus making it possible for black women to continue to draw on extended community support in combining work and family commitments (1990: 58). Notably too, "At all moments in time between 1880 and 1925 – that is, from an adult generation born in slavery to an adult generation about to be devastated by the Great Depression of the 1930s … the typical African-American family was lower class … and headed by two parents" (Gutman 1976: 455–456).

Although the recent expansion of the black middle class (e.g., Pattillo 2013; Wilson 1978: 144–152) has highlighted the increasing salience of class divisions among blacks, Collins argues that diversity of experience has always been part of black women's experience (1990: 23–24, 66). The challenge today, as Collins sees it, is for black feminist scholars "to rearticulate these new and emerging patterns of institutional oppression that differentially affect middle-class and working-class Black women." And she warns that "If this does not occur, each group may in fact become instrumental in fostering the other's oppression" (1990: 66).

CONTROLLING IMAGES OF BLACK WOMEN

Collins (1990: 67) underscores that "race, class, and gender oppression could not continue without powerful ideological justifications for their existence." In parallel fashion to Dorothy Smith's (1990b: 171) emphasis on how the discourse of femininity (through advertising, sitcoms, cosmetics displays, etc.) maintains women's presentation of self as an object for (and inferior to) men, Collins draws attention to the **controlling images** of black women that are used by the white male status quo in an attempt to suppress black women's vocal resistance to their subjugation and inequality. She argues:

> Portraying African-American women as stereotypical mammies, matriarchs, welfare recipients, and hot mommas has been essential to the political economy of domination fostering Black women's oppression. As part of a generalized ideology of domination, these controlling images of Black womanhood take on special meaning because the authority to define these symbols is a major instrument of power. In order to exercise power, elite white men and their representatives must be in a position to manipulate appropriate symbols concerning Black women. (Collins 1990: 67–68)

Rather than being allowed to define themselves, a definition that would likely draw on the diversity of black women's experiences and their active struggles against domination, black women are stripped of these experiences and portrayed in ways that distort the rich complexity of their diversity. They become defined as "Other" (see Said 1978), a threatening strangeness that needs to be controlled, suppressed, excluded. This depiction of Otherness, in its various guises, provides ideological justification for black women's gender, racial, and class oppression (Collins 1990: 68).

CULTURAL OPPRESSION

How do these controlling images maintain black women's oppression? The black *mammy* is the faithful, obedient servant, who loves her white family more than her own and thus, according to Collins, "symbolizes the dominant group's perceptions of the ideal Black female relationship [of subordination] to elite white male power" (Collins 1990: 71). One consequence of this stereotype is that today black women professionals and executives are also expected to be nurturant and subservient, even though the corporate workplace financially rewards the opposite traits, i.e., instrumental and autonomous behavior (1990: 71). The *matriarch* symbolizes the "bad" black mother; "as overly aggressive, unfeminine women, Black matriarchs allegedly emasculate their lovers and husbands" (1990: 74), causing them to desert the family and thus exacerbating the social problems associated with single-parent families/households. As women who work outside the home, matriarchs are seen as failing to "fulfill the traditional 'womanly' duties" (1990: 74). Thus matriarchs – rather than structural inequality – are blamed for black children's poor school performance and their continuing economic impoverishment (1990: 73–75). If black women did not work outside the home, however, their children would have access to even fewer economic resources (given the continued economic disadvantage experienced by black men) and this in turn would contribute to the spiral of black poverty and inequality.

The *mammy* and the *matriarch* are powerful images, but perhaps not as ideologically controlling of the tripartite, race–class–gender matrix as that of the *welfare mother*. The welfare mother captures the deeply embedded racial stereotype of blacks as lazy and as the source of their own poverty, relying on government welfare rather than their own work ethic to compensate for their "uncontrolled" fertility. The ideological intertwining of poverty and fertility directs attention away from the structural sources of poverty, while simultaneously reaffirming the traditional white view that black fertility should be controlled because it produces too many economically unproductive and costly children. Additionally, the welfare mother, typically portrayed as a single mother, "violates one cardinal tenet of Eurocentric masculinist thought: she is a woman alone. As a result, her denigration reinforces the dominant **gender ideology** positing that a woman's true worth and financial security should occur through heterosexual marriage" (Collins 1990: 77).

And the fourth image, the *hot momma*, the whore, the sexually aggressive Jezebel, Collins argues (1990: 77), provides "a powerful rationale for the widespread sexual assaults by white men" on black women. In short, Collins argues, white men can tolerate only the desexed black woman, the *mammy* (who can nanny their children), and must control the sexuality of the matriarch, the teenage mother, and the Jezebel (1990: 78).

BLACK FEMINIST THOUGHT

Black women have a long history of actively resisting these controlling images and articulating alternative definitions of their reality. However, because black women's experiences have historically been excluded from the traditional sites of knowledge – government agencies, academia, mass media, etc. – black women have voiced their knowledge of their reality in different sites: in everyday conversations with family, friends, and neighbors; through literature, poetry, art, music, and independent documentary films; and in the call-and-response discourse of church meetings (see Collins 1990: 91–114). **Black feminist thought** is thus produced by black feminist sociologists such as Collins. Importantly, it is also produced by all black women who vocalize their experiences of and responses to the cultural contradictions they encounter as black women, caught between two histories of oppression, those of race and gender (1990: 14–15). The popularity of Toni Morrison's novels, Maya Angelou's poetry, and Beyonce's songs, concerts, and video albums (such as "Lemonade") show that when black women have the opportunity to speak and to act, many blacks and whites, women and men, want to hear and are moved by what they say and do.

Black feminist thought, somewhat akin to white women's knowledge, is outside the paradigm of objective knowledge, that is, that which Smith (1987: 1) and Collins (1990: 201–206) debunk as the allegedly universal knowledge created from the standpoint of (Eurocentric white) men. Collins further underscores, however, that "Black feminist thought, like all specialized thought, reflects the interests and standpoint of its creators" (1990: 201). Therefore, whereas all women share a standpoint by virtue of their historical oppression as women, black feminist thought comes from a different standpoint than that of white feminist thought. It is knowledge that has a distinct African historical consciousness: "Black societies reflect elements of a core African value system that existed prior to and independently of racial oppression … Moreover, as a result of colonialism, imperialism, slavery, apartheid, and other systems of racial domination, Black people [whether living in the UK, Europe, North America, South America, the Caribbean, or Africa] share a common experience of oppression," though their specific histories differ (1990: 206). Therefore, "Because Black women have access to both the Afrocentric and the feminist standpoints, an alternative epistemology used to rearticulate a Black feminist standpoint should reflect elements of both traditions," and by highlighting the points of contact between the two, enrich understanding of how the experiences of subordinate groups "create knowledge that fosters resistance" (1990: 207).

SOCIAL INTERSECTIONALITY

Although emphasizing the specific standpoints from which knowledge is created, Collins calls for appreciation of the concrete **intersectionality** of all experiences – how experiences are shaped, interpreted, and talked about on the basis of the interlocking and interacting gender, race, social class, and other factors situating individuals. Different intersectional contexts give rise to different experiences and to different contradictions, and moreover, to how these contradictions are and can be negotiated. In Appalachia, West Virginia, a region in the US with a long history of poverty, women miners in the male-dominated coal mines experience harassment. But black women miners experience different forms of harassment than white women miners, a racial-and-gender harassment of which white women are unaware – they literally don't see skin color as a source of discrimination (Tallichet 2006).

Postcolonial theorists have long argued that who is Other and what it means to be Other are always grounded in relational and societal inequalities (Fanon 1967; Said 1978; see chapter 12). Further, as Goffman elaborates, who is "normal" and who is stigmatized depends on a given social relational context. Similarly, Collins observes:

> Privilege becomes defined in relation to its other … Race, class and gender represent the three systems of oppression that most heavily affect African-American women. But these systems and the economic, political and ideological conditions that support them may not be the most fundamental oppressions, and they certainly affect many more groups than Black women. Other people of color, Jews, the poor, white women, and gays and lesbians have all had similar ideological justifications offered for their subordination. (Collins 1990: 225)

Whatever the sources of oppression, Collins argues, it is their intersectionality that matters. In everyday life, one is not just a woman, or black or Latina, or working class, or poor or an immigrant, but typically, some combination of these subordinated statuses. The determining impact of such intersectionality on everyday experiences and life outcomes is institutionalized in the US stratification system: white men and black men, respectively, have higher median incomes than white women; and Latina women are at the bottom of the income ladder (Andersen and Collins 1995: 66). Different structural locations, therefore, interact and crisscross to produce different lived experiences, different power relations, and different conditions for the transformation of inequality and oppression. Collins thus pushes us to move beyond dichotomous either/or analyses of Otherness (e.g., women *or* men, black *or* white, gay *or* straight) and to instead examine racism and other social formations in terms of their "multiple, complex social inequalities" and their coexistence as and with other structural inequalities (Collins 2015: 5). This approach opens up our awareness of the multilayered ways in which identities and the social relations that they produce are structured and experienced. As Collins notes, although "white women are penalized by their gender, they are privileged by their race; thus depending on the context, an individual may be an oppressor, a member of an oppressed group, or simultaneously oppressor and oppressed" (Collins 1990: 225).

ACTIVIST KNOWLEDGE

The **activist knowledge** generated from within intersecting matrixes of resistance is emancipatory – it empowers individuals to take action against their oppression. Thus, Collins argues, although African-American women are victims of oppression, they are also active resistors of oppression: giving voice to oppression is an act of resistance, and resistance matters even if its voices are ignored by those in power. The interplay between oppression and activism is core to black feminist thought, Collins argues, and as such it advances the politics of empowerment:

> [Black feminist] thought views the world as a dynamic place where the goal is not merely to survive or to fit in or to cope; rather it becomes a place where we feel ownership and accountability … there is always choice, and the power to act, no matter how bleak the situation may appear to be. Viewing the world as one

in the making raises the issue of individual responsibility for bringing about change. It also shows that while individual empowerment is key, only collective action can effectively generate lasting social transformation of political and economic institutions. (Collins 1990: 237)

Speaking out with others of similar experience is a crucial step not only of resistance but of forcing accountability. Black feminist thought, therefore – knowledge derived from the daily experiences and activism of oppressed black women – is a knowledge that can be used by other oppressed people, whatever the intersecting sources of their marginality, to collectively transform the conditions of their daily existence (see Topic 10.2).

Topic 10.2   Intersectionality, activist knowledge, and social justice

We get a glimpse of what Collins means by activist knowledge and its empowering of social justice (Collins 2015; Collins and Bilge 2016) in the collective organizing efforts of domestic workers in the US. The workers – housekeepers, nannies, and caregivers – many of whom are women of color and immigrants from Mexico, Central and South America, the Caribbean, the Philippines, and India, convened in New York in June 2008 for a weekend of story-sharing and strategizing at the first National Domestic Workers Congress. At the congress, they told of their own experiences and, as representatives of domestic workers' groups in about ten US cities, also recounted the experiences of others like them. They shared stories of physical abuse by their employers – one was slammed into a wall, another was struck as she hand-polished the floor. They also talked of the long days they worked, of being paid far less than the minimum wage, about their lack of health benefits, and their generally poor working conditions. Using their experiences of exploitation, they came together to build alliances with other domestic workers with a view to securing better rights and improved working conditions for all domestic workers. The political necessity of giving visibility to domestic workers' everyday/everynight experiences is captured by one worker who commented: "Many women feel they are alone … and don't dare to come out in the light and speak" (Buckley and Correal 2008). In an effort to give voice to the plight of domestic workers, the National Domestic Workers' Alliance (NDWA) was founded in 2007, and its grassroots organizing is making a dent in improving their lives. By 2017, they had achieved protective legislative victories in New York, Massachusetts, Connecticut, Oregon, California, Illinois, and Hawaii. Despite the critically important roles they play in their employers' lives, domestic workers are still among the most vulnerable and invisible of workers, and federal law prevents them from joining a union. In 2012, a study documented their working conditions and experiences:

- One in four was paid less than minimum wage.
- Only 4 percent had employer-provided health insurance, and only 65 percent had any health coverage.
- Over a third (37 percent) were unable to pay their rent or mortgage on time in 2011.
- One fifth (20 percent) were unable to afford food for their own households in the prior month.
- Over a third (35 percent) reported working long hours with no breaks.
- Close to a third (29 percent) reported work-related back injuries in the year prior.

For more details, see the website of the National Domestic Workers' Alliance; www.domestic workers.org.

BLACK BODIES AND SEXUALITY

In *Black Sexual Politics*, published in 2004, Collins moves beyond her earlier emphasis on the oppressive intersectionality of gender, race, and class to address the intersectionality of gender, race, and *sexuality* in shaping black oppression and the possibilities for its transformation. She argues that "moving from an exclusive focus on Black women to a broader one that encompasses how the politics of gender and sexuality frame the experience of women and men alike creates new questions for investigation and, perhaps, a new antiracist politics that might follow" (Collins 2004: 8). She asks: "What good is the empowerment of African American women if it comes at the expense of Black men?" (2004: 9) – indicated, for example, by the disproportionately high rates of black men who are in prison, who lack a college education, who have AIDS, or who are embroiled in black-on-black violence as perpetrators and victims (2004: 7) (see also chapter 12, Box 12.1).

In Collins's view, the pursuit of antiracist policies cannot be successful unless black women and men confront intertwined questions of gender and sexuality, and in particular the oppressive ideology depicting them as the "embodiment of deviant sexuality" (Collins 2004: 35). She elaborates:

> Black gender ideology … draws upon widespread cultural beliefs concerning the sexual practices of people of African descent. Sexuality is not simply a biological function; rather, it is a system of ideas and social practices that is deeply implicated in shaping American social inequalities. Because ideas about sexuality are so integral to understandings of Black gender ideology [of femininity and masculinity] as well as broader gender ideology in the United States, neither Black masculinity nor Black femininity can be adequately understood let alone transformed without attending to the **politics of sexuality**. (Collins 2004: 6)

Whereas Collins (1990) previously elaborated on the politics of black women's sexuality apparent in the controlling images used by white male elite culture to maintain black women's inequality, she extends her attention to the need for blacks themselves to rethink and reclaim their sexuality. This involves what she calls "the sexual autonomy of **honest bodies**," in contrast to the "Black gender ideology that encourages Black people to view themselves and others as bitches, hoes, thugs, pimps, sidekicks, sissies, and modern mammies" (Collins 2004: 282). This ideology tends to be promulgated in some of the song lyrics and videos of top-selling black (and white) rappers. Many male rappers, like Tupac and Dr. Dre, for example, articulate a politics of resistance to the police and the government, and insightfully name the institutionalized urban ills that seriously undermine the life chances of economically disadvantaged blacks. Yet these same rappers also tend to reproduce the denigrating, stereotypical images of black women as sexual objects, bitches, and whores, and of black men whose virtue is defined by a hypermasculine virility focused on incessant sexual conquest (e.g., Dr. Dre's song "Ed-Ucation").

SEXUAL HONESTY

Reclaiming "honest bodies," – that is, a sexual identity and sexual feelings and experiences that are real for the people involved rather than a distortion of sexuality by those who oppress black women (and black gays) – presents a number of challenges. One of the challenges identified by Collins is that of integrating or rejoining "mind, soul, and body" (Collins 2004: 286), that is, recognizing that bodies are not simply objects but embody the feelings, desires, and expressivity of individuals. In this view, sex is not a commodity to be distorted, packaged, and sold in songs, videos, movies, advertising, and prostitution, but a desire and practice at the heart of relationships that are (or ought to be) based on mutual intimacy and love. A related "honest bodies" challenge is the "ability to select one's own sexual orientation," a challenge compounded by the heterosexism in society and its accentuation in black communities (Collins 2004: 286; Fields et al. 2015). In this regard it is noteworthy, for example, that in the US, blacks (51 percent) are less likely than Hispanics (60 percent) and whites (64 percent) to support same-sex marriage (Pew Research Center 2017: 4). Collins argues that black homophobia in turn produces a silence about risky heterosexual and gay sexual behavior and the denial, for example, that HIV/AIDS affects African-Americans (2004: 288–295). (I further discuss heterosexism and gay sexuality in chapter 11.) In the US, black men, black women, and black youth are disproportionally affected by HIV/AIDS. African American gay and bisexual men are the only group who did not experience a decline in HIV infections in the past decade, and young African American gay and bisexual men aged 13–24 had an 87 percent increase in diagnoses (Tavernise 2016; www.hiv.gov).

The reclaiming of sexual autonomy/honest bodies also challenges the association of eroticism with sexual violence and the extent to which intimate and family relationships involve violence (Collins 2004: 288). Compared to 37 percent of white and 34 percent of Hispanic women, 45 percent of African-American women experience intimate-partner violence, including rape, physical assault, or stalking (www.cdc.gov). And as ethnographic studies document, sexual harassment and violence are particularly prevalent in the everyday experiences of poor black women (e.g., Burton et al. 2015; Jones 2010; Miller 2008). Collins suggests that the entanglement of sex and violence may also be used, in part, to think about forms of violence beyond intimate relationships such as black male-on-male street violence. And she wonders whether some of this violence may mask the repression of homoerotic feelings in the homophobic black community (Collins 2004: 288), as Kimmel also suspects (2005: 25–42). Collins concludes that "African Americans certainly need to 'ready up for some honesty' in intimate love relationships" (2004: 292). The perpetuation of sexual oppression does violence not only to racial equality but also to the gender and sexual differences among blacks, undermining the building of solidarity within the black community between men and women, gay and straight. She warns: "As systems of oppression, racism, sexism, class exploitation, and heterosexism all gain power by denying sexual autonomy and annexing the power of the erotic for their own ends. In this context, reclaiming love and sexuality constitutes a necessary first step" (2004: 292–293). She also emphasizes: "At the same time, love and sexuality are insufficient for confronting the economic exploitation, political powerlessness, and sexual violence of the **new racism**" (2004: 293). This new racism does not displace the old. Rather, it refers (as I elaborate in chapter 12) to the changing cultural contours and symbols of racial inequality in media content and public discourse, and through which racism is denied or mass awareness of its ongoing insidiousness is undercut (2004: 54; see also Gilroy 2000: 32).

SOCIOLOGY OF EMOTION

Through much of its history, sociological theory was relatively inattentive to emotion, though theorists did not completely ignore it. Georg Simmel (1921/1971) wrote about love and more generally highlighted the centrality of emotion in social-collective behavior (e.g., mass feelings and mass appeal; 1917/1950: 34–36). Max Weber recognized emotion as a significant motivator of social action, and saw Calvinists' fears about the afterlife, for example, as a crucial component in the rationalization process accelerating modern capitalism. Overall, however, Weber emphasized emotion's secondary status vis-à-vis rational action; the cultural contribution of the Protestant ethic is, in part, its suppression and disciplined, methodical control of emotion (see chapter 3). Emile Durkheim gave more detailed attention to emotion, seeing the collective effervescence that emerges during ritual celebrations as a potent social force (see chapter 2). Nevertheless, in his analysis of the modern division of labor, his focus was not the emotional bonds but the functional interdependence that builds (organic) solidarity among individuals. More surprisingly, perhaps, Mead's focus on the practical consequences of face-to-face interaction essentially ignored the significance of emotion, instead emphasizing the cognitive aspects of interpretive action (see chapter 8).

At mid-twentieth century, Parsons's pattern variables confined emotion to the family sphere (see chapter 4), and if emotion presented itself in the public realm, it was largely a nonrational strain on social action (e.g., the mob contagion effect of "hostile outbursts" in collective behavior; Smelser 1962: 222–269). In sum, emotion was not something that many mainstream sociologists emphasized in their theory and research even as sociology of the family, of crime, and of health and illness, for example, all flourished – domains in which emotion surely matters. One exception was Goffman, but he emphasized the ritualization, rather than the *feeling*, of emotion in the signaling and performance of gender and other subordinated social statuses (see chapter 8). Emotion continues to be marginalized by influential contemporary theorists such as Habermas (see chapter 5).

BIOGRAPHICAL NOTE

Arlie Hochschild was born in 1940. She received her PhD in sociology from the University of California, Berkeley, and spent her entire faculty career there until her retirement in 2006. A prolific researcher and writer, Hochschild has focused much of her attention on themes of intimacy and the binds of home and work. Her major impact on the field, especially on feminist scholarship and qualitative research, has been widely recognized with several awards including, in 2000, the American Sociological Association's Award for furthering the public understanding of sociology. She is married to Adam Hochschild, a writer, and they have two children. Her most recent book, *Strangers in Their Own Land: Anger and Mourning on the American Right* (2016) was a finalist for the National Book Award.

ARLIE HOCHSCHILD: EMOTIONAL LABOR

Arlie Hochschild turned the sociological spotlight on emotion. Her landmark book *The Managed Heart* (1983) succeeded in making sociologists recognize that feelings and emotions are of core relevance to societal processes. Today, the sociology of emotions is a well-established subfield within the discipline (see, e.g., Stets and Turner 2006), and emotions are increasingly incorporated within several other fields of sociological inquiry too (e.g., social movements; e.g., Polletta 2006). This transformation is largely due to the pioneering efforts of Hochschild and other feminist sociologists.[3]

Although most of us tend to think of emotion as a natural reflection of how we are feeling at a given moment, Hochschild makes us think about emotions as work. She highlights the **feeling rules** that determine emotion and emphasizes that emotion is a socially structured, patterned way of feeling and of acting on feeling. We are socialized into learning how to recognize, and how and when to feel, certain emotions. We recognize a feeling rule, Hochschild explains,

> by inspecting how we assess our feelings, how other people assess our **emotional display**, and by sanctions issuing from ourselves and from them … Sanctions common to the social scene – cajoling, chiding, teasing, scolding, shunning – often come into play as forms of ridicule or encouragement that lightly correct feeling and adjust it to convention … What is taken for granted … is that there are rules or norms according to which feelings may be judged appropriate [or inappropriate] to accompanying events. (Hochschild 1983: 57)

GENDERED DIVISION OF EMOTIONAL LABOR

Hochschild argues that "both men and women do **emotion work**, in private life and at work" (1983: 162), but that "our culture invites women, more than men, to focus on feeling rather than action" (1983: 57). There is a socially and culturally structured, gendered specialization – a division of labor – in emotion work. Women are more responsible for smiling, being nice, celebrating others and empathizing with others, whereas men are expected to do the aggressive emotional tasks (1983: 163–165). By extension, when women engage in emotion work that is culturally unexpected of their gender (e.g., being angry), they are denigrated, and their credibility and femininity are called into question, even in professional-corporate contexts where "aggressiveness" is generally rewarded. Underscoring the gender contradictions in society, if women display stereotypically female emotions (e.g., crying), their professional credibility is questioned. Additionally, as Hochschild observes, because of their subordination to men in a patriarchal society, women tend to have a "weaker 'status shield' against the displaced feelings of others" (1983: 163). Hence, they are more likely than men to be the object of emotional ridicule and attack.

Emotion work is, in a sense, easier for men: they are more protected from the negative emotions of others, and they have less emotion management to do; they have more freedom to smile or be angry if it suits them. This is changing somewhat with the so-called sharing economy: Uber and Lyft drivers, for example, are rated by users on their friendly service (see Topic 1.2). It would be interesting to study whether the ratings vary depending on the sex of the driver and the user. Increasingly too (notwithstanding hegemonic masculinity), men can occasionally, or even routinely, cry in public, as Andy Murray did when he lost in the Wimbledon tennis championship in July 2012 (to Roger Federer), when he won Olympic gold in August 2012 (beating Roger Federer), and when he finally won his first Wimbledon championship in July 2013. Similarly, Roger Federer cried when he won the Wimbledon championship in 2017 – his eighth Wimbledon win and the most for any male tennis player – and Marin Cilic, who lost to him that day, also cried. Some feminist scholars, such as the psychologist Carol Gilligan (1982), argue that women *are* more emotional than men. In this view, women are seen as having a "natural," gender-specific way of accessing emotions and hence as more emotional and relational than men. Men, by contrast, are seen as being more readily suited to tasks that are abstract, strategic, and rule centered and to operating in contexts that marginalize emotion and relationships. This is the same idea, or stereotype, that got a male Google engineer fired in 2017; see Topic 4.3). Hochschild and other sociologists fully acknowledge that emotion involves physiological and biological processes. Emotions get displayed in physiological actions (crying, grimacing, shaking hands, etc.), "thus when we manage an emotion, we are partly managing a bodily preparation for a consciously or unconsciously anticipated deed" (Hochschild 1983: 220). But sociologists also stress that the organization of emotion work is socially and culturally, not biologically, determined. Thus the gendering of emotion and of emotional tasks is not based on biology, but on society's evaluation of biological sex differences and their translation into social structures and cultural processes. It is not biology itself but socially structured gender differences in emotion specialization and social status that frame women as being less rational and overemotional. Women are therefore seen as difficult to vote for or to promote, or simply hard to deal with, whether in romantic relationships or in the executive suite. As Hochschild observes, "Women's feelings are seen not as a response to real events but as reflections of themselves as 'emotional' women" (1983: 173).

Gendered feeling rules and habits also vary by, and interact with, social class. Hochschild explains:

> Especially in the American middle class, women tend to manage feeling more because in general they depend on men for money, and one of the various ways of repaying their debt is to do extra emotion work – especially emotion work that affirms, enhances, and celebrates the well-being and status of others … The emotion work of enhancing the status and well-being of others is … an unseen effort, which like

housework, does not quite count as labor but is nevertheless crucial to getting other things done. As with doing housework well, the trick is to erase any evidence of effort, to offer only the clean house and the welcoming smile. (Hochschild 1983: 165, 167)

PAID EMOTIONAL LABOR

As wives and mothers, women do a lot of emotion work. And, they are also more likely than men to do emotion work for pay, to engage in **emotional labor**. As "more accomplished managers of feeling in private life, women more than men have put emotional labor on the market, and they know more about its personal costs" (1983: 11). This is a core concern for Hochschild. She gives particular attention to the production and control of human emotion not just *as* work, but *at* work. She calls this the **commercialization of feeling**. Thus emotion work is not just the emotion management done in the home, typically for people with whom one has deep and continuous reciprocal relationships (children, spouse, parents, etc.), and where it is useful for maintaining relationships and gaining affirmation, respect, or gifts (i.e., has use-value). Emotion work also includes the work done by those whose labor-force participation (i.e., paid employment) is contingent on their continuous production of specific emotions as required by the marketplace. Hochschild explains:

> I use the term *emotional labor* to mean the **management of feeling** to create a publicly observable facial and bodily display; emotional labor is sold for a wage and therefore has *exchange value*. I use the synonymous terms *emotion work* or *emotion management* to refer to these same acts done in a private context where they have *use value*. (Hochschild 1983: 7)

THE MANAGEMENT OF FEELINGS

Hochschild's definition of emotional labor is influenced by Marx, by C. Wright Mills, and by Goffman. From Marx's discussion of the commodification of labor (see chapter 1), Hochschild construes emotions as commodities; they can (and must) be exchanged for money, that is, bought and sold on the market. Like the physical labor power that wage-workers in a factory sell to their employer, professional and service workers sell their emotional labor power to employers. And, once bought for a wage – i.e., its commercial or exchange-value in the occupational marketplace – the worker's emotional labor is used by the (capitalist) employer to produce profit for the employer (as a result of the difference between the worker's exchange-value and the surplus value it creates for the employer, i.e., the difference between the value of the emotion to the worker and its value to their employer; see chapter 1).

Once we sell our smile we no longer own it, and hence we must produce useful (i.e., profit-oriented) smiles as required by our employer. This is what flight attendants and waitresses typically do. Jobs that call for emotional labor "require face-to-face or voice-to-voice contact with the public; … [they] require the worker to produce an emotional state in another person – gratitude or fear, for example; [and] they allow the employer, through training and supervision, to exercise a degree of control over the emotional activities of employees" (Hochschild 1983: 147).

In today's postindustrial, **information economy** (where we are as likely to buy and sell information and personal services as factory-manufactured material goods), a broad range of professional, clerical, and service workers engage in emotional labor. A core component of their everyday job is the controlled presentation of feelings; this is especially true of the many service workers whose duties include the greeting and personal care of (paying) customers, a point observed by C. Wright Mills (1951) in his discussion of the "personality market" and the commercial masking of feelings (see chapter 6). Receptionists, retail workers, waitresses, air stewards, and childcare workers are among the emotional laborers who readily come to mind. Their labor power resides primarily in their smile and their repertoire of "niceness." They sell the ability to manage their emotions, irrespective of the feelings they are personally experiencing at any given moment.

Increasingly, too, as Hochschild's book *The Outsourced Self* (2012) documents, the commercialization of human feeling is becoming its own industry. It penetrates the sphere of intimate relationships as various paid experts and for-profit organizations package, market, and sell the emotional services that in the past were performed by family members and friends. Among these emotional outsourcing services are "Rent a friend" whereby customers can pay to hire someone to act as their dinner or movie companion (without sex), and more intimate services such as "love coaches" who guide their shy clients "on what to do and how to feel at each step of online dating" (Hochschild 2012: 11).

GOING BEYOND SYMBOLIC INTERACTIONISM

Hochschild's emphasis on emotion management is also very close to Goffman's theorizing (see chapter 8). Indeed, some textbooks include Hochschild's work as part of symbolic interactionism (SI). This categorization makes sense on one level: the fact that everyone who engages in face-to-face inter-action must maintain a front in order to project a particular definition of the situation. Hochschild's contribution, however, though influenced by Goffman, extends beyond SI in two major ways. First, as Hochschild points out, Goffman's analysis of social actors does not pay any attention to the actor's inner feelings and to how social actors actively name and manage inner feelings. She argues: "In Goffman's theory, the capacity to act on feeling derives only from the occasions [settings/situations], not from the individual. The self may actively choose to display feelings in order to give outward impressions to others. But it is passive to the point of invisibility when it comes to the private act of managing emotion" (Hochschild 1983: 218). Goffman takes it for granted that social actors manage the display of emotion in their self-presentation. He is not interested in the feelings beneath or behind the role performance, but in role performance irrespective of the actors' feelings.

Second, Goffman's analysis does not probe why emotion work is required in a capitalist (or socialist) society, nor how it is produced and regulated. Instead, Goffman is primarily interested in the social rules and implications (e.g., embarrassment) of face-to-face interaction, and not in how self-presentation rituals may vary depending on their structural context or their commercial value. By contrast, Hochschild argues that the habits individuals have or acquire in managing emotion vary by gender, social class, age, religion, and other sociocultural locations (1983: 214–218; see also Hochschild 2003: 7, 91). Additionally, she probes beneath the inner feelings of the social actor and beyond the actor to the cultural and orga-nizational rules determining emotion management and emotional labor.

Emotion work as self-alienation

In line with Marx's analysis of the alienation of labor (see chapter 1), and C. Wright Mills's (1951: 182–184) discussion of the standardized "personality market" that characterizes the service economy (see chapter 6), Hochschild argues that emotional labor constitutes self-estrangement or **self-alienation**. Drawing on observation research she conducted at Delta Airlines' training sessions, and interviews she conducted with Delta flight attendants, training supervisors, and company executives, she uses the flight attendant as the quintessential exemplar of emotional labor. She explains:

> [the labor done in a factory calls for coordination] a coordination of mind and arm, mind and finger, and mind and shoulder. We refer to it simply as physical labor. The flight attendant does physical labor when she pushes heavy metal carts through the aisles, and she does mental work when she prepares for and actually organizes emergency landings and evacuations. But in the course of doing this physical and mental labor, she is also doing something more ... emotional labor. This labor requires one to induce or suppress feeling in order to sustain the

outward countenance that produces the proper state of mind in others – in this case, the sense of being cared for in a convivial and safe place. This kind of labor calls for a coordination of mind and feeling, and it sometimes draws on a source of self that we honor as deep and integral to our individuality. Beneath the difference between physical and emotional labor there lies a similarity in the possible cost of doing the work: the worker can become estranged or alienated from an aspect of self – either the body or the margins of the soul – that is *used* to do the work … The company lays claim not simply to her physical motions – how she handles food trays – but to her emotional actions and the way they show in the ease of a smile. The workers I talked to often spoke of their smiles as being *on* them but not *of* them. They were seen as an extension of the make-up, the uniform, the recorded music, the soothing pastel colors of the airplane décor … The final commodity is not a certain number of smiles to be counted … For the flight attendant, the smiles are a *part of her work*, a part that requires her to coordinate self and feeling so that the work seems effortless. To show that the enjoyment takes effort is to do the job poorly. Similarly, part of the job is to disguise fatigue and irritation, for otherwise the labor would show in an unseemly way, and the product – passenger contentment – would be damaged. (Hochschild 1983: 6–8)

Emotional labor: External control of inner states

Manual workers engaged in physical labor can feel whatever (socially learned) emotions they feel like feeling and they can act on those feelings by smiling or frowning. From a capitalist viewpoint, it doesn't matter whether the chicken deboner is smiling or grimacing; she is not paid to feel, but to debone 42 chickens a minute (see chapter 1, Topic 1.5). Emotional labor is different. Hochschild argues that the emotional laborer's feelings must be given over to the work; they no longer belong to the person but to the employer who has purchased them for use in the creation of profit. Specific emotions must be produced by the worker as part of their labor, and they must be produced authentically and seem genuine so that they induce the correct emotional state in the customer. As she notes, "The airline passenger may choose not to smile [despite nudging from American Airlines!; see Topic 8.2], but the flight attendant is obliged not only to smile but to try to work up some warmth behind it" (1983: 19). (Of course, airline passengers too are required to do a certain amount of emotional labor; see Topic 8.2.)

Not all emotional labor is about smiling. The flight attendant's smiling empathy must produce a sense of emotional security and feelings of welcome in the airline passenger, but the bill collector's gruffness and hostility must produce feelings of fear and shame in the bill defaulter. Irrespective, however, of the specific emotion that the emotional laborer must produce, emotional laborers no longer "own" their own emotions; they are owned by others (the employer) and regulated by others (the customers; e.g., the airline passenger who despite being disruptive for the duration of a five-hour flight still expects the attendant to smile warmly at him as she reminds him for the third time to buckle his seat belt in preparation for landing).

Emotional laborers are thus trained to produce required emotions whose production is perceived as being sincere, not put on. Organizations and corporations train their workers to take an instrumental stance toward feeling, to see their feelings as a resource and thus to suppress the wrong feelings or induce the correct feelings, irrespective of how the worker is actually feeling. Hochschild (1983: 55) explains:

[Acting] in a commercial setting, unlike acting in a dramatic, private or therapeutic context, makes one's face and one's feelings take on the properties of a resource. But it is not a resource to be used for the purposes of art, as in drama, or for the purposes of self-discovery, as in therapy, or for the pursuit of fulfillment, as in everyday life. It is a resource to be used to make money.

Unlike actors in the theater, who know, and whose audience knows, that they are acting, and temporarily feeling whatever emotions the acting part requires, emotional laborers are supposed to *feel* the required emotions and to make sure that their customers feel that these emotions are real and sincere. The line between "surface acting" (in the theater) and the "deep acting" (inducing a specific felt emotion) required by the commercialization of feeling becomes blurred. Consequently, Hochschild argues, it is very difficult for the emotional laborer to know what is authentic to her own inner feeling state and what is phony. This split between felt and produced emotion weakens the worker's ability to relate on a deep emotional level to others and can adversely affect her own intimate relationships. A social theory of emotion, she contends, "must take into account that these emotional dues can be costly to the self. Institutional rules run deep but so does the self that struggles with and against them. To manage feeling is to actively try to change a preexisting emotional state" (Hochschild 1983: 219).

Most of us engage in deep acting occasionally as we try to really enter into feeling a particular emotion (of pride, sadness, gratitude, disappointment). But it is still we who are controlling the emotion and its expression. With the commercialization of feeling, however, Hochschild (1983: 49) argues, it is corporate organizations that dictate to employees how to feel: "some institutions have become very sophisticated in the techniques of deep acting; they suggest how to imagine and thus how to feel."

Emotion training

As Hochschild saw at Delta Airlines, trainees undergo arduous training. They and other airlines' trainees are screened for a "certain type of outgoing middle-class sociability" and for the ability "to project a warm personality" (Hochschild 1983: 97). The particular type of sociability required varies, with some airlines screening for more graciously reserved attendants and others wanting them to be more sexy and brassy – depending on the corporate image of the airline itself (1983: 97). Once screened, recruits are then systematically trained in how to "act as if the airline cabin (where she works) were her home (where she doesn't work)," and thus to act with the deep, inner-felt desire to treat passengers as family or friends (1983: 105). As Hochschild notes, "Recruiters understood that they were looking for a 'certain Delta personality' … The general prerequisites were a capacity to work with a team … interest in people, sensitivity, and emotional stamina," though the trainees themselves believed that they were chosen "because they were adventurous and ambitious" (1983: 98). Additionally, she explains,

> The trainees, it seemed to me, were also chosen for their ability to take stage directions about how to "project" an image. They were selected for being able to act well – that is, without showing the effort involved. They had to be able to appear at home on stage … they were constantly reminded that their own job security and the company's profit rode on a smiling face … There were many direct appeals to smile: "Really work on your smiles." "Your smile is your biggest asset – use it." And "Relax and smile," the trainees were instructed, in responding to troublesome passengers. (Hochschild 1983: 105)

In short, flight attendants are trained to manage and modify their felt feelings. And like others in the service sector (e.g., waitresses, sales assistants), they must do this emotional labor while being relatively unshielded from customers who angrily abuse them (Hochschild 1983: 163) for failings over which typically they have no control (e.g., delays in the flight taking off, cramped seats). In the UK, for example, the 2017 annual survey of retail staff conducted by the Union of Shop, Distributive and Allied Workers (Usdaw), found that a half of all shopworkers were verbally abused by customers in the past year and 29 percent were threatened with violence (see www.usdaw.org.uk).

HOCHSCHILD'S CONTRIBUTIONS TO FEMINIST AND LABOR THEORIES

By focusing on emotional labor, Hochschild makes a twofold feminist contribution. First, she redresses the male bias in sociology that downplays the social significance of emotion. She demonstrates that emotions matter, and they matter not only in the domestic sphere but in the workplace – they are an essential, and rationally instrumental, part of the commodities produced and sold in an ever-expanding service economy[4]. Second, as Hochschild (1983: 11) notes, women comprise a disproportionately large number of workers employed in service occupations requiring a substantial amount of emotional labor. Focusing on emotional labor, therefore, directly accesses the everyday experiences of women, whether at home or in the workplace.

Further, Hochschild's attentiveness to the personal and social costs of emotional labor makes a significant contribution not only to sociologists' understanding of the social and gendered contexts of emotion, but to broadening our understanding of occupations and labor-market processes. She makes a strong case that emotional labor is more costly to the self and social relationships than is manual-physical labor (because of the deep acting it requires). Of course, many manual laborers, especially the low-wage migrant and immigrant women workers (e.g., hotel maids and housekeepers) in the global service economy (e.g., Sassen 2007), also pay a steep emotional price. Many of them, for example, along with nurses and other service professionals leave their children behind in their home countries and deprive themselves of the everyday emotional satisfaction of family life in order for their families back home to subsist (e.g., England 2005: 392). In Ireland, for example, the health services sector is heavily reliant on immigrant Filipino nurses, many of whom can't afford to bring their children and other family members with them, thus intensifying the bifurcated emotion work they must do as nurses and as physically-absent mothers.

SUMMARY

Like society as a whole, sociology has been transformed by the changes in the status of women. Feminist theorists have challenged the discipline's marginalization of women's realities so that sociology can in fact be what it claims to be: a theory about society, one that recognizes that social processes and institutions shape, and are shaped by, the different gendered, racial, and other intersecting locations of individuals. Early feminist scholars such as Harriet Martineau and Charlotte Perkins Gilman observed the contradictions between women's lives and the male world that defined and curtailed them. Among contemporary theorists, Dorothy Smith and Patricia Hill Collins underscore how women's everyday experiences challenge the dominant ways of categorizing knowledge and organizing institutional life, and Arlie Hochschild demonstrates how emotion work varies by social context and by gendered and other socially differentiated statuses embedded in and determining institutional relations. Just as a feminist standpoint on social life challenges the dominant ways in which knowledge, experiences, and institutional practices are understood, sociologists have also opened up our understanding of masculinity. R. W. Connell, in particular, draws attention to the fact that masculinity expectations and practices vary by class, race, and sexuality and are positioned in relations of subordination vis-à-vis a dominant form of masculinity.

POINTS TO REMEMBER

Feminist standpoint theory (Smith):
- Challenges the male bias in allegedly objective knowledge
- Focuses attention on women's everyday/everynight knowledge and experiences
- Argues that sociological knowledge must begin from *within* the context of the people studied

- Women who move between the domestic and the public worlds develop a bifurcated consciousness of the split between objectified knowledge and women's everyday, localized experiences
- Standpoint theory opens up awareness and knowledge not only of women's diverse experiences but also of the experiences of all marginalized groups, including men whose masculinities contravene the hegemonic masculinity (Connell)
- There are multiple and varied, though hierarchically ordered, masculinities
- Hegemonic masculinity celebrates a macho heterosexuality and suppresses any signs of femininity in the male self

Black women's standpoint (Collins):
- Highlights the specific racial history of oppression black women collectively share
- Ideologically controlling images (e.g., mammy, matriarch, welfare mother, whore) continue to define and oppress black women
- Black feminist thought produces activist knowledge from black women articulating their experiences of, and responses to, the everyday contradictions they encounter as black women oppressed by race, gender, and other intersecting, marginalized statuses
- Attentiveness to sexual politics highlights how ideologies of femininity and masculinity are variously used to disempower all subjugated groups in society, including black gay and straight men
- An "honest bodies" project rejects the black gender ideology and commodification processes that subjugate black women
- "Honest bodies" require the reclaiming of authentic sexual identities and sexual feelings, especially by black women and black gay men

Emotional labor (Hochschild):
- The expression/display of feelings and emotion is socially regulated
- Women do more emotion management than men both in the home and at and as work
- Emotional labor is commodified; it has exchange- and profit value
- Involves face-to-face or voice-to-voice contact with the public
- Requires the worker's production of an emotional state in another person
- Is specified, supervised, and managed by employers

GLOSSARY

activist knowledge knowledge generated from within oppressed groups' lived experiences; empowers individuals to resist and take action against their oppression.

alternative sociology starts from the lived experiences and the standpoint of women and other minority groups rather than claiming an objectivity that largely cloaks male-centered knowledge; leads to the empowerment of women and men.

androcentric culture institutional practices and ideology whereby maleness defines humanity and the social reality of men and women.

bifurcation of consciousness knowledge that emerges from the contradictory realities women experience because of the split between objectified knowledge and the public world of work etc. and women's everyday, localized experiences (in the home, as mothers, etc.).

black feminist thought knowledge voiced by black women from within their lived experiences and across the different sites of their everyday reality.

black women's standpoint the common experiences that all African-American women share as a result of being black women in a society that denigrates women of African descent.

commercialization of feeling the training, production, and control of human emotions for economic profit.

controlling images demeaning images and representations of, for example, black women circulated by the largely white-controlled mass media and other social institutions.

discourse of femininity images, ideas, and talk in society informing how women should present themselves and behave vis-à-vis men and society as a whole.

domestic world home–neighborhood sphere of women's activity in a man-made world; deemed inferior to the public world in which men work, rule, and play.

emotion work control or management of feelings in accordance with socially and culturally defined feeling rules.

emotional display socially learned and regulated presentation of emotional expression.

emotional labor emotion work individuals do at and as work, for pay; has exchange-value.

everyday/everynight world continuous reality of women's lives as they negotiate the gendered responsibilities of motherhood, marriage, work, etc.

feeling rules socially defined, patterned ways of what to feel and how to express emotion in social interaction and in responding to and anticipating social events.

femininity (man-made) societal ideals and expectations informing how women should think and act in a society that rewards masculinity and male control of women.

feminist revolution transformation of knowledge and of social and institutional practices such that women are considered fully equal to men.

feminist theory focuses on women's inequality in society and how that inequality is structured and experienced at macro and micro levels.

gender ideology a society's dominant beliefs elaborating different conceptualizations of women and men and of their self-presentation, behavior, and place in society.

hegemonic masculinity – the dominant and most authoritative culture of masculinity in society; affirms heterosexuality, physicality, competitiveness, and the suppression of emotional vulnerability.

honest bodies rejection of sexual exploitation and degradation (e.g., of women and gays) and the affirmation of sexual images, desires, and practices that recognize the emotional-relational context of sexual expression.

information economy dominance of information or service commodities, produced and exchanged for profit.

institutional ethnography an investigation that starts with individual experiences as a way to discover how institutions work and how they might work better for people.

intersectionality multiple crisscrossing ways in which different histories and diverse structural locations (based on race, gender, class, sexuality, etc.) situate individuals' experiences and life chances.

knowing from within the idea that sociological knowledge must start from within the lived realities of the individuals and groups studied.

management of feeling control of emotion via the creation of a publicly observable and convincing display, irrespective of one's inner feelings.

masculinity societal expectations and practices governing the self-presentation and behavior of men; accentuates characteristics and traits of domination that are the opposite of femininity (subordination).

multiple masculinities the idea that masculinity expectations and practices vary by class, race, and sexuality and are positioned in relations of subordination and marginalization to the hegemonic masculinity.

new racism symbols and ideas used (in politics, pop culture, the mass media) to argue that race-based (biological) differences no longer matter even as such arguments reinforce racial-cultural differences and stereotypes.

patriarchal society one in which white men have a privileged position by virtue of the historically grounded, man-made construction of social institutions, texts, and practices.

politics of sexuality focus on the various ways in which ideas about sex and sexuality are used to create and contest divisions between and within particular social groups based on gender and sexual orientation differences.

public world the nondomestic arena; domains of work, politics, sports, etc., the sphere given greater legitimacy in society.

relations of ruling institutional and cultural routines that govern and maintain the unequal position of women in relation to men within and across all societal domains.

ruling practices array of institutional and cultural practices that maintain unequal gender relations in society.

ruling texts core man-made texts (e.g., Bible, US Constitution, laws, advertising) that define gender and other power relations in society.

self-alienation produced as a result of emotional laborers' splitting of internal feelings and external emotion management.

standpoint a group's positioning within the unequal power structure and the everyday lived knowledge that emerges from that position.

QUESTIONS FOR REVIEW

1   Identify one specific way in which gender inequality is manifested in the workplace, at church, at home, in sports, in television entertainment, in advertising, in politics, in sociology. In each instance, explain the processes of its reproduction. What are the ruling practices and the ruling texts that seem to matter in each case?
2   Given the strides in women's equality since 1990 (when Smith's books were published), does the construct of women's "bifurcated consciousness" still make sense? Why/why not?
3   How does a social intersectionality framework advance the understanding of gendered realities? How does intersectionality work in institutional processes and in everyday realities?
4   How can sociologists study and understand the lives and experiences of those who are different to us? What does it really mean to study social life "from within"? And what do we gain from doing so? Are standpoint knowledge and activist knowledge scientifically valid knowledge?
5   How can emotions that appear so "natural" be considered social, and even more specifically, gendered? What is emotional labor? Where can we see it? Is it hard work?

NOTES

1   Outside of sociology, other influential and Marx-inspired feminist standpoint theorists include political theorist Nancy Hartsock (1998) and philosopher of science Sandra Harding (e.g., 1987, 1991).
2   Although Collins capitalizes "Black," the convention in sociology today is not to capitalize color words for race (black, white); I follow this convention.
3   Nancy Chodorow (1978), using a psychoanalytical framework, has also made very important contributions to the understanding of emotion in gender-role reproduction.

4   Hochschild notes that service work is a requirement in capitalist and socialist economies. "Any functioning society makes effective use of its members' emotional labor. We do not think twice about the use of feeling in the theater, or in psychotherapy, or in forms of group life that we admire. It is when we come to speak of the exploitation of the bottom by the top in any society that we become morally concerned" (Hochschild 1983: 12).

REFERENCES

Andersen, Margaret, and Patricia Hill Collins. 1995. *Race, Class, and Gender: An Anthology*. Belmont, CA: Wadsworth.

Bernard, Jessie. 1998. "My Four Revolutions: An Autobiographical History of the ASA." Pp. 3–20 in Kristin Myers, Cynthia Anderson, and Barbara Risman, eds. *Feminist Foundations: Toward Transforming Sociology*. Thousand Oaks, CA: Sage.

Buckley, Cara, and Annie Correal. 2008. "Domestic Workers Organize to End an 'Atmosphere of Violence on the Job.'" *New York Times* (June 9).

Burton, Linda M., Diane Purvin, and Raymond Garrett-Peters. 2015. "Longitudinal Ethnography: Uncovering Domestic Abuse in Low-Income Women's Lives." Pp. 29–47 in Julia Hall, ed. *Female Students and Cultures of Violence in Cities*, volume 9. New York: Routledge.

Cannon, Katie. 1985. "The Emergence of a Black Feminist Consciousness." Pp. 30–40 in Letty Russell, ed. *Feminist Interpretations of the Bible*. Philadelphia: Westminster Press.

Chodorow, Nancy. 1978. *The Reproduction of Mothering: Psychoanalysis and the Sociology of Gender.* Berkeley: University of California Press.

Collins, Patricia Hill. 1990. *Black Feminist Thought: Knowledge, Consciousness, and the Politics of Empowerment.* New York: Routledge. 2nd edition 2000.

Collins, Patricia Hill. 2004. *Black Sexual Politics.* New York: Routledge.

Collins Patricia Hill. 2015. "Intersectionality's Definitional Dilemmas." *Annual Review of Sociology* 41: 1–20.

Collins, Patricia Hill, and Sirma Bilge. 2016. *Intersectionality.* Malden, MA: Polity Press.

Connell, R.W. 1983. *Which Way Is Up? Essays on Sex, Class, and Culture.* Sydney: Allen & Unwin.

Connell, R.W. 1987. *Gender and Power: Society, the Person and Sexual Politics.* New York: Cambridge University Press.

Connell, R.W. 1995. *Masculinities.* New York: Cambridge University Press.

Cott, Nancy. 1987. *The Grounding of Modern Feminism.* New Haven, CT: Yale University Press.

De Beauvoir, Simone. 1949/1953. *The Second Sex.* Harmondsworth: Penguin.

DeVault, Marjorie, ed. 2008. *People at Work: Life, Power, and Social Inclusion in the New Economy.* New York: New York University Press.

England, Paula. 2005. "Emerging Theories of Care Work." *Annual Review of Sociology* 31: 381–399.

Fields, Erroll Lamont, et al. 2015. "'I Always Felt I Had to Prove My Manhood': Homosexuality, Masculinity, Gender Role Strain, and HIV Risk Among Young Black Men Who Have Sex With Men." *American Journal of Public Health* 105: 122–131.

Fanon, Frantz. 1967. *Black Skin, White Masks.* Translated by Charles Lam Markmann. New York: Grove Press.

Gilligan, Carol. 1982. *In a Different Voice.* Cambridge, MA: Harvard University Press.

Gilman, Charlotte Perkins. 1903/1972. *The Home: Its Work and Influence.* Introduction by William O'Neill. Urbana, IL: University of Chicago Press.

Gilman, Charlotte Perkins. 1911. *Man-Made World or Our Androcentric Culture.* New York: Charlton.

Gilroy, Paul. 2000. *Against Race: Imagining Political Culture Beyond the Color Line.* Cambridge, MA: Harvard University Press.

Gutman, Herbert. 1976. *The Black Family in Slavery and Freedom, 1750–1925.* New York: Pantheon.

Harding, Sandra, ed. 1987. *Feminism and Methodology.* Bloomington: Indiana University Press.

Harding, Sandra. 1991. *Whose Science? Whose Knowledge? Thinking from Women's Lives.* Ithaca, NY: Cornell University Press.

Hartsock, Nancy. 1998. *The Feminist Standpoint Revisited and Other Essays.* Boulder, CO: Westview Press.

Hochschild, Arlie. 1983. *The Managed Heart: Commercialization of Human Feeling.* Berkeley: University of California Press.

Hochschild, Arlie. 2003. *The Commercialization of Intimate Life: Notes from Home and Work.* Berkeley: University of California Press.

Hochschild, Arlie. 2012. *The Outsourced Self: Intimate Life in Market Times.* New York: Henry Holt and Company.

Hochschild, Arlie. 2016. *Strangers in Their Own Land: Anger and Mourning on the American Right.* New York: New Press.

Hochschild, Arlie, with Anne Machung. 1990. *The Second Shift.* New York: Avon Books.

Jones, Nikki. 2010. *Between Good and Ghetto: African American Girls and Inner City Violence.* New Brunswick, NJ: Rutgers University Press.

Kimmel, Michael. 2005. *The Gender of Desire: Essays on Male Sexuality.* Albany, NY: SUNY Press.

Laslett, Barbara, and Barrie Thorne, eds. 1997. *Feminist Sociology: Life Histories of a Movement.* New Brunswick, NJ: Rutgers University Press.

Miller, Jody. 2008. *Getting Played: African American Girls, Urban Inequality, and Gendered Violence.* New York: New York University Press.

Mills, C. Wright. 1951. *White Collar: The American Middle Classes.* New York: Oxford University Press.

Myers, Kristin, Cynthia Anderson, and Barbara Risman, eds. 1998. *Feminist Foundations: Toward Transforming Sociology.* Thousand Oaks, CA: Sage.

O'Neill, William. 1972. "Introduction to This Edition." Pp. vii–xviii in Charlotte Perkins Gilman. 1903/1972. *The Home: Its Work and Influence.* Urbana: University of Illinois Press.

Pascoe, C.J. 2007. *Dude, You're a Fag: Masculinity and Sexuality in High School.* Berkeley: University of California Press.

Pattillo, Mary. 2013. *Black Picket Fences: Privilege and Peril among the Black Middle Class.* 2nd edition. Chicago: University of Chicago Press.

Pence, Ellen, and Martha McMahon. 2003. "Working From Inside and Outside Institutions: How Safety Audits Can Help Courts' Decision Making around Domestic Violence and Child Maltreatment." *Juvenile and Family Court Journal* 54: 133–147.

Pence, Ellen, and Michael Paymar. 1993. *Education Groups for Men who Batter: The Duluth Model.* New York: Springer.

Pew Research Center. 2017. *Support for Same-Sex Marriage Grows, Even Among Groups That Had Been Skeptical.* Washington, DC: Pew Research Center.

Polletta, Francesca. 2006. *It Was Like a Fever: Storytelling in Protest and Politics.* Chicago: University of Chicago Press.

Rankin, Janet, and Marie Campbell. 2006. *Managing to Nurse:*

Inside Canada's Health Care Reform. Toronto: University of Toronto Press.

Ray, Raka. 2006. "Is the Revolution Missing or Are We Looking in the Wrong Places?" *Social Problems* 53: 459–465.

Said, Edward. 1978. *Orientalism*. New York: Random House.

Sassen, Saskia. 2007. *A Sociology of Globalization*. New York: Norton.

Simmel, Georg. 1917/1950. *The Sociology of Georg Simmel*. Translated, edited, and with an introduction by Kurt Wolff. Glencoe, IL: Free Press.

Simmel, Georg. 1921/1971. *On Individuality and Social Forms*. Edited and with an introduction by Donald Levine. Chicago: University of Chicago Press.

Smelser, Neil. 1962. *Theory of Collective Behavior*. Glencoe, IL: Free Press.

Smith, Dorothy. 1987. *The Everyday World as Problematic: A Feminist Sociology*. Boston: Northeastern University Press.

Smith, Dorothy. 1990a. *The Conceptual Practices of Power: A Feminist Sociology of Knowledge*. Boston: Northeastern University Press.

Smith, Dorothy. 1990b. *Texts, Facts, and Femininity: Exploring the Relations of Ruling*. New York: Routledge.

Smith, Dorothy. 2005. *Institutional Ethnography: A Sociology for People*. Lanham, MD: AltaMira/Rowman & Littlefield.

Stets, Jan, and Jonathan Turner. 2006. *Handbook of the Sociology of Emotions*. New York: Springer.

Tallichet, Suzanne. 2006. *Daughters of the Mountains: Women Coal Miners in Central Appalachia*. University Park: Pennsylvania State University Press.

Tavernise, Sabrina. 2016. "Black Americans, Living Longer, Reduce Disparity in Life Spans." *New York Times* (May 9).

Tuchman, Gaye. 2011. *Wannabe U: Inside the Corporate University*. Chicago: University of Chicago Press.

Wallace, Ruth. 1989. "Introduction." Pp. 7–19 in Ruth Wallace, ed. *Feminism and Sociological Theory*. Newbury Park, CA: Sage.

Wilson, William Julius. 1978. *The Declining Significance of Race*. Chicago: University of Chicago Press.

CHAPTER ELEVEN

SEX, BODIES, TRUTH, AND POWER
MICHEL FOUCAULT, STEVEN SEIDMAN, AND QUEER THEORY

KEY CONCEPTS

disciplinary practices	genealogy	essentialist view of sexuality
surveillance	confession	constructionist view of
docile bodies	regime of truth	sexuality
Panopticon	politics of truth	semiotic code
bio-power	ritual of discourse	queering the text
discourse	power	queer theory
techniques of bio-power	heterosexist	

CHAPTER MENU

Introduction to Sociological Theory: Theorists, Concepts, and Their Applicability to the Twenty-First Century,
Third Edition. Michele Dillon.
© 2020 John Wiley & Sons Ltd. Published 2020 by John Wiley & Sons Ltd.
Companion website: www.wiley.com/go/dillon

The principal figure who transformed the body from a biological or physiological subject to an object of social inquiry was the late French philosopher **Michel Foucault.** He wrote extensively on philosophical questions probing the nature of knowledge, truth, and power. At the time of his death in 1984, he was regarded as "the most famous intellectual figure in the world" (Ryan 1993: 12). Foucault's fame derived from the wide range of topics he covered (see e.g., Power 2011 for a review) and the audacious challenge he posed to what we tend to think of as the "natural" order of things; how, for example, societal definitions of sexuality are not natural or preordained categories but human-social creations, and thus *social* constructions (cf. Berger and Luckmann, see chapter 9).

BIOGRAPHICAL NOTE

Michel Foucault was born in Paris, France, in 1926. He studied at the highly prestigious École Normale in Paris and wrote his dissertation on the history of psychiatry, later published as *Madness and Civilization* (1965). Foucault held many distinguished academic positions including a faculty appointment at France's most prestigious university, the Collège de France. For many years he was also a visiting professor at the University of California, Berkeley, and was famously involved in the gay culture of San Francisco from the mid-1970s until his death in 1984, allegedly from AIDS, then a disease emerging into public notice (Eribon 1991). Many of Foucault's books were best sellers in Europe and North America, and he wrote extensively about politics and culture for French newspapers and magazines.

DISCIPLINING THE BODY

Foucault investigated how institutional practices evolved so as to make control and regulation of the body, and hence the subjugation of individuals and society, a core preoccupation. Although "the body" is frequently associated with feminist scholarship, Foucault would not be considered a feminist. In fact, he is heavily criticized by feminist scholars for his intellectual abstraction and disregard for the subjectively lived experiences of embodied individuals (e.g., Hartsock 1998: 215–221; Hekman 1996; Taylor and Vintges 2004). His work, nevertheless, is of particular relevance to sociologists interested in the body – and especially in institutional processes – because much of his writing is devoted to uncovering how the body came to have several **disciplinary practices** imposed upon it. The "birth" of the prison, of madness, the clinic, the asylum, and sexuality – each of these topics converge in underscoring Foucault's focus on how society develops ways of regulating and controlling, that is, disciplining, the body/bodies. Therefore, despite his lack of attention to how disciplining practices are gendered and impact women and men differently (e.g., Bartky 1998), he stimulates us to think about the body and about social processes in new ways.

When we see the word "discipline" in a sociological text, we may well think of Max Weber, who drew attention to how the Protestant ethic's requirement of personal discipline and self-control provided the cultural-motivational energy for the expansion of capitalism (see chapter 3). Weber was interested in discipline insofar as it reflected and reinforced the increased rationality of modern society. Unlike Foucault, however, he did not discuss the body as an object of rationality in and of itself.

For Foucault, the history of civilization is the ever-expanding increase in rational **surveillance** of and over the body (bodies); modern, civilized society monitors, reins in, and disciplines the body. And although, historically, slavery regulated the body as a whole, Foucault argues that modern disciplinary practices target body details: "Discipline is a political anatomy of detail" (Foucault 1979: 139), wherein body desires, movements, gestures, attitudes, and behavior are subject to "a policy of coercions that act upon the body" with calculated manipulation (1979: 137–138). The physical-spatial layout, time scheduling, and supervisory and other organizational practices used in prisons, hospitals, asylums, military academies, and schools produces **docile bodies**: "A body is docile that may be subjected, used, transformed and improved" (1979: 136). Thus, from our earliest days in preschool, we learn (or are coerced) to sit attentively in a disciplined manner in class, and this body self-regulation continues as we grow: "No slouching!"; "Sit down and be still!"; "Keep your hands to yourself!"; "No looking around!" are the commands of parents, teachers, and coaches.

Foucault used the **Panopticon**, a model of a prison proposed by Jeremy Bentham in the eighteenth century, to illustrate how disciplinary power works, to underscore how its continuous penetrating surveillance gives the individual no respite. The Panopticon is a large spatial area with a tower in the center, surrounded by rows of buildings, and divided into multilevel cells with windows; the cells act as "small theatres in which each actor is alone, perfectly individualized and constantly visible" (Foucault 1979: 200). The inmate is an object, constantly observed, and constantly an object of information (derived from their constantly monitored actions), and visible only and at all times to the supervisor. The inmate cannot be seen by other inmates nor have contact with inmates in other cells (1979: 200). The power of the Panopticon also lies in the fact that the inmate cannot see whether the supervisor is present or not, and hence must act as if they are being observed at all times. The supervisors, too, moreover, are enmeshed in the localization of power: "they observe, but in the process of so doing, they are also fixed, regulated, and subject to administrative control" (Dreyfus and Rabinow 1983: 189). In today's world, the reach of technological and electronic surveillance – the various uses of sensors and GPS tracking technology, and the electronic monitoring of blogs, e-mail, Google searches, and Facebook (as noted in chapter 5) – might be seen as the new Panopticon. Such electronic surveillance is perhaps even more controlling; it transcends any localized geographical space and its visibility is more subtle than the presence of a human supervisor or a concrete structure (e.g., a watchtower).

BIO-POWER

Foucault (1978: 140–141) argues that **bio-power**, that is, the linking of biological processes (or body practices) to economic and political power, coincided with industrialization and capitalist growth in the eighteenth and nineteenth centuries and in the related expansion of the nation-state and other social institutions. He argues that although we associate the Victorian era (the nineteenth century) with sexual repression and silence (1978: 1–5, 17), that era, in fact, was one in which sex was a major preoccupation. It saw the transformation of sex into **discourse**, into something to be talked about, interrogated, and categorized. This transformation of sex, however, is not a liberation from repression as we might be inclined to think. Rather, Foucault argues that it produces a discourse that regulates and controls sex and the body.

He elaborates how, for example, the census of population – the great demographic data resource that many sociologists use, and that government officials and policymakers rely on – became one of a number of **techniques of bio-power**. It became an instrument for monitoring and controlling the practices of the body/bodies:

> One of the great innovations in the techniques of power in the eighteenth century was the emergence of "population" as an economic and political problem: population as wealth, population as manpower or labor capacity, population balanced between its own growth and the resources it commanded. Governments perceived that they were not dealing simply with subjects, or even with a "people," but with a population, with its specific phenomena and its peculiar variables: birth and death rates, life expectancy, fertility, state of health, frequency of illnesses, patterns of diet and habitation … At the heart of this economic and political problem of population was sex: it was necessary to analyze the birth rate, the age of marriage, the legitimate and illegitimate births, the precocity [e.g., age of sexual initiation] and frequency of sexual relations, the ways of making them fertile or sterile, the effects of unmarried life … the impact of contraceptive practices. (Foucault 1978: 25–26)

In other words, demographers had to categorize, document, analyze, and publicize all those acts that people did with their bodies (as do medical doctors, medical insurance companies, etc.) – their various sexual habits and arrangements, and those "secrets" of sex that were already familiar to the people engaged in varied sexual practices/relationships. Foucault adds that although it was long accepted that countries needed to be populated if they wished to be prosperous,

> this was the first time that a society had affirmed, in a constant way, that its future and its fortune were tied not only to the number and the uprightness of its citizens, to their marriage rules and family organization, but to the manner in which each individual made use of his sex … It was essential that the state know what was happening with its citizens' sex, and the use they made of it, but also that each individual be capable of controlling the use he made of it. Between the state and the individual, sex became an issue, and a public issue no less; a whole web of discourses, special knowledges, analyses, and injunctions settled upon it. (Foucault 1978: 26)

THE INVENTION OF SEXUALITY

Accordingly Foucault argues, biopolitics invented sexuality through various technologies, that is, its ethods, categories, and procedures. Through the census, for example, we have invented the categories by which we come to label and enumerate different sexual circumstances and behaviors. Foucault argues that how society categorizes sex (or anything else) is highly arbitrary, and to make his point he uses a humorous historical example – the categorization of animals taken, he says, from a "certain Chinese encyclopedia." He summarizes, "Animals are divided into: (a) belonging to the Emperor, (b) embalmed, (c) tame, (d) sucking pigs, (e) sirens, (f) innumerable, (k) drawn with a very fine camelhair brush, (l) et cetera, (m) having just broken the water pitcher, (n) that from a long way off look like flies." Foucault comments: "In the wonderment of this taxonomy, the thing we apprehend in one great leap, the thing that … is demonstrated as the exotic charm of another system of thought, is the limitation of our own, the stark impossibility of thinking *that*" (Foucault 1974: xv). It is easy for us to express wonderment at this peculiar Chinese set of animal categories. And Foucault pushes us to have the same wonderment with regard to our own society's categorizations, categories that seem natural and normal, but which Foucault argues are arbitrary and, perhaps, nonsensical.

Thus there is nothing natural about the census definitions or categories; they are administrative-bureaucratic constructs and, as such, are relatively arbitrary ways by which we describe and carve up the use of sex and, also, how society controls sex. If you look at the census of population today (see Box 11.1) you will readily see that the government makes several distinctions inferred from individuals' sexual identities, habits, and arrangements; who does what with whom and under what particular circumstances. The government uses this information in making and administering policy decisions about the allocation of economic, health, social welfare, and other resources. Once created, these categories make available to us ways of thinking about sex and what we can do or should do with sex. We categorize ourselves (i.e., where we fit in terms of these categories), and if our sexual habits and arrangements are not included in these lists, we wonder about the normalcy of our identities and practices. The US Census, for example, does not give people the option of identifying as transgender. In short, sex is not only categorized but defined, prescribed, and regulated by society.

Box 11.1   Keeping a tab on bodies: Census categories

Marital status
- Currently married
  - *Spouse present*
  - *Spouse absent*
- Widowed
- Divorced
- Separated
- Never married

Households
- Married couple households
- Unmarried partner households
- Opposite-sex partners
  - With own children
  - With own and/or unrelated children
- Same-sex partners
  - With own children
  - With own and/or unrelated children

Births
- To teenage mothers
- To unmarried mothers

THE PRODUCTION OF BODY DISCOURSE

Historically, the biopolitical production of discourse on sex (e.g., census data and its particular categories) meant that, like sex, the body too became something to be regulated and controlled. It produced a "constant alertness" among institutional authorities as to what was "normal" and "pathological" regarding both sex and the body (Foucault 1978: 28). Teachers, doctors, psychiatrists, psychotherapists, and workers in the criminal justice system, among others, became experts in investigating, discovering, categorizing, and (allegedly) remedying sexual peculiarities and perversions (1978: 30–31). These experts produced discourses on sex "undertaking to protect, separate, and forewarn, signaling peril everywhere, awakening people's attention, calling for diagnoses, piling up reports, organizing therapies. These [institutional] sites radiated discourse aimed at sex, intensifying people's awareness of it as a constant danger, and this in turn created a further incentive to talk about it" (1978: 30–31). See also Topic 11.1.

Topic 11.1   The birth of obesity

Amidst today's biopolitics (seen in public debates over abortion, stem-cell research, sex education, physician-assisted suicide, etc.), we are witnessing "the birth of obesity," as the government, working in tandem with the medical profession, researchers, and the health insurance industry, is imposing a new body category, obesity, one that is (and must be) institutionally monitored, tracked, and controlled. In 1998, the US government-funded National Institutes of Health (NIH) created guidelines defining and regulating obesity. Individuals whose body mass index (BMI) rating is between 18.5 and 24.9 are categorized as "normal," a rating between 25 and 29.9 makes you "overweight," and you are considered "obese" if your BMI is 30 or higher. By these standards, 38 percent of American adults and 20 percent of American youth are obese. The UK has the highest obesity rates in Europe but, at 27 percent for adults and 15 percent for youth, they are lower than in the US. Obesity rates have increased in several Western countries over the last decade and are projected to continue to grow (OECD Obesity Update, 2017; https://www.oecd.org/els/health-systems/Obesity-Update-2017.pdf). The "birth of obesity" has produced a vocabulary of obesity permeating everyday life such that many schools monitor students' weight and send obesity reports to parents documenting their children's BMI score, as well as an outline of recommended corrective dieting and exercise actions they should take to remedy their obesity. The birth of obesity has also led to the establishment of specialized centers for obesity research, national and international reports on rates and future projections of obesity, "Fat Studies" as a scholarly field, and specialized summer camps and spas catering to obesity reduction. Additionally, quite apart from obesity discourse, bodies are also highly regulated by everyday advertising, the fashion and cosmetology industries, and mass media content reminding us that particular kinds of bodies are better and more attractive than others (see also chapters 8, 10, and 12). And to help us be mindful of (and control) our bodies, we have smartphone apps to monitor our body particulars and what we are doing with and to our bodies any time every day, including our body fat percentage, our BMI, and our weight as well as our fitness and our sexual and menstrual activity (see also chapter 5, Topic 5.2).

CONFESSING SEX

The incitement to talk about the body and about sex, Foucault argues, has a sociohistorical **genealogy** originating in the sixteenth century. This was when the Catholic Church (as part of the Counter-Reformation reforms accentuating its theological differences from the emerging Protestant Church) gave increased emphasis to the obligatory ritual of **confession**. Because of the Catholic prohibition on sex outside of marriage, sex became the core topic of confessional interrogation; the Church made "sex into that which above all else, had to be confessed" (Foucault 1978: 35). Thus the Catholic confession became a major technique of bio-power; its procedures sought to extract truth about something that was omnipresent – sexual desire – yet repressed because of its sinful aura. The Church targeted not only sexual acts but sexual *desires*:

> The scope of the confession – the confession of the flesh – continually increased … [It] impose[d] meticulous rules of self-examination … attributing more and more importance in penance … to all the insinuations of the flesh: thoughts, desires, voluptuous imaginings, delectations, combined movements of the body and the soul; henceforth all this had to enter, in detail, into the process of confession and guidance. According to the new pastoral [the Catholic Church's instructions regarding confession], sex must not be named imprudently, but its aspects, its correlations, and its effects must be pursued down to their slenderest ramifications: a shadow in a daydream, an image too slowly dispelled, a badly exorcised complicity between the body's mechanics and the mind's complacency: everything had to be told. (Foucault 1978: 19)

By interrogating and requiring the self-examination of every intricate and fleeting sexual desire, the confession shifted

> the most important moment of transgression from the act itself to the stirrings – so difficult to perceive and formulate – of desire … Discourse, therefore, had to trace the meeting line of the body and the soul, following all its meanderings … Under the authority of a language that had been carefully expurgated so that it was no longer directly named, sex was taken charge of, tracked down as it were, by a discourse that aimed to allow it no obscurity, no respite. (Foucault 1978: 20)

In short, the confessing individual was obliged to "transform desire, every desire into discourse" (Foucault 1978: 21), through the self-examination of conscience, a process advanced during confession upon further interrogation by a priest and the inquisitorial language at his disposal.

PRODUCING TRUTH

Discourse, therefore, according to Foucault, the ways in which we categorize things, and talk (and remain silent) about what we do and what we desire, produces truth. This "truth" is not some lofty philosophical or religious truth, but a truth produced by the institutional apparatuses operating in a given society. Foucault argues that every society has its **regime of truth**. Just as we in the West refer to nondemocratic, authoritarian governments as *regimes*, so too we can think of Foucault's *regime of truth* as indicating what he sees as the systemic, authoritarian, and controlling ways in which modern society produces particular truths. For Foucault, the confessional discourses extracted by the church, and the various discourses produced by the state, the military, the medical and the criminal justice systems (and also by schools) are used not to establish some pure, disembodied truth but to categorize, govern, and regulate bodies. These are the institutional regimes that produce truth. Hence truth is not something that is independent of society, of the political and institutional contexts in which it is produced. Rather, Foucault argues, the history of ideas shows that knowledge has many imperfections and uncertainties. Knowledge has an archaeology (Foucault 1972) and a genealogy (Foucault 1984), a history that is built upon various pieces of bedrock. There are many discontinuities and shifts, therefore, in what is accepted as knowledge and in the ways of categorizing and formalizing knowledge and its related practices (evident, for example, if you compare changes over time in how criminologists and psychiatrists categorize crimes or illness). In Foucault's view, the truths and categories and knowledges produced – whether in literature, philosophy, psychiatry (Foucault 1965), medicine (Foucault 1975), criminology (Foucault 1979), or sexuality (Foucault 1978) – are coerced and power ridden. In sum, truth is entangled in politics and power and is far from pure. As Foucault reminds us,

> Truth isn't outside power, or lacking in power: contrary to a myth whose history and functions would repay further study, truth isn't the reward of free spirits, the child of protracted solitude, nor the privilege of those who have succeeded in liberating themselves. Truth is a thing of this world: it is produced only by virtue of multiple forms of constraint … Each society has its regime of truth, its general **politics of truth**: that is, the types of discourse which it accepts and makes function as true … The political question, to sum up, is not error, illusion, alienated consciousness, or ideology; it is truth itself. (Foucault 1984: 72–73, 75)

SEX AND THE CONFESSING SOCIETY

Foucault argues that confession as a technique of truth/power subsequently expanded beyond the religious sphere (Foucault 1978: 63), and alongside the development of scientific techniques and institutional discourses (of demography, medicine, psychiatry etc.):

> The confession became one of the West's most highly valued techniques for producing truth. We have since become a singularly confessing society. The confession has spread its effects far and wide. It plays a part in justice, medicine, education, family relationships, and love relations, in the most ordinary affairs of everyday life, and in the most solemn rites; one confesses one's crimes, one's sins, one's thoughts and desires, one's illnesses and troubles; one goes about telling with the greatest precision, whatever is most difficult to tell. One confesses in public and in private, to one's parents, one's educators, one's doctor, to those one loves; one admits to oneself, in pleasure and in pain, things it would be impossible to tell to anyone else, the things people write books about. One confesses – or is forced to confess. When it is not spontaneous or dictated by some internal imperative, the confession is wrung from a person by violence or threat; it is driven from its hiding place in the soul or extracted from the body. Since the Middle Ages torture has accompanied it like a shadow, and supported it when it could go no further: the dark twins. The most defenseless tenderness and the bloodiest of powers have a similar need of confession. Western man has become a confessing animal. (Foucault 1978: 59)

Figure 11.1   The disciplined body. Church, state, mass media, social media, and everyday conversation regulate bodies, body talk, and body desire. Source: Author.

The desire to confess, and the expectation that we should confess and coerce the confessions of others permeates contemporary everyday life. It is body practices, moreover, that still comprise confessional discourse. Politicians, Hollywood celebrities, sports stars, and even national governments (e.g., Australia, Canada, South Africa for their treatment of minority populations) engage in ritualistic confessions. These confessions invariably revolve around the body – what individuals do with and to their bodies, and with and to other bodies. And many of these public confessions are typically not spontaneous but coerced by the threat that particular sexual and body secrets will be exposed by either old or new media surveillance (e.g., the *National Inquirer*, TMZ website, Twitter photos), and lead to punitive consequences.

THE PRODUCTION AND CIRCULATION OF POWER

Though it may unburden the confessing individual or organization, confession is essentially a power-ridden discourse:

> The confession is a **ritual of discourse** in which the speaking subject is also the subject of the statement; it is also a ritual that unfolds within a power relationship; for one does not confess without the presence (or virtual presence) of a partner who is not simply the interlocutor [the person(s) with whom we are speaking] but the authority who requires the confession, prescribes, and appreciates it, and intervenes in order to judge, punish, forgive, console, and reconcile; … a ritual in which the expression alone, independently of its external consequences, produces intrinsic modifications in the person who articulates it: it exonerates, redeems, and purifies him; it unburdens him of his wrongs, liberates him, and promises him salvation. (Foucault 1978: 61–62)

For Foucault, **power** is relational rather than consolidated in specific institutional locations as it is for Weber (e.g., in the state and bureaucracy; see chapter 3). For Foucault, power does not flow in a top-down, hierarchical fashion but has many sources and points of shifting impact and resistance. He states:

> Power is everywhere; not because it embraces everything, but because it comes from everywhere … power is not an institution, and not a structure … Power is not something that is acquired, seized, or shared, something that one holds on to or allows to slip away; power is exercised from innumerable points, in the interplay of nonegalitarian and mobile relations … Power comes from below; that is, there is no binary and all-encompassing opposition between rulers and ruled at the root of power relations … We must not look for who has the power in the order of sexuality (men, adults, parents, doctors) and who is deprived of it (women, adolescents, children, patients); nor for who has the right to know and who is forced to remain ignorant. (Foucault 1978: 93, 94, 99)

In other words, in Foucault's framing, power is not contained in any specific location, person, or social status; it is omnipresent and has no one anchor but continuously flows in all directions. Its pervasiveness is further underlined by the fact that all discourses are constituted and permeated by power. Remember that for Foucault, the transformation of sex into discourse was a biopolitical strategy: a population's body practices (including desires) are documented, interrogated, and categorized (e.g., births outside of marriage), and in the process translated into a problem that needs to be administered and controlled. Power thus works through discourse; the very discourse produced on sex – even though it may seem liberating to us that we can talk so freely about sex – is a strategy to demarcate what is sinful, normal, weird, etc.

Although the interrogator (especially when using physical torture) may seem to have more power than the interrogated person, the discursive process of confession is not a zero-sum game. The questions asked by the interrogator (whether a priest, Oprah Winfrey, or a journalist) are not spontaneously chosen by the interrogator but are determined externally by the discourse itself, by a given society's ways of naming and inquiring into what it is that is being interrogated. Power permeates all that is said, and not said. Similarly, the redemption and purification that derive from confessing further control the individual to think, desire, and behave within particular categories of normalcy. Both the interrogator and the interrogated are docile bodies, used and/or improved, that is, controlled, by the confessional discourse (cf. Foucault 1978: 136).

MASKING POWER

The circulation of power as discourse is all the more controlling because it is essentially masked in and through discourse. When we are flagged down by a police officer for driving above the speed limit, we know we are looking at power (in the Weberian sense) and that we are in an unequal power relationship with an authority figure. But when we are talking with our friends about the sex lives of celebrities we are not aware that the very discourse we use is itself subjecting *us* to a particular, regulated way of thinking/talking about, categorizing, and practicing sex. We think we are just talking about sex, but we are really engaged in reproducing bio-power. Thus

> it is in discourse that power and knowledge are joined together … we must not imagine a world of discourse divided between accepted discourse and excluded discourse, or between the dominant discourse and the dominated one … Discourse transmits and produces power; it reinforces it, but also undermines and exposes it, renders it fragile and makes it possible to thwart it. In like manner, silence and secrecy are a shelter for power, anchoring its prohibitions; but they also loosen its holds and provide for relatively obscure areas of tolerance. (Foucault 1978: 100, 101)

Therefore, although we use a more explicit sexual vocabulary today, our discourse also contains many silences about sex and the body. We are relatively silent about the human costs of sexual exploitation, including prostitution and sex trafficking, for example; these topics tend to receive little public attention unless there is a whiff of political or celebrity scandal. Hence Patricia Hill Collins (2004) challenges us to create "honest bodies" (see chapter 10). Our silences about sex are an inherent part of discourse and how it works. Foucault argues that silence is not the opposite of discourse; rather, silence "functions alongside the things said, with them and in relation to them within overall strategies … silences permeate discourses" (Foucault 1978: 27).

For example, until the policy was changed in 2011, the US military's "Don't ask, don't tell" rule allowed gays to serve in the military as long as they kept their sexuality secret. The policy may have expanded career opportunities for gay soldiers and increased tolerance of them in the military. At the same time, however, the necessary silence required their closeted invisibility and contributed to reproducing the stigma of being gay. Such policies reinforce the idea that gays are different – they have a special secret that must be repressed – and that somehow, despite a long history of closeted gays in the military (e.g., Berube 1990) and a long history of gays serving openly in the British military, gay sexuality detracts from the ability to be a good soldier. In the US, President Trump's July 2017 reversal of a 2016 government policy allowing transgender individuals to serve in the US military reignited public debate about the silencing of gender/sexual identities. Underscoring, however, the recent advances made in LGBT equality (see Topic 11.2), his decision was heavily criticized by both Republican and Democratic lawmakers as well as by civil rights groups, all of whom argued that the ability to serve should be based on current medical and fitness standards, not on gender/sexual status.

RESISTING/REPRODUCING POWER

The military, the state, and other institutions (the church, school, medicine, the criminal justice system) certainly use bio-power. As Foucault documents, their everyday practices revolve around disciplining the body and regulating populations. These are not the only agents and locales of power. According to Foucault, we are all engaged in the ongoing production of power, whether we want to or not. Discourse *is* power and we cannot escape from producing it even as we try to thwart it. Individuals and groups are always within relational power struggles, struggles that are fluid but also never-ending.

Thus, "there is no point where you are free from all power relations" (Foucault 1984/1994: 167). Resistance itself is critical to the ongoing circulation of power, but not to its elimination or its transformation into something else. Resistance is critical, not because it produces political opportunities for change, but because it maintains the circulation of power (1984/1994: 167).

This is where Foucault's understanding of discourse/power may make us feel entrapped and frustrated, though he says that it is more correct to think of power as a (never-ending) struggle than as entrapment (Foucault 1984/1994: 167). Nevertheless, we cannot use silence or language to reject power, even though it might seem to us that we can, and indeed must if, for example, we wish to mobilize against social inequality and create a just society (e.g., Hartsock 1998: 221). This is because, for Foucault – unlike Habermas who affirms the emancipatory potential of reasoned argumentation (see chapter 5) – language is itself compromised by power. Because language comes out of and is conditioned in sociohistorical contexts characterized by unequal power relations, it is impossible to change power structures and relations; the only discourse that we can use against power is itself riddled with power. Therefore, although some arguments and silences may seem like resistance, ultimately they reproduce power. Foucault emphasizes that all arguments and the language in which they are framed are impotent against power. Silence is also impotent because silence itself is part of discourse/power. Thus, neither talk nor silence can disrupt power; it continues to circulate and flow. Although for Foucault, discourse (including silence) is power, from a traditional sociological perspective it is ultimately impotent power. This is because we cannot use it to get out of, or transform, the relations of economic, gender, racial, and sexual domination that, as Marx-inspired and feminist theorists highlight, are structured into society.

SEX AND QUEER THEORY

Not surprisingly, given Foucault's emphasis on both the historical-institutional *invention* of sexuality and the arbitrariness of all categories, he was highly influential among individuals attentive to sexual politics. Feminist theorists, as we discussed (chapter 10), challenge the alleged objectivity and neutrality of (white male) sociological and other ruling knowledges in society. In similar fashion, **Steven Seidman** and sociologists interested in sexuality (e.g., Connell 1987, 1995; Kimmel 2005; see chapter 10) seek to redress the long-time silence in social theory regarding sexuality. Seidman notes that despite the many sexual issues (e.g., divorce, homosexuality, prostitution, pornography, etc.) dominating public debate in the US and Europe at the beginning of the twentieth century, and the simultaneous rise of psychoanalysis, psychiatry, and Freudian theory – all of which gave prominence to sexuality – classical social theory ignored it.

BIOGRAPHICAL NOTE

Steven Seidman is professor of sociology at the State University of New York (SUNY) at Albany. He received his undergraduate education at SUNY-Brockport, his MA from the New School for Social Research, New York, and his PhD in sociology from the University of Virginia (in 1980). Seidman has written several important books on sexuality and on social theory and has been a highly influential scholar in elaborating a sociological interpretation and application of queer studies.

SOCIOLOGY'S HETEROSEXIST BIAS

Seidman states: "Despite their aim to view the human condition as socially constructed, and to sketch a social history of the contours of modernity, the classical sociologists [Marx, Durkheim, Weber] offered no accounts of the social making of modern bodies and sexualities" (Seidman 1996: 3). This silence fed into what Seidman sees as sociology's **heterosexist** bias, a bias stemming from the presumed naturalness of the founding fathers' "privileged gender and sexual social position" as heterosexual men. He elaborates:

> They took for granted the naturalness and validity of their own gender and sexual status the way, as we sociologists believe, any individual unconsciously assumes as natural those aspects of one's life that confer privilege and power. Thus, just as the bourgeoisie asserts the naturalness of class inequality and their rule, individuals whose social identity is that of male and heterosexual do not question the naturalness of a male-dominated, normatively heterosexual social order. It is then hardly surprising that the classics never examined the social formation of modern regimes of bodies and sexualities. Moreover, their own science of society contributed to the making of this regime whose center is the hetero/homo binary and the hetero-sexualization of society. (Seidman 1996: 4; see also Seidman 1997: 81–96)

Similarly, Kimmel argues that it was "not just 'man' as in generic mankind" that the classical theorists had in mind, "but a particular type of masculinity, a definition of manhood that derives its identity from participation in the marketplace, from interaction with other men in that marketplace – in short, a model of masculinity for whom identity is based on homosocial competition" (Kimmel 2005: 27), that requires and rewards the hegemony of an aggressive, competitive, virile masculinity (see chapter 10).

In other words, when we read social theory we take it for granted that when theorists write about "man in society" – whether the capitalist or the wage-worker, the bureaucrat or the Calvinist, the socially unmoored suicidal individual or the emotionally neutral doctor – they are assuming a heterosexual man whose sexuality is a given and about which there is nothing problematic. It is telling that Erving Goffman (1963), the one theorist who wrote about "the homosexual," did so to illuminate the self-presentation strategies that "abnormal" stigmatized individuals must use to pass as normal.

Figure 11.2 The legalization of same-sex marriage in many countries reflects a transformation in the understanding of sexual orientation and in society's acceptance of the normalcy of gay and lesbian relationships. Source: Author.

NORMALIZING LGB SEXUALITY

The social movements of the 1960s and 1970s that transformed consciousness about gender and racial inequality also chipped away at the privileging of heterosexuality as the only normal sexuality. This political activism coincided with the emergence of scholarly histories of sexuality, pioneered by Foucault, and with the influence of Berger and Luckmann's analysis of the social construction of reality (see chapter 9). The public activism of the gay and lesbian movement for acceptance of gay sexuality and for equal rights for gays and lesbians helped shift attention to the idea that they were more "normal" than many people, including themselves, had assumed (i.e., had learned from society). Gays and lesbians argued that their everyday reality as gays and lesbians was indeed real, a paramount "here-and-now" reality (see chapter 9) as relevant to them as the different realities experienced as real by heterosexual members of society. Rather than closeting this reality, the LGBT movement argued for legal and institutional changes that would recognize their realities.

In fact, writing in 2004 before the recent significant advances in gay rights (see Topic 11.2), Seidman offered a generally positive assessment of the struggle for equality. He comments:

> Heterosexuality remains very definitely normative and homosexuality is still freighted with connotations of moral pollution … concealment and disclosure decisions, and sexual identity management are still part of the lives of lesbians and gay men in America. Homosexuals still suffer and, for many, the closet and coming out remains not merely a phase of their lives but its center. Yet, [in individual lives, politics, and popular culture] … a trend toward normalization and social routinization seems to be one prominent current in contemporary America. (Seidman 2004: 259)

Topic 11.2   The normalization of sexual equality

June 2015 was a watershed month in the advancement of LGB equality. People in Ireland voted in a public referendum to legalize same-sex marriage, and in the US the Supreme Court ruled (in Obergefell versus Hodges) that there is a constitutional right to same-sex marriage, thus extending the right to all Americans, not just those living in states that had already legalized it (e.g., Massachusetts, which did so in 2005; and Connecticut, New York, Iowa, and Maryland, among others). Same-sex marriage is also legal in England, Wales, and Scotland (but not Northern Ireland), and in Canada, New Zealand, France, Belgium, the Netherlands, Norway, Spain, Argentina, and South Africa. Additionally, gay civil unions are legal in several countries, including Uruguay, Colombia, and Ecuador, and the Mexican Congress is developing legislation to legalize same-sex marriage. The shift in public support for gay marriage has been astonishing: from a third of Americans in 2001 to two-thirds today (Pew Research Center 2017: 12–13). The increased visibility of the normalcy of gay relationships is reflected in many ways, including the rise in gay households (estimated by the US Census Bureau to be 700,000), and gay families with children.

In addition to the political effects of organized gay activism, the coming-out of a wide range of public figures like Tim Allen (CEO of Apple), Elton John, Ellen DeGeneres, Anderson Cooper, country and western singer Chely Wright, hip-hop singer Frank Ocean, and the NFL football player Michael Sam; the visibility of gays on television shows (e.g., *Glee, Modern Family*); and the public support for gay rights and gay marriage, expressed by ideologically diverse politicians (e.g., Barack Obama, David Cameron, Nick Clegg, Dick Cheney, Michael Bloomberg), and by corporate retailers (e.g., Bloomingdale's) and investment banks (e.g., Goldman Sachs) helped to make being gay a less stigmatized identity. See also Topic 11.3.

There is still discrimination against LGBT individuals, couples, and families, however (e.g., Bruni 2017). The bullying of LGBT teenagers is of particular concern on both sides of the Atlantic, so much so that the Catholic bishops of England and Wales introduced an antibullying campaign in the 2017–2018 school year. Despite pockets of resistance against LGBT equality, the momentum is in its favor. This is especially evident among younger cohorts. For example, three-quarters of American millennials (those born after 1980) and two-thirds of Gen X (born 1965–1980) support gay marriage (Pew Research Center 2017: 3). Further evidence of the normalization of sexual equality is found in church. For example, the Episcopal Church in the US has allowed same-sex marriages since 2015, and on August 1, 2017 the first gay marriage in an Anglican church in Britain took place in Scotland, at St. John's Episcopal Church in Edinburgh (same-sex church marriages are not allowed by the Anglican Church of England & Wales, nor by the Catholic Church). Anglican national churches in Brazil, South Africa, New Zealand, South India, and Canada have taken steps to approve and celebrate same-sex weddings, and some US evangelical leaders who had argued that gayness was a temporary psychosexual condition that could be cured, have renounced their view.

PROBLEMATIZING SEXUALITY

In the 1980s and 1990s, sociologists, LGB activists, and others debated the nature of sexuality. Theoretically innovative, it illuminated the social origins of sexuality and how sociohistorical context shapes the definition and institutionalization of sexuality (e.g., Foucault 1978). This "sexual turn" in social theory ended the sociological silence on sexuality and challenged the conventional sociological view of sex as an ascribed, that is, biologically inherited, role status (see Parsons, chapter 4). It also helped legitimate and normalize LGB sexuality.

Essentialist view of sexuality

The debate on LGB sexuality has many strands but it has revolved around two contrasting perspectives (e.g., Epstein 1987). On the one hand are those who argue that sexuality is a biological given. In this view, frequently narrated in research interviews with gays and lesbians, gay people are born gay, something they long sense in their desires and experience as an essential part of their nature. This **essentialist view of sexuality** posits a core, natural difference between homosexuals and heterosexuals, a difference used by some to advocate a separatist identity politics that reinforces difference. The essentialist view is also used to support the political claim that because gay people are born gay, it is not their "fault"; it is a natural orientation, they cannot do anything about it, and, therefore, they should not be discriminated against by social rules that exclude gays (e.g., from marriage to another gay person, church membership, sports, etc.).

Constructionist view of sexuality

The social **constructionist view of sexuality** avoids discussion of the biological basis of sexual desire. It instead emphasizes that all labels and categories in society and the meanings attached to them come out of a particular sociocultural and historical context. In other words, they are socially defined and not prescribed by nonhuman forces (see Foucault earlier in the chapter; and, more broadly, Berger and Luckmann, chapter 9). Sexuality, homosexuality, heterosexuality, bisexuality (and all categories) are human-made social creations. In this framing, there is no one type of sexuality that is "natural." Rather, the meanings we assign to sexuality and what is "normal" and "less normal" vary across societies, and within any one society, across time.

Social constructionism sees sexuality more as an identity choice than a biologically given natural state. In this view, people learn how to present themselves as gay by internalizing what society labels as gay behavior; they seek out social ties with others whom they perceive to be gay, and form various gay subcultures. This perspective on sexual identity has parallels with how we commonly understand ethnic identity. Although ethnic identity can have a biological, genetic basis, in societal terms ethnicity is understood by individuals' patterns of association with others of similar ethnicity, and by the group's shared practices and meanings. Constructionists argue that gay and lesbian identity can be similarly thought of as another ethnosocial, subcultural identity; thus, like ethnic groups, LGBT individuals should be regarded as behaving in particular, meaningful ways that reflect and nurture their particular social identity (see Epstein 1987). The social constructionist view of sexuality, though popular among sociologists, is increasingly challenged today by cognitive psychologists and socioevolutionary biologists who, in searching to demonstrate the genetic basis for many social characteristics and personality traits (e.g., shyness), talk about "the homosexual gene."

Irrespective of whether being LGB is seen in essentialist (biological) or social constructionist terms, activists and feminist and sexuality scholars argue that it is a legitimate sexuality/identity and should not be grounds for discrimination. This, increasingly, is also the view of the public-at-large (see Topic 11.2).

One's sexuality is simply another source among the intersecting statuses that variously shape people's everyday existence (as noted by Patricia Hill Collins, see chapter 10). In some contexts, moreover, an individual's sexuality can be paramount, whereas in another context their economic, racial, and/or regional, political, and religious identities may be of greater salience.

Topic 11.3   Gay sexual freedom in China

Homosexuality was decriminalized in China in 1997 and was deleted from the health ministry's list of mental illnesses in 2001. Recent years have seen a "blossoming of gay life" there and a slow but perceptible increase in the public visibility of gays (Jacobs 2009). China's first gay pride festival took place in 2009, in Shanghai, organized by Shanghai Pride. The weeklong festival included events such as a "Hot Body" contest and a silent auction to benefit AIDS orphans. Festival "celebrants were self-assured, unapologetically gay and mostly under 30," though increased tolerance is also making it easier for some older gays, after "a lifetime of unrequited desire," to acknowledge their sexual identity (Jacobs 2009). In 2013, government censors permitted websites and newspapers to discuss LGBT issues and there are now several online gay dating services. And in 2016, the first Chinese gay-themed movie, "Looking for Rohmer," was approved by the government for public release. Although no well-known public figures have come out as gay, a wedding between two gay men (Internet entrepreneurs) celebrated in a public park in Beijing received a lot of positive media attention, and gay couples are also using the courts to challenge the right of government agencies to deny gay marriage. More and more LGBT individuals are coming out to their friends, but family pressure makes many, especially men, reluctant to do so. A 2016 survey of LGBT Chinese found that only 3 percent of male and 6 percent of female respondents described themselves as completely out; a third of gay men, but just 6 percent of lesbians said they were in the closet. There are no LGBT antidiscrimination laws and given the family stigma around LGBT issues, the legalization of same-sex marriage is not expected any time soon (*The Economist*, "Rohmer-therapy," April 30, 2016, p. 39).

THE QUEERING OF SOCIAL THEORY

Moving beyond essentialist/social constructionist ideas about the nature of sexuality and who fits into the category of "the homosexual," Steven Seidman proposed the *queering* of social theory. This turn is influenced by scholars outside of sociology and social science and whose theoretical background and methodology are very different from sociology. Most queer theorists are in the humanities, and they approach social categories and social identities just as they would the language used in literary texts. They regard the language used to categorize social behavior as a **semiotic code** – language used not simply to denote a particular reality but as a signifier, or an indicator, of a more deeply structured and culturally understood context of meaning. Thus, **queering the text** is an analytical approach that rereads novels (and all kinds of other textual material) looking for clues conveying a more fluid understanding of sexuality than that previously associated with a given author (e.g., Ernest Hemingway, Jane Austen).

Through socialization we learn language, the words and symbols used to name and give meaning to all those things in our environment. We learn what goes with what, how things go together (salt and pepper, for example) in a socially meaningful way (in setting the table, or seasoning our food). Words have the property of turning the external reality into binary categories (salt, not salt). Queer theorists argue that reality is not binary; it is more complicated and fluid (e.g., there are multiple shades of color and flavor between (white) salt and (black) pepper. And we lose recognition of this fluidity when we insist on its "either/or" binary classification. This is perhaps part of the phenomenal appeal and originality of the singer/musician Prince. He questioned the descriptive applicability of binary thinking, rhetorically asking "Am I black or white?/Am I straight or gay?" in his best-selling song "Controversy." For **queer theory**, the key binary that needs to be rejected is that of heterosexuality/homosexuality. Queer theorists argue that political and scholarly debates about the biological or social nature of homosexuality simply reproduce the dominance of the binary, either/or categories we use to think about sexuality. They maintain that sexuality is far more fluid than allowed by the heterosexual/homosexual binary; that it encapsulates a flowing continuum of variation. All binary categories contain an implicit hierarchy of difference or of Otherness. Dichotomized categories of opposites (e.g., heterosexual/homosexual; male/female) overstate differences as well as projecting the presumption that one element of the binary has greater significance and value than the other. Such binaries are not simply descriptive of differences but are, in fact, political and prescriptive. Thus heterosexuality is still more valued (and connotes more symbolic and material power) than LGB sexuality; male is more valued (and has more power) than female. And these categorical differences get translated and embedded into various institutional practices (in schools, churches, movies, music videos, laws, social policies, etc.).

The homosexual/heterosexual binary, queer theorists argue, reinforces the idea of sexuality as involving basic foundational differences (e.g., of sexual desire, attraction). Yet Arlene Stein (1997: 56) observes that being lesbian is not simply about sexual desire but about woman-identification and the development of a lesbian consciousness. Binary thinking also ignores the many social differences in lived experience that invariably characterize those singularly defined as gay or lesbian. This obscures recognition that among gays, just as among nongays, there are differences of social class, race, generation, religion, etc. In other words, there are many intersecting differences that make talk of and knowledge about "the homosexual" rather superficial, as if gays are essentially gay, with no other relevant, socially grounded identities and experiences.

Topic 11.4   The muxe as a separate gender category

Many individuals experience their sexual and/or gender realities in more fluid ways than captured by the binary categories of male/female and homosexuality/heterosexuality typically used in official and everyday discourse. The prevalence of gender-crossing highlights this fluidity (e.g., Talbot 2013). Whether motivated by biological or/and by social reasons, individuals can remove themselves from the census sex classification (male/female) assigned at birth on the basis of body-physiological characteristics, and cross into a different category; indeed, an estimated 1,600 to 2,000 people a year undergo sex-change surgery in the US. In Canada, individuals have the option of a third sex category (x) on their passports. One place in which there is cultural acceptance of the fluidity of gender/sexual identity is in indigenous communities in Oaxaca, a state in southern Mexico. There, the native Zapotec people recognize a third gender category, the muxes (derived from the Spanish word *mujer*, "woman"), which is used to refer to males who from boyhood have felt themselves female. However, though they dress in women's clothes, for the most part they do not publicly identify as women or consider changing their bodies. Muxes tend to occupy social roles in the community that are traditionally associated with women (as embroiderers or home-helpers) and increasingly they seek integration into university and professional settings. Acceptance of mixed gender identities has a long history among the Zapotec, as indicated by ancient Mayan gods who were simultaneously male and female. However, debate in the US about transgender rights is complicating local conversations in Oaxaca about how this third gender should be defined, whether, for example, one can be both muxe and transgender, and whether there should be separate public bathrooms for muxes (Burnett 2016; Lacey 2008).

THE REBELLIOUS INTENT OF QUEER THEORY

Queer theory thus pushes for a move away from and beyond the homosexual/heterosexual categorization, whether on campus, at nightclubs, or in academic and policy debates. Sociologists provide compelling research studies about the coming-out experiences of gays and lesbians, or how LGBTQ individuals negotiate the hurdles at work or in the legal system, or how they deal with illness and bereavement and other life transitions. These studies, however, according to queer theorists – rrespective of whether the findings indicate LGBTQ emancipation or/and continuing discrimination – ultimately reproduce and reinforce how we conceptualize sexuality and thus how we conceptualize and reaffirm the differences we impute to the categories of homosexual and heterosexual. See Topic 11.4.

Seidman explains that queer theory seeks to "shift the debate somewhat away from explaining the modern homosexual to questions of the operation of the hetero/homosexual binary" (Seidman 1996: 9). Accordingly, as he elaborates:

> Queer theorists have criticized the view of homosexuality as a property of an individual or group, whether that identity is explained as natural or social in origin. They argue that this perspective leaves in place the heterosexual/homosexual binary as a master framework for constructing the self, sexual knowledge, and social institutions. A theoretical and political project which aims exclusively to normalize homosexuality and to legitimate homosexuality as a social minority does not challenge a social regime which perpetuates the production of subjects and social worlds organized and regulated by the heterosexual/homosexual binary … Moreover, in such a regime homosexual politics is pressured to move between two limited options: the liberal struggle to legitimate homosexuality in order to maximize the politics of inclusion and the separatist struggle to assert difference on behalf of a politics of ethnic [or homosexual] nationalism. (Seidman 1997: 148–149)

The queering of social theory, then, aims to be disruptive. It is rebellious, "a theoretical sensibility that pivots on transgression or permanent rebellion" (Seidman 1996: 11). It challenges the very use of such words as "the closet" and "coming out" because these terms, whether used by gays and lesbians or by social researchers, yield power to the ascribed differences between homosexuals and heterosexuals institutionalized in cultural norms, laws, and everyday practices (Seidman 2004: 263). Queer theory contests this foundation, that is, the culturally embedded definition of sexuality that permeates our society and informs our knowledge of society (Seidman 1996: 22). Seidman (1996: 11) states: "I take as central to Queer theory its challenge to what has been the dominant foundational concept of both homophobic and affirmative heterosexual theory: the assumption of a unified homosexual identity. I interpret Queer theory as contesting this foundation and therefore the very telos [progress/ agenda] of Western homosexual politics."

Queer theory thus aims to decenter the normalcy of our categories and assumptions – whether "the homosexual" is a category used to discriminate against gays or as a social identity by gays to celebrate their difference and/or to claim equal rights with heterosexuals. It rejects all such packaged categorizations. Though sympathetic, Seidman (1996: 22) is also critical of queer theorists for failing to recognize the institutional reality in which categorizations are anchored and that structure individuals' life experiences and life chances. As sociologists emphasize, social reality is not solely about categories and language, but includes robust social structures and cultures that cannot simply be deconstructed by changing linguistic-semiotic codes.

Though queer theory's arguments can be abstract, in practical terms its rebellious challenge to sociology has very specific implications. Stein and Plummer elaborate, for example, on its implications for stratification and occupational mobility:

> How can sociology seriously purport to understand the social stratification system … while ignoring quite profound social processes connected to heterosexism, homophobia, erotic hierarchies, and so forth … What happens to stratification theory as gay and lesbian concerns are recognized? What are the mobility patterns of lesbians? How do these patterns intersect with race, age, region, and other factors? What happens to market structure analysis if gays are placed into it? … We need to reconsider whole fields of inquiry with differences of sexuality in mind. (Stein and Plummer 1996: 137–138)

Queer theory thus requires sociologists to alter how we think not only about sexuality but about all social dynamics – how we study stratification, crime, family, urban and rural life, religion, etc. The very use of the word "queer" captures its disruptive strategy. It was traditionally used to refer to homosexuals in a pejorative way (as queers), and subsequently reappropriated by gay activists in the 1980s and 1990s at the height of the AIDS epidemic in their fight to redress gay discrimination. They chanted: "We're here and we're queer." Queer theorists then inject this "disrespectable" word into respectable social theory. In sum, queer theory seeks to destabilize the homosexual/heterosexual distinction and how it is used to reproduce power and inequality, and in sociology, to destabilize the discipline's heterosexist assumptions and knowledge.

How effective queer theory can be in disrupting the heterosexist bias in sociology is uncertain. Not many sociologists use its framework or tend to use it in ways that fall short of its disruptive meaning. Moreover, the writings of queer theorists such as Judith Butler's (1990) *Gender Trouble* are dense and highly abstract despite the value in their argument that gender and sexual identities are not fixed but fluid. Nevertheless, the very radicalness of the idea of *queering* social theory is itself a contribution. Queer theory "aspires to transform homosexual theory into a general social theory or one standpoint from which to analyze social dynamics" (Seidman 1996: 13). It is another strand that makes us stop, if only momentarily, to reassess the language and categories we use to apprehend social reality. This can stimulate a broader reflection on how the master narratives we know and rely on – narratives regarding the foundation of sociology, Great Britain, the US, the Catholic Church, the Olympics, etc. – may obfuscate particular biases while simultaneously reproducing the language and rules that underlie the multiple forms of domination in our society. Queering, and querying, these narratives can disrupt our scholarly and everyday understandings of difference, such that we might eventually move beyond the differences that divide us.

SUMMARY

Michel Foucault insightfully elaborated on the many ways in which the body is institutionally and discursively controlled in modern society. As part of his wide-ranging analysis, he focused on the historical invention of sexuality, a theme that has significantly advanced scholarly and public understanding of sexuality. Among sociologists interested in sexual politics, Steven Seidman has played a lead role in bringing queer theory to mainstream attention.

POINTS TO REMEMBER

Foucault: The body and sexuality:
- The body has been a targeted object of institutional surveillance and regulation especially since the sixteenth century
- The transformation of sexual desire and sexual behavior into discourse was first accomplished by the Catholic confession and subsequently extended by the state (e.g., the census) for administrative and economic purposes
- Discourses of sex/the body are imbued with, and add to the circulation of, power
- Debates about sexuality contrast essentialist biological and social constructionist perspectives

Queer theory:
- Introduced to sociology by Steven Seidman
- Another standpoint from which to analyze social relations
- Rejects the binary, homosexual/heterosexual categories we use to think about and organize sexuality, instead emphasizing the fluidity of sexuality
- Focuses attention beyond sexual categories onto how sexuality and assumptions about it are embedded in institutional and everyday practices across all societal domains

GLOSSARY

bio-power the institutional use of bodies and body practices for purposes of political, administrative, and economic control.

confession production of discourse as a result of the interrogation of the self (by the self or others, real and imagined), typically with regard to body practices.

constructionist view of sexuality the idea that sexuality and what it means to be LGB vary across history and social context; contrasts with an essentialist, biological view.

disciplinary practices institutional practices (through schools, churches, clinics, prisons, etc.) used to control, regulate, and subjugate individuals, groups, and society as a whole.

discourse categorizations, talk, and silences pertaining to social practices.

docile bodies produced as a result of the various institutional techniques and procedures used to discipline, subjugate, use, and improve individual (and population) bodies.

essentialist view of sexuality the idea that being LGB, and the social characteristics associated with being gay, are a natural (essential) part of the LGB individual's biology.

genealogy (of knowledge/power) interconnected social, political, and historical antecedents to, and context for, the emergence of particular ideas/social categories.

heterosexist presumption that heterosexuality is normative (and normal) and that other sexual feelings and practices are socially deviant.

Panopticon model (invoked by Foucault) to highlight how disciplinary power works by keeping the individual a constant object of unceasing surveillance/control.

politics of truth idea emphasizing that truth is not, and can never be, independent of power; that all truths are produced by particular power-infused social relationships and social contexts.

power an ongoing circulatory process with no fixed location or fixed points of origin, possession, and resistance.

queer theory rejects the heterosexual/homosexual binary in language, culture, and institutional practices; shifts attention from LGBTQ inequality in (heterosexist) society to instead focus on the fluidity of all sexuality and its implications.

queering the text refers to the way in which, in light of current understandings of the fluidity of sexuality, we reread or look anew at earlier literary, artistic, and other cultural products (e.g., television shows, advertisements) to see whether we can identify elements that can be interpreted as suggesting a more disruptive understanding of sexuality than assumed at the time of their publication/authorship.

regime of truth institutional system whereby the state and other institutions (government agencies, the military, medical and cultural industries) and knowledge producers (e.g., scientists, professors) affirm certain ideas and practices as true and marginalize or silence alternative practices and interpretations.

ritual of discourse society's orderly, routinized, and power-infused ways (e.g., confession) of producing subjects talking about socially repressed secrets and practices.

semiotic code cultural code or meanings inscribed in language and other symbols in a given societal context.

surveillance continuous monitoring and disciplining of bodies by social institutions across private and public domains.

techniques of bio-power exertion of control over the body/bodies through institutional procedures (e.g., classroom schedules, census categories) and practices (e.g., confession).

QUESTIONS FOR REVIEW

1   What is bio-power? And why, and how, does it matter? Where can we see bio-power in action today?
2   What does it mean to say that sexuality is constructed? How can one reconcile an individual's personal feeling that their sexuality is natural or essential to who they are, and the constructionist perspective that what we label and call a particular type of sexuality changes over time, and across different societal contexts?
3   What are rituals of discourse? Do you agree that we have become a "confessing" society? What are the reasons for your assessment? What does confession do/accomplish?
4   What is queer theory? What does it help us to see that we might not otherwise think about from within the existing canon of sociological theory?

REFERENCES

Bartky, Sandra Lee. 1998. "Foucault, Femininity, and the Modernization of Patriarchal Power." Pp. 25–45 in Rose Weitz, ed. *The Politics of Women's Bodies*. New York: Oxford University Press.

Berube, Allan. 1990. *Coming Out Under Fire*. New York: Free Press.

Bruni, Frank. 2017. "The Worst (and Best) Places to be Gay in America." *New York Times* (August 26).

Burnett, Victoria. 2016. "Bathroom Debate Complicates a Town's Acceptance of a Third Gender." *New York Times* (June 23).

Butler, Judith. 1990. *Gender Trouble: Feminism and the Subversion of Identity*. New York: Routledge.

Collins, Patricia Hill. 2004. *Black Sexual Politics*. New York: Routledge.

Connell, R.W. 1987. *Gender and Power: Society, the Person and Sexual Politics*. New York: Cambridge University Press.

Connell, R.W. 1995. *Masculinities*. New York: Cambridge University Press.

Dreyfus, Herbert, and Paul Rabinow. 1983. *Michel Foucault: Beyond Structuralism and Hermeneutics*. Chicago: University of Chicago Press.

Economist. 2016. "Rohmer-Therapy." (April 30), p. 39.

Epstein, Steven. 1987. "Gay Politics, Ethnic Identity: The Limits of Social Constructionism." *Socialist Review* 93–94: 9–54.

Eribon, Didier. 1991. *Michel Foucault*. Cambridge, MA: Harvard University Press.

Foucault, Michel. 1965. *Madness and Civilization: A History of Insanity in the Age of Reason*. New York: Random House.

Foucault, Michel. 1972. *The Archaeology of Knowledge*. London: Tavistock.

Foucault, Michel. 1974. *The Order of Things*. London: Tavistock.

Foucault, Michel. 1975. *The Birth of the Clinic: An Archaeology of Medical Perception*. New York: Pantheon.

Foucault, Michel. 1978. *The History of Sexuality*, volume 1. New York: Random House.

Foucault, Michel. 1979. *Discipline and Punish: The Birth of the Prison*. New York: Penguin.

Foucault, Michel. 1984. "Truth and Power." Pp. 51–75 in Paul Rabinow, ed. *The Foucault Reader*. New York: Pantheon.

Foucault, Michel. 1984/1994. "Sex, Power, and The Politics of Identity." Pp. 163–173 in Paul Rabinow, ed. *Michel Foucault: Ethics, Subjectivity and Truth*. New York: New Press.

Goffman, Erving. 1963. *Stigma: Notes on the Management of Spoiled Identity*. New York: Simon & Schuster.

Hartsock, Nancy. 1998. *The Feminist Standpoint Revisited and Other Essays*. Boulder, CO: Westview Press.

Hekman, Susan, ed. 1996. *Feminist Interpretations of Foucault*. University Park: Pennsylvania State University Press.

Jacobs, Andrew. 2009. "Gay Festival in China Pushes Official Boundaries." *New York Times* (June 15), p. A6.

Kimmel, Michael. 2005. *The Gender of Desire: Essays on Male Sexuality*. Albany, NY: SUNY Press.

Lacey, Marc. 2008. "A Lifestyle Distinct: The Muxe of Mexico." *New York Times* (December 8).

Pew Research Center. 2017. *Support for Same-Sex Marriage Grows, Even Among Groups that Had Been Skeptical*. Washington, DC: Pew Research Center.

Power, Michael. 2011. "Foucault and Sociology." *Annual Review of Sociology* 37: 35–56.

Ryan, Alan. 1993. "Foucault's Life and Hard Times." *New York Review of Books* (April 8), pp. 12–17.

Seidman, Steven, ed. 1996. *Queer Theory/Sociology*. Oxford: Blackwell.

Seidman, Steven. 1997. *Difference Troubles: Queering Social Theory and Sexual Politics*. New York: Cambridge University Press.

Seidman, Steven. 2004. "Are We All in the Closet? Notes Toward a Sociological and Cultural Turn in Queer Theory." Pp. 255–269 in Roger Friedland and John Mohr, eds. *Matters of Culture*. New York: Cambridge University Press.

Stein, Arlene. 1997. *Sex and Sensibility: Stories of a Lesbian Generation*. Berkeley: University of California Press.

Stein, Arlene, and Kenneth Plummer. 1996. "'I Can't Even Think Straight': Queer Theory and the Missing Sexual Revolution in Sociology." Pp. 129–144 in Steven Seidman, ed. *Queer Theory/Sociology*. Cambridge, MA: Blackwell.

Talbot, Margaret. 2013. "About a Boy: Transgender Surgery at Sixteen." *New Yorker* (March 18), pp. 56–65.

Taylor, Dianna, and Karen Vintges, eds. 2004. *Feminism and the Final Foucault*. Urbana: University of Illinois Press.

CHAPTER TWELVE
POSTCOLONIAL THEORIES AND RACE

KEY CONCEPTS

slavery
Otherness
colonialism
race segregation
apartheid
postcolonial theory
empire
decolonize sociology
Southern theory

hegemony of the global
   metropole
affirmative action
race
racism
cultural identity
identity politics
whiteness
black underclass

politics of conversion
black cultural democracy
political race
culture lines
new racism
crisis of raciology
planetary humanism

CHAPTER MENU

Introduction to Sociological Theory: Theorists, Concepts, and Their Applicability to the Twenty-First Century,
Third Edition. Michele Dillon.
© 2020 John Wiley & Sons Ltd. Published 2020 by John Wiley & Sons Ltd.
Companion website: www.wiley.com/go/dillon

Timeline 12.1	Major events in the historical evolution of racial equality (1791–present)
1791	William Wilberforce's motion to dismiss the slave trade approved by British Parliament
1792	Slavery abolished in Dutch colonies
1794	Slavery abolished in French colonies
1808	US federal government prohibits import of slaves into the country
1837	US Congress passes gag law suppressing debate on slavery
1861–1865	American Civil War: fought over individual states' rights to slavery
1863	Emancipatory Proclamation of President Abraham Lincoln
1865	President Lincoln assassinated
1866	US Congress passes Civil Rights Act granting citizenship and equal civil rights for Negro freedmen
1866	US Congress passes Southern Homestead Act, providing public land for sale to freedmen at relatively low prices
1909	Founding of National Association for the Advancement of Colored People (NAACP) in the US
1944	Establishment of United Negro College Fund in the US; its well-known slogan is "A mind is a terrible thing to waste"
1954	US Supreme Court, in *Brown versus Board of Education of Topeka*, rules that racial segregation in schools violates Fourteenth Amendment to US Constitution
1957	Civil Rights Act passed in US; violence in Little Rock, Arkansas, against school integration
1962	Jamaica becomes independent from the UK; Algeria becomes independent from France
1963	Kenya becomes independent from the UK
1964	Race riots in US as result of enforcement of civil rights laws
1965	The UK passes Race Relations Act

1967	US Supreme Court, in *Loving versus Virginia*, rules that state laws banning interracial marriage are unconstitutional
1968	The UK passes Commonwealth Immigration Act imposing restrictions on immigrants
1968	Martin Luther King, Jr, leader of civil rights movement in US, assassinated
1986	*Oprah Winfrey Show* goes into national syndication
1994	Dr Lonnie Bristow first African-American president of American Medical Association (AMA)
2001–2005	Colin Powell first African-American US secretary of state
2007	African-Americans CEOs/CFOs at several major corporations including American Express, McDonald's USA, Aetna, Time Warner, Sears, Boeing, Xerox, Merrill Lynch
2007	Tony Dungy first African-American to coach winning NFL Super Bowl team (Indianapolis Colts defeated Chicago Bears)
November 2008	Barack Obama elected the forty-fourth president of US, first African-American to hold the office; he won over 50 percent of the popular vote and several states that had voted Republican in the past
2012	Gabby Douglas (age 16) at the London Olympics became the first black gymnast to win the all-around gold medal
2012	Barack Obama reelected President of the United States
2014	Pegida anti-immigration movement comes to prominence in Germany
2015	Black Lives Matter movement emerges in protest against the shooting of unarmed black men by police
May 2016	Sadiq Khan, a Muslim born to Pakistani immigrant parents, is elected Mayor of London
January 2017	President Trump bans admission to the US of all refugees, and of all individuals from seven Muslim-majority countries
May 2019	Robert F. Smith, a black billionaire finance and technology executive, told the graduating class at Morehouse College that his family would pay the entire amount of their student loan debt.

RACIAL OTHERNESS: EDWARD SAID, FRANTZ FANON

The hierarchies embodied in racial distinctions have a long and complicated history and continue to persist in social structures and everyday practices across the world. They are visible, for example, in the US, where **slavery** institutionalized a core rupture in black–white relations (see Box 12.1); and in the UK and a broad swath of countries where the British Empire institutionalized the **Otherness** of the populations it colonized. The black/white divide is not the only racial division that exists either historically or today. Tensions between whites and Arabs, among Arabs, between whites and Asians, among Asians, and between blacks and Hispanics are among the race-based and race-infused divisions evident across several different countries.

The profound and multifaceted legacy of the specifically racial history of slavery, especially for people of African descent, continues to resonate. World slavery institutionalized whites and Arabs as masters and blacks as slaves (e.g., Patterson 1982). And as Winant (2001: 20) argues, the modern world-system (elaborated by Wallerstein; see chapter 14), that is, the development and expansion of capitalism, cannot be understood without taking full account of the centrality of race "as *both* cause and effect" in its origins and development. Slavery – the coerced "chattelization" of others – was central to capitalist expansion; the trade in slaves, slaves' labor power, and the commodities the slaves produced provided the resources for a geographically and economically expanding industrial capitalism (Winant 2001: 294, 25).

Slavery's impact on racial formation is thus core to modernity's intermeshing of history, economics, and culture. Winant argues that any analysis of society must apprehend the historical and continuing significance of race:

> Race has been fundamental in global politics and culture for half a millennium. It continues to signify and structure social life not only experientially and locally, but nationally and globally. Race is present everywhere: it is evident in the distribution of resources and power, and in the desires and fears of individuals from Alberta to Zimbabwe. Race has shaped the modern economy and nation-state. It has permeated all available social identities, cultural forms, and systems of signification. Infinitely incarnated in institutions and personality, etched on the human body, racial phenomena affect the thought, experience, and accomplishments of human individuals and collectivities in many familiar ways, and in a host of unconscious patterns as well … Race must be grasped as a fundamental condition of individual and collective identity, a permanent, although tremendously flexible, dimension of the modern global social structure. (Winant 2001: 1)

Box 12.1   Slavery as social death

Following Marx (see chapter 1) and Du Bois (see Introduction), Orlando Patterson (1982) argues that slavery must be understood as a relation of domination, and more specifically as an extreme instance of such relations. Based on his comparative-historical analysis of slavery across many different types of societies (including the US, Europe, Asia, the West Indies, and Arab countries), he underscores the centrality of *coercion* in the master–slave relationship and the heavy social-psychological and cultural costs it imposed on slaves. Slavery, he argues, is in essence, a form of "social death."

> Slavery is one of the most extreme forms of the relation of domination, approaching the limits of total power from the viewpoint of the master, and of total powerlessness from the viewpoint of the slave. Yet, it differs from other forms of extreme domination in very special ways … It is unusual … both in the extremity of power involved … and in the qualities of coercion that brought the relation into being and sustained it … In his powerlessness the slave became an extension of his master's power … Perhaps the most distinctive attribute of the slave's powerlessness is that it always originated … as a substitute for death, usually violent death … The condition of slavery did not absolve or erase the prospect of death. Slavery was not a pardon; it was, peculiarly, a conditional commutation. The execution was suspended only as long as the slave acquiesced in his powerlessness. The master was essentially a ransomer. What he bought or acquired was the slave's life, and restraints on the master's capacity wantonly to destroy his slave did not undermine his claim on that life. Because the slave had no socially recognized existence outside of his master, he became a social nonperson. (Patterson 1982: 1, 2, 4–5)

Additionally, Patterson shows, slaves were denied all ties to their family and blood relatives and to their cultural ancestry; they were dispossessed of their "community of memory," cut off from any meaningful understanding of their historical, social, and cultural genealogy. As such, the slave's dishonoring – the "absence of any independent social existence" apart from ties to the slave-owner, the fact that "he had no name of his own to defend" – had severe emotional and psychological consequences for slaves. Their loss of a social identity contributed to producing the slave's "servile personality," the "crushing and pervasive sense of knowing that one is considered a person without honor and that there simply is nothing that can be done about it" (Patterson 1982: 10–12).

Patterson acknowledges that slaves had informal social relations with one another – something that Durkheim (see chapter 2) would see as functional to their societal integration notwithstanding the degrading conditions of their daily lives. But Patterson, using a Marxist framing, emphasizes that the slaves' social relations were denied legitimacy; their legitimacy consisted solely that which they did in servitude for their master. Thus slaves' sexual and parenting relationships were not socially recognized (i.e., not recognized in law as marriages or as families; Patterson 1982: 6). Similarly, despite the fact that they had a past, had a history (1982: 5), the conditions of their enslavement did not allow them to process and integrate this past as we, for example, would do in telling our family story, the narrative of our family tree. In all of these ways, therefore, slaves were considered social nonpersons and treated as such; "The slave was the ultimate human tool, as imprintable and as disposable as the master wished" (1982: 7).

THE COLOR LINE

In 1903, W.E.B. Du Bois, a pioneer sociologist (see Introduction), wrote:

> The problem of the twentieth century is the problem of the color-line, – the relation of the darker to the lighter races of men in Asia and Africa, in America and the islands of the sea … the question of Negro slavery was the real cause of the [US Civil War] conflict … No sooner had Northern armies touched Southern soil than this old question, newly guised, sprung from the earth, – What shall be done with negroes? (Du Bois 1903/1969: 54–55)

One hundred and twenty years later, the color lines of race and racism still matter in determining social, economic, and cultural status, political participation and everyday experiences. **Colonialism** has ended; laws mandating **race segregation** in schools, neighborhoods, cafeterias, hotels, and swimming pools have disappeared; the most persistent form of **apartheid** ended in South Africa in 1994; and black men and women are among those who have achieved the highest levels of success in government, law, business, academia, literature, television, sports, and music (see Timeline 12.1).

What then is the color-line problem? It is the persistence of racism in the everyday lived experiences of nonwhites as they go about finding a job, securing a promotion, getting a bank loan, hailing an Uber ride, making an Airbnb reservation, driving, or simply hanging out with friends in a park. Their life-chances and their life outcomes are constrained in particular and systematic ways by their racial or ethnic identity. In the UK, for example, individuals of Caribbean and of Pakistani ancestry have substantially lower levels of educational attainment than whites; and they have a higher risk of unemployment compared to whites with a similar level of education (e.g., Heath et al. 2008: 216, 218).

The "color-coding" society in which we live means that the "anonymous black male" in particular is the object of police surveillance, due to the cultural coding of black and male with criminality (Anderson 1990: 190; 2003). Such everyday racism is captured in "Driving while black," a phrase conveying the stronger probability that black (and increasingly Hispanic) motorists will be stopped more frequently than whites simply for driving in a normal manner. Leading scholars including Cornel West (1993: x) attest to their personal experience of being ignored while signaling for a taxi because they are black. "Shopping while black" similarly captures the routine ways in which racism penetrates everyday life – it refers to the tendency of blacks (including celebrities) to be frisked for possible shoplifting in upscale neighborhood stores and delicatessens.

Although there is no overarching sociological theory of race and racism, several contemporary scholars address the interrelated historical, economic, social, and cultural dimensions of these forces. I have already discussed Du Bois's writings (see Introduction), and Patricia Hill Collins's analysis of the intersectionality of race and gender (see chapter 10). This chapter introduces the key ideas of other scholars, many of whom are associated with **postcolonial theory**, a term used to refer to the critique of the continuing legacy of Western imperialism and colonialism on social relations, knowledge, and power inequalities.

COLONIALISM: THE CREATION OF OTHERNESS

The idea of Otherness, and specifically of racial Otherness, of racial difference, was given prominence by the Palestine-born, American literary and postcolonial theorist Edward Said (pronounced *Sai-eed*). His writings on literature, culture, and imperialism elaborated arguments infused with theoretical strands from Karl Marx and Michel Foucault. In his book *Orientalism* (1978), Said argues that the Orient, the East (e.g., the Middle East, Turkey), is not simply a geographically defined category of place, but an *idea*, a form of representation, of imagining and accentuating cultural difference. Drawing on examples from European literature and art, Said argues that Westerners/Europeans imagine the Orient as an exotic and strange place and describe and relate to it in stereotypical and mythical ways. These ideas/images (imaginings) serve to accentuate and reinforce the Orient's difference from the West, a difference that simultaneously informs, derives from, and legitimates the West's colonization and rule over the East. Thus Said argues, following Foucault (see chapter 11), that language, discourse, the categories of the Orient (the East) and the Occident (the West), are not innocent words on a page but are produced by and imbued with power. The West sees the Orient not only as different from, but as *inferior* to, it. In parallel fashion to how social scientists and economic policy makers (e.g., the World Bank) distinguish between developed ("first world") and developing ("third world") countries (see chapter 6), all distinctions, Said argues, are relative, not absolute; they are entwined with particular relational histories and politics: "As much as the West itself, the Orient is an idea that has a history and a tradition of thought, imagery, and vocabulary that has given it reality and presence in and for the West. The two geographical entities thus support and to an extent reflect each other" (Said 1978: 5).

Said argues that the relationship between the West and the East is a relationship of power and domination. This relationship is rooted in their shared history, and in what Marx (see chapter 1) would identify as the lived material existence of the colonizer and the colonized in their relations with one another. As Said emphasizes, the Orient is not just geographically "adjacent to Europe; it is also the place of Europe's greatest and richest and oldest colonies" (Said 1978: 1). This history has political and cultural consequences; it means that "ideas, cultures and histories cannot be seriously understood or studied without … their configurations of power … also being studied" (1978: 5). Central to this relationship is the West's casting of the East as Other (as different, inferior); its invocation and reinforcement of its Otherness reproduces the cultural superiority of the West and its attendant political power to colonize (literally and metaphorically) the East. Thus Orientalism is not simply an idea or a geographical tag; it is "a cultural and political fact" (1978: 13).

Otherness, therefore, is not simply a benign way to acknowledge difference but a political and cultural representation (Said 1978: 26–28) that constructs a hierarchy of difference, with Others defined as inferior. What – and who – are deemed Other are subjugated by those who are not-Other, for example, the West vis-à-vis the East, whites vis-à-vis Arabs, blacks, and Hispanics. In short, all racial (and ethnic) categories and representations make sense only in terms of the political and cultural histories (e.g., colonialism, slavery) that have produced particular kinds of Otherness, particular kinds of difference.

Topic 12.1 Muslims as Others

Across Western Europe – in the UK, Denmark, France, Italy, Switzerland, Belgium, Germany – and in the US and Quebec, there are recurring instances of public opposition to Islam's increasing visibility. In addition to the rise of "anti-Islamization" movements (e.g., Pegida in Germany), localized controversies range from pork as a school-menu item to the location of new mosques. Whatever the specific issue, the arguments articulated tend to convey that Muslims are a threat to the culture of democratic society and that Islamic religious practices and food and alcohol prohibitions are counter to a given (Western) country's "way of life" and "national identity." Yet, when democratic societies – nations built on principles of equality and freedom of expression – curb the religious expression of a minority group, it can signal the Otherization of those who look and act in ways that are different to the mainstream culture. Thus opposition to the building of mosques and Islamic centers, to the visibility of minarets, and to Muslim women wearing head scarves, veils, and burkinis may signal cultural racism, that is, seeing Muslims as a racial and religious Other.

Ironically, the Otherization of Muslims is especially apparent in France, the revolutionary cradle of the Enlightenment and equal rights. France is home to approximately 5 to 6 million Muslims, the largest Muslim population of any European country; Muslims have been migrating to France from North Africa since the early twentieth century. Yet in France, the values of freedom of expression and racial equality clash with that of cultural integration and with France's disavowal of multiculturalism in favor of its emphasis on the cultural oneness of France as a secular, republican society. This ideal sits uncomfortably with the visibility of French women wearing traditional Muslim veils on fashionable streets, in supermarkets and municipal buildings, and in schools and workplaces. In 2011, the French parliament made the wearing of veils in public illegal, and violators are fined approx. $250 and/or required to take citizenship classes. Many Muslim women say that for various reasons (e.g., personal security and autonomy, fashion), they like wearing the veil and some use it to bridge their intersecting identities as French and Muslim, British and Muslim, or American and Muslim (e.g., Haddad 2007; Williams and Vashi 2007). This claiming of a plural identity is emblematic of the dynamism of postcolonial cultural identities.

Others, however, mostly non-Muslims, see the veil as a visceral affront to women's equality, a sign of their subordination, and a regressive remnant of an earlier time when women were denied the basic freedoms guaranteed by law to men. As a French court ruled in 2014: "Banning the burqa helped preserve 'the conditions of living together.' In other words, a woman wearing the burqa in public infringed 'the rights and freedoms of others' who might be offended by it" (Uddin 2016). The dilemmas presented are not easily resolved. This was underscored in France in the summer of 2016. A ban on the burkini, "a full-body bathing suit designed to accommodate Islamic modesty codes," resulted in police officers patrolling several French beaches and ordering Muslim women sunbathers to either remove their burkini or leave the beach. Some onlookers applauded the police and jeered the modestly dressed women. Others condemned the police actions and the ban and accused the authorities of sexism in regulating what women wear (Rubin 2016). The vexing issue of Otherness remains, and it extends beyond beaches and streets: Is it culturally racist to view veiled Muslim women as an affront on women's equality? Or, is the ban on public Muslim dress a culturally racist tactic to suppress the identity of a cultural minority Other and simultaneously reassert the (assumed) superiority of the dominant culture?

THE PHENOMENOLOGY OF OTHERNESS

The phenomenological reality of Otherness, how the everyday/everynight, here-and-now reality (see chapters 9 and 10) is different for racially different individuals, is eloquently voiced by **Frantz Fanon**, a Caribbean-born writer and medical doctor. As Fanon (1967: 109) phrases it, "the fact of blackness" overrides all the other attributes of a person (or a neighborhood or a country). The fact of blackness is imbued with Otherness and, as with all who are categorized as Other (Latinos, Arabs, Indians, etc.), the fact of Otherness is invariably experienced as a "battered down" identity (1967: 112). In the overarching stigma system that race is, if "the normals" in Goffman's terms are white, then people of color are "less than human" (see chapter 8). Their Otherness is not simply a matter of difference but of inferiority, an inferiority that is collectively imposed (by whites) and collectively felt (by blacks, Arabs, Asians, Latinx, etc.) in subtle and not so subtle ways every day.

BIOGRAPHICAL NOTE

Frantz Fanon was born in 1925 in Martinique, a Caribbean island colonized and still controlled by France. During World War II, he left Martinique and enlisted in the army with the Free French Forces (following the fall of France to the Nazis in 1940). After the war, he returned to Martinique, where he received his undergraduate degree, and then moved to France, where he studied medicine and psychiatry. Soon thereafter, he moved to Algeria (a French colony) and was living and working there during the Algerian War of Independence (1956–1962) against France. Fanon traveled extensively in Algeria and through other countries in Africa and, as in Martinique, he observed first-hand the impact of colonialism on subjugated individuals' everyday lives. His writings have had a major impact in establishing colonialism/postcolonialism as a legitimate area of cultural and social scientific inquiry. Fanon was being treated for leukemia in the US in 1961 when he died; in recognition of his efforts on behalf of colonized people, his body lay in state in Tunisia prior to its burial in Algiers.

Fanon recounts his experience of blackness while working as a medical doctor in the then French-controlled colony of Algeria in the 1940s and 1950s:

> The white world, the only honorable one, barred me from all participation. A man was expected to behave like a man. I was expected to behave like a black man – or at least like a nigger. I shouted a greeting to the world and the world slashed away my joy. I was told to stay within bounds, to go back where I belonged … My blackness was there, dark and unarguable. And it tormented me, pursued me, disturbed me, angered me. Negroes are savages, brutes, illiterates. But in my own case I knew that these statements were false … We [blacks] had physicians, professors, statesmen. Yes, but something out of the ordinary still clung to such cases … It was always the Negro teacher, the Negro doctor; brittle as I was becoming, I shivered at the slightest pretext. I knew, for instance, that if the physician made a mistake it would be the end of him and of all those who came after him. What could one expect, after all, from a Negro physician? … The black physician can never be sure how close he is to disgrace. I tell you, I was walled in: No exception was made for my refined manners, or my knowledge of literature, or my understanding of the quantum theory. I requested, I demanded explanations. Gently, in the tone that one uses with a child, they introduced me to the existence of a certain view that was held by certain people, but I was always told "We must hope that it will very soon disappear." What was it? Color prejudice … It was hate; I was hated, despised, detested, not by the neighbor across the street … but by an entire race. (Fanon 1967: 114–115, 117–118)

NEW DIRECTIONS IN THE SOCIOLOGY OF COLONIALISM: R. W. CONNELL

Sociology has been slower than literary studies in specifically identifying postcolonialism as a central focus. This is largely because the various hierarchies and inequalities brought into sharp relief by a postcolonial lens have tended to be incorporated by sociological theorists using different conceptual frameworks and with theoretical objectives beyond or not confined to postcolonial relations. These include Marx's analysis of capitalism and his emphasis on the economic expansionist interests of the bourgeoisie beyond national borders (chapter 1); Weber's analysis of nations and their territorial and cultural interests vis-a-vis other (weak and strong) states, as well as his analyses of bureaucracy, authority, and stratification (chapter 2); the processes and "cultural lags" identified by modernization scholars (chapter 4): the sociology of dependency and underdevelopment in Latin America (chapter 6); Smith's focus on the particularism of knowledge standpoints (chapter 10); Collins's elaboration of the matrix of domination across multiple and intersecting unequal identities and relations of power (chapter 10); Bourdieu's attentiveness to social hierarchies (chapter 13), including colonial domination (see Go 2013); and world-systems theory (cf. Wallerstein, chapter 14). Historical and political sociologists, moreover, have a long history of empirical case studies focusing on colonizing and decolonized states and societies (e.g., Burawoy 1972; Hechter 1975; Steinmetz 2007; Williams 1990).

Recent years, nonetheless, have seen more systematic attention to "the sociology of empires, colonies, and postcolonialism" (Steinmetz 2014). **Empires** are "expansive, militarized, and multiethnic political organizations that significantly limit the sovereignty of the peoples and polities they conquer" (Steinmetz 2014: 79). For example, the British Empire at the height of its power in the nineteenth century included Ireland, Canada, Australia, India, and several African and Caribbean countries. And colonialism is the process by which a politically and/or militarily controlled population is not only stripped of its political and economic sovereignty, but systematically constructed as being inferior –. in legal, social, cultural, and biological/racial terms (e.g., Burawoy 1974; Said 1978; Williams 1990). The sociological analysis of empires and of colonial power and resistance tends to focus on six major analytical dimensions or interrelated causal mechanisms. As summarized by Steinmetz (2014) these are (1) capitalism; (2) geopolitics, war and violence; (3) cultural images/representations; (4) resistance and/or collaboration by the colonized; (5) bureaucratic administrative procedures and policies and (6) variation in the origins and autonomy of the administrative class (civil servants). Because of the broad and varied historical, geographical, and cultural contexts across which various forms of colonial rule were implemented, the empirical investigation of colonialism and of postcolonialism can yield much variation in processes and experiences, as underscored by Stuart Hall (discussed later). Similarly, as Connell et al. (2017: 31) point out,

> Brazil, South Africa and Australia are all post-colonial countries not part of a 'third world'; indeed each is a regional hegemon in economic terms. They have very different demographic and class structures, and though in all three class is interwoven with racial hierarchy, the different dynamics of race and class reflect three different histories and of colonization and post-colonial development.

They and other postcolonial scholars emphasize, however, that diversity of experiences should not be used to obscure the inequalities at the heart of the colonial/postcolonial relation.

SOUTHERN THEORY

Just as feminist standpoint theory (e.g., Dorothy Smith, see chapter 10), forces attention on the male biases institutionalized in sociology's in its ruling concepts, methods, and everyday disciplinary practices – a postcolonial lens unveils the role of Western sociologists (along with other knowledge producers such as priests, teachers, missionaries, lawyers, accountants, etc.) in supporting colonialism (e.g., Connell et al. 2017: 24). This body of writing points to the need to **decolonize sociology**. As Julian Go (2017) explains, this project is not simply about enhancing the demographic diversity within the discipline – though this is important, as initiatives by the American and British Sociological Associations and other professional associations emphasize. It also entails acknowledgement of sociology's role in colonialism and – more challenging – a fundamental rethinking of the Western basis of sociology's knowledge (or epistemic) categories and hierarchies. R. W. Connell (see bio, chapter 10) is at the forefront of such efforts – as are theorists who nudge a "multiple modernities" perspective in contrast to the deeply ingrained intellectual assumption that there is one single and universal modernity, that is, Western modernity (see chapter 15).

Connell (2007; Connell at al. 2017) argues for what she calls **Southern Theory**. This perspective gives center stage to the standpoints of those in the global South and in doing so seeks to contest the **hegemony of the global metropole** and the Northern bias in the production of knowledge. It thus seeks to redress the colonization of knowledge that has for so long been the privilege of Western/ Northern academics. Thus scientific and other knowledge practices in the postcolonial world are dominated by the metropole such that knowledge workers "learn the concepts and methods of metropolitan science, travel to the metropole for advanced training, seek to publish in metropolitan journals…and become embedded as subordinate players in a Northern-centered knowledge formation…. workers in peripheral countries primarily cite the texts of authors from the global North, while workers in the North mostly cite each other, and mostly ignore the ideas and studies produced by workers in the global South" (Connell at al. 2017: 26). One consequence of this is that local, indigenous, and activist knowledges (see Collins 2015; Topic 10.2) are marginalized in the articulation and solving not only of local but of global problems (e.g., HIV/AIDS, climate warming, economic inequality). Illustrating how "the long shadow of colonial history falls across whole domains of knowledge" and interpenetrates North–South relations in complex ways, Connell at al. (2017: 29) note that the initial treatment and prevention of HIV was compromised in the US by the institutionalized racist view that the virus was "an alien import originating in Africa" and undermined in developing countries by its association with gay sex and Western decadence.

RACE AND RACISM

Though the color line continues to exist today and to matter in everyday life, there are nuances and ambiguities in how, and where, that line is drawn and in how its meanings vary across different contexts. The black legal scholar and civil rights activist Lani Guinier elaborates on the multidimensionality of race. She emphasizes that

> Race is many things, not just a single thing. It can be stigmatizing, but it can also be liberating. If we think in categories, and think about race only as if it were a single category, we conflate many different spheres of racial meaning. We fail to specify if we mean biological race, political race, historical race, or cultural race. (Guinier and Torres 2002: 4)

Because of the many changes in the status of blacks since World War II (e.g., the civil rights movement in the US; the ending of apartheid in South Africa; **affirmative action** policies in the US), there is a tendency (especially but not exclusively among whites) to think that the task of achieving racial equality is no longer pressing. The sociologist Howard Winant (2001: 8) notes: "There is a prominent, indeed growing tendency to consider this task as largely accomplished: to operate, in other words, as if racial oppression had already been largely overcome, as if the errors of white supremacy had already been corrected".

He (and other scholars and activists) argue, however, that in the post-1960s, postcolonial world, race and racism have not disappeared – their meanings have changed (Winant 2001: 307). As **Paul Gilroy** (1987: 110) emphasizes: "Racism does not … move tidily and unchanged through history. It assumes new forms and articulates new antagonisms in different situations." Thus, in America, for example, "there are two languages of race" (Blauner 2001: 195): blacks and whites have different interpretations of social change and different understandings of whether and how race matters in everyday social reality.

BIOGRAPHICAL NOTE

Paul Gilroy was born in London, England, in 1956 to a Guyanese father and English mother. He received his BA from Sussex University and his PhD from Birmingham University, where he studied with Stuart Hall at the Centre for Contemporary Cultural Studies. Gilroy spent the early part of his career at various English universities, and in 2000, he was awarded an endowed professorship at Yale University in sociology and African-American studies. He returned to England in 2005 as the first holder of the Anthony Giddens Professorship in Social Theory at the London School of Economics.

What do sociologists mean then when they invoke such multilayered terms as "race" and "racism"? **Race**, Winant (2001: 317) argues, is "a concept that signifies and symbolizes sociopolitical conflicts and interests in reference to different types of human bodies"). To focus on race is to study yet another analytically separate but intersecting dimension of the systematic patterning of social inequality, stratification, and conflict. Although we see the fact of someone's blackness as, and through, body color, what we do with blackness (and with any body color) – how we use it to differentiate and regulate what particular types of bodies can and cannot do in society – is not a predetermined biological outcome. It is the product, rather, of particular societies making particular decisions about body color at particular historical moments. These decisions come to encrust themselves upon our culture and social institutions. As such, racial inequality – the fact of blackness, for example (Fanon 1967) – is not just something that is subjectively experienced by an individual, but something that gets objectively structured into social institutions and everyday culture. Race, therefore, and racial categorization, are an engine of, and mechanism reproducing, inequality, whether we focus, following Marx (see chapter 1), on economic relations, or more broadly, following Weber (see chapter 3), on economic inequality, social status, and cultural worldviews.

Winant (2001: 317) argues that although race "appeals to biologically based human [physical] characteristics … [the] selection of these particular human features for purposes of racial signification is always and necessarily a social and historical process." Just as gender and sexuality categories are used to impose, legitimate, and reproduce distinctions that appear determined by biological characteristics but that are, in fact, distinctions used as a veil for maintaining the power of one group at the expense of another, so too is race. And racism parallels sexism in the multiple and multilayered ways in which a society's institutional practices and everyday language and attitudes signify that one group (blacks, women) is inferior to another (whites, men).

Although the word "racism" only began to be used in the 1960s (Blauner 2001: 196), the "ideas and practices it denotes" have been part of the modern era for centuries (Winant 2001: 317). Winant acknowledges that what is entailed in **racism** is complex, but that it can "be provisionally defined as inhering in one or more of the following: 1. signifying practice that essentializes or naturalizes human identities based on racial categories or concepts; 2. social action that produces unjust allocation of socially valued resources, based on such significations; 3. social structure that reproduces such allocations" (2001: 316).

Paul Gilroy explains racism in more specific, everyday cultural terms:

> The idea that blacks comprise a problem, or more accurately, a series of problems, is today expressed at the core of racist reasoning. It is closely related to a second idea which is equally pernicious, just as popular and again integral to racial meanings. This defines blacks as forever victims, objects rather than subjects, beings that feel yet lack the ability to think, and remain incapable of considered behavior in an active mode. The oscillation between black as problem and black as victim has become today the principal mechanism though which "race" is pushed outside of history and into the realm of natural inevitable events [e.g., blacks' high rates of non-marital births]. This capacity to evacuate any historical dimension to black life remains a fundamental achievement of racist ideologies … Seeing racism in this way, as something peripheral, marginal to the essential patterns of social and political life can, in its worst manifestations, simply endorse the view of blacks as an external problem, an alien presence visited on Britain [or some other colonizing country] from the outside … Racism rests on the ability to contain blacks in the present, to repress and to deny the past. (Gilroy 1987: 11–12)

Topic 12.2   Affirmative action in Brazil

Brazil, host to the 2014 FIFA World Cup and the 2016 Summer Olympics, has more people of African descent than any other nation outside of Africa. Its 2010 Census showed that of its 196 million people, over half identify themselves as black or mixed race. Economic inequality is a major problem, and much of it correlates with nonwhite racial status, notwithstanding the extensive interracial mixing and tolerance that is part and parcel of everyday Brazilian life. As in other countries, education is widely seen as the pathway to socioeconomic success (see Topic 13.2, chapter 13). Racial quotas have been used for several years by some Brazilian universities (e.g., the University of Brasilia) to ensure greater representation in college – and subsequently in professional and business careers – of students from poor and nonwhite racial backgrounds. Demonstrating a strong commitment that "the blacks in Brazilian society can make up for lost time," in August 2012, the government enacted an ambitious affirmative action law that requires all public universities to reserve half of all their admission spots for poor and racial minority students. The number of spots assigned varies depending on the racial composition of each of Brazil's 26 states and the region of its capital, Brasilia. The law received almost unanimous support across the political spectrum, though some (as in debates elsewhere about how to ensure equality of opportunity) expressed reservations about the most effective way to bridge the race-based education and occupational mobility gaps in Brazil. Sociologist and ex-Brazilian President Fernando Cardoso (see chapter 6), for example, cautioned against replicating US policies in a country where race and race histories are different than in the US. Nonetheless, with a longstanding and deep commitment to promoting "racial democracy," political leaders and policymakers are optimistic that the new law will make a significant dent in narrowing racial and economic inequality in Brazil (Romero 2012: A4).

CULTURAL HISTORIES AND POSTCOLONIAL IDENTITIES: STUART HALL

Gilroy and other scholars (e.g., Bhabha 1994; Guinier and Torres 2002; Hall 1992, Roediger 2002; Winant 2001) emphasize that the construct of race is flexible in that racial categories and their meanings change over time and across different societal contexts. Large-scale social forces, such as colonialism, immigration, postcolonialism, and globalization, invariably affect the societal and cultural context in which race is defined and lived out by particular racial groups vis-à-vis one another, amidst relations and representations of domination and subordination. In this view, racial and ethnic identities (like other forms of identity) are dynamic, and they are especially contingent on the varied and multifaceted precolonial, colonial, and postcolonial histories of specific racial/ethnic groups. As **Stuart Hall** elaborates:

> **Cultural identity** … is a matter of "becoming" as well as of "being." It belongs to the future as much as to the past. It is not something that already exists, transcending place, time, history and culture. Cultural identities come from somewhere, have histories. But, like everything which is historical, they undergo constant transformation. Far from being eternally fixed in some essentialised past, they are subject to the continuous "play" of history, culture and power … identities are the names we give to the different ways we are positioned by, and position ourselves within, the narratives of the past. (Hall 1990: 225)

BIOGRAPHICAL NOTE

Stuart Hall was born in Kingston, Jamaica, in 1932 and moved to England in 1951. He was a Rhodes Scholar at Oxford University, from where he received his MA. He was among the pioneers of cultural studies and in the mid-1960s joined Birmingham University's highly influential Centre for Contemporary Cultural Studies (CCCS), which he subsequently directed. He conducted several analyses of the mass media; his research demonstrating the active interpretive cultural work that audiences do. After many years at the CCCS, Hall was appointed in 1979 as professor of sociology at the Open University in England. Until his death in 2014, at age 82, he continued to write extensively and was a frequent commentator in the British media on culture and politics.

The "traumatic character" of slavery and of colonialism for black people and black experiences can begin to be understood, Hall argues, only by recognizing how different subordinated groups internalize a particularized identity of themselves. The cultural particularity among blacks emerges out of the ongoing interaction between their varied precolonial histories of difference. In other words, slaves came from different villages, different tribal communities, different countries and different cultures, and hence did not have a shared precolonial history or cultural background. And yet at the same time, the context of their colonization and treatment by the colonizers, such as the British, gave them a shared cultural experience (Hall 1990: 225–228).

This interplay between cultural differences and similarities, between discontinuities and continuities, highlights the difficulty of talking about *the* colonial experience or *the* postcolonial experience as if there was just one, or one that captures the experiences of all subordinated racial-ethnic groups. Hall alerts us that these cultural differences (and similarities) are not simply between blacks of African compared to Caribbean descent; rather, within the Caribbean, for example, Jamaicans differ from Martinicans

(Hall 1990: 227). Similarly, Homi Bhabha (1994) argues that representations of Orientalism, such as Said's (1978) critique (discussed previously), ignore the ambiguities and contradictions with which Western literature imagines the colonial subject (e.g., as both docile and aggressive). In parallel fashion, black feminist scholars (e.g., Collins 1990, 2015) make the point that sociological understanding is severely limited when discussion of "women's experience" does not take account of how racial, ethnic, and other intersecting differences complicate generalizations about gender (see chapter 10).

In any case, the end of colonialism does not mean the end of colonial ties and relationships, as underscored by immigrant population flows especially from the (previously) colonized to the colonizing society. Thus, for example, Britain since the 1950s has become a visibly multicultural society, one in which whole communities of Jamaicans, Indians, Pakistanis, Chinese (from Hong Kong) and other groups have settled (seeking economic opportunity) and in the trans-generational process have become part of the cultural fabric of British society. Today, therefore, "being Black and British," as Hall (1990) argues, is a new cultural identity, one crafted out of the postcolonial diaspora.

Being black and British changes not just what it means to be black but also what it means to be British. Black is no longer necessarily an identity of "Otherness" – an otherness defined against and marginalized by white British colonial power – but one that is constitutive of both the past and the present British societal history and collective identity. In this reading, therefore, British identity can no longer be assumed to signify whiteness. What was previously unthinkable – being black *and* British – is now a de facto postcolonial reality, and one that must be incorporated into the imagining of what it means to be part of the British nation/culture. This point was highlighted in 2015 when the *Great British Bake Off* television cooking show was won by Nadiya Hussein, an English-born, hijab-wearing Muslim woman whose Bangladeshi parents came to the UK in the 1970s. And her winning "classic British cake" was a lemon wedding cake that she decorated with jewels from her own wedding and a wide ribbon in the colors of

Figure 12.1   Nadiya Hussein, winner of the Great British Baking Contest, featured here with Queen Elizabeth, conveys the symbolic power (and reality) of being black and British. Source: John Stillwell - WPA Pool/Getty Images International UK.

the Union Jack. The challenges in enacting a new cultural identity, however, are highlighted by Gilroy (1987), who reminds us that "there ain't no black in the Union Jack" (the title of one of his books). He thus reminds us that color lines and symbolic and material histories do not disappear with the formal end of colonialism or of slavery – or, for that matter, by winning a popular television contest.

Cultural identity tasks vary by sociopolitical context and the particular history of colonial subjugation. In generalized terms, however, black **identity politics** entails blacks' collective recovering and remembering of a shared history (of oppression), and their simultaneous pursuit of policies implementing black equality. This translates into a political agenda that compels white society to institutionalize laws and public policies that affirm blacks' social, political, and economic equality with whites, while simultaneously acknowledging blacks' history of difference.

CONSTRUING WHITENESS

Theorizing about race necessarily includes attention to the construal of **whiteness**. This is because both "white people and people of color live racially structured lives" (Frankenberg 1993: 1). Thus scholars engaged in "whiteness studies" remind us that white people are "colored white" (Roediger 2002: 15–16). Accordingly, the sociology of race (and of ethnicity) is not just about the experiences of blacks or other minority racial (or ethnic) groups. It also requires attention to whites and their relations to nonwhites. Ruth Frankenberg (1993: 1) explains that "whiteness is [first] a location of structural advantage, of race privilege. Second, it is a 'standpoint,' a place from which white people look at ourselves, at others and society. Third, whiteness refers to a set of cultural practices that are usually unmarked and unnamed." These practices include for example, the taken-for-granted presumption that whites hire black nannies, not the inverse; and that whiteness is what pervades fashion, mass media, and religious images, for example, representations of Christ (e.g., Roediger 2002: 27–43).

The task for the sociologist is to problematize the taken-for-grantedness of whiteness, to investigate how its meanings change in different social-historical contexts (e.g., Roediger 1991, 2005; Jacobson 2006), and to probe how whiteness matters in determining white people's everyday lives and their race consciousness (Frankenberg 1993: 18). David Roediger, using a neo-Marxist analysis, argues that in the US, whiteness became a sought-after identity for *white* working-class European immigrants (e.g., Irish and Italians) in Boston and other northern industrial cities in the nineteenth century (see also Williams 1990). Considered "nonwhite" because they were ethnically, culturally, and economically inferior to the capitalist class of (largely) English, Protestant origin, these low-wage workers affirmed their whiteness as a way to gain social status by differentiating themselves from, and as superior to, blacks. Fearing economic dependence (against the backdrop of a slave-owning society and the relations of black inferiority it created), the white working class constructed blacks, and not the white capitalist class, as Other, as a racially inferior outgroup. This sowed the seeds of the long and continuing complex history of racial prejudice among working-class whites (e.g., McDermott 2006).

RACE AND CLASS: WILLIAM J. WILSON, CORNELL WEST

THE BLACK MIDDLE CLASS

Increasingly sociologists talk about the black middle class (e.g., Pattillo 2005, 2013). The black middle class, however, is not a new phenomenon. In the mid-1950s, E. Franklin Frazier, a highly influential black sociologist and president of the American Sociological Association (in 1948), wrote about "the new Negro middle class" (Frazier 1955/1968: 256–266), composed primarily of those working in white-collar professional and supervisory occupations. Frazier noted that

> The changes which occurred in the economic and social organization of the United States as the result of two world wars brought into existence a new middle class group among Negroes. The primary cause of this new development was the urbanization of the Negro population on a large scale. Prior to World War I about nine-tenths of the Negro population was in the South, and less than 25 per cent of Southern Negroes lived in cities … The migration to Northern cities was especially crucial since it created large Negro communities in an area that was relatively free from the legal and customary discriminations under which Negroes live in the South. (Frazier 1955/1968: 258)

The effects of this migration, Frazier argued, were to expand the educational, occupational, and political opportunities for blacks, changes that intertwined to lay the economic and cultural basis of the new black middle class (Frazier 1955/1968: 258).

Despite the emergence of a flourishing black middle class, however, Frazier was very critical of what he observed to be its anti-intellectualism, its disavowal of its religious and other traditions, and its ostentatious search for social status. Frazier argued that the cultural characteristics of the black middle class stemmed from and reflected the racial divide, the chasm that existed between the black and the white middle classes. This divide, Frazier argued, led the black middle class to reject its own history and collective pride in that history, while seeking acceptance from its economic peers in the white middle class, an acceptance that had not been forthcoming. Consequently, the black middle class occupied a netherland, cut off from its racial roots and with unrealized cultural aspirations. Frazier elaborates:

> During its rise to its present position, the [black] middle class has broken with its traditional background and identification with the Negro masses. Rejecting everything that would identify it with the Negro masses and at the same time not being accepted by white American society, the [black] middle class has acquired an inferiority complex that is reflected in every aspect of its life … The middle-class Negro shows the mark of oppression more than the lower class Negro who finds a shelter from the contempt of the white world in his [traditions] … and in his freedom from a gnawing desire to be recognized and accepted. Although the middle-class Negro has tried to reject his traditional background and racial identification, he cannot escape from it. Therefore, many middle-class Negroes have developed self-hatred. They hate themselves because they cannot escape from being identified as Negroes. (Frazier 1955/1968: 263, 265)

THE BLACK CLASS DIVIDE

By contrast with the racial divide that separated the black middle class from the white middle class in the 1950s and 1960s, many sociologists argue that today social class is driving intraracial divisions. William Julius Wilson argues that the contemporary black class structure makes it "increasingly difficult to speak of a single or uniform black experience" (Wilson 1978: 144). In *The Declining Significance of Race*, he argues that as a result of economic and policy changes since the 1970s, and of shifts that have occurred in economic and occupational mobility patterns, "class has become more important than race in determining black life-chances in the modern industrial period" (1978: 150). He elaborates:

> The recent mobility patterns of blacks lend strong support to the view that economic class is clearly more important than race in predetermining job placement and occupational mobility. In the economic realm, then, the black experience has moved historically from economic racial oppression experienced by virtually all blacks to economic subordination for the **black underclass** … a deepening economic schism seems to be developing in the black community, with the black poor falling further and further behind middle- and upper-income blacks. (Wilson 1978: 152)

Drawing attention to the growing economic divide among blacks, he argues, moreover, that racial strife today has more to do with sociopolitical issues than with economic opportunities per se. Although race continues to matter in regard to decisions about the public funding of schools and municipal services, for example, it has significantly less importance in determining access to jobs and economic competition and conflict in general (Wilson 1978: 152).

Wilson is not arguing that racial problems derive from fundamental economic problems inherent in the capitalist structure, as a Marxist analysis would claim. He argues, instead, that it is "the intersection of class with race" that is crucial (1978: ix). Therefore, notwithstanding income differences between blacks and whites in a particular occupation or economic sector, and notwithstanding barriers against blacks in some elite occupations (e.g., NFL coaches, fashion models, corporate CEOs), in the economic sphere overall he maintains, "class has become more important than race in determining black access to privilege and power" (1978: 2).

Further, he argues, the economic stagnation of the black underclass has more to do with changes in the structure of the economy (e.g., the decline of manufacturing and service jobs in city neighborhoods as a result of globalization) than with racial discrimination per se (Wilson 1978: 1–2). In other words, the economic barriers encountered by the black underclass today – unlike in the past when there were (race-based) barriers against virtually all blacks – "have racial significance only in their consequences, not in their origins" (1978: 2). Of particular consequence, the rising strength of the black middle class means that there is a growing gap between rich and poor blacks in income and associated life chances (e.g., college education, living in a safe neighborhood, having a stable family household, having better health, living longer). Further, these differences are driving a cultural wedge among blacks, just as socioeconomic differences have long been a source of cultural division among whites.

However, notwithstanding the gains made by the black middle class, their lives still differ from those of white middle-class Americans. Mary Pattillo (2005) highlights the continuing racial divisions in lived experience among the middle class and the continuing need for affirmative action policies that recognize these differences. Using US Census data on race and neighborhood patterns, she argues that:

> Although more advantaged than poor blacks, middle-class blacks live [in neighborhoods] with more crime, more poverty, more unemployment, fewer college graduates, more vacant housing and more single-parent families than similar whites, and indeed than much poorer whites. Moving to the suburbs makes residential life a little more comfortable, but it does not erase the racial disadvantage. These disparities alone underscore the continuing need for affirmative action, for ignoring the importance of race would have college admissions officers, for example, assume that a middle-class black student has it better than a working-class white student. (Pattillo 2005: 323)

SCARRING OF BLACK AMERICA

Cornel West highlights the social-psychological scarring and resultant anger caused by the economic and cultural battering of blacks and black identity:

> This *angst* resembles a kind of collective clinical depression in significant pockets of black America. The eclipse of hope and collapse of meaning in much of black America is linked to the structural dynamics of corporate market institutions that affect all Americans. Under these circumstances black existential *angst* derives from the lived experience of ontological wounds [i.e., wounds that rupture the individual's basic sense of self, and his or her trust in people and social institutions] and emotional scars inflicted by white

supremacist beliefs and images permeating US society and culture. These beliefs and images attack black intelligence, black ability, black beauty, and black character daily in subtle and not-so-subtle ways … The accumulated effect of the black wounds and scars suffered in a white-dominated society is a deep-seated anger, a boiling sense of rage, and a passionate pessimism regarding America's will to justice. (West 1993: 17–18)

The battering of black communities is underscored by the high rates of incarceration of black men, the fragility of blacks' interpersonal and social relationships, and the attendant violence among blacks: Black-on-black homicides, rapes, and domestic violence are higher than for other groups in the US (see Box 12.2). The social disintegration in black communities cultivates the sense that blacks are "permanent outsiders" whose status in the US is difficult to transform (Patterson 2009: A25).

Box 12.2   Facts of blackness

In the US, blacks' life expectancy today is far higher than it was in the 1970s, and though it trails that of whites by 3.4 years this is down from a gap of 7 years in 1990:

- Life expectancy of blacks: 75.6 years; of whites: 79 years
- Life expectancy of black males: 71.8 years; of white males: 78.7 years
- Life expectancy of black females: 78.1 years; of white females: 81.1 years

Despite gains in racial equality:

- Black babies born in America are more than twice as likely as white babies to die before their first birthdays (Riddell et al. 2017)
- Black women are more likely than white women to be victims of intimate partner violence (see chapter 10)
- Black women with breast cancer are on average 40 percent more likely to die than their white counterparts (Freeman 2014)

Blacks are less likely than whites to:

- Graduate from either high school or college
- Receive recommended medical screening tests (for breast cancer, diabetes, heart disease)
- Receive bank approval for a housing mortgage
- Own their own homes
- Receive a job promotion.

Blacks are more likely than whites to:

- Live below the poverty line
- Be victims of homicide – by a ratio of 6 to 1
- Be incarcerated – by a ratio of 8 to 1
- Be diagnosed with HIV
- Develop heart failure – at a rate 20 times higher than whites; blacks in their thirties and forties have the same rate of heart failure as whites in their fifties and sixties.

(See the National Center for Health Statistics; www.cdc.gov/nchs)

RACIAL POLITICS AND DEMOCRACY

West argues that any discussion of race must begin with an analysis of the structural and cultural conditions that perpetuate racial inequality: "We must begin not with the problems of black people but with the flaws of American society – flaws rooted in historic inequalities and longstanding cultural stereotypes" (West 1993: 3). Blacks, he maintains, are the "them" in society who must fit in with "us" – with white America. Yet white America, he argues, resists "fully accepting the humanity of blacks" (1993: 3). Similarly, Manning Marable points out: "The greatest casualty of racism is democracy. Afro-Americans have understood this for many decades, and their leaders have attempted to redefine the American political system for the benefit of all citizens, regardless of race, gender, and social class" (Marable 1986: 1). The politics of racial division and the Otherness underpinning them are also variously apparent in European and other countries (e.g., see Topic 12.1 and Topic 15.3).

A new **politics of conversion**, West argues, requires a prophetic commitment to new ways of thinking and reasoning about racial identity – about what it means to be black – and new ways of organizing racial politics, new approaches that move beyond a narrow understanding of racial identity and interracial competition (West 1993: 23–32). He urges blacks to form coalitions with nonblacks and to nurture the antiracist strands that can be found among whites, Jews, Latinos, and Asians (notwithstanding the varied, historically based racist tensions between and among all these groups). In addition to building solidarity across races, he argues that conversion must work to produce an authentic solidarity among blacks themselves. He stresses, in particular, the imperative of working toward the achievement of **black cultural democracy**, a state of affairs in which blacks would respect each other across their own differences, a point also emphasized by Du Bois and by Patricia Hill Collins (see chapter 10). "Instead of authoritarian sensibilities that subordinate women or degrade gay men and lesbians, black cultural democracy promotes the equality of black women and men and the humanity of gay men and lesbians. In short, black cultural democracy rejects the pervasive patriarchy and homophobia in black American life" (West 1993: 29).

Figure 12.2   African American sports stars such as LeBron James play a prominent role in highlighting racial injustice. Source: © Al Bello - Getty Images Sport/Getty Images.

Topic 12.3   The postracial vision and racial awareness of Barack Obama

Like many people, Barack Obama has a complex racial and cultural identity. He has a mixed racial background, a white Kansas mother and a black Kenyan father; a childhood upbringing in Indonesia; and elite educational and professional credentials (e.g., Harvard law graduate). His presidency (2009–2017) stoked political attention to his Otherness (e.g., Kristoff 2008), as well as illuminating the ambiguities in how color lines and racial identities are drawn.

In a public speech on race and race relations that he gave in 2008, Obama articulated what might be considered a postracial political agenda. He stressed his confidence in Americans' ability to move beyond the racial wounds of the past while simultaneously making progress in committing to social and economic policies that would advance opportunities for all Americans, irrespective of race. Obama urged African-Americans to embrace the burdens of their past without becoming victims of their past; and he urged white Americans to recognize America's history of racial discrimination while committing not just to words but to deeds that will help remedy past injustices that excluded blacks from the "ladders of opportunity" available to whites. He urged all Americans to realize that: "Your dreams do not come at the expense of my dreams, that investing in the health, welfare and education of black and brown and white children will ultimately help all of America prosper" (see, e.g., Navarro 2008; Zeleny 2008).

Racial divisions, however, continue to matter a great deal in the US (see Box 12.2) and elsewhere, and racism persists. Nonetheless, public discussion of racism is fraught with tension. Trayvon Martin, an unarmed black US teenager, was shot and killed in February 2012 by "neighborhood watch" volunteer George Zimmerman, who trailed him around the Florida neighborhood in which they both lived and shot him because he suspected Trayvon was a criminal. Responding to the protests and public controversy sparked by the criminal jury's verdict in July 2013 that Zimmerman was acting in self-defense, President Obama commented on the pain caused to people of color by the widespread suspicion that all young black men are criminals. He stated: "Trayvon Martin could have been me 35 years ago," and he recounted his own earlier experiences of the "humiliations borne by young black men," including being followed while shopping in a department store and witnessing people locking their car doors as he crossed a street (Landler and Shear 2013: A1, 11). Racial divisions are deeply polarized, as underscored in ongoing public debates fueled by a continuing pattern of fatal shootings by police of unarmed black men like Michael Brown, in Ferguson, Missouri (see Sanneh 2015).

Guinier and Torres (2002) use the term **political race** to describe a vision whereby "racialized identities may be put to service to achieve social change through democratic renewal" (2002: 11). Like West, they envision this project as being cross-racial, and involving critique and transformation of the sociopolitical system that enables the perpetuation of racial and other forms of inequality. They emphasize that the inequalities most acutely experienced by racial minorities are inequalities reflecting "social justice deficiencies in the larger [societal] community....Racialized communities signal problems with the ways we have structured power and privilege" (2002: 12). Although recognizing that racial and other sources of group identity can motivate individuals to join particular identity-based social movements (2002: 80), Guinier and Torres emphasize the need for a transracial commitment to social change; "Political race seeks to construct a new language to discuss race, in order to rebuild a progressive democratic movement led by people of color but joined by others" (2002: 12).

CULTURE AND THE NEW RACISM: PAUL GILROY

Paul Gilroy also argues for new racial politics, though he takes a somewhat different tack than other scholars (e.g., Collins 2004; West 1993; Guinier and Torres 2002). In his book *Against Race* (2000), he argues against the idea that the color line matters in modern times. Instead of color lines, Gilroy argues, it is **culture lines** that are critical to the production of conflict and inequality, and to how culture and power get intertwined in ways that divide and subdivide humanity. As an immigrant West Indian growing up in London in the wake of World War II (Gilroy 2000: 2–5), he became sensitive to the subtle ways in which Nazi and Fascist symbolism (in graffiti, for example, and in the fashion and style adopted by white youth gangs such as Teddy Boys and skinheads; e.g., Hall and Jefferson 1976), and ethno-nationalist ideologies in general, use race and racial distinctions for destructive ends.

Figure 12.3 Drawing on the lived experience of economic and racial inequality, many popular rappers with cross-racial appeal like Fabolous celebrate their rise "From Nothin' to Somethin." Source: Author.

Gilroy argues that the affirmation of racial differences and the symbolic glorification of the uniqueness of discrete racial cultures seen, for example, on ethnic festive days and at ethnic festivals – the "currently fashionable obligations to celebrate incommensurability [distinctiveness] and cheerlead for absolute identity" (Gilroy 2000: 6–7) – convey the message that every race is beautiful. This, of course, is not quite true in an unequal society where race differentiates life chances and life outcomes. This celebration, moreover, simultaneously distracts from the routine ways in which racism permeates the state, schools, public housing, and other social institutions (2000: 5). When white suburban teenagers emulate black street culture and fashion (e.g., black rap music and style), their "acting black" might be seen as an effort to cross over and transcend racial differences. However, it may also contribute to reinforcing the cultural (and economic) divisions between blacks and whites (Roediger 2002: 212–240). Whites can act black, but, unlike blacks, they invariably do so with the secure knowledge that they can stop acting black whenever they choose and that their chances of economic success (or of being arrested) will be unaffected by acting black. Blacks do not have this assurance. Further, although "acting black" has symbolic value (a source of status) among white peers, the inverse is not true. Black students who strive to do well in school – recognizing education as a pathway to socioeconomic mobility – are often denigrated by their black friends for "acting white," thus dampening their motivation to succeed (e.g., Ogbu 2003).

More generally, Gilroy is concerned that race has become commercialized; e.g., we are drawn to advertisements proclaiming the glamor of racial differences (e.g., "Black is beautiful"). Consumer culture increasingly sees all bodies, and especially black bodies, as commodities to be reworked and manipulated (Gilroy 2000: 22–23; see also Collins 2004). The commodification of the body by (black and white) celebrities themselves – e.g., Beyonce's visually rich, elaborate self-presentations in music videos, etc., and by others (such as Madame Tussaud's "whitening" of Beyonce despite Beyonce's own celebration of blackness), feeds the commercialization of race. This commodification, Gilroy argues, detracts from and "do[es] nothing to change the everyday forms of racial hierarchy". To the contrary, an "actively de-politicized consumer culture … of racialized appearances" (Gilroy 2000: 23, 21), blurs the boundaries of racial difference. A consequence of this superficial blurring is the creation of new political tensions from the anxiety that takes hold when individuals and groups cannot draw the clear binary (racist) lines of racial difference and of everyone "knowing their (unequal) place" in the social-racial hierarchy (see also Roediger 2002).

Gilroy argues that race as such – race as a persistent source of political and social inequality – becomes secondary to the primary purpose of using black bodies and black popular culture to make cultural statements about consumption, beauty and adornment, even as this adornment conveys reminders about the historical inferiority of blacks (e.g., Tupac's "Thug Life" tattoos; Gilroy 2000: 22–23). In sum, Gilroy argues, the biological basis for socially categorizing racial differences on the basis of body color has now been displaced by a cultural colonization, one that racializes bodies in ways that fit market and consumption criteria.

NEW RACISM

The commercialization of race is part of the broader culturation of racial differences, and both are components of what is referred to as the **new racism**: the racism that emerges when a dominant racial-cultural group attributes core *cultural* (not biological) differences to the worldviews and ways of being of minority racial groups. The new racism rejects the old grounds for racism, that is, the view that "biology was both destiny and hierarchy" (Gilroy 2000: 32). Instead, it presumes that "nature, history, and geopolitics dictated that people should cleave to their own kind and be most comfortable in the environments that matched their distinctive cultural and therefore nationalist modes of being in this world" (2000: 32).

A racism based on cultural separateness, of keeping people with their "own kind," was the ideological justification for apartheid in South Africa and is a justification similarly used to uphold racial discrimination in other social contexts. Princeton University, for example, unlike Harvard and Yale, "long had a systematic policy of excluding blacks" (Karabel 2005: 232). In the 1940s, when it was debating whether to admit blacks, leading Princeton faculty "claimed that a concern for the well-being of blacks was the source of their opposition to admitting them" (2005: 234–235). And students who opposed change (over half the student body) similarly argued that "blacks would not be happy at Princeton" (2005: 235).

Thus, rather than saying that members of a minority racial or ethnic group are biologically inferior to the dominant race, the new racist tendency is to emphasize that "these people" are culturally different. In other words, their ways of being are at odds with the cultural purity of the dominant group and its ways of organizing and ordering society – e.g., "that their criminality is an expression of their distinctive culture" (Gilroy 1987: 69, 109). By extension, the (racist) argument is that they would be better off in their own country, neighborhood, or college residence hall among people like themselves. At the same time, however, amid cultural change and resentment against racial equality, the biological casting of race is still a force in contemporary racist politics. As Orlando Patterson (1997: 65) elaborates, the historical, biological-based "one-drop" rule is used by white nationalists (who see one drop of black ancestry as sufficient to contaminate racial purity) as grounds to justify "pernicious legal, social, and political injustices against Afro-Americans."

New racism and genetic technology

The new racism, the accentuation/clarification of racial-cultural separateness and difference, is abetted by advances in DNA testing technology, a technology that promises to determine an individual's exact racial composition. Many individuals today aspire to claim (and some to negate) a cultural identity that is based on a particular racial genetic inheritance. But, as in the complex relation between technology and societal processes in general (see chapter 5), technology in and of itself does not resolve the contradictions and inequalities in society. On the one hand, DNA technology can help people discover their roots and reconstruct racial histories and genealogies that were buried with enslavement (see Patterson 1982) or that went undocumented by public officials and by generations of black illiteracy. This is a goal of "The Root," a website for black culture, politics, and genealogy (www.theroot.com).

At the same time, however, genetic mapping and its diagnostic and forensic uses in medicine and law, for example, can resurrect traditional racist arguments about group inferiority and deviant propensities (see Duster 2015). Further, the expectation of scientific clarity on racial composition/identity also exacerbates what Gilroy (2000: 25) refers to as the **crisis of raciology**. The crisis surrounding the boundaries between the races – between what comprises and doesn't comprise a particular racial identity – may be further muddied rather than illuminated by technology. Just as the commercialization of the glamor of black bodies (e.g., Beyonce) complicates the representation of race and the boundaries between racial categories, technological innovations may have a parallel effect. The medical imaging of DNA, instead of clarifying what exactly race is genetically and what exact racial composition a given individual has, instead yields a surprise: "Current wisdom seems to suggest that up to six pairs of genes are implicated in the outcome of skin 'color.' They do not constitute a single switch" (Gilroy 2000: 49).

In any case, we continue to be perplexed by both the culturally visible and the biologically invisible dimensions of race, as we seek to understand the elements of a shared racial and cultural heritage (while also being aware differences of generation, social class, gender, nation, etc. that characterize any collectivity). As Gilroy observes – and as public discussion of Barack Obama's racial identity highlighted – these varied differences "challenge the unanimity of racialized collectivities. Exactly what, in cultural terms, it takes to belong, and more importantly, what it takes to be recognized as belonging, begin to look very uncertain" (Gilroy 2000: 24–25).

Rethinking racial and other differences

Gilroy offers a way out of this uncertainty by challenging us to think differently about race. He rejects both the biological and the cultural foundations of (old and new) racist thinking; he rejects "the foundational oscillation between biology and culture" and the closed circuit it has become (Gilroy 2000: 52). In their place, he advises a move toward what he calls a nonracial **planetary humanism** (2000: 2). A planetary humanism would require the abandonment of the exclusionary ways in which race and all group differences (based on gender, nationality, etc.) are construed. It would, by extension, also require the abandonment of the militaristic and other aggressive and symbolic means used to affirm and defend group identities and group differences.

This is a utopian recommendation (as Gilroy admits). It requires us to abandon the stubbornness with which we cling to notions of race, whatever our various motivations for doing so – whether as "the beneficiaries of racial hierarchies [who] do not want to give up their privileges" or because, as members of subordinated racial groups, we have developed "complex traditions of politics, ethics, identity, and culture" in our efforts to resist the racial categories imposed upon us (Gilroy 2000: 12). It is a utopian vision worth our consideration, however, if we are to move beyond the inhumane ways often used to evaluate and punish the Other. Gilroy tells us that we have to "refigure humanism" such that we stop using race (and gender and other differences) "to categorize and divide mankind" (2000: 17). It is not that we have to renounce the embodied realities of our existence. But in thinking beyond race (and gender, sexuality, etc.), we are empowered to begin to recognize the humanity we share with people whose bodies are (biologically and culturally) different from ours. As he notes, with a refigured humanism,

> The constraints of bodily existence (being in the world) are admitted and even welcomed, though there is a strong inducement to see and value them differently as sources of identification and empathy. The recurrence of pain, disease, humiliation and loss of dignity, grief, and care for those one loves can all contribute to an abstract sense of human similarity powerful enough to make solidarities based on cultural particularity appear suddenly trivial. (Gilroy 2000: 17)

Gilroy's vision of a universal human solidarity fits well with the cosmopolitan turn in social theory, a topic I discuss in chapter 15.

SUMMARY

The Otherness of race continues to matter a great deal in contemporary society. Racial differences persist across a broad range of institutional sectors and practices as well in the routines of everyday life. They are complex, with different histories and cultural manifestations depending on the geopolitical, national, and local contexts being studied. The sociology of colonialism focuses attention on postcolonial power inequalities and highlights what postcolonial realities mean for racialized social relations as well as for the production of knowledge. Sociologists variously focus on the economic, political, and cultural circumstances that create, reproduce, and transform the significance of race and its intersection with other forms of inequality and power. The meanings attached to racial categories and the consequences and implications of racial differences pose many complex questions that the scholars discussed in this chapter help us to disentangle.

POINTS TO REMEMBER

- Colonialism, and the race-segregated structures of Otherness that it created, were the critical economic-political-cultural force subjugating the lives, life chances, and social identities of colonized peoples
- The sociology of colonialism, among other aims, seeks to contest the hegemony of western and northern biases in sociology and other forms of knowledge production
- Postcolonial identities illuminate both the persistence of inequality and the changing and dynamic nature of cultural identities (e.g., "being Black *and* British" changes what it means to be black, and what it means to be British and to be white) Scholars emphasize the sociohistorical variation in how race and racism are construed
- There is increasing attention to whiteness as a racial identity and its impact on race consciousness
- Slavery was the most extreme form of black subjugation
- There is greater recognition today than in the past that there is no single or uniform black cultural or black economic experience

- Sociologists studying inequality document the significant intersection of race with class and gender
- There is an ever-expanding gap in income and related life chances between the black middle class and the black underclass
- Many scholars emphasize the need for a new racial, and transracial, politics of equality
- Scholars highlight the blurring of racial differences apparent in the commodification of the black body
- Technological advances in genetic testing complicate rather than clarify racial composition, and have potentially racist uses

GLOSSARY

affirmative action laws and public policies that seek to redress historical discrimination against blacks and other minority groups in access to education, voting, jobs, housing, etc.

apartheid system of laws and public policies that maintains discriminatory practices against blacks (e.g., white settlers in South Africa against indigenous blacks and people of mixed race).

black cultural democracy the idea that within black communities, men and women need to create equality in their social relationships with other blacks whom they demean (e.g., women, LGBT individuals).

black underclass segment of the black community experiencing persistent chronic poverty.

colonialism political control by an imperial power over a separate geographical area and its population (e.g., Great Britain over India and the Caribbean; Portugal over Brazil; etc.), and its construal of the colonized population as economically, culturally, legally, and biologically/racially inferior.

crisis of raciology contemporary blurring of racial boundaries and of the economic and political meanings and implications of racial categories.

cultural identity the historically grounded origins of, and ongoing transformation in, a particular group's sense of who they are and their status vis-à-vis other cultural groups.

culture lines accentuation of the symbolic, cultural, and social (as opposed to biological or physical) differences between groups.

decolonize sociology a new awareness in sociology that the discipline's history is entwined with colonialism and that its Western (and Northern) knowledge biases and practices need to be systematically rethought in ways that acknowledge its parochialism and incorporate non-Western (and Southern) knowledge, knowledge categories, and lived experiences.

empire the expansive control by a political, military, and economic power of a broad swath of territories and populations (e.g., the British Empire in the nineteenth century).

hegemony of the global metropole just as geographical empires were ruled from an imperial power's political center or metropole (e.g., London was the metropole of the British Empire), sociological theory and research (and other knowledge-production) in the world today is controlled by Western/Northern universities and academics and largely consented to by those situated in non-Western and southern locations.

identity politics strategic use of particular cultural and social identities (based on race, gender, sexuality, ethnicity, etc.) to resist discrimination and/or to gain political advantage.

new racism (1) symbols and ideas used (e.g., in politics, pop culture, the mass media) to argue that race-based (biological) differences no longer matter even as such arguments reinforce racial-cultural differences and stereotypes. (2) the invocation of cultural and symbolic (rather than biological) criteria of difference to legitimate the societal exclusion or marginalization of particular racial/ethnic groups.

Otherness social construction of racial, ethnic, and/or geographical differences as inferior to a dominant historical and political power (e.g., the West's construction of Orientalism).

planetary humanism idea that society can transcend its racial, cultural, and other group differences to recognize and realize its collectively shared humanity.

political race invocation of race-based experiences of social inequality to mobilize and expand cross-racial alliances toward the achievement of social and institutional change.

politics of conversion grassroots and institutional activism based on new ways of thinking about racial identity, and intraracial and interracial competition, with a focus on the equality of all people.

postcolonial theory critiques the legacy of Western imperialism for the cultural identities of previously colonized peoples.

race symbolization of social differences based on assumed or perceived natural (innate) differences derived from differences in physical body appearance.

race segregation legal and systematically imposed divisions in everyday life based on racial differences; for example, existence of separate schools and swimming pools for blacks and whites in the US until the 1950s.

racism implicit or explicit imposition of exclusionary boundaries and discriminatory practices based on racial appearance or racial categories.

slavery historical institutionalization of coercive, discriminatory, and dehumanizing practices against a subordinate group; typically legitimated on grounds of racial difference.

Southern theory seeks to redress the Northern (and Western) bias in knowledge production, including in sociology; it is part of the effort to redress or decolonize postcolonial, unequal power relations in the knowledge production and everyday practices of sociology and other disciplines.

whiteness term used to underscore that all racial categories, including historically dominant ones (e.g., being white), are socially constructed categories of privilege whose meanings and implications change over time.

QUESTIONS FOR REVIEW

1   What does it mean to say that race is a multidimensional thing?
2   What historical, social, and cultural factors contribute to the Otherization of members of minority racial groups?
3   How does sociology as a discipline reproduce postcolonial power inequalities?
4   Does the commodification of racial bodies dilute or exacerbate everyday racism? How so? In what ways?
5   How does social class complicate racial experiences and the life outcomes of individuals in minority racial and ethnic groups?
6   What institutional practices and cultural expectations would need to change for a sociologist to be able to say that the US, the UK, Australia, or South Africa are postracial societies? What would life in such a society be like?

REFERENCES

Anderson, Elijah. 1990. *Streetwise*. Chicago: University of Chicago Press.

Anderson, Elijah. 2003. *A Place on the Corner*. 2nd edition. Chicago: University of Chicago Press.

Bhabha, Homi. 1994. *The Location of Culture*. London: Routledge.

Blauner, Robert. 2001. *Still the Big News: Racial Oppression in America*. Philadelphia: Temple University Press.

Burawoy, Michael. 1972. *The Color of Class on the Copper Mines: From African Advancement to Zambianization*. Manchester: Manchester University Press.

Collins, Patricia Hill. 1990. *Black Feminist Thought: Knowledge, Consciousness, and the Politics of Empowerment*. New York: Routledge. 2nd edition 2000.

Collins, Patricia Hill. 2004. *Black Sexual Politics*. New York: Routledge.

Collins Patricia Hill. 2015. "Intersectionality's Definitional Dilemmas." *Annual Review of Sociology* 41: 1–20.

Connell, RW. 2007. *Southern Theory: The Global Dynamics of Knowledge in Social Science*. Sydney: Allen and Unwin.

Connell, Raewyn, Fran Collyer, Joao Maia, and Robert Morrell. 2017. "Toward a Global Sociology of Knowledge: Post-Colonial Realities and Intellectual Practices." *International Sociology* 32: 21–37.

Du Bois, W.E.B. 1903/1969. *The Souls of Black Folk*. Introductions by Nathan Hare and Alvin Poussaint. New York: New American Library.

Duster, Troy. 2015. "A Post Genomic Surprise. The Molecular Reinscription of Race in Science, Law and Medicine." *British Journal of Sociology* 66: 1–27.

Fanon, Frantz. 1967. *Black Skin, White Masks.* Translated by Charles Lam Markmann. New York: Grove Press.

Frankenberg, Ruth. 1993. *White Women, Race Matters: The Social Construction of Whiteness.* Minneapolis: University of Minnesota Press.

Frazier, E. Franklin. 1955/1968. "The Negro Middle Class." Pp. 239–279 in E. Franklin Frazier, *On Race Relations: Selected Writings.* Edited and with an introduction by G. Franklin Edwards. Chicago: University of Chicago Press.

Freeman, Harold. 2014. "Why Black Women Die of Cancer." *New York Times* (March 14), p. A21.

Gilroy, Paul. 1987. *"There Ain't No Black in the Union Jack": The Cultural Politics of Race and Nation.* London: Hutchinson.

Gilroy, Paul. 2000. *Against Race: Imagining Political Culture Beyond the Color Line.* Cambridge, MA: Harvard University Press.

Go, Julian. 2013. "Decolonizing Bourdieu: Colonial and Postcolonial Theory in Pierre Bourdieu's Early Work." *Sociological Theory* 31: 49–74.

Guinier, Lani, and Gerald Torres. 2002. *The Miner's Canary: Enlisting Race, Resisting Power, Transforming Democracy.* Cambridge, MA: Harvard University Press.

Haddad, Yvonne Y. 2007. "The Post 9/11 *Hijab* as Icon." *Sociology of Religion* 68(3): 253–267.

Hall, Stuart. 1990. "Cultural Identity and Diaspora." Pp. 222–237 in Jonathan Rutherford, ed. *Identity: Community, Culture, Difference.* London: Lawrence & Wishart.

Hall, Stuart, 1992. "What Is This 'Black' in Black Popular Culture?" Pp. 21–32 in Gina Dent, ed. *Black Popular Culture.* Seattle: Bay Press.

Hall, Stuart, and Tony Jefferson, eds. 1976. *Resistance through Rituals: Youth Subcultures in Post-War Britain.* London: Hutchinson.

Heath, Anthony F, Catherine Rothon, and Elina Kilpli. 2008. "The Second Generation in Western Europe: Education, Unemployment, and Occupational Attainment." *Annual Review of Sociology* 34: 211–235.

Hechter, Michael. 1975. *Internal Colonialism: The Celtic Fringe in British National Development, 1536-1966.* Berkeley: University of California Press.

Jacobson, Matthew Frye. 2006. *Roots, Too: White Ethnic Revival in Post-Civil Rights America.* Cambridge, MA: Harvard University Press.

Karabel, Jerome. 2005. *The Chosen: The Hidden History of Admission and Exclusion at Harvard, Yale, and Princeton.* Boston: Houghton Mifflin.

Kristoff, Nicholas. 2008. "The Push to 'Otherize' Obama." *New York Times* (September 21), Wk. Rev., p. 9.

Landler, Mark, and Michael Shear. 2013. "Obama Takes on Florida Killing and Race in US." *New York Times* (July 20) pp. A1, A11.

Marable, Manning. 1986. *W.E.B. Du Bois: Black Radical Democrat.* Boston: Twayne.

McDermott, Monica. 2006. *Working Class White: The Making and Unmaking of Race Relations.* Berkeley: University of California Press.

Navarro, Mireya. 2008. "Who Are We? New Dialogue on Mixed Race." *New York Times* (March 31), pp. A1, 15.

Ogbu. John. 2003. *Black American Students in an Affluent Suburb: A Study of American Disengagement.* Mahwah, NJ: Lawrence Erlbaum.

Patterson, Orlando. 1982. *Slavery and Social Death: A Comparative Study.* Cambridge, MA: Harvard University Press.

Patterson, Orlando. 1997. *The Ordeal of Integration: Progress and Resentment in America's 'Racial' Crisis.* Washington, DC: Perseus Books.

Patterson, Orlando. 2009. "A Job Too Big for One Man: The Limits of What Obama Can Do for Race." *New York Times* (November 4), p. A25.

Pattillo, Mary. 2005. "Black Middle Class Neighborhoods." *Annual Review of Sociology* 21: 305–329.

Pattillo, Mary. 2013. *Black Picket Fences: Privilege and Peril among the Black Middle Class.* 2nd edition. Chicago: University of Chicago Press.

Riddell, Corinne, Sam Harper, and Jay Kaufman. 2017. "Trends in Differences in US Mortality Rates Between Black and White Infants." *JAMA Pediatrics* 171: 911–913.

Roediger, David. 1991. *The Wages of Whiteness: Race and the Making of the American Working Class.* London: Verso.

Roediger, David. 2002. *Colored White: Transcending the Racial Past.* Berkeley: University of California Press.

Roediger, David. 2005. *Working Toward Whiteness: How America's Immigrants Became White: The Strange Journey from Ellis Island to the Suburbs.* New York: Basic Books.

Romero, Mary. 1992. *Maid in the USA.* New York: Routledge.

Rubin, Alissa. 2016. "Backlash Wells up as the French Police Enforce 'Burkini' Ban." *New York Times* (August 25), pp. A1, 7.

Said, Edward. 1978. *Orientalism.* New York: Random House.

Sanneh, Kelefa. 2015. "Don't Be Like That: Does Black Culture Need to Be Reformed?" *New Yorker* (February 9), pp. 62–68.

Steinmetz, George, 2007. *The Devil's Handwriting: Precolonial Ethnography and the German Colonial State in Qingdao, Samoa, and Southwest Africa.* Chicago: University of Chicago Press.

Steinmetz, George. 2014. "The Sociology of Empires, Colonies, and Postcolonialism." *Annual Review of Sociology* 40: 77–103.

Uddin, Asma. 2016. "The Swimsuit as Security Threat." *New York Times* (August 24), p. A19.

West, Cornel. 1993. *Race Matters*. Boston: Beacon Press.

Williams, Rhys H., and Gira Vashi. 2007. "*Hijab* and American Muslim Women: Creating Space for Autonomous Selves." *Sociology of Religion* 68: 268–287.

Williams, Richard. 1990. *Hierarchical Structures and Social Value: The Creation of Black and Irish Identities in the United States*. New York: Cambridge University Press.

Wilson, William Julius. 1978. *The Declining Significance of Race*. Chicago: University of Chicago Press.

Winant, Howard. 2001. *The World Is a Ghetto: Race and Democracy since World War II*. New York: Basic Books.

Zeleny, Jeff. 2008. "Obama Urges U.S. to Grapple with Race Issue." *New York Times* (March 19), pp. A1, 14.

CHAPTER THIRTEEN

PIERRE BOURDIEU
CLASS, CULTURE, AND THE SOCIAL REPRODUCTION OF INEQUALITY

KEY CONCEPTS

structure
culture
social classes
economic capital
class fractions
cultural capital
cultural competence

social capital
symbolic capital
institutional field
religious capital
educational capital
taste
habitus

symbolic goods
aesthetic disposition
game of culture
collective misrecognition
economy of practice

CHAPTER MENU

Introduction to Sociological Theory: Theorists, Concepts, and Their Applicability to the Twenty-First Century,
Third Edition. Michele Dillon.
© 2020 John Wiley & Sons Ltd. Published 2020 by John Wiley & Sons Ltd.
Companion website: www.wiley.com/go/dillon

Pierre Bourdieu is "the most influential and original French sociologist since Durkheim… at once a leading theorist and an empirical researcher of extraordinarily broad interests and distinctive style" (Calhoun 2000: 696). Like Durkheim, Bourdieu emphasized the thoroughly social nature of social life and how it is that a certain social order gets maintained. But unlike Durkheim, Bourdieu made social hierarchies and inequality a key focus. In particular, he underscored how the objective **structure** of social class and class relations conditions the individual's (and differently situated social groups') everyday **culture** and social interaction. His approach to conceptualizing inequality and stratification shows the influence of Marx, and especially Weber. Unlike Marx, who regarded economic capital as the basic source of inequality in society, Bourdieu saw economic capital as just one, though a very important, dimension of inequality. Like Weber, he conceptualized inequality as having multiple dimensions. Specifically, he identified the inequality stemming from individuals' and classes' differential amounts of what he termed economic capital, social capital, and cultural capital. In his later years, Bourdieu engaged in public debates about globalization, economic inequality, and human suffering (e.g., Bourdieu 1999). And in recent years his early ethnographic research in Algeria has been used to highlight his contribution to the sociology of colonialism (e.g., Go 2013).

BIOGRAPHICAL NOTE

Pierre Bourdieu was born into a lower-middle-class family in a small town in southwestern France in 1930. He excelled academically and made a career at the highly distinguished Collège de France, Paris (as did Durkheim). In the mid-1950s, Bourdieu completed required military service in Algeria (following the French–Algerian war) and subsequently worked at the University of Algiers; while there he conducted an ethnographic study of social relations in the province of Kabylia. He was a highly productive researcher and writer; across his many publications, he elaborated concepts based on his extensive empirical qualitative and quantitative research studies. Bourdieu died in 2002 at age 72 (Calhoun 2000).

SOCIAL STRATIFICATION

Bourdieu argues that we should think of society as being hierarchically organized (stratified) as a three-dimensional social space characterized by different types of capital (or power). This is "a space whose three fundamental dimensions are defined by volumes of capital, composition of capital, and change in these two properties over time (manifested by past and potential trajectories in social space)" (Bourdieu 1984: 114). Within the social space (any society) there are many different classes and class subcomponents. But all of them are primarily distinguished by "their overall volume of capital, understood as the set of actually usable resources and powers – economic capital, cultural capital and also social capital" (1984: 114). The distribution of **social classes,** therefore, is a function of differences in ownership and use of "the different types of capital (or power, which amounts to the same thing)" (Bourdieu 1986: 243). It "thus runs from those who are best provided with both economic and cultural capital to those who are most deprived in both respects" (Bourdieu 1984: 114).

ECONOMIC CAPITAL

What comprises **economic capital** is straightforward and easy to measure: money in the bank, home ownership and other property, investment assets, etc. It is relatively easy for most individuals and families to make a tally of the volume or amount of their economic capital. And there are ways that we can readily see how our volume of economic capital compares to others; after graduation you can compare your starting salary with that of your friends, knowing that your economic capital, though it may vary over time, is going to largely determine your long-term, postcollege lifestyle. We are reminded of acute differences in economic capital when we read details of the earnings and other economic assets of top corporate executives or watch television shows that peek into the lifestyles of the rich.

Although we tend to think of the wealthy as a homogeneous group, Bourdieu highlights the differences within economic groups – that is, among those who occupy a broadly similar social class position. He argues that economic – and cultural and social capital – varies and is a source of competition between what he calls **class fractions**, subcomponents of social classes. Thus, for example, there are competitive economic and lifestyle differences between the very rich and the super-rich whether in California's Silicon Valley or in Kensington, London.

CULTURAL CAPITAL

Bourdieu's concepts of social capital and cultural capital follow a logic of acquisition, use, and exchange that is parallel to how we think of economic capital. These concepts, however, are more difficult to define and measure. "**Cultural capital** can exist in three forms: in the embodied state, i.e., in the form of long-lasting dispositions of the mind and body; in the objectified form of cultural goods (pictures, books, dictionaries, instruments, machines, etc.) … and in the institutionalized state, a form of objectification … [such as conferred by] educational qualifications" (Bourdieu 1986: 243). Cultural capital thus has parallels with Weber's conceptualization of social status and lifestyle (see chapter 3). Additionally, Bourdieu is interested in how formal education *and* informal everyday cultural habits and experiences enhance an individual's **cultural competence**. This competence includes the ease and familiarity with which individuals carry themselves – whether at a party, in a fancy restaurant, in an art museum, or at a football game – how they display a certain cool or detached practical sense of how to behave.

Each social class (and class fraction) has its own culture, and individuals regardless of social class have a certain cultural competence. By the same token, different social contexts vary in the value placed on specific cultural competencies (self-presentation at a car rally requires a different cultural competence than at a golfing event). Nevertheless, in the objectively stratified order in society as a whole, some competencies are more highly valued than others. Specifically, it is upper-class culture that is the most highly valued – it is the *legitimate* culture. This is the case not because the things and dispositions that the upper class value have greater value in and of themselves. Rather, it is because the upper class uses strategies of exclusion and inclusion made possible by their privileged location in society (e.g., country club or art gallery membership, attendance at elite schools, etc.), and that enable them to institutionalize hierarchical distinctions between their culture and the tastes they don't value (Bourdieu 1984: 23–28).

In any case, unlike the balance sheet we can read detailing our stock of economic capital, it is more difficult to itemize and make a tally of individuals' cultural capital. We can easily count an individual's years of education, but formal education is only one part of what comprises cultural capital. Assessing the extent of our own, or of someone else's, stylistic comfort and the ease with which they make ordinary everyday choices (e.g., chicken wings or Brie? Fish and chips or smoked salmon?), calls for a subtle system of classification and evaluation. Moreover, any class schema of everyday cultural taste in the US, for example, would need to incorporate the greater ideological emphasis on popular (mass-democratic) than on elite culture, notwithstanding the importance of class distinctions in the US (e.g., Lamont 1992). The antielitism in US culture is reflected, for example, in the tendency of Republican politicians (despite their own affluence) to publicly belittle their Democratic rivals as being out of touch with "ordinary folk" because they allegedly prefer wine to beer and windsurfing to duck-hunting, etc.

SOCIAL CAPITAL

Social capital, for Bourdieu, is

> the aggregate of the actual or potential resources which are linked to possession of a durable network of more or less institutionalized relationships of mutual acquaintance and recognition – or in other words to membership in a group – which provides each of its members with the backing of the collectivity-owned capital, a "credential" which entitles them to credit, in the various senses of the word … The volume of the social capital possessed by [individuals] … depends on the size of the network of connections [they] can effectively mobilize and on the volume of the capital (economic, cultural, or symbolic) possessed in [their] own right by each of those to whom [the individual] is connected. (Bourdieu 1986: 248–249)

Thus social capital refers to individuals' social connections, the social networks and alliances that link them in all sorts of direct as well as indirect and informal ways to opportunities that can enhance their stock of capital (whether economic, social, or cultural capital, and any combination thereof). In the US, college fraternities and sororities are good sources of durable social capital; such connections frequently open doors to members' first college internship, first postcollege job interview and first job, and assure members that when they move or travel to other places they have a ready-made social network (for life). In assessing social capital, the volume is contingent not just on the number of people you know but on how important the people you know are, that is, how much economic, cultural, and social capital the people you know have and are willing to share with you, and which in turn you can use to expand your volume of economic, cultural, and social capital.

As with economic capital, the accumulation of social and cultural capital takes time, and although each is distinct, there are multiple links among all three.

ECONOMIC AND CULTURAL CAPITAL IN STRATIFYING SOCIETY

Bourdieu focuses on how economic and cultural capital produce and reproduce social inequality. Economic and cultural capital are analytically independent (though interrelated) resources. Thus, an individual can have a lot of economic capital and not much objectively valued cultural capital or can have a lot of cultural capital and relatively little economic capital. Many newly rich business executives and investment-fund managers have a large volume of economic capital, but are low on cultural capital – they experience anxiety in their high socioeconomic circles because they do not have the cultural competencies to move with ease in the art and cultural worlds that are part of the upper-class social scene. Thus super-rich families who hire butlers to signify their high social status (see chapter 3), also have the opportunity to enroll in courses that teach the rules of formal dinner etiquette so that they know these rules themselves. The Butler-Valet School in Oxfordshire, England, for example, offers four-week courses at a cost of 8,000 pounds sterling (approx. $12,000) where employers can learn, among other things, that port should always be passed to the left, regardless of the rank of the person sitting next to you.

Because all types of capital are exchangeable, an individual can use one type of capital to gain more of another type. This is exactly what many economically rich people do – they pay to acquire cultural capital. Its acquisition, however, is not based automatically on an economic exchange: Money can quickly earn an individual some cultural capital – if, for example, they purchase an expensive piece of art. But the *ease* of art appreciation that is so intrinsic to showing one's cultural competence/cultural capital means that it is advisable for them to also use their economic capital (money) to get immersed and spend time in the art world. Thus some hire art consultants who teach them about different types of art and guide them in gallery visits so that eventually they will feel more at ease in making their own art choices, discussing them at elite social gatherings, and receiving approval for them. This new knowledge and individuals' ease in displaying it, in turn, increases their cultural capital, and importantly too, their **symbolic capital** (an individual's reputation) that in turn (if positive) dynamically consolidates and enriches their other forms of capital. The individual's art purchases (and their newly acquired art reputation) can translate into additional economic capital if, for example, they subsequently sell for profit one of their acquired pieces of art.

By the same token, art historians, although they have high cultural capital, may be relatively low on economic capital. But they can use their art expertise to advise rich clients and hence over time increase their economic capital, as well as further consolidating their cultural and social capital if they are able to enhance their reputation – that is, their symbolic capital (Bourdieu 1984: 291) – in the **institutional field** of art and culture as competent, accomplished, and sought-out art advisers. Bourdieu thus sees a very dynamic relation between the different types of capital and the conditions for their exchange and accumulation within and across particular institutional fields (e.g., art/culture, banking/finance). Bourdieu's construal of an institutional field is somewhat similar to how sociologists more generally discuss specialized domains of institutional behavior (e.g., economy, politics, family, law, education, culture, religion). Innovatively, however, Bourdieu highlights how the particular practices – the logic, competencies, and organizational composition and interrelations – within any one field may vary from those of other fields. Notwithstanding this variation, he also shows how all institutional fields work to reproduce inequality within their respective field and within society as a whole. Bourdieu's (1991, 1998) analysis of the religious field, for example, highlights that religion, like all symbolic systems (e.g., art, education), is an instrument of communication and knowledge and hence of classification. Its (arbitrary) divisions and distinctions impose boundaries of inclusion and exclusion that structure and reproduce inequality in **religious capital**, that is, practical mastery and competence in church doctrine and its interpretation. He highlights the struggle between "religious specialists" who seek to monopolize the production and dissemination of religious goods, and those whom they dispossess of religious capital. Thus in the specific religious institutional field of Catholicism, the structurally dispossessed laity (ordinary Catholics) are engaged in an ongoing dynamic struggle with the bishops who seek to be recognized (or misrecognized) as "the exclusive holders of the specific competence necessary for the production and dissemination of a deliberately organized corpus of secret (and therefore rare) knowledge" (Bourdieu 1991: 9; see also Dillon 2001). Religious capital too is converted into other forms of capital, such as through the economic capital provided to the clergy by the sacrificial (unpaid) labor the laity do for the church at their behest (and which as a practice also in turn reproduces the structured inequality in the Church). In summary, for Bourdieu, each type of capital is and has to be usable. All forms of capital are resources that can be accumulated and/or converted into other forms of capital, and/or traded, exchanged, and transmitted to others (including as an inheritance or a gift). They are also resources that might and can be underused or only partially converted into other types of capital. Bourdieu (1984: 105) stresses that there is nothing automatic about the relationship between economic capital and cultural capital, for example; rather, there is autonomy or agency in how any particular family or individual chooses to use their economic (or their cultural) capital. This is readily apparent when you see intrafamily cultural or economic differences among those who nonetheless have the same shared family background and social class origins. In short, capital is not simply something that an individual or family, or a social class or class fraction *has*. It is also something they *use* and (must) use to show, establish, or change their positioning in and among the economic-social-cultural hierarchies that comprise society. (See also Box 13.1.)

Box 13.1   Erotic capital

An interesting extension of Bourdieu's analysis of diverse forms of capital is the idea of erotic capital outlined by Catherine Hakim (2010), a British scholar. She argues that erotic capital (sexual attractiveness, energy, and competence) should be considered a personal capital asset that, like other forms of capital, can be translated into and used to acquire economic, social, and cultural capital. In Hakim's framing, erotic capital is multifaceted and can include (1) beauty; (2) sexual attractiveness; (3) social interaction skills such as charm and grace (parallel to Hochschild's emotional labor; see chapter 10); (4) liveliness/social energy and good humor; (5) style of dress and self-presentation; and (6) sexuality itself which includes sexual competence, erotic imagination, playfulness. She argues that women have more erotic capital than men; that it is advantageous in mating, marriage, and the labor market; and it has "greater value when it is linked to high levels of economic, cultural, and social capital" (2010: 503). Hakim acknowledges that erotic capital is difficult to measure objectively, and that its elements may vary across cultures and social contexts. Not surprisingly, the construct is controversial. Despite decades of feminist resistance to the equation of women as sexual objects, erotic capital explicitly focuses on the "special assets" that women (though not only women) may possess as a result of their sexual-erotic skills and attributes. Nonetheless, it taps into everyday empirical realities and highlights how differences in erotic assets are consequential in everyday life (at work, at home, in public).

FAMILY AND SCHOOL IN THE PRODUCTION OF CULTURAL CAPITAL

Bourdieu underscores the significance of the family of origin in determining an individual's access to capital. Someone from a relatively poor family can, through educational qualifications (what Bourdieu calls academic or **educational capital**), subsequently gain a considerable amount of capital (economic, social, and/or cultural); indeed, many empirical studies document such patterns of upward occupational and social mobility in the US and the UK (e.g., Fischer and Hout 2006; Heath et al. 2008) Nonetheless, there is a close positive relationship between socioeconomic background and educational capital. This means that children who grow up in families of high socioeconomic status – that is, families that have relatively large amounts of economic and/or cultural capital – are more likely than children from families of low socioeconomic status to go to and succeed in college (i.e., acquire educational capital) and subsequently achieve occupational-economic success (e.g., Rivera 2015).

Consequently, as Bourdieu argues, "the educational capital held at a given moment expresses, among other things, the economic and social level of the family of origin" (Bourdieu 1984: 105). Academic capital is contingent on (though also somewhat autonomous of) the cultural capital inherited within the family (1984: 22–23). This insight is influential in sociolinguistics, which recognizes that language skills and vocabulary are determined not alone by formal cognitive learning but also by experiences within the family-social context in which children grow and play and learn. And, as sociologists document, family environments are further mediated by varied gender, ethnic, and social class differences (e.g., Lareau 2003).

Therefore, although we might think of the educational system as a social institution whose functioning and effectiveness sets it apart from other institutions, such as the family and the economy, this is not the case. Bourdieu argues that the cultural disposition required and rewarded by schools is one that emphasizes the student's familiarity with a general culture that can be transmitted only by families who already have cultural capital. What he means by this is that children who grow up in families with cultural capital are exposed to everyday cultural experiences (reading, travel, visiting restaurants and art museums, etc.) and habits (e.g., punctuality, task completion, an emphasis on knowledge appreciation and on the normalcy of reading, visiting museums, etc.) that cultivate in them the "natural" disposition and habits necessary for success at school – success both in the classroom and, importantly too, among one's peers on the playing fields and in other daily activities.

These cultivated habits are conducive to success in terms of the formal curriculum and the school's "scholastically recognized knowledge and practices" (Bourdieu 1984: 23). Academic success, in turn, gives the individual the necessary credentials that are the gateway to occupational-economic opportunities and success (Bourdieu 1996: 336). These habits are also crucial to developing the individual's more general "cultivated disposition" (Bourdieu 1984: 23), their ability to be at ease with the everyday cultural requirements of being a member of the upper class to which academic credentials are a conduit.

Both the family and the school are engaged in cultural transmission (Bourdieu 1984: 23), and these institutions entwine to reinforce the dispositions and practices that constitute and facilitate the accumulation of cultural and economic capital. The school is the one institution in society, Bourdieu argues, that reproduces social divisions both objectively, through its impact in credentializing and positioning individuals in the occupational-social class hierarchy; and subjectively, by inculcating individuals with ways of perceiving and evaluating the social world (Bourdieu 1996: xix). In particular, "It is largely through the crucial role it plays in individual and collective transactions between employers … and employees … that the educational system directly contributes to the reproduction of social classifications" (1996: 121).

> ### Topic 13.1   College education, economic mobility, and social well-being
>
> A college education gives students from lower-income families in the US almost a one-in-five chance of joining the top one-fifth of earners, and almost a two-out-of-three chance of joining the middle class or better (Hauser 2009). These are good odds. However, individuals from the lowest-income bracket are far less likely than others to go to college: 11 percent, compared to 53 percent of children from families among the country's highest earners. The majority of children from high-earning families who graduate from college maintain their family's high socioeconomic status (SES) in adulthood. Further, almost one in four of the children who come from the top income bracket are likely to remain within that bracket in adulthood even if they do not graduate from college. In sum, college education significantly enhances the economic opportunities of children from low-income families. And for those from high-income families, family SES cushions against the absence of a college degree. Despite intersecting social class and racial disparities in access to education (Rich et al. 2016), its economic and social value is well documented. Based on examination of a wide range of data, the sociologist Michael Hout (2012: 400) concludes: "Education makes life better. People who pursue more education and achieve it make more money, live healthier lives, divorce less often, and contribute more to the functioning and civility of their communities than less educated people do."

BOURDIEU'S IMPACT ON THE SOCIOLOGY OF EDUCATION

Bourdieu's insights into the interlinking of family and school culture have been influential in orienting research and debates within the sociology of education. In the post-World War II era, the expansion of education, especially university education, in the US and Western European countries was a critical institutional mechanism promoting economic growth and the expansion of the middle class. Education was widely seen by sociologists and policymakers as a highly effective system for transmitting the knowledge and values required in a high-functioning society, securing individual upward mobility, and advancing societal modernization and social progress (e.g., Smelser 1968; see chapter 4).

This functionalist view was well represented in the research of James Coleman (1961), who stressed the significance shared norms and values (among teachers, parents, students, and peers) in ensuring effectively functioning school (and other) communities (see chapter 7). This perspective dominated the field until the 1980s, though it drew criticism from scholars using a Marxist framework. Most notably, Bowles and Gintis (1976) argued that the organization and the authority and rewards system (e.g., grades, competition) of the school (as part of the capitalist superstructure; see Marx; chapter 1) basically perpetuate the economic and class inequality of the larger society.

Autonomy of economic and cultural capital

It was not until the 1980s, however, that sociologists had a new way of thinking about the place of school in society. Bourdieu offered a much more dynamic and nuanced analysis of how schools work. His theorizing argued against Parsons's emphasis on the functionality of schools in determining individuals' positioning within the occupational and stratification subsystems of society; and against the Marxist view of schools as an arm of capitalist structure and ideology. Highlighting the analytical and empirical independence of different types of capital, i.e., that cultural capital can be autonomous of economic capital, Bourdieu pushed recognition that schools produce and transmit cultural capital – e.g., academic credentials and a general cultivated disposition – and do so somewhat independent of the family and of social class. Equally significant, his emphasis on the linkages between economic and cultural capital, and between family/social class and school, is crucial. It highlights that although the school (or education as an institutional field) has some autonomy from the economy and from family, it is nonetheless positioned to reproduce the socioeconomic inequalities that antecede, are reflected in, and extend beyond the school. Importantly, however, this reproduction effect is not automatic; the analytical separateness of cultural and economic capital fosters dynamic openings and tensions in the reproduction of both privilege and inequality.

Further, because of the autonomy of cultural and economic capital, Bourdieu's analysis also illuminates how educational capital itself becomes a force in interclass competition (rather than simply a mechanism of upward class mobility). Interclass competition is fueled by the expansion of educational opportunities and the attendant increase in university enrollments of students from lower-class families. It is also pushed by the related emphasis on merit and academic credentials in securing access to well-paying jobs. He argues:

> When class fractions who previously made little use of the school system enter the race for academic qualifications, the effect is to force the groups whose reproduction was mainly or exclusively achieved through education to step up their investments so as to maintain the relative scarcity of their qualifications and consequently, their position in the class structure. Academic qualifications and the school system which awards them thus become one of the key stakes in an interclass competition which generates a general and continuous growth in the demand for education and an inflation of academic qualifications. (Bourdieu 1984: 133)

Bourdieu's insights are based on empirical studies he conducted of schooling in France (Bourdieu and Passeron 1971; Bourdieu 1996). Although the educational and social class system in France is more highly stratified and more competitive than in the US, empirical studies in the US support his theorizing (e.g., Karabel 2005; Lareau 2003; Lareau and Weininger 2003). They show the strong influence of family background on educational capital and the impactful role of schools in the transmission and reproduction of cultural and economic capital. This is especially true of elite colleges (e.g., Harvard, Yale) that, by continuing to give preferential treatment to the admission of children of alumni, operate a relatively closed system of upper-class status reproduction, notwithstanding their admission also of students from middle- and lower-income families (Karabel 2005: 548–549).

SOCIAL POLICY IMPLICATIONS OF BOURDIEU'S ANALYSIS

From a social policy perspective, Bourdieu's findings highlight the challenge entailed in efforts to reduce inequality. Although his framework allows for upward (and downward) mobility, the significance of family cultural capital in determining an individual's class position, independent of school, puts a damper on liberal democratic policies that seek to expand access to education for economically disadvantaged families. One implication of his analysis is that access to education, in the absence of the cultural competencies that come with a high social class background, will fall short of making a substantial dent in equalizing the economic and cultural differences between social classes (e.g., MacLeod 2008; Willis 1977).

For example, a lower-class individual who is the first in their family to go to college is also likely to come from a neighborhood where comparatively fewer students go to college. Once in college – not only a new educational but also a new social class and cultural environment – this student will not be as *familiar* as middle-class students with the expectations and practices that characterize college everyday reality; they will feel as "strangers," less "at home" there, than the middle class students (see chapter 9). They will not already know that certain study habits and certain seminars, majors, and summer internships are "better" than others in positioning a student for college and postcollege success. Equally important, a lower-class student – feeling out of place in a middle- (and upper-) class environment – may be shyer or feel less entitled about interacting with professors and getting help (and thus getting a higher grade). Working-class students who graduate from college are likely to have much greater economic success than their social class peers who don't go to college (e.g., Haskins et al. 2009; Hout 2012). On average, however, they may not do as well in college and after college as middle-class students. This is because they are disadvantaged by working-class culture and family/ neighborhood experiences that inhibit the "self-assurance of legitimate membership and the ease given by familiarity" (Bourdieu 1984: 81) with the middle-class culture required, affirmed, and rewarded by schools. Nevertheless, school is still *the* one crucial mechanism facilitating upward mobility (see Topics 13.1 and 13.2).

Topic 13.2   "I'm First-Gen"

Reflecting Bourdieu's insight that success at school and college is not merely a matter of gaining admission but of having the cultural competence, that is, the feel for how to navigate campus life, many colleges are actively engaged in outreach to "first-generation" students. As children of parents who did not go to college, first-gen students (and their parents) are often intimidated by the unfamiliar world of campus life and have a higher risk of dropping out. Programs to attract and retain first-gen students include (i) Special Welcome Week orientations for them and their parents; (ii) financial aid packages tailored in recognition of the fact that such parents are not only often squeezed by the costs of college but are more fearful than college-educated parents of taking on debt; (iii) organized faculty and first-gen student social gatherings; and (iv) specifically targeted Pathway programs for both college and career success. There is also recognition that first-gen is another enriching source of intersecting diversity on campus. Indeed, some colleges are tackling the social isolation and stigma frequently experienced by first-gen students by celebrating it as an identity. With students wearing bright tee-shirts proclaiming "I'm first-gen," the hope is that social class background will come to be seen as an interesting part of a student's life narrative and not an impediment to either academic success or making friends.

TASTE AND EVERYDAY PRACTICES

THE CLASS CONDITIONING OF TASTE

Bourdieu's analysis of education and cultural capital is part of his larger interest in how ordinary everyday habits reflect and reproduce social class differences. He emphasizes the social class conditioning of **taste** in all the "ordinary choices of everyday existence" (Bourdieu 1984: 77). Although we think of our taste in clothes and food and music, as uniquely ours, Bourdieu argues that individual tastes are patterned along social class lines. No matter how natural some of our tastes may seem to us, we like what we like as a consequence of what it is we have learned to like or to appreciate, or to think is cool, as a result of the social conditions and class culture in which we live and in which we have been brought up.

These dispositions and tastes are not the result of formal learning, even though at school and college we learn "the linguistic tools and references which enable aesthetic preferences to be expressed and to be constituted by being expressed" (Bourdieu 1984: 53). And we can learn to discover and acquire new tastes. Formal learning aside, taste is part of our cultural **habitus**. The habitus, for Bourdieu essentially refers to the everyday tastes we actively and literally (though unconsciously) *embody*; the relatively enduring schemes of perception, appreciation, and appropriation of the world that we absorb and act on. We acquire our cultural habitus from the repetitive, everyday habits that we experience (and enact or practice) within our family of origin, a sociocultural context that itself is conditioned by social class and by the particular everyday habits that distinguish each social class (1984: 101). These embodied experiences make certain dispositions appear natural to us. (See also Box 13.2.)

In emphasizing the habitus as culturally and physically embodied, Bourdieu means that the tastes we have are not just cognitively learned habits; they are also deeply grounded in the smells, looks, and sounds that surrounded and infused the habits in our homes and families while we were growing up. Judgments of taste

impress themselves through bodily experiences which may be as profoundly unconscious as the quiet caress of beige carpets or the thin clamminess of tattered, garish linoleum, the harsh smell of bleach or perfumes as imperceptible as a negative scent. Every interior expresses, in its own language, the present and even the past state of its occupants, bespeaking the elegant self-assurance of inherited wealth, the flashy arrogance of the nouveaux riches, the discreet shabbiness of the poor and the gilded shabbiness of "poor relations" striving to live beyond their means. (Bourdieu 1984: 77)

Tastes in food and how we eat

Similarly, we learn – quite readily, almost naturally, as a result of our own family's class-conditioned and gender-mediated habits – to *embody* cultural expectations of what "people like us" eat and do. Writing in generalized terms about class differences in France, he states:

Tastes in food … depend on the idea each class has of the body and of the effects of food on the body, that is, on its strength, health, and beauty; and on the categories it uses to evaluate these effects, some of which may be important for one class and ignored by another, and which different classes may rank in different ways. Thus, whereas the working classes are more attentive to the strength of the (male) body than its shape, and tend to go for products that are both cheap and nutritious, the professions prefer products that are tasty, health-giving, light and not fattening. (Bourdieu 1984: 190).

He further elaborates:

The whole body schema, in particular the physical approach to the act of eating, governs the selection of certain foods. For example, in the working classes, fish tends to be regarded as an unsuitable food for men, not only because it is a light food, insufficiently "filling," which would only be cooked for health reasons, i.e., for invalids and children, but also because, like fruit (except bananas) it is one of the "fiddly" things which a man's hands cannot cope with and which make him childlike … but above all, it is because fish has to be eaten in a way which totally contradicts the masculine way of eating, that is, with restraint, in small mouthfuls, chewed gently, with the front of the mouth, on the tips of the teeth (because of the bones). The whole masculine identity – what is called virility – is involved in these two ways of eating, nibbling and picking, as befits a woman, or with whole-hearted male gulps and mouthfuls [as befits a man]. (Bourdieu 1984: 190–191)

Therefore it is not just the foods chosen, but "the treatment of food and the act of eating" itself that reaffirm and reproduce the different class habits and cultures (Bourdieu 1984: 197). Hence, the working class, concerned with eating as a functional task – something necessary to nourish and replenish the body – prefer large portions of heavy foods like meat and stews and don't pay much attention to the meal's presentation. By contrast, the upper class deny eating's primary bodily function, thus preferring small portions of light food (e.g., salad, fish) (1984: 197–198), and instead of nourishment construe the meal as "a social ceremony" (1984: 196).

Box 13.2   Norbert Elias: The civilizing process

The German social theorist Norbert Elias (1897–1990) used the term "habitus" to refer to the socializing/civilizing process, that is, the social prohibitions whereby certain everyday social habits and manners (e.g., how to hold your knife and fork) are ingrained in the "civilized" individual, such that habits of "self-restraint" (e.g., "Don't stuff your mouth") become "second nature," i.e., operating against the individual's "conscious wishes" (Elias 1978: 129). He elaborates: socially imposed civilized manners "appear to [individuals] as highly personal, something 'inward,' implanted in them by nature … later it becomes more and more an inner automatism, the imprint of society on the inner self, the superego, that forbids the individual to eat in any other way than with a fork" (1978: 128–129).

Elias's analysis of the evolution of manners is part of his larger interest in how society changes over time and, with social change, how the individual is construed and how group life is regulated. His inquiry parallels Durkheim's focus on the shift from traditional to modern society and how the structure, rules, and bonds of community change. It also parallels Weber's focus on the gradual rationalization of societal processes (e.g., religion, economy, bureaucratization). Thus Elias addresses the increased emphasis on individualization associated with modernity, the emergence and expanding regulatory power of the nation state, and the changing social class structure and its associated competitive tensions (e.g., away from monarchy and aristocracy to a more differentiated social class formation). He probes how these macro-level changes converge over time to produce new civilizing movements; new understandings of what a civilized individual and a civilized society should look like and how they should behave; and the development of new interrelated structures (e.g., institutions and norms) that define and regulate "civilized" behavior. His focus on the sociology of civilizing processes and the context in which they take hold has renewed relevance today as we witness the modernization of Asian societies (e.g., China, South Korea, India). It will be interesting to see the extent to which Western and non-Western understandings of etiquette and manners will be mutually reworked and incorporated into a cosmopolitan habitus (see chapter 15). (See Mennell and Goudsblom [1998] for an introduction to Elias's writings.)

GENDERED TASTES, GENDERED BODIES

Bourdieu also elaborates on the class-mediated gender differences in the disposition toward food and the body: "There is also the principle of the division of foods between the sexes, a division which both sexes recognize in their practices and their language. It behooves a man to drink and eat more, and to eat and drink stronger things," to eat meat rather than fish, and to have seconds rather than women's

Figure 13.1 What looks good, smells good, and tastes good is conditioned by our everyday social class and family habits and practices. Source: Author.

single and smaller portion (Bourdieu 1984: 190, 192). Thus, talking about the "abundance" of the working-class meal, he notes:

> Plain speaking, plain eating: the working class meal is characterized by plenty ... and above all by freedom... "abundant" dishes are brought to the table – soups or sauces, pasta or potatoes ... and served with a ladle or spoon, to avoid too much measuring and counting, in contrast to everything that has to be cut and divided, such as roasts [of meat]. This impression of abundance, which is the norm on special occasions, and always applies, so far as is possible, for the men, whose plates are filled twice (a privilege which marks a boy's accession to manhood), is often balanced, on ordinary occasions, by restrictions which generally apply to the women, who will share one portion between two, or eat left-overs of the previous day; a girl's accession to womanhood is marked by doing without. (Bourdieu 1984: 194–195)

And, as we know from the prevalence of women who diet and who are diagnosed with anorexia, women (somewhat independent of class) tend to "do without." This cultural message is further reinforced by fashion models and a fashion industry that requires extreme thinness (i.e., below size 0).

In sum, our judgments of taste are conditioned and structured by the intersecting family and social class context in which we are socialized. We internalize and act on these conditionings through an array of everyday practices – for example, by what our family eats for dinner and how; who cooks it and washes up; and whether and how we talk about sports, work, music, or politics over dinner. These practices are explicitly prescribed by "the semi-legitimate legitimizing agencies" (Bourdieu 1984: 77), including women's and "ideal home" magazines, websites, and neighborhood grocery stores, reminding us that this is what people like me (and us) eat, buy, and like (see also Smith's discussion of the ruling discourse of femininity in chapter 10). And, it is through these everyday practices that the macro structures of society – stratification, gender, family, religion, for example – get institutionalized and reproduced in the individual's everyday life and in society.

Gender divisions, for example, get reproduced through the parallel divisions between home and work and between women and men (see chapter 10), that the family habitus and its everyday habits (e.g., eating family meals) enact (and that socialize us). Decisions of taste and of fashion are, by and large, established as women's domain. It is women, Bourdieu argues, who are responsible for the consumption of **symbolic goods** – for the buying, displaying, and gift-giving of those goods that reproduce the family's good taste/status reputation, or what can also be called the "production of the signs of distinction" (Bourdieu 2001: 101). The symbolic goods people buy and place on display objectify their (socially conditioned) "personal" taste, that is, their cultural capital, and position them hierarchically in relation to others (Bourdieu 1984: 282). And, because of women's responsibility for the "conversion of economic capital into symbolic capital within the domestic unit," they are the ones in the vanguard of the competitive cultural practices that characterize intra- and interclass status competition. Women "are predisposed to enter into the permanent dialectic of pretension and distinction for which fashion offers one of the most favourable terrains and which is the motor of cultural life as a perpetual movement of overtaking and outflanking" (Bourdieu 2001: 101).

The sociological pairing of women and fashion is not new. At the beginning of the twentieth century, Georg Simmel (1904/1971: 309, 313) argued that women were fashion's "staunchest adherents." He maintained that this was because it compensated for their lack of professional career and that, in fact, "emancipated women" were indifferent to fashion. Similarly, Charlotte Perkins Gilman (1903/1972) argued that if women could claim economic equality and be released from the home burdens of "domestic art," they would not need to be so subjugated to fashion.

Bourdieu is not saying that women are naturally (biologically) inclined toward fashion. He is arguing rather that their objective positioning as women within the gender hierarchy of a stratified society requires them to use their (socially conditioned) taste for fashion to acquire and use symbolic capital that will reproduce their class, family, and (unequal) gender status. He recognizes that gender hierarchies are arbitrary; they are not biologically determined but "*historical* mechanisms responsible for the *relative dehistoricization* and *eternalization* of the structure of the sexual division and the corresponding principles of division" (Bourdieu 2001: vii–viii). These gendered structures are institutionalized and reproduced in and through everyday practices. For Bourdieu, nonetheless, gender is analytically relevant mostly insofar as it mediates class reproduction and helps explain symbolic and other capital accumulation processes. He observes for example that in societies where economic assets are scarce, women are used as objects of capital accumulation:

> When – as is the case in Kabylia [province in Algeria] – the acquisition of symbolic capital and social capital is more or less the only possible form of accumulation, women are assets which must be protected from offence and suspicion and which, when invested in exchanges, can produce alliances, in other words social capital, and prestigious allies, in other words, symbolic capital. (Bourdieu 2001: 45)

Understandably, he affirms the political significance of the women's movement and its efforts to resist masculine domination and transform women's subordination into gender equality (Bourdieu 2001: 88–90).

UPPER-CLASS TASTE

Because taste is conditioned by social class conditions, each social class produces its own distinctive class habitus, a set of taste dispositions that can be seen in the choices made (and not made) by class inhabitants. Bourdieu argues that the upper-class habitus is marked by an **aesthetic disposition** that requires the upper class to admire a work of art or music for its stylistic form rather than any practical function it might have; and similarly regarding clothes, food, furniture, and other everyday objects. The aesthetic disposition signals both economic and cultural capital and their merging as a result of freedom from economic necessity.

The aesthetic disposition, a generalized capacity to neutralize ordinary urgencies and to bracket off practical ends, a durable inclination and aptitude for practice without a practical function, can only be constituted within an experience of the world freed from urgency and through the practice of activities which are an end in themselves such as ... the contemplation of works of art. (Bourdieu 1984: 54)

Such engagement in practices that have no practical function is itself produced (and required) by the upper class's economic power, which, as Bourdieu notes,

is first and foremost a power to keep economic necessity at arm's length. This is why it universally asserts itself by ... conspicuous consumption, squandering, and every form of gratuitous luxury ... Material or symbolic consumption of works of art constitutes one of the supreme manifestations of *ease*, in the sense both of objective leisure and subjective facility [cultural competence]. (Bourdieu 1984: 55)

THE CULTURE GAME

The (established) upper class, therefore, play the **game of culture** with the playful seriousness (Bourdieu 1984: 54) that comes only from familiarity with its rules. As in any game, this includes the spoken and also, importantly the unspoken rules, that is, the insider's knowledge of and feel for the game. Like accomplished basketball players on the court, the upper class know the right moves, the insider subtleties that are not necessarily written down anywhere; where to seamlessly position themselves, and when to score and how to score with ease and finesse, thus enhancing their good reputation (symbolic capital), and likely too, adding to their economic capital. Just as the game-playing of accomplished athletes seems natural to us, so too does that of the upper class; they convey their "natural" claim on the game – even though, as in sports, we know that notwithstanding any natural talent, the best players also train and practice a lot.

The different social classes and class fractions play the culture game through their everyday practices of taste and consumption, practices that serve to distinguish the classes from one another (Bourdieu 1984: 250). The culture game – and the hierarchical positioning games played in other institutional fields (e.g., the religious field; Bourdieu 1998) – "like all social stakes, simultaneously presupposes and demands that one take part in the game and be taken in by it" (Bourdieu 1984: 250). We misrecognize the *arbitrariness* of the game's structure and rules; to play is to be taken in by the game. All games are symbolic struggles over the appropriation of scarce goods; only the winners get trophies, that is, objects, or economic and status rewards, that affirm their symbolic capital, their reputation as a "winner."

Bourdieu argues that **collective misrecognition** of the arbitrariness of the social hierarchies and evaluative categories that structure everyday practices is the process which necessarily sustains unequal social relations across all institutional fields (culture, education, art, law, religion). As he states, "there is no way out of the game of culture" (Bourdieu 1984: 12). Hence we variously engage in practices that we tacitly know are arbitrary (e.g., why should visiting an art museum be considered more culturally worthy than visiting a sports museum?), but that, if we were to explicitly acknowledge them as arbitrary, would lose their symbolic power, that is, the symbolic power necessary to maintain unequal class and other unequal social relations (e.g., gender hierarchies in the Catholic Church that exclude women from ordination).

WORKING-CLASS TASTE

In contrast to the upper-class habitus, the working-class habitus, Bourdieu argues, produces a taste and style that are dictated by economic and cultural necessity: "Necessity imposes a taste for necessity which implies a form of adaptation to and consequently acceptance of the necessary, a resignation to the inevitable" conditions of class and the choices it allows in ordinary everyday existence (Bourdieu 1984: 373). Necessity produces a working-class habitus whereby, for example, manual workers indicate an appreciation for clothes that are "good value for money," that are cheap and long lasting, practical or functional, and not stylistically risky. Their choices are not determined by their volume of economic capital alone, though this clearly is an important dimension of necessity. Their choices are codetermined by the coincidence of economic and cultural necessity: Among the working class, conformity rather than personal autonomy is valued.

As Bourdieu points out, this functional disposition toward buying clothes (or toward food) is a *reasonable strategy* for the working class given the economic and cultural capital (and time) that buying more fashionable clothes would require. Moreover, the symbolic capital (the gains to their reputation) that would ensued from such an investment would be low (at least while at work, given the nature of their work) compared, say, to clerical workers, whose taste in fashion can enhance their reputation among peers and supervisors at work (Bourdieu 1984: 377–378).

There is thus what Bourdieu calls an **economy of practice** in working-class taste; and a similar logic applies to the practices of all social classes. Given what they've got – given the economic and cultural capital they have – each class makes reasonable strategic investments in order to expand and maximize their symbolic capital. Thus, Walmart's consumer categories are not only an effective market-control strategy (see Topic 5.4, chapter 5); they also make good cultural sense: "Value-price shoppers," "brand aspirationals," and "price-sensitive affluents" are each composed of class-situated individuals who are making the most economically and culturally of what they have got (economically and culturally). Bourdieu states:

> The interest the different classes have in self-presentation, the attention they devote to it, their awareness of the profits it gives and the investment of time, effort, sacrifice and care which they actually put into it are proportionate to the chances of material or symbolic profit they can reasonably expect from it. (Bourdieu 1984: 202)

WHO WANTS TO BE A MILLIONAIRE?

Further, because taste is produced in and by a class-conditioned habitus, its relatively enduring system of judgments and dispositions means that the individual's taste does not change just because they win the lottery. "Having a million does not in itself make one able to live like a millionaire; and parvenus [the newly arrived rich] generally take a long time to learn that what they see as culpable prodigality [excessive self-indulgent spending] is, in their new [economic] condition, expenditure of basic necessity" (Bourdieu 1984: 374). To live like a millionaire, or as an upwardly mobile rich person, requires the acquisition of a new class disposition such that the individual can be at ease in claiming as their own that which they can (unexpectedly) afford. They thus need to learn to appreciate with ease that one person's extravagance is another person's necessity (1984: 375), a distinction whose nuances are often apparent in the lifestyles and purchases of residents in the same affluent community. It is likely that such nuances can be traced to differences in their class/family origins (notwithstanding their current shared affluence).

The cultural competence projected in being at ease with one's new-found wealth - the "self-assurance of legitimate membership and the ease given by familiarity" (Bourdieu 1984: 81) – requires, Bourdieu argues, following Goffman, a certain amount of role distance. One cannot self-present as being ever so excited to have all this new money (or to be in a museum or an expensive restaurant for the first time); one has to act as if this is what you are used to, as if this is your habitus (1984: 54). Thus,

> to appreciate the "true value" of the purely symbolic services which in many areas (hotels, hairdressing etc.) make the essential difference between luxury establishments and ordinary businesses, one has to feel oneself the legitimate recipient of this bureaucratically personalized care and attention and to display

vis-à-vis those who offer it the mixture of distance (including "generous" gratuities) and freedom which the bourgeois have toward their servants. (Bourdieu 1984: 374)

TASTE IN THE REPRODUCTION OF SOCIAL INEQUALITY

The different, economically conditioned class cultures of everyday life reinforce the objective distinctions and boundaries between the classes (i.e., in how they act and where they come from). They also reinforce the dispositions that class-situated individuals subjectively feel about crossing class boundaries. One structural consequence of this system of distinction is the reinforcement of class inequality. The familiarity and comfort individuals feel in their own class habitus, with their own culture's ways of doing things, means that working-class individuals, for example, feel less attracted, less entitled, to entering and participating in institutional spaces such as universities whose culture – *the* legitimate culture – they perceive to be so different from own everyday culture. This becomes both an objectively structured, and subjectively felt, impediment, therefore, to the educational success and upward mobility of children from working-class families (as discussed previously). Once they make this break, however, then their own children, born into a higher class fraction, can be more at ease with (upper-class) legitimate culture.

In sum, Bourdieu (1984: 6) argues, we distinguish ourselves by the distinctions we make. Taste reveals our social class conditioning as well as our current position in social space. Embodied as it is in our everyday habits, it reproduces and extends the social class differences that characterize everyday cultural choices and their evaluation. Thus taste

> unites and separates. Being the product of the conditionings associated with a particular class of conditions of existence, it unites all those who are the product of similar conditions while distinguishing them from all others. And it distinguishes in an essential way, since taste is the basis of all that one has – people and things – and all that one is for others, whereby one classifies oneself and is classified by others … Aversion to different life-styles is perhaps one of the strongest barriers between the classes; class endogamy is evidence of this … Objectively and subjectively aesthetic stances adopted in matters like cosmetics, clothing or home decoration are opportunities to experience or assert one's position in social space, as a rank to be upheld or a distance to be kept. (Bourdieu 1984: 56–57)

In short, "Taste is what brings together things and people that go together" (Bourdieu 1984: 241).

LINKING MICRO ACTION AND MACRO STRUCTURES

Bourdieu's discussion of everyday taste highlights his larger theoretical emphasis that micro-level individual action matters in society, and at the same time, individual choices are invariably conditioned by and work back on macro-structural processes (e.g., inequality in society, at work, in gender relations). There is a tendency in sociology to counterpoise micro-level with macro-level perspectives, and similarly to contrast approaches that emphasize individual or collective agency with those that focus on explaining social action in terms of structural and institutional processes. Bourdieu's conceptualization of how we should analyze and understand society transcends these polarities.

His writing points to the agency of individuals in everyday life – the individual makes choices every day about what food to buy, what clothes to wear, what music to listen to, what church to attend, what political party to support, what gift to buy, etc. Yet, at the same time, no matter how avant-garde or autonomous, the individual does not act alone or in some sort of existential vacuum. Ordinary everyday habits are infused by society; we cannot escape from its structural and cultural forces. Individual agency is always constrained (always structured) by formal education, social class, family habits, and the distinctive (and unequal) cultural codes and practices that these contexts teach us and which we reproduce, more or less, through our everyday preferences and habits. Thus in Bourdieu's framework, individuals embody the habits and attitudes – the culture and the cultural strategies and practices – of those around them, and act back on that culture in everyday social life with a certain degree of individual autonomy (e.g., choosing chicken or fish). Yet the cultural options available to the most agential of individuals are themselves constrained by an objective class (and racial and gender) structure wherein the distribution of economic and cultural resources makes certain options more culturally (and economically) reasonable or "natural" (though arbitrary) than others. It is through such ordinary everyday actions as food shopping and eating that we as individuals reproduce the objective structural order, even though we have a certain amount of latitude in the choices and distinctions we make.

ENDLESS STRATIFICATION

Some readers may find Bourdieu's emphasis that we cannot escape the game of culture – that is, that we cannot escape distinguishing ourselves by the (arbitrary but class-conditioned) taste distinctions we make every day – an exaggeration of the importance of hierarchies in social life; that everything we do – every taste we express – reflects and feeds into a system of stratification. This is an understandable response. Yet, by making us think about taste as a socially conditioned and socially conditioning set of practices, Bourdieu alerts us to the many small (as well as big) ways in which class divisions – and gender divisions too – get reproduced. These are important contributions. His detailed focus on the minutiae of different habits as socially conditioned and socially contextualized individual choices and tastes, alerts us that social inequality is found and reproduced ubiquitously. It is not just in the institutional arenas where we might expect to find inequality – in schools, business, sports – but also in what we might think of as relatively benign everyday sites (e.g., the dinner table) and everyday activities (e.g., having a picnic).

Feminists (e.g., Martineau, Gilman, Smith, Collins, Hochschild) have long identified the kitchen and the home as sites for the reproduction of gender inequality. The gender division of labor is visible in who cooks, who cleans, who smiles, and who doesn't get to leave the home for the economic-public world (see chapter 10). Additionally, Nancy Chodorow (1978) highlights the social-psychodynamic forces that reproduce gendered patterns in the taste or desire for mothering. Bourdieu adds to the sociological understanding of how and why structures of inequality are so resilient. He illuminates how individuals acting on their own (socially conditioned) taste in making everyday choices about apparently mundane things are really enacting practices and habits that are grounded in, reflect, and reproduce society's institutionalized social hierarchies. This does not mean that people do not have individual agency, or that we cannot change the structures and cultural practices that reproduce inequality. But it cautions us that change in the social order is a long and slow process. This is largely because of the ways in which everyday practices embody cultures of hierarchy (e.g., social class) and domination (e.g., hegemonic masculinity) and do so across the intersecting institutions (e.g., the state, the economy, the home, the university, mass media, advertising, sports, the church) that make such practices of inequality appear normal and necessary though they are arbitrary (Bourdieu 2001: viii).

SUMMARY

Bourdieu's overarching focus is on social inequality – on stratification in schools, art, clothes, food, etc. – and on how inequality gets reproduced across diverse institutional and cultural domains. He outlines the details of individual choices in the micro contexts of everyday life, but overall analytical framing is more concerned with macro structures and processes than with micro relations. His conceptualization of the habitus shows how micro practices are conditioned by and reproduce macro structures (e.g., of class inequality), and how objective macro structures (e.g., the educational system, the social class system) get internalized into individuals' everyday habits and dispositions. His approach thus exemplifies how sociologists must necessarily attend to the interplay of micro and macro processes.

Although Bourdieu discusses the strategic choices made by individuals and the fact that, for example, there are economic efficiencies in working-class tastes (dictated by necessity), he does not regard individual choices as motivated by the same individual self-interested, utilitarian motives elaborated by rational choice theorists (see chapter 7). For Bourdieu, individual choices are invariably located within a class-conditioned cultural habitus and thus are structured by a particular social, economic, and cultural context.

POINTS TO REMEMBER

Pierre Bourdieu
- Focuses on the reproduction of inequality in society
- Inequality is due to class-conditioned differences in volume of capital (economic, social, cultural capital)
- He gives special attention to the links between economic and cultural capital
- School is a major transmitter and reproducer of cultural and economic capital
- Everyday taste is socially conditioned by the social class habitus
- Different social classes construe the body, food, and eating differently
- Different social classes and genders have a (socially conditioned) taste for different cultures, and different everyday habits and practices
- Taste reproduces social hierarchies, including gender hierarchies; we distinguish ourselves by the distinctions we make
- Different institutional fields (e.g., education, art, etc.) have their own respective logics of symbolic differentiation and inequality

GLOSSARY

aesthetic disposition the class-inculcated attitude that allows and requires the upper class to admire art, clothes, etc., for style rather than practical function.

class fraction differentiated, hierarchical subcomponents (e.g., the lower-middle class) of broadly defined social classes (e.g., the middle class); the economic and cultural capital of class fractions varies.

collective misrecognition immersion in a particular habitus or set of everyday practices whereby we (necessarily) fail to perceive the arbitrary, though highly determining ways in which those practices reproduce inequality.

cultural capital familiarity and ease with (the legitimate) habits, knowledge, tastes, skills, and style of everyday living; education is one institutional field that requires, transmits, produces, and reproduces cultural capital; can be used to acquire economic and social capital and to accumulate additional cultural capital.

cultural competence possessing the appropriate family and social class background, knowledge, and taste to display (and acquire additional) cultural capital.

culture dispositions, tastes, evaluative judgments, and knowledge inculcated in and as a result of class-conditioned, embodied experiences (including but not limited to formal education).

economic capital amount of economic assets an individual/family has; can be converted into social and cultural capital and to acquire additional economic capital.

economy of practice individuals' and social classes' use of the economic and cultural capital they have to make reasonable strategic investments that expand and maximize their economic, cultural, and symbolic capital.

educational capital competencies acquired through school; can be converted into economic and cultural capital.

game of culture participation in the evaluative and taste practices that confer style or distinction as if "naturally" rather than due to class conditioning; reproduces social class differences.

habitus relatively enduring schemes of perception, appreciation, and appropriation of things, embodied in and through class-conditioned socialization and enacted in everyday choices and taste.

institutional field specific institutional spheres (e.g., education, culture, religion, law) characterized by institution-specific rules and practices reproducing inequality.

religious capital practical mastery and competence in church doctrine and its interpretation

social capital individuals' ties or connections to others; can be converted into economic and cultural capital and into additional social capital.

social classes broad groups based on objective differences in amounts of economic, social, and cultural capital.

structure objective ways in which society is organized; for example, the social class structure exists and has objective consequences for individuals independent of individuals' subjective social class feelings and self-categorization.

symbolic capital one's reputation for competence, good taste, integrity, accomplishment, etc.; has exchange-value, convertible to economic, social, and cultural capital.

symbolic goods goods we buy, display, and give to distinguish ourselves from others; signal and reproduce taste, status, social hierarchy, social class inequality.

taste social class- and family-conditioned, ordinary, everyday preferences and habits; socially learned ways of appreciation, style.

QUESTIONS FOR REVIEW

1   What are the different types of capital analyzed by Bourdieu? What does each type consist of and accomplish? What is the interrelation among the different types?
2   What is the role of school (formal education) in the reproduction of class inequality? Is knowledge acquired outside of the classroom valuable in increasing a person's cultural capital? Explain why/why not.
3   How do everyday food preferences and food habits reflect, illuminate, and reproduce social class differences?
4   How do gender hierarchies get manifested in and reproduced through taste? How is the body implicated in social class and in gender hierarchies?

REFERENCES

Bourdieu, Pierre. 1984. *Distinction: A Social Critique of the Judgment of Taste*. Cambridge, MA: Harvard University Press.

Bourdieu, Pierre. 1986. "The Forms of Capital." Pp. 241–258 in John Richardson, ed. *Handbook of Theory and Research for the Sociology of Education*. New York: Greenwood Press.

Bourdieu, Pierre, 1991. "Genesis and Structure of the Religious Field." *Comparative Social Research* 13: 1–44.

Bourdieu, Pierre. 1996. *The State Nobility: Elite Schools in the Field of Power*. Stanford, CA: Stanford University Press.

Bourdieu, Pierre. 1998. *Practical Reason: On the Theory of Action*. Stanford, CA: Stanford University Press.

Bourdieu, Pierre. 1999. *The Weight of the World: Social Suffering in Contemporary Society*. Stanford, CA: Stanford University Press.

Bourdieu, Pierre. 2001. *Masculine Domination*. Stanford, CA: Stanford University Press.

Bourdieu, Pierre, and Jean-Paul Passeron. 1971. *Reproduction: In Education, Culture, and Society*. Beverly Hills, CA: Sage.

Bowles, Samuel, and Herbert Gintis. 1976. *Schooling in Capitalist America*. New York: Basic Books.

Calhoun, Craig. 2000. "Pierre Bourdieu." Pp. 696–730 in George Ritzer, ed. *The Blackwell Companion to Major Social Theorists*. Oxford: Blackwell.

Chodorow, Nancy. 1978. *The Reproduction of Mothering: Psychoanalysis and the Sociology of Gender*. Berkeley: University of California Press.

Coleman, James. 1961. *The Adolescent Society*. Glencoe, IL: Free Press.

Dillon, Michele. 2001. "Pierre Bourdieu, Religion, and Cultural Production." *Cultural Studies: Critical Methodologies* 1: 411–429.

Elias, Norbert. 1978. *The Civilizing Process: The History of Manners*. Translated by Edmund Jephcott. New York: Urizen Books.

Fischer, Claude, and Michael Hout. 2006. *Century of Difference: How America Changed in the Last One Hundred Years*. New York: Russell Sage Foundation.

Gilman, Charlotte Perkins. 1903/1972. *The Home: Its Work and Influence*. Introduction by William O'Neill. Urbana, IL: University of Chicago Press.

Go, Julian. 2013. "Decolonizing Bourdieu: Colonial and Postcolonial Theory in Pierre Bourdieu's Early Work." *Sociological Theory* 31: 49–74.

Hakim, Catherine. 2010. "Erotic Capital". *European Sociological Review* 26(5): 499–518.

Haskins, Ron, Harry Holzer, and Robert Lerman. 2009. *Promoting Economic Mobility by Increasing Postsecondary Education*. Washington, DC: Brookings Institution and Pew Charitable Trusts.

Hauser, Robert. 2009. "On 'Quality and Equity in the Performance of Students and Schools.'" Center for Demography and Ecology Working Paper No. 2009-06. Madison: University of Wisconsin.

Heath, Anthony F., Catherine Rothon, and Elina Kilpli. 2008. "The Second Generation in Western Europe: Education, Unemployment, and Occupational Attainment." *Annual Review of Sociology* 34: 211–235.

Hout, Michael. 2012. "Social and Economic Returns to College Education in the United States." *Annual Review of Sociology* 38: 397–400.

Karabel, Jerome. 2005. *The Chosen: The Hidden History of Admission and Exclusion at Harvard, Yale, and Princeton*. Boston: Houghton Mifflin.

Lamont, Michele. 1992. *Money, Morals, and Manners: The Culture of the French and the American Upper-Middle Class*. Chicago: University of Chicago Press.

Lareau, Annette. 2003. *Unequal Childhoods*. Berkeley: University of California Press.

Lareau, Annette, and Elliot Weininger. 2003. "Cultural Capital in Educational Research: A Critical Assessment." *Theory and Society* 32: 567–606.

MacLeod, Jay. 2008. *Ain't No Makin' It: Aspirations and Attainment in a Low-Income Neighborhood*. 3rd edition. Boulder, CO: Westview Press.

Mennell, Stephen, and Johan Goudsblom. 1998. "Introduction." Pp. 1–45 in Norbert Elias, *On Civilization, Power, and Knowledge: Selected Writings*. Edited and with an introduction by Stephen Mennell and Johan Goudsblom. Chicago: University of Chicago Press.

Rich, Motoko, Amanda Cox, and Matthew Bloch. 2016. "In Schools Nationwide, Money Predicts Success." *New York Times* (May 3), p. A3.

Rivera, Lauren A. 2015. *Pedigree: How Elite Students Get Elite Jobs*. Princeton: Princeton University Press.

Simmel, Georg. 1904/1971. *On Individuality and Social Forms*. Edited and with an introduction by Donald Levine. Chicago: University of Chicago Press.

Smelser, Neil. 1968. *Essays in Sociological Explanation*. Englewood Cliffs, NJ: Prentice Hall.

Willis, Paul. 1977. *Learning to Labour: How Working Class Kids Get Working Class Jobs*. Farnborough: Saxon House.

CHAPTER FOURTEEN

ECONOMIC AND POLITICAL GLOBALIZATION
WALLERSTEIN, SKLAIR, GIDDENS, SASSEN, BAUMAN, CASTELLS

KEY CONCEPTS

globalization
disembeddedness
glocalization
transnational practices
capitalist world-system
geographical division of
    labor
world-economy
core states
peripheral areas
semiperipheral areas

crisis
capitalist globalization
socialist globalization
global systems theory
financial sector
financial capitalism
global cities
class polarization
transnational capitalist class
denationalized class
geopolitical

world military order
new imperialism
dialectical nature of
    globalization
distant proximities
postnational
denationalized state
network society
deepening of democracy
antiglobalization movement
global social democracy

CHAPTER MENU

Introduction to Sociological Theory: Theorists, Concepts, and Their Applicability to the Twenty-First Century,
Third Edition. Michele Dillon.

Timeline 14.1	Major globalizing economic and political events (1450–present)
1450–1640	Emergence of capitalism in Europe
1815–1917	Accelerated expansion of capitalism
1884	Drawing of Africa's colonial boundaries at Berlin conference
1914–1918	World War I, first global war
1939–1945	World War II
1944	The International Monetary Fund (IMF) is created close to the end of World War II to help nations rebuild their economies and to oversee and bring stability to the international monetary system (e.g., exchange rates), headquartered in Washington, DC
1945	World Bank Group established, headquartered in Washington, DC
1945	United Nations (UN) founded. Headquartered in New York City, with its European headquarters in Geneva, Switzerland. It has 185 member countries; 18 specialized agencies; and a number of programs, councils, and commissions
1945	At the end of World War II, Korea was divided into two regions, with the US occupying the South and the USSR (Soviet Union) occupying the North

1946–1991	Cold War between US and Soviet Union
1947	General Agreement on Tariffs and Trade (GATT) formed; precursor to World Trade Organization (WTO)
1948	Organization of American States (OAS; US, South and Central America, Caribbean) founded, headquartered in Washington, DC
1948	South Korea proclaims its political independence as a democratic Republic
1948	UN Economic Commission for Latin America and the Caribbean (ECLAC) established
1948	World Health Organization (WHO; part of the UN) established
1949	North Atlantic Treaty Organization (NATO) formed, headquartered in Brussels, Belgium
1949	Fourth Geneva Conventions ratified, giving protection to prisoners of war
1950	Korean War; invasion of the South by the North; US assisted South Korea
1957	Treaty of Rome agreed, founding of European Economic Community (EEC), now the EU
1957	International Atomic Energy Agency (IAEA) established, headquartered in Vienna, Austria
1960	International Development Association (IDA) instituted, headquartered in Washington, DC
1960	Organization of Petroleum Exporting Countries (OPEC) created, headquartered in Geneva, Switzerland, then in Vienna, Austria
1960s–1980s	Though a democracy, South Korea's government is controlled by military dictators
1961	Organisation for Economic Cooperation and Development (OECD) established, headquartered in Paris, France
1963	Organization of African Unity (OAU) founded, headquartered in Addis Ababa, Ethiopia
1967	Association of Southeast Asian Nations (ASEAN) established, headquartered in Jakarta, Indonesia
1968	Organization of Arab Petroleum Exporting Countries (OAPEC) established, headquartered in Safat, Kuwait
1971	China joins the United Nations
1975	Latin American Economic System (SELA) founded, headquartered in Caracas, Venezuela (27 members; Central and South America, Caribbean)
1976	OPEC Fund for International Development established, headquartered in Vienna, Austria
1980	China begins decollectivization and the expansion of industry and entrepreneurship; beginning of its economic modernization
1981	Cooperation Council for the Arab States of the Gulf, also known as Gulf Cooperation Council (GCC), founded, headquartered in Riyadh, Saudi Arabia
1987	Military dictatorship in South Korea ends, replaced by elected civilian government
1988	US–Canada Trade Agreement signed
1989	Collapse of Berlin Wall

1989	Asia-Pacific Economic Cooperation (APEC) established, headquartered in Singapore
1991	Persian Gulf War
1991	South Korea joins the United Nations
1992	European Community becomes European Union (EU)
1994	Euro launched as official currency of some EU member states (not including UK and Denmark)
1994	North American Free Trade Agreement (NAFTA) established between US, Canada, and Mexico
1995	The World Trade Organization (WTO) comes into being to facilitate multilateral trade relationships and practices. Countries that had already signed the General Agreement on Tariffs and Trades (GATT) automatically became members (including the US, UK, Ireland, European countries, Central and South American countries, some African countries, Australia, South Korea)
1997	Hong Kong reverts from British colonial rule to administrative and sovereign control by China
2001	Terrorist attacks on World Trade Center Towers, New York City
2001	China joins the WTO
2002	Chinese Taipei joins the WTO
2003	US invades Iraq
2004	Cambodia joins the WTO
2005	Saudi Arabia joins the WTO
2008	Summer Olympics in Beijing, China
2008	Russia invades ex-Soviet Republic Georgia
Winter 2008	Start of US and global economic recession
2012	Russian Federation, and Montenegro join the WTO
2012	Summer Olympics in London, England
2014	Winter Olympics in Sochi, Russia; FIFA World Cup Soccer Tournament, Brazil
2014	ISIS (the Islamic State) terrorist group comes to prominence
2014	Ebola epidemic kills over 11,000 people in West Africa and infects Western travelers to the region
January 2015	"Charlie Hebdo" terrorist attacks in Paris
April 2015	Earthquake in Nepal kills 8,000 people
June 2015	Pope Francis release his encyclical on climate change, *Laudato Si'*, in which he defines climate change and poverty as an interrelated societal crisis
June 2016	The majority of people in the UK vote to leave the European Union (EU)

July 2016	Summer Olympics in Rio de Janeiro, Brazil
2016	Zika virus prevalent in Brazil and other Central and South American countries
2017	China has more Internet users than any other country: approx. 730 million (mostly using smartphones)
2018	Winter Olympics in South Korea
2020	Summer Olympics in Tokyo, Japan; FIFA World Cup Soccer Tournament in Russia

Social action today is increasingly impervious to geographical-national borders. You get a sense of this flow from Topic 14.1. As this box highlights, **globalization** is not any one thing but is composed of several interrelated economic, political, social, and cultural processes (e.g., Giddens 1990; 1991; Ritzer 2007; Robertson 1992; Sklair 2002). Globalization processes are not driven by any one single mechanism, and they don't affect global, national, or local society in any single or predetermined way. Further, as the word conveys, globalization involves forces and issues that span the whole *globe*, and as such it is qualitatively different from the inter*national* relationships, trade relations, migration patterns, and political interactions that have long existed between particular regions and countries.

Globalization, therefore, requires a shift in sociological perspective from the tendency to think of society as coinciding with, or happening within and between, specific geographical-national territories. Although there is no single sociological theory of globalization, different theoretical strands help us to make analytical sense of what globalization entails and its implications for social institutions, social change, and everyday life.

Topic 14.1   Global flows

- More than one-tenth of all the goods and services produced in New York City, and 1 in every 20 jobs, are supplied by companies controlled by foreign investors.
- General Electric (US) has research centers in Munich (Germany), Shanghai (China), and Bangalore (India).
- Stretching from China to Europe, China's investment initiative "One Belt, One Road" encompasses 60 countries and covers six major international economic corridors including Central Asia (e.g., Kazakhstan), South Asia (e.g., Pakistan), and North Africa (e.g. Egypt). Indian companies are outsourcing jobs to workers in Mexico, Brazil, Chile, and Uruguay.
- Thomas the Tank Engine (created by an English clergyman in 1946 and owned by Mattel) is introducing new and more ethnically diverse train characters reflecting its popularity in Mexico (Carlos), India (Ashima), China (Yong Bao), and Brazil (Raul).
- Every year, American, Chinese, and Japanese visitors travel to South Korea, Mexico, India, and Thailand for surgery and medical care.
- "Gangnam Style" by the South Korean pop musician Psy has vast global popularity; it was the first YouTube video to reach one billion views.
- The Chinese government and Middle Eastern families have substantial investments in American-based financial companies, hotels, and resorts.
- Walmart is expanding in China and India.

- American universities have branch campuses in Doha (Qatar), Dubai (United Arab Emirates), and Singapore, and joint programs (e.g., Navitas) with Chinese and Indian universities.
- The Louvre, the renowned Paris museum, has sold rights to the use of its name to a museum in Abu Dhabi, the capital city of the United Arab Emirates, in a deal worth approx. $1.3 billion.
- In UK Premier League Football (soccer), Manchester United Football Club is owned by an American family; Manchester City Football Club is owned by a sheik who lives in Abu Dhabi; and Chelsea Football Club is owned by a Russian billionaire; there are eight nationalities on the Chelsea team's starting lineup (of 11 players), with just three from England.
- Los Angeles is home to the largest number of Mexicans, Guatemalans, and Koreans outside of their own countries; 40 percent of its total population was born outside of the US
- 70 percent of the apple juice, 80 percent of the tilapia, and over 40 percent of the processed mushrooms consumed in the US are imported from China.

WHAT IS GLOBALIZATION?

Globalization can be defined in general terms as "the *process* of integrating nations and peoples – politically, economically, and culturally – into larger communities" (Eckes and Zeiler 2003: 1). This process is one that is not linear or incremental but "dynamic, transformational, and synergistic" (2003: 1). Thus, just as Durkheim emphasized that society is greater than the sum of the individuals who comprise it (see chapter 2), we should think of globalization as being more than the cumulative sum of the nations and populations comprising the globe. It has its own reality, and as such creates social processes and dynamics that cannot be reduced to the economic, political, or cultural actions of any one nation or to any combined alliance of nations. In Durkheimian language, globalization is an objective social fact with its own external and constraining force in society. This should not be interpreted to mean that globalization is independent of society or driven by some invisible, nonsocietal force; rather it is produced by society and affects other forces in society (e.g., nationalism, inequality, smoking patterns). And it spans and affects both macro and micro processes. (e.g., Robertson 1992: 61–84)

BIOGRAPHICAL NOTE

Anthony Giddens was born into a lower middle-class family in London in 1935. The first in his family to go to college, he received his PhD from Cambridge University, where he subsequently spent much of his prolific career. In the 1990s, he became an influential advisor to British prime minister Tony Blair and is widely acknowledged for elaborating the "third way" social-democratic approach that was central to Blair's and the Labour Party's political agenda (and that is often also used to characterize the policies of the Clinton presidency in the US). Giddens has been widely recognized for his academic and policy contributions, and in 2004 was awarded a peerage. He currently sits in the British House of Lords and continues to advocate for social democratic policies as a way to incorporate the changes associated with globalization.

What is new about globalization is the simultaneous circulation and flow of people (migration); of money; of things, including illicit things such as drugs; of ideas (e.g., about gender equality); and of information (e.g., via the Internet) about all sorts of people and things, between and among all sorts of people. Globalization processes are driven by, among other factors, advances in communication technology and especially the continuing advances in Internet and digital technology. Their accessibility and benefits are uneven, as reports on the digital divide highlight (e.g., UNCTAD 2017). But for those who have access, such technologies free us, or disembed us, from the constraints of time and space; from the physical, geographical, economic, political, cultural, and social boundaries that define and demarcate our immediate, place-based context.

As elaborated by **Anthony Giddens** (1991), the **disembeddedness** of time and space is our current social experience. The physical centers of money, power, and knowledge that characterized past times are increasingly complemented if not displaced by multiple digitalized platforms and networks. These advances allow for flexibility, fluidity, and mobility, rather than requiring us to be anchored in, or to, a particular space and bound by a particular clock. We, and individuals in places far distant from us, can take online college courses, watch online our favorite sports teams and sporting events, e-shop, e-bank, e-pray, e-date, e-trade, e-mail. Such disembedded practices inhere in and simultaneously accelerate globalizing processes. Giddens argues that globalization is "best understood as expressing fundamental aspects of time–space distanciation. Globalisation concerns the intersection of presence and absence, the interlacing of social events and social relations 'at distance' with local contextualities" (Giddens 1991: 21).

The ongoing dynamic between local "here-and-now" realities and their intertwining and interdependence with global processes (e.g., financial markets on a different geographical continent) give prominence to the notion of **glocalization** (Robertson 1992). This concept recognizes the fact that in our increasingly disembedded era of globalization and digitalization, the local and the distant can no longer be considered independent of each other. Rather, globalization changes the dynamics of life across all spheres of social interaction. As defined by Leslie Sklair, globalization is "a particular way of organizing social life across existing state borders," and as such gives rise to distinctively **transnational practices** – transnational economic, political, and cultural practices (Sklair 2002: 8). These practices are not dictated or determined by technology but are shaped by the interaction of multiple economic, political, and cultural forces. Although digital and wireless technology expands the possibilities for how to organize institutional and everyday practices, these decisions are not foreclosed by the technology itself. Indeed, Christian Fuchs argues, "Global network capitalism is characterized by an economic antagonism between proprietary and open space, a political antagonism between dominated and participatory space, and a cultural dynamic between one-dimensional and wise space" (2008: 120).

ECONOMIC GLOBALIZATION

Much of what we hear about globalization focuses on its economic aspects. Though global trade is not a new phenomenon, "globalization" was first used in in an article in 1983 (Eckes and Zeiler 2003: 1) to basically refer to the expansion of the world economy such that trade in consumer products increasingly extends beyond a particular country's borders. This is precisely the process predicted by Karl Marx when he spoke of the ever-increasing pressure on capitalists to expand profits by finding and conquering new world markets for their products (see chapter 1). And at the time he wrote in the late nineteenth century there was already plenty of movement of capital, trade, and people around the world, but it came to a halt with the outbreak of World War I (1914–1918) (e.g., King 2017).

Economists have a different perspective than sociologists on how society works. They focus primarily on the economic mechanisms and consequences of globalized trade in commodity, labor, and capital markets, and they generally do so without regard to its social and cultural implications (e.g., Bordo et al. 2003). They tend to regard capitalism as effectively regulated by *natural* forces of demand and supply and to see globalization through this same lens. Thus the deputy editor of the influential news magazine *The Economist* states, "Globalization has a powerful economic momentum of its own. Technological progress, left to its own devices, promotes [economic] integration ... [Economic] integration seems in many ways a natural economic process, which can only be reversed, if at all, when policies are deliberately framed to that end" (Cook 2003: 549).

Further, economists see global trends in *intra*national (within-country) inequality as a result of "the fact that the opening to trade and foreign investment was incomplete," concentrated in select cities and provinces at the expense of rural and other areas (Lindert and Williamson 2003: 255). By extension, in this view, global inequality is a result of "differential access to the benefits of the new economy" and of particular countries' and regions' failures to participate in globalization (2003: 263).

Sociologists apply a very different framework to the economic aspects of globalization. They fully recognize the expansion of new markets that is entailed in globalization and emphasize, as Giddens notes (1990: 76), the many advances made after World War II in expanding global relations of economic interdependence. This includes the opening up of new geographical centers of industrial production and the emergence of newly industrializing countries in the third world (1990: 76). Subsequently, the rise of a postindustrial information and service economy (see chapter 6) and today's transnational informational economy (e.g., Fuchs 2008) further expanded world markets as well as the transnational social and political relationships that this expansion necessitates. But, in highlighting these globalizing forces, sociologists also emphasize the historical, geographical, and structural *unevenness* of globalizing economic processes (Wallerstein 2004), and their weakening effects on local subsistence economies (e.g., Giddens 2003: 17).

IMMANUEL WALLERSTEIN: THE MODERN WORLD-SYSTEM

Any sociological discussion of economic globalization must necessarily engage the theorizing of the American sociologist **Immanuel Wallerstein**. He argues that the association of globalization with relatively open economic frontiers between countries is part of a much longer "cyclical occurrence throughout the history of the modern world-system," a world-system in which economic logic is the primary driver (Wallerstein 2004: 93). Wallerstein was influential in establishing the idea of a **capitalist world-system**. In his three-volume historical analysis of "the creation of the modern world" (Wallerstein 1974: 3), he detailed the formation of capitalism as a bounded, historically unique, and economically distinctive world-system that emerged in Europe in the sixteenth century.[1] Although his focus anticipates the globalization dominant in contemporary society, his long historical perspective on the development of capitalist processes makes him skeptical of talk of globalization. He "rarely if ever uses the word globalization" (Sklair 2002: 42) and on his Yale University website, refers to it as "so-called globalization."

Using language similar to Talcott Parsons, who conceptualized society as a social system (see chapter 4), Wallerstein states that a "world-system is a social system, one that has boundaries, structures, member groups, rules of legitimation, and coherence" (Wallerstein 1974: 347). Unlike Parsons, Wallerstein is a neo-Marxist. Strongly influenced by Marx's analysis of capitalism, he emphasizes the centrality of unequal relations of production to capital accumulation. And extending Marx, he emphasizes the **geographical division of labor** in the historical emergence of capitalism (1974: 349). In this view, we cannot understand the contemporary manifestations of (global) capitalism and its various problems and crises without appreciating the geographical dynamics of its historical evolution. Let us explore what this entails.

BIOGRAPHICAL NOTE

Immanuel Wallerstein was born in New York in 1930. He received his undergraduate and graduate education in sociology at Columbia University and spent most of his career at the State University of New York, Binghamton, where he was also the founding director of the Fernand Braudel Center for the Study of Economies, Historical Systems, and Civilization. He is currently a senior research scholar in the sociology department at Yale University. A renowned expert on Europe and Africa, he is a prolific and wide-ranging author (including collaboration with Andre Gunder Frank). Wallerstein was a founding member of the *Journal of World-Systems Research*, and of the American Sociological Association (ASA) section for the Political Economy of the World System. He was president of the International Sociological Association (1994–1998), and in 2003, received the ASA's Career of Distinguished Scholarship Award.

MODERN WORLD-ECONOMY

Taking the world-system rather than any particular country (e.g., US, England, Argentina) as the unit of analysis, Wallerstein analyzes how the relations of production and capital accumulation characterize countries relative to one another in the world-system's capitalist **world-economy**. According to Wallerstein, world-economies are independent of political boundaries and are structurally divided into **core states**, **peripheral areas**, and **semiperipheral areas**. And between and among these, there is an unequal flow of capitalist resources. He specifically talks about peripheral and semiperipheral *areas* rather than states, precisely because these geographical regions are characterized by indigenous weak states (Wallerstein 1974: 349). A world-system, he argues, is

> one in which there is extensive division of labor. This division is not merely functional – that is, occupational – but geographical. That is to say, the range of economic tasks is not evenly divided throughout the world-system. In part, this is the consequence of ecological considerations [e.g., population distribution, natural resources], to be sure. But for the most part, it is a function of the social organization of work, one which magnifies and legitimizes the ability of some groups within the system to exploit the labor of others, that is to receive a larger share of the surplus [wealth/profit]. (Wallerstein 1974: 349)

The corresponding links between the geographical and the occupational division of labor in the world-economy are decisive in reproducing inequality:

> The division of a world-economy involves a hierarchy of occupational tasks, in which tasks requiring higher levels of skill and greater capitalization are reserved for higher-ranking areas [geographical regions] … Hence, the ongoing process of a world-economy tends to expand the economic and social gaps among its varying areas in the very process of its development. (Wallerstein 1974: 350)

In short, in the world-system, the core tends to dominate the periphery (Wallerstein 1974: 129). The determining force of the unequal geographical distribution of economic production roles (e.g., industrialization in the core, agriculture in the periphery) is such that core and peripheral areas develop "different class structures ... different modes of labor control" (1974: 162), and different state structures, whereby strong states at the core protect their various economic interests against other relatively strong states, and especially against (weak) states in peripheral areas, and do so in ways that effectively maintain the (unequal) world-system (1974: 354–355).

Moreover, Wallerstein sees culture as a servant of economic interests (similar to Marx, see chapter 1), and argues that "any complex system of ideas can be manipulated to serve any political or social objective" (Wallerstein 1974: 152). Noting that Protestantism came to dominate in the core and Catholicism in the periphery, he maintains that this geographical religious distribution was a function of world-system economic forces and not, as Weber argues, driven by differences in cultural ideas (e.g., Calvinism; see chapter 3). Wallerstein argues that because the transnational Catholic Church "was threatened by the emergence of an equally transnational economic system which found its political strength in the creation of strong state machineries in certain (core) states" "it threw itself wholeheartedly" into opposing modernity. The Church thus consolidated its power in peripheral countries (e.g., Poland, Ireland), and, paradoxically, its success in the periphery "ensured the long-term success of the European world-economy" (Wallerstein 1974: 156).

WORLD-SYSTEMS IN CONTRAST TO WORLD-EMPIRES

Although Wallerstein's world-system may seem like another way of talking about empires, this is not the case. World-systems are not the same as empires, though they share some features in common. They may each cover a large spatial area and encompass diverse languages, religions, and cultures (e.g., the British Empire; see chapter 12) The distinctive feature of the modern world-system is its world-economy. Wallerstein explains: "It is a 'world-system' not because it encompasses the whole world, but because it is larger than any juridically-defined political unit. And it is a 'world-*economy*' because the basic linkage between the parts of the system is economic" (Wallerstein 1974: 15). A world-empire, by contrast, is essentially a political and administrative unit.

Unlike an empire, which is a political unit ruled by a single ruler from a centralized political location, the world-economy encompasses many states, several of which have different forms of political organization (Wallerstein 1974: 15). And whereas an empire relies on a large administrative staff in place in its varied geographical locations to enforce its economic coercion (e.g., tax collection, property rules), world-systems function by virtue of the (unequal) economic relations among the states. Thus,

> Political empires are a primitive means of economic domination. It is the social achievement of the modern world, if you will, to have invented the technology that makes it possible to increase the flow of the surplus [wealth/profit] from the lower strata to the upper strata, from the periphery to the center, from the majority to the minority, by eliminating the "waste" of too cumbersome a political superstructure. (Wallerstein 1974: 15–16)

DISTINCTIVE CHARACTERISTICS OF THE MODERN WORLD-SYSTEM

Wallerstein argues that "the modern world-system (or the capitalist world-economy) is merely one system among many" (Wallerstein 1996: 294). It does not refer to the noncapitalistic systems that have existed over time, nor to those system(s) that might replace the existing one (Wallerstein 2004: 76–90). What is distinctive is that the capitalist world-system has managed to destroy all of its historically contemporaneous systems, such as long-dominant empires, and, moreover, no other historical system was based on "the structural pressure for the ceaseless accumulation of capital" (1996: 295). Earlier systems engaged in long-distance trade but, Wallerstein notes, this was primarily trade in luxuries and *between* center (e.g., Great Britain) and periphery systems (e.g., India, Egypt), rather than trade in necessities and *within* a given system, specifically within the modern capitalist world-system (1996: 294). Consequently, earlier forms of trade did not have the same structural imperative toward capital accumulation and profit so fundamental to modern capitalism (see Marx, chapter 1).

Wallerstein (1974: 10) argues that modern capitalism originated as a distinctive world-system or world-economy in sixteenth-century Europe, that this system became consolidated between 1640 and 1815, and that it aggressively expanded during the following hundred years (1815–1917). The so-called Age of Discovery (sixteenth century) is regarded as the beginning of modern capitalism. European explorers such as Vasco da Gama chartered new Atlantic ocean trade routes from Europe to India, Africa, and the Americas and brought back exotic goods (including pepper and other spices). There was nothing natural or miraculous about the development of modern capitalism. Instead, as Wallerstein (1974) argues, it was contingent on, among other factors, (1) the economic opportunities for exploitation and expansion created by the ebb and flow of industrial cycles of growth, overproduction, and decline; (2) the financial and political imperatives for competing monarchies (e.g., England, the Netherlands, Spain, and Portugal) to explore distant lands for new goods and revenue sources, and thus to maintain their political-economic hegemony; (3) far-reaching political struggles and alliances between countries; (4) the emergence of stronger and more autonomous states freed from religious influences; (5) timely alliances between church and state at various critical moments; (6) class alliances among varied social strata (e.g., landed gentry, aristocrats, bureaucrats) within countries; and (7) economic, cultural, and political opportunities presented by both the outbreak and the resolution of various wars.

THE STATE IN THE EXPANSION OF CAPITALISM

Wallerstein highlights the technological accomplishments of capitalism and its ability to progressively produce more goods for more profit. Nonetheless, he underscores that capitalism does not proceed because of some invisible hand of the market acting naturally or alone (as free market economists would contend). His analysis shows, rather, that it is bolstered by strong states that "serve the interests of some groups and hurt those of others" (Wallerstein 1974: 354). From a detailed review of the history of European capitalism, he concludes: "The state's role in capitalist development has been constant throughout modern history" (1974: 127).

The typical historical narrative of social change emphasizes the transformative effect of late eighteenth-century industrialization and its political revolutions in advancing economic and political freedom. Wallerstein's thesis—that the modern capitalist system is historically specific and dates further back, to sixteenth century Europe— challenges that notion:

> None of the great revolutions of the late eighteenth century – the so-called industrial revolution, the French Revolution, the settler independences of the Americas – represented fundamental challenges to the world capitalist system. They represented its further consolidation and entrenchment. The popular [mass democratic] forces were suppressed, and their potential in fact constrained by the political transformations. (Wallerstein 1989: 256)

Most sociologists and historians would likely argue that we should still regard the late eighteenth century as a time of critical transformation in society. At the same time, however, Wallerstein's argument reminds us that history is usually more complicated than an event-oriented calendar can fully capture. In other words, social change, including globalization, does not happen out of the blue. Some of its manifestations and dimensions may be unexpected, but once we trace the precursors of any sociohistorical shift, we can usually find that even the most unexpected or tumultuous events and processes (e.g., democratization) were preceded by multiple social, cultural, economic, and political tremors.

CHANGING CONTEXT OF THE CORE–PERIPHERY WORLD

Another important characteristic of the world-system perspective is that it expects change within the system. Although the world-system is a self-contained and coherent system (Wallerstein 1974: 347), it also has its own internally generated tensions and contradictions. These include migration and other demographic shifts and (following Marx) crises of overproduction and competitive struggles between companies and nations in conquering new markets (1974: 347). The structure of the capitalist world-system, therefore, Wallerstein argues, is not set once and for all time by historical events. Geographical boundaries can expand such that areas external to the system can become incorporated into it, typically into new periphery or semiperiphery areas (mostly, historically, due to colonization of peripheral areas; e.g., Williams 1990). By the same token, particular regions may change their role in the system, such that "core states can become semi-peripheral and semi-peripheral ones peripheral" (Wallerstein 1974: 350). Although core states have an advantage over others, their status is not assured across a long period of time; and they necessarily encounter challenges from other core states as to which will be "top dog." Wallerstein suggests we should think of this process as a structural "circulation of the elites in the sense that the particular country that is dominant at a given time tends to be replaced in this role sooner or later by another country" (1974: 350).

Currently, we can think of the US as among the core states, and we might think of Bangladesh as on the periphery. But its recent economic growth (averaging more than 6 percent annually between 2007 and 2017), just as the post-1990s economic transformation in previously "peripheral" countries such as India and China, underscores the theoretical and empirical difficulty in assigning countries/regions within Wallerstein's schema. How many years of continuous economic growth, for example, are necessary for a country to be considered core? Should it more accurately be seen as semi-peripheral? As Wallerstein notes, the semiperiphery is not an artificial or residual category; like core and periphery, it too "is a necessary structural element in the world-economy" (Wallerstein 1974: 349). But it is also a little murky; semiperipheral areas constitute a sort of middle area, functioning as "collection points of vital skills that are often politically unpopular. These middle areas … partially deflect the political pressures which groups primarily located in peripheral areas might otherwise direct against core states and the groups which operate within and through their state machineries" (1974: 349–350). Further, being on the semi-periphery means that countries/states are "located outside the political arena of the core states, and find it difficult to pursue the ends in political coalitions that might be open to them were they in the same political arena" (1974: 350).

This definition thus further complicates who belongs where. A semiperipheral designation would obscure the core role that India and Brazil are playing in today's global trade markets as well as their increased weight in world politics. Therefore, although Wallerstein emphasizes the world-system's accommodation of change, its conceptual categories may be somewhat limited, weighed down by past history rather than readily adaptable to current developments.

WORLD-ECONOMY CRISIS

Wallerstein contends that because the capitalist world-system is historically unique and has its own internal tensions, that its historical life cycle will come to an end. This view parallels Marx's prediction of capitalism's displacement by an alternative system of economic and social organization (i.e., communism). Wallerstein argues, in fact, that the capitalist world-economy is undergoing a systemic **crisis** (Wallerstein 1996: 295; 2004: 76–90). The crisis has multiple causal sources, including the escalation of production costs, market speculation, and environmental pollution. Particularly significant, for Wallerstein, is the expanding gap in economic resources between core and periphery despite the unprecedented economic growth in the system as a whole (Wallerstein 2004: 84). This is a "true crisis" such that its difficulties "cannot be resolved within the framework of the system," but can be "overcome only by going outside of and beyond the historical system of which the difficulties are a part" (2004: 76).[2] The instability resulting from the crisis "may go on another twenty-five to fifty years" (2004: 77), Wallerstein states, and its resolution will depend on the collective choices society makes about what future system(s) it wishes to construct.

CONTEMPORARY GLOBALIZING ECONOMIC PROCESSES

Wallerstein's emphasis on the geographical patterns in economic inequality permeates sociologists' and policymakers' assessments of current globalization trends (e.g., Sklair 2002), even though they do not necessarily embrace his conceptual categories. A recent report from the United Nations Conference on Trade and Development (UNCTAD) affirms the ongoing relevance of geographical nuance regarding the impact of globalization (UNCTAD 2017). Although documenting the positive ways in which digital technology (e.g., Internet and mobile phones) is enhancing the economic prosperity of local communities, countries, and companies throughout the world, UNCTAD also warns that a big gulf remains between rich and poor countries. For example, whereas 83 percent of the population in developed countries (e.g., US, Europe, Australia) use the Internet, this is true of 55 percent in Latin America, 49 percent in Asia, and only 20 percent in Africa. Similarly, 81 percent of business firms in developed countries use the Internet, and a large proportion of firms in Asia (60 percent) and Latin America (75 percent) do so too, but far fewer in Africa (45 percent), thus stalling the impact of the digital economy (UNCTAD 2017: 189). It is these inequalities and the larger structural context shaping global economic inequality in its various forms that many sociologists focus on.

THE TRANSNATIONAL CORPORATION

As a general analytical principle, sociologists emphasize the significance of social structures – as opposed to economic momentum alone – in shaping the global economy and its impact. In following Weber's emphasis on the expansion of bureaucracy, Giddens argues that "corporations are the dominant agents within the world economy" (Giddens 1990: 71). He notes, however, that although corporations are powerful, their power does not go unchecked. Transnational or multinational economic corporations must contend with the state, and with the expanding range of nongovernmental organizations (NGOs), many of which are global too, such as Greenpeace, Oxfam, and Amnesty International.

Leslie Sklair, a neo-Marxist sociologist, gives greater emphasis than Giddens to the centrality of the capitalist corporation to globalization. He argues, first of all, that although it is common to think of globalization as essentially meaning **capitalist globalization**, we should in fact recognize that capitalist globalization is simply one form of globalization, one based on a capitalist mode of production. And, he maintains, it is possible to conceive of alternative modes, such as **socialist globalization**, a system that would require a shift from capitalist corporate ownership toward the creation of local producer–consumer cooperatives (Sklair 2002: 299–321).

BIOGRAPHICAL NOTE

Leslie Sklair is retired from the sociology faculty at the London School of Economics, where he was also associated with the Centre for the Study of Human Rights. He has written several books and journal articles on issues of economic development and globalization.

Sklair (2002: 7) argues for a **global systems theory**. This emphasizes a dialectical synthesis between states and transnational globalizing forces and institutions. It thus transcends what he sees as inadequacies in current approaches: the tendency to adopt either an international, state-centered approach to globalization (most readily seen in political science; cf. Eckes and Zeiler 2003) or a transnational approach that emphasizes globalism with little reference to national states (seen in economics).

Sklair argues that the "major transnational corporations are the most important and most powerful globalizing institutions in the world today" (Sklair 2002: 7). For Sklair, the state is complicit in securing transnational interests. As he notes, transnational corporations (e.g., IBM, Microsoft, Philip Morris, General Motors, Walmart, Exxon Mobil, Sony) have not only "grown enormously in size in recent

Figure 14.1   Coca-Cola – a quintessentially American brand – is among the world's largest and most recognizable transnational corporations, with business operations, staff, and sales in more than 200 countries. Source: Author.

decades, but their global reach has expanded dramatically" (2002: 36). He argues, moreover, that although many transnational corporations are legally domiciled and/or headquartered in the US and Europe, this should not obscure the fact that their economic interests, both objectively and as described by the corporations themselves (in annual reports, etc.), are truly globalizing in scope (2002: 38).

GLOBAL FINANCIAL CAPITALISM

A major transformative change in the global economy today is the centrality of finance, and the related exponential expansion of the financial sector and its infrastructure (e.g., Carruthers and Kim 2011). These developments are themselves reflective of and accelerated by the disembeddedness of time and space that Giddens (1991) identifies as core characteristics of our contemporary experience. Although sociological interest in money and the economy is long standing, going back especially to Marx, Weber, and Simmel, the subfield of "economic sociology" is relatively recent (e.g., Smelser and Swedberg 2005). Nonetheless, testifying to the increased interest among sociologists in economic sociology, membership of the American Sociological Association's (ASA) section on economic sociology increased from 439 members in 2001 to 771 in 2017. Many of these sociologists focus on the major ways in which the financial sector has been transformed and the implications it has for globalizing economic processes, as well as for the micro- and macro-organization of society as a whole (Carruthers and Kim 2011).

The **financial sector** includes a broad range of actors and institutions. It includes large-scale retail and investment banks; insurance and pension funds; traders, brokers, and financial advisors; stock exchanges; venture capital, private equity and hedge fund firms; credit card companies; and credit rating agencies (e.g., Moody's). It also includes the institutions that regulate these actors, including the Securities and Exchange Commission (SEC in the US), the Financial Conduct Authority and the Prudential Regulation Authority (both in the UK), the Federal Reserve Bank, the European Central Bank, and individual countries' central banks. We get a sense of the scale of the transformation of the role of the financial sector just by considering the fact that finance has displaced manufacturing in terms of gross domestic product (GDP, a measure of a country's aggregate economic activity). In 1960, finance accounted for 15 percent of the US's GDP; currently it accounts for more than 25 percent. In short, industrial capitalism has given way to **financial capitalism.**

Much of the change in the financial sector is related to the global diffusion of market economies (Simmons et al. 2008). In the 1980s, one heard about the Dow Jones Industrial Average (Wall Street/ US) and the City of London's FTSE stock market indexes. Currently, the *Economist* magazine lists over 40 major stock markets, a list that simultaneously underscores the financialization and the globalization of capitalism. Because of the globally interconnected nature of economic events – and of expectations and rumors about market behavior – the DAX (Germany), the BVSP (Brazil), the Nikkei (Japan), the Hang Seng (Hong Kong), and multiple other stock indexes affect ordinary people in multiple ways (e.g., college

Figure 14.2 The expansion of financial capitalism is reflected in the prominent visibility of new financial offices in global cities. Source: © majaiva/iStockphoto.

loan rates, and individuals' access to jobs, to goods, and to credit). Further, the interdependence of financial markets across the globe means that a recession in Spain or high unemployment in the UK are not just national domestic problems for Spain and the UK, but directly affect the rest of Europe, as well as the US, China, and Russia, and the global economy as a whole. In short, national borders and transnational alliances cannot keep financial threats at bay. See also Topic 14.2.

Topic 14.2   Global openness

The transnational flows of financial capital, trade, technology, consumer goods, workers, and ideas are the engines of today's globalizing economy and society. Despite antiglobalization sentiments (seen in the Brexit vote and among President Trump's supporters), this is the current reality. Global openness contrasts with the economic protectionist policies of the past when nations restricted what products they imported and exported and with whom they traded, a protectionism that was also evident in immigration restrictions. The ratification of the North Atlantic Free Trade Agreement (NAFTA; in 1994) by the US, Canada, and Mexico was a significant step in both acknowledging and building a changing, transnational marketplace. Earlier, the formation of the European Economic Community (EEC, currently the EU) was an innovative effort to open markets and to forge a more integrated transnational European community. It was initially based on six member countries, and extended to nine in 1973, when the UK, Ireland, and Denmark joined their continental neighbors (West Germany, France, Italy, the Netherlands, Belgium, and Luxembourg). In 2019, prior to the finalization of the UK's proposed exit, the EU has 28 member countries. Shared EU membership has been critical to the growth of many small European economies and opened up the flow of trade, capital, workers, and ideas in multiple directions across all member countries' geographical borders. Indeed surveys show that despite some concerns about the EU, and despite the economic populism/nationalism that partly motivated Brexit, large majorities in various EU countries favor staying in the EU. For example, over 80 percent of people in Germany, Spain, and Poland and three-quarters of the French and the Swedes want to remain in the EU; somewhat fewer, but still a majority, in Greece (58 percent) and Italy (54 percent) favor staying (Meichtry, Troianovski, and Walker 2017).

- The changes that have occurred in the global economy over the last three decades are highlighted by the 2018 KOF Index of Globalization (published by the KOF Swiss Economic Institute; www.kof.ethz.ch). Ireland, for example, is ranked at number 13, even though prior to the 1970s it had a history of economic and social protectionism. Note, too, that some of the countries that have very strong economies such as the UK (8), Germany (9), and the US (19) are not necessarily as globally open as some smaller economies; this is largely because of the latter's reliance on direct foreign capital investment. Reflecting the multiple dimensions of globalization, the index takes account of economic, social, and political globalization, and its rankings highlight how a country can be ranked higher on economic than on political globalization, for example, or equally high on economic and social but lower on political. Globalization indices use various definitions and a mix of measures. Economic globalization is typically measured by such indicators as openness to trade (e.g., business-friendly environment; low and predictable tax rates; relative absence of trade barriers), capital flows (success in attracting large amounts of high foreign direct investment), and income payments to foreign nationals (immigrant employees)

Social globalization includes:

- Cross-border flow of information and ideas; and includes such measures as the proportion of telephone, television, and Internet users; and trade in books
- International tourism
- Foreign-born residents as a percentage of the country's total population

Political globalization includes:

- Foreign embassies in a country
- Membership in international organizations
- Participation in the UN Security Council Missions
- International Treaties (e.g., the Paris Climate Accord)

In addition to those noted here, the overall ranking (taking account of economic, social, and political indicators) of other select countries are Belgium (1), Switzerland (3), Sweden (4), Denmark (6), France (7), Finland (10), Norway (11), Canada (14), Portugal (17), Italy (18), Australia (22), Poland (26), New Zealand (27), Japan (30), South Korea (31), Israel (32), Chile (38), Turkey (42), Russia (48), South Africa (54), Costa Rica (67), Mexico (70), China (71), Brazil (73), Tunisia (81), Jamaica (85), Ghana (97), India (107), and Pakistan (113).

HIGH-SPEED, AUTOMATED, AND FLUID FINANCE

The global flows and implications of financial capital are accelerated by high-speed computerized networks and the quantification of super-large financial information data sets that this technology allows (Zaloom 2006). The so-called quantification of finance (and the hiring of "quants" – college graduates who majored in math or physics) provides a continuous, flowing analysis of detailed information about banking and market activities and stock estimates. It also propels high-speed and high-frequency *automated* trading and hedging decisions that instantaneously move enormous amounts of money within and between diverse types of funds all around the globe.

The intensity and speed with which complex financial products are bought and sold may make transactions and markets more efficient. They also carry the risk, however, that an excessively risky trade or its unanticipated negative effects cannot subsequently be controlled by the traders and investors directly involved in the process – yet another manifestation of how Giddens's (1991) concept of disembeddedness matters. In the spring of 2012, for example, JPMorgan Chase incurred a $5.8 *billion* loss resulting from a *single* trade made by one of its investor units in London. Another company, MF Global, declared bankruptcy after losing $1.6 billion of customer money (much of it from farmers and other middle-class investors), and not long before MF Global's collapse, a UBS trader in London lost his firm $2.3 billion. Further, the increasing reliance on high-speed automated trades means that a single software glitch in a single trading office can cause mayhem in stock prices, further underscoring the regulatory challenges in the financial sector. One such glitch at Knight Capital, a New Jersey trading firm that specializes in high-speed stock trading, cost the firm $10 million a minute on August 1, 2012, and accrued to a total loss of $460 million. This did not lead to the collapse of Knight Ridder, however; the high-speed/high-frequency trading giant merged at the end of 2012 with Getco, another leader in computerized trading, thus consolidating their weight and the normalcy of automated trades in the financial sector.

GLOBAL CITIES AS FINANCIAL CAPITALS

The visibility of the financial sector is most apparent in what **Saskia Sassen** (2007) calls **global cities**. She explains:

> The global economy needs to be produced, reproduced, serviced, and financed … [Its operational functions] have become so specialized that they can no longer be contained in the functions of corporate headquarters. Global cities are strategic sites for the production of these specialized functions to run and coordinate the global economy. Inevitably located in national territories, global cities are the organizational and institutional space for the major dynamics of denationalization. (Sassen 2007: 73; see also Sassen 1991)

Global cities "accumulate immense concentrations of economic power" (Sassen 2007: 111), and unlike world cities (e.g., Paris, Rome) that have existed through time, global cities are distinctively new: "They are the terrain on which multiple globalization processes assume material and localized forms" (2007: 23–24). She lists New York, London, Tokyo, Frankfurt, Zurich, Amsterdam, Los Angeles, Toronto, Sydney, Hong Kong, Bangkok, Taipei, São Paulo, and Mexico City as geographical spaces that "bind the major international financial and business centers" in the network of global cities (2007: 111). Global cities constitute a new geography, one that is no longer demarcated by a North/South division but as this list highlights, incorporates several strategic cities in the southern hemisphere (2007: 24). This list is not set for all time. After Brexit disrupted London's centrality to global finance, other lesser-known financial cities such as Dublin seek to be global financial hubs.

BIOGRAPHICAL NOTE

Saskia Sassen was born in The Hague, the Netherlands, in 1949. She received her PhD in sociology from the University of Notre Dame, Indiana, and is currently professor of sociology at Columbia University, New York. She has written extensively on globalization, particularly its technological, cultural, and socioeconomic dimensions, and is active professionally in several organizations, including the Council on Foreign Relations and the newly formed Information Technology, International Cooperation and Global Security Committee of the Social Science Research Council. She is married to the sociologist Richard Sennett.

CLASS INEQUALITY

Sociologists also emphasize the persistence of class inequality notwithstanding the economic gains in individuals' and countries' standards of living. Giddens highlights the profit logic and attendant class inequalities that inhere in global markets, stating:

> In their trading relations with one another, and with states and consumers, companies (manufacturing corporations, financial firms and banks) depend upon production for profit. Hence the spread of their influence brings in its train a global extension of commodity markets, including money markets. However, even in its beginnings, the capitalist world economy was never just a market for the trading of goods and services. It involved, and involves today, the commodifying of labour power in class relations which separate workers from control of their means of production … [a] process … fraught with implications for global inequalities. (Giddens 1990: 71–72)

In other words, as first emphasized by Marx, even as wages improve, they do not reduce the inherent structural gap between workers and business owners/executives in access to money and other resources. And, the poorer the country (e.g., India), the more blatant the gap between its corporate class and its indigenous workforce (see Topic 14.3).

The increased global flow in trade and consumer products, whereby, for example, Chinese manufacturers and suppliers – of fashion apparel, children's toys, fish, or flowers – are major players in the global economy, is typically at the expense of workers laboring under dangerous, sweatshop conditions to meet production demands. These inequalities fester, in part, because the expansion of the middle class in China (and elsewhere) is based on a labor system that relies on young migrant workers who come from rural villages to spend lengthy intervals (e.g., two or three years) working in urban plants, hoping to make enough money before returning home and starting a family. Economic globalization thus exacerbates on a global level the class-based inequalities found in local economic markets. Giddens (2003: xxix) and other Weber-inspired sociologists (e.g., Held 2004: 164–165), who see the state as an actor that can intervene to ensure a more equitable distribution of market resources, thus argue for the institutionalization of reforms (e.g., labor and occupational safety laws) that would protect workers' rights.

Sklair acknowledges that the standard of living of millions of people across the globe has been vastly improved by capitalist globalization in ways unimaginable to an earlier generation. But he emphasizes that this achievement has not eliminated class inequality. Rather, in a Marxist framing, Sklair argues that "capitalist globalization produces **class polarization**" (Sklair 2002: 27, 26). Unlike Giddens and Held, Sklair contends this polarization is not correctable within the current capitalist globalization system. Rather, it is a crisis of globalization: "the distinctiveness of the class polarization thesis is that it recognizes both increasing emiseration [poverty] and increasing enrichment, thus in all countries, rich and poor, privileged communities are to be found" (2002: 50). Class polarization is evident in access to education, health care, and the Internet, etc. (2002: 48–53), and is visibly underscored by the emergence of gated affluent communities, whether in Los Angeles, Mexico City, or Mumbai, that are geographically separated from ghettos and factories (2002: 51). Further, Sklair argues, the **transnational capitalist class** – composed of "corporate executives, world leaders, those who run the major international institutions, globalizing professionals, the mainstream mass media" – accepts and colludes in the perpetuation of class inequality (2002: 56). This economically and politically powerful class, working from "the material base" provided it by transnational corporations, "unquestionably dictates economic transnational practices, and is the most important single force in the struggle to dominate political and cultural-ideology transnational practices" (2002: 9).

Topic 14.3　Class polarization in India

Although India has experienced enormous economic growth since the early 1990s and has become a major player in global economic production, it is a country in which class polarization is highly visible. In Guragon, for example, a booming town in the northern part of India, the highly affluent, cosmopolitan professional class who live within gated communities encounter an everyday reality that is far different from that of the many servants, nannies, and chauffeurs who serve them round the clock. The flat-screen televisions, air conditioning, and other modern amenities of the newly rich are not affected by the water and electricity outages that last an average of 12 hours a day in the slums right outside their gates. Immaculately-groomed gated communities not only provide residents with their own utilities; they also have their own private schools, health clinics, and cricket clubs. Poverty in India has significantly declined, but one in five remain poor (subsisting on roughly $1.25 a day); 80 percent of the poor live in rural areas with few basic amenities. Overall, only 6 percent of poor people have access to tap water, and 42 percent of Indian children are clinically malnourished. (Sengupta 2008; 2009; World Bank 2016, www.worldbank.org/en/news/infographic/2016/05/27/india-s-poverty-profile).

Sassen (2007: 168) takes a more differentiated approach to the class inequality produced by globalization. She argues that globalization produces a new form of stratification, a **denationalized class** of global workers. This is a heterogeneous class composed of three class groups whose occupational conditions and lifestyles vary considerably. It includes (1) a transnational professional and executive class of cosmopolitans who work and move between the global financial centers in London, New York, Tokyo, Frankfurt, etc.; (2) a class of transnational government officials and experts (a class that includes many midlevel workers, e.g., immigration and police officers); and (3) an emergent class of disadvantaged, resource-poor workers and activists, many of whom live in transnational immigrant communities (2007: 168–169; see also Miraftab 2017).

Sociologists, therefore, like economists, recognize the "integration" of commodity, labor, and capital markets that economic globalization entails. But sociologists emphasize that market integration is part of a long, though changing, historical-geographical process. This is a process that is neither seamless nor apolitical, and is characterized by considerable economic disparities between and within countries/ regions. Sociologists further underscore that economic globalization includes and is accompanied by the expanding power of transnational corporations, the exponential growth in and transformation of the financial sector, the emergence of global cities, new forms of class composition and stratification, and economic inequality and polarization.

GLOBALIZING POLITICAL PROCESSES: THE CHANGING AUTHORITY OF THE NATION-STATE

Another major analytical focus of globalization scholars is the role of the nation-state in the new global order. Recall that Max Weber underscored the significance of the state as the embodiment of bureaucratic, rational legal authority in modern society (see chapter 3). It and its various bureaucracies regulate society, including the economy (see Giddens and Held discussed previously) and other social institutions; maintain order and security; and protect state borders. Globalization scholars disagree about the significance and authority of the state in a globalizing society wherein national borders are increasingly less salient. The autonomy of the nation-state to act based on its own interests is curtailed by free trade between countries; transnational political, economic, and cultural alliances (e.g., the European Union [EU]); transnational military alliances (e.g., NATO); and the global flow of Internet and satellite information that is relatively impervious to national boundaries and state control. Additionally, transnational citizenship (e.g., among member states of the EU) and transnational laws and legal forums (e.g., the European Court) further challenge the discrete political, legal, and cultural power of the nation-state.

In Sklair's (2002) Marxist-derived analysis of capitalist globalization, the state has little institutional autonomy. As discussed previously, for Sklair the main political actor is the transnational capitalist class; and specifically those who are members of the capitalist class in the most powerful (capitalist) states (2002: 7). Although he concedes that the nation-state cannot be ignored, he maintains that a state-centered focus obscures the decreased relevance of state territorial borders; the system of global relationships; and the changing power dynamics between states and nonstate actors, including transnational corporations (2002: 8). Thus, for example, he argues that the terrorist attacks of 9/11 highlight the importance of a transnational rather than a nation-state approach to understanding within-state/ global occurrences (2002: 11). We can readily see that 9/11 was not the result of a war between one state and another (or of one state alliance against another, as in World War II, for example), but of a transnational terror alliance against one location of capitalist globalization.

Unlike Sklair, Giddens (influenced mostly by Weber) identifies the nation-state as a key actor in globalization dynamics. He argues that although there is overlap between the political and economic dimensions of globalization, each sphere has its own institutional autonomy:

> The main centers of power in the world economy are capitalist states ... The domestic and international economic policies of these states involve many forms of regulation of economic activity, but ... their institutional organization maintains an "insulation" of the economic from the political. This allows wide scope for the global activities of business corporations, which always have a home base within a particular state but may develop many other regional involvements elsewhere. (Giddens 1990: 70; see also 2003: xxv)

Giddens (1990: 70) recognizes that many business corporations – e.g., Coca-Cola, Nike, Microsoft – exert a great deal of economic and political power within their own home countries as well as across the world. But he also makes the important point that corporations lack certain powers that states have. Specifically, they lack, as Weber noted, "territoriality and control of the means of violence within their own territories. No matter how great their economic power, industrial corporations are not military organizations (as some of them were during the colonial period) and they cannot establish themselves as political/legal entities which rule a given territorial area" (Giddens 1990: 70–71).

The global **geopolitical** order is also complicated by the global diffusion of military power. In fact, Giddens sees what he calls the **world military order** as a discrete analytical dimension of globalization (Giddens 1990: 74). He emphasizes that military power often overlaps, but does not always correlate, with a country's positioning within the world capitalist and the nation-state system. As he points out, many economically weak "third world" countries are militarily powerful: "In an important sense there is no 'Third World' in respect of weaponry, only a 'First World', since most countries maintain stocks of technologically advanced armaments," including, in some cases, nuclear technology (1990: 74–75). Hence countries such as Iran, Pakistan and North Korea are important players in complex geopolitical networks(see chapter 7).

ECONOMICS AND POLITICS: A NEW IMPERIALISM

The consolidated force of strong economic and strong military power preoccupies David Harvey (2003). Looking at the varied military, political, and economic globalizing forces in play today, he argues for what he calls the **new imperialism**. Though noting a dynamic tension between state territorial-political interests and capitalist economic interests, Harvey tends to see the triumph of a capitalist economic logic (2003: 30, 33). He argues that although the traditional understanding of imperialism saw "an easy accord" between territorial and economic interests (e.g., the British Empire), the current global situation, exemplified by the US invasion of Iraq and its related move toward creating new allies in the Middle East (e.g., Saudi Arabia), Eastern Europe, and Turkey, is driven more by economic than political-territorial interests (2003: 198–199). For Harvey, "The fundamental point is to see the territorial and the capitalist logics of power as distinct from each other" (2003: 29). In other words, economic and political interests can be antagonistic and certainly do not always coincide. This includes the fact that a country's internal politics (2003: 211) are frequently conflicted over global economic policies (e.g., anti-NAFTA sentiment in the US; Brexit debate in the UK) and political-territorial goals (e.g., antiwar opinion).

Nevertheless, Harvey argues, the global geopolitical agenda of the US is "all about oil" (Harvey 2003: 18). Its primary economic interests intertwine with military-territorial interests, such that it consolidates a

> vital strategic bridgehead ... on the Eurasian land mass that just happens to be the centre of production of the oil that currently fuels (and will continue to fuel for at least the next fifty years) not only the global economy but also every large military machine that dares to oppose that of the United States. This should ensure the continued global dominance of the US for the next fifty years. (Harvey 2003: 198–199)

THE STATE'S NEGOTIATION OF LOCAL AND GLOBAL FORCES

Although Giddens emphasizes the nation-state's territorial and policing-military rights, he does not present the state solely in terms of its strategic economic and security-military interests. Rather, he argues: "The material involvements of nation states are not governed purely by economic considerations ... They do not operate as economic machines but as 'actors' jealous of their territorial rights, concerned with the fostering of national cultures, and having strategic geopolitical involvements with other states or alliances of states" (Giddens 1990: 72). The state, to be sure, has economic and territorial and national security interests, but, Giddens argues, it is also has an interest in protecting its own particular cultural identity, and all of these interests intertwine in shaping its geopolitical engagement.

The multiple and varied interests of the state show themselves in what Giddens refers to as the **dialectical nature of globalization**, namely, the push and pull between centralizing, interstate (or transnational) tendencies and the assertion of state sovereignty (Giddens 1990: 73). We see many examples of this push–pull among states that are members of the European Union. On the one hand, most EU states share a single financial currency (the euro) and want taxation and trade policies facilitating the free flow of goods and people among member countries. This is the push of centralization. But at the same time, individual countries protest against policies that threaten their country-specific economic interests and the interests of their various internal business and other constituencies. The assertion of state sovereignty over and against the pull of common European interests (e.g., EU financial security) is highly apparent in ongoing EU discussions as member countries (e.g., Spain, Greece) act to protect their own nation's economic and political interests in the face of austerity constraints imposed by the EU. Various push–pull dynamics play out elsewhere. India, for example, strongly embraces the pull toward the international capitalist economy; at the same time, it ignores localized demands to bolster its existing national infrastructure, especially the need to build more schools despite their obvious necessity to Indians' success in the local–global economy.

Globalization also coincides with the emergence of new nationalist or ethnonationalist movements underpinned by a mix of political, economic, and cultural motivations (e.g., Scottish nationalism and Catalonia's pursuit of independence from Spain). Indeed there is irony, or sociological complexity, in the fact that globalization, celebrated in part as the triumph of the decreased relevance of borders (e.g., in economic trade, Internet communication, the free movement of people), also coincides with the drawing of new territorial borders that undermine the societal cohesiveness of an established national identity. This is part of a postcolonial legacy whereby previously colonized or subordinated states, regions, or ethnic groups reclaim an identity that is no longer defined solely in terms of the Other (Said 1978; see chapter 12). This process is evident in the relatively rapid transformation of Ukraine and Georgia (former Soviet republics) into politically and economically independent countries; e.g., Georgia joined the World Trade Organization (WTO) in 2000, and Ukraine in 2008, and did so against the objections of Russia (which became a member in 2012). The creation of new nations, such as the split of Czechoslovakia, for example, into Slovakia and the Czech Republic, or Kosovo's declaration of independence from Serbia, points to the reclaiming of territory, and of a national and cultural identity, that can stand alone without being defined by its relation to the dominant country. James Rosenau argues that globalization as a concept is insufficient to capture the full dynamic complexity of the political alignments and tensions that characterize our current era. He suggests the notion of **distant proximities** as a way to think about the intertwining of the global and the local in world affairs. He explains,

The best way to grasp world affairs today requires viewing them as an endless series of distant proximities in which the forces pressing for greater globalization and those inducing greater localization interactively play themselves out … Distant proximities encompass the tensions between core and periphery, between national and transnational systems, between communitarianism and cosmopolitanism, between cultures and subcultures, between states and markets, between urban and rural, between coherence and incoherence, between integration and disintegration, between decentralization and centralization, between universalism and particularism, between pace [speed/flow] and space, between the global and the local … All of these tensions are marked by numerous variants; they take different forms in different parts of the world, in different countries … in different communities … in different cyberspaces, with the result that there is enormous diversity in the way people experience the distant proximities of which their lives are composed. Whatever the diversity, however, locating distant proximities … enables us to avoid the trap of maintaining an analytic separation between foreign and domestic politics. (Rosenau 2003: 4–5)

Figure 14.3 Despite the success of the European Union in building a more integrated political, economic, and cultural community of nations, it is frayed by tensions between national and transnational interests. Source: © David Callan/iStockphoto.

In emphasizing the need to avoid the either/or conceptual binary (local/global) in discussing globalization, Rosenau references the work of the postcolonial theorist Stuart Hall, who, as I discuss in chapter 12, elaborates the co-occurrence of difference and similarity in racial histories and identities (e.g., being black *and* British). Whatever the topic of our research, attentiveness to the intermingling of the local and the global in specific social, political, and cultural contexts offers a fruitful way to apprehend the varied manifestations and consequences of globalization in our everyday lives.

THE IMPOTENT POSTNATIONAL STATE

Zygmunt Bauman (2000, 2013) offers a more pessimistic view than Giddens and Rosenau of the place of the state in the globalizing world. He sees the state as being increasingly limited in its ability to function as a powerful, sovereign actor on behalf of its own people and its own national interests due to the increasing dominance of supranational forces – global trade, global currencies, global military alliances (e.g., NATO), and economic-political alliances (e.g., the EU). He argues that in a global world where global processes affect whole societies irrespective of national boundaries, the nation can no longer be considered the core economic, political, or military unit.

BIOGRAPHICAL NOTE

Zygmunt Bauman was born in Poland in 1925 to Jewish parents. He studied philosophy at the University of Warsaw and subsequently received his MA in sociology. He moved to England, to the University of Leeds, in the early 1970s, partly as a result of the anti-Semitism experienced by his family, and he established a prolific career there as a professor of sociology. He wrote extensively on various aspects of modernity and identity until his death in 2017.

Bauman (2000) chooses the phrase "liquid modernity" to refer to the fluidity (as opposed to the solidity) of contemporary globalizing processes. He highlights how fluidity affects the role of the nation-state in an era that we need to think of as "after the nation-state" (Bauman 2013). Bauman argues that we are orphaned in this new **postnational** order, unprotected by the state and its institutions, against the powerful forces of globalization and economic and social change. He concludes that if a nation tries to protect its citizens from unemployment and other economic losses (e.g., loss of pension benefits), its failure to play by the global economic rules will result in further economic punishment:

> The orphaned individual [can no longer] huddle under the nation's wings … The freedom of state politics is relentlessly eroded by the new global powers … Insubordinate governments, guilty of protectionist policies or generous public provisions for the "economically redundant sectors" of their populations and of recoiling from leaving the country at the mercy of "global financial markets" and "global free trade," would be refused loans and are denied reduction of their debts; local currencies would be made global lepers, speculated against and pressed to devalue; local stocks would fall head down on the global exchanges; the country would be cordoned off by economic sanctions and told to be treated by past and future trade partners as a global pariah; global investors would cut their anticipated losses, pack up their belongings and withdraw their assets, leaving local authorities to clean up the debris and bail the victims out of their added misery. (Bauman 2000: 185–186)

Thus Bauman sees the state as a victim of globalization. Sklair, by contrast, sees the state – and "the globalizing elements in governments and bureaucracies who are members of the transnational capitalist class" – as being complicit in globalization: "Often governments will go along with globalization not because they cannot resist it but because they perceive it to be in their own interests" (Sklair 2002: 6).

Another postnationalist consequence is that the relevance of a nation's territoriality itself is called into question. Bauman argues that, whether in the pursuit of economic or military power, the fluidity of force and the accelerated speed at which it can target its object and achieve its objectives make for a world in which territoriality is less and less desired. Rather than being prized, territory can become a burdensome constraint (Bauman 2000: 188) – it can literally bog down the invading country (e.g., the US in Vietnam). Thus the *electronic* waging of war facilitated by technological advances in "smart bombs," drones, remotely piloted surveillance airplanes and missile firing systems reduces (or suppresses) the on-the-ground consequences of military action for the aggressor. Responsibility both for the war and for its aftermath gets displaced amidst the fluidity of force and space. This is so notwithstanding the fact that war invariably occurs in some localized on-the-ground setting; in other words, smart bombs generally target people and communities, not other smart bombs. Bauman explains that key feature of liquid modernity is the ability to "escape local commitments":

> The cumbersome jobs of ground occupation, local engagements and managerial and administrative responsibilities, [are] quite out of tune with liquid modernity's techniques of power. The might of the global elite rests on its ability to escape local commitments, and globalization is meant precisely to avoid such necessities, to divide tasks and functions in such a way as to burden local authorities, and them only, with the role of guardians of law and (local) order. (Bauman 2000: 188)

However, as we saw in Iraq, the US was unable to avoid the local complications of its territorial (and electronically waged) invasion. It was unable to avoid the many administrative, civic, and political dilemmas and the attendant errors and financial costs encountered in literally rebuilding a working society. The ensuing problems thus further add to the perception of the civil-political impotence of the state in contemporary society.

THE DENATIONALIZED STATE

Contrary to Bauman, who sees the state's erosion of power as an inevitable consequence of globalization; contrary to Sklair and Harvey who see the state as complicit in globalization; and contrary to Giddens, who sees it as adapting more or less to the push and pull of globalization, Sassen argues that sociologists need to think of the **denationalized state**. In this framing, globalization causes the state to lose some aspects of authority within its national territory, because of transnational trade and human rights agreements and transnational laws. Yet, at the same time, the state can also increase its authority beyond the nation; it does this through, for example, participation in "governing the global economy in a context increasingly dominated by deregulation, privatization, and the growing authority of non-state actors" (Sassen 2007: 49). Thus the state, she argues, is "one of the strategic institutional domains in which critical work on the development of globalization takes place" (2007: 4).

Sassen (2007: 51), therefore, frames the state as an actively engaged institutional actor that can proactively attempt "to link into the global economy, to claim jurisdiction over the various tasks involved in globalization, thereby securing [its] own power." The state, after all, is "the ultimate guarantor of the rights of global capital" (2007: 54). It has, for example, the legal and political authority to regulate financial corporations and to approve or reject corporate mergers. Moreover, it encounters new regulatory opportunities, as evidenced by policy debates over its role in outlining Internet access and security standards. Despite the frequently voiced emphasis on the autonomy of digitalized technology and its avoidance of national territorial restrictions, it is still the case that states have the power to enforce a particular kind of Internet-digital environment within and beyond their own national territory (e.g., Sassen 2007: 82–96). Cyberspace attacks on one country's Internet infrastructure by another are increasingly frequent occurrences, and incidents of Internet-based economic and political theft and espionage have become major strategic concerns and sources of tension between states (e.g., between the US and China). Government blackouts on citizens' access to the Internet (see Topic 5.1, chapter 5), and governments' legally privileged access to users' e-mail, phone, and digital traffic in the name of national and international security (highlighted by the US National Security Agency employee Edward Snowden), further underscore the state territoriality and control of Internet space and its use. States also use cyber weapons, implanting technologically sophisticated computer viruses and worms to impede the strategic and militaristic goals of enemy states as, for example, the virus implantation by the US and Israel in Iran's nuclear program in June 2012. And the sophisticated hacking of the US Democratic Party during the 2016 presidential election is widely believed by spying and intelligence agencies to have been committed by hackers closely allied with Russia's President Putin (e.g., Khatchadourian 2017).

Sassen argues that although we commonly think of globalization as the growing interdependence of the world and the formation of global institutions (e.g., the WTO) and global processes (global financial markets), it is also necessary to recognize that "the global partly inhabits the national" (Sassen 2007: 3). For example, the services that are essential to the globalizing economy (e.g., financial markets and their corporate-professional infrastructure) are invariably located in national-geographical spaces; global cities/financial capitals (discussed previously) are situated in state-controlled national territory (2007: 49), even as their products, operations, and impact transcend any one nation. In sum, sociologists vary in their assessment of the role and power of the state in and amidst globalization. The extent to which the state becomes relatively powerless, or instead acquires new institutional significance as a denationalized actor, is an empirical question that remains to be answered over the next few decades. In the meantime, the unprecedented intervention of national governments in the US and in European countries, in rescuing banks and financial markets from further collapse during the recession of 2008–2009, and their continuing attempts to restore and bolster financial stability within national (e.g., Greece, Spain) and global markets suggests that the power of the nation-state and its various bureaucratic organizations is not likely to soon diminish, notwithstanding transnational alliances (e.g., EU) as well as, for example, the pushback from banks and financial firms against the government's regulatory, oversight role.

MIGRATION AND POLITICAL MOBILIZATION IN A TRANSNATIONAL WORLD

Global cities are not just the location for the transnationalization of capital. They are also the location for the transnationalization of the labor that sustains the economic and corporate services and the everyday infrastructure of the global economy. The transnational labor market is a highly stratified one; as Sassen observes, it includes cosmopolitan professionals as well as midlevel government and low-wage workers (Sassen 2007: 168–169). The latter group, in particular, is composed of many migrants and immigrants. A major feature of our global age is immigration, and it is truly a worldwide phenomenon. We are currently witnessing unprecedented population flows, with an estimated 200 million people classified as migrants. Among these are "Latvian mushroom workers in Ireland … Tajik construction workers in Russia, farmhands from Burkina Faso who pick Ghanaian crops, and the Peruvians who take jobs left behind by Ecuadorean workers who have emigrated to Spain" (DeParle 2008: A11).

New trends in the transnationalization of labor, Sassen argues, mean that we need to be attentive to the new processes entailed in social identity formation. She argues that the (old) analytical "language of immigration … overlooks the transnationalization in the formation of identities and loyalties among various population segments that explicitly reject the imagined community of the nation. With this rejection come new solidarities and notions of membership" (Sassen 2007: 122–123). In other words, although sociologists have tended, in accord with Durkheim, to emphasize the nation as a unit of collective-societal identity (with a shared culture and common beliefs), or, following Weber, to emphasize shared territoriality, this framing tends to marginalize those within a given nation who have more transitory cultural-geographical histories. As Stuart Hall argues, such singular notions of identity do not capture the complexity of postcolonial identities (see chapter 12). Nor do they jibe with contemporary transnational trends. For many individuals and groups today, the nation is no longer an overarching source of social or political identity. People move, literally, between nations (e.g., between Mexico or Brazil and the US; between Poland and Ireland), and their identities, solidarities, and commitments are not tied exclusively to any one nation. Transnational identities are thus increasingly affecting individuals' economic, religious, and political resources and family relationships in varied and multilayered ways (e.g., Menjivar et al. 2016).

Much of this transnational identity formation can be seen in cities. Cities, as Sassen emphasizes, are

strategic sites for both the transnationalization of labor and the formation of transnational identities. In this regard, they form a site for new types of politics, including new types of transnational politics. Cities are the terrain on which people from many countries are most likely to meet and a multiplicity of cultures can come together. The international character of major cities lies not only in their telecommunications infrastructure and international firms; it lies also in the many cultural environments in which their workers exist. (Sassen 2007: 123)

Consequently, Sassen is optimistic that the very presence in global cities of structurally disadvantaged workers, especially "women, immigrants, people of color, groups with a mostly troubled relation to the national state," has the potential to make global cities the sites for political change and increased social equality.

This is because, she argues, the economic, social, and political forces in global cities are less bound up with any one particular nation-state (notwithstanding the local nationalized territory in which these cities are located). Hence they are more autonomous of the institutional mechanisms upholding the status quo. In contrast to Bauman, who sees globalization as further marginalizing economically disadvantaged groups who cannot rely on the state to protect them (or itself) from globalization (discussed previously), she sees the possibility of political ferment among transnational, disadvantaged workers who are not politically tied to any one state.

BIOGRAPHICAL NOTE

Manuel Castells was born in Barcelona, Spain, in 1942. He received his PhD in sociology from the University of Paris, where he was subsequently a professor. He spent most of his career as professor of sociology and city and regional planning at the University of California, Berkeley, and in 2003, accepted a distinguished chair at the University of Southern California. Castells is widely recognized for his academic and policy expertise on the information society, and has received numerous international awards. He continues to lecture widely and to write on the challenges posed by the network society.

Other scholars argue that the Internet-electronic age makes opportunities for political engagement more accessible. **Manuel Castells**, a neo-Marxist scholar, suggests that the **network society** is more conducive to challenging the hierarchies institutionalized into social life. In *The Information Society*, a three-volume, empirically detailed study, Castells (1997) argues that the network society emerged during the last quarter of the twentieth century as a result of the convergence of (1) the information technology revolution; (2) the restructuring of capitalism and of nation-states; and (3) the political and cultural effectiveness of the social movements of the 1960s and 1970s. These changes influenced the emergence of more *decentralized* forms of social organization, political and religious movements, and social relationships. We see such decentralization in many computer software companies. Apple, Uber, and Facebook, for example, all have impressive futuristic corporate headquarters and their open-plan interiors accentuate worker mobility and spontaneous interaction and collaboration. In contrast to the bureaucratized structures of assigned offices and assigned desks in government, finance, and many other sectors, "fluid" workspaces are considered more conducive to creative thinking and problem solving. We should also note that some, like Google and Microsoft, also provide extensive leisure and dining amenities for their employees, a strategy that maintains them on *campus* (as these sprawling sites are called) amidst blurred work–leisure boundaries that keep them not only at work but working, despite the apparently relaxed and egalitarian atmosphere. Castells notes,

> For the first time in history, the basic unit of economic organization is not a subject, be it individual (such as the entrepreneur) … or collective (such as the capitalist class, the corporation, the state) … *the unit is the network*, made up of a variety of subjects and organizations relentlessly modified as networks adapt to supportive environments and market structures. (Castells 1997: 198)

Castells (2000: 695) argues that new, digitalized information technology enhances networks' decentralized flexibility and the efficient performance of complex and wide-ranging tasks. As in the pre-Internet era, it is largely an *economic* logic that influences network composition. Thus, all regions in the world may be linked into the global economy, but only to the point where they add value to the value-making function of this economy, by their contribution in human resources, markets, raw materials, or other components of production and distribution. If a region is not valuable to such a network, it will not be linked up; or if it ceases to be valuable, it will be switched off, without the network as a whole suffering major inconvenience. (Castells 2000: 695)

Nonetheless, Castells argues, noneconomic values and goals can also, in principle, be programmed into the network. Just as the social movements of the 1960s and 1970s used the public square (public streets and parks) to mobilize and protest against the established institutional powers, so too, but with much greater efficiency, flexibility, and reach, the social change movements of today can set emancipatory goals and mobilize global support for particular causes through the creation of global communication networks (e.g., Castells 2000: 695; 1997: 470).

As such, the Internet can be seen as a crucial resource facilitating the **deepening of democracy** envisioned by Giddens (2003: 75). This is necessary, he states, because: "The old mechanisms of government don't work in a society where citizens live in the same information environment as those in power over them" (2003: 75). Giddens argues that, whether in advanced democratic or socialist and authoritarian societies, the varying degrees of secrecy and the backstage political alignments of the past can no longer withstand the onslaught of a currently resurging citizen involvement in politics and in policymaking, and the desire to build strong democratic institutions (2003: 75–82). He is optimistic that these changes can be used to control what might appear as a "runaway world" propelled by unprecedented, globalizing change (2003: xxxi).

Digital social media (e-mail blasts, Twitter, Facebook) have become a major part of the campaign and election strategies of politicians, and even of some leaders' governing strategies (e.g., President Trump's intense use of Twitter). They have also gained widespread use in protest movements (e.g., the Occupy movement), mass demonstrations (e.g., in Turkey, Egypt, and the US), and as mobilization tools across an array of issues (see Topic 5.5). These new trends have many diverse implications; technology can be used either to bully and/or to help emancipate people. Nevertheless, in terms of the deepening of democracy, the fact remains that electronic networks are highly accessible to individuals who might not otherwise participate in political activities, and are giving digital media and their users a new, influential role in local, national, and global politics (e.g., Earl and Kimport 2011; Kreiss 2012), even as governments and hackers alike can control their content and use.

ANTIGLOBALIZATION MOVEMENTS

Today, the **antiglobalization movement**, a broadly defined and relatively loose association of various groups and initiatives, is at the forefront of efforts to redefine societal values about economic growth, socioeconomic equality, and the relations of individuals to one another and to their natural environment. Sklair argues that the movement's success to date lies in its strategic ability to make connections between the twin crises of capitalist globalization: class polarization and ecological sustainability/environmental issues (Sklair 2002: 278). The antiglobalization movement challenges the globalization practices of transnational corporations, the activities of the state and the transnational capitalist class, and the culture and ideology of consumerism (2002: 278). Many antiglobalization efforts are highly localized (e.g., opposition in particular towns/neighborhoods to Walmart and to other "big box" stores). However, as Sklair contends, "Precisely because capitalist globalization works mainly through transnational practices, in order to challenge these practices politically, the movements that challenge them have to work transnationally too" (2002: 280). This entails political confrontation with local, national, and transnational politicians and officials as well as political activism centered on strategic national and international symbolic sites (e.g., the WTO; the G20 summit and World Bank meetings; and annual World Economic Forum meetings at Davos, Switzerland). One such transnational activist channel is the ("antiglobalization") World Social Forum (WSF), in which Wallerstein, concerned about the globalization crisis (discussed previously), is active. The WSF sees itself as a counterforce against the "pro-globalization" World Economic Forum of the financial and political elite. It points to the systemic need to expand social equality such that the rights of all individuals and groups, majorities and minorities, are recognized, even though, as Wallerstein (2004: 88–90) acknowledges, the question of whose rights should be given precedence in any given sphere is not easily settled.

ALTERNATIVE VISIONS OF GLOBALIZATION

The antiglobalization movement, with the help of Irish-born world celebrities Bob Geldof and Bono, has had some success in getting human rights and social justice issues – poverty, AIDS, women's rights, environmental sustainability – on the agenda of global financiers and politicians (e.g., Evans 2005). In view of feminist theorists' emphasis on the importance of women's standpoint in the crafting of new institutional realities (e.g., Smith; Collins; see chapter 10), it is noteworthy that women have been at the forefront of antiglobalization activism. They have a strong presence in local grass-roots movements, community organizations, and in transnational forums on women's equality (e.g., Desai 2016; Naples and Desai 2002).

Some sociologists warn that transnational activism and the transnational "exchange" of ideas and scholarship should not be a one-sided reproduction of the dominance of American/European ideas and experiences as the only valid or best framework (e.g., Ray 2006: 463). This bias informed Parsons's modernization theory (see chapter 4); and, Gunder Frank argues, it is also present in Wallerstein's Eurocentric world-system perspective – as if European capitalism is the only valid historical model of economic development (Gunder Frank and Gills 1996b: 4). Attentiveness to non-US/non-European ideas and practices may, however, be difficult to implement; one of the products and drivers of globalization is the expansion of so-called "global universities," that is, branches of American universities in non-Western societies (e.g., the Middle East, Singapore), teaching American-based and Eurocentric curricula.

Yet highlighting the variation in globalization processes and outcomes, Manisha Desai reports that among activist women forging "transnational feminist solidarities" in local sites and via networks and world conferences, "the flow of ideas and activism is no longer unidirectional, from the North to the South, but multidirectional" (Desai 2002: 15). There is unevenness in women's experiences of globalization; for example, an increase in women's work opportunities in Ghana, and a decrease in women's labor force participation in post-Soviet countries (Desai 2002: 16–18). Women, moreover, are overrepresented in low-paying manual work (Sassen 2007: 112). Nonetheless, Desai argues, women are successful in resisting globalization and creating counter-hegemonic structures:

> Many activist women's efforts focus, to varying degrees and in various ways, on developing concrete economic alternatives based on sustainable development, social equality, and participatory processes, though such economic initiatives have not been as successful at the transnational level … These counter-hegemonies have succeeded in transforming the daily lives of many women at the local level. (Desai 2002: 33; see also Desai 2016)

It may seem odd to talk about the "success" of antiglobalization protests and initiatives, or to listen to the critiques of globalization occasionally voiced by leading globalizers (e.g., Microsoft's Bill Gates), amidst the ever-increasing reach of globalizing forces. Yet, Sklair maintains:

> The significance of these public demonstrations of divisions over globalization is that they send messages of confusion to the public at large, and the anti-globalization movement can use them to great advantage … [to co-opt and maybe even] … actually convert some influential members of the transnational capitalist class to their views on important issues. (Sklair 2002: 282, 283)

Sklair himself believes that capitalist globalization cannot resolve its ecological and class polarization crises; hence his suggestion that a possible alternative lies in socialist globalization (discussed previously).

In a somewhat similar vein, though less economically radical, David Held argues for a **global social democracy** to underpin the new global economy. This project, he explains:

> is a basis for promoting the rule of international law; greater transparency, accountability and democracy in global governance; a deeper commitment to social justice; the protection and reinvention of community at diverse levels; and the transformation of the global economy into a free and fair rule-based economic order. The politics of global social democracy contains clear possibilities of dialogue between different segments of the "pro-globalization/anti-globalization" political spectrum, although it will, of course, be contested by opinion at the extreme ends of the spectrum. (Held 2004: 163)

He thus envisions the regulation and taming of global markets (2004: 164–167), rather than, as Sklair does, the restructuring of their ownership. Both agree, however, that the systematic, global implementation of the ethics of human rights and social justice is imperative. (See chapter 15.)

THE OCCUPY MOVEMENT

Political mobilization against the excesses of global capitalism came to the fore in the fall of 2011 when hundreds of protesters took to the streets of lower Manhattan, the site of Wall Street and the stock exchange, to rally against the stark inequality in contemporary society. The protesters took over and maintained occupancy of Zuccotti Park, a publicly accessible park owned by a corporate giant, and remained there until they were forcibly removed by the New York City police. Occupy Wall Street, as the movement became quickly known, created a stir and a new model of activism. Occupy groups sprung up in public spaces across the US, including Boston, Chicago, and Los Angeles, and across the world: London, Melbourne, Sydney, Taipei, Tokyo, and Hong Kong, as well as even in China. One of the London sites was St. Paul's Cathedral, the sacred space of the Church of England, itself beholden symbolically to the monarchy and the political status quo; it became a focal space of angry contestation and put into sharp relief the religious and ethical questions that overhang the structuring of economic inequality.

In all occupied spaces, the protesters' visibility made their protest, that is, "We are the 99 percent," difficult to ignore. The Occupy movement included students, recent unemployed graduates, laid-off middle-aged professional and skilled workers, and older people concerned about their pensions and health insurance Occupy groups received considerable media attention, and the Occupiers themselves relied heavily on cell phones and Twitter to connect with one another, to make collective decisions, and to get their messages out. Sympathizers from far-away places tweeted their support and some sent Internet-ordered gifts of hot meals and toiletry supplies to the protesters.

The Occupy movement is unlikely to bring about significant changes in Wall Street practices and global finance (given the structural and ideological forces inherent in capitalism, as discussed in chapter 1, including the growing power of transnational corporations, discussed previously). It still matters, nonetheless, and can be seen as an instance of the deepening of democracy. It shows that although capitalism may be stronger than democracy in terms of its impact on (unequal) wealth distribution, it is not strong enough to purchase political indifference and apathy. Moreover, even if the Occupy movement will be regarded historically as just a flash in the pan, at the time it was seen as sufficiently threatening and disruptive that its activities in the US were closely monitored by counter-terrorism agents working for the FBI (the Federal Bureau of Investigation). See also Topic 14.4.

Topic 14.4   Curbing excess in the financial sector

Although public protests such as the Occupy movement may have a limited impact on financial practices, there is some evidence of increased oversight of financial companies both from within companies themselves and from external regulators.

- In 2016, the average bonus paid by Wall Street companies to employees was $138,200, down 28 percent from its peak in 2006 before the financial crisis.
- Lloyd Blankfein, CEO of Goldman Sachs, received $24 million in pay for 2017, much less than he received in 2007 ($68 million).
- Libor, the benchmark interbank lending rate, that became a symbol of Barclays' and other banks' rate-rigging and other risky practices during the 2007–2008 financial crisis, was phased out by the UK regulator in 2017 and replaced with more transparent procedures.
- In August 2017, the British government announced new rules on executive pay, requiring companies, for example, to publish the ratio of bosses' to average workers' pay; and for remuneration committees to consider employee wages when they are setting executive salaries.
- The Royal Bank of Scotland agreed to pay $5.5 billion (in July 2017) to settle claims brought by the US Federal Housing Finance Agency relating to risky mortgages sold by the bank between 2005 and 2007
- There is also shame: Conscious of the damage caused to their public reputation by financial scandals, Morgan Stanley, Citigroup, Bank of America, Credit Suisse, Barclays, and Deutsche Bank have cut back on company-sponsored holiday parties.

SUMMARY

The historical-geographical context for the emergence of economic globalizing processes has long been a focus of Immanuel Wallerstein. In this chapter, therefore, we first discussed his modern world-system perspective and then explored how other sociologists conceptualize globalization and its implications. By contrast with economists, who tend to affirm economic autonomy as the main driver of globalization, sociologists are sensitive to the crisis tendencies in global financial capitalism, and they focus on the structures and particular forms of social organization that shape and result from globalizing processes. Sociologists are attentive to the expansion of economic corporations, the impact of the globalizing division of labor on geographical-regional inequality and class polarization, the rise of global cities, and the role of the nation-state amid new transnational economic processes and relationships. They also highlight the new opportunities and resources for political mobilization and activism.

As in other areas of sociology, there is a divergence in emphasis among globalization theorists. Sklair uses a Marxist perspective, for example, to underscore the primacy of economic profit, transnational corporations, and the transnational capitalist class, as well as the class polarization and ecological crises that globalization exacerbates. Giddens, by contrast, tends to apply a Weberian perspective, emphasizing the continuing significance of the state and of its relations with other bureaucratic actors, including economic corporations. Sassen too leans toward Weber, especially in highlighting the socio-economic differentiation among transnational workers and in envisioning an active role for the state in regulating and influencing globalization processes.

POINTS TO REMEMBER

- Globalization entails multidimensional economic, political, social, and cultural processes.
- Globalization flows and processes are accelerated by advances in Internet and digital technology and the disembeddedness of time and space that they facilitate and produce.

Wallerstein's world-system perspective emphasizes:
- Globalization is yet another cyclical occurrence in the history of the modern world-system
- Capitalism emerged as a world-system in sixteenth-century Europe and subsequently expanded
- The capitalist world-system is distinguished by its capitalist world-economy
- The world-system is characterized by a geographical division of labor in the production of capitalist profit
- The capitalist world-economy comprises core states and peripheral, and semi-peripheral areas
- The world-system is currently in a state of systemic crisis
- The crisis is exacerbated by increasing economic core–periphery inequality, and by systemic failures to institutionalize social equality

Sociologists who study globalization emphasize:
- The impact of the globalizing expansion of the division of labor on increasing living standards/quality of life *and* economic inequality
- The expansion of transnational corporations
- The global expansion of financial capitalism
- The emergence of global cities as part of the corporate infrastructure of global finance
- The expansion of class polarization within both highly advanced and newly industrializing countries and regions
- The emergence of transnational workers whose life-chances and experiences vary widely, especially those between the cosmopolitan professionals/executives and low-wage, resource-poor workers
- The continuing, though changed – and disputed – relevance of the nation-state in transnational economic and political processes
- The emergence of new political and economic alignments
- The emergence of transnational social and political identities
- In a globalized network society, electronic networks can be programmed to reproduce existing inequality, and/or to accomplish alternative goals (e.g., social equality)
- The emergence and political significance of antiglobalization movements (e.g., Occupy Wall Street), and the articulation of alternative forms of globalization
- The vanguard role of women in forging transnational feminist solidarities and new forms of economic and social organization

GLOSSARY: WALLERSTEIN

capitalist world-system the historical emergence of the modern capitalist economy in sixteenth-century Europe.

core states those at the center of world economic production (e.g., the US, UK, Germany).

crisis idea that the current problems of the capitalist world-economy cannot be resolved within the framework of the capitalist world-system.

geographical division of labor the idea that specific countries/world regions emerged as core drivers of the historical emergence of capitalist trade and economic expansion.

peripheral areas those areas marginal but necessary to world economic production.

semiperipheral areas those structurally necessary to the world-economy but outside its core political and economic coalitions.

world-economy the capitalist world-system economy; an economic unit independent of political and administrative boundaries; it is divided into core, peripheral, and semiperipheral geographical areas among which there is an imposed, unequal flow of resources.

GLOSSARY: OTHER RELEVANT CONCEPTS

antiglobalization movement broad array of local and transnational social movement organizations, community groups, and political activists opposing various aspects of globalization.

capitalist globalization emphasis that the current era of globalization represents one specific, historically dominant type or mode of production, that is, capitalist, not socialist, globalization.

class polarization result of the increase in both extreme poverty and extreme affluence in all globalizing countries.

deepening of democracy the free flow and public accessibility of information as a result of the Internet and social media means that ordinary citizens have new resources with which to track the activities and decisions of political elites and to challenge the status quo.

denationalized class global workers (professionals/executives, government bureaucrats, and low-skilled service workers) necessary to the coordination and maintenance of the globalized financial and service infrastructure.

denationalized state a state that wields authority within and beyond its own national geographical territory and on globalization issues that implicate it and other nation-states.

dialectical nature of globalization push and pull between local and global interests; for example, between centralizing, transnational interests (e.g., the EU) and the assertion of state sovereignty.

disembeddedness unmooring of individuals and of institutional practices from specific locales, traditions, and time/space constraints.

distant proximities local and globalizing tendencies that forcefully interact across contemporary society.

financial capitalism increasing prominence of financial services, products, and transactions as a major driver of economic activity.

financial sector includes banks and other financial firms and their employees (e.g., traders), stock exchanges, financial rating agencies (e.g., Moody's) and the institutions that regulate these firms/institutions (e.g., the Securities and Exchange Commission).

geopolitical axis along which a country's (or group of countries') political-economic and geographical or regional interests coincide.

global cities cities in which the core organizational structures and workers necessary to the functioning of the global economy are located.

global social democracy vision of globalized society underpinned by principles of fair play, participatory democracy, and social justice.

global systems theory analytical approach emphasizing the dialectic between states/international alliances and transnational globalizing forces and institutions.

globalization interrelated transformation in economic, political, social, and cultural practices and processes toward increased global integration (notwithstanding unevenness in the reach and impact of these processes).

glocalization the recognition that in contemporary society, one in which the forces of disembeddedness, globalization, and digitalization are highly prevalent, local and global realities are not independent of each other.

network society one in which information technology networks are the dominant shapers of new, decentralized, economic and social organizations and relationships.

new imperialism the idea that a country's geopolitical and military strategies today are driven primarily by capitalist economic interests.

postnational the current era of transnational political organizations (e.g., the EU) and other globalizing forces, with the nation-state no longer considered the core or most powerful political unit.

socialist globalization form of globalization that would gradually eliminate privately owned big business, establish local producer–consumer cooperatives, and implement social equality/human rights.

transnational capitalist class composed of corporate executives/professionals and political, institutional, and media leaders who play a dominant role along with transnational corporations in advancing capitalist globalization and inequality.

transnational practices the idea that (capitalist) globalizing processes require and are characterized by specific transnational economic, political, and cultural-ideological practices or ways of being.

world military order the idea that the distribution of military power in the world is empirically and analytically independent of the distribution of economic power (e.g., Pakistan's and North Korea's nuclear power is considerable despite their considerably weaker economic position relative to the US and Europe).

QUESTIONS FOR REVIEW

1   In what ways are contemporary economic globalizing processes different from the emergence of the modern capitalist world-system?

2   What is the impact of global economic processes on (1) access to resources, (2) class inequality, (3) migration, and (4) cities within your particular country and across the world? What accounts for the patterns you observe?

3   How is the nation-state affected by globalizing economic processes? What role, if any, does it have in shaping the nature and consequences of economic globalization?

4   What does it mean to describe contemporary times as an era of financial capitalism? How does financial capitalism differ from industrial capitalism?

5   Some scholars have described globalization as a juggernaut. Is there any evidence that its force is resisted and/or modified in either local or world contexts?

NOTES

1   Although Gunder Frank sets his analysis of the development of underdevelopment within the contemporary capitalist world system (see chapter 6), for him the use of the term "world system" (without a hyphen) simply connotes the world – the existence of the same world system that has been in existence for 5,000 years (Gunder Frank and Gills 1996b: 3; see also Amin et al. 1990). Rather than identifying a unique *capitalist* world-system, Gunder Frank sees capitalism and socialism as part of the one *same* world system (Gunder Frank and Gills 1996a: xvii). For Gunder Frank, contemporary capitalism is not so different from earlier forms of economic organization and domination reaching further back than sixteenth-century Europe – the context that for Wallerstein marks the emergence of a distinctive capitalist world-system or world-economy.

2   Wallerstein's definition of a world capitalist systemic crisis has parallels with that of Habermas (see chapter 5), notwithstanding their different theoretical frameworks and concerns; as noted, Wallerstein is neo-Marxist, whereas Habermas is more interested in the redemption of capitalism (see also chapter 15). See Wallerstein (1980) for an elaborated assessment of the "crises" that have characterized the development of capitalism.

REFERENCES

Amin, Samir, Giovanni Arrighi, Andre Gunder Frank, and Immanuel Wallerstein. 1990. *Transforming the Revolution: Social Movements and the World-System.* New York: Monthly Review Press.

Bauman, Zygmunt. 2000. *Liquid Modernity.* Cambridge: Polity.

Bauman, Zygmunt. 2013. *Globalization: The Human Consequences.* Oxford, UK: Wiley.

Bordo, Michael, Alan Taylor, and Jeffrey Williamson, 2003. "Introduction." Pp. 1–10 in Michael Bordo, Alan Taylor, and Jeffrey Williamson, eds. *Globalization in Historical Perspective.* Chicago: University of Chicago Press.

Carruthers, Bruce G., and Jeong-Chul Kim. 2011. "The Sociology of Finance." *Annual Review of Sociology* 37: 239–59.

Castells, Manuel. 1997. *The Rise of the Network Society*, volume 1. 2nd edition. Oxford: Blackwell.

Castells, Manuel. 2000. "Toward a Sociology of the Network Society." *Contemporary Sociology* 29: 693–699.

Cook, Clive. 2003. "Globalization in Interdisciplinary Perspective." Pp. 549–552 in Michael Bordo, Alan Taylor, and Jeffrey Williamson, eds. *Globalization in Historical Perspective.* Chicago: University of Chicago Press.

DeParle, Jason. 2008. "A Tiny Staff, Tracking People across the Globe." *New York Times* (February 4), p. A11.

Desai, Manisha. 2002. "Transnational Solidarity: Women's Agency, Structural Adjustment, and Globalization." Pp. 15–33 in Nancy Naples and Manisha Desai, eds. *Women's Activism and Globalization: Linking Local Struggles and Transnational Politics.* New York: Routledge.

Desai, Manisha. 2016. *Subaltern Movements in India: Gendered Geographies of Struggle Against Neoliberal Development.* New York: Routledge.

Earl, Jennifer, and Katrina Kimport. 2011. *Digitally Enabled Social Change: Activism in the Internet Age.* Cambridge, MA: MIT Press.

Eckes, Alfred, and Thomas Zeiler. 2003. *Globalization and the American Century.* New York: Cambridge University Press.

Evans, Peter. 2005. "Counterhegemonic Globalization: Transnational Social Movements in the Contemporary Political Economy." Pp. 655–670 in Thomas Janoski, Robert Alford, Alexander Hicks, and Mildred Schwartz, eds. *Handbook of Political Sociology.* New York: Cambridge University Press.

Fuchs, Christian. 2008. *Internet and Society: Social Theory in the Information Age.* New York: Routledge.

Giddens, Anthony. 1990. *The Consequences of Modernity.* Stanford, CA: Stanford University Press.

Giddens, Anthony. 1991. *Modernity and Self-Identity: Self and Society in the Late Modern Age.* Stanford, CA: Stanford University Press.

Giddens, Anthony. 2003. *Runaway World: How Globalization is Reshaping our Lives.* New York: Routledge.

Gunder Frank, Andre, and Barry Gills. 1996a. "Preface." Pp. xv–xxii in Andre Gunder Frank and Barry Gills, eds. *The World System: Five Hundred Years or Five Thousand?* New York: Routledge.

Gunder Frank, Andre, and Barry Gills. 1996b. "The 5,000-Year World System." Pp. 3–55 in Andre Gunder Frank and Barry Gills, eds. *The World System: Five Hundred Years or Five Thousand?* New York: Routledge.

Harvey, David. 2003. *The New Imperialism.* Oxford: Oxford University Press.

Held, David. 2004. *Global Covenant: The Social Democratic Alternative to the Washington Consensus.* Cambridge: Polity.

Khatchadourian, Raffi. 2017. "Man Without a Country: Julian Assange, WikiLeaks, and the Election." *New Yorker* (August 21), pp. 36–61.

King, Stephen, 2017. *Grave New World: The End of Globalization, the Return of History.* New Haven, CT: Yale University Press.

Kreiss, Daniel. 2012. *Taking Our Country Back: The Crafting of Networked Politics from Howard Dean to Barack Obama.* New York: Oxford University Press.

Lindert, Peter, and Jeffrey Williamson. 2003. "Does Globalization Make the World More Unequal?" Pp. 227–271 in Michael Bordo, Alan Taylor, and Jeffrey Williamson, eds. *Globalization in Historical Perspective.* Chicago: University of Chicago Press.

Menjivar, Cecilia, Leisy Abrego, and Leah Schmalzbauer. 2016. *Immigrant Families.* Malden, MA: Polity Press.

Miraftab, Faranak. 2017. *Global Heartland: Displaced Labor, Transnational Lives and Local Placemaking.* Bloomington, IN: Indiana University Press.

Meichtry, Stacy, Anton Troianovski, and Marcus Walker. 2017. "Europe's Populists Rethink Approach." *Wall Street Journal* (August 22), pp. A1, 8.

Naples, Nancy, and Manisha Desai, eds. 2002. *Women's Activism and Globalization: Linking Local Struggles and Transnational Politics.* New York: Routledge.

Ray, Raka. 2006. "Is the Revolution Missing or Are We Looking in the Wrong Places?" *Social Problems* 53: 459–465.

Ritzer, George, ed. 2007. *The Blackwell Companion to Globalization*. Oxford: Blackwell.

Robertson, Roland. 1992. *Globalization: Social Theory and Global Culture*. London: Sage.

Rosenau, James. 2003. *Distant Proximities: Dynamics beyond Globalization*. Princeton, NJ: Princeton University Press.

Said, Edward. 1978. *Orientalism*. New York: Random House.

Sassen, Saskia. 1991. *The Global City*. Princeton, NJ: Princeton University Press.

Sassen, Saskia. 2007. *A Sociology of Globalization*. New York: Norton.

Sengupta, Somini. 2008. "Inside Gate, India's Good Life; Outside, the Servants' Slums." *New York Times* (June 9), A1, 9.

Sengupta, Somini. 2009. "As Indian Growth Soars, Child Hunger Persists." *New York Times* (March 13), pp. A1, 10.

Simmons, B.A., Frank Dobbin, and G. Garret, eds. 2008. *The Global Diffusion of Markets and Democracy*. Cambridge: Cambridge University Press

Sklair, Leslie. 2002. *Globalization: Capitalism and Its Alternatives*. Oxford: Oxford University Press.

Smelser, Neil, and Richard Swedberg. 2005. *The Handbook of Economic Sociology*. Princeton, NJ: Princeton University Press.

UNCTAD. 2017. *World Investment Report, 2017: Investment and the Digital Economy*. Sales No. E.17.II. D. 3. Geneva: United Nations.

Wallerstein, Immanuel. 1974. *The Modern World-System I: Capitalist Agriculture and the Origins of the European World-Economy in the Sixteenth Century*. New York: Academic Press.

Wallerstein, Immanuel. 1980. *The Modern World-System II: Mercantilism and the Consolidation of the European World-Economy, 1600–1750*. New York: Academic Press.

Wallerstein, Immanuel. 1989. *The Modern World-System III: The Second Era of Great Expansion of the Capitalist World-Economy, 1730–1840s*. New York: Academic Press.

Wallerstein, Immanuel. 1996. "World System Versus World-Systems: A Critique." Pp. 292–296 in Andre Gunder Frank and Barry Gills, eds. *The World System: Five Hundred Years or Five Thousand?* New York: Routledge.

Wallerstein, Immanuel. 2004. *World-Systems Analysis: An Introduction*. Durham, NC: Duke University Press.

Williams, Richard. 1990. *Hierarchical Structures and Social Value: The Creation of Black and Irish Identities in the United States*. New York: Cambridge University Press.

Zaloom, Caitlin. 2006. *Out of the Pits: Traders and Technology from Chicago to London*. Chicago: University of Illinois Press.

CHAPTER FIFTEEN

MODERNITIES, RISK, COSMOPOLITANISM, AND GLOBAL CONSUMER CULTURE

KEY CONCEPTS

contrite modernity
postsecular society
multiple modernities
compressed modernity
risk society
First Modernity
reflexive modernization
Second Modernity

cosmopolitan imperative
cosmopolitan modernity
methodological nationalism
empathy walls
flexible citizenship
unicity
McDonaldization
cultural imperialism

remix
aestheticization of reality
sheer commodification
simulacra
hyperreality
dilemmas of the self

CHAPTER MENU

Introduction to Sociological Theory: Theorists, Concepts, and Their Applicability to the Twenty-First Century,
Third Edition. Michele Dillon.
© 2020 John Wiley & Sons Ltd. Published 2020 by John Wiley & Sons Ltd.
Companion website: www.wiley.com/go/dillon

As highlighted in chapter 14, globalizing economic and political forces are exacerbating ongoing social problems (e.g., economic class polarization) and presenting new challenges. In a sense, to borrow from Charles Dickens's *A Tale of Two Cities*, we are living in the best of times and the worst of times. On the one hand, the global pooling of information, for example, means that we have instant high-speed access to information about all sorts of things and we can form friendships with all kinds of people all across the globe. On the other hand, the global forces that make the world seem smaller and faster also accelerate the computer viruses and cyberattacks that can disrupt major national security and financial networks and other aspects of a country's infrastructure. Similarly, globalizing economic forces accelerate the migration of people but also accelerate the global flows of infectious disease, international terrorism, human sexual trafficking, and climate change.

Modernity, it seems, is a mixed bag. Its gains are readily apparent (e.g., affluence, freedom) but so too are its problems (e.g., climate change, nuclear accidents, poverty). Thus sociologists today are taking a second look at modernity, and rethinking its characteristics and consequences. They are also showing greater awareness of the "modernities" apparent in non-Western countries. This chapter explores these developments, as well as discussing risk society and cosmopolitanism, and contemporary perspectives on global consumer culture.

JÜRGEN HABERMAS: CONTRITE MODERNITY

Although deeply committed to Enlightenment ideals of reason and social progress (see this book's Introduction and chapter 5), Jürgen Habermas (2006: 25) acknowledges that the Enlightenment project of modernization has gone somewhat awry. In particular, he points to financial crises and mismanagement, economic inequality, cultural polarization, and political indifference toward these problems (2006: 25).

For Habermas (2001: 67), the threat posed by current globalizing forces to potentially "degrade the capacity for democratic self-steering" both within and across nations makes the need for reasoned public debate all the more necessary. Going beyond the principles outlined in his construal of the ideal speech situation (see chapter 5), he looks to discover new or underappreciated, cultural resources that can be used for the revitalization of reasoned public debate and democratic participation. In a countermove against his earlier marginalization of religion, he now concedes that moderate public religious traditions (e.g., Catholicism) may have relevance in helping to remediate the problems of modernity. He argues that a **contrite modernity**, one characterized by several social problems that need fixing, may benefit from religious-derived norms and ethics: "A contrite modernity can find help in letting itself out of its [economic and political] dead-end only through a religious orientation toward a transcendent [nonmaterial] point of reference" (Habermas 2006: 26). Such religious-ethical resources, he suggests, can help human society deal with "social pathologies" (e.g., poverty), the "failures of individual life projects" (e.g., due to the lack of opportunities for educational and occupational advancement), and broken personal relationships and a lack of meaning (2006: 26).

POSTSECULAR SOCIETY

Habermas's evolving regard for religion, expressed across several venues since 2001, leads him to use the term **postsecular society**. He uses *postsecular* to demarcate the current moment as one in which religion has not only not disappeared (as Enlightenment thinkers presumed would happen), but in fact continues to have public relevance in and to secular society (where religion has lost a lot but not all of its authority). As he notes, religion continues to be important even in highly secular societies (e.g., UK, France, US). For Habermas, the label can be applied to *secularized* societies where "religion maintains a public influence and relevance, while the secularistic certainty that religion will disappear worldwide in the course of modernization is losing ground" (Habermas 2008: 4). Postsecular society thus "has to adjust itself to the continued existence of religious communities in an increasingly secularized environment" (2008: 3). In short, he calls for a revised understanding of the relevance and place of religion in modern – secular – Western societies (Habermas 2010: 18–19). He argues for a new understanding that balances acceptance of the public value of nonfundamentalist religious-based ideas with simultaneous acceptance of the fact that secularization (the decline of religious belief and authority) is the settled reality.

Postsecularity as a normative idea requires religious and secular citizens in secular society not only to tolerate but talk with one another. Each is expected to be reflexively self-conscious of their own beliefs. This requires them to recognize that, in a pluralistic society, different individuals and communities have different understandings of various issues and that their view of things can be tempered as a result of mutually engaged conversation with others. Further, because secularization is the settled reality, Habermas (2006: 27) argues that when "religious citizens" participate in public debate they must translate or rework their religious-based ideas into a secular vocabulary that is culturally resonant and accessible to a broad array of individuals irrespective of their religious background. He acknowledges that "the persons who are neither willing nor able to divide their moral convictions and their vocabulary into profane [i.e., secular] and religious strands must be permitted to take part in political will formation even if they use religious language" (Habermas 2008: 11). The core expectation, nonetheless, is that when religious individuals participate in public debate, they should discard specifically religious vocabularies and sources of authority. For their part, "secular citizens" are expected "to meet their fellow religious citizens as equals" in civil society (2008: 11). In other words, they have to sincerely engage in reciprocal conversation with them and not dismiss religious-based arguments (translated into a culturally resonant vocabulary) as simply irrational or irrelevant. Although there are tensions in Habermas's construal of religion and postsecularity (see Dillon 2012), his acknowledgement of the cultural relevance of moderate religious ideas and values in reorienting public debate about societal ills is important. For example, religious-based arguments such as Pope Francis's discussion of climate change and economic inequality, draw attention to the ethical and political urgency of dealing with these interrelated global problems (Dillon 2018).

S.N. EISENSTADT: MULTIPLE MODERNITIES

Habermas's reappraisal of religion and modernity is an important theoretical development (given the Enlightenment view of religion as a nonrational and nonprogressive force). Yet his theorizing is very much grounded in the framework of Western modernity. The longstanding, dominant view in social theory and in western intellectual thought more generally is that there is only one modernity, and (1) that its origins lie in the Enlightenment (which was itself a thoroughly Western phenomenon), (2) that its trajectory is evident in and unique to the West, and (3) that its contents and manifestations are what we know as the one and only modernity.

This understanding of modernity has been tempered in recent years by the concept of **multiple modernities**. It emphasizes that modernity can take different forms other than what is denoted by Western modernity. The idea was introduced by S.N. Eisenstadt (1923–2010), a Polish-born Israeli sociologist who, influenced by Parsons, wrote extensively about modernization in the 1960s and 1970s. He adopted a strong comparative historical approach (following Max Weber's example) and gave far greater acknowledgement than Parsons to the enduring relevance of tradition in modernizing processes (see Eisenstadt 1973). Outliving Parsons by more than 30 years, and having been able to witness the many divergent ways in which diverse societies embrace and institutionalize change, Eisenstadt came to argue for multiple modernities – the "ongoing reconstructions of multiple institutional and ideological [cultural] patterns … carried forward by specific social actors … pursuing different programs of modernity" (Eisenstadt 2000: 2). As he emphasized, the term "multiple modernities" highlights that "modernity and Westernization are not identical, that the Western patterns of modernity are not the only 'authentic' modernities, though they enjoy historical precedence and continue to be a basic reference point for others" (2000: 2–3).

Figure 15.1   Although the manifestations of modernity vary across the world, the sites and symbols of consumer choice are increasingly universal. Source: © oasistrek/iStockphoto.

Thus Eisenstadt argues, world civilizations other than the Western tradition alone matter in how different societies accomplish modernity. He also notes, however, that the basic Western model of modernity is still far-reaching. The Western model is highly influential in how modernity gets institutionalized, notwithstanding the important and innovative ways in which different cultures and societies encounter modernity and give their own particularized understanding to it. He states:

> Modernity first moved beyond the West into different Asian societies – Japan, India, Burma, Sri Lanka, China, Vietnam, Laos, Cambodia, Malaysia, Indonesia – to the Middle Eastern countries, coming finally to Africa. By the end of the twentieth century, it encompassed nearly the entire world, the first true wave of globalization. In all these societies the basic model of the territorial state and later of the nation-state was adopted; so were the basic premises and symbols of Western modernity. So, too, were the West's modern institutions – representative, legal, and administrative [bureaucratic]. But at the same time the encounter of modernity with non-Western societies brought about far-reaching transformations in the premises, symbols, and institutions of modernity – with new problems arising as a consequence. (Eisenstadt 2000: 14)

The partial rather than wholesale appropriation of the cultural ideas and institutions of Western modernity thus "served to encourage and accelerate the transposition of the modern project" in ways that simultaneously found resonance with the cultural and political traditions of non-Western societies (Eisenstadt 2000: 15). The notion of multiple modernities is thus an important corrective to the enduring tendency (especially of those of us in the West) to equate the "real" modernity with what we see and know as modernity, that is, its manifestations in North America, Europe, and Oceania (Australia and New Zealand). Of course, even without the term multiple modernities, we have long known that modernization – including in the West – is uneven; that tradition (including religious traditions) still matter; and that modernity despite its great advances also gives rise to many new problems (e.g., climate change, identity theft), while at the same time failing to remedy old problems (e.g., poverty, inequality).

CHINESE MODERNITY

Evidence of the fact that modernities vary and that there are structural (institutional) breaks within any one modernity, can be seen in the case of China. As highlighted throughout the book, China has experienced rapid economic growth over the last three decades; it is currently the world's second largest economy (after the US) and has a booming consumer market. The sociologist Yunxiang Yan (2010) points out that state-led, market-oriented reforms not only expanded the Chinese economy but also led to increased awareness of individual rights among the Chinese people. Interestingly, this expansion was first propelled by Maoist socialist reforms in the 1950s – social engineering reforms that, for example, allowed the Chinese to choose their own spouses rather than defer to arranged marriages.

In more recent decades, from the late 1970s onwards, social change (e.g., the gradual adoption of Western ideas/practices) was driven by Chinese rural migrants who, when they came to the cities to meet the accelerated labor market demand, had to rely (at least initially) on their own individual resources rather than on the social anchors of family and their home community (Yan 2010: 497–498). As Yan points out, it was among peasants in rural China that economic decollectivization or market privatization first took hold. It was peasants who defied state laws and surreptitiously worked parcels of land for their own individual/family income, a shift that was eventually accepted by the state once it saw that the "privatization" of agriculture was profitable. Self-employment and "individual career development" eventually spread to the cities as workers chose to spend their spare time working in second jobs (e.g., at McDonald's) to secure additional income as well as new skills. The significant role played by rural migrants and rural regions in propelling modernization and individualization (i.e., an emphasis on the freedom of individuals to determine the course of their lives) contrasts with Western modernity where typically we associate cities as the locus of social progress and increased individualism. In China, it was rural people, and subsequently their urban counterparts, who were able to remake their biographies; choosing alternative employment and careers to those mandated by state planning and state control of the occupational market (Yan 2010: 502). The new selves that have emerged, however, are to a large extent "market driven selves" (2010: 505), not unlike the selves in the West.

Individualization is a very Western concept (partly rooted in Calvinists' beliefs about self-reliance and self-determination; see Weber, chapter 3), and it is increasingly apparent in how ordinary Chinese people think about and craft their lives. For example, a 25-year-old woman, one of 164,000 employees at Foxconn's (iPhone) electronics manufacturing factory in Chengdu, responded very positively to reforms implemented to improve employees' working conditions. She was able to avail herself of a high-backed chair on which to sit while assembling parts, and she also took leisure courses on knitting and sketching offered by the factory. Convinced that a better life for herself was within reach, she also strayed from her parents' expectations about whom she should marry. Rather than settling with a man from her own geographical region, she became attracted to someone from another province and, defying her parents' wishes, began dating him. Commenting on the changes in her work and personal life, she stated, "There was a change this year. I'm realizing my value" (Bradsher and Duhigg 2012: A10). Valuing one's own individual self and giving it priority over the contrary pull of the authority of family and other traditional structures echoes the American and Western sense of individualization.

Individualization processes, however, are uneven in China. Unlike Western modernity, it maintains a centralized economy largely controlled by the Chinese state and the political elite rather than by free-market, capitalist principles. Nor does China have a culture of democracy and a well-grounded infrastructure of political rights and procedures (Yan 2010). As underscored by, for example, the restrictive controls it imposes on free speech and on Internet content and use, economic growth and consumerism in China are not accompanied by a (Western) cultural ethos of individual political freedom and the right to political self-determination.

SOUTH KOREAN MODERNITY

The modernization process in South Korea also presents some unique characteristics. The term **compressed modernity** is used to capture the dynamics of societal change occurring there. South Korea's economic modernization was encouraged by the US at the end of World War II (1939–1945), as it was emerging from colonial domination by Japan. State bureaucrats and state-run organizations within the country, as well as individual entrepreneurs, were influential in initiating change. Its economy experienced rapid economic growth between the 1960s and the 1990s, reliant to a large extent on the manufacturing and export of electronics and cars. South Korea's economic transformation is labelled compressed modernity because industrial capitalism and the related shift away from agriculture, as well as urbanization and democratization, all simultaneously occurred in a remarkably condensed time interval (Chang 2010). However, notwithstanding this rapid and internally driven economic-social-political transformation, much of the traditional culture of South Korea remained in place and is at times at cross-purposes with South Korea's new modernity. This type of cultural lag – the gap between economic modernization and traditional values – is also variously found in Western countries at particular junctures (e.g., Ireland in the 1980s; Dillon 1993). In South Korea, Chang and Song (2010) argue, the family in particular has been both the receptacle for and the driver of compressed modernity, and it is currently showing the strains of this overload. Women are in the vanguard of efforts to resist what they experience as the oppressive reach of family responsibilities imposed by a patriarchal family structure and culture. Consequently they are delaying or postponing marriage; remaining unmarried; and if married, choosing to have fewer children as well as readily embracing the option of divorce. "By radically deferring, forgoing or ending marriages, by sternly refusing to produce more than one or two offspring (or to procreate at all), or by courageously rejecting family relations beyond the nuclear [primary or traditional family] unit, South Korean women have taken their society – and to some extent, the world – by surprise" (Chang and Song 2010: 540). These trends are evidence of an increased individualization in South Korea. They are also a source of concern to policymakers that women's retreat from traditional family-formation patterns provides a "potential threat to the social sustainability of the national economy, and that of the nation itself" (2010: 540). The compressed or rapid nature of modernization in South Korea has accentuated the tensions resulting from the mismatch between economic and social progress and the pull of traditional collective identities ("the family"; "the nation"). Such tensions, however, are not confined to South Korea. They are also implicit in Western societies in policy debates about fertility decline, gender equality, and gendered work and family roles.

Topic 15.1   Is China changing the world?

"The world has changed China. And China is now changing the world." This heading in a one-page advertisement in the *New York Times* (December 10, 2012, p. A9) was sponsored by CCTV2, one of China's state-run television organizations. It seems an apt characterization of the reflexivity of modernization whereby countries mutually impact one another and can do so in various asymmetrical ways. The US, long regarded as the exemplar of modernity and for many decades the world's largest economy, is expected to be eclipsed economically by China by 2030. Increasingly too, the US and the West are paying attention to China's growing geopolitical and militaristic influence. A major way in which China's modernity differs from the West is its suppression of human rights and democratic freedoms. Democracy is absent in China, and freedom of speech and of the press is highly restricted. China's state-run media organizations not only dominate in China but are increasingly visible in other countries; for example, its state-run news agency Xinhua, sponsors one of the biggest and flashiest billboards in Times Square, New York. In 2016, President Xi Jinping told Chinese media officials that: "All news media run by the [Communist] party must work to speak for the party's will and its propositions, and protect the party's authority and unity" (Wong 2016). Apple, Amazon, and Western newspapers and other publishers, including academic presses, are restricted from publishing and distributing content online in China, and social media and Internet search engines are frequently blocked by the government (and WhatsApp is banned). These and other restrictions (e.g., on freedom of religion and on peaceful dissent, as exemplified by the imprisonment of Nobel laureate, Liu Xiaobo who, prohibited from traveling abroad for cancer treatment, died in July 2017), seek to keep Western influences from undermining the power of the Communist Party (and its leaders). This cultural atmosphere, however, as well as the problems associated with unchecked economic development (e.g., pollution), are prompting many educated, professional workers and their families to leave China for more open and stable societies (e.g., Australia, US; e.g., Johnson 2012). China is changing the world in many ways. However, a modernity that resists the institutionalization of the individual rights and freedoms of Western modernity is indeed a different modernity.

ULRICH BECK: GLOBAL RISK SOCIETY

The persistence of old social problems and the emergence of new problems across the world suggest that incarnations of modernity, whether in the West or in Asia, the Middle East, and Africa, are increasingly demarcated by the prevalence of risk. The everyday ubiquity of risk is such that the German theorist Ulrich Beck (1992) refers to contemporary society as **risk society**. Our advanced modernity(ies) have provided individuals and whole countries with unprecedented individual freedom and prosperity. They have also foregrounded risk and uncertainty and anxiety about how to deal with them. Risk is created, in large part, by society – especially by the accelerated push toward economic prosperity and progress (Beck 1992: 40). But this does not make it any less threatening. For example, while we can travel the globe in a relatively efficient manner today, the same efficiency also applies to the travel time for the global circulation of contaminated foods and of disease, with the effect that illness spreads more rapidly (e.g., Ebola, SARS), and diseases appear (or reappear) in places where they were thought not to occur or to have disappeared (e.g., tuberculosis in the US).

By the same token, as a result of advances in scientific technology, we have new inventions creating increased risk (e.g., military-nuclear armament technology) and new ways of detecting and treating various risks (e.g., nuclear medicine). We also have more information and greater access to information (e.g., genetic profiling, WebMD) making us aware of the risks that surround us (e.g., of getting cancer, living in a polluted city, etc.). All of this technology and information, however, does not resolve – as Weber (see chapter 3) and critical theorists (see chapter 5) would point out – how we should deal with and negotiate among the risks and the risk information we encounter. For example, individuals who discover from newly developed medical prognostication tests that they have an elevated risk of cancer still have to decide which course of action (surgery or radiation) prior to the onset of symptoms might ensure a better outcome. Moreover, in our globalized world they also have to decide among transnational, geographically diverse medical venues where to receive (buy) treatment – whether at a distant medical-tourist resort in Mexico or at a more locally situated clinic. In any event, the assessment of risk is economically costly, as well as stressful. Angelina Jolie underwent a preventive, double mastectomy after she discovered from a highly specific genetic test that she had a high risk of getting breast and ovarian cancer. Her public disclosure alerted other women to wonder whether they too had risky genes and whether they should undergo the same testing procedure. The gene evaluation test, however, costs patients approximately $4,000 (Agus 2013: A21). Such risk assessment options, therefore, impose a big expense, especially for women who are not economically well off and who do not have health insurance. And, further, the new awareness that the risk exists (whether one tests for it or not) adds to women's risk anxiety.

Risk is not new; all societies through time have encountered risk. But Beck (1992), and Giddens (2003), emphasize that today our detailed knowledge of risk and its possible outcomes is unprecedented. Yet, we frequently cannot control or eliminate the uncertainties surrounding the probable outcomes of various risks. Consequently, as individuals, as local communities, and as large-scale societies we are afflicted by risk and its uncertainties (Beck 1992: 23–24). Thus, although we "are creating something that has never existed before, [i.e.,] a global cosmopolitan society," at the same time, globalization "is shaking up our existing ways of life, no matter where we happen to be … It is not settled or secure, but fraught with anxieties" (Giddens 2003: 19).

Risk, moreover, as Beck (1992) argues, is a fate universal in scope rather than unevenly distributed along economic class lines. Toxic industrial accidents may initially have a more immediate impact on particular economically and socially disadvantaged communities because of the geographical concentration of factories and power plants and oil refineries, in poorer neighborhoods and in poorer global regions. Yet, Beck argues, in the risk society everyone is at risk, including the rich (even though the rich can better afford personal risk assessment genetic and medical tests, and medical and home and car insurance, etc.). Risk's inclusivity is further underscored by changes in the natural environment. Hurricane Harvey, for example, "took aim at rich and poor alike," having an equally devastating impact on affluent and poor people's homes and neighborhoods in Houston and the surrounding area (Turkewitz and Burch 2017). Floods are a global risk in every sense of the term: That same month (August 2017), a mud slide in Sierra Leone killed over one-thousand people; and monsoon floods are a recurring problem in India, Bangladesh and Nepal, leaving millions homeless (*The Economist*, "How to cope with floods," September 2, 2017, p. 9). Additionally, there is risk and uncertainty as a result of global terrorism, and from sophisticated cyberattacks (e.g., computer viruses and hacking) that disrupt financial systems, customer data bases, electrical grids, and political campaigns. Beck elaborates:

> Risk positions are not class positions. With the globalization of risks a social dynamic is set in motion, which can no longer be composed of and understood in class categories. Ownership implies non-ownership and thus a social relationship of tension and conflict, in which reciprocal social identities can continually evolve and solidify – "them up there, us down here." The situation is quite different for risk positions. Anyone affected by them is badly off, but deprives the others, the non-affected, of nothing. Expressed in an analogy: the "class" of the "affected" does not confront a "class" that is not affected. It confronts at most a "class" of not-yet-affected people. The escalating scarcity of health will drive even those still well off today (in health and well-being) into the ranks of the "soup kitchens" provided by insurance companies tomorrow, and the day after tomorrow into the pariah community of the invalid and the wounded. (Beck 1992: 39–40)

In short, "freedom from risk can turn overnight into irreversible affliction" (Beck 1992: 40). And this is a fate that, for all the achievements of modernity, cannot be overcome by individual achievement. Modern individuals, notwithstanding their resources and their freedom to make decisions about so many aspects of their life, stand relatively powerless against the uncertainties of risk society. Beck states: "Now there exists a kind of *risk fate in developed civilization*, into which one is born, which one cannot escape with any amount of achievement … we are *all* confronted similarly by that fate" (1992: 41).

What then are individuals and society to do? Clearly, many individuals and collectivities are quite planful and creative in trying to minimize risk. For example, the US Olympic delegation to Beijing, worried about drug and pesticide contaminants in Chinese products and the increased risk both of illness and of athletes testing positive for (prohibited) prescription drugs, had 25,000 pounds of lean protein shipped from the US to China in advance of the 2008 Olympic Games. The pervasiveness of risk is such, however, that even a meal at your local Chipotle (or any other) restaurant can lead to a serious foodborne illness (as many American college students discovered in 2016).

Topic 15.2   Risk and resentment in the digital economy

Amid the many societal changes propelled by advances in digital technology, the computerization of more tasks and services (see Topics 1.2 and 5.2) is adding uncertainty to how individuals and communities envision their economic and social well-being. Driverless cars (and ships) will likely reduce the risk of injuries and deaths from traffic accidents. But they also put a lot of jobs at risk: There are 1.7 million truck drivers in America and many others drive taxis, ambulances, and other vehicles for a living. Self-driving vehicles will have a major impact on these occupations and will require current employees to get training and skills that are more suitable for the e-economy, a challenge especially for older workers (Leubsdorf 2017). Beyond self-driving vehicles, the acceleration of digitalized, "smart" computer automation will decrease demand for, if not eliminate, an array of occupations, including telemarketers; accountants and auditors; retail salespeople; technical writers; real-estate sales agents; typists; and machinists (*The Economist*, "Artificial Intelligence: Special Report," June 25, 2016, p. 9). The economic populism variously seen in the Brexit vote, in support for President Trump and for the Alternative Germany party, and in anti-immigration movements in general (e.g., Pegida and France's Marion Le Pen supporters) is partly attributed to the resentment of native-born and working class voters (e.g., Hochschild and Hout 2017). For several years, they have felt that they are missing out on the economic opportunities available to others (including immigrants) as well as being belittled by the cosmopolitanism (e.g., environmental sustainability, LGBT equality) celebrated by urban elites. The displacement of manufacturing jobs with a service, financial and information economy has certainly been disruptive. But the transformation of everyday life by the sharing economy (e.g., Uber, Airbnb; Heller 2017; see Topic 1.2), the Internet of things, and ever-smarter computerization (including artificial intelligence, see Topic 5.2) are undoubtedly brining new risks, uncertainties and vulnerabilities. And, as Beck (1992) would predict, they are universal in scope, not confined to any one social class or political or cultural group.

COSMOPOLITAN MODERNITY

There is no panacea for dealing with the legacies of modernity or with the risks, challenges, and crises of the current moment. These challenges are all the more varied in part because there has not been a convergence of modernity experiences across the world; modernity in Asia is different to modernity in the West (see previous section, Multiple Modernities). As Beck and other scholars emphasize, there are "a plurality of modernization paths" (Beck and Grande 2010: 412; Therborn 1995), and this pluralization is not simply variation on the theme of Western modernity. Rather, there are different paths in, to, and through modernity (Therborn 1995; Beck and Grande 2010: 414). Importantly too, this also means that there can be "discontinuous societal change *within* modern societies" (Beck and Grande 2010: 215).

Beck and Grande (2010: 215) argue that the structural and organizational principles of modern societies can be distinguished from traditional and premodern societies (as Durkheim and Weber also emphasize). Additionally, they argue, the structures and principles of modernity "can be institutionalized in very different ways." They differentiate between a **First Modernity** and a Second Modernity. The premises of a First Modernity include those structures that the Western concepts of industrialization and modernization typically encompass (see Weber and Parsons). Among these are the nation-state, the market economy, and principles that define a socially-anchored individualism, scientific rationality, and functional differentiation (2010: 415). Building upon and extending his risk society thesis, Beck argues that the "basic social institutions of the First Modernity have become ineffective or dysfunctional for both society and individuals" (2010: 15). Institutional failures push individuals toward an increased individualization away from the First Modernity structures that they had come to rely on (the state, the occupational structure, the anchor of family expectations, gender roles, political parties, etc.), and consequently they are compelled "to design their biographies in terms of permanently individualized endeavors, pursuits, and life courses" (2010: 15). This is a process of **reflexive modernization** whereby individuals and whole societies critically examine the legacy of modernization and deliberately seek awareness of its pitfalls and failures. And, in turn, they respond to them by implementing societal changes that seek to transform the threat of modernity's collapse into a more sustainable society/modernity. (This idea is similar to Habermas's notion of a contrite modernity.) Reflexive modernization, Beck argues, thus marks the transition into and characterizes Second Modernity. Again, Beck emphasizes that there are different varieties of **Second Modernity**; the transition is not the same for all societies, "but breaks and reflects itself in different contexts, paths, thresholds, etc." (2010: 15).

COSMOPOLITAN IMPERATIVES

According to Beck:

> the theory of reflexive modernization argues that modern societies – Western and non-Western alike – are confronted with qualitatively new problems which create "**cosmopolitan imperatives**." These cosmopolitan imperatives arise because of global risks: nuclear risks, ecological risks, technological risks, economic risks created by insufficiently regulated financial markets, etc. These new global risks have at least two consequences: firstly, they mix the "native" and the "foreign" and create an everyday global awareness; and secondly therefore, they create chains of interlocking political decisions and outcomes among states and their citizens, which alter the nature and dynamics of territorially defined governance systems. These risks link the global North [e.g., the US and Europe] and the global South [e.g., South America, Africa] in ways that were unknown hitherto ... these risks produce new cosmopolitan responsibilities, cosmopolitan imperatives, which no one can escape. What emerges, is the universal possibility of "risk communities" which spring up, establish themselves and become aware of their cosmopolitan composition – "imagined cosmopolitan communities" which come into existence in the awareness that dangers or risks can no longer be socially delimited in space and time. In light of these cosmopolitan imperatives a reformulated theory of reflexive modernization must argue that nowadays we all live in a Second, **Cosmopolitan Modernity** – regardless of whether we have experienced First Modernity or not. (Beck and Grande 2010: 417–418)

In cosmopolitan modernity – one in which the boundaries of space and time are no longer limiting or constraining (or from which we are disembedded; cf. Giddens, chapter 14), our consciousness of risk and its consequences must encompass a global, world society, not just our own local community and our own particular interests and uncertainties. Further, because cosmopolitan modernity has a plurality of pathways and structures, it gives rise to competition "between ways and visions of modernity and new types of cosmopolitical conflict and violence" with which we must deal (Beck and Grande 2010: 419). As the word cosmopolitan suggests, cosmopolitan modernity is premised not simply on acceptance of the idea that a plurality of modernities exist, but that our worldview and social practices must encompass an inclusive and reflexive engagement with these multiple ways of being. Thus cosmopolitan modernity (or cosmopolitan modernization) not only

> highlights the existence of a variety of different types of modern society, it also emphasizes the dynamic intermingling and interaction between societies ... Cosmopolitization relates and connects individuals, groups and societies in new ways, thereby changing the very position and function of the "self " and the "other" ... cosmopolitization is not, by definition, a symmetrical and autonomous process; it may well be the product of asymmetries, dependencies, power and force, and it may also create new asymmetries and dependencies within and between societies. (Beck and Grande 2010: 418)

In light of a cosmopolitan modernity, Beck argues that sociologists need to expand their frameworks for studying society. He strongly cautions us to avoid making the categorical error "of implicitly applying conclusions drawn from one society to society (in general), which then becomes a universal frame of reference" (Beck and Grande 2010: 411). This tendency is something that, he argues, is true of "most of the dominant theories in contemporary sociology," – including those discussed in this book including Beck's own "risk society" thesis (2010: 411). It is understandable that sociology is accused of displaying a **methodological nationalism** – that is, that we tend primarily to theorize about and to conduct research on our own national society and to generalize from that knowledge to "modern society" and to societal processes in general. Although Max Weber set a strong example for sociologists to engage in comparative research (evident in his studies of world religions, for example), successive generations of sociologists have tended to shy away from in-depth comparative studies. This too is understandable given that, phenomenologically, our own (national) society is our here-and-now reality and trying to understand even one society is itself a complicated and time-consuming task. Nevertheless, we can avoid some of the pitfalls of a methodological nationalism if, although not actually studying other societies, we at least expand our immersion in sociological studies of societies other than our own. This is all the more necessary given globalization and the many ways in which contemporary opportunities and lived experiences are affected by the flow of social, economic and political developments that occur independent of national borders (see also chapter 14).

THE GLOBAL EXPANSION OF HUMAN RIGHTS

By changing contemporary experiences of modernity, globalization is also contributing to the acceleration and expansion of human rights. The Enlightenment and the dawn of modernity marked a watershed in the recognition of human reason and individual rationality. This brought forth a recognition of individual human rights, specifically, the rights associated with political participation (e.g., voting, free speech), and collective self-governance (see Introduction). Western democratic societies exemplified modern political citizenship. It was initially partial and uneven (e.g., restricting political rights to property-owning men), but eventually extended voting rights to women and racial minorities. The mid-twentieth century saw an expansion of political rights in countries that had been colonized by European powers (e.g., the Caribbean, North Africa); and subsequently, democratic rights and procedures (e.g., direct elections) were institutionalized at a varied pace in South America, Asia (e.g., South Korea in 1987), and in Eastern European countries (following the collapse of the Berlin Wall in 1989 and the breakup of the Soviet Union).

In the West, from the early decades of the twentieth century onward, we see a progressive commitment to complementing the rights of political citizenship with the crafting of social citizenship: An emphasis on the inclusivity of all groups, including subordinate minorities, within the state. The rise of the welfare state (e.g., Marshall 1950) was a systematic effort to reduce economic and social inequalities (e.g., with policies to help the unemployed, the poor, widows, occupationally disabled individuals, etc.). Social Security and Medicare in the US, and welfare state legislation providing universal health care and social services in Western European countries, institutionalized the recognition that personal suffering and socioeconomic vulnerability required a commitment from society at large to ensure the well-being of disadvantaged individuals and groups. More recent decades, has seen increased recognition that sexual, cultural, and ethno-based identities are also worthy of state-societal respect and protection. The legalization of same-sex marriage and antidiscrimination LGBT legislation are particularly noteworthy (see chapter 11, Topic 11.2).

> **Topic 15.3   Empathy walls and opportunity barriers in Europe**
>
> The plight of over ten million refugees and asylum-seekers fleeing violence and poverty in Syria, Afghanistan, and Africa continues to roil political debate in several developed countries and especially the EU. Though knocking at EU borders, the refugees' suffering is made more distant by their cultural otherness as mostly Arab and African Muslims (see chapter 12, Topic 12.1). The Organisation for Economic Cooperation and Development (OECD, 2017) reports that in 2016 alone there were more than 1.6 million asylum requests. The **empathy walls** (Hochschild 2016: 5) impeding appreciation of their plight are bolstered in Europe by its history of relative homogeneity. Compared to some other rich countries, Europe has fewer foreign-born residents (Porter 2015). According to OECD figures, Australia (28 percent) and New Zealand (22 percent) have the most foreign born, followed by Canada (20 percent) whose hospitality was highlighted by the Syrian refugee crisis and its early commitment to accept 25,000 displaced people. Welcoming a group of new Syrian arrivals at the airport, Prime Minister Pierre Trudeau said: "Tonight they step off the plane as refugees, but they walk out of this terminal as permanent residents of Canada" (Austen 2015). Europe has fewer foreign-born residents though the proportions vary across countries: Sweden (16 percent), Ireland (16 percent; high, partly due to returning Irish immigrants whose children were born overseas), Norway (14 percent), Germany (13 percent), Spain (13 percent), France (12 percent), Britain (12 percent), Italy (9 percent), and Denmark (9 percent). In the US, a country historically used to welcoming the world's "tired, hungry and poor," as inscribed on the Statue of Liberty, approximately 13 percent of the current population are foreign born. Beyond the refugee crisis, Europe's relative lack of diversity dampens immigrants' opportunities. Economic analyst Eduardo Porter (2015) comments: "It is harder for immigrants to get a job in an EU country than in most other rich countries." More surprisingly, perhaps, "it is also harder for their European-born children, who report even more discrimination than their parents and suffer much higher rates of unemployment than the children of the native-born." The political, economic, and cultural challenges entangled in diversity are unlikely to dissipate soon. The UN projects a global population of 10 billion people by 2050, and most of this growth "will come from the poor, strife-ridden regions of the world that have been sending migrants scrambling to Europe in search of safety and a better life" (Porter 2015). As Porter (2015) concludes: "The choice is clear. Europe's best shot at prosperity is to build upon the diversity that immigration will bring."

WHO IS MY NEIGHBOR?

The values, obligations, and rewards associated with being a "good citizen" prompt discussion of "Who is my neighbor?" This is so regardless of whether the focus is on one's local neighborhood or society at large. What does it mean to be a good neighbor? And what is entailed in showing concern for others? These questions, and the scope, meaning, and implications of citizenship come into even sharper relief as a result of globalization. The global flow of information such as the television and Internet images of war, violence, famine, forest fires, tsunamis, and earthquakes; the global flow of ideas about equality and personal and political freedom; and the transnational migration flow of people sharpen awareness that one's neighbor, and especially a neighbor in need (e.g., victims of war and natural disasters), is not circumscribed by one's geographical or national community. Increasingly, rather, talk of "the common good" requires awareness that all individuals are members, however passively or invisibly, of a transnational, global community, bound by a human solidarity amid and across differences (reminiscent of Paul Gilroy's notion of planetary humanism; see chapter 12).

The cosmopolitan imperatives of today include deference to the force of a cosmopolitan bond. This means that we have a moral/societal obligation to think not only about exercising our own individual political rights and protecting the social rights of particular groups who are familiar to us (e.g., children, or LGBTQ, elderly or physically disabled people). Additionally, we are required to respond to "distant suffering" (e.g., Boltanski 1999), to appreciate the experiences and suffering, and make efforts to protect the rights, of culturally distant Others. This is a challenge, as underscored by political controversies over accommodating refugees (see Topic 15.3). Beck and Sznaider (2012: 636–637) argue that there is a

> new need for a hermeneutics of the alien other in order to live and work in a world in which violent division and unprecedented intermingling coexist, and danger and opportunity vie. This may influence human identity construction, which need no longer be shaped by the opposition to others, in the negative, confrontational dichotomy of "we" and "them."

Bridging the "we" and the "them" is necessary, and it is an ongoing task. We can enjoy the same consumer goods as a person 5,000 miles from where we live, and yet have difficulty fully recognizing the humanity of an ethnically different neighbor or classmate. Episodes of ethnic or tribal conflict whether in Northern Ireland, India, Kenya, or Myanmar highlight the inability of groups to appreciate the rights of Others even when the groups involved share many points of cultural similarity. Further, among similarly situated individuals and groups we witness what appear as irreconcilable differences over contested rights issues. Women's rights, for example, continue to be ambiguous in many countries around the world; sexual and other forms of violence against women are recurring problems, and the rights of women to control reproduction decisions continue to be fraught with political and cultural tensions.

Figure 15.2   The cosmopolitan imperative requires us to think of ourselves and of local and distant Others as all part of the one shared humanity. © Andrew Wink/Michele Dillon.

Globalization processes shift the territorial basis of human rights and also draw attention to the fact that the citizens in question do not necessarily "belong" to any single nation. Consequently, as Aihwa Ong (1999) argues, transnational migration and the emergence of multiple cross-cutting transnational identities require a notion of **flexible citizenship**. This entails ensuring that individuals and groups who migrate back and forth across a number of different countries/jurisdictions have their human rights protected regardless of their mobile or transitory status within a particular jurisdiction/territory. Similarly, the global flow of ideas about rights and accountability and the global flow of information about human rights atrocities, require individual nations and transnational entities (e.g., the UN) and organizations (e.g., Amnesty International) to work to ensure that justice is pursued, if not always secured, across multiple national jurisdictions (e.g., Sikkink 2011).

Topic 15.4   One Love: Bob Marley, a cosmopolitan figure

Bob Marley's face and iconic dreadlocks adorn tee-shirts, mugs, plates and many other commodities available for purchase the world over. The profit-driven promotion and availability of all things Marley is, in many respects, an exemplar of the global unicity of consumer culture and the commodification of body and place (i.e., Jamaica). But one can also see in Marley the promise of the cosmopolitanism to which we are all called in today's cosmopolitized world, a world in which the moral imperative of an ethic of care for the Other transcends nation, place, race, culture, and class. Paul Gilroy argues that Marley's "unchanging face now represents an iconic, godly embodiment of a universal struggle for justice, peace, and human rights, a prefiguration of more positive forms of global interconnection" (Gilroy 2010: 88). "The history of Marley's continuing worldwide appeal reveals a distinctive blend of moral, spiritual, political, and commercial energies" (2010: 89). Notwithstanding the clever commercial marketing of his images and music, and notwithstanding his conservative views on gender (e.g., Hsu 2017), he is a figure whose voice and lyrics speak to some extent to a utopian politics. "Marley can be judged to have become a brand, as well as a symbol of resistance and resilience … Canonised, he retains a unique moral authority" (2010: 91), to move us to take responsibility for, and commit to building, a solidarity based on shared humanity rather than shared blood, history, or place.

An additional challenge to the global articulation and accountability of human rights lies in the fact that cosmopolitization complicates and dislocates the point of reference such that cultural minorities may change the cultural majority, or at least are expected to have a reciprocal engagement with and impact on the cultural majority. The cosmopolitan imperative pushes global society toward an ideal of mutuality that was largely absent in the past, when it was taken for granted that it was solely the migratory or the minority or dominated cultural group that was changed, that is, for all intents and purposes, culturally colonized, by the dominant majority. Cosmopolitanism is not at all equivalent to inverse or reverse colonization. It requires a whole new perspective. It requires that all cultures, all modernities, notwithstanding their variation, be equally present to one another. It is not about triumphalism but humility in the face of diverse experiences and how they should be interpreted.

GLOBAL CONSUMER CULTURE

Though there are significant differences in how different societies experience modernity and in the extent to which they institutionalize respect for human rights, one point of convergence across the world is the appearance of shared cultural, and specifically, consumer icons (e.g., Apple, Coca-Cola, Abercrombie & Fitch). The "pooling of knowledge" via the Internet and social media is one of the main engines of cultural globalization (Giddens 1990: 76). One way of thinking about the impact of the global pooling of information – whether stock prices or celebrity gossip – and of the culture it transmits, is the concept of **unicity**, introduced by Roland

Robertson (1992). He argues: "Globalization has to do with the movement of the world as a whole in the direction of unicity – meaning oneness of the world as a single sociocultural place" (Robertson 2005: 348). The concept seeks to convey the multiple interconnectedness of individuals, places, experiences, ideas, and institutions in a globalized society; but as he points out it is not to be confused with global societal integration or unification. He acknowledges, moreover, that unicity is a fuzzy concept insofar as there are no criteria for deciding when it has been achieved (2005: 348).

CULTURAL HOMOGENIZATION

Oneness of culture has long been demarcated by a community's shared symbols and the shared meanings given to those symbols (see Durkheim, chapter 2). As sociologists are well aware today, the meanings given to any specific symbol can vary considerably within a given community or societal context. Nonetheless, a oneness of global culture is conveyed by the world's shared recognition of consumer icons and pop cultural figures (e.g., Bob Marley).

The golden arches – the McDonald's sign that greets us in Galway, Paris, Seattle, Liverpool, Shanghai, Perth, or Dubai – is a centerpiece of a shared global vocabulary that transcends national languages and local accents. It is a "global icon" (Ritzer 2000: 1–7). The **McDonaldization** of society, as phrased by George Ritzer (2000), captures the convergence and homogenization of culture across the globe, notwithstanding the simultaneous significance of local cultural differences. McDonald's offers the world a standardized cultural experience (Ritzer 2000: 22–26); its Big Mac tastes more or less the same no matter where we buy it. But McDonald's also bows to cultural differences. Even though some of its local adaptations may be driven, as Sklair (2002: 185–186) contends, by "commercial opportunism," it nonetheless adjusts its menu and advertising to enhance its appeal to local-national consumers. At McDonald's restaurants in Australia, for example, you can have a lamb burger, reflecting the dominance of sheep farming and lamb cuisine in Australia and New Zealand, whereas in India the menu is modified to be beef free, reflecting the Hindu religion's prohibition on eating beef. Local adaptations also attest to the continuing salience of gender inequality. In Riyadh, Saudi Arabia, for example, McDonald's has separate sections for men and for completely covered women, a regional and political practice that stands immune to the global diffusion of ideas about gender equality.

Figure 15.3   Cultural globalization often means cultural homogenization. The ideal for many Asian women is a Caucasian face, a standard of beauty promoted by the cosmetics industry globally, as advertised by Chanel in Seoul, South Korea. Photo courtesy of Chulsoo Kim.

The ubiquity of the golden arches – McDonald's is present in 119 countries – underscores that cultural globalization is especially apparent in consumption. The fact that it and other American brands (e.g., Nike, Abercrombie & Fitch), are well known beyond American borders might be seen as simply an expansion of American **cultural imperialism**. This concept captures the one-way flow of American ideas and products to the rest of the world; it gained prominence in the post-World War II decades with the surging global popularity of Disney characters, Coca-Cola, and other American cultural icons and products (e.g., Tunstall 1977). Today, however, the one-way flow of American culture overseas is tempered somewhat by the indigenous development of cultural industries in, for example, India, Mexico, and Brazil; even though they tend to imitate American movies and soap operas, and the locally produced programs are consumed primarily by their home-country residents rather than by more globally dispersed audiences (Sklair 2002). The one-way flow is also tempered by the greater global visibility of non-American shops and brands – Louis Vuitton, Prada, Chanel – in affluent cities and urban pockets around the world, and the general availability of a greater array of everyday "ethnic" foods, propelled in part by global migration patterns. Global consumer trends are also driven, as Sklair (2002) underscores, by transnational advertising agencies, which actively promote the first world (especially Americanized) consumer lifestyle in the third world. Given the extensive promotion of cigarettes and other products considered unhealthy in the West (Sklair 2002), it is not surprising that a recent World Health Organization (WHO) report documents a soaring increase in cigarette sales in poor and middle-income countries, a trend that coincides with the implementation of smoking bans in bars, restaurants, and other public places in Europe and the US. In line with a Marxist–critical theory analysis of the media-advertising industry (see chapter 5), Sklair notes that the consumer culture promoted in third world countries sharply contrasts with the everyday material existence of the people living there, an existence which for many borders on starvation. He thus suggests that we "pause to distinguish the effects of consumerism in societies where affluence is the norm (though even here some people may be without the necessities of life) and societies where poverty is the norm (though some people may be very affluent)" (2002: 187).

EVERYDAY CULTURAL REMIX

One of the characteristics of everyday culture today is the mixing together of fragments of many different things – the **remix** splicing of songs, video clips, photos, and images that come from multiple and varied sources, traditions, and eras. Remix opens up all kinds of possibilities and gives us freedom to mix and match all kinds of everything in all kinds of ways. One effect of this, however, is that at times it is hard to decipher what is real; what is the original, and what is simulated; what is artificially created and imposed on the original; what is the remix, and what exactly has been mixed. Thus remix, with its blending of incoherent or dissociated and disembedded bits and pieces, exemplifies the decentering and fluidity of our digitalized age (e.g., Bauman 2000; Giddens 1991).

Beyond music and art, we see mixed and remixed fragments in all sorts of places, and especially in the consumer images we encounter every day. They bombard us with multiple possibilities, multiple simultaneous desires and imaginings. The neo-Marxist cultural theorist **Fredric Jameson** argues that our current era is one in which commodities, and the process of commodification, are all encompassing. Everything, he argues, including the most banal, the most natural, and the most sacred of things, is eyed with a view toward wondering how it can be commodified, that is, how it can be used for economic gain. The "sphere of commodities" seems infinite, as we witness "a quantum leap in … the **'aestheticization' of reality** (… a prodigious exhilaration with the new order of things, a commodity rush, our 'representations' of things tending to arouse an enthusiasm and a mood swing not necessarily inspired by the things themselves)." Hence, what we are witnessing and participating in "is the consumption of **sheer commodification** as a process" (Jameson 1991: ix–x).

The "aestheticization of reality" is a difficult phrase. But we can understand it as referring essentially to the unabashed packaging and explicit re-presentation of something ordinary and real as something spectacular ("aesthetic" is another word for art/artistic sensibility). It is the culturing or the remaking – the "beautifying" – of some ordinary element of reality – a particular thing, place, or idea – into a commodity to be sold for profit and celebrated and consumed in its newly cultured form, as a cultural package. With clear reference to Marx's discussion of commodity fetishism (see chapter 1) and critical theorists' focus on the entanglement of culture and economics (see chapter 5), Jameson notes that with the aestheticization of reality, the cultural and the economic "collapse back into one another and say the same thing" (Jameson 1991: xxi).

BIOGRAPHICAL NOTE

Fredric Jameson was born in Cleveland, Ohio, in 1934. He was educated at Haverford College, Pennsylvania, and Yale University, where he completed a doctorate in philosophy. He has written extensively on Marxism and postmodernism, and is currently professor of comparative literature and director of the Duke Center for Critical Theory at Duke University.

For Jameson, the profit logic of capitalism is essentially "the cultural logic of late capitalism" (the title of his book). The equation of economic profit with the images and things that comprise everyday culture produces a commodity rush: it is the commodification of something that previously we did not think of as a commodity, but as something else; as something that had its own existence independent of our consumption. For example, the Olympics is not simply a sporting event, a celebration of athletic prowess; it is also a branding opportunity, an event or a visual-cultural text by which to market and sell commodities. This includes the copyrighted branding of the Olympics symbol itself (by the International Olympic Committee [IOC]), and the selling of the commercial rights so that only its sponsoring companies (e.g., Coca-Cola) and not some local merchant can make money from even playfully using the Olympics symbol. Thus during the London Olympics (in 2012), a butcher in England was told that he could not place sausages in his shop window that he had assembled into a shape mimicking the five rings of the Olympics symbol; his creative and humorous act infringed on the Olympics brand, and the right of the IOC to make profit from it. The commodification of the Olympics also includes the commodification of gold-medal and other winning athletes: Their bodies are used (and paid) to wear and promote the coveted brands licensed by the IOC, and in the process adding to the allure of the Olympics, its array of commodities, the specific brands featured, and the athletes' bodies. "Shopping is not a sport on the Olympic programme," winks a sign outside the entrance to the gift shop at the Olympics museum in Lausanne, Switzerland. But it certainly is an everyday sport and one promoted by the Olympics! In short, we live in a time of sheer commodification; everything can be packaged (see Topic 15.5). Thus,

> Everything can now be a text ... (daily life, the body, political representations), while objects that were formerly "works" can now be reread as immense ensembles or systems of texts of various kinds, superimposed on each other by way of the various intertextualities, successions of fragments, or ... sheer process (henceforth called textual production or textualization). (Jameson 1991: 77)

(On commodified bodies, see also chapter 12 on "Culture and the New Racism.")

Topic 15.5   Smart water: Liquid gold

Water, that most natural and flowing of resources is commodified, packaged into different types and brands, and sold for profit. The global market for bottled water has grown annually by 9 percent in recent years and is worth $147 billion. No wonder *The Economist* (2017a) calls it "liquid gold." Sales and consumption of bottled water in the US, for example, increased from approx. 28 gallons per person in 2006 to 40 gallons per person in 2016. Though it is a natural resource, a raw material that does not need to be "produced" or manufactured, bottled water is increasingly marketed as sourced from exotic places and packaged as a luxury product. A bottle of Svalbardi, sourced from Norwegian icebergs that are up to 4,000 years old, costs 80 pounds sterling ($99) at Harrods upscale department store in London. Perrier and Evian are also well-known premium brands, with Evian using the tag "Live young." And Coca-Cola, with the help of Jennifer Aniston (one of Hollywood's highest paid actresses), advertises "inspirational" SmartWater for successful people.

JEAN BAUDRILLARD: THE AESTHETICIZATION OF REALITY

The process of textualization or commodification is highly visible in Las Vegas – in the *production* of a "lavish Las Vegas." What is exciting about Las Vegas is the seemingly endless possibilities and redefinitions that it offers. We can, as an advertisement for the Venetian hotel tells us: "Experience Venice in Vegas – Only at the Venetian. Discover the spirit and passion of Venice at the world's largest four-star and four-diamond resort hotel. Enjoy Venezia, our hotel within a hotel … as grand as Venice itself." "Venezia," moreover, is copyrighted as a commodity trademark; the hotel owns the name; it has

Figure 15.4   In Las Vegas, newly built, lavish replicas of unique world-famous sites dazzle us. They prompt us to wonder which one is true, more real, more impressive – the original or its recreated spectacle? Source: © Kim Steele/Photographers Choice RF/Getty Images.

bought and paid for Venezia/Venice. Las Vegas has taken the Real – that is, Venice (Italy) – as well as other real places and real, historically significant monuments (e.g., the Eiffel Tower, the Great Sphinx) and recreated them lavishly for us to enjoy, to consume in Las Vegas. We do not need to visit and experience the (real?) Venice in Venice. In Las Vegas, the lavishly recreated world tourist sites are more real, that is, more sumptuous, than the original; they are better than real.

In other words, in contemporary culture, as **Jean Baudrillard** argues, the **simulacra** – the simulated, lavishly imagined consumer realities – are what is real, and what they produce in fact is a **hyperreality**. In this view, spectacle, and whatever things (kitchens, bodies), places, events (war, political campaigns), or values (e.g., freedom) we choose to make spectacular become the reality. Writing in the late 1980s before the accelerated expansion of global capitalism and global consumerism, Baudrillard argued that hyperreality is especially apparent in America:

> America is neither dream nor reality. It is hyperreality. It is a hyperreality because it is a utopia which has behaved from the very beginning as though it were already achieved. Everything here [in the US] is real and pragmatic, and yet it is all the stuff of dreams too. (Baudrillard 1991: 28)

BIOGRAPHICAL NOTE

Jean Baudrillard was born in Reims, France in 1929. He studied sociology at the University of the Sorbonne in Paris and subsequently held a faculty position at the University of Paris. He was active in the French student protest movements of the 1960s and maintained a neo-Marxist critical disposition throughout his life. He wrote several books and newspaper commentaries analyzing the centrality of consumption as a signifier of wealth and coolness in contemporary Western and global society. He died in Paris in 2007.

Las Vegas crystallizes the subversion of order that we experience in dreams, but does so in a more intense, accelerated, and fluid way. It is an action-packed, free-flowing blurring, and remixing of odd fragments of the real and the re-created. As the hedonistic "entertainment capital of the world" ("What happens in Vegas stays in Vegas"), it mixes old-fashioned gambling fruit-machines and high-end poker tables. It mixes gambling culture, pop culture, and high culture – on display at the Guggenheim Heritage Museum (at the Venetian) and public art works by highly renowned contemporary artists and designers (on show at the spectacular Bellagio hotel). It also mixes in a diverse array of high-end restaurants; and "sumptuous spas" whose "new aesthetic based on Zen philosophies, boasts a variety of distinct treatments from Egyptian, Indonesian, Thai, Indian, Balinese, and native American traditions." The simultaneous co-occurrence of all these diverse fragments in a simulated hyperreality stimulates and feeds into our longing for sheer commodification.

All of these amenities – commodities – are not simply for sale; they "have become a key offering in the city's lavish new lifestyle." In today's culture of consumption, it is not just individuals and groups who have lifestyles (see Weber, chapter 3; Bourdieu, chapter 13); cities and suburbs and villages do too. Dubai is another example of the lifestyle city, a city in the desert that has manufactured itself into a spectacular global metropolis, one that has, among other things, indoor ski slopes.

This is the aestheticization of reality, the aestheticization of history and of culture. We commodify and repackage historic cities, villages, mills, and cathedrals into something spectacular; we convert the original thing, with its already interesting history, into an even more intriguing, Disney-like theme park. And in many instances, it seems, the commodified version of the real is (or may be) better, more fun, more exhilarating, more dazzling, more sumptuous than the original.

> **Topic 15.6**   Dubai: The aesthetic commodification of culture and place
>
> Dubai, an old, historically rich Muslim town, markets itself today as: "A futuristic city-state with imaginative and unusual landmarks, from man-made islands in the shape of a map of the world, to Dubailand, a massive theme-park development. Yet Dubai's new incarnation as an avant-garde frontier has only made its history all the more intriguing." "Tradition deliberately shines through the innovative designs of the construction boom. The Fairmont Dubai … is modeled after an Arabic wind tower … The Raffles Dubai is shaped like a pyramid, one of the earliest desert marvels, now updated as a hotel with a champagne bar." (These quotes are from advertisements for Dubai printed in *The New Yorker*, October 22, 2007; and *The New Yorker*, May 12, 2008.)

COMMODIFICATION AND SIMULATION

Baudrillard is highly critical of cultural commodification and what he sees as the excesses of consumption. He argues that it is as if images – signs of consumption – are more real, more glossy, more culturally significant than any given reality; it is the recreation or simulation of Dubai as a Disney-like Dubailand that is *the* reality. Thus "It is Disneyland that is authentic [in America]" (1991: 104), and we seek to make all realities, including the everyday banality of life in the suburbs, a Disney-like paradise (1991: 84–87, 98). We see community simulated in the bucolic names given to new housing developments and gated communities; having tampered with, if not destroyed, an existing natural habitat (by encroaching on an expanse of land, forestation, or dunes) to build the housing development, they then simulate the feelings of pastoral or coastal bliss by using signs – literally street signs - whose names are codes invoking a Paradise-like reality – Sycamore Drive, Willow Road, Palm Cove, etc.

This simulated, beautified reality, Baudrillard contends, eludes the pursuit of substance; that is, of living a meaningful life that is not so entwined with and dependent on the "orgy" of lavish consumption and consumer excess (Baudrillard 1991: 30–31). He argues that the overvaluing of "mind-blowing consumption" for the sheer sake of consumption "is America's problem and, through America, it has become the whole world's problem" (1991: 30–31). Thus, the pursuit of "endless consumption," and not the expansion of economic equality, becomes the high priority shared across the globe (1991: 19, 87); this is evident, for example, in India, where surplus wealth and affluent consumption coexist right alongside abject poverty (see Topic 14.2, chapter 14). For Baudrillard, the real realities of poverty get displaced by the hyperreality of lavish consumption; commodification blurs the line between what is real and what is illusory.

ANTHONY GIDDENS: DISEMBEDDEDNESS AND DILEMMAS OF THE SELF

Commodification disembeds things and places from their real or original location and mixes them into a new reality in ways that dazzle but also disequilibrate us. What is the real, we ask, and where is it, really? Such uncertainties are part of contemporary experience. And they coexist with and amid the many other uncertainties and anxieties of global risk society. There are many formal (e.g., safe food certification) and informal ways (e.g., avoiding bars that play exceptionally loud music) for managing risk. These strategies may fall short, however, in our efforts to deal with anxieties and choices about the self as we navigate the fluidity and mobility of everyday life(e.g., Elliott and Urry 2010). Personal relationships are highly fluid as we move from one love interest to another, even as, like the characters

Figure 15.5   Simulated trees in the mall enhance the naturalness of the mall as an aesthetic and cultural experience, as well as conveying the illusion that shopping is as natural as nature itself. Source: Author.

in HBO's *Girls*, we may occasionally long for greater emotional attachment. In the e-economy, occupational stability and insurance and other benefits are no longer guaranteed. Indeed, the routines of work are themselves increasingly mobile; teleworking (working for a company or an employer from home), gives us greater flexibility and control over our work and family schedule, but it may also isolate us from our coworkers and the informal and formal conversations that can nurture friendship as well as work innovation. Moreover, the intense and continuous flow of the wide-ranging choices available to us, and what to like and what to dislike – whether friends, songs, photos, restaurants, videos, TV shows, interactive games, clothes, sneakers – instantly accessible at the touch of a smartphone, do not guarantee that we will make smart choices (even if we drink smart water!). In fact, they contribute to our anxiety about making a good choice. Weber's question: "What should we do and how should we live?" (see chapter 3) thus continues to be highly salient as we try to carve meaningful lives amid the flux of the current moment.

Giddens (1990, 1991) highlights the dilemmas of self-identity that become accentuated for individuals in a globalizing society. For many, globalization, and the Internet in particular, brings an expansion of possibilities for the self. These new opportunities are liberating in many ways, but they can also add to personal insecurity. What gives us self-security – the feeling of being "at home," on one's own stomping ground and knowing what's what – is neither tied to nor necessarily produced in our local space and time. This is all part of the lack of grounding, the disembeddedness, of contemporary society that Giddens argues may weaken our sense of ontological security, that is, our sense of internal self-security and our trust in the world and the people with whom we interact. Thus, he argues, the individual must negotiate some middle ground in carving out a flexible but coherent self amidst the **dilemmas of the self** we necessarily encounter.

We have to negotiate (1) between a *unified* and a *fragmentary* self; (2) between the *powerlessness* one might feel against the juggernaut of global forces, on the one hand, and on the other, the knowledge that you too are free to *appropriate* the latest technology and, for example, post your own YouTube video; (3) between the *authority* the Internet gives you to directly access and read commentaries on Marxism, or reviews of a new pizza restaurant, and the *uncertainty* you experience when you see that there are several contradictory views on any topic – how can you know what to think, do, or believe amidst these contrasting evaluations? And, finally, there is the dilemma of negotiating (4) between what is truly an authentic *personalized* experience for you, and what you embrace because it is marketed or *commodified* as the latest fad. (Do you need to be in therapy because of persisting interpersonal conflicts in your life, or because Nicole Richie and Paris Hilton are in therapy?)

How we resolve such self-dilemmas has implications for our everyday, social-psychological functioning as individuals and will also contribute to shaping the kind of society we try to foster. If globalization, as Sassen (2007) argues, creates new political opportunities toward building a more egalitarian society, and, as Giddens (2003) suggests, demands a deepening of democracy (see chapter 14), then it seems important for individuals to develop a sense of self that is not fragmented and diffuse, but can authoritatively commit to specific values or general policy proposals. This sort of commitment would itself require an appropriate sense of empowerment, one that is aware of, but not intimidated by, social forces, such as thinking of globalization as a juggernaut against which one is helpless (cf. Giddens 2003). Instead, contemporary society – a contrite modernity with problems but also possibilities for their transformation - requires the active participation of individuals and groups in the public sphere; in local, national, and transnational forums where they debate the issues and explore action strategies to mitigate the problems at hand (e.g., global warming).

SUMMARY

This chapter reviewed different perspectives on modernity and its legacy, and introduced new concepts outlined as a way to make sense of changing world society(ies). There is a consensus that modernity has not eventuated quite as assumed by Enlightenment and modernization theorists who viewed it as the engine of economic prosperity, democratic political participation, and social equality. Theorists vary in the range of perspectives they offer, however, as to what to do with or about modernity. Habermas uses the notion of contrite modernity to emphasize a way forward from the current crises of modernity, notwithstanding the challenges this entails. Other scholars place emphasis on the multiplicity of ways in which different societies experience modernity. Scholars also emphasize the globalization of risk and the global expansion of human rights as well as the imperative to think differently about citizenship in a cosmopolitical world. Notwithstanding variation in how modernity has evolved across different societies, consumer culture is a point of convergence across many diverse countries. Although the increasing commodification of everyday culture may distract us from some of our social problems and personal anxieties, it may also accentuate the dilemmas of the self and the challenge of social inclusion in a complex world.

POINTS TO REMEMBER

- The promises, progress, and contours of modernity are increasingly being scrutinized in an attempt to reassess the nature of modernity/modernities and their implications
- The reassessment of modernity has spawned a number of reappraisals and new constructs that aim to capture current social realities: contrite modernity, multiple modernities, first modernity, second modernity, cosmopolitan modernity
- Habermas argues that a contrite modernity can be revitalized through the appropriation of moderate religion into reasoned public discourse
- The notion of multiple modernities draws attention to the fact there are many different pathways to and experiences of modernity (Eisenstadt)
- The structures and principles of modernity are not only institutionalized in different ways in different societies, but there can also be different types of, and structural discontinuities within, modernity (e.g., China, South Korea)
- Contemporary society is marked by the expansion of risk to such an extent that our current era can be described as "risk society" (Beck)
- Risk and its consequences and uncertainties are universal, prevalent across socioeconomic classes and across world society(ies)

- Reflexive modernization (e.g., awareness of the problems of modernity and the crafting of new ways to avoid or fix them) is such that countries can transition to second modernity without having undergone first modernity
- All societies today, irrespective of their modernity trajectory, can be construed as cosmopolitan
- Cosmopolitan modernity requires a new global awareness of, and global interconnectedness to deal with, global risks
- Globalization has accelerated the expansion of human rights while also challenging conceptually narrow notions of citizenship and social inclusivity
- Cosmopolitan citizenship requires an openness to the whole world as a social-moral unit and requires us to develop an empathic understanding of and engagement with culturally-different others
- Consumer culture anchors global culture; consumer icons, products, and experiences are standardized across societies that may otherwise differ
- Contemporary everyday culture celebrates the remix of disparate and contradictory elements
- The repackaging and commodification of the Real into simulated and hyperreal consumer realities is a dominant strand in contemporary culture (e.g., Las Vegas)
- Conflicting dilemmas of the self emerge as a result of the impact of disembedding forces (e.g., Internet, digitalized media) and mobilities on everyday life.

GLOSSARY

aestheticization of reality the cultural packaging and re-presentation of something ordinary as a commodified, spectacular thing for sale in the market.

compressed modernity the rapid industrialization, urbanization, and democratization of any given traditional society/country (e.g., South Korea) in a short (compressed) time interval; typically driven by proactive national economic development policies.

contrite modernity recognition that modernity has derailed from its intended path of economic, political, and social progress and is open to self-correction and revitalization.

cosmopolitan imperatives arise because of global risks (e.g., nuclear threats, financial crisis, global warming) across world society and require global awareness and global political alliances and solutions.

cosmopolitan modernity the idea that contemporary society(ies), Western and non-Western alike, are mutually entangled and interconnected and internalize one another's societal processes.

cultural imperialism the idea that the global distribution and sale of American-produced cultural content (e.g., movies, television shows, pop music, advertising, consumer ideology) constitutes a form of political-cultural control of other countries.

dilemmas of the self challenges encountered in negotiating a flexible yet coherent self amidst the many insecurities and opportunities confronting the individual in a globalizing, disembedded world.

empathy walls obstacles that impede a deep understanding of, and foster indifference or hostility toward, those who are different from us.

First Modernity refers to modernized societies characterized by the nation-state, industrial economy, scientific rationality, functional differentiation, and socially bound individualism.

flexible citizenship the idea that the rights of citizens can no longer be defined in a terms of a single national territory alone but must be broadened in recognition of the transnational flow of migrant workers and others across national and state boundaries.

hyperreality a glossy, lavish, cinematic, consumption driven, utopian reality dominated by spectacle (e.g., Las Vegas).

McDonaldization the thesis that cultural icons, products, and standards are increasingly similar across the world.

methodological nationalism criticism that sociologists theorize about and conduct research on their own national society and generalize from that specific society to society in general.

multiple modernities recognition that different societies experience modernity in different ways; challenges the prevailing idea that Western modernity is the only form of modernity.

postsecular society refers to the continuing public relevance of religion in and to secularized societies; challenges the secular presumption that religion necessarily declines or disappears with modernization; postsecularity requires mutual reflexivity and engagement between religious and secular actors.

reflexive modernization the process whereby societies critically examine the legacy of modernization (in one's own or other countries) and deliberately and selectively develop and implement structures and processes that seek to avoid the ills of modernization while creating a prosperous and sustainable society.

remix blending and reworking of several original sounds, themes, or ideas into a new reality.

risk society the global expansion, awareness, and impact of risk and of the insecurities and anxieties it produces in society.

Second Modernity demarcates societies that have reflexively modernized; cosmopolitan modernity.

sheer commodification the cultural or lifestyle packaging of everyday things, places, or experiences as images and commodities purely for the purpose of promoting consumption for the sake of consumption.

simulacra things that are glossy, polished representations and commodified imaginings of other things/realities; the simulated product/representation assumes a more real, more beautiful, more intense, more cinematic presence than the original.

unicity the idea that as a result of globalization processes, the world as a whole is moving toward sociocultural oneness.

QUESTIONS FOR REVIEW

1   Why are scholars reassessing modernity and its consequences? In your opinion, based on experiences in your own country or locality, is this reassessment necessary?

2   How would you summarize what is entailed by the notion of "multiple modernities"? How does this idea complicate what Talcott Parsons (see chapter 4), has argued about modernization? Where do we see evidence of different modernity pathways?

3   How is modernity affecting China and South Korea? How do their respective experiences of modernity vary from modernity as experienced in the West?

4   What are some of the main features of cultural globalization? To what extent are they visible in your home town? To what extent does global consumerism obscure, dilute, and/or exacerbate global risk?

5   What does cosmopolitanism entail, and what challenges and possibilities does it present to human society? And to you personally?

REFERENCES

Agus, David. 2013. "The Outrageous Cost of a Gene Test." *New York Times* (May 21): opinion editorial, p. A21.

Austen, Ian. 2015. "Canada Welcomes New Arrivals from Syria." *New York Times* (December 12), p. A4.

Baudrillard, Jean. 1991. *America*. 4th edition. London: Verso.

Bauman, Zygmunt. 2000. *Liquid Modernity*. Cambridge: Polity.

Beck, Ulrich. 1992. *Risk Society: Towards a New Modernity*. London: Sage.

Beck, Ulrich, and Edgar Grande. 2010. "Varieties of Second Modernity: The Cosmopolitan Turn in Social and Political Theory Research." *British Journal of Sociology* 61(3): 409–443.

Beck, Ulrich, and Nathan Sznaider. 2012. "New Cosmopolitanism in the Social Sciences." Pp. 635–652 in Bryan Turner, ed. *The Routledge International Handbook of Globalization Studies*. Abingdon, UK: Routledge.

Boltanski, Luc. 1999. *Distant Suffering: Morality, Media and Politics*. New York: Cambridge University Press.

Bradsher, Keith, and Charles Duhigg. 2012. "Signs of Changes Taking Hold in Electronics Factories in China." *New York Times* (December 27), pp. A1, 10, 11.

Chang Kyung-Sup. 2010. "The Second Modern Condition? Compressed Modernity as Internalized Reflexive Cosmopolitization." *British Journal of Sociology* 61(3): 444–464.

Chang Kyung-Sup and Song Min-Young. 2010. "The Stranded Individualizer under Compressed Modernity: South Korean Women in Individualization without Individualism." *British Journal of Sociology* 61(3): 539–564.

Dillon, Michele. 1993. *Debating Divorce: Moral Conflict in Ireland*. Lexington, KY: University Press of Kentucky.

Dillon, Michele. 2012. "Jürgen Habermas and the Post-Secular Appropriation of Religion: A Sociological Critique." Pp. 249–278 in Philip Gorski, David Kim, John Torpey, and Jonathan Van Antwerpen, eds. *Probing the Post-Secular*. New York: New York University Press/Social Science Research Council.

Dillon, Michele. 2018. *Postsecular Catholicism*. New York: Oxford University Press.

Economist. 2016. "Artificial Intelligence: Special Report." (June 25), pp. 3–16.

Economist. 2017a. "Liquid Gold." (March 25).

Economist. 2017b. "How to Cope with Floods." (September 2), p. 9.

Eisenstadt, S.N. 1973. *Tradition, Change, and Modernity*. Malabar, FL: Krieger.

Eisenstadt, S.N. 2000. "Multiple Modernities." *Daedalus* (Winter): 1–29.

Elliott, Anthony, and John Urry. 2010. *Mobile Lives*. New York: Routledge.

Giddens, Anthony. 1990. *The Consequences of Modernity*. Stanford, CA: Stanford University Press.

Giddens, Anthony. 1991. *Modernity and Self-Identity: Self and Society in the Late Modern Age*. Stanford, CA: Stanford University Press.

Giddens, Anthony. 2003. *Runaway World: How Globalization Is Reshaping our Lives*. New York: Routledge.

Gilroy, Paul. 2010. *Darker Than Blue*. Cambridge, MA: Harvard University Press.

Habermas, Jürgen. 2001. *The Postnational Constellation*. Cambridge, MA: MIT Press.

Habermas, Jürgen. 2006. In Virgil Nemoianu, "The Church and the Secular Establishment: A Philosophical Dialog between Joseph Ratzinger and Jürgen Habermas." *Logos* 9: 17–42.

Habermas, Jürgen. 2008. "Notes on Post-Secular Society." *New Perspectives Quarterly* 25(4): 17–29.

Habermas, Jürgen. 2010. *An Awareness of What Is Missing: Faith and Reason in a Post-Secular Age*. London: Polity.

Heller, Nathan. 2017. "The Gig is Up: Many Liberals Have Embraced the Sharing Economy. But Can They Survive It?" *New Yorker* (May 15), pp. 52–63.

Hochschild, Arlie. 2016. *Strangers in Their Own Land: Anger and Mourning on the American Right*. New York: New Press.

Hochschild, Arlie, and Michael Hout. 2017. "Was Trump a Meteor or a Volcano? Racial Resentment, Immigration, and the Environment Built Up as Strong Predictors of Whites' Votes Before the U.S. 2016 Presidential Election." Paper presented at the American Sociological Association Annual Meeting (August), Montreal.

Hsu, Hua. 2017. "Stir It Up: The Battle over Bob Marley." *New Yorker* (July 24), pp. 56–61.

Jameson, Fredric. 1991. *Postmodernism or the Cultural Logic of Late Capitalism*. Durham, NC: Duke University Press.

Johnson, Ian. 2012. "Wary of Future, Professionals Leave China in Record Numbers." *New York Times* (November 1), pp. A1, 3

Leubsdorf, Ben. 2017. "Driverless Cars May Alter 1 in 9 Jobs." *Wall Street Journal* (August 15), p. A2.

Marshall, Thomas. 1950. *Citizenship and Social Class*. Cambridge: Cambridge University Press.

OECD. 2017. *International Migration Outlook 2017*. Paris: OECD. https://data.oecd.org/migration/foreign-born-population.htm.

Ong, Aihwa. 1999. *Flexible Citizenship: The Cultural Logics of Transnationality*. Durham, NC: Duke University Press.

Porter, Eduardo. 2015. "A Migration Juggernaut Is Headed for Europe." *New York Times* (September 16), pp. B1, 7.

Ritzer, George. 2000. *The McDonaldization of Society*. Thousand Oaks, CA: Pine Forge Press.

Robertson, Roland. 1992. *Globalization: Social Theory and Global Culture*. London: Sage.

Robertson, Roland. 2005. "Globalization: Sociology and Cross-Disciplinarity." Pp. 345–366 in Craig Calhoun, Chris Rojek, and Bryan Turner, eds. *The Sage Handbook of Sociology*. Thousand Oaks, CA: Sage.

Sassen, Saskia. 2007. *A Sociology of Globalization*. New York: Norton.

Sikkink, Kathryn. 2011. *The Justice Cascade: How Human Rights Prosecutions Are Changing World Politics*. New York: Norton.

Sklair, Leslie. 2002. *Globalization: Capitalism and Its Alternatives*. Oxford: Oxford University Press.

Therborn, Goran. 1995. "Routes to/through Modernity." Pp. 124–139 in Mike Featherstone, Scott Lash, and Roland Robertson, eds. *Global Modernities*. Thousand Oaks, CA: Sage.

Tunstall, Jeremy. 1977. *The Media Are American*. New York: Columbia University Press.

Turkewitz, Julie, and Audra Burch. 2017. "Storm with 'No Boundaries' Took Aim at Rich and Poor Alike." *New York Times* (August 31).

Wong, Edward. 2016. "Chinese Leader's News Flash: Journalists Must Serve Party." *New York Times* (February 23), pp. A1, 8.

Yan, Yunxiang. 2010. "The Chinese Path to Individualization." *British Journal of Sociology* 61(3): 489–512.

GLOSSARY

accomplishment of social reality the idea that social reality does not have a pregiven objective order but needs to be achieved on an ongoing basis by societal members.

accounts how individuals categorize events, experiences, and everyday reality such that their accounts produce an ordered sequential reality that makes sense and is credible in a given societal context.

achievement versus ascription one of Parsons's five patterned value-orientations whereby, for example, modern society emphasizes achievement rather than ascriptive (e.g., inherited status) criteria.

actant the understanding in actor–network theory (ANT) that all human actors and nonhuman things (e.g., animals, avatars, physical objects, scientific discoveries) are coequal, agential social entities.

action–reward/punishment orientation behavior as motivated by the individual's perception of its likely rewards and punishments.

activist knowledge knowledge generated from within oppressed groups' lived experiences; empowers individuals to resist and take action against their oppression.

actors (1) general – any individual, collective, or institutional (e.g., the state) social unit engaged in social action. (2) dramaturgical – individuals performing roles.

adaptation economic function (or institutional subsystem) necessary in all societies and societal subunits (Parsons).

administered world bureaucratic-state regulation and control diminishing the political autonomy of individuals and the public sphere.

aesthetic disposition the class-inculcated attitude that allows and requires the upper class to admire art, clothes, etc., for style rather than practical function.

aestheticization of reality the cultural packaging and representation of something ordinary as a commodified, spectacular thing for sale in the market.

affirmative action laws and public policies that seek to redress historical discrimination against blacks and other minority groups in access to education, voting, jobs, housing.

agency individuals, groups, and other collectivities exerting autonomy in the face of social institutions, social structures, and cultural expectations.

alienated labor the objective result of the economic and social organization of capitalist production (e.g., division of labor): (a) alienation from products produced Wage-workers are alienated from the product of their labor; a worker's labor power is owned by the capitalist, and consequently the products of the worker's labor belong not to the worker but to the capitalist who profits from them. (b) alienation within the production

Introduction to Sociological Theory: Theorists, Concepts, and Their Applicability to the Twenty-First Century,
Third Edition. Michele Dillon.
© 2020 John Wiley & Sons Ltd. Published 2020 by John Wiley & Sons Ltd.
Companion website: www.wiley.com/go/dillon

process Wage-workers are actively alienated by the production process; labor is not for the worker an end in itself, freely chosen, but coerced by and performed for the capitalist; the worker is an object in the production process. (c) alienation of workers from their species being By being reduced to their use-value (capitalist profit), workers are estranged from the creativity and higher consciousness that distinguish humans from animals. (d) alienation of individuals from one another The competitive production process and workplace demands alienate individuals from others.

alternative sociology starts from the lived experiences and the standpoint of women and other minority groups rather than claiming an objectivity that largely cloaks male-centered knowledge; leads to the empowerment of women and men.

altruistic suicide results from tightly regulated social conditions in which the loss of close comrades, or an individual's loss of honor in the community, makes suicide obligatory.

analytical Marxism use of social scientific methods to highlight how the interest maximization strategies of individual and collective rational actors affect class formation, exploitation, and class alliances.

androcentric culture institutional practices and ideology whereby maleness defines humanity and the social reality of men and women.

anomic suicide results when society experiences a major disruption that uproots the established norms.

antiglobalization movement broad array of local and transnational social movement organizations, community groups, and political activists opposing various aspects of globalization.

apartheid system of laws and public policies that maintain discriminatory practices against blacks (e.g., white settlers in South Africa against indigenous blacks).

appearance signals indicating the individual's social statuses and "temporary ritual state" (e.g., a nurse dressed for work).

asceticism avoidance of emotion and spontaneous enjoyment as demonstrated by the disciplined, methodical frugality and sobriety of the early Calvinists.

audience individuals who witness our role performance and for whom we perform.

authority structures varied sources of legitimation, authority, or power in modern society; possible sources of ongoing normal conflict.

autopoiesis process in biology whereby living systems self-regulate and so too, according to Luhmann, social systems.

background knowledge an individual's stock of previous experiences and knowledge of reality; affects how they categorize and evaluate current experiences.

backstage staging area for front-region behavior, where actors do the preparatory work to ensure a successful performance.

behavior conditioning human behavior as determined (conditioned) as a function of previous experience of, and/or perceived future, rewards and punishments.

behaviorism strand in psychology emphasizing that humans behave in predictable ways in particular situations.

bifurcation of consciousness knowledge that emerges from the contradictory realities women experience because of the split between objectified knowledge and the public world of work, etc., and women's everyday, localized experiences (in the home, as mothers, etc.).

bio-power the institutional use of bodies and body practices for purposes of political, administrative, and economic control.

black cultural democracy the idea that in black communities, men and women need to create equality in their social relationships with other blacks whom they demean (e.g., women, LGBT individuals).

black feminist thought knowledge voiced by black women from within their lived experiences and across the different sites of their everyday reality.

black underclass segment of the black community experiencing persistent chronic poverty.

black women's standpoint the common experiences that all African-American women share as a result of being black women in a society that denigrates women of African descent.

body idiom information conveyed through body language/display.

bourgeoisie the capitalist class; owners of capital and of the means of production, who stand in a position of domination over the proletariat (the wage-workers).

breaching experiments designed to disrupt a particular micro-social reality in order to illustrate the fragility that underlies the order and routines of everyday reality.

bureaucracy formal organizational structure characterized by rationality, legal authority, hierarchy, credentialed and certified expertise, and impersonal rules and procedures.

calling intrinsically felt obligation toward work; work valued as its own reward, an opportunity to glorify God.

Calvinism theology derived from John Calvin; emphasis on the lone individual whose afterlife is already predestined at birth by God.

canon established body of core knowledge/ideas in a given field of study.

capital money and other (large-scale) privately owned resources (e.g., oil wells, land) used in the production of commodities whose sale accumulates profit for the capitalist.

capitalism a historically specific way of organizing commodity production; produces profit for the owners of the means of production (e.g., factories, land, oil wells, financial capital); based on structured inequality between capitalists and wage-laborers whose exploited labor power produces capitalist profit.

capitalist globalization emphasis that the current era of globalization represents one specific, historically dominant type or mode of production; that is, capitalist, not socialist, globalization.

capitalist world-system the historical emergence of the modern capitalist economy in sixteenth-century Europe.

celebrity mass media celebration of the public legitimacy and influence of actors and other media personalities irrespective of their credentials.

center–satellite the idea that some states/regions are dominant in (core to) world economic production whereas others are marginal or peripheral (e.g., the North–South divide).

charisma nonrational authority held by an individual who is perceived by others to have a special personal gift for leadership.

charismatic community group of individuals (disciples) who follow and defer to a charismatic individual's personal leadership authority.

Christianizing of secular society the thesis that Christian-derived values (e.g., Protestant individualism, the Golden Rule) penetrate the everyday culture and nonreligious institutional spheres of modern secular society.

church any community unified by sacred beliefs and ritual practices.

civil religion the civic-political symbols, ceremonies, and rituals that characterize society's public life and reaffirm its shared values.

civil society sphere of society mediating between individuals and the state, for example, informal groups, social movements, mass media.

civil sphere a sphere of activity with its own values (e.g., democracy, justice) and institutions (e.g., civic associations, social movements, popular media) focused on ongoing efforts to create an inclusive, just, and universally integrating solidarity in society (Alexander).

class individuals who share an objectively similar economic situation determined by property, income, and occupational resources.

class consciousness the group consciousness necessary if wage-workers (the proletariat) are to recognize that their individual exploitation is part and parcel of capitalism, which requires the exploitation of the labor power of all wage-workers (as a class) by the capitalist class in the production of profit.

class depoliticization growth in working-class affluence and consumerism reduces the (Marxist-assumed) class-based motivation to use the political process to protest against economic inequality.

class fraction differentiated, hierarchical subcomponents (e.g., the lower-middle class) of broadly defined social classes (e.g., the middle class); the economic and cultural capital of class fractions varies.

class polarization result of the increase in both extreme poverty and extreme affluence in all globalizing countries.

class relations unequal relations of capitalists and wage-workers to capital (and each other). Capitalists (who own the means of production used to produce capital/profit) are in a position of domination over wage-workers, who, in order to live, must sell their labor power to the capitalists.

classical theory the ideas, concepts, and intellectual framework outlined by the founders of sociology (Marx, Durkheim, Weber, Martineau).

collective conscience a society's collectively shared beliefs and sentiments; has authority over social conduct.

collective misrecognition immersion in a particular habitus or set of everyday practices whereby we (necessarily) fail to perceive the arbitrary, though highly determining ways in which those practices reproduce inequality.

collective representation the symbols and categories a society uses to denote its commonly shared, collective beliefs, values, interpretations, and meanings.

colonialism political control by an imperial power over a separate geographical area and its population (e.g., Great Britain over India and the Caribbean; Portugal over Brazil), and its construal of the colonized population as economically, culturally, legally, and biologically/racially inferior.

colonization of the lifeworld the idea that the state and economic corporations (including mass media) increasingly penetrate and dominate all aspects of everyday life.

commercialization of feeling the training, production, and control of human emotions for economic profit.

commodification of labor the process by which, like manufactured commodities, wage-workers' labor power is exchanged and traded on the market for a price (wages).

common-sense knowledge knowledge derived from individuals' everyday practices; what seems "natural" or obvious in their social environment.

communicative action the idea that social action should be determined by a rationally argued consensus driven by empirically grounded claims and rationally argued ethical norms rather than strategic partisan interests.

communicative rationality back-and-forth reasoned examination of the claims and counter-claims made by communication partners in a communicative exchange. The reasonableness of the arguments expressed rather than the power or social status of the communication partners determines the communicative outcome.

communism envisioned by Marx as the final phase in the evolution of history, whereby capitalism would be overthrown by proletarian class revolution, resulting in a society wherein the division of labor, private property, and profit would no longer exist.

compressed modernity the rapid industrialization, urbanization, and democratization of any given traditional society/country (e.g., South Korea) in a short (compressed) time interval; typically driven by proactive national economic development policies.

concepts specific ideas about the social world defined and elaborated by a given theorist/school of thought.

conceptual framework the relatively coherent and interrelated set of ideas or concepts that a given theorist or a given school of thought uses to elaborate a particular perspective on things; a particular way of looking at, framing, theorizing about, social life.

confession production of discourse as a result of the interrogation of the self (by the self or others, real and imagined), typically with regard to body practices.

conflict groups competing interest groups in society.

conformist individual who accepts cultural goals and institutionalized means toward their achievement.

constructionist view of sexuality the idea that sexuality and what it means to be gay varies across history and social context; contrasts with an essentialist, biological view.

contemporary theory the successor theories/ideas outlined to extend and engage with the classical theorizing of Marx, Durkheim, Weber, and Martineau.

contract society's legal regulation of the obligations it expects of individuals in their relations with one another; its regulatory force comes from society.

contradictory class locations employees, such as professionals, managers, and bureaucrats, whose objective location in the class-occupational structure as members neither of the capitalist nor of the proletarian class means that their economic interests are not *a priori* allied with any one particular class.

contrite modernity recognition that modernity has derailed from its intended path of economic, political, and social progress and is open to self-correction and revitalization.

controlling images demeaning images and representations of, for example, black women circulated by the largely white-controlled mass media and other social institutions.

conversation analysis detailed analysis of the specific, pragmatic steps in how language and speech are used in everyday conversation to create order.

conversation of gestures process by which our signals (or gestures) bring forth a meaningful response in another.

core states those at the center of world economic production (e.g., the US).

cosmopolitan imperatives arise because of global risks (e.g., nuclear threats, financial crisis, global warming) across world society and require global awareness and global political alliances and solutions.

cosmopolitan modernity the idea that contemporary society(ies), Western and non-Western alike, are mutually entangled and interconnected and internalize one another's societal processes.

crisis of raciology contemporary blurring of racial boundaries and of the economic and political meanings and implications of racial categories.

crisis (1) when the state or other social institutions are perceived as being structurally unable to respond to a particular societal problem due to limitations in how the structures themselves are constituted (Habermas). (2) idea that the current problems of the capitalist world-economy cannot be resolved within the framework of the capitalist world-system (Wallerstein).

critical theory theorists' critique of the one-sided, instrumental, strategic, or technical use of reason in democratic capitalist societies to advance economic, political, and cultural power and suppress critique of social institutions and social processes, rather than to increase freedom, social equality, and democratic participation. Critical theory highlights the irrational character of what society presents as rational; this perspective is most closely associated with theorists associated with the Frankfurt School.

cues verbal and nonverbal signs, signals, gestures, messages.

cultural capital familiarity and ease with (the legitimate) habits, knowledge, tastes, and style of everyday living; education is one institutional field that requires, transmits, produces, and reproduces cultural capital.

cultural competence possessing the appropriate family and social class background, knowledge, and taste to display (and acquire additional) cultural capital.

cultural goals objectives and values affirmed in a given society; e.g., economic success.

cultural identity the historically grounded origins of, and ongoing transformation in, a particular group's sense of who they are and their status vis-à-vis other cultural groups.

cultural imperialism the idea that the global distribution and sale of American-produced cultural content (e.g., movies, television shows, pop music, advertising, consumer ideology) constitute a form of political-cultural control of other countries.

cultural lag when societies that experience economic and social modernization experience a delay in adjusting their (traditional) values to accommodate change.

cultural system institutionalized norms, values, motivations, symbols, and beliefs (cultural resources).

cultural totalitarianism the repression of diversity in the expression of individual needs and opinions; accomplished by the restricted sameness of content and choices available in the economic, political, and cultural marketplace.

culture industry corporate economic control of the mass media and its emphasis on advertising and business rather than providing cultural content (e.g., ideas, story plots) that would challenge rather than bolster the status quo.

culture lines accentuation of the symbolic, cultural, and social (as opposed to biological or physical) differences between groups.

culture (1) beliefs, rituals, ideas, worldviews, and ways of doing things. Culture is socially structured, that is, individuals are socialized into a given culture and how to use it in everyday social action. (2) dispositions, tastes, evaluative judgments, and knowledge inculcated in and as a result of class-conditioned and embodied experiences (including but not limited to formal education) (Bourdieu).

decolonize sociology a new awareness in sociology that the discipline's history is entwined with colonialism and that its Western (and Northern) knowledge biases and practices need to be systematically rethought in ways that acknowledge its parochialism and incorporate non-Western (and Southern) knowledge, knowledge categories, and lived experiences

deepening of democracy the free flow and public accessibility of information as a result of the Internet and social media means that ordinary citizens have new resources with which to track the activities and decisions of political elites and to challenge the status quo.

definition of the situation socialization of individuals into a society's generalized expectations of behavior across an array of social settings (Thomas); crucial to how actors interpret and perform in a particular role-performance setting (Goffman).

democracy political structure derived from the ethos that because all individuals are endowed with reason and created equal they are entitled (and required) to participate in the political governance of their collective life in society.

democratization of conflict establishment of formally organized interest groups and of institutional mechanisms (e.g., labor courts, mediation panels) to regulate group conflicts.

denationalized class global workers (professionals/executives, government bureaucrats, and low-skilled service workers) necessary to the coordination and maintenance of the globalized financial and service infrastructure.

denationalized state a state that wields authority within and beyond its own national geographical territory and on globalization issues that implicate it and other nation-states.

dependence an underdeveloped or peripheral country's relation to a developed country due to the historical economic and structural inequalities between them.

development economic growth and related societal changes in previously undeveloped countries.

deviance the result of discrepancies between society's culturally approved goals and the institutional means toward their realization.

dialectic of Enlightenment the thesis that the ideas affirmed by the Enlightenment (e.g., the use of reason in the advancement of freedom, knowledge, and democracy) have been turned into their opposite (reason in the service of control, inequality, political passivity) by the instrumentally rational domination exerted by capitalist institutions (e.g., the state and financial, technological, and media companies).

dialectic of power and resistance ongoing conflicts (and changes) in society produced by group power inequalities and group resistance to those inequalities.

dialectical materialism the idea that historical change (i.e., material/economic change) is the result of conscious human activity emerging from and acting on the socially experienced inequalities and contradictions in historically conditioned (i.e., human-made) economic forces and relations.

dialectical nature of globalization push and pull between local and global interests; for example, between centralizing, transnational interests (e.g., the EU) and the assertion of state sovereignty.

diffuseness of expectations unspecified expectations characterize noneconomic and noncontractual social relationships (e.g., friendships).

dilemmas of the self challenges encountered in negotiating a flexible yet coherent self amidst the many insecurities and opportunities confronting the individual in a globalizing, dis-embedded world.

disciplinary practices institutional practices (through schools, churches, clinics, prisons, etc.) used to control, regulate, and subjugate individuals, groups, and society as a whole.

discourse categorizations, talk, and silences pertaining to social practices.

discourse of femininity images, ideas, and talk in society informing how women should present themselves and behave vis-à-vis men and society as a whole.

disembeddedness unmooring of individuals and of institutional practices from specific locales, traditions, and time/space constraints.

distant proximities local and globalizing tendencies that forcefully interact across contemporary society.

distorted communication ways in which current social, economic and political arrangements and cultural assumptions (e.g., free markets; hierarchical authority, individual self-reliance) impede communicative rationality.

division of labor the separation of occupational sectors, workers, and institutions into specialized spheres of activity; produces for Marx, alienated labor, and for Durkheim, social interdependence.

docile bodies produced as a result of the various institutional techniques and procedures used to discipline, subjugate, use, and improve individual (and population) bodies.

domestic world home–neighborhood sphere of women's activity in a man-made world; deemed inferior to the public world in which men work, rule, and play.

domination authority/legitimacy; the probability that individuals and groups will be persuaded/obliged to comply with a given command.

double-consciousness the alienation of blacks' everyday identity/consciousness as a result of slavery such that blacks invariably see themselves through the eyes of (superior) whites, the dominant race.

dramaturgical perspective using the metaphor of drama to describe social life.

economic base the economic structure or the mode of production of material life in capitalist society. Economic relations (relations of production) are determined by ownership of the means of production and rest on inequality between private-property-owning capitalists (bourgeoisie) and propertyless wage-workers. Economic relations determine social relations and social institutional practices (i.e., the superstructure).

economic capital amount of economic assets an individual/family has; can be converted into social and cultural capital (and additional economic capital).

economic efficiency purposive utility and resource rationality of a given course of action.

economy of practice individuals' and social classes' use of the economic and cultural capital they have to make reasonable strategic investments that expand and maximize their economic, cultural, and symbolic capital.

educational capital competencies acquired through school; can be converted into economic and cultural capital.

egoistic suicide results from modern societal conditions in which individuals are excessively self-oriented and insufficiently integrated into social groups/society.

emancipated society when previously marginalized individuals and groups are free to fully participate across all spheres of society; one in which freedom rather than domination is evident in social and institutional practices.

emancipatory knowledge the use of sociological knowledge to advance social equality.

emotion work control or management of feelings in accordance with socially and culturally defined feeling rules.

emotional action subjectively meaningful, nonrational social action motivated by feelings.

emotional display socially learned and regulated presentation of emotional expression.

emotional labor emotion work individuals do at and as work, for pay; has exchange-value.

empathy walls obstacles that impede a deep understanding of, and foster indifference or hostility toward, those who are different from us.

empire the expansive control by a political, military, and economic power of a broad swath of territories and populations (e.g., the British Empire in the nineteenth century).

empiricism use of evidence or data in describing and analyzing society.

encapsulated interest in exchange relations of mutual dependence, we trust individual, group, and institutional actors, believing that they sincerely appreciate our interests and merge (encapsulate) our interests with theirs.

encounter acts and gestures comprising communication about communicating (e.g., how we respond when we encounter a stranger on an elevator or unexpectedly meet an acquaintance on the street).

Enlightenment eighteenth-century philosophical movement emphasizing the centrality of individual reason, human equality, scientific rationality, and human-social progress and the rejection of nonrational beliefs and forms of social organization (e.g., monarchy).

essentialist view of sexuality the idea that being LGB, and the social characteristics associated with being gay, are a natural (essential) part of the LGB individual's biology.

ethnomethodology shared methods societal members use to make sense of everyday experiences across different settings.

everyday/everynight world continuous reality of women's lives as they negotiate the gendered responsibilities of motherhood, marriage, work, etc.

exchange network sets of actors linked together directly or indirectly through exchange relations.

exchange-value the price (wages) wage-workers get on the market for the (coerced) sale of their labor power to the capitalist; determined by how much the capitalist needs to pay the wage-workers in order to maintain their labor power, so that the workers can subsist and maintain their use-value in producing profit for the capitalist. The workers' exchange-value is of less value to the worker than their use-value is to the capitalist.

exploitation the capitalist class caring about wage-workers only to the extent that wage-workers have "use-value," that is, can be used to produce surplus value/profit.

externalization an aspect of the dynamic process by which individuals maintain social reality, whereby they act on and in regard to the already existing (human-created and externalized) objective reality (e.g., institutions, everyday practices in society).

false consciousness the embrace of the illusionary promises of capitalism.

false needs the fabrication or imposition of consumer wants (needs) as determined by mass media, advertising, and economic corporations in the promotion of particular consumer lifestyles; and which consumers (falsely) feel as authentically theirs.

feeling rules socially defined, patterned ways of what to feel and how to express emotion in social interaction and in responding to and anticipating social events.

femininity (man-made) societal ideals and expectations informing how women should think and act in a society that rewards masculinity and male control of women.

feminist revolution transformation of knowledge and of social and institutional practices such that women are considered fully equal to men.

feminist theory focuses on women's inequality in society, and how that inequality is structured and experienced at macro and micro levels.

fetishism of commodities the mystification of capitalist production whereby we inject commodities with special properties beyond what they really are (e.g., elevating an Abercrombie & Fitch shirt to something other than what is really is, that is, cotton converted into a commodity), while remaining ignorant of the exploited labor and unequal class relations that determine production and consumption processes.

financial capitalism increasing prominence of financial services, products, and transactions as a major driver of economic activity.

financial sector includes banks and other financial firms and their employees (e.g., traders), stock exchanges, financial rating agencies (e.g., Moody's) and the institutions that regulate these firms/institutions (e.g., the Securities and Exchange Commission).

First Modernity refers to modernized societies characterized by the nation-state, industrial economy, scientific rationality, functional differentiation, and socially bound individualism.

flexible citizenship the idea that the rights of citizens can no longer be defined in a terms of a single national territory alone but must be broadened in recognition of the trans-national flow of migrant workers and others across national and state boundaries.

frame simplifies reality by selectively interpreting and categorizing (and prioritizing) simultaneously occurring activities.

front the self-presentation maintained by the individual to project an intended definition of the situation in executing a particular role performance.

front-stage area where role performances are given.

functional analysis the combination of theory, method, and data to provide a detailed account of a given social phenomenon such that the description illuminates the phenomenon's particular social functions.

functionalism term used (often interchangeably with "structural functionalism") to refer to the theorizing of Durkheim (and successor sociologists, e.g., Parsons) because of a focus on how social structures determine and are effective in, or functional to, maintaining social cohesion/the social order.

functions necessary tasks accomplished by specific social institutions (e.g., family, economy, law, occupational structure) ensuring the smooth functioning of society.

functions of social conflict social integration due to the interdependent coexistence of conflict groups and social change resulting from institutional resolution of group conflict.

game of culture participation in the evaluative and taste practices that confer style or distinction as if "naturally" rather than due to class conditioning; reproduces social class differences.

game theory a scientific experimental method used mostly by economists to predict interest maximization decisions.

gender ideology a society's dominant beliefs elaborating different conceptualizations of women and men and of their self-presentation, behavior, and place in society.

genealogy (of knowledge/power) interconnected social, political, and historical antecedents to, and context for, the emergence of particular ideas/social categories (Foucault).

generalized other community or society as a whole.

geographical division of labor the idea that specific countries/world regions emerged as core drivers of the historical emergence of capitalist trade and economic expansion.

geopolitical axis along which a country's (or group of countries') political-economic and geographical or regional interests coincide.

global cities cities in which the core organizational structures and workers necessary to the functioning of the global economy are located.

global social democracy vision of globalized society underpinned by principles of fair play, participatory democracy, and social justice.

global systems theory analytical approach emphasizing the dialectic between states/international alliances and transnational globalizing forces and institutions.

globalization interrelated transformation in economic, political, social, and cultural practices and processes toward increased global integration (notwithstanding unevenness in the reach and impact of these processes).

glocalization the recognition that in contemporary society, one in which the forces of disembeddedness, globalization, and digitalization are highly prevalent, local and global realities are not independent of each other.

glossing practices shorthand ways in which language and speech utterances are used to communicate in particular social contexts.

goal attainment political function (or institutional subsystem) necessary in all societies and societal subunits (Parsons).

grand theory elaborate, highly abstract theory that seeks to have universal application.

group conflict emerges when the manifest interests of one group conflict with those of another.

habitus relatively enduring schemes of perception, appreciation, and appropriation of things, embodied in and through class-conditioned socialization and enacted in everyday choices and taste.

hegemonic masculinity the dominant and most authoritative culture of masculinity in society; affirms heterosexuality, physicality, competitiveness, and the suppression of emotional vulnerability.

hegemony the authoritative way in which certain cultural assumptions appear so normal and natural that we freely consent to them; for example, advertising and media culture orchestrate our consent to consumerism and more generally to the status quo and the dominant ideology (Gramsci).

hegemony of the global metropole just as geographical empires were ruled from an imperial power's political center or metropole (e.g., London was the metropole of the British Empire), sociological theory and research (and other knowledge-production) in the world today is controlled by Western/Northern universities and academics and largely consented to by those situated in non-Western and Southern locations.

here-and-now reality immediate pragmatic salience of individuals' everyday reality.

heterosexist presumption that heterosexuality is normative (and normal) and that other sexual feelings and practices are socially deviant.

historical materialism history as the progressive expansion in the economic-material-productive forces in society.

homogenization standardization of products, content, and choices in consumption and politics driven by the mass orientation (sameness) most profitable or advantageous to the culture industry and other corporate and political actors.

honest bodies rejection of sexual exploitation and degradation (e.g., of women and gays) and the affirmation of sexual images, desires, and practices that recognize the emotional-relational context of sexual expression.

human capital skills, education, health, and other competences/resources that individuals possess; influences their economic and social-psychological functioning.

human ecology geographical spaces (e.g., cities) can be understood in terms of competition among diverse population groups, the outcomes of which produce social change; there is a correlation between spatial relations and social relations.

hyperreality a glossy, lavish, cinematic, consumption-driven, utopian reality dominated by spectacle (e.g., Las Vegas).

"I" part of the self; the "I" is the (subjective) acting self, and is able to act only because it internalizes the attitudes toward the "Me" (as an object) received from others' behavior/responses toward the acting "I" (Mead).

ideal speech situation when communication partners use reason (communicative rationality) to seek a common understanding of a question at issue and to embark on rationally justified, mutually agreed, future action.

ideal type an exhaustive description of the characteristics distinctive to and expected of a given phenomenon (e.g., of bureaucracy).

identity politics strategic use of particular cultural and social identities (based on race, gender, sexuality, ethnicity, etc.) to resist discrimination and/or to gain political advantage.

ideology ideas in everyday circulation; determined by the ruling economic class such that they make our current social existence seem normal and desirable.

imagined community concept introduced by Benedict Anderson (1983) elaborating how the nation as a political community is imagined in the sense that the felt affinities toward diverse others with whom one shares a given legal-geographical national territory are imagined rather than based on personal ties to them. Although the nation is a significant communal unit, one may think of oneself as belonging to several different, imagined communities – for example, the Catholic community, the LGBTQ community.

impression management symbolic and strategic communicative work toward orchestrating a particular definition of the situation and a successful role performance.

inalienable rights Enlightenment belief that all individuals by virtue of their humanity and their naturally endowed reason are entitled to fully participate in society in ways that reflect and enrich their humanity (e.g., freedom of speech, of assembly, to vote, etc.).

individualism cultural ethos of individual independence, responsibility, and self-reliance.

inequality structured into the profit objectives and organization of capitalism whereby the exploited labor power of wage-workers produces surplus value (profit) for the capitalist class.

information economy dominance of information or service commodities, produced and exchanged for profit.

in-group particular community (or group/society) in which we are immersed, whose habits we have inherited, and with which we are "at home."

innovator individual who accepts cultural goals but substitutes new means toward their attainment.

institutional ethnography an investigation that starts with individual experiences as a way to discover how institutions work and how they might work better for people.

institutional field specific institutional spheres (e.g., education, culture, religion, law) characterized by institution-specific rules and practices reproducing inequality.

institutionalized means approved practices in society toward the achievement of specific goals (e.g., a college education as the means toward achieving a good career or economic success).

instrumental domination strategic use of reason (knowledge, science, technology) to control others.

instrumental rational action behavioral decisions or actions (of individuals, groups, organizations, etc.) based on calculating, strategic, cost–benefit analysis of goals and means.

integration regulatory function (or institutional subsystem; e.g., law) necessary in all societies (and societal subunits) (Parsons).

interaction rituals routinized ways of self-presenting/behaving in the co-presence of others (e.g., greeting rituals).

interdependence ties among individuals; for Durkheim, the individualism required by the specialized division of labor creates functional and social interdependence.

interest group any group whose members consciously share and express similar interests.

internalization an aspect of the dynamic process by which individuals create social reality such that, in experiencing an external, objective reality (e.g., institutional practices, social inequality), they translate (internalize) it into their own particular, subjectively experienced reality.

interpretive process interpretation of the meaning of individuals' verbal and nonverbal communication and of the meanings of other objects/things in the social environment is an ongoing activity.

interpretive understanding *Verstehen*; task of the sociologist in making sense of the varied motivations that underlie meaningful action; because sociology studies human lived experience (as opposed to physical phenomena), sociologists need a methodology enabling them to empathically understand human-social behavior.

intersectionality multiple crisscrossing ways in which different histories and diverse structural locations (based on race, gender, class, sexuality, etc.) situate individuals' experiences and life chances.

knowing from within the idea that sociological knowledge must start from within the lived realities of the individuals and groups studied.

language a socially shared symbol and meaning system.

latency (pattern maintenance) cultural socialization function (or institutional subsystem) necessary in all societies and societal subunits (Parsons).

latent functions unanticipated and unrecognized (functional or dysfunctional) consequences of an intended course of action.

latent interests unspoken, tacit interests of one group vis-à-vis another.

legal authority based on rational, impersonal norms and rules; imposed by the state and other bureaucratic organizations; dominant in modern societies.

legitimation crisis when national or other collectivities lose trust in the ability of the state (or other institutions) to adequately respond to major systemic disruptions in the execution of institutional tasks (e.g., the effective functioning of the banking system).

lifeworld from the German word *Lebenswelt*; the world of everyday life and its taken-for-granted routines, customs, habits, and knowledge.

looking-glass self self-perception and behavior contingent on our knowing (or imagining) how others (would) respond toward us.

macro analytical focus on large-scale social structures (e.g., capitalism) and processes (e.g., class inequality).

management of feeling control of emotion via the creation of a publicly observable and convincing display irrespective of one's inner feelings.

manifest functions intended and recognized consequences of a particular course of action.

manifest interests explicitly stated objectives.

manner signals which function to indicate the tone in the interaction role a performer expects to play in an oncoming situation (e.g., the sympathetic grief counselor).

marginal man a person who lives in and moves between two diverse (and possibly conflicting) cultural groups (Robert Park).

marginal utility extent to which one course of action rather than another proportionally increases an individual's resources or advances their interests.

masculinity societal expectations and practices governing the self-presentation and behavior of men; accentuates characteristics and traits of domination that are the opposite of femininity (subordination).

mass culture advertising and other mass mediated content delivered by a technologically sophisticated, profit driven, corporate culture industry.

mass society thesis idea that individuals in society are passive, unaware of and uninvolved in, politics.

maximization of utility behavior motivated by principles advancing self-interest.

McDonaldization the thesis that cultural icons, products, and standards are increasingly similar across the world.

"Me" part of the self; the self as object ("Me"); the internalization of the expectations and attitudes of others toward "Me" and to which "I" (as the acting subject) respond (Mead).

meaning significance given to particular symbols and objects/things in our environment.

means of production resources (e.g., land, oil wells, factories, corporations, financial capital) owned by the bourgeoisie and used for the production of commodities/profit as a result of the labor power of wage-workers.

mechanical solidarity social bonds and cohesion resulting from the overlapping social ties that characterize traditional societies/communities.

members individuals, that is, societal members; they accomplish social reality.

methodological nationalism criticism that sociologists theorize about and conduct research on their own national society and generalize from that specific society to society in general.

micro analytical focus on small-scale, interpersonal, and small group interaction.

microeconomic model presumes that individuals act to maximize their own self-interests and self-satisfaction.

middle-range theory generates theoretical explanations grounded in and extending beyond specific empirical realities.

mode of production how a society organizes its material-social existence (e.g., capitalism rather than feudalism or socialism).

modernization theory the thesis that all societies will inevitably and invariably follow the same linear path of economic (e.g., industrialization), social (e.g., urbanization, education), and cultural (e.g., democracy; self-orientation) progress achieved by American society.

moral community any group or collectivity unified by common beliefs and practices and a shared solidarity.

moral density the density of social interaction associated with encountering and interacting with a multiplicity of diverse others in modern society.

moral individualism individuals (as social beings) interacting with others for purposes other than simply serving their own selfish or material interests.

morality social life; the ties to group life that regulate individual appetites and attach individuals to something other than themselves, that is, to other individuals, groups, society; sociology's subject matter; can be studied with scientific objectivity.

multiple masculinities the idea that masculinity expectations and practices vary by class, race, and sexuality and are positioned in relations of subordination and marginalization to the hegemonic masculinity.

multiple modernities recognition that different societies experience modernity in different ways; challenges the prevailing idea that Western modernity is the only form of modernity.

mystique of science unquestioned presumption that the accumulation, application, and everyday use of scientific data and scientific advances are invariably good and that they should be automatically welcomed as evidence of social progress.

nation-state rational, legal, bureaucratic actor; has specific territorial interests; entitled to use physical force to protect and defend its internal and external security.

natural attitude the individual's orientation toward his or her social environment, a reality that seems natural because it is the everyday reality that he or she knows.

neofunctionalism refers to the approach of contemporary sociologists who embrace Parsons's theoretical perspective but who amend some of its claims.

neo-Marxist ideas derived from Marx's theory of capitalism but reworked in new ways and/or with new applications to take account of the transformations in capitalism.

net gain when the benefits of a course of action outweigh its costs.

network society one in which information technology networks are the dominant shapers of new, decentralized, economic and social organizations and relationships.

neutrality versus affectivity one of Parsons's five patterned value-orientations whereby, for example, modern societies differentiate between institutional spheres and relationships based on impersonality (e.g., work) rather than emotion (e.g., family).

new imperialism the idea that a country's geopolitical and military strategies today are driven primarily by capitalist economic interests.

new middle class the expanding sector of educated (but politically indifferent) salaried managers, professionals, and sales and office workers that resulted from the post-World War II expansion of bureaucracy and the consumer economy.

new racism (1) symbols and ideas used (e.g., in politics, pop culture, the mass media) to argue that race-based (biological) differences no longer matter even as such arguments reinforce racial-cultural differences and stereotypes. (2) the invocation of cultural and symbolic (rather than biological) criteria of difference to legitimate the societal exclusion or marginalization of particular racial/ethnic groups.

noncivil sphere the domains of state, economy, family, community, religion; each with particularized goals, interests, and structures (Alexander).

nonrational action behavior motivated by emotion and/or tradition rather than by reasoned judgment.

normative rationality evaluative use of reason to advance values (or prescriptive norms) of equality and freedom.

objectification the dehumanization of wage-workers as machine-like objects, whose maintenance (with subsistence wages) is necessary to the production of commodities (objects) necessary to capital accumulation/profit. The term is interchangeable with "alienation."

objective reality the social reality, including objectively existing social institutions (economic, legal, etc.), language, and social processes (e.g., gender/race inequalities), into which individuals are socialized.

objectivity (1) positivist idea (elaborated by Comte and Durkheim) that sociology can provide an unbiased (objective) analysis of a directly observable and measurable, objective social reality. This approach presumes that facts stand alone and have an objective reality independent of social and historical context and independent of any theories/ideas informing how we frame, look at, and interpret data. (2) term used by Weber to highlight the professional obligation of scientists, researchers, and teachers to report and discuss "inconvenient facts," that is, facts that disagree with or contradict their personal feelings and opinions.

one-dimensionality sameness, homogenization, or standardization; lack of meaningful alternatives in mass culture and politics.

on-the-ground observation systematic data gathering in the everyday social contexts or settings in which individuals interact; ethnography.

organic solidarity social ties and cohesion produced by the functional and social interdependence of individuals and groups in modern society.

organization assets specific skills and resources controlled by the class of professionals/bureaucrats/managers who have technical knowledge and expertise.

Otherness social construction of racial, ethnic, and/or geographical differences as inferior to a dominant historical and political power (e.g., the West's construction of Orientalism).

other-worldly nonmaterial motivations; for example, after-death salvation; the opposite of this-worldly.

out-group everyday reality of those who have different everyday habits to us and that to us seem "strange."

Panopticon model (invoked by Foucault) to highlight how disciplinary power works by keeping the individual a constant object of unceasing surveillance/control.

part aspect of a social role.

parties political groups or associations that seek to influence the distribution of power in society.

passing the impression management and self-presentation symbolic work an individual must do in order to cover up or secretly maintain a stigmatized identity.

patriarchal society one in which white men have a privileged position by virtue of the historically grounded, man-made construction of social institutions, texts, and practices.

pattern maintenance latency; socialization function (or institutional subsystem) necessary in all societies and societal subunits.

pattern variables Parsons's schema of five separate, dichotomously opposed value-orientations determining social action.

performance the idea that social life, society, is based on the socially structured, acting out (performance) of particular social roles.

peripheral areas those areas marginal but necessary to world economic production.

personality system the individual's inculcation of the values and habits necessary to effective functioning in a given society (e.g., ambitious, hardworking, and conscientious personality types favored in the US).

phenomenology focuses on the reality of everyday life and how individuals make sense of their everyday experiences.

physical density the number of people encountered in the conduct of everyday life.

planetary humanism idea that society can transcend its racial, cultural, and other group differences to recognize and realize its collectively shared humanity.

plausibility structure group and institutional settings (e.g., churches) and laws that affirm (make plausible) the objective reality of individuals' subjectively experienced realities.

pluralistic simultaneous coexistence of, and mutual engagement across, diverse strands (of thought, of research, of people).

political dependency dependence of citizens and economic and other institutions on the state to resolve problems and crises created, by and large, by the state and economic institutions.

political race invocation of race-based experiences of social inequality to mobilize and expand cross-racial alliances toward the achievement of social and institutional change.

politics of conversion grassroots and institutional activism based on new ways of thinking about racial identity and intraracial and interracial competition, with a focus on the equality of all people.

politics of sexuality focus on the various ways in which ideas about sex and sexuality are used to create and contest divisions between and within particular social groups based on gender and sexual orientation differences.

politics of truth idea emphasizing that truth is not, and can never be, independent of power; that all truths are produced by particular power-infused social relationships and social contexts.

positivist the idea that sociology as a science is able to employ the same scientific method of investigation and explanation used in the natural sciences, focusing only on observable data and studying society with the same objectivity used to study physical/biological phenomena.

postcapitalist society Dahrendorf's term; the result of transformations in the economy and in the occupational and class structures since the mid-twentieth century that make capitalist society structurally different from its late nineteenth-century incarnation (when Marx was writing about the capitalist structure and class relations).

postcolonial theory critiques the legacy of Western imperialism for the cultural identities of previously colonized peoples.

postindustrial society changes in economy and society resulting from the decline of manufacturing industry and the increased and growing importance of services and information as economic engines/sources of employment (basically refers to the same processes highlighted by Dahrendorf in his notion of postcapitalist society).

postnational the current era of transnational political organizations (e.g., the EU) and other globalizing forces, with the nation-state no longer considered the core or most powerful political unit.

postsecular society refers to the continuing public relevance of religion in and to secularized societies; challenges the secular presumption that religion necessarily declines or disappears with modernization; postsecularity requires mutual reflexivity and engagement between religious and secular actors.

post-truth society a term that has gained currency amid the whirl of misinformation and false statements disseminated on social media and by partisan news outlets; it conveys that objectively validated, evidence-based statements are displaced by distorted or contrary assertions adjusted to suit the interests of the individual or group making particular, untruthful claims.

power (1) the probability that a social actor (e.g., the state, an organization, an individual) can impose its will despite resistance (Weber). (2) an unequally divided, perpetual source of conflict and resistance (Dahrendorf). (3) an ongoing circulatory process with no fixed location or fixed points of origin, possession, and resistance (Foucault).

power dependence basis of power in an exchange relation; the power of actor A over actor B in the A–B relation is a function of B's dependence on A.

power elite upper echelon in the interlocking network of economic, political, and military decision makers; holders of power, prestige, and wealth in society.

power imbalances in any social exchange relation, interaction is contingent on differentiation between and among the actors in terms of who gets more out of the relationship.

practical knowledge knowledge needed to accomplish routine everyday tasks in the individual's environment.

pragmatism strand in American philosophy emphasizing the practicalities that characterize, and the practical consequences of, social action and interaction.

predestination Calvinist belief that an individual's salvation is already determined at birth by God.

presentation of self ongoing symbolic work the role-performing actor does to project an intended definition of a situation.

primary group has a crucially formative and enduring significance in child socialization (e.g., the primacy of the family).

private property the source and the result of the profit accumulated by capitalists and a source and consequence of the inequality between capitalists and wage workers.

profane ordinary, mundane, nonsacred things in society.

profit capitalists' accumulation of capital as a result of the surplus value generated by wage-workers' (exploited) labor power.

proletariat wage-workers who, in order to live, must sell their labor power to the capitalist class, which uses them to produce surplus value/profit.

promotional culture constant stream of consumer advertising dominating mass media content and public space (e.g., highways).

props objects and things in a setting that bolster (prop up) the actor's intended definition of the situation.

public sociology research addressing questions relevant to social activists and other audiences outside of academia and with the goal of critiquing existing knowledge and practices.

public sphere public, relatively informal spaces (e.g., coffee shops, public squares) and non-state-controlled institutional settings (e.g., mass media, voluntary and nonprofit organizations) where individuals and groups freely assemble and discuss political and social issues; produces "public opinion." *See also* civil society.

public world the nondomestic arena; domains of work, politics, sports, etc., the sphere given greater legitimacy in society.

Puritan ethic emphasis on disciplined and methodical work, sober frugality, and the avoidance of spontaneous emotion.

queer theory rejects the heterosexual/homosexual binary in language, culture, and institutional practices; shifts attention from LGBTQ inequality in (heterosexist) society to instead focus on the fluidity of all sexuality and its implications.

queering the text refers to the way in which, in light of current understandings of the fluidity of sexuality, we reread or look anew at earlier literary, artistic, and other cultural products (e.g., television shows, advertisements) to see whether we can identify elements that can be interpreted as suggesting a more disruptive understanding of sexuality than assumed at the time of their publication/authorship.

race symbolization of social differences based on assumed or perceived natural (innate) differences derived from differences in physical body appearance.

race segregation legal and systematically imposed divisions in everyday life based on racial differences; for example, existence of separate schools and swimming pools for blacks and whites in the US until the 1950s.

racism implicit or explicit imposition of exclusionary boundaries and discriminatory practices based on racial appearance or racial categories.

rational action a reason-based, logical, methodical, deliberate, and planful approach to social behavior.

rationality emphasis on the objective and impersonal authority of reason in deliberating about, and evaluating explanations of, social behavior/social phenomena.

reason human ability to think about things; to create, apply, and evaluate knowledge; and as a consequence, to be able to evaluate one's own and others' lived experiences and the sociohistorical context that shapes those experiences.

rebel individual who rejects cultural goals and institutionalized means and who substitutes alternative goals and alternative means toward attaining those goals.

recipe knowledge particular ways of doing things in a particular social environment.

reflexive modernization the process whereby societies critically examine the legacy of modernization (in their own or other countries) and deliberately and selectively develop and implement structures and processes that seek to avoid the ills of modernization while creating a prosperous and sustainable society.

regime of truth institutional system whereby the state and other institutions (government agencies, the military, medical and cultural industries) and knowledge producers (e.g., scientists, professors) affirm certain ideas and practices as true and marginalize or silence alternative practices and interpretations.

region any role-performance setting bounded to some extent by barriers to perception (e.g., walls divide a restaurant's kitchen from its dining area).

reification from the Latin word *res*, "thing"; process whereby we think of social structures (e.g., capitalism), social institutions, and other socially created things (e.g., language, technology, "Wall Street," "The City") as things independent of human construction rather than as social creations that can be modified and changed to meet a society's changing needs and interests and to accomplish particular normative or strategic goals.

relations of ruling institutional and cultural routines that govern and maintain the unequal position of women in relation to men within and across all societal domains.

religion a social phenomenon, collectively defined by the things, ideas, beliefs, and practices a society or community holds sacred; a socially integrating force (Durkheim).

religious capital practical mastery and competence in church doctrine and its interpretation

remix blending and reworking of several original sounds, themes, or ideas into a new reality.

retreatist individual who rejects cultural goals and institutionalized means, and who, by and large, withdraws from active participation in society.

risk society the global expansion, awareness, and impact of risk and of the insecurities and anxieties it produces in society.

ritual of discourse society's orderly, routinized, and power-infused ways (e.g., confession) of producing subjects talking about socially repressed secrets and practices.

ritualist individual who rejects cultural goals but who accepts and goes along with the institutional means toward their achievement.

rituals (1) collectively shared, sacred rites and practices that affirm and strengthen social ties, and maintain social order

(Durkheim). (2) routinized ways of face-to-face acting and interacting that reflect status differences and maintain social order (Goffman).

rituals of subordination signals in self-presentation (e.g., body posture of one actor vis-à-vis another) symbolizing or indicating status differences or social inequality.

routines socially prescribed, ordered ways of accomplishing particular tasks or establishing particular situational definitions and meanings in executing a role performance.

routinization of charisma the rational translation of individual charisma into organizational goals and procedures.

ruling class the class that is the ruling material force in society (capitalists/bourgeoisie) is also the ruling intellectual/ideological force, ensuring the protection and expansion of capitalist economic interests.

ruling ideas ideas disseminated by the ruling (capitalist) class, invariably bolstering capitalism.

ruling practices array of institutional and cultural practices that maintain unequal gender relations in society.

ruling texts core man-made texts (e.g., Bible, Constitution, laws, advertising) that define gender and other power relations in society.

sacred all things a society collectively sets apart as special, requiring reverence.

scarcity value determines power imbalances in any exchange relationship; a function of the relation between the supply of, and demand for, rewards.

scheme of reference stock of accumulated knowledge and experiences we use to interpret and make sense of new experiences.

scientific management industrial method introduced in the early twentieth century by Frederick Taylor to increase worker efficiency and productivity by controlling workers' physical movements and techniques.

scientific reasoning emphasis on the discovery of explanatory knowledge through the use of empirical data and their systematic analysis rather than relying on philosophical assumptions and faith/religious beliefs.

Second Modernity demarcates societies that have reflexively modernized; cosmopolitan modernity.

secularization the thesis that religious institutions and religious authority decline with the increased modernization of, and institutional differentiation in, society.

segregated audiences when role-performing actors are able to keep the audiences to their different roles separate from one another; facilitates the impression management required in a particular setting.

self reflexively active interpreter of symbols and meanings in the individual's environment; comprised of the "I" and the "Me."

self-alienation produced as a result of emotional laborers' splitting of internal feelings and external emotion management.

self-fulfilling prophecy individuals' (possibly false) perceptions of a given situation lead them to behave in ways that result in bringing about an objectively changed reality; known as the Thomas theorem.

self- versus collectivity orientation one of Parsons's five patterned value orientations whereby modern society emphasizes individual over communal interests.

semiotic code cultural code or meanings inscribed in language and other symbols in a given societal context.

semiperipheral areas those structurally necessary to the world-economy but outside its core political and economic coalitions.

setting the bounded social situation or context in which a social role is performed.

sheer commodification the cultural or lifestyle packaging of everyday things, places, or experiences as images and commodities purely for the purpose of promoting consumption for the sake of consumption.

simulacra things that are glossy, polished representations and commodified imaginings of other things/realities; the simulated product/representation assumes a more real, more beautiful, more intense, more cinematic presence than the original.

situations of dependency term used to highlight the social, historical, and economic variation that exists among developing economies.

slavery historical institutionalization of coercive, discriminatory, and dehumanizing practices against a subordinate group; typically legitimated on grounds of racial difference.

social capital individuals' ties or connections to others; can be converted into economic capital.

social classes broad groups based on objective differences in amounts of economic, social, and cultural capital.

social construction of reality social reality as the product of humans acting intersubjectively and collectively. Social reality exists as an objective (human-social) reality that individuals subjectively experience, to which they respond and, acting collectively, can change.

social control methodical regulation curtailing the freedom of individuals, groups, and society as a whole.

social disorganization the result of the co-presence of numerous interrelated social problems (e.g., unemployment and crime).

social exchange all forms of social behavior wherein individuals exchange resources with others in order to attain desired ends.

social facts external and collective social forces (structures, practices, norms, beliefs) regulating and constraining the ways of acting, thinking, and feeling in society.

social integration degree to which individuals and groups are attached to society. Individuals are interlinked and constrained by their ties to others.

social roles socially scripted role-performance behavior required of a person occupying a particular status and/or in a particular setting; individuals perform multiple social roles.

social solidarity social cohesion resulting from shared social ties/bonds/interdependence.

social structures forms of social organization (e.g., capitalism, democracy, bureaucracy, education, gender) in a given society that structure or constrain social behavior across all spheres of social life, including the cultural expectations and norms (e.g., individualism) that underpin and legitimate social institutional arrangements.

social system(s) interconnected institutional subsystems and relationships that comprise society and all of its subunits.

socialist globalization form of globalization that would gradually eliminate privately owned big business, establish local producer–consumer cooperatives, and implement social equality/human rights.

socialization process by which individuals learn how to be social – how to participate in society – and thus how to use and interpret symbols and language, and interact with others.

sociological theory the body of concepts and conceptual frameworks used to make sense of the multilayered, empirical patterns and underlying processes in society.

sociology of knowledge demonstrates how the organization and content of knowledge is a social activity contingent on the particular sociohistorical circumstances in which it is produced.

Southern theory seeks to redress the Northern (and Western) bias in knowledge production, including in sociology; it is part of the effort to redress or decolonize postcolonial, unequal power relations in the knowledge production and everyday practices of sociology and other disciplines.

species being what is distinctive of the human species (e.g., mindful creativity).

specificity versus diffuseness one of Parsons's five patterned value-orientations whereby, for example, modern society emphasizes role specialization rather than general competence.

stage specific setting or place where the role-performing actor performs a particular social role.

standardization imposition of sameness or homogenization in culture and politics.

standpoint a group's positioning within the unequal power structure and the everyday lived knowledge that emerges from that position.

standpoint of the proletariat the positioning of the proletariat vis-à-vis the production process, from within which they perceive the dehumanization and self-alienation structured into capitalism, unlike the bourgeoisie, who experience capitalism (erroneously) as self-affirming.

status social esteem or prestige associated with style of life, education, and hereditary or occupational prestige.

status differentials comprise social inequality (stratification); gap in achievement and rewards based on differences in individuals' achieved competence (doctor/patient) and ascribed social roles (male/female).

steering problems emerge when economic and political institutions do not work as functionally intended and as ideologically assumed (e.g., the market's "invisible hand" working to produce economic growth and social integration), thus causing problems (e.g., recession) whose resolution demands state intervention in the system (e.g., federal monetary policy).

stigma society's categorization or differentiation of its members as inferior based on the social evaluation and labeling of various attributes of undesired difference.

stock of preconstituted knowledge cumulative body of everyday knowledge and experiences that individuals have from living in a particular social environment.

stratification inequality between groups (strata) in society based on differences in economic resources, social status and prestige, and political power.

strong ties exist when people are closely bonded to others (e.g., cliques); can reduce interaction or sharing of information with individuals or groups outside the group; can be a source of community fragmentation.

structural-functionalism term used to refer to the theorizing of Durkheim and Parsons because of their focus on how social structures determine, and are effective in (or functional to) maintaining, the social order, society (social equilibrium).

structure objective ways in which society is organized; for example, the social class structure exists and has objective consequences for individuals independent of individuals' subjective social class feelings and self-categorization.

subjective reality the individual's subjective experience and interpretation of the external, objective reality.

subjectively meaningful action individuals and groups engage in behavior that is subjectively meaningful (or important) to them and that takes account of, and is oriented to, the behavior of others.

subsistence wage minimum needed to sustain workers' existence (livelihood) so that their labor power is maintained and reproduced for the capitalist class.

subsystems spheres of social (or institutional) action required for the functioning and maintenance of the social system (society) and its subunits (institutions, small groups, etc.).

subuniverses of meaning collectivities that share and objectify (or institutionalize) individuals' similarly meaningful experiences and interpretations of reality.

sui generis **reality** the idea that society has its own nature or reality – its own collective characteristics or properties that emerge and exist as a constraining force independent of the characteristics of the individuals in society.

superstructure noneconomic social institutions (legal, political, educational, cultural, religious, family) whose routine institutional practices and activities promote the beliefs, ideas, and practices that are necessary to maintaining and reproducing capitalism.

surplus value capitalist profit from the difference between a worker's exchange-value (wages) and use-value; the extra value over and above the costs of commodity production (i.e., raw materials, infrastructure, workers' wages) created by the labor power of wage-workers.

surveillance continuous monitoring and disciplining of bodies by social institutions across private and public domains.

symbol signs whose interpretations and meanings are socially shared; collective representations of a community's/society's collectively shared beliefs and values.

symbolic capital one's reputation for competence, good taste, integrity, accomplishment, etc.; has exchange-value, convertible to economic, social, and cultural capital.

symbolic goods goods we buy, display, and give to distinguish ourselves from others; signal and reproduce taste, status, social hierarchy, social class inequality.

symbolic interactionism sociological perspective emphasizing society/social life as an ongoing process wherein individuals continuously exchange and interpret symbols.

symbolic universes overarching meaning systems (e.g., religion, science) that integrate and order individuals' everyday realities.

systems of domination penetration of the regulatory control of the state and other bureaucratic and corporate entities into everyday life.

systems of trust establishment of organizations and groups to mediate transactions between social actors. These systems influence the decisions of self-interested actors to place trust and to be trustworthy in order to maximize gains.

taste social class- and family-conditioned, ordinary, everyday preferences and habits; socially learned ways of appreciation, style.

team when role-performers cooperate to stage a single routine or performance and project a shared definition of the situation.

technical rationality calculated procedures and techniques used in the strategic implementation of instrumental goals typically in the service of economic profit and/or social control.

techniques of bio-power exertion of control over the body/bodies through institutional procedures (e.g., classroom schedules, Census categories) and practices (e.g., confession).

technological determinism the assumption that the use of a particular technology is determined by features of the technology itself rather than by the dominant economic, political, and cultural interests in society.

this-worldly the material reality of the everyday world in which we live and work.

total institutions highly regimented settings (e.g., prisons) in which the barriers that customarily divide individuals' everyday functions (sleeping, eating, and working) are removed.

traditional action nonrational, subjectively meaningful social action motivated by custom and habit.

traditional authority derived from long-established traditions or customs; dominant in traditional societies but coexists in modern society with legal-bureaucratic and charismatic authority.

transnational capitalist class comprised of corporate executives/professionals and political, institutional, and media leaders who play a dominant role along with transnational corporations in advancing capitalist globalization and inequality.

transnational practices the idea that (capitalist) globalizing processes require and are characterized by specific transnational economic, political, and cultural-ideological practices or ways of being.

triangle of power the intersection of economic, political, and military institutions.

trust confidence in the reciprocity and sincerity of economic, professional, and other social relationships.

typifications customary (typical) ways in which an individual's intersubjective social environment is organized; how things, individuals (e.g., as role/status types), and institutions are presumed to work/behave.

underdevelopment economies in the third world whose development is hindered by their relational dependence on, and exploitation by, the economically developed first world.

uneven modernization when societies experience modernization more quickly in one sphere of society (e.g., the economy) than in another (e.g., in education, the failure to develop the educated workforce necessary to the changed economy).

unicity the idea that as a result of globalization processes, the world as a whole is moving toward sociocultural oneness.

unit act analytically, the core of social action; comprised of a social actor, a goal, specific circumstances, and a normative or value orientation.

universalistic versus particularistic one of Parsons's five patterned value orientations whereby, for example, modern society emphasizes impersonal rules and general principles rather than personal relationships.

use-value the usefulness of wage-workers' labor power in the production of profit.

utilitarianism idea from classical economics that individuals are rational, self-interested actors who evaluate alternative courses of action on the basis of their usefulness (utility) or resource value to them.

value neutrality the idea that scientists and researchers do not inject their personal beliefs and values into the conduct, evaluation, and presentation of their research.

value system shared value orientation (culture) that functions to maintain societal cohesion/integration.

value-rational action rational, purposeful behavior (of individuals/groups/organizations) motivated by commitment to a particular value (e.g., loyalty, environmental sustainability, education) and independent of the probability of its successful outcome.

values what a social actor (e.g., an individual, a group, an organization) values (such as equality, or environmental preservation); raises questions concerning the goals or ends that individuals, organizations, institutions, and societies should purposefully embrace and pursue.

Verstehen German for "understanding"; refers to the process by which sociologists seek interpretive understanding of the subjective meanings that individuals and collectivities give to their behavior/social action.

voluntaristic action social actors are free to choose among culturally constrained goals and the means to accomplish those goals.

weak ties when people have loose ties to acquaintances across several different social contexts. Weak ties expand individuals' access to information and opportunities and can facilitate community-oriented action.

whiteness term used to underscore that all racial categories, including historically dominant ones (e.g., being white), are socially constructed categories of privilege whose meanings and implications change over time.

wide-awakeness the practical consciousness and attentiveness required in attending to the "here-and-now" tasks and realities of everyday life.

working concepts general definitions or fames of reference that seek to specify what a particular social phenomenon is before empirically investigating it (e.g., specifying what "a gang" is).

world military order the idea that the distribution of military power in the world is empirically and analytically independent of the distribution of economic power (e.g., Pakistan's and North Korea's nuclear power is considerable despite their considerably weaker economic position relative to the US and Europe).

world system the world as a relational system comprised of structurally unequal, developed and underdeveloped economies.

world-economy the capitalist world-system economy; an economic unit independent of political and administrative boundaries; it is divided into core, peripheral, and semiperipheral geographical areas among which there is an imposed, unequal flow of resources.

SOCIOLOGICAL THEORISTS AND SELECT KEY WRITINGS

Theodor Adorno [chapter 5]
The Dialectic of Enlightenment (1972; with Max Horkheimer)

Jean Baudrillard [chapter 15]
America (1991)

Zygmunt Bauman [chapter 14]
Liquid Modernity (2000)

Ulrich Beck [chapter 15]
Risk Society: Towards a New Modernity (1992)
"Varieties of Second Modernity: The Cosmopolitan Turn in Social and Political Theory Research" (2010; with Edgar Grande)
"New Cosmopolitanism in the Social Sciences" (2012; with Nathan Sznaider)

Peter Berger [chapter 9]
The Sacred Canopy: Elements of a Sociological Theory of Religion (1967)
The Social Construction of Reality: A Treatise in the Sociology of Knowledge (1966; with Thomas Luckmann)

Peter Blau [chapter 7]
Exchange and Power in Social Life (1964)
On the Nature of Organizations (1974)

Herbert Blumer [chapter 8]
Symbolic Interactionism: Perspective and Method (1969)

Pierre Bourdieu [chapter 13]
Distinction: A Social Critique of the Judgment of Taste (1984)
"The Forms of Capital" (1986)
"Genesis and Structure of the Religious Field" (1991)
The State Nobility: Elite Schools in the Field of Power (1996)
Practical Reason: On the Theory of Action (1998)
The Weight of the World: Social Suffering in Contemporary Society (1999)
Masculine Domination (2001)

Fernando Cardoso [chapter 6]
Dependency and Development in Latin America (1979; with Enzo Faletto)

Manuel Castells [chapter 14]
The Rise of the Network Society, volume I (1997)
"Toward a Sociology of the Network Society" (2000)

James Coleman [chapter 7]
The Adolescent Society (1961)
Foundations of Social Theory (1990)
Equality of Educational Opportunity (1966)

Introduction to Sociological Theory: Theorists, Concepts, and Their Applicability to the Twenty-First Century, Third Edition. Michele Dillon.
© 2020 John Wiley & Sons Ltd. Published 2020 by John Wiley & Sons Ltd.
Companion website: www.wiley.com/go/dillon

Patricia Hill Collins [chapter 10]

Black Feminist Thought: Knowledge, Consciousness, and the Politics of Empowerment (1990)

Black Sexual Politics (2004)

"Intersectionality's Definitional Dilemmas" (2015, *Annual Review of Sociology*)

Auguste Comte [Introduction]

The Positive Philosophy (1855)

The Catechism of Positive Religion (1891)

R.W. (Raewyn) Connell [chapters 10 and 12]

Gender and Power: Society, the Person and Sexual Politics (1987)

Masculinities (1995)

"Masculinities in Global Perspective" (2016, *Theory & Society*)

"Toward a Global Sociology of Knowledge" (2017, *International Sociology*)

Karen Cook [chapter 7]

Cooperation Without Trust? (2005; with Russell Hardin and Margaret Levi)

Whom Can We Trust? (2009; with Margaret Levi and Russell Hardin)

Ralf Dahrendorf [chapter 6]

Class and Class Conflict in Industrial Society (1959)

Essays in the Theory of Society (1968)

Alexis de Tocqueville [Introduction]

Democracy in America (1835–1840)

William Edward Burghardt Du Bois [Introduction]

The Souls of Black Folk (1903/1969)

Black Reconstruction in America (1934/2007)

Emile Durkheim [chapter 2]

The Division of Labor in Society (1893)

The Rules of Sociological Method (1895)

Suicide (1897)

The Elementary Forms of Religious Life (1912)

"The Dualism of Human Nature and Its Social Conditions" (1914)

S.N. Eisenstadt [chapter 15]

Tradition, Change, and Modernity (1973)

"Multiple Modernities" (2000)

Richard Emerson [chapter 7]

"Power and Dependence Relations" (1962)

"Exchange Theory, Part I. A Psychological Basis for Social Exchange. Exchange Theory, Part II. Exchange Relations and Network Structures" (1972)

Frantz Fanon [chapter 12]

Black Skin, White Masks (1967)

Michel Foucault [chapter 11]

Madness and Civilization: A History of Insanity in the Age of Reason (1965)

The Order of Things: An Archaeology of the Human Sciences (1970)

The Archaeology of Knowledge (1972)

The Birth of the Clinic: An Archaeology of Medical Perception (1975)

The History of Sexuality, volume 1 (1978)

Discipline and Punish: The Birth of the Prison (1979)

"Truth and Power" (1984)

"Sex, Power, and the Politics of Identity" (1984)

Anthony Giddens [chapters 14 and 15]

The Consequences of Modernity (1990)

Modernity and Self-Identity: Self and Society in the Late Modern Age (1991)

Runaway World: How Globalization Is Reshaping our Lives (2003)

Charlotte Perkins Gilman [chapter 10]

The Home: Its Work and Influence (1903)

Man-Made World or Our Androcentric Culture (1911)

Paul Gilroy [chapter 12]

"There Ain't No Black in the Union Jack": The Cultural Politics of Race and Nation (1987)

Against Race: Imagining Political Culture Beyond the Color Line (2000)

Darker than Blue (2010)

Erving Goffman [chapter 8]

The Presentation of Self in Everyday Life (1959)

Asylums: Essays on the Social Situation of Mental Patients and Other Inmates (1961)

Stigma: Notes on the Management of Spoiled Identity (1963)

Behavior in Public Places: Notes on the Social Organization of Gatherings (1963)

Interaction Ritual: Essays in Face-to-Face Behavior (1967)
Strategic Interaction (1969)
Relations in Public (1971)
Frame Analysis: An Essay on the Organization of Experience (1974)
Gender Advertisements (1979)

Andre Gunder Frank [chapter 6]
Capitalism and Underdevelopment in Latin America (1996)
The 5,000-Year World System (1996; with Barry Gills)

Jürgen Habermas [chapters 5 and 15]
Knowledge and Human Interests (1968)
Legitimation Crisis (1975)
The Theory of Communicative Action, volume 1(1984)
The Theory of Communicative Action, volume 2 (1987)
The Structural Transformation of the Public Sphere (1989)
Between Facts and Norms: Contributions to a Discourse Theory of Law and Democracy (1996)
"Notes on Post-Secular Society" (2008)

Stuart Hall [chapter 12]
"Cultural Identity and Diaspora" (1990)
"What Is This Black in Black Popular Culture?" (1992)

Arlie Hochschild [chapter 10]
"Emotion Work, Feeling Rules, and Social Structure" (1979)
The Managed Heart: Commercialization of Human Feeling (1983)
The Commercialization of Intimate Life: Notes from Home and Work (2003)
The Second Shift (1990; with Anne Machung)
The Outsourced Self (2012)
Strangers in Their Own Land: Anger and Mourning on the American Right (2016)

George Caspar Homans [chapter 7]
The Human Group (1950)
Social Behavior: Its Elementary Forms (1961)
"Fundamental Social Processes" (1967)

Max Horkheimer [chapter 5]
The Dialectic of Enlightenment (1972; with Theodor Adorno)

Fredric Jameson [chapter 15]
Postmodernism or, the Cultural Logic of Late Capitalism (1991)

Bruno Latour [chapter 7]
Science in Action (1987)
Reassembling the Social (2005)

Herbert Marcuse [chapter 5]
One-Dimensional Man: Studies in the Ideology of Advanced Industrial Society (1964)

Harriet Martineau [Introduction]
Society in America (1837)
How to Observe Morals and Manners (1838)
The Positive Philosophy of Auguste Comte (1855)

Karl Marx [chapter 1]
"Alienation and Social Classes" (1844)
Economic and Philosophical Manuscripts of 1844
The German Ideology (1846/1932; with Engels)
The Communist Manifesto (1848; with Engels)
"The Eighteenth Brumaire of Louis Bonaparte" (1859)
"Preface to 'A Contribution to the Critique of Political Economy'" (1859)
Capital (*Das Capital*; 1867)

George Herbert Mead [chapter 8]
Mind, Self, and Society (1934)

Robert Merton [chapter 4]
Social Theory and Social Structure (1949)

C. Wright Mills [chapter 6]
The New Men of Power: America's Labor Leaders (1948)
White Collar: The American Middle Classes (1951)
The Power Elite (1956)
The Sociological Imagination (1959)

Talcott Parsons [chapter 4]
The Structure of Social Action (1937)
Essays in Sociological Theory (1949/1954)
The Social System (1951)
Sociological Theory and Modern Society (1967)
The System of Modern Societies (1971)

Henri Saint-Simon [Introduction]
Selected Writings on Science, Industry, and Social Organization (1807–1813)

Saskia Sassen [chapter 14]
The Global City (1991)
A Sociology of Globalization (2007)

Alfred Schutz [chapter 9]
Collected Papers (1962)
On Phenomenology and Social Relations (1970)

Steven Seidman [chapter 11]
Queer Theory/Sociology (1996)
Difference Troubles: Queering Social Theory and Sexual Politics (1997)
"Are We All in the Closet? Notes Toward a Sociological and Cultural Turn in Queer Theory" (2004)

Georg Simmel [chapters 1 and 2]
The Sociology of Georg Simmel (1903)
On Individuality and Social Forms (1907)

Leslie Sklair [chapter 14]
Globalization: Capitalism and Its Alternatives (2002)

Dorothy Smith [chapter 10]
The Everyday World as Problematic: A Feminist Sociology (1987)
The Conceptual Practices of Power: A Feminist Sociology of Knowledge (1990)
Texts, Facts, and Femininity: Exploring the Relations of Ruling (1990)
Institutional Ethnography: A Sociology for People (2005)

Immanuel Wallerstein [chapter 14]
The Modern World-System I: Capitalist Agriculture and the Origins of the European World-Economy in the Sixteenth Century (1974)

The Modern World-System II: Mercantilism and the Consolidation of the European World-Economy 1600–1750 (1980)
The Modern World-System III: The Second Era of Great Expansion of the Capitalist World-Economy 1730–1840s (1989)
"World System Versus World-Systems: A Critique" (1996)
World-Systems Analysis: An Introduction (2004)

Max Weber [chapter 3]
The Protestant Ethic and the Spirit of Capitalism (1904–1905)
Economy and Society (1909–1920)
From Max Weber: Essays in Sociology (1946)
"The Social Psychology of the World Religions" (1915)
"Politics as a Vocation" (1919)
"Science as a Vocation" (1919)
The Methodology of the Social Sciences (1903–1917)

Erik Olin Wright [chapter 7]
"A General Framework for the Analysis of Class Structure" (1984)
Class Counts: Comparative Studies in Class Analysis (1997)

INDEX

Page references to Boxes are followed by the letter 'b, Figures are followed by the letter 'f'; references to Notes are followed by the letter 'n' following the Note and references to all Glossary entries are in **bold.**

academic capital *see* educational capital
accomplishment of social reality 292, 293, **301**, 477
accounts 290, 292–297, 299, 300, **301**, **477**
achievement versus ascription 161, 163, 167, **175**, **477**
actant 242, 243, **252**, **477**
action/social action
   action–reward/punishment orientation 233, **251**, **477**
   compartmentalized social activity 17
   instrumental rational *see* instrumental rational action
   Parsons on 153, 156
   phenomenology 283
   physical-biological activity 17
   rational 128, 490
   subjectively meaningful 116, 146, 283, 493
   traditional 144, 493
   and utilitarianism 156
   voluntaristic 156, 174, 494
   Weber on 115, 124–130, 144
     emotional action 144, 145, 482
     instrumental rational action *see* instrumental rational action
     nonrational action 126, 128, 145, 487
     traditional action 144, 146, 493
     understanding 116–117

     value-rational action 124–126, 128, 144, 146, 494
activism
   activist knowledge 327–328, 338, 477
   symbolic universes 291
   uberization of 66
actor-network theory (ANT) 242–244, 251
   actant 242, 243, 252, 477
   definition 252, 477
actors
   see also actor-network theory (ANT); theatrical performance metaphors
   deep acting 335–336
   definition 276, 477
   impression management 269
   in social exchange 232–234
   surface acting 335
   symbolic interactionism 263
   theater 335
adaptation 154, 155, 172b, **175**, **477**
Addams, Jane 151
administered world 201, **207**, **477**
Adorno, Theodor 183–188, 191, 193, 196, 200, 495
   see also critical theory
   biographical aspects 184
   Dialectic of Enlightenment 184

Introduction to Sociological Theory: Theorists, Concepts, and Their Applicability to the Twenty-First Century, Third Edition. Michele Dillon.
© 2020 John Wiley & Sons Ltd. Published 2020 by John Wiley & Sons Ltd.
Companion website: www.wiley.com/go/dillon